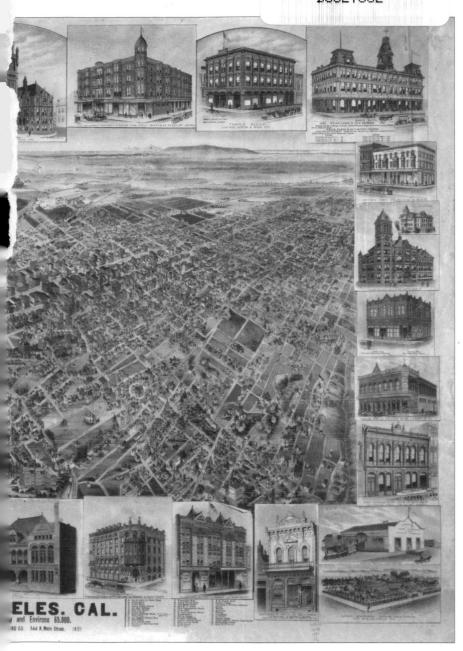

ELES. CAL.
and Environs 65,000.
ND CO.   344 N. Main Street.   1891

LOS ANGELES
ATTRACTIONS

MUSEON

PUBLISHING

www.museonbooks.com

COPY EDITORS: Laurence Vittes, Alexandria Nabatoff
PHOTOGRAPHERS: Borislav Stanic, Mihailo Stanic
MAPS: Suzana Sumrah, Darko Stetin
COVER DESIGN: Marek Djordjevic

First American Edition
5 4 3 2

Printed in China

Published in the United States by
Museon Publishing
P O Box 17095
Beverly Hills, CA 90209-2095

ISBN 978-1-889224-11-4   2007922504
512pp. Includes index

Bulk purchases of this book are available at special discounts
for sales promotions or premiums. Custom editions can be
provided with personalized covers and corporate imprints for
special needs. For more information write to the publisher at
the address above.

Every effort has been made to ensure accuracy of the information in this book. All contents are based on data available
at the time of publication. However, time brings change and
the publisher can accept no responsibility for any loss or
inconvenience sustained by any visitor as a result of
information contained in this book.

Readers are invited to write to the publisher with their
comments, suggestions and ideas.

ILLUSTRATIONS:
front endpaper: *Los Angeles* (1891) by Elliott
rear endpaper: *Los Angeles* (1894) by B W Pierce
p1: *Crossroads* (1990) by Frank Romero
p6: *Discovery* (1932) by Dean Cornwell (detail)
p12: *Founding of Los Amgeles* (1932) by Dean Cornwell
(detail)
p13: *Pink Landscape* (1984) by Frank Romero
p47: *Freeway Wars* (1990) by Frank Romero
p71: *Norm's La Cienega on Fire* (1964) by Ed Ruscha
p99: *Olive Hill* (1987) by Frank Romero

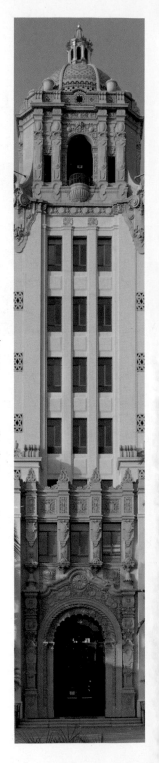

LOS ANGELES
ATTRACTIONS

Borislav Stanic

MUSEON
PUBLISHING

Acknowledgments

Every effort has been made to contact copyright holders and we apologize for any errors and omissions. Museon Publishing would be pleased to insert appropriate acknowledgments in future editions of this guide.

We are grateful to the following authors, publishers and agencies for permission to include their material in this book:

Oil! by Upton Sinclair, Copyright ©1997 The Regents of the University of California. Reprinted by permission of the University of California Press: 72
Golden Land by William Faulkner, Copyright ©1935 by Random House. Reprinted by permission of Random House, Inc: 73
Double Indemnity by James M Cain, Copyright ©1936 by James M Cain. Reprinted by permission of Random House, Inc: 73
The Mattress by the Tomato Patch by Tennessee Williams, Copyright ©1948 by the University of the South. Reprinted by permission of Random House, Inc: 74
The Day of the Locust by Nathanael West. Copyright ©1939 by Nathanael West. Reprinted by permission of Amereon/Signet: 75
What Makes Sammy Run?, Copyright ©1941, renewed 1969 by Budd Schulberg. Reprinted by permission of Miriam Altshuler Literary Agency, on behalf of Budd Schulberg: 76
The Labyrinth of Solitude, Copyright ©1961 by Grove Press. Reprinted by permission of Grove/Atlantic, Inc: 76
The Little Sister by Raymond Chandler, Copyright ©1949 by Raymond Chandler. Reprinted by permission of Random House, Inc: 77
Local Color: Hollywood by Truman Capote, Copyright ©1950 by Truman Capote. Reprinted by permission of Random House, Inc: 77

The position of photographs on a page has been abbreviated in the following manner: t = top; tr = top right; tl = top left; tbl = top below left; tbr = top below right; c = center; ct = center top; ca = center above; car = center above right; cal = center above left; cr = center right; crb = center right bellow; cl = center left; clb = center left below; cb = center below; cba = center below above; b = bottom; ba = bottom above; br = bottom right; bl = bottom left; bla = bottom left above; bra = bottom right above; bc = bottom center.

All photographs taken especially for this book are by Borislav and Mihailo Stanic. Museon would like to thank the following institutions and individuals for permitting the reproduction of their photographs in this publication:

Academy of Motion Picture Arts and Sciences (AMPAS): 48l, 48-49c, 112c, 112bl, 150t, 196cl, 216t, 234t, 234b, 235c, 236t, 238t, 239b, 240b, 245c, 245bl, 245br, 273b, 312b, 335tr, 394cl
Antelope Valley Indian Museum: 14bl
Aquarium of the Pacific: 404t, 404c
Archdiocese of Los Angeles: 39tr
Archivo General de Indias, Sevilla, Spain: 17t
ARCO Photography Collection: 253tr
Asprey London: 51tr
Beverly Hills Hotel: 463, 484t
Biltmore Hotel: 255br, 485b, 485t/photo by Alex Vertikoff
Bison Archives: 42cr, 42-43c, 171t, 196t, 215c, 231b, 462c, 466cl, 468tr, 468c, 469cl
Collection of Dr and Mrs Edward H Boseker: 21t, 84cl, 84b
Bowers Museum of Cultural Art, Santa Ana, California: 21cr
Buena Vista Pictures Distribution: 110b
Burbank Glendale Pasadena Airport: 322t
Cabrillo Marine Aquarium/photo by Gary Florin: 61br
Cartier: 52cr
Charmlee Nature Preserve: 358t
Chaya Brasserie: 484b
Chevron Corporation: 39c, 55t
Columbia TriStar/Photofest: 197br
Courtesy of DeRu's Fine Arts, Laguna Beach: 85b
©2000 Lucia Eames/Eames Office (www.eamesoffice.com): 373tl
Courtesy of Patricia Faure Gallery: 89t
Courtesy Joycie Fickett: 344b, 403
Fox Village Theatre: 443tl, 443tr
Courtesy of the J Paul Getty Museum: 70, 429-431
Griffith Observatory: 164ca, 164b
Griffith Park Merry Go Round/© Tom Henderson: 162t
©David Hockney: 87t
Hollywood Entertainment Museum: 53cal
Hotel Bel Air: 482t
Huntington Library, San Marino, California: 26cr, 26-27c, 30cl, 31cl, 32br, 37cr, 103t, 289, 290, 291bl, 291br, 352-53t
Japanese American National Museum: 267b
Kodak Theatre: 116b
Courtesy of Koplin Del Rio Gallery, Los Angeles: 88b, 89c
Courtesy of La Luz de Jesus Gallery: 89b

LACMA: 86t, 205b, 206, 207
Courtesy of Lawrence Rubin Greenberg van Doren Fine Art, New York: 87b
Courtesy of Margo Leavin Gallery, Los Angeles: 88t
Library of Congress: endpapers
Lily, Beverly Hills: 51tl
Lockheed: 41c
Loews Santa Monica Beach Hotel: 481b
Los Angeles County Sheriffs' Museum: 25cr
Los Angeles Dodgers: 175t
Metro Goldwyn Mayer/United Artists: 414t, 415t
Metropolitan Transportation Authority: 33b
Courtesy of Tobey C Moss Gallery: 86c
Norton Simon Museum: 302t, 302bl
Orange County Museum of Art: 18-19c
Paramount Pictures: 137t
Pasadena Civic Auditorium: 297b
Petersen Automotive Museum: 204t
Queen Mary: 406
Ramona Museum of California History: 20-21c
©Nancy Reddin Kienholz: 56bl
©Nancy Reddin Kienholz, photo courtesy of LA Louver, Venice, California: 87c
Regent Beverly Wilshire: 458t, 482b
Courtesy of Frank Romero: 1, 13, 47, 88c, 90
Franklin D Roosevelt Library, Hyde Park, New York: 22-23c
Courtesy of Ed Ruscha: 86b, 71
Santa Monica Public Library Image Archives, photo by Russ Saunders: 353br
Seaver Center for Western History Research: 24cl, 28-29c, 37br, 354-55t
Courtesy Julius Shulman: 97c, 97b
Sony Pictures Entertainment: 232clb, 416-17c, 417b, 418t
Southwest Museum: 14t, 14bl, 14tbr, 14ca, 14br, 15bc, 15bl, 15bra, 15bla, 15cl, 15cr, 15ct, 15cba, 19tr, 177b
Courtesy of George Stern Fine Arts: 85t, 85c
Sunset Tower: 483
Tournament of Roses: 300b, 301c
Courtesy of Track 16 Gallery: 63clb
20th Century-Fox: 451t
Universal Studios: 333t, 335br, 336cl, 336bl, 337cr, 337ba, 337b
Valentino USA Inc/photo by Steven Meisel: 198c
Warner Bros Pictures: 329t
Delmar Watson Photography Archives: 41tl
Will Rogers State Park/photo by Herm Falk: 371tr
Courtesy of Robert Williams: 56br

How to Use This Book

This guide invites you to explore one of the most unusual and exciting cities in the world. To help you cope with the city's geography, Los Angeles has been divided in this book into 12 sightseeing areas. The guide is organized to be as useful to the reader as possible, containing all the necessary information for both visitors and residents. From recognized tourist sights, historic and cultural landmarks, to annual events, movie studio tours and tapings of TV shows, it provides a cross section of the best Los Angeles has to offer. Useful practical information about hotels, restaurants, entertainment and the arts is also included.

Location:
Each entry is clearly indicated with an individual heading and map reference for quick and easy location.
Entries are described in detail and listed in order, following the numbers on the area map.

Maps:
Each section of the book is preceded by its own map. The numbers on the map correspond to the numbers of the text entries, indicating the location of a specific sight featured in the section.

Information:
The book features a description of every sight, with interesting historical and architectural details

Details:
Addresses, telephone numbers, websites, hours of operation, admission charges and other useful information are all included in our listings.

The key to the special symbols used in this guide:

☎	Telephone	♠	Haunted place
⊕	Hours	ⓦ	Crime scene/death site
☛	Tours	⚑	Film/TV location
Ⓢ	Admission	◆	Literary site
ⓘ	Information	NRHP	National Register of
→	See page		Historic Places

Contents

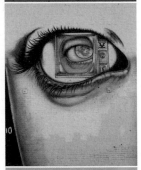

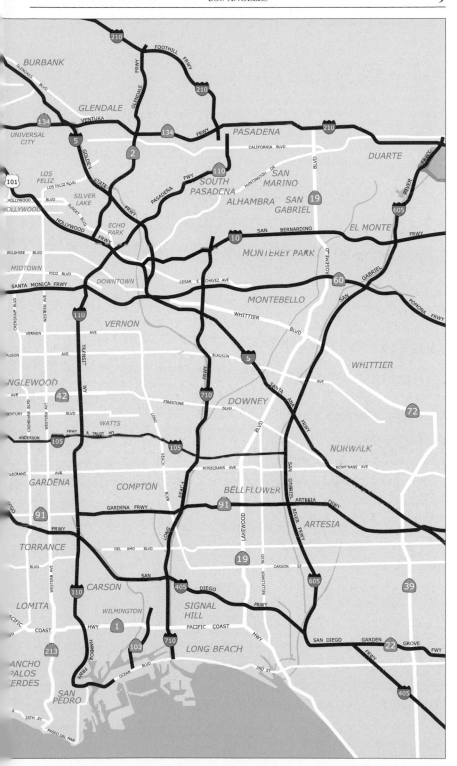

Introduction

In the minds of the millions who arrive every year, Los Angeles is associated with palm trees and permanent sunshine, sandy beaches packed with hard bodies, year-round surfing on perfect

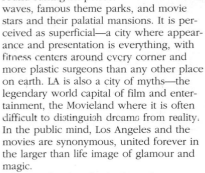

Vanity license plate

waves, famous theme parks, and movie stars and their palatial mansions. It is perceived as superficial—a city where appearance and presentation is everything, with fitness centers around every corner and more plastic surgeons than any other place on earth. LA is also a city of myths—the legendary world capital of film and entertainment, the Movieland where it is often difficult to distinguish dreams from reality. In the public mind, Los Angeles and the movies are synonymous, united forever in the larger than life image of glamour and magic.

Greater Los Angeles is situated on a vast coastal plain, facing the Pacific Ocean and surrounded by mountains. It covers more than 4,900 square miles (12,500 km²) and has a population of 11 million. LA enjoys an enviable climate of mild winters and warm, dry summers that supports outdoor activities and stimulates a relaxed, casual atmosphere. Not even the constant threat of earthquakes, fires, floods and mudslides can stop exuberant LA in its tracks.

Not a traditional city in the usual sense, Los Angeles is an enormous urban sprawl lacking a real center or characteristic area, a conglomeration of some 90 independent municipalities. With their mosaic of cultures, customs and cuisines, these separate neighborhoods give the city its distinctive charm and ambience. LA is also home to immigrants from 140 countries, who speak more languages here than in any other American city. This remarkable ethnic and cultural diversity brings crime, social ills and racial tensions that occasionally erupt in riots.

A conglomerate of creative types—artists, filmmakers, musicians, dancers and writers—as well as eccentrics and weirdoes of all kinds, it is unconventional by any standard and accommodates every conceivable lifestyle. Its tolerant, free-spirited and stimulating atmosphere radiates a sense of possibility, giving birth to trends and styles in art, architecture, music and fashion widely embraced and copied around the world.

Complex like no other metropolis, Los Angeles is a place of extremes too confusing to be quickly comprehended. It is frequently dismissed by many outsiders who judge it at first sight, not understanding its multiple personalities. The city of countless contradictions, it appears frighteningly vast and elusive, its disparate parts lacking any unifying feature. No wonder perplexed visitors try in vain to answer seemingly the impossible question, which is the real LA?

For those following the ultimate tourist draw—movie star homes—we have provided addresses and descriptions of some of the most famous celebrity dwellings. As they frequently move or own second or third homes, some of the stars are mentioned several times throughout the book. Many houses had multiple celebrity owners as they often sell to each other due to marriages and divorces, or career ups and downs. Regardless of whether actual stars still live at particular homes at the present time, they are private residences and should be viewed only from the public sidewalk. Visitors should not at any time trespass on private property or disturb the privacy of occupants.

This book will help those wishing to visit the final resting places of their favorite celebrities and pay their respects. For easier orientation, maps of cemetery grounds show the exact location of each star's grave, together with the name of the section and lot number. Photographs of the plaques are also provided. Visitors should always respect the burial places and observe common decency.

If you plan a longer stay and wish to survey local attractions at length, a car is a must. Due to LA's immense size, it is the only efficient means of transportation. If you intend to stay within certain neighborhoods, local public transportation is sometimes sufficient.

Beyond obvious tourist draws, it is worth your time to explore other, less known Los Angeles, with its world-class museums and art galleries, beautiful parks and gardens, astonishing mix of cutting-edge and historical architecture, its superb orchestras and innovative fusion cuisine.

Over 1,000 entries, numerous maps and nearly 1,800 fine photographs, most taken specifically for this book, make *Los Angeles Attractions* the most complete guide to the city ever written.

History of Los Angeles

Ring and pin game

...hat is now the ...re members ...noshonean ...ne area for ...efore the Euro- ...long their neighbors ...sh, who occupied the ...between Malibu and ... the Tataviam, who lived ...e San Fernando Valley.

Between five and ten thousand Tongvas were living in villages scattered over the region. This peaceful and friendly people had melted away so completely by 1910, however, that of all their culture just a few everyday objects remained. Their heritage is visible today only in Indian place-names that are still used: Cahuenga, Malibu, Topanga, Cucamonga, Pacoima.

...l native peoples of North ...merica, California Indians were the most skillful basket makers. Baskets were indispensable in everyday life and were used for a variety of purposes, including food collecting, cooking and storage. Water bottles were woven so tightly that they could hold water without leaking.

Mortar and pestle
California Indians did not farm. They gathered a large variety of wild food, such as fruits, nuts, berries, roots, seeds and leaves. Their diet also included seafood, small game, birds, reptiles and grasshoppers. Acorn meal mush was the favorite dish. The shelled acorns were ground in a mortar with a pestle. To remove bitter tannin, acorn meal was repeatedly leached by pouring warm water over it.

Baskets were used for food collecting, cooking and storing water

Gathering Acorns, a drawing by Charles Nahl (1862)

Shell bead necklace
Indian tribes traded among themselves to obtain goods unavailable in their own domains. Beads made of *olivella* shells were used as a form of money.

Shredded bark skirt
The mild southern California climate required little clothing. Men usually went naked, while women wore skirts and aprons of buckskin, grass or shredded bark

Chumash Indian village (1542). The Indian houses in southern California had a circular floor plan and were typically conical or dome shaped. Willow stick frames were covered with sea grass, tule or brush. The island Chumash used whale ribs for the main framework of their houses. Smaller huts usually provided shelter for one family, while the largest of these structures could house up to 50 people.

Hunters used bows and arrows, javelins, slings, curved throwing sticks and various snares and traps to hunt deer, foxes, rabbits and birds. They sometimes wore decoy deer headdresses to approach their game without startling it. Fishing gear included abalone shell fishhooks, line and sinker, harpoons, fish spears and nets. They caught fish, sharks, seals and sea otters.

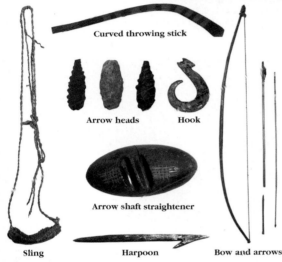

Curved throwing stick

Arrow heads   Hook

Arrow shaft straightener

Sling   Harpoon   Bow and arrows

Steatite effigies, mainly in the form of marine mammals and water birds, were considered power objects and used as talismans

The Tongva (Gabieliño) Indians built three types of watercraft: the plank canoe, the dugout and the tule balsa canoe. Coastal Indians of southern California were the only native people in North America who built seagoing plank canoes. Propelled by double-bladed paddles and holding from 2 to 12 people, their well-fashioned canoes were able to reach offshore islands.

A shaman, or medicine man, was responsible for curing illness. The shaman gained his special power from a guardian spirit who appeared to him through a dream or trance. To perform healing, shaman used herbal remedies and sang sacred songs, sometimes wearing feather skewers (left). They were paid well for their services, usually with fancy baskets or other valuable items (right).

Bone whistles and flutes were played during important rituals and ceremonies (above), while participants wore special ceremonial skirts (below)

...lonization

...n Rodríguez Cabrillo, a Por-
...gator in service to the Spanish
...1 in the summer of 1542 with two
...1 from Navidad, Mexico. On Sep-
...3, he sailed into San Diego Har-
...king that date the official "discov-
...California. Cabrillo anchored
...y in San Pedro Bay, what is
...y Los Angeles Harbor, and named
...*bahia de los Fumos* (the Bay of
...nokes). The smoke he was referring
...o probably originated from brush fires
set by Indians while hunting rabbits.
The following year Cabrillo died of

**Spanish helmet
(ca. 16th c.)**

an infection from a wound after a battle with
Indians. Sixty years later Sebastián Vizcaíno
sailed along the California coast, giving Santa
Catalina Island its modern name. For the
next 150 years, Spain did not show
much interest in the Pacific coast.

In the middle of the 18th century,
however, the growing presence of
Russia and England posed a threat
to Spanish dominance along the Pacific coast. To deter their rivals, the Spanish organized several expeditions by
land and sea, trying to colonize the
land and secure it for the Crown.

**Felipe de Neve (1728-84),
Spanish Governor of the Californias (1775-82), organized
the expedition from Mexico
that founded Los Angeles and
laid out the town in 1781.
On the orders of King Carlos
III of Spain, Governor Neve
selected a site near the present-day Los Angeles River,
eight miles west of the San
Gabriel Mission (just north of
the present Plaza).**

Discovery (1932) by Dean Cornwell represents a highly romanticized version of this important event in California history

**Spanish explorers sailing
along the Pacific coast in the
16th century believed that
they had found a mythical
island called California, mentioned in a novel by Garcí
Rodríguez de Montalvo. The
book, *Las Sergas de Esplandi-
an* (The Adventures of Esplan-
dian), was first published in
1510 and stated that a beautiful black queen Calafiá ruled
"an island named California,
which was very close to the
earthly Paradise."
On this early map of the New
World California is depicted as
an island.**

The Spanish came to the New World equipped with heavy armor suitable for European warfare. During the early years of the California conquest, they realized it was inconvenient for the region's climate and too cumbersome for clashes with lightly-armed Indians. The Catalonian volunteers and other Spanish soldiers in California were known as *soldados de cuera*, or leather-jacket soldiers. Their garment was made of six or seven layers of tanned buckskin which served as a protection against Indian arrows.

Carlos III, King of Spain (1759-88), issued an edict in 1769 that established permanent colonies in California. He granted the first municipal charter to the City of Los Angeles in 1781.
In the American Revolution he entered the war in 1779 on the American side and regained Florida, previously lost to England in the Seven Years War.

A small group of 44 *pobladores* (settlers), recruited by Felipe de Neve in Sinaloa and Sonora, Mexico, arrived at San Gabriel Mission after a 300-mile (480-km) journey through the desert that lasted 100 days. The party that founded the new pueblo called *Reina de Los Angeles*(Queen of the Angels) consisted of 11 men, 11 women and 22 children. As to their race, records show that the original adult founders were enlisted as: two Spaniards, one mestizo, two negroes, eight mulattos and nine Indians.

Mission Period

Spanish plans for the colonization of Alta (Upper) California included the establishment of *missions* (churches), *presidios* (forts) and *pueblos* (towns). Father Junípero Serra of Captain Portolá's expedition was the founder of Alta California's Franciscan mission chain. The first mission was estab-

Monstrance

lished at San Diego in 1769 and over the next 50 years 21 missions were built along the coast all the way to San Francisco Bay. San Gabriel Mission was founded on September 8, 1771, as the 4th in the chain, while the 17th, Mission San Fernando, was built in 1797.

Father Junípero Serra (1713-1784) established Alta California's chain of missions. He was a driving force in the Spanish conquest of California. Despite the romanticized picture of mission life that persists to this day, the *padres* faced significant resistance to forced labor and conversion. Indians continued to practice their ancestral customs and armed resistance was common.

"Why, you make me think that if one were to give you a young bull, a sheep and a *fanega* (1.5 bushels) of grain every day, you would still be yearning for your mountains and your beaches."
        —Fray Fermin Lausen
"What you say is true, Father."
        —the neophyte's response

***San Gabriel Mission* (ca. 1832) by Ferdinand Deppe**

The first American to reach California by land was Jedediah Strong Smith. Leading a group of 15 half-starved fur trappers from the Missouri frontier settlements over the Rocky Mountains and across a vast desert, he arrived at the San Gabriel Mission in November of 1826. Though he was well received by the padres and given much-needed supplies, the governor refused to give him permission to go northward along the coast, ordering him instead to leave by the route over which he had come.

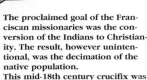

The proclaimed goal of the Franciscan missionaries was the conversion of the Indians to Christianity. The result, however unintentional, was the decimation of the native population.
This mid-18th century crucifix was brought to California from Mexico by one of the colonizing families.

Tongva Indian Rogerio Rocha, the last of the San Fernando Mission Indians. When he died in 1904, he was reportedly 103 years old. After being forcibly evicted from his adobe house by a white man, he spent the last years of his life living in a canyon.

The missions were built entirely with forced native labor, described by some foreign travelers as slavery. After San Gabriel and San Fernando missions were established, most of the local Indians were forcibly relocated around them and converted. The *neophytes* (baptized Indians) were called Gabrieliños and Fernandeños, after the mission with which they were associated. The Spanish mission system had a devastating impact on the natives, leading eventually to their destruction. By the end of the mission period in 1821, their numbers were reduced from 70,000 to 18,000. Hard labor, unbearable living conditions, a new and insufficient diet, and European diseases such as measles, smallpox and syphilis decimated the Indians.

Restored interior of San Gabriel Mission church. With its holdings of 1.5 million acres (600.000 ha), Mission San Gabriel (called the "Queen of the missions") was the largest and richest of all Alta California missions. Tens of thousands of cattle, sheep and horses grazed on its pastures. It produced a bounty of agricultural products, such as corn and beans, and supplied soap and candles to other missions. The mission had the oldest and largest winery in California and was famous for its vineyards and fine wines.

chos

1784 Governor Pedro Fages awarded to e of his former soldiers the first permits graze cattle and horses in California, in eas near the pueblo of Los Angeles. This vas the beginning of the *ranchos*, vast cattle-raising domains, which left a distinctive mark on California history and gave Los Angeles its contemporary name: the "Queen of the Cow Counties."

In 1821 Spanish rule came to an end and in 1834 the secularization of the

Spur

Franciscan missions began. Under the decree of the Mexican Government, half of the mission lands were to be distributed among the Indians. However, most of the land was granted to the prominent *Californio* families (Mexicans born or living in California), and the natives received almost nothing. At San Gabriel Mission, out of 1.5 million acres, Indians received only 203! Most of the natives continued to work for their new masters.

Rodeo was a periodic roundup held to count, separate and brand the stock. The *vaqueros* who gathered and slaughtered cattle "were almost constantly on horseback, and as horsemen excel." The California *vaquero* was a predecessor of the American cowboy, one of the West's most popular figures.

A highly idealized picture of pastoral life in Spanish California, the silent film *The Mark of Zorro* (1920) features Douglas Fairbanks as Don Diego Vega, a wealthy landowner who transforms into the masked avenger Zorro. He takes up arms to defend the oppressed against a corrupt government, embodied by the evil Captain Ramon.

Native Californians Lassoing a Bear (1873) by Felix Octavius Carr Darley.
On a moonlit night *vaqueros* trap a grizzly and rope it with their lassoes. The practice, together with undiscriminating hunting, helped drive the California grizzly to extinction.

In the *pueblo* plaza the bear would be matched against the bull in one of the favorite sports of the day. In these fights to the death, the bear would usually win. Current stock exchange terms "bear and bull market" have their origin in this hideous pastime.

Mexican Cattle Drivers in Southern California by William Hahn (1883).
Californios raised cattle mainly for hides. Known as "California bank notes," cattle hides were traded for manufactured goods brought by Yankee merchant ships. The rancho period reached its heyday during the Gold Rush (1848-59), when southern California beef was in greatest demand. Valued $1 to $2 before the rush, a single head of cattle brought as much as $200 in the northern mines in the 1850s.

Francisco Serrano

Don José Sepúlveda by Henri Penelon (1856). A prominent California *ranchero* astride his famous racehorse Black Swan. As was customary with all rich landowners, called *Silver Dons*, Don Sepúlveda is outfitted in resplendent attire, with golden spurs, bridles with silver chains, and silver-studded saddle and stirrups.
During the 1850s the *rancheros* prospered as never before. They acquired considerable wealth and were able to spend money on luxury goods previously nearly impossible to obtain.

Members of the influential Lugo family in front of their adobe on rancho San Antonio in present-day Bell Gardens (ca. 1890). The house, with its thick walls and wide veranda, was well-suited to the area's Mediterranean climate. The Lugos were the wealthiest and most prominent family in the Southland in the 1850s. California *rancheros* usually maintained two houses: the rancho house was the main family residence, and the townhouse, built near the Plaza, served as a second home when they visited the *pueblo*.

American Conquest

The first white American to permanently settle in California was Joseph Chapman, a seaman who arrived in 1818 and was briefly imprisoned as a "pirate." Other settlers, mostly merchants, soon followed on trading ships. In 1846, a group of Americans at Sonoma proclaimed a short-lived "Republic of California." The Anglo-American invasion began with the Gold Rush of 1848, when tens of thousands of settlers flooded the region. During the Mexican War (1846-1848), *Californios* in the southern part of the territory resisted American conquest. After a number of battles, the *pueblo* of Los Angeles was finally occupied by American forces on 10 January, 1847, when the conquest of California was completed. In 1850, California was admitted to the United States as the 31st state of the Union.

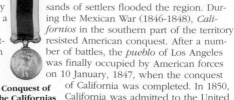

Conquest of the Californias medal

General John C Frémont (1813-1890) accepted the surrender of California by General Andrés Pico in the Mexican War. Frémont became the first US Senator from California and was the first nominee of the Republican Party for President in 1856.

American dog-locked pistol (late 18th c.)

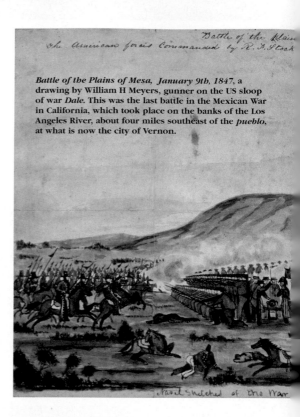

Battle of the Plains of Mesa, January 9th, 1847, a drawing by William H Meyers, gunner on the US sloop of war *Dale*. This was the last battle in the Mexican War in California, which took place on the banks of the Los Angeles River, about four miles southeast of the *pueblo*, at what is now the city of Vernon.

The adobe house on the Cahuenga rancho was the site where Frémont and Pico signed the treaty that ended hostilities between American forces and the *Californios* on January 13, 1847 (→ p332). California was formally acquired by the United States on February 2, 1848, when the Treaty of Guadalupe Hidalgo was signed. Under the terms of this treaty, Mexico lost more than half its territory to the United States, ceding the vast area now comprising California, Nevada, Utah, Arizona, New Mexico, Texas and parts of Colorado and Wyoming.

Signing of Cahuenga Treaty, a mural by Hugo Ballin (1931)

Pío Pico (1801-1894), the last governor of Mexican California, with his wife Maria Ignacio Alvarado de Pico and her nieces, Marianita Alvarado (left) and Trinidad Ortega (right). In a speech before the Departmental Assembly in 1846, he said: "We find ourselves suddenly threatened by hordes of Yankee immigrants, who have already begun to flock into our country, and whose progress we cannot arrest . . ."

In the decisive battle for Los Angeles, American forces successfully repelled the cavalry charge of the Mexican lancers under the command of José María Flores. The next day Americans, under the command of Commodore Robert F Stockton and General Stephen W Kearny, marched into Los Angeles and took it over.

General Andrés Pico (1810-1876), brother of Pío, led the *Californio* forces which inflicted a disastrous defeat to the Americans at the Battle of San Pasqual, on December 6, 1846. He negotiated the Treaty of Cahuenga with Frémont and later became a prominent American citizen. He was elected four times to the Assembly and became a state Senator.

Mexican officer's sword (1813)

Large Spanish and Mexican land grants did not have precise boundaries and often depended on features of the land to describe them on documents. After the American takeover, many Mexican *rancheros* had great difficulties defending their rights under the US Land Law of 1851. Eventually, most of them lost title to their lands to lawyers and creditors. Americans seized these holdings, mostly illegally, through ruinous interest rates, tax debts, lawyers' fees and other machinations. Vast Mexican *ranchos* were turned into huge agricultural domains; others were broken up and sold as farm fields or subdivided into small plots.

The Old Spanish and Mexican Ranchos of Los Angeles County, a mural by Lucien Labaudt (1938)

Hell Town

During the two decades between 1850 and 1870, Los Angeles became a magnet for outlaws, gamblers, saloon keepers and prostitutes, many of them driven out of northern towns by vigilante committees. Lawlessness ruled in *Los Diablos* (the Devils), as it was nicknamed—social banditry, robberies, knife fights, shootings, lynchings and violence of all kinds. Referred to as "the den of thieves," the town did not have law enforcement agencies that could cope with the overwhelming amount of criminal activity.

Deringer pistol (1860s)

The result was that Los Angeles was the most violent American city at the time. Describing Los Angeles of that era, Wyatt Earp, the pioneer US marshall, said: "Tombstone was but a Sunday school by comparison."

Another famous name of the Old West, the outlaw Emmett Dalton, also made Los Angeles his home. The youngest brother of the Dalton Gang, notorious for a series of bank and train robberies, tried his luck in the movies, often playing himself.

Frontiersman—one of thousands of the backwash from the mines who flooded Los Angeles in the years following the Gold Rush, which included drifters, thieves and con men of all kinds

Cuffs used by local law enforcement

In a California version of a final solution to the race problem, remaining Indians who survived decades of exploitation at local missions or random killings by white settlers, were sold at the local slave mart as day laborers. After being given *aguardiente* (firewater) Saturday night, they were arrested and Sunday morning offered for sale, as slaves for the week. The ranchers paid their fine for public drunkenness in return for a week's labor. The vicious cycle was repeated week after week, until all the Indians in the town perished.

An $8,000 reward was offered for the head of Tiburcio Vásquez (left), the notorious *bandido* who terrorized Los Angeles for 20 years. Although feared across California, Vásquez (whose supporters considered him a fighter for social justice and a resister against Yankee tyranny) was not without influence over the fair sex. Many of his female admirers, including some Anglo ladies, came to his prison with flowers. Even schools closed so that pupils could come and see Vásquez in jail. This picture was taken the day before his hanging on March 19, 1875.

Gambling (right) was a popular pastime in Los Angeles, which was packed with gambling halls, monte parlors, saloons and brothels. A traveler recorded: "The pueblo . . . is the noted abode of the lowest drunkards and gamblers of the country."

The hanging of murderer Miguel Lachenais, December 17, 1870. He was one of the last victims of the Los Angeles vigilantes, who lynched 37 men during the first two decades of American rule. There were also 40 legal hangings during the same period. Organized to deal with crime and violence, the first vigilance committee in California was formed in Los Angeles on 7 April, 1836. Their first action was aimed at a wife and her lover, accused of killing a husband. A mob of vigilantes took the pair from jail and shot them.

Los Angeles, California 1857 by Kuchel & Dresel.
This early lithograph shows the pueblo looking north from First Street; Main Street is on the left, Los Angeles Street on the right. The highest buildings in town were two-story, flat-roofed adobes. "The houses have flat roofs, covered with bituminous pitch, brought from a place within four miles of the town, where this article boils up from the earth. As the liquid rises, hollow bubbles, like a shell of large size, are formed. When they burst, the noise is heard distinctly in the town."
— *Los Angeles in 1824* by trapper James Ohio Pattie

A sheriff's life expectancy was short during this turbulent era due to the enormous dangers connected with the job. Although offering a high salary, the sheriff's office would often remain vacant for months. In 1877, James F Burns (above), a county sheriff's deputy, pursued the murderer Stephen "Buckskin Bill" Samsbury all the way to Baja California. After finally catching his prey, Burns killed him and brought back the man's well-known six toed foot preserved in mescal as proof to collect the reward money.

Calle de los Negros, or Nigger Alley, was only a block long, but earned a reputation of being "the wickedest street on earth." It was packed with gambling places, saloons and brothels, and fights and shootings occurred almost daily. It was noted that "an officer would not have had the temerity to attempt an arrest in Nigger Alley, at that time." It was the scene of the infamous Chinese Massacre in 1871. An angry mob of 400, interfering in a feud between two tongs over a woman, lynched at least 19 Chinese men and boys.

Transportation

Since the days of the first Spanish settlers, the only means of transportation into Los Angeles was either on horseback or in the crude, ox-drawn wagon called a *caretta*. The first Butterfield Overland stagecoach reached Los Angeles on October 7, 1858, establishing the first direct transportation link with the East. The route was the longest in the world, and the 20-day journey from St.

Caretta

Louis was rough and perilous. It was obvious that the isolated city needed a more reliable link to the outside world. In 1876 the Southern Pacific Railroad connected Los Angeles to San Francisco and the rest of the country. Proven to be the cheapest and fastest way of transportation, the railroad brought tens of thousands of newcomers to the region within a few years.

Filling in Secret Town Trestle by Carleton E Watkins—the construction of America's first transcontinental railroad. On May 10, 1869, Central Pacific met Union Pacific at Promontory Point, Utah, linking the Pacific Coast with the rest of the continent. Seven years later, the Southern Pacific Railroad arrived at Los Angeles, opening up the city to the Eastern United States.

A cartoon of the Southern Pacific as the "Octopus" in the satirical magazine *The Wasp* (1880). The monopolistic railroad is depicted holding free enterprise in California in its tentacles.

Concord Stagecoach (ca. 1865), built by Abbott, Downing & Co of Concord, New Hampshire. In 1852 Phineas Banning and D W Alexander started the first stage line between the Port of San Pedro and the city. Their drivers mounted races between two stages up to Los Angeles, to the great amusement of citizens who placed large bets.

After the arrival of the railroads, the stagecoach's role was reduced to providing local service between hotels and railroad depots. Taken in 1871, this photograph shows in the foreground a Lafayette Hotel stage coach. The building behind is the Coronel Block, the site of the Chinese Massacre; on the right is Calle de los Negros (Nigger Alley).

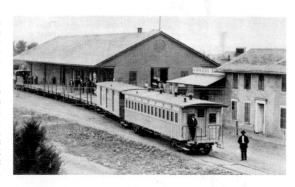

The first railroad in Southern California was completed in 1869. The twenty one-mile Los Angeles and San Pedro Railroad line connected downtown with the city of Wilmington and later San Pedro. Passengers were charged $2.50 one way; freight rates were $6 per ton for dry goods and $5 per ton for groceries. The first railroad terminal in LA (right), which stood at Alameda and Commercial streets, served both as freight house and passenger depot.

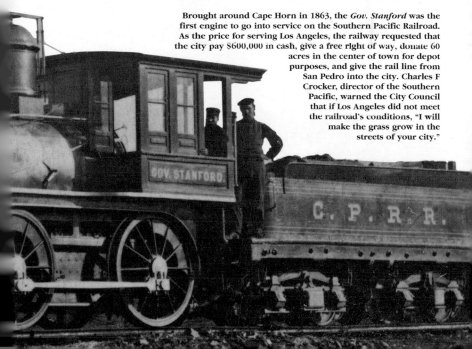

Brought around Cape Horn in 1863, the *Gov. Stanford* was the first engine to go into service on the Southern Pacific Railroad. As the price for serving Los Angeles, the railway requested that the city pay $600,000 in cash, give a free right of way, donate 60 acres in the center of town for depot purposes, and give the rail line from San Pedro into the city. Charles F Crocker, director of the Southern Pacific, warned the City Council that if Los Angeles did not meet the railroad's conditions, "I will make the grass grow in the streets of your city."

Population Booms

On 29 November, 1885, after a decade of the Southern Pacific's monopoly, the Santa Fe Railroad entered Los Angeles on its own tracks. The arrival of a second railroad sparked a rate war that drastically lowered passenger rates. Reduced fares brought tens of thousands of immigrants to Los Angeles from the East.

Locomotive steam whistle

The great Boom of the Eighties peaked in 1887, only to collapse the following year, when local banks declined to accept real estate as collateral. Many broken would-be settlers left the town; thousands, however, remained, marking the beginning of the city's rapid expansion into a future metropolis.

Monrovia land auction in 1886, during the wild real estate boom.
Many newcomers arrived with land options purchased with their train tickets. Others were lured into new towns by real estate agents offering a seductive "free ride and a free lunch," together with brass bands and circus performers. At the height of the frenzy in 1887, real estate prices rose 400 to 500 percent.

During the 1870s, newspaper articles and books such as Charles Nordhoff's *California for Health, Pleasure and Residence*, advertised the region as a health resort. Lured by boosters promoting the benefits of Southern California's mild climate, countless invalids flocked to the area seeking a cure for a myriad of ailments. Special sanitariums, such as this one in Glendale, were built across the region to accommodate the visitors seeking promised land.

The arrival of the Southern Pacific "emigrant cars" from the Midwest during the boom of the 1880s. Packed with passengers, these trains were described as "mere boxcars with cooking facilities." A rate war between competing railroads reduced fares from Kansas City to Los Angeles from $100 to $25 and, finally, although for just one day in the spring of 1886, to an absurd $1! Over 120,000 settlers flooded the area in 15 years.

General Phineas Banning (1830-1885) was called the father of Los Angeles transportation and the father of Los Angeles Harbor. He was instrumental in all major developments in the city from 1851 to 1885. Banning established the first stage lines in the area and built the first railroad in Southern California. He was also the first promoter for a free harbor at San Pedro. His residence in Wilmington is now a museum (→ p91).

A promotional poster advertising the auction sale of lots in Garvanzo, one of many new paper towns with fanciful names. Of more than one hundred such towns plotted during the boom years, almost two-thirds disappeared without a trace as the entire speculative scheme collapsed after peaking in 1888.

During the boom of the 1920s, promotional photographs like this one were used to boost visitor attendance. The "gamblers" were Miss Venice beauty contestants who posed in a mock card game for this publicity stunt.

Urban Transit

The mass rapid transit system in Los Angeles began on July 1, 1874, when the first horse-drawn cars appeared on city streets. The line, one and one-half miles in length, was remarkably popular. The fare was 10 cents, or 5 tokens for 25 cents. The city saw its first cable car in operation in 1885. Although the LA cable car system was one of the finest and most modern in the world, it lasted only seven years.

Yellow Car (1921)

The cable railway was gradually replaced with speedy electric trolleys. Los Angeles adopted the new electric railways more quickly and earnestly than any other city in the nation. Rapid development of both city and interurban electric lines, most of which were installed to promote the sale of real estate, resulted in the transformation of Los Angeles into the megalopolis we know today.

"I am a foresighted man. I believe that Los Angeles is destined to become the most important city in the country, if not in the world. It can extend in any direction, as far as you like; its front door opens on the Pacific, the ocean of the future."

— Henry Huntington

Henry Huntington (1850-1927) was a nephew of Collis P Huntington, one of the founders of the Central Pacific and Southern Pacific railroads. Shortly after his uncle's death in 1900, Henry sold his own and inherited stock and invested this enormous fortune ($50 million) in Los Angeles' trolley systems, electric power systems and real estate. He considered efficient public transportation only an aid in the promotion of the huge land holdings he owned. Huntington made tremendous profits in real estate speculation by knowing exactly where the next real estate boom would occur (he built his own rails). He owned the Los Angeles Railway, or "Yellow Cars," as well as the Pacific Electric interurban system, or "Big Red Cars." Huntington became one of the city's greatest philanthropists, founding the world-famous art and rare book collections at his San Marino estate (➔ p289).

The first electric railway on the Pacific Coast began operation in Los Angeles in January of 1887. Over a period of two decades, more than 20 different companies operated streetcars in the city. In 1910, after a series of mergers, Henry Huntington's narrow-gauge Los Angeles Railway (LARY), or "Yellow Car" system, gained total control of local transit. In its peak in the mid-1920s, LARY owned more than 1,200 electric streetcars and was the second largest urban transit system in the United States. The influence of the street railways is still visible in Los Angeles. Major arteries, such as Vermont Ave and Venice Blvd, were developed along rail tracks to serve customers who traveled by streetcar.

The open bench cars were the earliest form of trolleys in Los Angeles. This streetcar was built by the St Louis Car Company in 1889 for the Electric Rapid Transit Company of Los Angeles. In the early 1900s, the open bench cars were modified or replaced with more fashionable cars that had enclosed seating.

The Los Angeles cityscape as envisioned by an artist in 1913. A futuristic transit system, which included a monorail and people mover, would provide "relief of overcrowded streets." This conception of sci-fi transportation never materialized, as the city rejected elevated railways and subway lines in the 1920s.

A classic scene from the 1930 movie *Hog Wild.* Famous comedy duo Laurel and Hardy found themselves in "another fine mess," trapped in a Ford Model T crushed between two trolley cars in central Los Angeles. Streetcar-automobile accidents like this one were common at the time. Trolley cars regularly appeared as backdrops in Hollywood two-reel comedics of the 1920s and 1930s.

A Pacific Electric Railway pamphlet promoting special sightseeing trolley trips.
The first streetcar lines were built to sell and develop real estate. The best way to make rural land skyrocket in value was to connect it with the city center via a trolley line. Prices soared when the Big Red Cars, traveling at speeds of 45 to 55 mph (72-88 km/h), made outlying properties within easy reach of commuters. An electric railway slogan of the early 1900s, "Live in the Country and Work in the City," stimulated land sales, epitomizing the ideal of suburban living. Pacific Electric's interurban system enormously contributed to the city's dispersed pattern of settlement, making Los Angeles a conglomeration of many smaller communities.

Since its first recorded trial, which took place on April 25, 1869, the bicycle became enormously popular among Angelenos. By the end of the 1890s, there were more bicycles in Los Angeles than in any other city in the world. In 1895 cyclists even petitioned the city to sprinkle the streets after 8 am, so they could arrive at work with clean and dry clothes. The proud wheelmen on this photograph were the city champions of 1888.

When the first two horse-drawn streetcars appeared on Los Angeles streets in 1874, *The Star* newspaper described them as "splendid and easy-riding omnibuses." Some lines gave horses and mules a well-deserved lift downhill after they loyally pulled streetcars uphill. On this photograph from the 1870s, horse power gets a free ride (in a special compartment) on Euclid Avenue. The last horse car line was closed in 1901.

Demise of Rail Transit

The Los Angeles' transit system, with its Yellow Cars connected with interurban Big Red Cars, was regarded as one of the best urban transportation networks in the country. However, as Angelenos fell in love with the automobile, railway passengers declined in number, routes were abandoned and travel time increased. Fares had to rise to

**Big Red Car
(1922)**

make up for losses and as a result, ridership dropped even further. It was clear that the deteriorating railway system could no longer be operated profitably. The last of the Big Red Cars completed its final run on April 8, 1961. The last Yellow Car retired from service on March 31, 1963, ending a streetcar era nearly nine decades long.

Hand-painted dash signs announced the streetcar's destination to the passengers. Mounted on the front dash of each car, these double-sided signs were turned around upon reaching the end of the line.

Pacific Electric "Hollywood Car" 637 (1922).
At its heyday in the 1920s, the Pacific Electric Railway had 1,164 miles of track and operated 6,000 scheduled cars daily. The Pacific Electric was larger than the transit systems of the next five major American cities combined. Its electric trolleys, called "Big Red Cars" by passengers and employees, were the finest and largest interurban cars anywhere. Operating under the slogan "comfort-speed-safety," the Pacific Electric boasted that it was the "world's greatest electric railway."

The first freeway in California, the Arroyo Seco Parkway, now the Pasadena Freeway, was opened on December 30, 1940. As the support for a network of freeways grew, the streetcars first lost their rights of way, and when they were finally denied routes down the median strips of new freeways, the collapse of the trolley system was imminent.

The first Pacific Electric buses appeared on Los Angeles streets in the early 1920s as a supplement to the local rail transport. After that buses were used whenever the company expanded service, and by the late 1930s buses began to replace trolley cars. It soon became obvious that public transport was no match for the private automobile in speed or convenience. By 1923, one third of the city's workers were commuting in their own automobiles.

In a decade between 1920 and 1930, the number of registered vehicles in Los Angeles County increased from 160,000 to over 840,000. As the automobile became increasingly popular, it brought about congestion and traffic conflicts, and accidents became more common. The railways lost their great advantage as roads cut through their rights of way and the number of grade crossings increased, further slowing down trolley cars.

The demise of rail transit in Los Angeles was blamed on car manufacturers, tire companies and oil lobbyists, including General Motors, Standard Oil and Firestone Tire. They were accused of trying to monopolize ground transportation through a corporation called National City Lines, which took over and dismantled the local streetcar system. However, the ailing rail system was already in a long decline, plagued by inefficiency and aging technology. The Los Angeles public clearly chose the automobile over the streetcar.

MTA 1999 weekly transit passes for buses and the Metrorail featuring original artwork from vintage passes issued by the Los Angeles Railway and Los Angeles Transit Lines from 1934 to 1947

The alleged corporate conspiracy to replace streetcars with automobiles and buses underlies the plot of the live action/animation film *Who Framed Roger Rabbit?* (1988). Playing 1930s gumshoe Eddie Valiant, Bob Hoskins exclaims, "Who needs a car in Los Angeles? We've got the best transportation in the world." He discovers a scheme by a villain named Judge Doom who envisioned "wonderful, wonderful billboards reaching as far as the eye can see" along the Pasadena freeway.

Water

Situated in a semi desert region with little rainfall, Los Angeles was constantly striving to obtain adequate supplies of water. At the turn of the 20th century it was recognized that the local water supply (wells and the Los Angeles River) was not sufficient. If the city was to grow, additional source of water had to be found. And it was found—the Owens River in the eastern Sierra Nevada, more than 200 miles to the north.

Plans to build the aqueduct were kept secret so that farmers in the Owens Valley would sell their water rights without knowing the city's real intentions. When the last parcel of land necessary to obtain control was purchased, the *Los Angeles Times* announced on July 29, 1905: "The titanic project to give the city a river." Owens Valley residents were furious, claiming that their water had been looted. The controversy, called the Owens Valley Water War, lasted almost 25 years.

In September 1905, Los Angeles voters, by a margin of 14 to 1, approved the sale of $1.5 million in bonds to buy land and water rights in Owens Valley. In July 1907, by a 10 to 1 majority, voters passed a second bond issue of $23 million for aqueduct construction (left). Irish immigrant William Mulholland arrived in Los Angeles in 1877 with $10 in his pocket. A self-taught man who studied engineering at night from public library books, he began his career as a ditch tender, or *zanjero,* and rose to the position of chief water engineer for the city of Los Angeles (right).

52-mule team hauling 20 tons of steel pipe into position. 6,000 mules were used to transport large sections of pipe during the construction of the First Los Angeles Aqueduct (1908-13).

The aqueduct construction involved 5,000 workers and new technologies over a five-year period. This enormous task was successfully completed within Mulholland's original time and cost estimate. When it was finished in 1913, the 233-mile (375-km) aqueduct was the longest in the world. Its unique feature is that water flows through steel pipe, open culverts and 142 tunnels entirely by gravity; not a single pump had to be used. The aqueduct was considered one of the greatest engineering wonders of modern times, second only to the Panama Canal

Jawbone Siphon, the largest of 23 inverted siphons on the Los Angeles Aqueduct. (An airtight siphon draws the water back up after it has fallen into the canyon 850 feet (260 m) deep.)

Zanjero by Hernando Villa
To provide the pueblo with water, the first Spanish settlers dug open irrigation ditches called *zanjas*. Water was so important to the city that in the 1860s, the water commissioner received a higher salary than the mayor of Los Angeles, a tradition that still goes on.

In the early 1900s, ten wealthy and powerful Angelenos formed a syndicate and bought up almost fifty thousand acres of dry land in San Fernando Valley. When water from the Sierras arrived, real estate prices skyrocketed and speculators sold the land, making over $100 million in profits. Roman Polanski's classic detective film *Chinatown* (1974) was loosely based on these events. Jack Nicholson plays private eye J J Gittes who is drawn into a complex case of murder and land machinations.

On 5 November 1913, the aqueduct was completed and 40,000 spectators gathered to see the first rush of water at the cascades in the San Fernando Valley. Mulholland delivered his famous laconic speech: "There it is. Take it."

Agriculture

Agriculture has been the main economic venture in the Los Angeles basin since the mission days. Because of the area's mild climate and fertile soil, almost all kinds of produce could be grown. The Southland lead the nation in introducing new crops, and its greatest success was the orange—"the gold nugget of Southern California."

California oranges

Between 1909 and 1949 Los Angeles County was the largest agricultural producer in the United States. It lost first place only after the post World War II housing boom made the farmland more valuable as residential lots. Los Angeles did not became completely urbanized until the 1950s, when immense orchards were finally divided into small housing tracts.

Bright colors and the eye-catching design of crate labels, used to identify and advertise the brand name, played a vital role in selling citrus fruit. Promoted by the LA-based cooperative, later named Sunkist, the orange was transformed from an exotic fruit into one of life's essentials. In one of the most successful marketing campaigns ever, Sunkist introduced a new habit—a glass of fresh orange juice in the morning, changing American breakfast patterns forever.

A stereoscopic card showing 10,000 acres of navel orange groves in San Gabriel Valley (1903). The California citrus industry started in 1873 with the introduction of two trees of a new variety of orange from the Brazilian jungle, known as the navel orange. Within 15 years, more than 1 million navel orange trees had been planted, revolutionizing agriculture in the Southland.

In *It's a Gift* (1934), W C Fields plays a small town grocer who buys a Los Angeles orange grove by mail and moves west with his family in a car. Throughout this great comedy of disasters, in spite of endless setbacks and frustrations, he never stops pursuing his agricultural dream. Created by city boosters, the myth of "gentleman farming" in sunny California promised an idyllic image of the farmer as "middle-class horticulturist."

Wheat and barley crops were a major industry in the San Fernando Valley from the 1870s until 1913, when the Owens Valley water made production of other, more lucrative crops, possible.

Oranges and Snow, the Winter of California. Thousands of picture post cards like this one immortalized the cliché of the sunny San Gabriel Valley that was advertised around the world. This bucolic scene of bright-colored oranges against snow-covered mountain peaks appealed to generations of Americans. Promoters boosted the pleasures of Southern California's Mediterranean climate to affluent Easterners. Why go to Italy when America had its own garden of Eden on the Pacific shores?

-More than 10,000 Acres of Navel Orange Groves, San Gabriel Valley, Cal., U. S. A.

Promotional events such as the 1886 Southern California Citrus Fair in Chicago widely publicized Los Angeles and its citrus industry. In 1884 Southern California oranges won the first prize at the International Exposition in New Orleans. Visual presentations of the area's bounty, held in every major fair in the Midwest, lured more settlers to California than the Gold Rush.

California—The Cornucopia of the World, promotional poster for Pacific Fruit Express. The transcontinental railroad brought the eastern fruit market within reach of California producers. Another boost to the trade was the invention of the refrigerated rail car in 1890. Railroads joined the marketing effort in 1906, their fruit trains running across the country with huge banners that read: "Oranges for Health, California for Wealth."

After ostriches were introduced to the area in the 1880s, several successful farms were opened and the birds became an instant tourist attraction. The gentleman in this post card enjoys a joy ride at Cawston's Ostrich Farm in South Pasadena, ca. 1910. Among other period fads were alligator farms, Belgian hare farms and pigeon farms.

The first commercial shipment of California oranges to an eastern market was sent in 1877. The trip to St. Louis took a month, but the fruit arrived in good shape. In 1910 California growers shipped 40,000 rail cars of fruit to the East. Enough, however, left for local consumption, as this photograph of a picnic in Exposition Park from 1917 shows.

Oil

It was predicted in the mid 19th century that Los Angeles had no future because it had no sources of energy within easy reach. The city lacked timber or coal, and there was no close by falling water for hydropower. Los Angeles, however, was sitting on a sea of oil, which did not pass entirely unnoticed. The tar (*brea* in Spanish) from the area was used by the Indians to

caulk their canoes and later by white settlers to cover the flat roofs of their adobes. But it was not until 1864 that oil was commercially utilized, and an oil boom in 1892 marked the turning point that changed the city forever. Oil provided Los Angeles with a source of cheap and clean energy, making possible the rise of new industries.

Rocking-arm pump

It's a gusher—a tower of oil streams high above the new well. Edward L Doheny's discovery of an oil field near the city's center started a frenzy of exploration in a quiet residential neighborhood. Frantic homeowners were suddenly digging holes in their lawns and backyards in hope of striking "black gold." Neatly maintained gardens were turned into muddy, greasy messes, soil was saturated with oil and wells were dug in every empty lot. Sometimes even houses were torn down to make more room for additional derricks. Three thousand oil wells were crammed into a four square-mile area. In 1907 the Echo Park Lake (➔ p174) was so saturated with oil from nearby wells that it caught fire and burned for days.

Los Angeles County still has more than 40 producing oil fields. They lie under downtown, East LA, West LA, Beverly Hills, Inglewood, Torrance, El Segundo and Long Beach. About 2,900 active wells produce some 80,000 barrels of oil daily.

In June 1921, an oil gusher erupted in on Signal Hill in Long Beach. Almost 15,000 people rushed to the scene to watch the roaring monster send a column of oil 250 feet (76 m) in the air. Alamitos No. 1, as it was called, proved the richest oil field in American history. Oil production in the area jumped from 3 million barrels in 1917 to 157 million barrels in 1923.

Signal Hill (below) turned Los Angeles into the fifth largest oil producer in the world. The forest of black derricks transformed the county's skyline and changed the destinies of locals for good (➔ p72). The value of real estate on Signal Hill skyrocketed. A house previously estimated at $15,000 was worth more than $150,000 on the first morning after the strike.

The Pioneer Oil Company stock certificate.
The company was founded in January of 1865, during the city's first oil boom. It was promoted in local newspapers as capable of generating "incalculable fortunes" for its shareholders. The boom was, however, short-lived. Of more than 70 oil companies formed between 1864 and 1867, all but one went out of business.

Carleton E Watkins's photo of California Star Oil #4 (Pico No. 4), June 26, 1877.
Designated a National Historic Landmark, the well is located in Pico Canyon in the now ghost town of Mentryville in the Santa Susana Mountains. Tapped in September 1876, this was the first commercially successful oil well in the western United States. When No. 4 was capped in September 1990, it was the longest continuously operating oil well in the world.

Edward L Doheny discovered oil in the center of Los Angeles, near the present intersection of Second St and Glendale Blvd. His find triggered the city's second oil boom and made Los Angeles the petroleum capital of the country. After Doheny found the site by following a trail of greasy sand, he and his partner, Charles Canfield, started digging a shaft with picks and shovels. They later switched to a primitive drill in the form of a sharpened eucalyptus tree trunk and finally struck oil at 200 feet (60 m) on April 20, 1893.
By the late 1910s, Doheny's vast holdings in the United States and Mexico were rumored to produce $1 million of oil every week. Edward L Doheny became one of the richest men in the world.

Aviation

Los Angeles' industrial growth was driven from the beginning by innovation and technological experimentation. More than anywhere else, this was apparent in the infant aircraft industry. Adventurous and glamorous, aviation instantly appealed to the young city. The climate was a great advantage, allowing the rising industry year-round outdoor manufacturing. High visibility and good weather meant the planes could be flight-tested throughout the year. Additional advantages were the abundance of land for fields and plants, skilled labor and visionary engineering. The aerospace industry, along with the movies, changed the city more than any other activity and contributed substantially to Southern California's economic predominance.

P-51 Mustang

The World War II fighter plane P-51 Mustang (left) was manufactured at the North American Aviation plant in Inglewood.

The Times described the meet at Dominguez Hills as "the greatest sporting event the world has, perhaps, ever witnessed."
A huge grandstand was packed with 20,000 curious observers each day. Los Angeles was fascinated with the pioneers' aerobatics and their frail devices, as the competition continued for ten days. Over $80,000 in prize money was distributed. French pilot Louis Paulhan set records in altitude with 4,165 feet (1.272 m) and endurance (1 hour, 49 minutes). Aviator Glenn Curtiss broke the world's speed record by flying 16 miles in less than 24 minutes (approximately 40 miles per hour or 64 km/h).
Not all planes, balloons and dirigibles shown on this composite photograph were in the air at the same time.

Dominguez Air Meets: the poster announcing the country's first international air show, which took place on the grounds of the Dominguez Ranch from 10 to 19 January 1910. The meet attracted 175,000 spectators and tremendously popularized the airplane.

The Douglas World Cruiser *New Orleans*, one of the original biplanes that circled the globe for the first time.
On March 17, 1924, four airplanes built by Donald Douglas took off on the first around-the-world flight from Santa Monica airport, then known as Clover Field. Two of the aircraft completed the six-month flight on September 28.

Spruce Goose, a unique Howard Hughes design, was an experimental, eight-engine plywood flying boat. With its 320-foot (98-m) wingspan, 219-foot (67-m) length and weight of 200 tons, it was the world's largest airplane. The giant ship was intended as a troop carrier, with a capacity of 750 passengers, but was never used. Its only flight took place on November 2, 1947 in Long Beach harbor, when Howard Hughes piloted it for about a mile.

A controversial billionaire industrialist, inventor and movie producer, Howard Hughes was one of the greatest aviators in American history. In the 1930s he founded Hughes Aircraft Company, which became an important defense contractor. As a test pilot for planes of his own design, Hughes set several aviation world records, including a world speed record in 1935, the transcontinental air record in 1937 and a record for around-the-world flight in 1938.

His life story is told in Martin Scorsese's biopic *The Aviator* (2004), with Leonardo DiCaprio in the title role.

The outdoor manufacturing of the twin-engine fighter Lockheed P-38 Lightning. The plane inspired the legendary automobile tail fins, which were introduced by Cadillac in 1948 (➜ p55). By 1941 Los Angeles had become a major manufacturing center. Industrial output tremendously increased under the demands of World War II. Douglas, Lockheed, Northrop, North American, Hughes and other local manufacturers furnished approximately one-third of all American aircraft produced. In a 1943 report, the Department of Labor stated, "Los Angeles has become the Detroit of the aircraft industry."

In 1920, aeronautical engineer Donald Douglas started his own company with $600 in the back room of a Santa Monica barber shop. Douglas Aircraft Company produced the Cloudster, the first airplane in history to lift a useful load exceeding its own weight. The most famous of Douglas aircraft was, however, the DC-3. During the World War II, the company manufactured more than 10,000 of these planes. It became the work horse of commercial aviation and carried freight and passengers all over the world for more than five decades.

Douglas DC-3

The Birth of Hollywood

The name Hollywood became the symbol of the American film industry and its global dominance. It all started in 1907, when the Selig Polyscope Company sent director Francis Boggs from Chicago to complete the outdoor scenes for *The Count of Monte Christo*. It was the first professional film to be shot in California.

Southern California's ideal climate and the exceptional variety of scenic backgrounds—deserts, mountains, beaches, countryside and city streets, as well as cheap rents and inexpensive labor, were all reasons moviemakers

**Nestor Company
film can**

were drawn to Los Angeles. Another, not less important reason was that some of the independents wanted to escape the armed agents of Thomas Alva Edison and his New York-based Motion Picture Patents Company, which was trying to enforce its monopoly on the various patents on film technology. Having grown steadily from humble beginnings, Hollywood quickly reached remarkable supremacy and by 1920 more than 90 percent of US feature films were produced in the Los Angeles area.

Poster for the 1922 reissue of D W Griffith's *The Birth of a Nation* (1915) promotes the movie as an "American Institution." Based on a novel about the American Civil War, the film was widely acclaimed as the first masterpiece of cinema. It turned out to be a tremendous financial success as well and the most profitable silent feature ever. The Los Angeles Chamber of Commerce claimed that *The Birth of a Nation* made "Los Angeles the permanent and recognized seat of the motion picture industry."

Director Cecil B DeMille (seated on running board) and actor Dustin Farnum (hatless, in the middle) during the filming of *The Squaw Man*. The film was released on February 15, 1914 and is considered the first feature-length motion picture filmed in Hollywood. Its cost of $47,000 was way over budget, but the five-reel picture ultimately grossed $245,000. Although no print survives, the movie's astonishing success launched DeMille's directorial career and assured a bright future for the studio, the Jesse L Lasky Feature Play Company (one of the parent companies of present day Paramount Pictures).

The converted Blondeau Tavern at 6101 Sunset Blvd served as Hollywood's first motion picture studio

The first motion picture studio in the Hollywood area was formed by the short-lived Nestor Film Company in October 1911. The English brothers David and William Horsley rented the old Blondeau Tavern, closed earlier by local sobriety boosters, at Sunset Blvd and Gower St (now the site of CBS, → p120). The brothers produced popular comedies and westerns with Al Christie as a director before the company was acquired by Universal in 1912. Their first picture in Hollywood was *The Law of the Range* (1911).

Cecil B DeMille (in the center, wearing riding boots and a light suit) during the filming of *The Squaw Man* in 1913. The photo shows the entire cast of the film in front of a rented horse barn in Hollywood (→ p152), where the picture was made. Indoor scenes were filmed outside on an improvised wooden stage, with white muslin canopies to diffuse the sun's rays. Film stock available at the time was not sensitive enough to permit indoor shooting under artificial light.

❮ The first permanent film facility in Los Angeles was built by the Chicago-based Selig Polyscope Company in 1908. The studio was set up downtown, on a vacant lot behind the Sing Loo Chinese laundry on Olive St, between Seventh and Eighth streets. The company made *The Heart of a Race Tout* there, the first full-length motion picture to be shot entirely in California.

During the 1910s a process of consolidation took place in Hollywood, with smaller pre-war companies either disappearing completely or merging into huge conglomerates. These new giant studios, which still dominate the movie industry, used the tactic of vertical integration in order to ensure their dominant position. They controlled not only movie production, but also distribution and exhibition through ownership of first-run theaters in major cities. The power in these companies remained in the hands of a small number of bosses (who all started as independent exhibitors), fabled as "movie moguls." The old "Hollywood system" broke up in the 1950s, when government action forced studios to sell off their theater chains.

World War I disrupted film production in France, Italy and Germany, practically removing European competition from the international market. Obtaining an effective monopoly by the end of the war, the US emerged as the world's leading movie producer, a position it maintains to the present day. With its enormous production capabilities, Hollywood lured a number of prominent European film professionals. Among the major creative figures (who brought with them European styles) were directors Erich von Stroheim (above), Victor Sjöström, Ernst Lubitsch and actors Charlie Chaplin, Greta Garbo and Bela Lugosi.

Hollywood Dream Factory

By the 1920s, Hollywood was firmly established as the cinema capital of the world. "The Dream Factory" was associated in the public mind with glamour and luxury, as well as scandal and pomposity. Magnificent "picture palaces" transposed moviegoers to a world of fantasy, and films offered them escape from reality to daydreams, if only for a brief 90 minutes.

Movie camera

The widely publicized lifestyles of Hollywood stars had significant influence on domestic living, fashion and style, romancing and sex. The mystique and seductive magic of the silver screen became a unique cultural phenomenon which penetrated all aspects of everyday life in America and around the world.

Tracing its beginnings to circus and theatrical productions, film posters were created when exhibitors discovered they could lure crowds into theaters by using the name or face of a movie star. They advertised the film's story and its dramatic qualities, as seen on this poster for *The Son of the Sheik* (1926) starring Rudolph Valentino as the prince of the desert.

A Hollywood-style premiere was the most glamorous and thrilling phenomenon in the world of show business. These glittering spectacles filled Hollywood streets with thousands of fans, tourists and locals alike, waiting for a glimpse of the movie stars attending the show. Bleachers were filled with spectators, searchlights pierced the skies and reporters and gossip columnists noted every arrival of celebrities in their limos, as shown in this photograph of the film premiere of the first American collaboration between Marlene Dietrich and Josef von Sternberg—*Morocco* (1930)—at Grauman's Chinese Theatre.

The original auditorium of Grauman's Egyptian Theatre, with a massive proscenium arch decorated with ancient hieroglyphics

During the 1920s and 1930s were commissioned some of the most elaborate and extravagant movie palaces ever built. Decorated in an amazing variety of exotic styles, they provided a glamorous setting for an extraordinary moviegoing experience. In their imposing first-run theaters, major studios showcased their movies in a standard program that lasted three hours and included a newsreel, shorts, a live show and a main feature.

In the early years of the American cinema the actors' true names were not revealed to the public—by mutual consent. Producers feared that the most famous players would demand a big increase in salaries. Actors, on the other hand, requested anonymity because work on film was regarded as a sign of failure in the live theater.

In 1910 producer Carl Laemmle revealed the true name of actress Florence Lawrence (left), who was formerly known only as "the Biograph Girl," announcing that she was working for his company, the IMP (Independent Motion Picture Company). This is regarded as the introduction of the star system, the dominant element in film publicity ever since.

With the creation of a star system newspapers began publishing articles on "picture personalities." The *Los Angeles Times* was the first major newspaper to run a gossip column (called "The Preview"). *The Times* writer, Stella the Stargazer, was the first gossip columnist of the film business. The first fan magazine, *Photoplay*, appeared in 1911, marking the birth of a new subsidiary industry. Other titles soon followed, feeding the insatiable need of movie fans for the news, gossip, conflicts and details of the personal lives of movie stars.

In the days before the arrival of radio and television, the popularity of top movie stars reached mythic proportions, the extent of which is difficult to imagine today. An Italian landscape gardener turned movie star, Rudolph Valentino, was the silent era's most famous screen lover. At the time of his untimely death in 1926, he enjoyed unprecedented worldwide fame which ensured him a unique place in cinema history.

Theda Bara, the first artificially created screen personality, is shown here as the heroine of *Cleopatra* (1917). Born Theodosia Goodman, her professional name was said to be an anagram of "Arab Death." Daughter of a Cincinnati tailor, she was launched by mogul William Fox, who circulated bizarre stories about her exotic origin—supposedly she was born in the desert in the shadow of the Sphinx. He also created for her the term "vamp" (from vampire). The buxom, full-figured actress became the first screen sex goddess, fascinating American audiences as a man-devouring *femme fatale* and provoking early censorship.

Lifestyles

Oscar®

The Oscar is the most valuable but least expensive item of worldwide public relations ever invented by any industry.
— **Frank Capra, director, 1936**

The Academy Awards—or Oscars, as they are traditionally called—have captured the world's imagination like no other prize ever since 1929, when the first Awards of Merit were presented. During a banquet held in the Blossom Room of the Hollywood Roosevelt Hotel (→ p115) on May 16, 1929, Academy of Motion Picture Arts and Sciences President Douglas Fairbanks officially presented the awards in twelve categories.

Oscars are today awarded for outstanding individual or collective achievements of the year in more than 20 categories. All voting for the Academy Awards is conducted by secret ballot of the entire Academy membership. Results of the balloting are tabulated by an impartial auditing firm and are kept in secret. They are not revealed until the sealed envelopes are opened on stage during the awards ceremony, followed by the famous announcement: "And the winner is . . ."

Attendance at the Annual Academy Awards at present is by invitation only. No tickets are put on public sale.

© AMPAS ®

On May 11, 1927, 300 of the most prominent names in the burgeoning movie industry gathered at a banquet in the Biltmore Hotel's Crystal Ballroom to mark the official founding of the Academy of Motion Picture Arts and Sciences (→ p216, 255). That same night, 230 of the attendees became the first members of the new organization. Among the guests were moguls Louis B Mayer and Jack Warner, directors King Vidor and Cecil B DeMille, and stars Mary Pickford and Douglas Fairbanks. Legend has it that Oscar was born during that dinner when Cedric Gibbons, MGM art director, sketched the figure on a hotel linen napkin. That sketch was later used as a model for the Oscar statuette.

The gold-platted Oscar statuette, designed in 1928 by Cedric Gibbons in the streamlined moderne style, has become one of the most famous symbols of Hollywood. It is made of brittanium and represents a knight holding a crusader's sword standing on a reel of film. The statuette is 13 1/2 inches (34 cm) tall and weighs 8 1/2 pounds (3,8 kg). The nickname "Oscar" was born in the early 1930s when the Academy's librarian Margaret Herrick supposedly remarked, "It looks like my Uncle Oscar." Actress Bette Davis and columnist Sidney Skolsky have also claimed credit for the name. The first individual to actually receive an Oscar was Emil Jannings, who was named best actor for his roles in *The Last Command* and *The Way of All Things*.

Leonardo DiCaprio and Kate Winslet star in *Titanic* (1997)

The most honored motion pictures in the history of the Academy Awards are *Ben-Hur* (1959), *Titanic* (1997) and *The Lord of the Rings: The Return of the King* (2003). Each of them received a total of eleven Academy Awards.

The most honored individual is Walt Disney, personally credited with 26 Awards. The most honored performer is Katharine Hepburn, winner of four Academy Awards for acting, all of them in the best actress category. The most honored director is John Ford, with four Awards.

The Day After: a fiberglass Oscar statue is moved after the Academy Awards ceremony. The giant statue is 24 feet (7,3 m) high and weighs 1,200 pounds (540 kg).

Telecasting brings the Awards program throughout the world to more than one billion viewers in over 100 countries. However, a couch seat is no substitute for several hundred die-hard movie fans who want to sense the full flair and glamour of the show. Those who travel from all over the globe to watch the arrivals from the bleachers and catch a glimpse of their favorite star must submit an application in advance and agree to be subject to a background check. For more information, visit www.oscars.org.

Tightly grasping her Oscar statuette for having made the outstanding picture of the year, Janet Gaynor (portraying actress Esther Blodget) gives her acceptance speech in *A Star Is Born* (1937). In real life, Gaynor made history by winning the first Academy Award ever given in the best actress category (for the 1927-28 season).

The Academy Awards are featured in numerous Hollywood films, including *A Star Is Born* (1937 and 1954), *California Suite* (1978) and *Naked Gun 33 1/3: The Final Insult* (1994).

Fashion

> I want clothes that will make people gasp when they see them. Don't design anything anybody could possibly buy in a store.
>
> — Cecil B DeMille, director

From the early days of the silent screen, movies have had an enormous impact on fashion trends around the world. During the peak era of Hollywood glamour, its top stars appeared on the covers of fashion magazines and had a great impact upon the way movie fans dressed in their everyday lives. A large number of movie costumes were copied by clothing manufacturers, who often collaborated with studios in promoting the newest trends to coincide with the release of a film.

Among the iconic looks that Hollywood invented were Greta Garbo's berets, Jean Harlow's tight satin gowns, Marlene Dietrich's trousers, Katharine Hepburn's high-necked dresses, Rita Hayworth's strapless dresses and elbow-length black satin gloves, and Esther Williams's lightweight swimsuits.

Publicity photo of Jean Harlow in a satin gown on a reclining board during filming of *Dinner at Eight* (1933).
In Hollywood costume design, look was the only thing considered; comfort and practicality were of no significance. Jean Harlow was notorious for wearing her skin-tight sheaths of bias-cut satin without underwear. Her signature gowns were often glued to her body and steamed off after filming. She had to use a padded reclining board to rest between takes without wrinkling the costume.

Of all Hollywood leading ladies, Joan Crawford had the greatest influence on women's wardrobe. The sensational ruffled-shoulder dress, designed by MGM's Adrian, which she wore in *Letty Lynton* (1932), was widely copied and so popular that Macy's department stores sold 50,000 copies. The dress influenced a fashion trend that lasted for years and was periodically revived ever since—shoulder pads.

***Femme fatale* Rita Hayworth** sings her famous song *Put the Blame on Mame* from *Gilda* (1946), while peeling off her shoulder-length satin gloves. Her iconic strapless black satin gown became the look of the decade and was reborn as Paris couture after Yves Saint Laurent saw it in the movie.

Marilyn Monroe's famous dress which billowed up over the subway vent in *The Seven Year Itch* (1955) became one of the most recognizable movie icons. The white halter-neck pleated dress was an instant hit, its versions regularly reintroduced by Bloomingdale's stores and still available today.

Glorified as the most beautiful woman of the century and famous for her clothes and world-class jewelry collection, Elizabeth Taylor left a remarkable influence on film fashion. The strapless white evening dress she wore in *A Place in the Sun* (1951) caused a sensation, and its designer, Paramount's Edith Head, received an Oscar for costume design. Department stores throughout the United States sold so many copies that a fashion writer noted, "Go to any party this summer and you'll see at least ten of them."

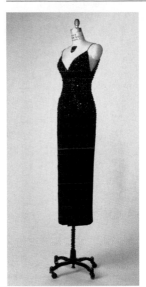

Portraying Rose in *Titanic* (1997), Kate Winslet wore *Heart of the Sea*—a fake necklace designed to look like an impossibly rare blue diamond. As it captured the imagination of romantics all over the world, Asprey London, the jeweler of England's royal family, made an original based on the film imitation. Featuring a 170-carat, heart-shaped sapphire with 65 diamonds, each 30 carats, the necklace created a sensation when Celine Dion wore it at the 1998 Academy Awards as she sang *My Heart Will Go On*—the theme song from *Titanic*. It was later auctioned for the Diana, Princess of Wales Memorial Fund, raising $2.2 million for charity.

During the 47 years of his amazingly successful career, Los Angeles-based James Galanos gained a reputation as one of the world's finest fashion designers. This self-conscious perfectionist, who won every important fashion award in the world, created glamorous ready-to-wear clothes for some of the America's most famous celebrities and socialites. Marlene Dietrich, Dorothy Lamour, Judy Garland, Loretta Young, Rosalind Russell and Diana Ross all wore Galanos.

In her Oscar-winning role as a high-class prostitute in *Butterfield 8* (1960), Liz Taylor wore a beautiful tight slip, turning this traditional garment into the hottest fashion item.

One of the most innovative and controversial American designers, Austrian-born Rudi Gernreich made one of the greatest sensations in American fashion history in 1964. From his Santa Monica Boulevard headquarters, Gernreich and his model Peggy Moffitt launched a stunning topless bathing suit. Although designed as a social statement aimed to free women of body-restraining clothes, the suit was widely criticized as scandalous and banned around the world. It united Kremlin and Vatican for the first time, after both *Izvestiya* and *L'Osservatore Romano* condemned the suit, agreeing that it was immoral.

Realizing that Hollywood stars have so much power to influence fashion, Giorgio Armani introduced an entirely new strategy in the 1980s when he proposed to dress celebrities for the Academy Awards. Jodie Foster, Michelle Pfeiffer, Anjelica Huston, Faye Dunaway and other stars dressed in his sleek designs, signaling the return of the old Hollywood glamour. Los Angeles became so essential to the fashion business that the Council of Fashion Designers of America declared the Academy Awards "the world's most glamorous fashion show."

Designers are well aware that the red carpet exposure could mean immediate global recognition and millions of dollars in sales. When Oscar-nominated actress Uma Thurman wore this stunning gown by an unknown company in 1995, the name Prada instantly became famous worldwide.

The 1977 smash hit *Saturday Night Fever* started a global disco craze and turned street fashion into a world-wide phenomenon. John Travolta's famous disco suit, as reported by *Newsweek* in 1978, took the place of jeans as men's leisurewear of choice. The original white polyester suit was purchased in 1980 by the film critic Gene Siskel for $2,000. When it was auctioned at Christie's in the early 1990s, it brought in $150,000.

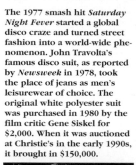

In the 1950s teenagers, who became Hollywood's most important audience, rejected the classic look of their parents and invented their own. In *The Wild One* (1955), Marlon Brando personified a "bad boy" look wearing blue jeans and leather jackets.

His T-shirts in *A Streetcar Named Desire* (1951) were so popular that he declared: "I could've made more money if I'd sold torn T-shirts with my name on them . . . they would have sold a million."

The rebellious image of the 1950s was epitomized by James Dean's casual look in *Rebel Without a Cause* (1955). His simple red jacket had great impact as his disregard for fashion influenced menswear for decades.

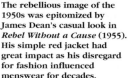

Rudolph Valentino wears his signature Cartier Tank wristwatch in *The Son of the Sheik* (1926). Cartier Tank watches were inspired by World War I tanks and appeared on the market in 1919. They achieved great popularity in the late 1920s, when the movie made people who wore the cumbersome pocket watch suddenly switch to the watch on their wrist.

When Clark Gable showed his bare chest in *It Happened One Night* (1934) revealing that he is not wearing a T-shirt, sales of men's undershirts dropped by 75 percent. In another example of a film's influence on American society, Claudette Colbert, the film's leading actress, helped popularize pajamas for women.

American Gigolo (1980) caused a fashion revolution, launching the Armani look internationally and reestablishing a well-tailored suit as a status symbol and an indispensable part of a man's wardrobe. Giorgio Armani's glamorous costuming for Richard Gere introduced a new standard of how a stylish man is supposed to dress.

Max Factor

With his background as cosmetician to the Russian Imperial Court, young immigrant Max Factor opened a small shop in downtown's theater district. During his long career, he came up with more makeup "firsts" than anyone else in the history of cosmetics. Factor devised many of the trademark looks that made movie stars famous: Phyllis Haver's

Supreme Greasepaint

false eyelashes, Jean Harlow's platinum blonde hair and Clara Bow's "Cupid's Bow Lips." Max Factor revolutionized Hollywood glamour and inspired the world-wide craze for cosmetic products with such innovations as the principle of "Color Harmony," lip gloss, lipstick, "Pan-Cake" make-up, false eyelashes created of human hair, and body makeup.

Max Factor created the first wig fashioned completely of human hair used in a motion picture. When actor Dustin Farnum fell in the water wearing it during the shooting of *The Squaw Man* (1914) and nearly drowned, the wig was saved first. Factor's revolutionary hairlace wigs created the illusion of natural-looking hairlines for the first time.
The company hand made over 2,000 wigs for the period spectacle *Marie Antoinette* (1938), including 18 wigs made of pure white human hair for Norma Shearer in her title role.

When Joan Crawford wanted to change her flapper screen image, Max Factor smeared lipstick across her lips creating a style called "Hunter's Bow Lips," which became the actress's trademark look

A mechanical osculator, called "the kissing machine," was designed in the 1930s to test the relative adhesive powers of experimental lipstick formulas.

Max Factor checking the make-up of actress Paulette Goddard. In 1914 Max Factor perfected "Supreme Greasepaint," the first make-up designed specifically for the movies. It was in cream form, thin and very flexible, allowing slapstick comedians (its first customers) greater facial expression. Film actors previously were dependent on the heavy stick make-up designed for theatre use, which quickly dried and cracked under strong artificial lights. Factor was the first to introduce to the general public items which were available only for film professionals, such as lip gloss and lip brush, and eyeshadow and eyebrow pencil. Almost every cosmetic product on the market today was developed for the film industry.

The beauty calibrator, a face-measuring device invented in 1932, enabled Hollywood make-up artists to pinpoint facial corrections that had to be made. Although Max Factor measured hundreds of screen beauties, he never found a perfect face,

When Max Factor began distribution of his make-up products to the general public, he promised middle-class American women the look of movie stars. Countless Hollywood celebrities provided invaluable endorsements (for the incredible sum of one dollar!), fulfilling their contractual obligations to the studio. The ads featured actresses applying Max Factor make-up and also promoted their latest film.

Los Angeles and the Automobile

Los Angeles is the only major city fundamentally shaped by the automobile. The advent of the motor car had an extensive impact on the city's growth and continues to influence the development of the whole region. In 1915 LA County became the world's leader in per capita automobile ownership. Today, with some 9 million cars and trucks distributed among its 11 million residents, it still leads the world. The automobile transformed LA from a city with a dominant central business district to a decentralized metropolitan area with several commercial centers. Although the automobile enhanced personal freedom and improved mobility, car dependence brought numerous side-effects, including legendary smog pollution and traffic congestion, as well as drive-by shootings and carjacking.

Richfield gas pump

In 1920, when real estate developer A W Ross acquired 18 acres (7 ha) of bean fields to build the first shopping center not located on the trolley line, his venture was called "Ross's Folly." Yet, Ross successfully assumed that shoppers would drive four miles to stores to avoid downtown traffic congestion. Known as the Miracle Mile, this stretch of Wilshire Boulevard between La Brea and Fairfax avenues was the first shopping district in the world specifically designed for customers arriving by car. Providing ample off-street parking, Miracle Mile stores were the first to turn their principal entrances to back parking lot rather than to the sidewalk (➔ p217).

The main entrance to the Bullocks Wilshire department store, viewed from the parking lot

Although the concept did not originate here, freeways represent the single most important feature of the Los Angeles cityscape. Since the opening of the Arroyo Seco Parkway in 1940, the city's freeways have expanded into a complex network, extending for hundreds of miles over the LA basin. An amazingly innovative and much photographed four-level interchange in downtown LA was opened in 1953. The "stack" was the first in the world to integrate freeway travel in four different directions. Today it carries about 350,000 vehicles a day.

The Martian attack in the movie *War of the Worlds* (1953) was staged on this interchange.

Because Los Angeles adopted the automobile as its principal means of transportation earlier than most other cities, it quickly established its reputation as a leader in automobile-related innovations. One of the most important local inventions was the super service station. In addition to the sale of gas and oil, this new concept offered considerable convenience to customers, such as repair services, lubrication and sale of tires, batteries and other accessories. Another local innovation was the "Gas-a-teria," a self-service gas station which was quickly copied throughout the state and the country.

The trendy design and convertible roof of this 1959 Cadillac Eldorado perfectly served the independent and casual lifestyle of Southern California. It sported stylish accessories, such as chrome bumpers, the wrap-around windshield and white sidewall tires.

Legendary tail fins, introduced by Cadillac in 1948, were the brain child of Harley Earl, a Los Angeles native and head of styling for General Motors for over three decades. He was inspired by a World War II fighter plane, the Lockheed P-38 Lightning, which was manufactured locally (→ p41). The tail fins grew from relatively modest beginnings to enormous size, appearing on almost every line of cars between 1948 and 1965.

The first automobiles fit exceptionally well to the Los Angeles area's climate and topography. Open and unheated cars could be used year round, and the relatively flat terrain was ideal for early vehicles, which had a hard time driving uphill. Recreational touring was the first widespread function of cars. Southern California was promoted as a tourist heaven and the automobile replaced the street car as the favored recreational vehicle.

A tourist car on this vintage post card drives through the water at Eastlake Park, demonstrating the region's capabilities as a winter resort (ca. 1910).

Chapman Park Market (→ p214).

During the 1920s, a completely new concept was developed locally that revolutionized retail business. Called drive-ins, hundreds of these establishments catering to motorists were built in the LA area, more than anywhere else in the world. There were drive-in restaurants, drive-through florists and dry cleaners, drive-up churches and bank teller windows (the nation's first bank designed as a drive-in was built in Vernon). The word "motel" was first used in 1925 by a local architectural firm and the word "supermarket" was coined here in 1927.

Los Angeles Car Culture

Nowhere else is America's love affair with the automobile more visible than in Los Angeles. Car ownership is an integral part of an Angeleno's identity and the type of vehicle one drives became an important expression of individuality. During the 1950s and 1960s a popular new movement developed, as young people raced in dragsters, customized their cars

parking meter

and cruised LA boulevards listening to their loud car radios. It was the subject of numerous movies, including *Rebel Without a Cause* (1955) and the 1964 cult film *Kustom Kar Kommandos*. The local car culture, as it was depicted in motion pictures, contributed to the idealized image of the city and influenced popular imagination around the world.

To attract the attention of motorists in fast-moving cars, advertisers started to rely on roadside billboards of enormous size. This new form of advertising, whose scale perfectly fitted the LA cityscape, conveyed a commercial message directly to passengers and permanently changed the appearance of the city.

Back Street Dodge '38 (1964) by Ed Kienholz. Probably the most famous of Edward Kienholz's works, this assemblage features an actual 1938 Dodge automobile whose body had been cut down and foreshortened. On the back seat are life-size figures of a couple in a sexual embrace, with empty beer bottles scattered around. The work reflects the artist's own adolescent experience from the 1940s when he used his father's car for the same purpose. When first exhibited at LACMA in 1966, the work caused a huge controversy—an enraged county supervisor threatened to shut the museum down. Again in 1999, a museum docent was fired for showing the work to fifth-grade girls, but was later reinstated.

Hot Rod Race (1976) by Robert Williams. Southern California car culture became a favorite theme with many local artists who were fascinated with the world of speed and powerful machines. As one of the genuine visual forms of the 20th century, the automobile has inspired painters, sculptors, designers and photographers who utilized a variety of media to create widely diversed works of art.

Lowriding originated in Latino communities in the years following World War II. Instead of being "fast and furious" like hot-rodders, lowriders distinguished themselves by driving "low and slow." The cars were so lowered that their bumpers almost touched the ground. (Before elaborate hydraulics was developed, this was achieved by filling the trunk with bags of cement.) Considered by some to be works of art, lowriders feature mural-like paintings, glass etchings, chromed parts and upholstered interiors. Their enduring popularity made them status symbols among Mexican-Americans.

One of the most awarded lowriders is El Corazón, the apple-red 1951 Chevrolet Coupe built by Mario DeAlba Sr.

One of the cult youth films of the fifties, *Rebel Without a Cause* (1955), depicts restless teenagers engaged in various forms of physical combat, including a deadly "chicken run." Racing in stolen automobiles toward the brink of a cliff, the first driver to jump out of his car was considered a "chicken" or coward.

The celebrated 1951 Mercury Club Coupe (above) was customized by Sam and George Barris for customer Bob Hirohata. The car's top was chopped and all doors, hood and trunk corners were rounded, thus achieving a smooth, streamlined look. Stripped of all excessive ornamentation, it was finished with several coats of hand rubbed lacquer paint in foam green and organic toners.

In the early 1960s, Barris introduced his own line of paint featuring the distinctive translucent, metal-flecked look. Called Kandy Kolors, with names such as Kandy Apple Red and Kandy Tangerine, the lavish paint was immortalized in this description:

"The main thing you notice is the color—tangerine flake. This paint—one of Barris' Kandy Kolor concoctions—makes the car look like it has been encrusted with chips of some kind of semi-precious ossified tangerine, all coated with a half-inch of clear lacquer."

— Tom Wolfe,
The Kandy-Kolored Tangerine Flake Streamlined Baby (1965)

One of the most famous artists associated with the Southern California car culture was Kenny Howard, universally known as Von Dutch. He is considered the father of freestyle pinstriping. Inspired by painted decorations on World War II fighter planes, he was the first artist to paint flames on cars and motorcycles. People from all over the country came to him to have their cars "Dutched." His logo—a bloodshot winged eyeball—today adorns the Von Dutch fashion line.

Cars as Stars

Famous director Cecil B DeMille noted that both the automobile and the movies captured Americans' special "love of motion and speed." Already established as a part of everyday life when the film industry arrived, the automobile has always been one of its favorite subjects. Movie screens around the country and the world showed everything that took place on the LA street scene, influencing the ways people used their cars everywhere. The automobile became a routine part

Cobra hood ornament

of the Hollywood lifestyle beginning in the early days of the film industry. Hollywood's publicity machine required that actors project to the public the celebrity image, and that included driving some of the most spectacular and desirable automobiles ever made. From Clark Gable in his 1935 Duesenberg SJ roadster, Marilyn Monroe in 1955 Lincoln Capri to Arnold Schwarzenegger in his Hummer, stars could always be spotted driving their luscious cars along Los Angeles boulevards.

A local passion for speed was manifested in early road and track races, the first of which took place in 1908 in Playa del Rey. Hot-rodding was born in Los Angeles in the 1920s out of a desire to gain maximum acceleration and speed from "stock" automobiles.

In the 1930s and 1940s another sport gained popularity in Southern California—racing on the dry lake beds of the Mojave desert. Illegal street racing, popular during the 1940s, was abandoned after the establishment of the first regular drag-strips, another local novelty.

In Los Angeles the sport of midget auto racing was also pioneered, a forerunner of today's stock-car racing.

Drag racing was born on the streets of Southern California in the 1940s. The concrete bed of the Los Angeles River was the frequent stage for drag racers' competitions.

In the film *Grease* (1978), set in the late 1950s, John Travolta as a high school "greaser" takes part in a hot rod race on the concrete channel of the Los Angeles River

The first drive-in movie theater was built in Camden, New Jersey, in 1933. Los Angeles, however, quickly followed and built the second example of this union of cars and movies.

Located at the corner of Pico and Westwood boulevards, the Picwood Theater (above), as it was called, lured motorists to "sit in your car, see and hear talking pictures on the world's largest screen." Merging comfort and entertainment in a uniquely American fashion, the drive-in theater reached the peak of its popularity in the 1950s and 1960s. During that period one-quarter of film profits came from drive-ins.

1923 Avions Voisin C5 Sporting Victoria, owned by silent film star Rudolph Valentino.
The custom-bodied car was purchased in Paris at the cost of $14,000. Valentino kept it at his mansion, Falcon Lair in Beverly Hills (→ p466), until his death in 1926.
The car's most distinguished feature is a silver-plated, coiled cobra hood ornament (→ p58), said to be a gift from celebrity friends Douglas Fairbanks and Mary Pickford. It was presented to Valentino upon the completion of his film *Cobra* (1925). Widely regarded a publicity stunt to promote the movie, it quickly became one of the most prominent hood ornaments of its time.

Clark Gable, posing by his 1940 Hudson, demonstrates movie stars' affection for gorgeous cars

Los Angeles leads the world in the number of bizarre and eccentric cars seen on its streets. One of the unusual examples is this 1948 Chrysler Town and Country convertible, specially modified for Leo Carrillo, the star of *The Cisco Kid* television show. Custom touches include a hood-mounted steer head with eyes that light and specially mixed paint to match the color of Carillo's palomino pony. The actor drove this car frequently in parades and to publicity events.

The art of car body customizing was born in LA, originating with the Southern California hot rod scene and reaching its peak in the decade after World War II. Those who admired the sheer look (and wanted their automobiles to appear unique and expensive) had their cars customized at small local shops, which produced an amazing range of fantasy vehicles. One of the most famous pioneers was George Barris, best known as the King of the Kustomizers. He is credited with the first use of the word custom spelled with a "K". Among his legendary achievements were General Lee from *The Dukes of Hazzard*, famously upholstered Mustangs for Sonny and Cher, the Porsche in which James Dean was killed, as well as hundreds of other cars designed for movies, TV shows or extravagant owners. (→ p339).

Designed by George Barris, Batmobile II was driven by Michael Keaton in *Batman* (1989) and *Batman Returns* (1993). The hood-mounted intakes were formed from parts of a Rolls-Royce jet engine and turbine blades in the nose piece were scavenged from a British Harrier fighter jet.

Life's a Beach

Los Angeles County's 70 miles (112 km) of coastline and 31 miles (50 km) of life-guarded beaches attract more than 60 million people each year. The remarkable geographical diversity of local coast—sandy beaches, rocky cliffs, secluded coves, towering bluffs, wetlands and tide pools—is well worth exploring.

Life preserver

The beach is the most enduring symbol of the relaxed, carefree lifestyle widely associated with Los Angeles. To the rest of the world, the city is a year-round playground for glamorous young men and women who show off their tanned bodies under the perpetually sunny skies.

The Los Angeles County lifeguard force consists of 137 full-time and some 600 seasonal guards. Millions of annual beachgoers keep lifeguards busy performing on the average 10,000 rescues every year. Lifeguards give information about the surf conditions and provide safety instructions and first-aid treatment. For young and inexperienced swimmers, usually the safest precaution is to play in the water nearest to lifeguard towers. Several hundred of these distinctive grey huts dot the county coastline. They have been made famous around the world by the popular TV beach drama *Baywatch*. For safety tips and precautionary measures, call lifeguards at ☎(310) 577-5700, or visit their web site at www.lacofd.org.

Stretching along the rocky shorelines, tide pools are a diverse marine habitat that offer a perfect hiding place from predators to such sea creatures as crabs and small fish. When the water recedes, a search through the tide pools can reveal a variety of aquatic life including many species of sea stars, sea urchins, sea anemones, octopus, mussels, as well as algae and sea grass. Among the most popular spots for tide pooling are Cabrillo Beach, the coast of the Palos Verdes Peninsula, Leo Carrillo State Beach and Paradise Cove Beach. Also see Aquarium of the Pacific and Cabrillo Marine Aquarium, which conducts guided tours of the tide pools. For information on daily low and high tide times, call ☎(310) 457-9701.

Popular whale tail license plates raise funds for coastal preservation, coastal access trails and wetland restoration

During the 1960s, a series of movies was made that depicted the Southern California youth subculture. This artificial, utopian world was an ideal setting for youthful romance, dreams of freedom and a jovial life. The best-known of these beach frolic films is *Beach Blanket Bingo* (1965), starring teen favorites Frankie Avalon and Annette Funicello.

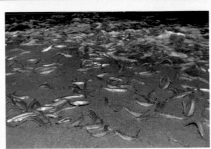

These small, silvery fish are famous for their extraordinary mating ritual, which occurs on sandy beaches between late February and early September. Grunion (*Leuresthes tenuis*) come ashore to spawn, but only during the highest tides of the month, two to six nights after the full and new moons. The female digs her body into the wet sand and lays between 1,600 and 3,600 eggs. Several males curve around her and release milt, which fertilizes the eggs.

Grunion may be collected by hand only; persons 16 years and older need a valid California fishing license. For future run dates and more grunion facts visit www.dfg.ca.gov (Department of Fish and Game). Cabrillo Marine Aquarium offers a grunion run program (→ p400).

During the winter, California coastal waters are the site of the longest natural migration in the world: the Pacific gray whale's annual round trip of up to 14,000 miles (22,000 km). In December and January, nearly 26,000 sea mammals travel from their summer feeding grounds in the chilly seas near Alaska all the way down to Mexico's Baja California. In the warm waters of Baja's lagoons, they give birth and nurse their newborns, and from February to early April, they swim back north. The whales can be seen from several observation points on the shore or during whale watching boat cruises which depart daily from harbors in the LA area. For more details, call the American Cetacean Society at ☎(310) 548-6279 or visit www.acs-la.org.

Surf's Up

Surfing was an ancient Hawaiian sport practiced for 400 years by the island's royalty and nobility. It was introduced to California in 1907 by Hawaiian surfer George Freeth. He was hired by Henry Huntington, the owner of the Pacific Electric Railway, to draw the masses to Redondo Beach, the final destination on his newly opened trolley line. Here Freeth

Surfboard

delighted crowds conducting surfing demonstrations on his 10-foot (3-m), 200-pound (90-kg), solid wood board. Dormant for decades, the sport boomed in the 1950s when new synthetic materials made the surfboard lighter. Surfing culture as a California phenomenon was widely popularized by countless songs, films and television productions.

Gidget (1959) was the landmark movie that started the surfing craze and generated several sequels and popular TV series. The film was based on the novel by Frederick Kohner, who described the experiences his daughter had as a young surfer and beach groupie in Malibu. *Big Wednesday* (1978), the cult film among the surfers themselves, is a story of three friends growing up in Malibu during the 1960s, waiting for the ultimate wave. *Point Break* (1991) is the surfer thriller about a cop infiltrating the beach community in search of bank robbers.

Heal the Bay

The environmental group Heal the Bay regularly monitors and rates water quality at Southern California beaches. Their annual report card, that assigns each beach a letter grade of A to F, is available online at www.healthebay.org or call ☎(800) 432-5229.

Danger signs posted along the waterfront warn swimmers to enter the surf at their own risk. Water quality plummets when rains cause sewage spills and wash pollutants down storm drains and out to the ocean. Health officials recommend that beachgoers avoid contact with coastal water during rainstorms and for three days afterward.

For beach safety tips check www.cslsa.org (California Surf Lifesaving Association).

Inspired by the idyllic youth culture, the new sound originated in Los Angeles in the early 1960s. Created by Dick Dale and his Del-Tones, this style of rock and roll was widely popularized by such local bands as the Beach Boys and Jan & Dean. Although the Beach Boys spearheaded the surf-dancing craze and were the most popular of all surf bands, Jan & Dean were the most durable. Cover art for Dick Dale's first album introduced the images which later became icons of Southern California beach culture—surfboards, bikinis and "woodies."

Lobby card for *Gidget* (1959)

California law guarantees public access to any beach seaward of the "mean high tide line." To protect their privacy, some wealthy homeowners put up "private property" signs and hire security guards on all-terrain vehicles to harass beachgoers. Since only the State Lands Commission can establish where the exact line in the sand is, the boundaries these signs proclaim are irrelevant for enforcement purposes. Many of them even stand on properties that have public easements, so dedicated by the owners in exchange for permissions to expand or remodel their homes. So do not get intimidated by these questionable signs and enjoy your public beaches.

The California Coastal Commission posts detailed information about exact location of "public access easements" on its website, www.coastal.ca.gov.

Pink Whale (1987) by Peter Schroff.
In this unusual piece surfing found its way into art as the artist converted a 15-foot-long board into a home entertainment center complete with a radio, a TV and an aquarium.

During the late 1950s and 1960s, wood-bodied cars became the utility vehicle of choice for young California surfers. Bought inexpensively as used cars, they quickly became synonymous with easygoing beach lifestyle. Woodies were particularly convenient for carrying long surfboards and other bulky gear.

Kite surfing (also called kite boarding) is the newest craze to hit Los Angeles beaches. Powered by strong winds and kites that resemble parachutes, the riders are carried through the swells at speeds that can reach 50 mph (80 km/h).

Maneuvering his kite which flies 120 ft (40 m) overhead, a kite surfer glides across the waters at Topanga State Beach. Other popular beaches among kite surfers are Leo Carrillo, Point Dume, Zuma and Belmont Shore in Long Beach.

Events and Festivals

Los Angeles offers a myriad of events throughout the year. There is something for everyone—including more than 170 ethnic festivals that celebrate different heritages and traditions, reflecting the unparealled diversity of the city. There is also an enormous array of cultural events, from visual arts, literature, dance and folk art to international film and music festivals.

The following are some of the most popular events; a free booklet *Los Angeles Festival Guide* offers a comprehensive listing. For information call ☎(213) 473-7700 or visit **www**.culturela.org.

January

Tournament of Roses Parade and Football Game
Jan 1, Pasadena.
The historic festival featuring floral floats, equestrian units and marching bands is followed by the Rose Bowl football game (➔ p306).

Whale watching
Jan-Mar, coastal area.
This is the peak season for watching the gray whales' annual migration (➔ p61).

February

Chinese New Year
Feb, Chinatown.
☎(213) 680-0243.
www.chinatownla.org

The festival includes the Golden Dragon parade featuring magical lion and dragon dancers, decorated floats and a beauty pageant.

Pan African Film and Arts Festival
Feb, Baldwin Hills.
☎(213) 896-8221.
www.paff.org

The largest Black film festival in America screens over 100 films from all over the world. Also featured are art exhibits, children's events, poetry readings and fashion shows.

Mardi Gras
Feb, Olvera Str, downtown.
☎(213) 485-9769
www.cityofla.org/elp/olvera.html

Celebrations of traditional "Fat Tuesday" include music, singing, dancing and a colorful parade.

March

Academy Awards
Early Mar, Kodak Theatre.
The world-famous ceremony takes place at its new home in Hollywood (➔ p116).

Los Angeles Marathon
Early Mar, citywide.
☎(310) 444-5544.
www. lamarathon.com

The Cardinal blesses the animals as they go by in a procession

This street-clogging extravaganza draws 30,000 runners and a million spectators.

California Poppy Reserve
Mid-Mar to May, Antelope Valley.
☎(661) 723-6077.
www.poppyfestival.com

Staggering panoramas of red and orange wildflower fields await visitors during the poppy blooming season.

Blessing of the Animals
Day before Easter, downtown.
☎(213) 680-2525.

Continuing a Mexican tradition, the Cardinal of Los Angeles sprinkles with holy water all kinds of domestic animals and pets.

Chinese New Year celebration in Chinatown

Masked participants of the Mardi Gras parade

Traditional Thai dancers performing at Songkran Festival

Venice Art Walk
May, Venice.

This self-guided tour through artists' studios raises funds for the Venice Family Clinic (➔ p390).

Van Nuys Airport Aviation Expo
Jun, Van Nuys Airport,

One of the most popular air shows in the country features rare vintage aircraft as well as some of the most advanced flying machines in the arsenal today (➔ p348).

April

Songkran Festival
Apr, Hollywood Blvd.
☎(818) 913-8999.
www.thainewyear.com

The Thai New Year celebration features traditional ceremonies, a cultural parade, stage performances and Thai boxing demonstrations.

A dancer at Cinco de Mayo

Toyota Grand Prix
Apr, Long Beach.
☎(562) 981-2600.
www.longbeachgp.com

The largest race car competition in the United States draws top American and international drivers.

Festival of Books
Apr, UCLA campus.
☎(800) 528-4637.

A weekend-long gathering of writers, poets, publishers and storytellers celebrates the love of reading.

May

Cinco de Mayo
May 5, El Pueblo de Los Angeles Historic Monument, downtown.
☎(213) 485-9769.
www.cityofla.org/elp/olvera.html

This is one of the most widespread festivals in Los Angeles, celebrating Mexico's victory over the French forces in Puebla in 1862. It includes countless fiestas with mariachi, folklorico bands, puppets and carnivals.

Pacific Islander Festival
May, Wilmington.
☎(714) 968-1785.
www.hiccsc.org/members/picc

Communities from Hawaii, Samoa, Tonga, Fiji, Guam, Tahiti, New Zealand, Cook and Marshall Islands celebrate their indigenous cultures with traditional music, dance, and arts and crafts.

F-117A stealth fighter on display at the Van Nuys Airport Aviation Expo

Mariachi USA Festival
Jun, Hollywood Bowl.
☎(800) MARIACHI II
www.mariachiusa.com

One of the largest mariachi festivals in the world, this is a spectacular celebration of Mexican culture and tradition featuring the finest mariachi music, ballet folklorico and special performances. The extravaganza culminates with a breathtaking fireworks finale.

A mariachi band performs at the annual festival

Re-creation of LA's first Independence Day celebration in 1847

African Marketplace and Cultural Faire
Aug, Rancho Cienega Park.
☎(323) 734-1164.
www.africanmarketplace.org.

This annual celebration of the African diaspora features festivals and performances that represent 20 Pan African cultures and 40 countries.

September

Watts Towers Day of the Drum and Jazz Festival
Sep, Watts Towers Arts Center.
☎(213)847-4646.
www.wattstowers.com

Costumed participant in the Nisei Week Grand Parade

July

Independence Day
July 4, Hill Str, downtown.
History buffs dressed as soldiers in period garb re-create the first Independence Day celebration in Los Angeles in 1847. As part of a holiday celebration, there are some 50 fireworks displays across the city.

Festival of the Chariots

Lotus Festival
Jul, Echo Park.
☎(213) 485-1310.
www.laparks.org
Celebrating the people and cultures of Asia and the Pacific Islands, the festival features a carnival, a variety of cultural entertainment and dragon boat races.

Blessing of the Cars
Jul, Verdugo Park, Glendale.
www.blessingofthecars.com

As with the Blessing of the Animals, car-loving Angelenos bring any vehicle that can be moved to this event.

August

Nisei Week
Aug, Little Tokyo, downtown.
☎(213) 687-7193.
www.niseiweek.org
Los Angeles' oldest ethnic festival celebrates Japanese culture and heritage. Major events include the Grand Parade, Queen coronation and Taiko drumming.

Festival of the Chariots
Aug, Venice Beach Pavilion Park.
☎(310) 836-2676.
www.festivalofchariots.com
Based on a 2,000-year-old Hindu ceremony, the three colorful chariots drawn in the parade represent effigies of Krishna and his siblings.

This extravaganza features a wide range of international drumming, including Afro-Cuban folkloricos, Jamaican steel drummers, Afro-Brazilian percussion ensembles, East Indian tabla players and American jazz drummers.

A performer at Day of the Drum and Jazz Festival

October

The International Festival of Masks
Oct, Hancock Park.
☎(323) 937- 4230.
www.culturela.org

This annual festival honors and celebrates traditional mask making, with contibutions from over 75 communities throughout Los Angeles

West Hollywood Halloween Costume Carnival
Oct, Santa Monica Blvd.
☎(310) 289-2525.
www.visitwesthollywood.com

Halloween Costume Carnival

Participants dressed in drag and other eccentric costumes join comedians, musicians and entertainers for this street celebration.

Día de los Muertos
Oct, Olvera Str, downtown.
☎(213) 624-3660.
www.cityofla.org/elp/olvera.html

The traditional candlelight procession of Las Posadas

Day of the Dead is celebrated with decorated altars, ceremonial dances, walking skeletons (*calavera*) and a candlelight procession. This annual Mexican ritual honoring the dead takes place all over the city.

November

Sejat Spirit Pow Wow
Nov, Santa Fe Springs.
☎(562) 946-6476

This celebration of Native American culture pays tribute to the Tongva, a local indigenous tribe. Dancers, drummers and singers from Navajo, Pueblo and Luiseño nations also participate.

Doo Dah Parade
Nov, Pasadena.
This spoof at the Rose Parade features such favorites as the Lounge Lizards and drag cheerleaders from West Hollywood (➔ p301).

December

Hollywood Christmas Parade
Dec, Hollywood.
☎(323) 469-2337.
www.hollywoodchristmas.com

This traditional event features B-list celebrities, equestrians, marching bands, floats and, of course, Santa Claus.

A dancer at Pow Wow

Las Posadas
Dec, El Pueblo de Los Angeles Historic Monument, downtown.
☎(213) 485-9769.
www.cityofla.org/elp/olvera.html

This annual candlelight procession reenacts the biblical story of the nine-day search of Mary and Joseph for lodging in Bethlehem before the birth of Jesus. The centuries-old tradition features participants dressed in typical festive costumes, singing hymns and songs as they go door to door seeking shelter.

Day of the Dead is celebrated with faces painted like skeletons

Jamie Foxx

Paris Hilton

Stargazing

In this ultimate celebrity town, it is not difficult to spot a star. A great place to catch them in action is at movie premieres. Another surefire place is a major studio, where you can attend a taping of a TV show. Shop along Rodeo Dr, Montana Ave and at the Grove and you will probably run into someone famous. Celebrities will pop up at power lunch or dinner at hot spots such as Spago, The Ivy, Matsuhisa and Mortons. You are sure to see a star if you go to their favorite hotels and clubs (the obvious

Reese Witherspoon

Demi Moore

Alicia Keys

Kristin Davis

Jennifer Lopez

Mena Suvari

Tom Cruise

choices are the Beverly Hills Hotel, Hotel Bel Air and Château Marmont). You may watch celebrities receive stars on the Hollywood Walk of Fame. You may also attend gallery openings, book signings and charitable events, all frequented by celebrities. Location filming on the streets of Los Angeles is another opportunity to view famous faces up close.

For more information, check www.seeing-stars.com—the best guide to star spotting and celebrity-studded events.

Brooke Shields

Charlize Theron

Scarlett Johansson

Ziyi Zhang

Jake Gyllenhaal

Nicole Kidman

Kate Beckinsale

Sharon Stone

Salma Hayek

Culture

Los Angeles in Fiction

Los Angeles fiction traces its beginnings to Helen Hunt Jackson and her novel *Ramona* (1884), a highly romanticized version of life in early California. The greater part of fiction about the city was created by writers who came here from other parts of the country. The booming film industry attracted many famous names, including F Scott Fitzgerald, William Saroyan and Norman Mailer, who came to Hollywood to work as screenwriters.

By the eve of World War II, a diverse group of European intelectuals also found their home in LA. Among the prominent novelists were Englishmen Christopher Isherwood and Aldous Huxley, and German exiles Bertolt Brecht and Thomas Mann, who conceived and wrote his major work, *Doctor Faustus* (1947), while residing here. The presence of such outstanding figures helped establish Los Angeles as a major literary center.

Upton Sinclair (1878-1968)

A prolific journalist and author of ninety books, Sinclair was a vocal advocate for socialist causes. He even ran for governor of California in 1934, but was defeated after a smear campaign spearheaded by Harry Chandler of the *Los Angeles Times* and MGM head, Louis B Mayer. Inspired by the oil scandals of the 1920s, Sinclair's novel *Oil!* (1927) traces the rise and fall of independent oil operators during the Signal Hill oil boom (➜ p38).

There she came! There was a cheer from all hands, and the spectators went flying to avoid the oily spray blown by the wind. They let her shoot for a while, until the water had been ejected; higher and higher, way up over the derrick—she made a lovely noise, hissing and splashing, bouncing up and down!

It was just at sundown, and the sky was crimson. "Lights out!" Dad kept calling—nobody must even start a motor-car while she was spouting. Presently they shut her off, to try the valve of the casing-head; they worked on, late into the night, letting her spout, and then shutting her off again; it was mysteriously thrilling in the darkness. At last they were ready to "bring her in"—which meant they would screw up the "flow-line" between the casing-head and the tank, and let the oil run into the latter. Just as simple as that—no show, no fuss, you just let her flow; the gauge showed her coming at the rate of thirty thousand gallons every hour, which meant that the first tank was full by noon the next day.

Yes, that was all; but the news affected Beach City as if an angel had appeared in a shining cloud and scattered twenty-dollar gold pieces over the streets. You see, Ross-Bankside No. 1 "proved up" the whole north slope; to tens of thousands of investors, big and little, it meant that a hope was turned into glorious certainty. You couldn't keep such news quiet, it just didn't lie in the possibility of human nature not to tell; the newspapers bulletined the details—Ross-Bankside was flowing sixteen thousand barrels a day, and the gravity was 32, and as soon as the pipe-line was completed—which would be by the end of the week—its owner would be in possession of an income of something over twenty thousand dollars every twenty-four hours.

Oil! (1927) by Upton Sinclair

A vintage post card depicting California oil wells on fire

William Faulkner (1897-1962)

The great novelist, who won the Nobel Prize for Literature in 1949, first came to Los Angeles to write for the movies in 1932. Although he deplored Hollywood, calling it "a kind of purgatory, a place where it was necessary to come from time to time to do penance," he went back and forth many times between LA and his home in Mississippi. Faulkner made notable contributions to such Howard Hawks films as *To Have and Have Not* (1945) and *The Big Sleep* (1946). Several of his own works were brought to the screen, including *Intruder in the Dust* (1949), *Tarnished Angels* (1957), an adaptation of his novel *Pylon*, and *The Reivers* (1969).

He laughed, short and harsh. "I'd like to see the Los Angeles servant you could get for five hundred dollars a year. But what—" He stopped laughing, looking down at her.

"That would be at least five thousand dollars," she said.

He looked down at her. After a while he said, "Are you asking me again for money?" She didn't answer nor move, her hands picking slowly and quietly at one another. "Ah," he said. "You want to go away. You want to run from it. So do I!" he cried, before he could catch himself this time; "so do I! But you did not choose me when you elected a child; neither did I choose my two. But I shall have to bear them and you will have to bear all of us. There is no help for it." He caught himself now, panting, quieting himself by will as when he would rise from bed, though his voice was still harsh: "Where would you go? Where would you hide from it?"

"Home," she said.

"Home?" he repeated; he repeated in a kind of amazement: "home?" before he understood. "You would go back there? with those winters, that snow and all? Why, you wouldn't live to see the first Christmas. don't you know that?" She didn't move nor look up at him. "Nonsense," he said. "This will blow over. In a month there will be two others and nobody except us will even remember it. And you don't need money. You have been asking me for money for years, but you don't need it. I had to worry about money so much at one time myself that I swore that the least I could do was to arrange your affairs so you would never even have to look at the stuff. I must go; there is something at the office today. I'll see you tomorrow."

Golden Land (1935) by William Faulkner

James M Cain (1892-1977)

Cain came to Hollywood in 1931 to work as a screenwriter for Paramount, but his dislike for movies eventually led him to pursue his literary ambitions. With his first novel, the tremendously popular sordid tale of lust and murder, *The Postman Always Rings Twice* (1934), Cain set the tone for all his subsequent works. With their bleak atmosphere, violence and obsession with sex, his fast-moving crime books became a principal inspiration for film *noir*. Besides *Postman*, which was filmed in 1946 and 1981, two other Cain's hard-boiled novels became into classics of the genre: *Double Indemnity* (1936, filmed 1944) and *Mildred Pierce* (1941, filmed 1945).

I drove out to Glendale to put three new truck drivers on a brewery company bond, and then I remembered this renewal over in Hollywoodland. I decided to run over there. That was how I came to this House of Death, that you've been reading about in the papers. It didn't look like a House of Death when I saw it. It was just a Spanish house, like all the rest of them in California, with white walls, red tile roof, and a patio out to one side. It was built cock-eyed. The garage was under the house, the first floor was over that and the rest of it was spilled up the hill any way they could get it in. You climbed some stone steps to the front door, so I parked the car and went up there. A servant poked her head out. "Is Mr. Nirdlinger in?"

"I don't know, sir. Who wants to see him?"

"Mr. Huff."

"And what's the business?"

"Personal."

Fred MacMurray, portraying an insurance salesman, and Barbara Stanwyck, playing a client's wife, plot to murder her husband and collect his insurance money in the classic *Double Indemnity* (1944)

Getting in is the tough part of my job, and you don't tip what you came for till you get where it counts. "I'm sorry, sir, but they won't let me ask anybody in unless they say what they want."

It was one of those spots you get in. If I said some more about "personal" I would be making a mystery of it, and that's bad. If I said what I really wanted, I would be laying myself open for what every insurance agent dreads, that she would come back and say, "Not in." If I said I'd wait, I would be making myself look small, and that never helped a sale yet. To move this stuff, you've got to get in. Once you're in, they've got to listen to you, and you can pretty near rate an agent by how quick he gets to the family sofa, with his hat on one side of him and his dope sheets on the other.

"I see. I told Mr. Nirdlinger I would drop in, but—never mind. I'll see if I can make it some other time."

Double Indemnity (1936) by James M Cain

Tennessee Williams (1911-1983)
The great American dramatist lived in Santa Monica during the summer of 1943 after being fired from MGM, where he was briefly employed as a screenwriter. While staying in an apartment building on Ocean Avenue, Williams worked on his play *The Glass Menagerie* (1944), which would be his first major success. Fifteen of his plays, including the Pulitzer Prize-winner *A Streetcar Named Desire* (1947) and *Cat on a Hot Tin Roof* (1955), were made into films.

This resurrected day is a Saturday and all afternoon pairs of young lovers have wandered the streets of Santa Monica, searching for rooms to make love in. Each uniformed boy holds a small zipper bag and the sunpinked-or-gilded arm of a pretty girl, and they seem to be moving in pools of translucent water. The girl waits at the foot of steps which the boy bounds up, at first eagerly, then anxiously, then with desperation, for Santa Monica is literally flooded with licensed and unlicensed couples in this summer of 1943. The couples are endless and their search is unflagging. By sundown and long after, even as late as two or three in the morning, the boy will bound up steps and the girl wait below, sometimes primly pretending not to hear the four-letter word he mutters after each disappointment, sometimes saying it for him when he resumes his dogged hold on her arm. Even as daybreak comes they'll still be searching and praying and cursing with bodies that ache from pent-up longing more than fatigue.

Terrible separations occur at daybreak. The docile girl finally loses faith or patience; she twists violently free of the hand that bruises her arm and dashes sobbing into an all-night cafe to phone for a cab. The boy hovers outside, gazing fiercely through fog and window, his now empty fist opening and closing on itself.

The Mattress by the Tomato Patch by Tennessee Williams

Nathanael West (1903-1940)

Upon his arrival in Hollywood in 1933, West, a New York native, was employed as a screenwriter by Columbia Pictures, Republic Pictures and later RKO. Although he wrote only four novels during his brief career, he left a lasting mark with his original, satirical depiction of the disintegration of the American dream in the 1930s. He was killed in a car crash with his wife, Eileen McKenney, the heroine of Ruth McKenney's novel *My Sister Eileen.* West's *The Day of the Locust* (1939) is considered by many critics one of the best novels about Hollywood ever written. It depicts the world on the fringes of the movie industry's dream machine, populated with the hosts of hopefuls, disillusioned and outcasts—wannabe actresses, prostitutes, dwarfs and con artists. It was made into a movie in 1975.

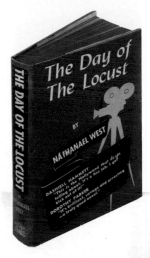

He had learned this just in time. During his last year in art school, he had begun to think that he might give up painting completely. The pleasures he received from the problems of composition and color had decreased as his facility had increased and he had realized that he was going the way of all his classmates, toward illustration or mere handsomeness. When the Hollywood job had come along, he had grabbed it despite the arguments of his friends who were certain that he was selling out and would never paint again.

He reached the end of Vine Street and began the climb into Pinyon Canyon. Night had started to fall.

The edges of the trees burned with a pale violet light and their centers gradually turned from deep purple to black. The same violet piping, like a Neon tube, outlined the tops of the ugly, hump-backed hills and they were almost beautiful.

But not even the soft wash of dusk could help the houses. Only dynamite would be of any use against the Mexican ranch houses, Samoan huts, Mediterranean villas, Egyptian and Japanese temples, Swiss chalets, Tudor cottages, and every possible combination of these styles that lined the slopes of the canyon.

When he noticed that they were all of plaster, lath and paper, he was charitable and blamed their shape on the materials used. Steel, stone and brick curb a builder's fancy a little, forcing him to distribute his stresses and weights and to keep his corners plumb, but plaster and paper know no law, not even that of gravity.

The Day of the Locust (1939) by Nathanael West

A film premiere in Hollywood explodes into a cataclysm of destruction as a mob gone mad lynches the excentric hick played by Donald Sutherland in the finale of *The Day of the Locust* (1974)

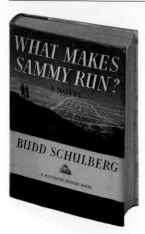

Budd Schulberg (b. 1914)

Schulberg's upbringing in Hollywood—his father was production chief at Paramount Studio—provided him with firsthand
experience of the film industry he later depicted in his works.
He achieved an immediate success with his first novel, *What
Makes Sammy Run?* (1941), which chronicles the meteoric rise
of unscrupulous Sammy Glick from office boy to studio head.
Schulberg wrote screenplays for several films and in 1954 won
an Academy Award for his screenplay *On the Waterfront.*

Sammy's apartment was in the fashionable Colonial
House just off the Sunset Strip. The names of the tenants
underneath the mail boxes at the entrance read like a list
of Hollywood's most eligible bachelors.

Sammy's place was one of the smallest in the building
and even that must have been way beyond his means for
those early days, but he wrote off only part of the
expense to shelter, the rest to prestige.

The apartment was furnished with an elegance that
didn't seem to fit Sammy, at least not yet, with a bed-
room that opened off a long living room with a fireplace at one end. Sammy brought
out Courvoisier. I wondered where he picked up all those little tricks, and then Billie
and I started playing records and doing a little slow dancing, while Sammy and Sally
Ann took over the big couch.

As we danced, hardly moving together, I heard the sound and silence of held kisses,
several shrill, half-giggled Sammy, don'ts! and then Sammy started giving her the business about putting her in the movies. It was hardly more than kidding, and Sally Ann
knew it, but you could tell from the way she kidded back how much that meant to her.
It was all so naked that I wished I were drunker or not there. It was no secret to anybody that she was working out on him and he was working out on her, each one want-
ing something and not quite admitting it. Some people call that the Hollywood tug of
war, though that concept is a little narrow. Hollywood may be one of its most blatant
battlegrounds, but it is really a world war, undeclared.

What Makes Sammy Run? (1941) by Budd Schulberg

Octavio Paz (1914-1998)

Mexican poet and essayist, winner of the 1990 Nobel Prize for Literature, Paz came to California in
the late 1940s on a Guggenheim Fellowship. In the first essay of his *The Labyrinth of Solitude*
(1950), Paz described the Mexican-American community in Los Angeles. Insecure about their identity, these *pachucos* did not belong to Mexico any more, but were not accepted into mainstream
American culture either, living on the edges of society.

When I arrived in the United States I lived for a while in Los Angeles, a city inhabited
by over a million persons of Mexican origin. At first sight, the visitor is surprised not
only by the purity of the sky and the ugliness of the dispersed and ostentatious buildings, but also by the city's vaguely Mexican atmosphere, which cannot be captured in
words or concepts. This Mexicanism—delight in decorations, carelessness and pomp,
negligence, passion and reserve—floats in the air. I say "floats" because it never mixes
or unites with the other world, the North American world based on precision and efficiency. It floats, without offering any opposition; it hovers, blown here and there by the
wind, sometimes breaking up like a cloud, sometimes standing erect like a rising skyrocket. It creeps, it wrinkles, it expands and contracts; it sleeps or dreams; it is ragged
but beautiful. It floats, never quite existing, never quite vanishing.

Something of the same sort characterizes the Mexicans you see in the streets. They
have lived in the city for many years, wearing the same clothes and speaking the same
language as the other inhabitants, and they feel ashamed of their origin; yet no one
would mistake them for authentic North Americans. I refuse to believe that physical features are as important as is commonly thought. What distinguishes them, I think, is their
furtive, restless air: they act like persons who are wearing disguises, who are afraid of a
stranger's look because it could strip them and leave them stark naked. When you talk
with them, you observe that their sensibilities are like a pendulum, but a pendulum that
has lost its reason and swings violently and erratically back and forth. This spiritual condition, or lack of a spirit, has given birth to a type known as the *pachuco.*

The Labyrinth of Solitude (1950) by Octavio Paz

Raymond Chandler (1888-1959)

Renowned writer of mystery novels, notable for his elegant style, striking dialogue and vivid descriptions, Chandler is considered one of the leading figures in "hard-boiled" detective fiction. He began writing for magazines but gained fame for his seven mystery novels, all of which were set in LA. Called the father of "Los Angeles Noir," Chandler captured a dark aspect of the city, an endless urban sprawl brimming with crime and corruption, like no other writer.

The protagonist of all Chandler's novels, the archetypal private eye Philip Marlowe, was characterized as a lone-wolf, cynical, hard-drinking anti-hero. He has been portrayed in various films based on Chandler's works by such stars as Dick Powell, Humphrey Bogart, Robert Montgomery, Elliott Gould and Robert Mitchum.

Chandler's first project as a Hollywood screenwriter was a collaboration with director Billy Wilder on a film version of James M Cain's novel, *Double Indemnity* (1944). His other scripts include *The Blue Dahlia* (1946) and *Strangers on a Train* (1951). Almost all of Chandler's novels were made into films, the most popular being *noir* classics *Murder, My Sweet* (1945) and *The Big Sleep* (1946).

Malibu. More movie stars. More pink and blue bathtubs. More tufted beds. More Chanel No. 5. More Lincoln Continentals and Cadillacs. More wind-blown hair and sunglasses and attitudes and pseudo-refined voices and waterfront morals. Now, wait a minute. Lots of nice people work in pictures. You've got the wrong attitude, Marlowe. You're not human tonight.

I smelled Los Angeles before I got to it. It smelled stale and old like a living room that had been closed too long. But the colored lights fooled you. The lights were wonderful. There ought to be a monument to the man who invented neon lights. Fifteen stories high, solid marble. There's a boy who really made something out of nothing.

So I went to a picture show and it had to have Mavis Weld in it. One of those glass-and-chromium deals where everybody smiled too much and talked too much and knew it. The women were always going up a long curving staircase to change their clothes. The men were always taking monogrammed cigarettes out of expensive cases and snapping expensive lighters at each other. And the help was round-shouldered from carrying trays with drinks across the terrace to a swimming pool about the size of Lake Huron but a lot neater.

The Little Sister (1949) by Raymond Chandler

Truman Capote (1924-1984)

A favorite writer of the fashionable high society between the 1950s and the 1970s, Capote (➔ p445) developed a journalistic approach to fiction writing which was called the "nonfiction novel." Among several of his own works which have been produced as motion pictures, the most famous was *Breakfast at Tiffany's* (1958, filmed 1961). He also wrote for the movies, contributing to such screenplays as *Beat the Devil* (directed by John Huston in 1953) and *The Innocents* (1961).

Approaching Los Angeles, at least by air, is like, I should imagine, crossing the surface of the moon: prehistoric shapes, looming in stone ripples and corroded, leer upward, and paleozoic fish swim in the shadowy pools between desert mountains; burned and frozen, there is no living thing, only rock that was once a bird, bones that are sand, ferns turned to fiery stone. At last a welcoming fleet of clouds: we have crept between a sorcerer's passage, snow is on the mountains, yet flowers color the land, a summer sun juxtaposes December's winter sea, down, down, the plane splits through plumed, gold, incredible air. Oh, moaned Thelma, I can't stand it, she said, and poured a cascade of Chiclets into her mouth. Thelma had boarded the plane in Chicago; she was a young Negro girl, rather pretty, beautifully dressed, and it was the most wonderful thing that would ever happen to her, this trip to California. "I know it, it's going just to be grand. Three years I've been ushering at the Lola Theatre on State Street just to save the fare. My auntie tells the cards, and she said—Thelma, honey, head for Hollywood 'cause there's a job as private secretary to a movie actress just waiting for you. She didn't say what actress, though. I hope it's not Esther Williams. I don't like swimming much."

Local Color (1950) by Truman Capote

Los Angeles Sound

Today considered the undisputed global capital of pop music, Los Angeles became a significant player on the rock scene in the early 1960s. During the 1970s, LA replaced New York as the center of the recording industry. Following "the new sounds," leading labels including Motown, Atlantic, Polydor and Elektra moved west, joining local record companies such as Capitol and A & M.

With its seductive mix of showbiz, sunshine and easygoing lifestyle, Los Angeles has been for decades a mecca for aspiring musicians, who flocked here in hope of making the big break. Hollywood, and especially the Sunset Strip (➔ p180), offered a variety of highly visible venues that attracted musical talent from all over the world.

The Beach Boys released their first single in 1961, launching the surf music craze inspired by the teen motifs of surfing, girls and hot rods. Noted for unsurpassed vocal harmonies created by the band's genius leader, Brian Wilson, their songs, such as *Surfin' USA, Help Me Rhonda, California Girls* and *God Only Knows*, epitomized the Southern California lifestyle. Between 1961 and 1966 they had 11 No. 1 hits, culminating with their ground-breaking album *Pet Sounds* (1966).

The Byrds

The seminal folk-rock band whose distinctive style defined by vocal harmonies and a jangling 12-string guitar had an enormous influence on the West Coast sound. They created a sensation in 1965 with their first No. 1 hit, a cover of Bob Dylan's *Mr Tambourine Man.*

Buffalo Springfield

Considered by many to be the most talented of all LA rock bands, this short-lived group forged a unique blend of folk, country and rock. Comprised of strong willed performers/songwriters, the band gained national reputation with their landmark 1967 single, *For What It's Worth.*

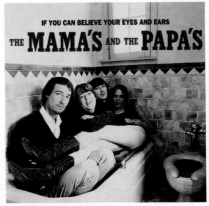

IF YOU CAN BELIEVE YOUR EYES AND EARS

THE **MAMA'S** AND THE **PAPA'S**

The Mamas and the Papas

During their brief career, the famous quartet popularized West Coast vibes and helped define the "California sound." Noted for their rich harmony style, they topped the charts in 1966 with their first single, *California Dreamin',* and reached US No. 1 with *Monday, Monday.*

Crosby, Stills, Nash and Young

Comprising former members of the Byrds (David Crosby) and Buffalo Springfield (Stephen Stills and Neil Young), this legendary folk-rock group reached cult status among the hippie generation. Their debut album *Déjà Vu* topped US charts in 1970. In various permutations, CSN&Y had numerous successful releases over the years.

Frank Zappa was one of the most colorful, original and controversial personalities of modern music. He was the founder and leader of the Mothers of Invention, the band which debuted with the landmark double album *Freak Out!* (1966) and gained notoriety for their provocative, ear-shattering stage performances.

The Doors

Their provocative, psychedelic mix of hard rock and heavy blues won them cult audiences across the globe and inspired countless followers. Their songs *Light My Fire* (1967) and *Hello I Love You* (1968) both reached US No. 1. Soon after the release of their album *L.A. Woman* (1971), which featured major hits *Love Her Madly* and *Riders on the Storm*, singer and rock idol Jim Morrison died mysteriously in Paris.

The Eagles

One of the top-selling groups of the decade, they established a harmonious, laid-back rock sound that mixed folk and country elements. They had a number of No. 1 hits, including *Hotel California*, the title track from the 1976 album.

Van Halen

Led by Eddie Van Halen, one of the most impressive guitarists in rock, this band is the chief representative of the LA hard rock sound of the late 1970s and remains one of the best in the genre. After their debut album *Van Halen I* (1978), they gained international fame, undertaking long world tours and playing before packed stadiums. Their reputation for sex, drugs and excess equaled only the legendary sprees of Led Zeppelin.

1985 homemade guitar played by Eddie Van Halen

Between the late 1970s and mid 1980s LA developed a violent style of punk called "hardcore." Among the emerging pioneers of the hardcore movement were **the Germs**, whose brief career was marked by savage performances and the destruction of the venues in which they played. The band that took hardcore to the extreme was **Black Flag**, with its dark, aggressive music and anti-establishment, nihilistic lyrics. Other prominent bands on the diverse LA punk scene included X, the all-girl Go-Go's and the Circle Jerks.

"Gangsta" rap originated in the Compton area of LA with the band **NWA** (Niggaz With Attitude), founded by seminal rappers Eazy-E, Dr Dre and Ice Cube (left). NWA attained national notoriety with the release of their debut album *Straight Outta Compton* (1988). Their lyrics about guns, violence and "bitches" spoke about the mindset of the dope-smokin', gun-tottin' ghetto subculture. Songs such as *Fuck Tha Police* and *Gangsta Gangsta* elevated the album to multi-platinum status, unintentionally helped by an FBI attempt to block its distribution.

Guns N' Roses

Considered by many the biggest rock band of the 1980s, Guns N' Roses burst on the scene with their US No.1 album *Appetite for Destruction* (1987), introducing unique energy and volatility. Their infamous offstage incidents involving drugs, alcohol, bar-room brawls and even fights with police were widely publicized. The band's hits were featured in a number of movies, including *You Could Be Mine*, used in the Arnold Schwarzenegger film *Terminator 2* (1991); *Welcome to the Jungle*, included in the Clint Eastwood Dirty Harry film *Dead Pool* (1988), in which the band appeared in a cameo spot; and their version of Bob Dylan's *Knockin' On Heaven's Door*, used in the Tom Cruise movie *Days of Thunder* (1990).

1999 Ibanez custom guitar played by Tom Morello

Rage Against the Machine

One of the most acclaimed rock bands of the 1990s, the Machine is known for some of the most explosive, politically charged live performances. Their music, which blends hardcore metal with elements of rap and punk, is famed for radical lyrics against the establishment and its various forms of repression. Guitarist Tom Morello summarizes their philosophy: "The band weaves political awareness through its music. We've always been about making our audience more conscious of the world around them and not blindly accepting what is forced on them."

Red Hot Chili Peppers

The pioneers of rock-funk sound which also incorporated influences of punk and metal, the Chili Peppers became one of the world's most popular rock bands of the 1990s. They earned their reputation as a unique live act, gaining notoriety for performing naked wearing only socks over their genitalia. The band's groundbreaking album *Blood Sugar Sex Magik* (1991) propelled them into stardom, and the smash hit ballad *Under the Bridge*, a nostalgic walk through the streets of Los Angeles, reached US No. 2 in 1992.

Los Angeles' Murals

Representing a significant part of the city's cultural identity, murals are probably the most common art form in Los Angeles. They have a long tradition in the region, dating back hundreds of years, to local Chumash Indians' cave paintings. The modern mural era in Los Angeles began in 1932, when Mexican artist David Alfaro Siqueiros painted his *América Tropical*. Many murals painted in the 1930s were specially commissioned, but the majority of those existing today were created since the 1960s and appeared spontaneously. Murals became a powerful means of self-expression, as amateur or self-trained artists used historical and social subjects to make public statements. With more than 1,500 public murals, Los Angeles has been proclaimed the "Mural Capital of the World."

América Tropical (1932) by David Alfaro Siqueiros. Italian Hall, 650 N Main St.
Built in 1907 as an Italian community center, the building contains an 18 x 80-foot (5,5 x 24-m) mural painted by the famed Mexican muralist David Alfaro Siqueiros (1896-1974). Called *América Tropical*, it was commissioned by an art dealer who had a gallery on the building's second floor. On the south-facing exterior wall, Siqueiros painted an Indian peon crucified on a double cross of the Church and imperialism. An American eagle is perched on top of the cross.

The controversial mural, recognized as an indictment of American imperialism and oppression, shocked officials who prompted its whitewashing. This drastic measure, however, actually saved the brilliantly colored mural, which would have certainly faded away over time had it not been painted over. Siqueiros's six-month visa was revoked and he was expelled from the United States.
The uncovering process is underway, conducted by the Getty Conservation Institute, and the restored mural will be displayed again.

The Story of Venice (1941, detail) by Edward Biberman. Post Office, 1601 Main St, Venice.
During the Depression of the 1930s, the United States government created five federal arts projects that commissioned unemployed artists to decorate public buildings across the country. In Los Angeles, more than 200 murals were painted in city halls, schools, libraries, post office buildings and other public sites between 1933 and 1943, when the art projects abruptly ended. Among the local artists who were hired under the auspices of this program were Hugo Ballin, Millard Sheets and Howard Warshaw.

Untitled (1970) by Millard Sheets.
In 1952 artist Millard Sheets received an invitation from Howard Ahmanson, chairman of Home Savings and Loan, to design for him two branch offices on Wilshire Boulevard. The initial success was so great that in the next 27 years Sheets supervised construction of over 40 of the company's branch offices. He also designed murals for these buildings, sometimes in collaboration with other artists, mainly with local history and home and family themes. After Washington Mutual's acquisition of Home Savings in 1998, the fate of many closed branch offices and their murals remains uncertain.

Ricochet (1994) by Roberto Salas, 405 fwy at Manchester Blvd.
During the 1970s, local governments and community organizations began to show wider support for public murals. Both the county and the city of Los Angeles began to fund public murals at that time. In 1974 a citywide mural project was initiated and in 1976 the Social and Public Art Resource Center (SPARC) was formed. This multicultural organization that produces, exhibits, distributes and preserves public artworks produced over 60 murals across the city, including the monumental mural *Great Wall of Los Angeles* (➔ p340). The city and the state sponsored murals honoring major sport events, such as the 1984 Olympics and World Cup Soccer 1994, provided broader recognition to the mural movement.
For more information, visit www.lamurals.org. The Metro Art Docent Council organizes free group tours of the murals and public art in LA's subway system; for information call ☎(213) 922-4ART, or visit www.mta.net/metroart.

Untitled (1946) by Alfredo Ramos Martinez.
One of nine panels of the 100-foot (30 m) long mural featuring flower vendors was painted on the Margaret Fowler Garden's wall on the campus of Scripps College in Claremont. The Mexican mural tradition played an important part in the history of wall art in Los Angeles. Mexican influence started during the 1930s when Diego Rivera, Alfaro Siqueiros and José Clemente Orozco, known as *Los Tres Grandes*, came to California to paint murals.

In the mid-1980s, a widespread practice of spray painting walls, fences, buses and other surfaces reached an alarming level. Graffiti art evolved from nicknames, called "tags," scrawled by youths looking for recognition, whether to mark gang territory or bring fame to their writers. Tagging is illegal, and to curb it the city banned the sale of spray cans to minors and introduced a penalty for graffiti. It didn't stop the notorious tagger of the 1990s, Daniel "Chaka" Ramos, who eluded police long enough to leave his mark 10,000 times before he was finally caught. The price tag for a cleanup of his signatures was $55,000.

Los Angeles in Art

The first artists who arrived in Los Angeles in the 1880s were inspired by its unique light, climate and the beauty of its landscapes. They painted in a variety of styles, including Romantic Realism, Tonalism and Impressionism. Ideas of Modernism arrived in LA in the 1930s, together with such European artists as Oscar Fishinger and Salvador Dalí, who worked for the film studios.

In the post-World War II era, and especially since the 1960s, the city's innovative artists, who experimented with new techniques and materials, drew wider attention. With its vibrant gallery scene, world-class museums and high-profile art schools, Los Angeles emerged as a major international art center which today produces the most exciting contemporary art in the world.

Henri Penelon (1827-1885)

The French-born Penelon was LA's first resident artist. Although without formal training, which is evident from the naiveté of his pompous works, he was popular with the city's most prominent citizens whose portraits he painted.

Don Vicente Lugo (ca. 1855) by Henri Penelon

San Gabriel Mission (1899) by Edwin Deakin

Edwin Deakin (1838-1923)

The English-born Deakin worked in the Romantic, picturesque style, specializing in painting crumbling California missions. He pictured them in a sad, deteriorating condition after they were abandoned following secularization. Deakin's interest in architectural detail is seen in this depiction of the portion of the church's unique south façade, with its buttressed walls and *campanario* (the bell-wall), with six bells hanging in arched openings of graduated size.

Franz Bischoff (1864-1929)

Born in Austria, where he studied ceramic decoration, Bischoff settled in Los Angeles in 1906 and built a home and studio in Arroyo Seco in Pasadena. Impressed by this natural surrounding, he painted many landscapes and scenes of everyday life here. Regarded as an outstanding colorist, Bischoff also painted Southern California's deserts, mountains and coastal areas, but is best-known for his still lives of flowers.

Arroyo Seco (1908) by Franz Bischoff

Cahuenga Pass (1912) by William Wendt

William Wendt (1865-1946)

A German-born landscape artist who settled in Los Angeles in 1906, Wendt was revered as the "Dean of California *plein air* painters." He painted from nature and often traveled to remote, uninhabited areas to capture the unspoiled beauty of the wilderness. He perceived it as a manifestation of God, which required his respect and faithful interpretation. Noted for good composition, his works in the early 1910s are characterized by broad brushstrokes and organic color.

Edgar Payne (1883-1947)

This basically self-taught artist, who settled in Los Angeles in 1911, is best known as one of the main painters of the High Sierras, where he occasionally spent months working. Even a lake at his favorite painting site in the mountains is named in his honor. Payne's early works use light, short brushstrokes, but later he employed a much broader and bolder brush and intense, bluish purple colors. His book *Composition of Outdoor Painting* is still used by artists, teachers, students and collectors around the world.

Altadena Hills (ca. 1925) by Edgar Payne

Arroyo Seco (n.d.) by Marion Kavanagh Wachtel

Marion Kavanagh Wachtel (1876-1954)

An acknowledged *plein air* landscape painter, Wachtel traveled extensively throughout the Southwest with her husband Elmer Wachtel, also a famous landscapist. They built a home in the Arroyo Seco section of Pasadena, the rustic canyon where artists, intellectuals and craftsmen in the Arts and Crafts movement were congregating. The wooded arroyos became a favorite subject of her work, noted for its lyrical tone and softly applied colors, predominantly pale blues and pinks. Later in her career Wachtel painted primarily with watercolors.

Millard Sheets (1907-1989)

Sheets was the widely recognized leader of LA's American Scene painting and an accomplished architect and muralist. His designs for over forty branch offices of Home Savings and Loan incorporated such decoration as sculptures, murals and mosaics.

In one of his best-known works, Sheets here depicts a working-class neighborhood inhabited with ordinary people engaged in everyday tasks. The painting's title is a reference to the short cable railway built to ascend a steep incline up Bunker Hill (➜ p262).

Edward Biberman (1904-1986)

An acknowledged painter of the city's urban landscapes, Biberman favored the flat surfaces and straight lines of Art Deco or International Style buildings. His architectural settings, brightly colored and flooded with intense Southern California light, invoke a distinctive mood, enhanced by their striking absence of people. Here he depicts a famous dance club in Hollywood (➜ p126).

Angels Flight (1931) by Millard Sheets

Ed Ruscha (born 1937)

An internationally acclaimed artist whose work blends Pop, Conceptual and Minimal elements, Ruscha is best known for his paintings of words. Here the HOLLYWOOD sign, the city's most prominent landmark, is set on a hilltop against a fiery dusk sky, presenting a dramatic interplay between word and image. The actual sign, which is in reality nestled mid-slope, started as an advertising gimmick for real estate development and eventually became the symbol of the Hollywood dream factory (➜ p165).

The Hollywood Palladium (1955) by Edward Biberman

Hollywood (1968) by Ed Ruscha

Beverly Hills Housewife (1966) by David Hockney

David Hockney (born 1937)

A British expatriate living in Los Angeles since the 1960s, David Hockney is a universally popular figurative painter, photographer, printmaker and stage designer. The city had a strong effect on him with its mild climate, easy-going lifestyle and houses with vast glass windows, patios and distinctive swimming pools.
In this painting Hockney places a lonely female figure in the typical architectural setting of a luxurious home in an affluent neighborhood.

Edward Kienholz (1927-1994)

Kienholz's drastically realistic and often shocking assemblages are created from everyday objects, with plaster-cast figures set in environments of room-size proportions. His primary concerns are social and cultural problems such as war, hypocrisy, cruelty, consumerism, sexuality, and the individual's failure to confront them.
The Beanery (1965) recreates a sleazy bar scene in a famous West Hollywood eatery called Barney's Beanery (➔ p193).

The Beanery (1965) by Edward Kienholz

Richard Diebenkorn (1922-1993)

An Abstract Expressionist painter who also experimented with figuration, Diebenkorn is best known for his large paintings of the *Ocean Park* series. Named after the beachside community in Santa Monica where he lived, these works resonate with the architectural shapes of the neighborhood and reflect the luminous colors and translucent light of Southern California.

Ocean Park Series No. 49 (1972) by Richard Diebenkorn

Same Old Paradise (1987) by Alexis Smith

City at Night (1992) by Frank Romero

Frank Romero (born 1941)

Romero captures the essence of Los Angeles with his signature rich, multiple coats of paint and bright colors inspired by Mexican heritage. With the cartoonish rendering of cars, freeways, palm trees and the city landmarks, Romero's paintings and numerous murals across the city bear his highly personalized commentary on the stereotypical images of Los Angeles. Concerned with social and political issues, especially gang violence and police brutality in East Los Angeles, Romero's work helped Chicano art achieve proper recognition.

Alexis Smith (born 1949)

Renown for collage and assemblage work that includes found objects combined with old photographs and texts clipped from magazines, Alexis Smith creates an intriguing interplay between past and present, old and new.

In this mixed media installation Smith presents a nostalgic view of the Garden of Eden in the form of the vast expanses of orange groves that once comprised Los Angeles, complete with a snake whose body suddenly metamorphoses out of the highway.

James Doolin (1932-2002)

A realist painter with a keen eye for detail, Doolin offered a fresh look at spaces that do not usually attract much attention from passerbys on their everyday routine, such as busy street corners, beaches, freeway onramps and neon signs. The artist is best known for the luminous quality of his urban landscapes, as evident in this dramatic depiction of a freeway during a windstorm.

East Wind (1991) by James Doolin

Rape of the Angels (1991) by Llyn Foulkes

Dante and Virgil Contemplate the Inferno (2003) by Sandow Birk

Llyn Foulkes (born 1934)

Known for his sharp social commentaries, the artist demystifies in his works widely accepted myths about American values. In this painting Foulkes exposes transactions of local real estate developers who "revitalized" the former residential neighborhood in downtown Los Angeles, transforming it into a corporate environment. The self-portrait of the artist on the right makes obvious his opinion about the dealings in the "balloon."

Sandow Birk (born 1962)

A poignant observer of utterly commercialized and decaying urban landscapes, the realist painter Sandow Birk is best known for his series called *In Smog and Thunder: The Great War of the Californias*. The project documents an imaginary war between Los Angeles and San Francisco in a cacophony of allegories, symbols and pop culture references. In this painting the artist places Dante's *Inferno* in contemporary Los Angeles, with two poets standing on the edge of a cliff under the HOLLYWOOD sign and watching the present-day version of hell below.

Jeff Soto (born 1975)

An artist who combines elements of painting, graffiti, signage and collage in his work, Soto offers here a futuristic view of the wasteland that might be Los Angeles after machines take over an environment destroyed by humans.

Los Angeles: Decay and Overgrowth (2002) by Jeff Soto

Architectural Styles

Los Angeles' architectural history began with the Spanish colonization in the late 18th century. European architectural styles usually arrived later to the West Coast, and were adapted to the specific conditions of the Southern California environment and the needs of local inhabitants. Los Angeles architecture is eclectic and inventive, the city being a hybrid of manifold styles. Although "pure" examples of all major styles exist, builders never

Tiled dome

hesitated to experiment, creating an immense variety of blends. The result is a staggering architectural diversity that makes Los Angeles unique among American cities.

The world's top architects, from Frank Lloyd Wright to Frank Gehry, found LA a fertile environment for testing their new ideas. The city is a trove of scattered architectural gems, many hidden in the hills, others lost amidst endless rows of nondescript residential buildings, strip malls and parking lots.

San Fernando Mission (Spanish Colonial, 1797). The most remarkable structure on the San Fernando Mission complex (➔ p345) is the 1822 *convento*, the least altered of the mission buildings, featuring four-foot adobe walls and a corridor with 21 Roman arches.

Leonis Adobe (Monterey, 1844), 23400 Calabasas Rd, Calabasas

Britt Residence (Georgian, 1910), 2141 W Adams Blvd, Exposition Park

Spanish Colonial (1769-1850)
The Spanish Colonial house was a one- or two-story structure built of adobe bricks or stone, its thick walls covered with a lime wash or plaster. Among the finest buildings from this period were 21 California mission complexes built by Native Americans for the Spanish Franciscan missionaries. Most of these structures fell into disrepair over the years or were damaged in earthquakes. A few, however, have been saved and restored, but during the process were altered so much that some of the original style characteristics were lost.

Monterey (1837-1860s)
Thousands of settlers coming to California during the Gold Rush in the 1850s and 1860s brought with them traditional East Coast styles. The Monterey style was created by Bostonian Thomas Larkin, who adapted Greek Revival to the California climate and indigenous building materials. These symmetrical adobe buildings featured two-story galleries and a low-hipped, wood shingle roof. The style derived its name from the state capital under Mexican rule.

Georgian (1700-1790)
This style was popular in the 18th-century during the reigns of England's first three kings named George. It was called the first true American style and went out of fashion with the Revolutionary War. The main features include balanced proportion, symmetrical composition, classical details and hipped roofs.

Greek Revival (1820-1860)

This style represents an adaptation of the ancient Greek temple, loosely based on the classic Greek orders: Doric, Ionic and Corinthian. Greek Revival's most prevalent feature was a triangular pediment supported by a columned portico. It became popular during the Greek War of Independence from the Turks, which was associated with the American Revolution. The style was linked to the democratic ideals of ancient Greece and therefore considered ideal for civic monuments.

Italianate (1840-1880)

This style is a free and unpretentious interpretation of 15th- and 16th-century Italian villas. An Italianate house in California was a wooden version of a brick or brownstone house popular on the East Coast. It was usually a two-story structure featuring a low-pitch hip roof, a bracketed cornice and a small porch. Other distinctive characteristics are tall, thin segmental windows, sometimes arched with eyebrow heads.

Gothic Revival (1830-1860)

Based on the English country cottage, the Gothic Revival style was used for a variety of buildings, from timber cottages and country villas to stone castles and churches. Its most striking characteristic was a steeply pitched gable roof, trimmed with wooden bargeboard decorated with Gothic motifs such as trefoils, quatrefoils or pointed arches. Other features include wall dormers, hood molds over the windows, and large ornamental chimneys.

Banning Residence (Greek Revival, 1864), 401 E "M" St, Wilmington

Perry Residence (Italianate, 1876), Heritage Square, 3800 Homer St (→ p177)

Collins Residence (Stick, 1881), 892 Kensington Rd, Echo Park

Stick (1860-1890)

The Stick style emphasized the "bones" of the building with its vertical and horizontal wood framing and diagonal boards. Although this stickwork, for which the style was named, was mostly decorative, it was intended to "honestly" express the structural character of the building. This style is characterized by its asymmetrical composition and vertical basic orientation. Other features include a pitched gable roof, bay windows, and large verandas and porches.

Doheny Mansion, (Gothic Revival, 1899). It features gabled red-tiled roofs with copper Gothic detail and a 12-sided tower topped with a heavily ornamented pavilion (→ p223).

Second Empire (1860-1880)

The Second Empire style derives from architecture developed in France during the reign of Napoleon III. Its signature feature is the use of the high mansard roof, named for the 17th-century French architect François Mansart. Consisting of a steep lower slope, occasionally gently convex or concave in form, and usually a flat top portion, it was an elegant way of adding another story to a house. Other features include use of tower pavilions and multi-colored slates for roof covering.

Eastlake (1870-1880)

This variant is a decorative style of ornamentation most frequently found on Queen Anne and Stick style houses. It was named for Charles Eastlake, an English architect and interior designer, whose writings and furniture designs provided the basis for this style. Eastlake, however, strongly disapproved the "Eastlake" style as practiced in California. The most distinctive features are curved eave brackets, massive porch posts and decorative knobs worked on a mechanical lathe.

Queen Anne (1880-1900)

The Queen Anne style was based on the works of English architect Richard Norman Shaw, but the name, however, does not refer to a historical period; Queen Anne reigned in the early 18th century. This picturesque style gained enormous popularity at the end of the 19th century and became what most people associate with the "Victorian house." It was incredibly varied and elaborate, incorporating a variety of forms, textures and materials. The asymmetrical house featured towers, turrets, steeped gables and encircling porches and verandas.

Valley Knudsen House (Second Empire, 1883), Heritage Square, 3800 Homer St (→ p177)

Eastlake Inn (Eastlake, 1887), 1442 Kellam Ave

Hale House (Queen Anne, 1887), Heritage Square, 3800 Homer St (→ p177)

Romanesque Revival (1870-1890)

Based on medieval European and English buildings, the Romanesque Revival was first introduced in Boston by young architect Henry Hobson Richardson in the early 1870s. The key identifying feature of this style was a semi-circular arch, used singly or in an arcade. Other features included squat columns, solid masonry with thick walls and square or polygonal towers.

Stimson House (Romanesque, 1891), 2421 S Figueroa St

Rindge Residence (Châteauesque, 1900), 2263 S Harvard Blvd

Osiris Apartment Building (Egyptian Revival, 1926), 430 S Union Ave

Herald-Examiner Building (Mission Revival, 1912), 1111 S Broadway (➔ p249).
This magnificent edifice, with its large central tower and two bellfries with colorfully tiled domes, is the work of Julia Morgan, who also designed the Hearst Castle in San Simeon.

Châteauesque (1890-1910)
The Châteauesque was loosely based on French castles built in the 15th and 16th centuries in a combination of the late Medieval and the early French Renaissance styles. The most distinguished features are steeply pitched hipped roofs, tall decorated chimneys and round corner turrets with conical roofs. Its elements were sometimes mixed with other styles.

Egyptian Revival (1830-1850; 1920-1930)
The first appearance of this style in the 19th century was associated with Napoleon's Egyptian Campaign of 1798. Later, it was triggered again by the discovery of King Tutankhamun's tomb in 1922, when all things Egyptian became immensely popular. Its key identifying features are distinctive columns, often with lotus flower capitals, and characteristic Egyptian cornices and ornaments. Other components include flat roofs and smooth exterior finishes which resembled the walls and gateways of ancient Egyptian temples.

Mission Revival (1890-1912)
Based on the early adobe missions of Franciscan padres, this style originated in California and was popularized across the country around the 1900s. It was used for a wide variety of buildings, including railroad stations, churches, city halls, hotels, apartment buildings and single-family houses. Characteristics include white, plain, stucco walls, low pitched tile roofs, round-arch openings, porches, arcades and bell-towers.

Gilbert Residence (Shingle, 1903), 1333 Alvarado Terrace (→ p221)

Higgins Residence (Colonial Revival, 1902), 637 S Lucerne Blvd

Raphael Residence (Tudor, 1903), 1353 Alvarado Terrace (→ p221)

Shingle (1880-1900)

Often called a truly American style, the Shingle began in New England as a revival of early colonial forms. It focuses on the so-called skin of the house, wrapping it from roof to stone foundation in a flowing covering of unpainted wood shingles. This uniform coating seemed to merge all irregular shapes into a smooth and continuous mass. The exterior of these buildings is typified by lack of excess decoration, standing in contrast to other late-19th-century styles.

Colonial Revival (1890-1915)

This style often combines characteristic features of various Colonial styles, such as large entry porticos or porches, gambrel roofs with wood shingles, columns and louvered shutters, with contemporary components. Colonial Revival was inspired by the Philadelphia Centennial of 1876, which celebrated the country's heritage, and became the most widespread architectural style in American history.

Tudor Revival (1900-1925)

Named for the English royal house that reigned during the 16th century, this style has its origin in village cottages and houses of England. Tudor buildings were picturesque, asymmetrical mansions, featuring the extensive use of decorative half-timbering. Other characteristics are high-pitched gables, tall chimneys and casement windows.

Spanish Colonial Revival (1915-1940)

This is the style for which Southern California is best known. It began with the buildings designed by architects Bertram Goodhue and Carleton M Winslow for the Panama California Exposition, held in San Diego in 1915. By the 1920s it was predominant in California, where it became the favorite style for Hollywood stars. It features irregular, picturesque buildings with stucco walls and low, round towers. Arcaded porches, window and balcony grilles were also common. Its distinctive characteristic were applied ornaments around doorways or windows, known as Churrigueresque for the 16th-century Spanish architect José Benito Churriguera.

Adamson House (Spanish Colonial Revival, 1929), 23200 Pacific Coast Hwy, Malibu (→ p365)

Trinity Auditorium Building (Beaux-Arts, 1923), 851 S Grand Ave

California Bungalow (1913), 1443 N Martel Ave

The Gamble House of Charles and Henry Greene represents the most elaborate and sophisticated expression of the Craftsman style, unequalled anywhere in the United States (→ p304)

Beaux-Arts (1890-1920s)

This style derives its name from the École des Beaux-Arts in Paris, where the first generation of California's trained architects had studied. It embodies elements of both Italian and French Renaissance, as well as Parisian Neo-Baroque and Roman Imperial architecture. Featuring symmetrical façades, projecting pavilions and monumental columns and flights of stairs, Beaux-Arts was regarded an ideal of urban beauty and became the predominant medium for public and institutional buildings.

Bungalow (1890-1930)

The typical bungalow is a one- or one-and-one-half story building with overhanging roof, ample porch and simplified interior. Although the majority of bungalows are Craftsman, many style variations were widely used, from Queen Anne to Spanish Colonial Revival to Prairie. The Los Angeles area is considered the real home of the bungalow. It still contains the largest collection of bungalows anywhere. As the bungalow fascination started in Southern California, this type of building was almost universally called a "California bungalow" at the time, regardless of where it was built.

Craftsman (1890-1920)

The Craftsman style represents a distinct American architectural development. Its source was the English Arts and Crafts movement, which rejected mass industrial production in favor of traditional handcraftsmanship. In America, this philosophy was widely publicized in *The Craftsman*, a popular magazine published between 1901 and 1916 by the businessman and furniture designer Gustav Stickley. The Craftsman was essentially a domestic style, related mainly to the suburbs and adapted to a middle-class requirement for affordable and attractive housing. It featured low-pitched roofs, open floor plans, porches, terraces, pergolas, and included finely crafted and detailed built-in features.

Prairie (1900-1920)

This indigenous American style was named for the prairies of the Midwest, where it originated in the early work of Frank Lloyd Wright. The Prairie house is a one- or two-story structure set on low foundations, incorporating Wright's basic premise that a building should appear to grow organically from its site. Reflecting the rolling, open space of the prairie, its horizontal lines were emphasized by a low-pitched roof with projecting eaves, casement windows, and large terraces and porches.

Art Deco (1925-1940)

Art Deco takes its name from the title of a 1925 Paris fair, *Exposition des Arts Décoratifs et Industriels Modernes*. Also called Zigzag Moderne, this style was characterized by prominent vertical elements, hard edges and stepped or set-back façades. It reached its ultimate expression in New York and Los Angeles skyscrapers and commercial buildings, which were ideally suited for angular, low-relief and highly stylized ornamentation. Various materials such as marble, terrazzo, colored terra cotta, chrome and ebony were often used for ornamental detailing.

Moderne (1930-1950)

The main feature of this variation, sometimes called Streamline Deco, is a striking streamlined look borrowed from the aerodynamic form of the automobile and the airplane. Fascinated with speed and glamour, Los Angeles eagerly adopted this new fad, which was implemented in various commercial buildings, airports and bus stations to an extent unequaled anywhere. Its key features are horizontal emphasis, smooth surfaces, circular bands of windows, rounded edges and flat roofs. Ornament was almost completely rejected, and when used, usually consisted of cement or metal panels.

Ebell Club (Praire, 1913), 131 S Avenue 57

Hollywood High School Science Building (Moderne, 1935), 1521 N Highland Ave

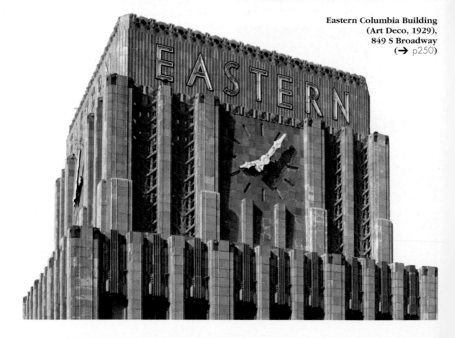

Eastern Columbia Building (Art Deco, 1929), 849 S Broadway (➜ p250)

International Style (1920-1950)

The ground-breaking show *Modern Architecture: International Exhibition*, organized in 1932 at MOMA in New York, gave the Modernist movement its name—the International Style. Developed in Europe, the style found its foothold in America in the early works of Austrian architects Rudolph Schindler and Richard Neutra. These two émigrés practiced architecture in Los Angeles and produced in the area some of the most important buildings in this style in America. The distinguishing features include flat walls without ornament or texture, and large expanses of glass.

Lovell House (International Style, 1929) (➔ p161)

Case Study Houses (1945-1966)

The internationally acclaimed Case Study House program represents a significant phenomenon in post-World War II American architecture. Designed by some of the most renowned architects of Southern California, including Raphael Soriano, Charles and Ray Eames, Craig Ellwood and Pierre Koenig, Case Studies comprise Los Angeles' single most important contribution to architecture. The program was created in 1945 by John Entenza, publisher of *Arts & Architecture* magazine. It intended to promote innovative and affordable residential housing based on new technology and materials. Using steel frames and large glass surfaces, Case Study houses were famous for their open-space designs and integration of indoor and outdoor areas. Influenced by the region's modernist tradition, 36 single-family homes were designed and most of them built over two decades, becoming synonymous with the California lifestyle.

Case Study House No. 21 (Pierre Koenig, 1958), 9038 Wonderland Park Ave (➔ p199). Photo by Julius Shulman.

Julius Shulman

Documenting Southern California architecture for over 65 years, Julius Shulman photographed buildings of almost all the leading architects. He started his career in the 1930s recording early modernism and became world famous for his coverage of the Case Study House program. Shulman is best-known for his method of "constructing" the view—his composition communicates not only the architect's idea about the building, but also places it within a specific time and space frame.

Shulman's work established architectural photography as an independent art form and helped create Los Angeles' reputation as an important architectural center. The American Institute of Architecture awarded him a Gold Medal for architectural photography in 1969. Shulman's most famous image is this 1960 photograph of the Case Study House No. 22. Capturing a stunning 240-degree view of the glass living room overlooking a nightly cityscape, the photograph conveys the glamorous image of the vibrating metropolis (➔ p198).

Samson Tire and Rubber Company Building (Morgan, Walls and Clements, architects, 1929). 5675 Telegraph Rd, City of Commerce.

Looking like an ancient Assyrian walled city, this imposing structure once housed the Samson Tire and Rubber Company, said to be the second largest tire manufacturing plant in the world. The company's name, which evokes Near Eastern associations, apparently was the inspiration for the building's elaborate decoration.

Its nearly third-mile-long (500-m) façade is embellished with 20-foot-tall (6-m) bas-reliefs of bearded warriors and winged creatures from Assyrian mythology and religion. The renovated building, which retains the original wall and main tower, serves today as a retail outlet mall, known as the Citadel.

Programmatic Architecture

During the early automobile age, and especially between 1925 and 1935, a thriving roadside architecture blossomed in Los Angeles. Located along the busy commercial strips, these vernacular buildings were designed to catch the eye of passing motorists and lure them off the street. Named "programmatic" by architects, some of these structures were shaped like a product they sold, while others mirrored the name or function of their business. Among the countless varieties of shapes and sizes, there were examples of ice-cream cones, chili bowls, coffee pots, milk cans, oranges, hotdogs, tamales, shoes, igloos, wigwams, windmills, owls, pigs, toads and dogs. Most of these architectural curiosities, called "California Crazy," have been razed and only a few remaining examples are presently standing as amusing landmarks.

Donut Hole (1968), 15300 E Amar Rd, La Puente. As they drive through the giant donut holes, motorists get their donuts without leaving the car.

Googie Architecture

During the 1950s, a new, futuristic design of commercial spaces such as coffee shops, drive-in restaurants and bowling alleys took hold in LA. These one-story buildings featured angular, glassed-off rooms, cantilevered roofs and cozy interiors with space-age motifs. Catering to the emerging car culture, the designs employed every trick to lure passing motorists, including wings, sharp angles, outrageous color schemes and flashy neon signs. Named after an establishment in West Hollywood called Googie's, which was designed by architect John Lautner in 1949 and since demolished, the term now epitomizes mid-century coffee shop style.

Norm's Restaurant (Armét and Davis, architects, 1956), 407 N La Cienega Blvd (➔ p71)

World's Oldest McDonald's (Stanley C Meston, architect, 1953), 10207 Lakewood Blvd, Downey. This streamlined drive-in is the third McDonald's ever built and the oldest in existence. Opened on August 18, 1953, the red and white tiled building remains virtually unchanged, with its signature pair of yellow neon arches. The towering, 60-foot (18-m) neon sign features Speedee the Chef, the old McDonald's mascot. Since the original owners got their franchise directly from the McDonald brothers, this is the only privately-owned restaurant in the world permitted to use the McDonald's name.

Exploring Los Angeles

Hollywood

"Friends, Hollywood is the bunk. There's no such place—it is a state of mind . . . Do not look for 'Hollywood' in Hollywood. You're more likely to find it in Beverly Hills."
— Lee Shippey, *The Times* columnist

To movie fans around the world Hollywood and the motion pictures became inextricably linked. Although strongly supported by the media, the image of Hollywood as the capital of glamour

Hollywood street sign

was never fully founded in reality. For the tourists who crowded the area, the "real Hollywood" was often a big disappointment. No stars could be seen on the streets. Those actors who made it left only their hand- and footprints in the cement sidewalk in front of Grauman's Chinese Theatre and were living elsewhere, mostly in Beverly Hills. Everyday Hollywood was home to the aspiring and the wannabes.

"When Todd reached the street, he saw a dozen great violet shafts of light moving across the evening sky in wide crazy sweeps . . . The purpose of this display was to signal the world premiere of a new picture."
—The Day of the Locust

The Hollywood Boulevard film premiere epitomized the image that millions of movie fans had of the motion picture capital of the world. Countless spectators witnessed the arrival of celebrities at Grauman's Chinese Theatre as the Hollywood staple—klieg searchlights—fanned the skies. The whole idea started when Otto K Oleson bought a war-surplus carbon arc lamp off a battleship. Mounted on wheels, it provided a powerful beam of light that became an essential publicity tool and unmistakable Hollywood attraction.
During the golden age of the movies—the 1920s and 1930s—Hollywood gained international fame as the glamour capital of the world. Hollywood Boulevard

became the main commercial artery, with its elegant shops, celebrated restaurants and lavish movie palaces. Hollywood nightclubs carried special allure as the playground of the stars, symbolizing the celebrities' wild and extravagant lifestyles.

The Earl Carroll Theatre was the Hollywood's most spectacular nightclub

The opening of the Earl Carroll Theatre (➔ p126), on December 26, 1938, was one of the most star-studded events in the history of Hollywood. The greatest movie stars, such as Clark Gable,

Carole Lombard, Marlene Dietrich, Errol Flynn and Tyrone Power, flocked to the premiere of the enormously popular show.
LA's first movie studios were located in Edendale (now southern Glendale) and Silver Lake, but Hollywood soon became the favored place for early filmmaking. As much as the locals were annoyed by the encroaching movie colony, visitors to Hollywood, who flocked from all over the world, were thrilled to see film people at work in the streets.
Hollywood remained a center of movie production until the early 1920s, when major studios began migrating to larger lots in Burbank and Culver City. After the studios (and the stars with them) left, Hollywood began a long and steady decline. Competition from television also contributed to the area's deterioration. Nightlife relocated to nearby Sunset Strip, and by the 1970s famed Hollywood Boulevard had become a seedy mix of shabby T-shirt and souvenir shops.

Portraits of film personalities are painted on roll-down security doors along Hollywood Blvd

A postcard of Hollywood Blvd in the 1920s shows a typical scene, complete with klieg lights

Hollywood Beginnings

In 1886 the ardent Kansas prohibitionist, Harvey Wilcox, bought a 120-acre (48-ha) tract of Rancho La Brea for $150 an acre. His wife, Daeida, had met a woman on a train while traveling to her old home in the East. The woman evocatively described her estate called Hollywood, and the name so appealed to Mrs Wilcox that, upon her return, she chose the same name for their ranch in the foothills.

Hollywood as it appeared in 1905, looking south from the hills above Orange Dr

The huge set built for *The Thief of Bagdad* (1924)

Hollywood was incorporated in 1903 as a conservative Methodist town. Liquor was banned and all the bars were shut down. Hotels and restaurants were not allowed to operate since they also represented a temptation to people of disputable character. This pastoral idyll was soon to change, forever, to the horror of God-fearing Hollywood citizens—with the coming of hordes of "movie people."

Since their arrival in 1906, moviemakers had been filming scenes all over Hollywood's quiet neighborhoods. Actors were jumping over fences; cowboys were shooting at trees and riding over well-manicured gardens; car-chasing scenes were filmed at intersections; wild animals were escaping from the movie zoos. Innocent bystanders were frequently herded from the sidewalks to enhance mob scenes. Hollywood residents had such antipathy toward the invaders that a sign, "No dogs or actors allowed," was tacked to many apartment buildings. Nonetheless, as the city continued to accumulate cash from local film productions, protests were disregarded and petitions were ignored. The temperance community was powerless to stop the making of movies.

Some magnificent sets, such as this enormous palace built for *The Thief of Bagdad* on Santa Monica Blvd, remained standing for years and were visible from a great distance (left, bottom).

The house with the cupola in the foreground is the only building in this photograph that still exists (left, top).

First Map of Hollywood (1887) was an advertisement for a real estate development. It is the first recorded use of the name.

Hollywood was founded during the real-estate boom of 1887 when realtor Harvey Wilcox filed his tract of land in the Cahuenga Valley for subdivision purposes. His ranch was laid out in a rectangular grid according to the cardinal points; the streets were lined with pepper trees. A map of the tract filed with the county recorder on February 1, 1887 bears the name Hollywood, being the first advertisement for the future valuable properties and the first recorded use of the famous name.

Castle Sans Souci

This extravagant building was erected in 1912 by Dr Alfred Guido Randolph Schlosser, a Chicago-born physician who had made his fortune in the Nevada silver mines. With its crenellated façade, leaded-glass windows, large turrets and dominating central tower, Castle Sans Souci became a major tourist attraction. In its 25 foot-high Gothic hall, the eccentric doctor, who was never seen without makeup and top hat, entertained both the city's social elite and visiting European royalty. In a practice that, in various forms, still continues in Hollywood to this very day, the doctor advertised a unique rejuvenating technique. It consisted of ingesting pellets derived from the glands of sheep and goats. After his therapy proved ineffective in reversing the aging process, the physician ventured into real estate. He razed Sans Souci in 1928 and built the Castle Argyle apartment building on the same spot, which now serves as a residence for senior citizens.

Castle Sans Souci ("without care"), one of the most excessive structures ever built in Hollywood, once stood at the northwest corner of Franklin and Argyle avenues. Today, the Castle Argyle apartment building stands on the site.

The HOLLYWOODLAND sign was erected in 1923

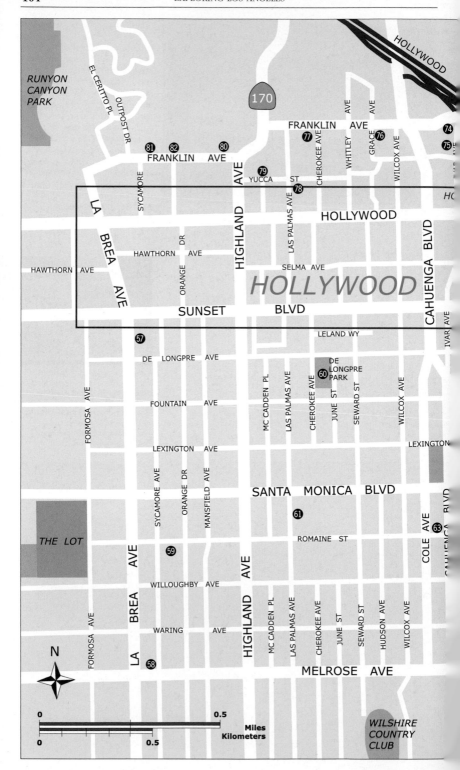

VINE ST
ARGYLE AVE
VISTA DEL MAR
BEACHWOOD DR
CHEREMOYA AVE
TAMARIND AVE
BRONSON AVE
BRIARCLIFF DR
LOS FELIZ BLVD

101 FRWY

73
72
FRANKLIN AVE
71

YUCCA ST
CARLOS AVE

70
CANYON
VAN NESS AVE
TAFT AVE
PL
GARFIELD PL
AVE

HOLLYWOOD BLVD

OOD BOULEVARD, see pp 106-7

BLVD
VINE ST
ARGYLE AVE
SELMA AVE
CARLTON WY
HAROLD WY
HAROLD WY
WILTON

SUNSET BLVD

46
AVE
VAN NESS AVE
DE LONGPRE AVL
67
FERNWOOD AVE
HOLLYWOOD
FOUNTAIN
SERANO AVE

DE LONGPRE AVE

FOUNTAIN AVE

65
EL CENTRO AVE
LODI PL
GOWER ST
BEACHWOOD ST
GORDON ST
TAMARIND AVE
BRONSON AVE
VAN NESS AVE
LEXINGTON AVE
SAINT ANDREWS
FRWY

HIST 66

SANTA MONICA

2

ELEANOR AVE
ROMAINE ST
BARTON AVE
WILLOUGHBY AVE
GREGORY AVE
64
WARING AVE
CAMERFORD AVE
VINE ST
GOWER
68
HOLLYWOOD FOREVER CEMETERY
PL
ROMAINE ST
AVE
WESTERN AVE

PARAMOUNT STUDIOS
69
VAN NESS AVE
RIDGEWOOD PL
WILTON

MELROSE AVE

66
GOWER ST
BRONSON AVE
AVE

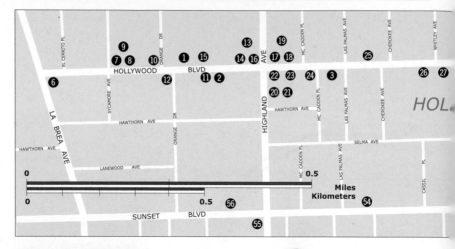

Winona Ryder's star dedication

Hollywood Walk of Fame

Hollywood Blvd, between Gower St and La Brea Ave; Vine St, between Sunset Blvd and Yucca St. ⓘ For a schedule of forthcoming dedication ceremonies contact the Hollywood Chamber of Commerce, 7018 Hollywood Blvd, ☎ (323) 469-8311. A brochure listing the names of honorees and their star locations on the Walk of Fame is also available.

The most famous sidewalk in the world, the Hollywood Walk of Fame, stretches more than two miles, lining both sides of Hollywood Blvd and Vine St. It consists of a series of stars set in a glittery sidewalk, each containing the name of the performer being honored. The Walk began as part of a plan to restore Hollywood's faded glamour and entice tourists to the area. It was the brainchild of Harry Sugarman, president of the Hollywood Improvement Association and owner of the Tropics restaurants in Beverly Hills and Hollywood. His idea for the Walk was inspired both by the hand- and footprints in the forecourt of Grauman's Chinese Theatre and the menu of his famous restaurants, which

Five emblems designate each recipient's field of endeavor

featured cocktails named after Sugarman's celebrity friends whose portraits were framed in gold stars. The first eight stars were installed in the sidewalk on the northwest corner of Hollywood Blvd and Highland Ave in September 1958. All of the recipients were movie stars, including Joanne Woodward and Burt Lancaster. A dedication ceremony was conducted on February 8, 1960, and within the next sixteen months, 1,558 celebrities had received a star on the famed sidewalk. Since then, approximately 15 to 20 stars have been added every year. There are now more than 2300.

Conceived as a permanent tribute to the personalities

View of Hollywood Blvd and the Walk of Fame. The famed sidewalk is embedded with 2300 stars

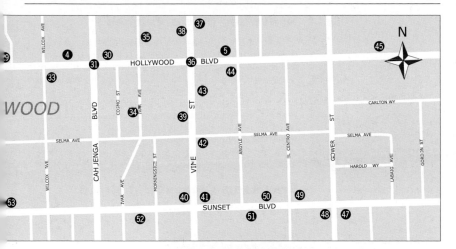

who helped make Hollywood the "Entertainment Capital of the World," the Walk honors recipients in five categories: motion pictures, television, radio, music recording and live theater. Besides the artist's name, each star contains one of five brass emblems representing the category in which the celebrity is being honored: a movie camera (film), a TV set with a rabbit ear antenna (television), a microphone (radio), a phonograph record (recording) and the masks of comedy and tragedy (theater).

The price of immortality, currently $25,000 per star, must be paid by the honoree. The celebrity must also guarantee that he or she will attend the dedication ceremony, which is traditionally well attended by the public.

Among the celebrities who did not thank the crowd in person when their star was dedicated were Mickey Mouse, Donald Duck, Snow White, Bugs Bunny, Big Bird and Godzilla. Lassie and Rin Tin Tin, the dog that saved Warner Bros from bankruptcy in the 1920s, have also been immortalized. King Kong is still waiting for his star. The four large stars at each of the corners of the Hollywood and Vine intersection are dedicated to the Apollo 11 astronauts who landed on the moon. Gene Autry has

A vintage post card depicting Hollywood stars of the 1930s

five stars on the Walk of Fame—more than anyone else. There even has been one celebrity casualty on the Walk: William Frawley (Fred from *I Love Lucy*) died here of a heart attack in 1966.

The visitors are encouraged to follow the sign markers posted along a self-guided Historic Hollywood Walking Tour. There are 46 orange-and-red signs posted along Hollywood Blvd and Vine St that explain the history of significant sites on the route. The tour takes about 2 1/2 hours to complete.

Stuff Hollywood stars are made of—the making of the Samuel L Jackson's star. The Walk of Fame is made of charcoal terrazzo squares embedded with brass stars filled with coral terrazzo.

Grauman's Chinese Theatre

Hollywood Movie Palaces

During the 1920s, some of the most elaborate movie theaters in the world were built in Hollywood. Known as movie palaces, they featured exotic façades, glittering marquees and neon spires outside, and sweeping stairways, wide aisles and plush seats inside. They thrived for decades, offering moviegoers an incomparable escapist experience, until financial pressures and changing moviegoing tastes pushed the big theater chains towards becoming look-alike multiplexes. Hollywood's El Capitan, the Pantages, the Chinese and the Egyptian are among the few reminders of single big-screen theaters of a flamboyant era.

Grauman's Chinese Theatre ❶

Meyer and Holler, architects (1927).
6925 Hollywood Blvd.
☎(323) 461-3331.
🔊a behind-the-scenes tour is available every day between 9:30am and the first show.
If you want to see a movie, make sure that it plays in the main auditorium and not in one of the smaller side theaters built later.
🕐call for showtimes. Ⓢ 🚩

Grauman's Chinese is probably the most famous movie theater in the world. Designed to resemble a Chinese temple, it became one of the most recognizable landmarks in cinema history. Envisioned to be "totally unexpected and spectacular," the theater remained virtually unchanged for more than 70 years. Its grand entrance is still overseen by a 30-foot (9-m) tall dragon and guarded by a pair of huge, stone-carved "Heaven Dogs." The entrance is flanked by a pair of red columns with black dragon-mask capitals which support the steep, pagoda-style copper roof. The large gong hanging over the entry once summoned audiences from the forecourt.

The Chinese was Sid Grauman's second movie palace in Hollywood. It opened on May 18, 1927, with Cecil B DeMille's *The King of Kings* screening for 2000 selected viewers. Besides being the host to more premieres than any other theater in Hollywood, the Academy Awards of 1944, 1945 and 1946 were held at Grauman's Chinese Theatre. Ingrid Bergman, Bing Crosby and Joan Crawford received their Oscars here.

The lavish interior of the 2,258-seat theater, designed to create an illusion of exotic Oriental opulence, is deco-

The attention to detail is visible in elaborate signage

The opulent auditorium of Grauman's Chinese Theatre

Many authentic artifacts in the theatre's lobby, such as bells, lanterns, vases and urns were imported with the permission of the Chinese government

Mary Pickford and Douglas Fairbanks pose with Sid Grauman before leaving their prints in the wet cement during the first ceremony in 1927

The legendary forecourt, with hand- or footprints and autographs of more than 160 movie stars, is one of Hollywood's largest tourist attractions

rated primarily in red. The auditorium features octagonal concrete columns and red-lacquered brick walls with an overlay of silver-painted Chinese motifs, including dragons, plants and birds. Its most dominant feature is an imposing, ornately-carved ceiling lantern. The attention to detail was visible in such niceties as dragon-shaped handles for the water faucets in the lavatories.

Hollywood's most successful showman, Sid Grauman, left an enduring legacy with his innovative publicity gimmick: concrete impressions of the movie stars. Contrary to common belief, silent screen star Norma Talmadge was not the first to implant her prints in the Grauman's Chinese forecourt. That fame belongs to Mary Pickford and Douglas Fairbanks.

There are numerous stories as to how this tradition got started. Legend has it that Grauman got the idea when Norma Talmadge accidentally stepped into fresh cement as she was getting out of her car. According to another version, Sid stumbled into wet concrete himself. Some say that the French mason working on the construction crew put his handprint in the cement, a sign that his ancestors used to leave in medieval cathedrals. Another story, reportedly told by Grauman himself, has it that Mary Pickford's dog Zorro first ran through wet cement, leaving tiny paw prints. Rumors circulate (denied by the management) that the theater's basement became a repository of a number of cement slabs signed by forgotten early stars, which were chiseled out from the courtyard to make room for new celebrities.

Intricate ornamentation on the façade includes small copper dragons whizzing down the gables

Some celebrities' immortalized imprints other than hands and feet include Sonja Henie's ice skates; Harold Lloyd's glasses; Harpo Marx's harp; William S Hart's guns; Jimmy Durante's and Bob Hope's noses; John Wayne's fist and one of Betty Grable's "million-dollar" legs. Among other oddities are Roy Rogers's horse Trigger and Gene Autry's Champion hoofprints; treadmarks left by *Star Wars* robots R2-D2 and C-3PO; and Donald Duck's webbed footprints, placed on his 50th birthday in 1984.

Janet Gaynor as aspiring actress Esther Blodgett in the classic *A Star Is Born* (1937) steps into the footprints of her favorite star and future husband, Norman Maine (Fredric March). A million curious tourists who visit the famous forecourt each year repeat the similar procedure daily.

The *Hell's Angels* premiere in 1930 attracted 50,000 people, the largest crowd ever assembled for a movie opening. At the premiere of *Hell's Angels*, as seen in *The Aviator* (2004), Howard Hughes (played by Leonardo DiCaprio) escorts young starlet Jean Harlow (Gwen Stefani) on the red carpet. The Chinese Theatre scenes in the movie were actually filmed on a set in Canada.

The elaborate marquee was added in 1942

Morgan, Walls and Clements, architects (1926).
6838 Hollywood Blvd.
☎(323) 467-9545; 467-7674
⏰call for showtimes. Ⓢ

The 20-foot (6-m) high box office foyer features molded plaster ceiling and ornate, wrought iron windows, entrance doors and poster cases

El Capitan Theatre ➋

Designed by the architectural firm of Morgan, Walls and Clements in the Spanish Colonial Revival style as a legitimate theater and office building, the El Capitan made its debut on May 3, 1926. Its Churrigueresque façade with East Indian detailing and ornate East Indian interior (designed by San Francisco architect G Albert Lansburgh) made it the most lavish legitimate theater in Hollywood. In its first decade more than 120 live plays were produced here, with stars such as Buster Keaton, Clark Gable, Henry Fonda, Will Rogers and Rita Hayworth among the top performers.

On May 9, 1941 (Orson Welles's twenty-sixth birthday), *Citizen Kane* made its world premiere here, after a long search for a venue whose owner would risk screening the movie William Randolph Hearst reviled. (The Welles's film contains allusions to the powerful newspaper magnate, who tried to stop its release at all costs.)

Due to faltering attendance, the El Capitan was converted to a movie house in 1942 and later renamed the Hollywood Paramount. Other famous movies that premiered here were *Sunset Boulevard* (1950), *Vertigo* (1958), *Gigi* (1958) and *Doctor Zhivago* (1965).

The theater's magnificent 1,550-seat auditorium originally had the proscenium ceiling, ornate opera boxes, sidewalls and organ grilles ornamented with cast plaster decorations covered with gold leaf. It was remodeled in 1942 as an Art Moderne movie house.

The El Capitan was superbly restored to its original splendor and opened in 1991 with the world premiere of *The Rocketeer*. It is now a showcase for first-run Disney movies, often accompanied by a live musical revue. Recent premieres include *The Lion King* (1994), *Pocahontas* (1995), *Toy Story* (1995), *Finding Nemo* (2003) and *The Incredibles* (2004).

The magnificently restored amphitheater of El Capitan Theatre

The grand 150-foot courtyard is restored with the help of old photographs

The Egyptian's restored auditorium with a gilded sunburst above the screen

Grauman's Egyptian Theatre ➌

The Egyptian Theatre was Sid Grauman's first movie palace in Hollywood, opened on October 18, 1922 with a gala premiere of Douglas Fairbanks' *Robin Hood*. It was the first-ever Hollywood premiere, a tradition originated by Sid Grauman with klieg spotlights, red carpet and celebrities arriving in limousines. Billing itself as the theater "where the stars see the movies," the Egyptian hosted countless movie premieres, from *The Thief of Bagdad* (1924) to *The Prince of Egypt* (1998).

The choice of Egyptian theme for the building is the result of the 1920s fascination with all things Egyptian. (King Tut was certainly not the inspiration—his tomb was discovered one month after the theater opening.)

After decades of neglect and damage, the theater was in a sad state of disrepair when the American Cinematheque bought it in the mid 1990s. After an extensive, $14-million restoration, it was re-opened on December 4, 1998 with a screening of DeMille's 1923 version of *The Ten Commandments*, which had premiered at the Egyptian 75 years ago to the day. As the Cinematheque's permanent home, the theater is one of the best venues in town for seeing foreign movies and documentaries, as well as classics and retrospectives.

Restored head of a pharaoh oversees the courtyard

The 1,760-seat auditorium originally featured a magnificent proscenium arch, together with massive twin Egyptian columns on each side, all richly decorated with ancient hieroglyphics (➔ p44). The ceiling was painted to represent an endless night sky, its constellations changing and shifting as the different lighting effects change and shift. These are all gone, but what remained is a splendid gilded sunburst above the screen.

Meyer and Holler, architects (1922)
6712 Hollywood Blvd.
☎(323) 466-FILM,
www.americancinematheque.com
www.egyptiantheatre.com
🎬 a behind-the scenes historic tour.
Film: A 55 minute documentary *Forever Hollywood*.
🕐 call for showtimes. Ⓢ

The Egyptian opened in 1922 with a premiere of *Robin Hood*

Sid Grauman hired an actor who patrolled the ramparts dressed as an ancient Egyptian guard and chanted the film's title luring passerbys. Even the usherettes (beautiful brunettes of the supposed Egyptian type) were clad as Cleopatra's handmaidens.

Warner Bros Hollywood Theater ❹

Famous San Francisco architect G Albert Lansburgh designed this movie palace, office and retail complex in a combination of styles, with a dominant Spanish Renaissance theme. The extravagant building was topped with two dirigible mast radio towers on the roof. It was opened as Warner Bros Theater on April 26, 1928, with a premiere of *Glorious Betsy*, starring Dolores Costello and Conrad Nagel. With more than 2,700 seats, it was at the time the largest movie theater in Hollywood. Carol Burnett started her show business career here as an usherette in 1951. Her star was later dedicated in the Walk of Fame in front of the same theater. With the installation of a huge semicircular screen in 1952, it became the first theater converted to Cinerama.

Warner Bros Theater was purchased in 1968 by Pacific Theaters chain, which partitioned it into a triplex, destroying much of the original interior in the process. Since 1999, the movie house has been leased by USC Entertainment and Technology Center, which is creating a state-of-the-art projection room and digital lab to research and test new movie technologies.

In the lobby is installed a plaque dedicated to Sam Warner, who conceived this theater as a showcase for sound technology and personally oversaw its construction. Sam convinced his brothers to venture into the sound process, and was involved in the production of the first sound film, *The Jazz Singer* (1927). He did not live to see his dream fulfilled, dying of a brain hemorrhage a day before the film premiered in New York on October 6, 1927. His spirit reportedly still haunts the theater.

Façade of Warner Bros Theater

G Albert Lansburgh, architect (1927)
6433 Hollywood Blvd.
Closed to the public. ♠

Crowds gather at the Warner Hollywood Theater for the gala premiere of John Wayne's *Operation Pacific* (1951)

The original auditorium of the Warner Bros Theater was designed as an opulent Spanish interior court, apparently opening to the sky and surrounded by a colonnade through which pictorial vistas, painted by prominent international artist Albert Herter, could be seen. Specially designed lighting produced changing cloud effects in the sky-like ceiling.

The Warner Theater's Moorish interior features a still intact, monumental semi-circular lobby, called the promenade, which surrounds the auditorium

Pantages Theatre ❺

Designed by famous theater architect B Marcus Priteca, this was the last and largest of three theaters he built for vaudeville impresario Alexander Pantages. Constructed at an enormous cost of $1.25 million and opened as part of the Fox theater chain, it was the last and most ornate of Hollywood's great movie palaces. Among the first movie houses built after the advent of talking pictures, the Pantages boasted the most advanced sound equipment in the world. The opening program, hosted by Master of Ceremonies Al Jolson on June 4, 1930, featured the world premiere of MGM's *The Florodora Girl*, starring Marion Davies.

When movie producer Howard Hughes, through his RKO Pictures, acquired the theater in 1949, it became the home of the Academy Awards presentations. The lavish ceremonies were held here for the next 10 years, including the first televised Oscars in 1953. Humphrey Bogart, Gary Cooper, Marlon Brando, Vivien Leigh, Grace Kelly and Frank Sinatra received their Oscars on this stage. The Pantages was also the site of many glamorous premieres and "spectaculars," including *Spartacus* (1959) and *Cleopatra* (1963). It has itself been the setting for numerous films, including *At Long Last Love* (1975) and *The Aviator* (2004).

The Pantages's Zigzag Moderne façade features large second-floor windows with bas-relief panels and elaborate grillwork, as well as an ornate marquee suspended on distinctive spiky chains. The theater's exterior box office lobby features ornate display cases and a magnificent, intricately carved domed ceiling. Its modest exterior does not prepare the visitor for the breathtaking Art Deco extravaganza that awaits inside; it was often described as one the most spectacular theater interiors ever built.

With its seating capacity of 2,812, the Pantages's auditorium was the largest in Hollywood. Its most staggering feature is the majestic blue ceiling with its ornate gold, silver and bronze geometric motifs, and massive central chandelier of frosted glass.

After a $10-million renovation, the interior was restored to its former grandeur and reopened for *The Lion King* musical in 2001.

The theater is said to be haunted by its former owner, Howard Hughes, whose apparition was reportedly seen on the second floor, where his office was once located.

B Marcus Priteca, architect (1929), Anthony Heinsbergen, interior.
6233 Hollywood Blvd.
☎(323) 468 1700.
🕐call for showtimes. Ⓢ 🏳 ♠

The Pantages's grand lobby is covered by a vaulted coffered ceiling that rests on magnificent zigzag column capitals. Flanked by twin grand stairways, it is adorned with gold, silver and bronze statues depicting characteristic Southern California themes such as filmmaking and aviation.

Overflowing with light, the famous mirrored women's powder room is a dazzling Art Deco spectacle

A curious visitor examines La Brea Gateway

La Brea Gateway ❻

SE corner of Hollywood Blvd and La Brea Ave.

Designating the western gateway to Hollywood Blvd, this sculpture/gazebo by Catherine Hardwicke is a homage to legendary women film stars: Anna May Wong, Mae West, Dolores Del Rio and Dorothy Dandridge. The Beatles' star on Hollywood Walk of Fame is placed nearby.

Garden Court Apartments (site) ❼

7021 Hollywood Blvd.

On this site stood one of the most exuberant apartment buildings ever built in the city. Opened in 1919, the magnificent Beaux-Art structure featured luxury suites furnished with Oriental carpets, grand pianos and fine oil paintings. Other amenities included two ballrooms, billiards room, pool and tennis courts. In its heyday, it was home to such luminaries as Louis B Mayer, Mae Murray, John Gilbert, Mack Sennett, Lillian Gish and John Barrymore.

The building later fell into disrepair and became known as "Hotel Hell." Although there were attempts by preservationists to save it, the building was torn down in 1985.

Hollywood Galaxy ❽

7021 Hollywood Blvd.
☎(323) 465-7900.

This $48-million mall opened in 1991, featuring a six-screen cinema complex. Standing on the site formerly occupied by Garden Court Apartments, it was the first movie theater built on the boulevard in five decades.

Hollywood Entertainment Museum ❾

7021 Hollywood Blvd.
☎(323) 469-7900.
🕘Thu-Sun 11am-6pm. Ⓢ
www.hollywoodmuseum.com

Each gallery in the museum, which reviews the history of Hollywood, offers displays that thematically revolve around the four components of the entertainment industry: film, television, radio and sound recordings.

The pictorial central gallery, called the Rotunda, houses the museum's permanent collection and is dominated by the 15-foot-tall Goddess of Entertainment.

On display is the Max Factor Collection, previously housed in the former Max Factor Museum. The star exhibit is the bridge of the Federation Starship USS *Enterprise*, complete with

A statue of comedian Buster Keaton as a cameraman

some of the artifacts used to create *Star Trek* for more than 30 years, including giant Klingon figures and alien masks.

C C Brown's Ice Cream (site) ❿

7007 Hollywood Blvd.

The famous chocolate shop and ice cream parlor was located at this site from 1929 to 1996. Frequented by movie stars (and crowded with fans seeking autographs), this was the place where the hot-fudge sundae was born. The locale is used today as a souvenir shop.

Masonic Hall

Masonic Hall ⓫

John C Austin, architect (1921)
6840 Hollywood Blvd. **NRHP**

This Neoclassical colonnaded temple was the work of the architect who also designed Los Angeles City Hall, the Shrine Auditorium and the Griffith Observatory. Erected in 1921, it was the headquarters of the Hollywood Freemasons for 60 years. Among the lodge's prominent members were early movie industry celebrities Cecil B DeMille, Oliver Hardy, Harold Lloyd, Douglas Fairbanks, W C Fields, D W Griffith and later Gene Autry, Glenn Ford and John Wayne. D W Griffith's memorial service was held here in 1948, attended by a number of celebrities.

A recent renovation restored the original fixtures and preserved much of the original décor. The building now features Disney's interactive exhibits and after the film receptions.

The bottom of the hotel's pool was painted by British artist David Hockney

Hollywood Roosevelt Hotel ⑫

Fisher, Lake and Traver, architects (1926).
7000 Hollywood Blvd.
☎(323) 466-7000. ♠ 🏴 NRHP

Named after Theodore Roosevelt, the 26th President of the United States, the hotel opened May 15, 1927. Financed by such industry greats as Mary Pickford, Douglas Fairbanks, Marcus Loew and Louis B Mayer, the hotel quickly became the gathering place of Hollywood's luminaries and the site of lavish post-premiere parties.

The first meetings of the Academy of Motion Picture Arts and Sciences were held in the hotel library. The famous Blossom Ballroom was the site of the first Academy Awards presentation, on May 16, 1929 (➔ p48).

Designed in 1926 and restored in 1985 and 2005, the hotel features an exquisite two-story Spanish Colonial lobby with painted beamed ceiling and wrought-iron grillwork. On the tile steps that lead to the mezzanine Bill "Bojangles" Robinson taught Shirley Temple how to do the staircase dance.

Among the hotel's famous guests were Charlie Chaplin, David Niven, Marilyn Monroe and Montgomery Clift. A two-story cottage on the grounds was once Clark Gable and Carole Lombard's love nest. During Prohibition, Errol Flynn allegedly used to mix his notorious gin concoction in the back of the hotel barbershop. Famous astrologer Linda Goodman wrote her best-selling books *Sun Signs* and *Love Signs* in suite 1217.

Both the patrons and the hotel's staff reported the presence of numerous ghosts at the hotel. While filming *From Here to Eternity* in 1952, actor Montgomery Clift used room 928 for three months. His spirit is frequently observed in the room and the hallway. The reflection of Marilyn Monroe has been seen in a mirror in suite 1200, where the actress often stayed.

Marilyn Monroe posed for her first ad (for suntan lotion) on the diving board of the hotel's swimming pool. British artist David Hockney painted the bottom of the pool with dark blue swirls in 1987.

The hotel's live cabaret, the Cinegrill, started as a jazz club in the early 1930s. It used to be a favorite of writers F Scott Fitzgerald and Ernest Hemingway, as well as Surrealist painter Salvador Dalí, who worked as a movie set designer at the time. Liberace was the headliner here for many years.

Both the strip tease show in *Beverly Hills Cop II* (1987) and Michelle Pfeiffer's sexy nightclub scene, in which she sings while crawling across the top of a piano in *The Fabulous Baker Boys* (1989), were filmed in the Cinegrill.

Hollywood Hotel
(site) ⑬
6811 Hollywood Blvd. 🏴

The northwest corner of Hollywood Blvd and Highland Ave was the site of the first major hotel in Hollywood. Built in Mission Revival Style in 1905 and owned by chocolate heiress Mira Hershey, it was extremely popular with tourists from the East. But it was such early movie stars as Greta Garbo, Douglas Fairbanks, Gloria Swanson, Pola Negri, Norma Shearer, Lon Chaney and others who brought the Hollywood Hotel its legendary fame. One of the celebrity regulars was Rudolph Valentino, who in 1919 checked in at the hotel with his first wife, Jean Acker. He reportedly wasn't allowed into their suite on the wedding night until he showed a clerk a marriage license. Story has it that the bride, a lesbian, threw Valentino out of their honeymoon suite on the same night.

During the 1930s, gossip columnist Louella Parsons brought the hotel to national prominence when she broadcast her popular radio show from the establishment. The 144-room hotel was razed in 1956 when it could not meet new safety standards.

Busby Berkeley's musical *Hollywood Hotel* (1938), which mocks both the film and the radio industries, took place at the hotel and generated the famous song, *Hooray for Hollywood*.

A vintage post card depicting Hollywood Hotel

The Hollywood and Highland retail and entertainment complex

Hollywood and Highland ⓮

Ehrenkrantz Eckstut & Kuhn Architects (2001).
Hollywood Blvd and Highland Ave.

Built at a cost of $615 million on the site of the original Hollywood Hotel, this retail and entertainment complex is the first and largest of several developments intended to help reinvigorate the area as a tourist magnet.

The design took its inspiration from D W Griffith's epic film *Intolerance* (1916), whose extravagant set was erected a few miles east (➔ p158). Two monumental columns topped by 33-foot (10-m) trumpeting elephants dominate the development's central courtyard, called Babylon Court. Looking through a recreated portal of the same set, visitors may even catch a glimpse of the HOLLYWOOD sign.

Called *Road to Hollywood*, the path in the courtyard is engraved with memorable quotes from determined filmmakers who made it in the movie mecca: "Louis B Mayer saw me in a film in Berlin and asked me to come to Hollywood if I was willing to lose some weight. 'We don't like fat girls in my country,' he said." (Greta Garbo)

Since 2002 the Kodak Theatre is the new home of the Oscars

Kodak Theatre ⓯

David Rockwell, architect (2001).
6801 Hollywood Blvd.
☎(323) 308-6379.
www.kodaktheatre.com.
☛for 30-minute behind-the-scenes tours, call (323) 308-6363. Ⓢ

The 3,600-seat Kodak Theatre is a state of the art performing arts venue, designed to meet all the requirements of the Academy of Motion Picture Arts and Sciences. Built primarily with television in mind as a broadcast and recording studio, it has three balcony levels stacked on top of one another, which provide unobstructed sight lines and bring the audience closer to the stage. The theater features 24 opera boxes; its stage is one of the largest in the US, measuring 113 ft wide and 60 ft deep (34 x 18 m).

Floating high above the seats is the theater's main design element, an imposing oval chandelier interlaced with several smaller ovals and coated in silver leaf. Called the tiara (Spanish for crown) by the architect, it was inspired by the floor pattern of Michelangelo's Campidoglio in Rome, as well as the endlessly changing forms choreographed by Busby Berkeley in the famous dance sequences of his musicals. Beside its decorative function, the tiara camouflages the ceiling riggings and the catwalks necessary to reach them.

The Kodak Theatre is the first "permanent" home of

Front entrance of the Kodak Theatre

the Academy Awards presentations since 1929, when the first Oscar ceremony took place at the Hollywood Roosevelt Hotel just down the street. As part of the deal with the Eastman Kodak Co, which will pay $75 million over 20 years for the venue-naming rights, the Oscars will stay here for two decades. The Academy Awards moved to the Kodak Theatre in March 2002, when the 74th annual ceremony was held at its new home amid heightened security.

For fans willing to go through the scrutiny of background checks to watch the celebrity arrivals from the bleachers, some 400 seats are made available by advance reservation only. The applications can be obtained on the Academy's web site, www.oscars.org, about six weeks before the event.

Hollywood and Highland subway station ⑯

Dworsky Associates, architects; Sheila Klein, artist (2000). ▸

With its blue ribs and pink central columns, the subway tunnel looks like the belly of a whale, reflecting the architect's intention to create an abstract representation of a Hollywood fantasy. In a hint at "Sin City" and female sexuality, the artist designed wall sconces in the form of splayed legs fanning out from the columns.

An iconic sequence in *The Italian Job* (2003) was filmed on location here, with three tiny Mini Coopers racing along a Hollywood Blvd sidewalk and down the actual stairwell to the subway station. Since the MTA did not allow gasoline-powered cars in its underground locations, BMW custom built three electric-powered Minis— the only ones in the world.

Hollywood and Highland subway station

with a 12-story octagonal tower with eight buttresses, the bank is decorated with motifs of the explorer Christopher Columbus and scientist Nicolaus Copernicus. The building served as the Daily Planet in the old *Superman* television series. The journalist turned hero took flight from its balcony.

Hollywood Wax Museum ⑱

6767 Hollywood Blvd.
☎ (323) 462-8860.
⏰ Sun-Thu 10am-12midnight; Fri-Sat 10am-1am. ⑤

This tourist attraction displays over 200 wax replicas, ranging from film and television stars to sports heroes, politicians and other celebrities. The most renowned part of the museum is the Chamber of Horrors, containing recreations of thrilling scenes from horror films.

Hollywood First National Bank

Hollywood First National Bank ⑰

Meyer and Holler, architects (1927) 6777 Hollywood Blvd. ▸

Designed in 1927, this was briefly the tallest building in the city—until the LA City Hall was built a year later. A striking white Gothic and Spanish Colonial structure,

Montmartre Café

(formerly) ⑲

6757 Hollywood Blvd.

In 1923, Eddie Brandstatter opened one of Hollywood's wildest and most famous nightspots on the second floor of the C E Toberman Italian Renaissance building. The long list of its celebrity patrons included Charlie Chaplin, Marion Davies, Clark Gable, Carole Lombard, Gloria Swanson and Winston Churchill. Rudolph Valentino tangoed here with Pola Negri, while Joan Crawford was discovered after she won a Charleston dance competition. Singer Bing Crosby performed here in the 1930s.

During the 1970s, the building was the home of the famous acting school, the Lee Strasberg Institute. Today, it houses the Stella Adler Academy of Acting and Theatres (6773 Hollywood Blvd, 2nd fl).

Mural on the Hollywood Wax Museum Building

Max Factor Studio Building (formerly) ⑳

S Charles Lee, architect (1935).
1668 N Highland Ave. 🏃

The building was Max Factor's (➔ p53) famed Hollywood Makeup Salon. It was originally constructed in 1915 and used as a warehouse until architect S Charles Lee remodeled it in 1935. Using pink and white marble, he created the Regency-style Art Deco façade suitable for the King of Hollywood Glamour.

Over 8,000 people attended the premiere opening of the Max Factor Studio, including every big name in the movie industry. Each celebrity was invited to sign a large genuine parchment, known as the Scroll of Fame, which became one of the largest collections of screen stars' autographs in existence.

The exterior of the building was featured in *Beverly Hills Cop II* (1987) as a jewelry shop robbed by Brigitte Nielsen.

Entrance to Max Factor Studio

Hollywood Museum ㉑

1660 N Highland Ave.
☎(323) 464-7776.
🕐Thu-Sun 10am-5pm. 💲

Located in the painstakingly restored landmark Max Factor Building, this new Hollywood attraction features four floors of displays, from the beginnings of the movie industry to today's international blockbusters.

Among the museum's highlights are four Max Factor make-up rooms, individually

Max Factor make-up room "For Brunettes Only," especially designed to demonstrate Factor's concept of color harmony

designed "For Blondes; Redheads, Brunettes; or Brownettes Only," which demonstrate Factor's concept of color harmony.

The museum's collection comprises rare photographs, movie posters, awards, original scripts, vintage equipment and Hollywood memorabilia, including a dazzling selection of sets, costumes and props from such productions as *Gladiator* (2000) and *Moulin Rouge* (2001). The dinosaur-hatching incubator from *Jurassic Park* (1993), the space ship from *Planet of the Apes* (2001) and Hannibal Lecter's jail cell, as seen in *The Silence of the Lambs* (1991), are also on display.

Extensive costumes exhibits include Marilyn Monroe's honeymoon gown, Shirley MacLaine's stage show outfits and the world's largest collection of costumes and personal items of Mae West, on permanent loan to the museum by her personal assistant.

Ripley's Believe It or Not! Museum ㉒

6780 Hollywood Blvd
☎(323) 466-6335.
🕐Sun-Thu 10am-10:30pm; Fri-Sat 10am-11:30pm. 💲

The museum displays over 300 unusual items collected around the world by Robert Ripley or his organization. Rarities include a genuine shrunken human head from the Jivaro Indians of Ecuador,

a 14-piece vampire killing kit and the Quarter Million Dollar Marilyn, sculpture made from over $260,000 in wornout dollar bills that the government had thrown in the garbage.

Guinness World of Records Museum ㉓

6764 Hollywood Blvd.
☎(323) 463-6433.
🕐daily 10am-12midnight.
💲 NRHP

Containing over five million pieces of information, the museum features the greatest facts, the wildest feats and the most outstanding achievements of all time. It is located at the former Hollywood Theater, designated a National Register Landmark, and Hollywood's oldest movie house still standing.

The former nickelodeon was opened in 1913. Its 1930s triangular neon marquee was among the first designed with side panels in order to be more easily seen by passing motorists.

A model T-rex tearing the roof off Ripley's Believe It or Not!

Christie Hotel

(formerly) ㉔

Arthur B Kelly, architect (1922).
6724 Hollywood Blvd.

This was the first of Hollywood's luxury hotels. It was built in 1922 by brothers Al and Charles Christie, who established the Nestor Studio, the first motion-picture studio in Hollywood. The hotel was designed in the Georgian style, a rarity in Hollywood, and featured a fashionable innovation not seen before in the area—private baths in every room. Today, the Church of Scientology owns the building.

Façade of the Christie Hotel

Musso and Frank Grill ㉕

6667 Hollywood Blvd.
☎(323) 467-7788. ↝ ⚑

Open since 1919, this is the oldest continuing restaurant in Hollywood, also considered by many to be its finest. The original location was at 6669, but in 1936 Musso's (as it has always been known) relocated to larger housing next door, where it is still standing. From the beginning it was extremely popular with movie celebrities, attracted by its casual atmosphere and dark-paneled, circular red leather booths. It is said that Charlie Chaplin used to sit in the booth located by the front-corner window, facing the boulevard.

Hollywood lore has it that Chaplin and Douglas Fairbanks once raced each other on horseback down the boulevard; the winner's prize was dinner at Musso's. During the 1930s and 1940s, the restaurant was the favorite hangout for hard-drinking novelists and screenwriters (who worked for movie studios), including William Faulkner, F Scott Fitzgerald, Raymond Chandler, John Fante, Dashiell Hammett, William Saroyan, Nathanael West and Budd Schulberg. Since the writers had their characters frequent Musso's too, it became one of the most regularly mentioned restaurants in California literature (➜ p72).

Marlon Brando's son Christian and his half sister Cheyenne had drinks here before heading to Brando's compound on Mulholland Dr (➜ p472), where Christian shot his sister's lover Dag Drollet to death in 1990.

In the film *Ocean's Eleven* (2001), George Clooney and Brad Pitt drive a convertible on Hollywood Blvd and make a right turn on Cherokee St as the sign of the restaurant appears. After leaving the car in the parking lot, they are seen again in one of the restaurant's signature red leather booths.

Musso and Frank Grill in the 1920s

Frederick's of Hollywood (formerly) ㉖

Edward F Sibbert, architect (1935).
6606-12 Hollywood Blvd.
☎(323) 466-8506.

Formerly S H Kress Department Store, this 1935 classic Art Deco building housed Frederick's of Hollywood flagship store. Its façade has been painted purple and pink probably to match the provocative lingerie that was sold inside. Frederick Mellinger started his company in 1946 with a motto: "Fashions may change, but sex appeal is always in style." Among his famous innovations were the first push-up bra and the first front-hook bra.

A small celebrity lingerie museum, first of its kind in the world, displayed Marilyn Monroe's bra from *Let's Make Love* (1960), Tony Curtis's black lace bra from the classic *Some Like It Hot* (1950) and Madonna's famous black bustier from the *Who's That Girl?* world tour (1987).

The store relocated to 6755 Hollywood Blvd in 2005.

Charlie Chaplin's booth at Musso and Frank Grill

Gaudy façade of Frederick's of Hollywood flagship store

The "five and dime" J J Newberry Building

J J Newberry Building ㉗

6600-04 Hollywood Blvd.

This colorful Art Deco building, designed by an anonymous staff architect in 1928, features turquoise, gold and yellow glazed terracotta arranged in a zigzag pattern of chevrons and squares.

Janes House

Janes House ㉘

6541 Hollywood Blvd.
Closed to the public

Built in 1905 on what was then known as Prospect Ave, this restored Queen Anne landmark structure is the last remaining private residence still standing on Hollywood Blvd. Between 1911 and 1926, the three daughters of the first owner, Herman Janes, operated a famed elementary school here. It was attended by the children of motion picture pioneers Cecil B DeMille, Jesse Lasky, Charlie Chaplin, Douglas Fairbanks, Thomas Ince and Carl Laemmle.

Hillview Apartments ㉙

6531-35 Hollywood Blvd.
Private residences.

Built in 1917 by movie mogul Jesse Lasky, this Mediterranean-style apartment building provided much-needed housing for movie actors close to the studios. Many landlords in Hollywood refused to accept members of the motion picture industry in their rooming houses, regarding them a nuisance and threat to morality.

Paul DeLongpre Home (site) ㉚

Hollywood Blvd and Cahuenga Blvd, NE corner.

Built in 1901 by French-born painter Paul DeLongpre, this palatial, Moorish-inspired estate was the first Hollywood tourist attraction. Brought by streetcars, 25,000 visitors every year flocked to DeLongpre's residence to see the famous artist, his studio and paintings, and to stroll through elaborate three-acre gardens that held 4,000 rose bushes.

Raymond Chandler Square ㉛

Hollywood Blvd and Cahuenga Blvd. ➥

The corner of Hollywood and Cahuenga boulevards was made famous by mystery novelist Raymond Chandler, who placed the seedy offices of his hero, private detective Philip Marlowe, on the sixth floor of the fictional "Cahuenga Building." It is widely believed that Security Trust and Savings Bank, at 6381-85 Hollywood Blvd, was Chandler's inspiration for the fictional building, mentioned in his novel *The Long Goodbye*.

Hollywood Murals

6542 Hollywood Blvd (mural on Schrader Ave, SW corner).
6440 Hollywood Blvd (mural on Wilcox Ave, SE corner).

The Muralists (1989) by Richard Wyatt ㉜
Comedians Stan Laurel and Oliver Hardy paint a mural of Laurence Olivier, Vivien Leigh, James Cagney and Lauren Bacall.
You are the Star (1983) by Thomas Suriya ㉝
In a role reversal, scores of Hollywood stars sitting in a movie theater look at the spectator.

A vintage post card depicts Paul DeLongpre Hollywood home

***The Muralists* (1989) by Richard Wyatt (top)**
***You are the Star* (1983) by Thomas Suriya (bottom)**

Frances Goldwyn Library ㉞

Frank O Gehry and Associates, architect (1986).
1623 N Ivar Ave.
☎(323) 467 1821.

When an arson fire destroyed the Hollywood Library and its 80,000 books in 1982, security played an important part in plans for the new structure.

Designed by famous local architect, Frank O Gehry, the building comprises three box-like pavilions well protected behind the 15-foot-high security walls. Second-story reading rooms, which offer views into the shallow reflecting pools, are splendid ly lit with diffused daylight.

The library specializes in reference materials about Hollywood and the movies.

Knickerbocker Hotel ㉟

E M Frasier, architect (1923).
1714 N Ivar Avenue.
Retirement home.

Opened in 1925 as a luxury apartment building, the Knickerbocker later became one of Hollywood's most glamorous hotels.

Among its early guests were Gloria Swanson, Dick Powell, Bette Davis and Cary Grant; later, Frank Sinatra and Jerry Lee Lewis also stayed here. When Errol Flynn arrived in Hollywood in 1935, the Knickerbocker was his first home. The hotel housed William Faulkner when he was writing the screenplay for *The Road to Glory* (1936). Marilyn Monroe used to sneak through the hotel's kitchen and into the bar to meet Joe DiMaggio in 1954. Elvis Presley, who called it "Heartbreak Hotel," stayed here while filming *Love Me Tender* (1956) and recording the *Elvis* album. On Halloween of 1936, Harry Houdini's widow, Bess, conducted a séance on the roof, unsuccessfully trying to communicate with her deceased husband's spirit. In 1948, celebrated silent film director D W Griffith died here in his room. After leaving a note apologizing to other hotel guests, famed MGM costume designer Irene jumped out of the window from the eleventh floor in 1962.

The hotel bar, which closed in the 1960s, was supposedly haunted the patrons reported seeing ghosts of former customers, including Marilyn's.

Once a popular hangout, the lounge area was used as a hotel bar where Benjamin (played by Dustin Hoffman) and Mrs Robinson (Ann Bancroft) rendezvoused in *The Graduate* (1967).

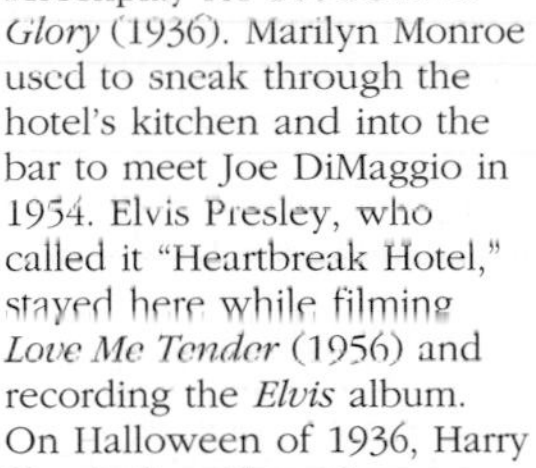

A vintage post card depicts Knickerbocker Hotel

The bar scene in *The Graduate* (1967) was filmed at the Knickerbocker Hotel

Hollywood and Vine ㊱

Called the most famous intersection in the world during the Hollywood golden age, it is most disappointing to today's visitor. It was often debated what made this unremarkable spot a symbol of Hollywood glamour. Was it the nearby Brown Derby restaurant, the epicenter of the Hollywood social scene, with its celebrities and crowds of tourists? Or the two-block stretch of Vine St, between Hollywood and Sunset boulevards, that became the center of the radio industry? The phrase "brought to you from Hollywood and Vine," a frequent opening to many radio shows, remained in the memory of millions of listeners.

The claim to fame certainly has its price—in 1920 four corner lots at Hollywood and Vine were estimated at $30,000; ten years later, an interested buyer could have purchased them for about $8,000,000.

Capitol Records ㊲

Welton Becket Associates (1954).
1750 N Vine St.
☎(323) 462-6252.

Designed in 1954, this famed Hollywood landmark was the first circular office building in the world. It was also the first fully air-conditioned office building in the country. It was said that the cylindrical structure was designed to resemble a stack of 45-rpm records on a phonograph, with a stylized rooftop needle. Not true, says its designer, Louis M Naidorf. As a young architect with the firm, he was assigned to a secret project without knowing who the client was. The beacon at the top flashes "Hollywood" in Morse code.

Capitol Records was started as Liberty Records in 1942 by the owner of Wallichs Music City, Glenn Wallichs, songwriter Johnny Mercer and executive producer at Paramount Pictures, Buddy DeSylva. The company was innovative from the beginning, providing disc jockeys with sample records of each new release. This coopera-

Hollywood Jazz, 1945-1972 by Richard Wyatt (1990)

tion with radio later became a standard practice of the recording industry. Among the label's top recording stars were Nat "King" Cole, Peggy Lee, Les Paul, Frank Sinatra, Dean Martin, Tina Turner, the Beatles and the Beach Boys.

Numerous gold records of Capitol's famous performers are displayed in the lobby.

John Lennon's star on the Walk of Fame is imbedded in front of the entrance.

Hollywood Jazz, 1945-1972
by Richard Wyatt (1990)

A mural painted on the south side of the building honors Capitol Records' star performers. From left: Chat Baker, Gerry Mulligan, Charlie Parker, Tito Puente, Miles Davis, Ella Fitzgerald, Nat "King" Cole, Shelly Manne, Dizzy Gillespie, Billie Holliday and Duke Ellington.

Palace Theater
(formerly) ㊳

1735 N Vine St.
☎(323) 462-8900.

Opened in 1927 as a legitimate theater known as the Hollywood Playhouse, this Spanish Colonial Revival building changed name several times and was used as a television and radio facility. It was a home for Ken Murray's Blackouts revue, which ran continuously from 1942 to 1949. With 3,844 performances, it became the longest running show in American history. The first nationally televised telethon, with Bing Crosby, Bob Hope and Frank Sinatra, took place here in 1952 to raise funds for the US Olympic team. It was at this theater that Raquel Welch started as a (Hollywood Palace) showgirl. It was here that Dean Martin insulted the Rolling Stones on his variety TV show in 1964. Among the artists who performed here were Frank Sinatra, the Beatles, Prince, Nirvana and Snoop Dogg.

Today called Avalon Hollywood, it operates as a concert venue and dance club.

Vine Street Theater ㊴

1615-29 N Vine St.

Formerly known as the Doolittle Theater, this venue, which opened in 1927, originally showcased live performances. It was later used as a movie house and for radio and television shows. From the mid-1930s to 1945, the famous Lux Radio Theater, hosted by Cecil B DeMille and featuring major movie stars as guests, was broadcast from here.

Capitol Records Building

Wallichs Music City (site) ⑳

1501 N Vine St.

One of the most famous music stores in the world, Wallichs pioneered the self-service concept to sell records. It was the first store to seal record albums in cellophane, the first to introduce display racks for browsing and the first to have demonstration rooms for customers to listen to the records in before purchasing. Frank Zappa was working here as a clerk in 1965. The store operated between 1940 and 1978. Its owner, Glenn Wallichs, was one of the founders of Capitol Records. What was considered the world's largest serve-yourself record store was demolished in 1982 for a mini-mall and a parking lot.

Lasky Feature Play Company used a horse barn as a studio (1915)

open to the public, which could take a close look of the facility during guided tours. Many nationally broadcast shows started here, including *The Jack Benny Show* and *The Bob Hope Show*.

Untitled (1970) by Millard Sheets and Susan Hertl
Erected on the site where Hollywood's first feature-length movie was made, the Washington Mutual (formerly Home Savings of America) bank building pays tribute to the pioneers of the movie industry. At the building's front and rear entrances are mosaic portraits of early movie stars such as Rudolph Valentino, Mary Pickford, Gloria Swanson, Gary Cooper and Charlie Chaplin. They are accompanied by hundreds of names of famous motion picture personalities inscribed in gold.
Inside the building, the murals show scenes from *The Squaw Man* (1914).

Greta Garbo, a detail of the mosaic *Untitled* (1970)

Jesse L Lasky Feature Play Company Studio (site) ㊷

SE corner of Vine St and Selma Ave.

This is the site where in 1914 Cecil B DeMille completed production of *The Squaw Man*, the first feature-length motion picture made by a major company in Hollywood. DeMille, Jesse Lasky and Samuel Goldfish (later Goldwyn) used a rented horse barn here as a set, office and dressing rooms. The movie's great success enabled Lasky to expand his studio to two city blocks within 18 months. It later merged with Adolph Zukor's Famous Players Corporation, forming the precursor to Paramount Pictures. In 1926, the barn was transported to the new Paramount lot and finally, in 1983, moved to its current site on Highland Ave (➔ p152).

NBC Radio City (site) ㊶

1500 N Vine St.

On the northeast corner of Sunset Blvd and Vine St stood from 1938 to 1964 one of the best-known Hollywood landmarks. Called the radio center of the world, NBC's Radio City complex housed eight expansive studios, shaped like live theaters to accommodate the audiences. Live broadcasts were

A vintage post card depicts NBC Radio City in 1940

THE BROWN DERBY RESTAURANT. — 1628 N. VINE ST., — HOLLYWOOD, CALIF.

The Brown Derby, known as "The Rendezvous of the Stars," was the gathering place of celebrities from the motion picture and radio, and the mecca of film fans and visitors to the film capital

Hollywood Brown Derby (site) ④③

1620-28 N Vine St.

This was the second branch in a chain of four restaurants bearing the same name (➜ p214). The Spanish Colonial Revival style structure was designed by Carl Jules Weyl, an Oscar-winning art director who created the unforgettable look of Rick's Café in *Casablanca* (1942). Founded by Herbert Somborn, one of Gloria Swanson's husbands, the Derby opened on Valentine's Day in 1929. Owing to its celebrity patrons and continual coverage by gossip columnists, it became the most famous restaurant in the world. Its close proximity to the movie and radio studios made it a gathering point of Hollywood celebrities—stars in costume could often be seen during lunchbreak. With its signature brown leather seats designed to be low enough to allow an unobstructed view of the room, this was the place to see and be seen. The Derby quickly became the glamorous heart of the Hollywood entertainment industry, as evidenced on its walls lined with hundreds of luminary caricatures. Clark Gable supposedly proposed to Carole Lombard here in booth #5.

The Derby originated a practice of providing telephones at the tables during mealtimes, so that stars and executives did not have to interrupt dining. Calls were relayed by loudspeakers, and the number of times a patron was paged became a measure of one's importance in Hollywood.

Damaged by fire and the Northridge earthquake, the building was demolished in 1994.

Hollywood and Vine subway station ④④

Miralles Associates, architect/ Gilbert "Magu" Lujan, artist (1999)

Taking inspiration from the idea of Hollywood as a "dream factory," the station's interior incorporates such details as a vaulted ceiling sheathed in blue 35mm film reels; movie projectors and a squat columns with palm leaf capitals made of green metal plates; and stairway railings reproducing the musical score from *Hooray for Hollywood*. A modified form of the yellow brick road from *The Wizard of Oz* runs along the floor. LA's car culture is reflected on the benches whose backs are shaped like classic cars.

Outside, on the street-level plaza, bus shelters are shaped like Grauman's Chinese Theatre, the Brown Derby restaurant and a white stretch limo.

Florentine Gardens ④⑤

Gordon Kaufmann, architect (1938) 5951 Hollywood Blvd. ☎(323) 464-0706. Ⓢ

During the 1940s, this was a downscale nightclub that featured such headliners as Al Jolson, Ozzie Nelson, Sophie Tucker and the Mills Brothers. Actress Yvonne De Carlo danced here before becaming a star. Famous strippers Sally Rand and Lili St Cyr also started their careers here. Although not frequented by celebrities, this large club that offered a trapeze circus act and beautiful, scarcely-clad girls as entertainment, packed its 500 seats every night. In June of 1942, sixteen-year-old Norma Jean Baker (later Marilyn Monroe) and her first husband, Jim Dougherty, celebrated their wedding here. Today, the club hosts hip-hop parties on weekends.

"Dream factory"-inspired interior of Hollywood and Vine station

Former Warner Bros Studio building is now home to independent television station KTLA

KTLA
(formerly **Warner Bros Studio**) 46

5858 Sunset Blvd.
☎(323) 460-5672. ⌖

Built in 1922, this long, colonnaded building served as the headquarters of the Warner Bros main studio until 1929. The back lot of this enormous facility included probably the largest shooting stages in the industry. It was the site of the filming of *Don Juan* (1926) and *The Jazz Singer* (1927), the first pictures with synchronized sound.

After Warner Bros moved its headquarters to Burbank, the building (affectionately called "Termite Terrace" by animators) was used for the production of Bugs Bunny, Porky Pig, Daffy Duck and other Warner Bros animated cartoons.

The facility was later bought by Paramount, which established its television station here. Sold to Gene Autry's Golden West Broadcasters in 1967, the building today houses the independent television station KTLA (Channel 5) and radio station KTZN.

Sunset-Gower Studios
(formerly **Columbia Pictures Studios**) 47

1438 N Gower St.
☎(323) 467-1001. ⌖

From 1925 to 1972 this was the site of Columbia Pictures, the only Poverty Row studio that ultimately succeeded.

Brothers Harry and Jack Cohn first rented and later acquired the former California Studios here and established their supremacy by buying up many of the smaller studios on the row. Among the notable movies created here were all Frank Capra's classics, including Columbia's first Oscar winner, *It Happened One Night* (1934), as well as *Mr Smith Goes to Washington* (1939), *Gilda* (1946) and *From Here to Eternity* (1953). During the 1960s, such celebrated television shows as *I Dream of Jeannie* and *Bewitched* were filmed on the lot.

In 1972 Columbia moved to the Burbank Studios and later to Culver City, where it now occupies a part of the former MGM lot (➔ p416).

With its 13 soundstages, Sunset-Gower is the biggest privately owned rental studio in LA. It has been used mostly for taping television shows such as *Married With Children*, *Fresh Prince of Bel Air* and *Six Feet Under*.

Gower Gulch 48
SW corner of Sunset Blvd and Gower St.

During the 1920s, a large number of small, struggling production companies occupied this particular stretch of Sunset Blvd, giving it the name Poverty Row. These studios attracted costumed cowboys and extras, who hung around the corner of Sunset and Gower, nicknamed Gower Gulch, awaiting a chance to play a bit part in low-budget westerns. Today a shopping center resembling a western town street pays homage to those early days.

Gower Gulch strip mall commemorates the area's history

A photograph from the 1930s shows Columbia Pictures Studios

Columbia Square

William Lescaze and E T Heitschmidt, architects (1937-38)
6121 Sunset Blvd.
☎(323) 460-3000; program 460-3366. 🎗

This is the site where the first motion picture studio in Hollywood, Nestor Film Company, was established in 1911 (➔ p.43). The company was sold to Universal next year, but the studio continued to produce short comedies as Christie Studios until 1936, when CBS razed it to make room for the Columbia Square radio complex.

Despite the remodeling, the main CBS Building remains a remarkable example of International Style Modern. It lies perpendicular to the street, and this unusual orientation makes both of its longer sides visible. George Burns and Gracie Allen broadcast their famous radio show from here.

Today, the complex houses KCBS-TV (Channel 2) and the KNX radio station.

CBS's West Coast home

Hollywood Palladium ⑩

6215 Sunset Blvd.
☎(323) 962-7600. ⑤ 🎗

Built by *Los Angeles Times* publisher Norman Chandler, the Palladium was once the largest dance club in the world. Lana Turner appeared at its groundbreaking ceremony with a silver shovel in hand. The club opened on October 31, 1940, with the Tommy Dorsey band and an unknown young singer named Frank Sinatra. It was the best place to hear famous names in jazz, swing and big band music, including Glenn

Miller and Benny Goodman. Among other stars who performed here were Judy Garland, Betty Grable and Marilyn Monroe. During the 1960s, the popular *The Lawrence Welk Show* was broadcast from the Palladium, and the club hosted the Emmy, Grammy and Golden Globe Awards. It also presented the Rolling Stones, David Bowie, the Who and the Grateful Dead. Today it is still used for regular concerts.

The Palladium appeared in a number of movies, including *The Day of the Locust* (1975) and *FIST* (1978). The famous concert scene in *The Blues Brothers* (1980) was also filmed here.

Earl Carroll Theatre
(formerly) ⑪

6230 Sunset Blvd.

Opened in 1938 as a home for Earl Carroll's Vanities revue (➔ p101), the theater featured guest stars and a cast of 60 scantily clad dancers, providing the best and the most popular entertainment in Hollywood. "Thru these portals pass the most beautiful girls in the world," read the neon motto outside the theater. Inside, 10,000 neon tubes lit the world's first double revolving stages and a dining area that could seat 1,100 guests (more than any other supper club in Los Angeles).

After Carroll's death in a plane crash in 1948, the place reopened as the Moulin Rouge in 1953. In the late 1960s, it was

renamed Kaleidoscope and featured the Doors, Jefferson Airplane, Canned Heat and many other acts. Later it became the Aquarius Theater, where the musical *Hair* ran in the 1970s. Today, it is a state of the art Nickelodeon Theater.

The impressive geodesic dome of the Cinerama Theater

Cinerama Dome Theater ⑫

Welton Becket, architect (1963)
6360 Sunset Blvd.
☎(323) 466-3401.

During the 1950s and early 1960s, Hollywood tried to lure audiences from television with short-lived novelties such as 3-D, Cinerama, CinemaScope and VistaVision. Cinerama was a unique three-camera, three-projector wide screen process that was eventually abandoned in 1966 due to high production costs and technical restrictions.

Completed in 1963, this impressive geodesic-dome theater, built exclusively for Cinerama, features a giant curved screen and remarkable sound system. The 900-seat theater is now one of only a few (less than 10) theaters in the world still capable of 3-projector Cinerama presentations.

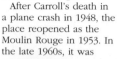

The Hollywood Palladium was once the world's largest dance club

Hollywood Athletic Club ⑤

Meyer and Holler, architects (1922)
6525 Sunset Blvd.
☎(323) 460-6360; 462-6262.

Designed by the architects of Grauman's Chinese and Egyptian theaters, this Spanish Colonial Revival building was opened on New Year's Eve 1923. One of the most lavish athletic clubs in the country at the time, it provided a full range of amenities for the mannerly athlete, including a swimming pool, a gymnasium, a barbershop and guest rooms. It was an exclusive men's retreat with celebrity members such as Rudolph Valentino, Charlie Chaplin, John Barrymore, Clark Gable, Bela Lugosi, Walt Disney and John Wayne (who threw billiard balls at cars on the street from the balcony).

Johnny Weissmuller was discovered here as a life guard, and Esther Williams was the only female ever allowed to swim in the club's pool. Silent screen legend Tyrone Power Sr died here in his room in 1931.

Today, the beautifully restored complex houses offices, restaurant and billiards parlor.

Hollywood Athletic Club was an exclusive celebrity retreat

Crossroads of the World ⑤

Robert V Derrah, architect (1936).
6671 Sunset Blvd. ⚑ NRHP

Opened in 1936 as the city's first pedestrian outdoor shopping mall, Crossroads of the World was designed by the same architect who built another Streamline Moderne nautical building in downtown, the Coca-Cola Bottling Plant. The central structure here resembles a ship, with a number of nautical features such as bridge, portholes and pipe railings. Its bow is surmounted by a 60-foot tall tower on which revolves an eight-foot globe. A variety of small cottages surround the ship, featuring Italian, French, Spanish, and Moorish

themes. Originally designed as a group of shops, the complex is today occupied by small offices.

The mall appeared in *Indecent Proposal* (1993) and the *noir* film *L.A. Confidential* (1997), where it is seen through the window in the opening scenes as the Hollywood journalist played by Danny DeVito drafts a gossip column on his typewriter.

Crossroads of the World

Top Hat Café (site) ⑤

1500 N Highland Ave.

This is the site of the former malt shop where 15-year-old high school student Lana Turner was discovered after she cut her typing class. According to Turner's autobiography, she was sipping a soda when *Hollywood Reporter* publisher Billy Wilkerson approached her, asking: "Do you want to be in the movies?" She responded:

"I don't know. I'll have to ask my mother." Her mother obviously agreed, but film historians could not agree on the exact location of the former soda fountain. Hollywood legend has it that it was located across the street from Hollywood High.

Hollywood High School ⑤

1521 N Highland Ave.
☎(323) 461-3891.

Opened in 1904, this is one of the oldest high schools in Los Angeles. Among its famous alumni are Norman Chandler, the former publisher of the *Los Angeles Times*, William Schockley, Nobel Prize winner for chemistry, and Warren Christopher, former Secretary of State. The long list of the school's graduates who made it in show business includes Judy Garland, Mickey Rooney, Jason Robards, Linda Evans, Carol Burnett, James Garner, Barbara Hershey, Stephanie Powers and Lana Turner.

Sheik playground

The Charlie Chaplin Studio today houses Jim Henson Productions

Charlie Chaplin Studio (formerly) 57

1416 N La Brea Ave.
☎(323) 802-1500. 📍

Looking like a picturesque English village, this Tudor Revival complex was built in 1918 by Charlie Chaplin as an independent studio. It was constructed behind his home, which used to face Sunset Blvd (southeast corner at La Brea), one year after the actor signed a million-dollar contract.

The Gold Rush (1925) was made at the Chaplin Studio

Chaplin made some of his most famous films here, including *The Kid* (1920), *The Gold Rush* (1925), *City Lights* (1931), *Modern Times* (1936) and *The Great Dictator* (1940).

Many of the original studio bungalows have survived, including Stage 3 with the embedded footprints of Chaplin's character the Little Tramp in the cement in front of it.

CBS owned this facility for a time and shot the popular television series *Perry Mason*

here. Herb Alpert and Jerry Moos of the A & M Records bought the complex in 1966 and turned it into a recording studio. Among the musicians who recorded here are the Carpenters, the Moody Blues, Eric Clapton, Joe Cocker, Sheryl Crow, Janet Jackson, Suzanne Vega and Sting.

In 1985, the song and video of *We Are the World* was recorded here, featuring such legends as Ray Charles, Bob Dylan, Michael Jackson, Bruce Springsteen and Stevie Wonder. More than 40 artists gathered at the A & M Studios to record the song which was an American response to the famine in Africa.

Today, the studio houses Jim Henson Productions. The statue of their signature character, Kermit the Frog, sporting the famous Little Tramp outfit, dominates the studio gate.

Danziger Studio 58

Frank O Gehry and Associates, architect (1965).
7001 Melrose Ave.
Private residence.

One of Frank Gehry's early designs, this minimalist structure was built as a house/studio for designer Lou Danziger. Viewed from Sycamore Ave, it looks like a blank stucco box broken by a garage door with a cube enclosing a window at the roof.

Howard Hughes Headquarters (formerly) 59

7000-7050 Romaine St. 📍

From this unassuming Art Deco (Zigzag) Moderne building, Howard Hughes ran the operations of enormous holdings that included aircraft factories, airlines, film studios and movie theaters. Also located here was his Caddo Company, a production company that turned out such hits as *Hell's Angels* (1930), *Scarface* (1932) and *The Outlaw* (1943). All three films were edited in this building.

Famous for his eccentricities, Hughes had his employees vacuum their clothes before going through a series of doors designed to prevent dust from entering his film printing room. The building is today used as a climate-controlled film and tape security storage.

The Howard Hughes Headquarters is featured in the biopic *The Aviator* (2004) as the facility where 25 miles of film shot during the production of *Hell's Angels* (1930) were edited

DeLongpre Park ⑥⓪

Cherokee Ave at DeLongpre Ave.

Named for well-known floral artist Paul DeLongpre, whose home and gardens stood nearby (→ p120), this small municipal park contains two monuments commemorating silent screen legend Rudolph Valentino. The 4-foot bronze statue of a nude male, named *Aspiration*, was designed by sculptor Roger Noble and dedicated on the anniversary of the actor's birth, May 16th, 1930. Erected with funds raised worldwide by Valentino's fans, the statue was stolen in the 1950s, but was recovered and reinstated in 1976. Next to the statue stands a bronze bust of Rudolph Valentino, the work of sculptor Richard H Ellis.

Metro Studios in 1918, before it became the Buster Keaton Studio

Rudolph Valentino (1978)
by Richard H Ellis

Hollywood Center Studios ⑥①

1040 N Las Palmas Ave.
☎(323) 469-5000. ☛

Established in 1919 as Jasper Hollywood Studios, this facility was rented out in the 1920s to independent moviemakers such as Harold Lloyd and Howard Hughes. Hughes filmed here parts of his spectacular *Hell's Angels* (1930), in which the platinum blonde Jean Harlow made her first film appearance. Young Shirley Temple also made her film debut here. In the 1950s and 1960s, under

the name of Hollywood General Studios, it was the home of the popular television series *I Love Lucy* and *The Beverly Hillbillies*. After the enormous success of *The Godfather* films, Francis Ford Coppola founded his independent Zoetrope Studios here in 1980, as an alternative to the Hollywood major studios. After *One From the Heart* (1982) and several other movies he produced proved to be financial failures, Coppola was forced to sell his studio in 1983.

Today the studio is used as a rental lot again. *Shampoo* (1975), *When Harry Met Sally* (1989), *Con Air* (1997) and numerous classic TV series, including *The Rockford Files*, *Everybody Loves Raymond* and *Jeopardy* game show, were all filmed here.

Buster Keaton Studio (site) ⑥②

1025 Lillian Way. ☛

The southwest corner of Eleanor Ave and Lillian Way was the location of the early Metro Studios before it merged with Goldwyn Pictures and Louis B Mayer Productions to form MGM. In 1916, the facilities were rented by the Chaplin-Mutual Studio. Under the contract with Mutual, Charlie Chaplin made 12 films here, including his memorable shorts *The Floorwalker* (1916), *Easy*

Street (1917) and *The Immigrant* (1917), before building his own studio (→ p128). In 1920, the plant became the

The General (1927) was made at the Buster Keaton Studio

Buster Keaton Studio, and in the next eight years some of the most brilliant comedies in the history of cinema were made here, including *The Navigator* (1924), *Sherlock, Jr* (1924) and *The General* (1927).

In a strange twist, the plaque commemorating the studio is erroneously placed on the northwest corner of Lillian Way and Eleanor Ave.

Commemorative plaque marking the site of the original Buster Keaton Studio

Television Center Studios ⑥

6311 Romaine St.
☎(323) 464-6638. ⌁

Between 1930 and 1975 this building served as the offices and a processing lab of Technicolor Inc. Devised mainly by Herbert Kalmus, Technicolor was the first widely accepted color film process and dominated the industry for decades. The first feature-length Technicolor film debuted in 1922. Originally a two-color process, its initial technical restrictions were overcome and in 1935 the first full-length feature using the superior three-strip Technicolor, *Becky Sharp*, was produced.

The building is now home to the UCLA Film and TV Archives. For information call ☎(323) 462-4921.

The Hollywood Studio Club was once Marilyn Monroe's home

Hollywood Studio Club ⑥

Julia Morgan, architect (1926).
1215 Lodi Place. ♠ NRHP

Designed in 1926 by Julia Morgan (architect of Hearst Castle in San Simeon), this Italian Renaissance-style building provided a home for the increasing number of actresses who came to Hollywood looking for stardom. The club's residents have included Rita Moreno, Donna Reed, ZaSu Pitts, Kim Novak and Sharon Tate. Marilyn Monroe stayed briefly in room 334 while working for Columbia in 1948.

The club, which was reportedly haunted, closed in 1975 and today is a YWCA jobs training center.

Raleigh Studios ⑥

650 N Bronson Ave.
☎(323) 466-3111. ⌁

Founded in 1914 as the Fiction Studios, this is one of the longest continuously operating studios in Hollywood.

Movie production started on this lot with Adolph Zukor's *A Girl of Yesterday* (1915), starring Mary Pickford. Raleigh still maintains Mary Pickford's little cottage on its lot. Later known as the Clune Studio, it rented to Douglas Fairbanks who filmed here his swashbucklers *The Mark of Zorro* (1920) and *The Three Musketeers* (1921). Ronald Reagan was host of the *Death Valley Days* television series here in the 1950s. Renamed Producers Studios in the 1960s, it was used for *What Ever Happened to Baby Jane?* (1962) and *In the Heat of the Night* (1967). It was also the home of the original *Superman* television series. Early in his Hollywood career, while he was still auditioning for parts, Kevin Costner worked here as a grip.

Raleigh Enterprises purchased the studio in 1980 and since it has been used for the features *The Naked Gun* (1988) and *Death Becomes Her* (1992), as well as music videos starring Madonna, Michael Jackson and Nirvana.

Television Center Studios

Hollygrove (site) ⑥

815 N El Centro Ave.

It was to this establishment, previously known as the Los Angeles Orphans Society, that Norma Jean Baker (later Marilyn Monroe) arrived in 1935 weeping, "I am not an orphan." Ten-year old Norma Jean stayed almost two years here while her mother was confined in mental institutions. The old building was razed in 1977 and a new one was erected on the site.

Façade of the reconstructed and expanded Raleigh Studios

Fox Studio

(formerly) ⑥⑦

5433 Fernwood Ave.
☎(323) 462-6171. ⚐

William Fox began producing films in Los Angeles in 1915 at the old Selig Studio in Edendale, located at 1845 Allesandro St (now Glendale Blvd). Two years later Fox Film Corporation moved into the five-and-a-half-acre lot of the old Thomas Dixon Studio, at the corner of Western Ave and Sunset Blvd. As production increased, Fox bought an additional eight acres directly across the street. During 1917, the studio made more than 100 movies.

Among Fox's major early stars who made their films here were Theda Bara, the first screen vamp, Janet Gaynor, the winner of the first best actress Oscar, cowboys Tom Mix, Buck Jones and Will Rogers, and John Wayne, who made his first screen appearance here in 1928. It was one of the most successful Hollywood studios until the stock market crash forced founder William Fox out of his company. In 1935 Fox merged with 20th Century, and soon after the new studio moved to a new lot in West Los Angeles (➔ p452).

The original Fox studio is today reduced to DeLuxe Laboratories ("Color by Deluxe"). The rest of the site is occupied by a huge discount supermarket.

View of the lake surrounding the family mausoleum of William A Clark Jr (1877-1934), founder of the Los Angeles Philharmonic

Hollywood Forever Cemetery ⑥⑧

6000 Santa Monica Blvd.
☎(323) 469-1181.
www.hollywoodforever.com.
⊕daily 8am-5pm.
♠ NRHP
⚐a map of the stars' graves is available at the gate. Private tours available. Art Deco Society hosts a walking tour each October; call ☎(310) 659-3326 for info.
www.adsla.org. ⑤

Founded in 1899 and formerly known as Hollywood Memorial Park Cemetery, this world-renowned landmark is the final resting place of a number of early Hollywood luminaries and prominent Los Angeles citizens. Dubbed Cemetery of the Immortals in the 1930s, the glamorous cemetery fell into neglect for years and had became dilapidated when the brothers Cassity bought it in January of 1998.

Now fully restored, this is the first cemetery in the world to offer specially created, high-tech services. The project, known as Forever, allows families to compile a personal archive of their departed made up of videotapes, recorded messages, photographs, letters and other memorabilia, and store

Stained-glass window in the Cathedral Mausoleum

this information in Forever's data bank. These multimedia biographies can be viewed on touch-screens at computer terminals at the cemetery or worldwide on the Internet.

To further cash in on the celebrity concept, the cemetery hosts open-air screenings among the mausoleums and headstones during the summer months, showing movies of the stars buried on the grounds. Film fans can get more info on www.cemeteryscreenings.com.

William Fox Studio as it looked in 1926

Hollywood Forever Cemetery

Columbarium, upper north wall, niche 7-8, tier 3 ①

Abbey of the Psalms, Shrine of Eternal Love, family room ②

Abbey of the Psalms, Sanctuary of Refuge, crypt 2081 ③

Abbey of the Psalms, Sanctuary of Light, crypt 2196 ④

"THAT'S ALL FOLKS"
MEL BLANC
MAN OF 1000 VOICES
BELOVED HUSBAND AND FATHER
1908 — 1989

Section 13, lot 149 ⑤

Section 8, lot 6 ⑥

Section 8 ⑦

JAYNE MANSFIELD
1938 — 1967
WE LIVE TO
LOVE YOU MORE
EACH DAY

Section 8, lot 218 ⑩

VIRGINIA RAPPE
1895 — 1921

Section 8, lot 257 ⑪

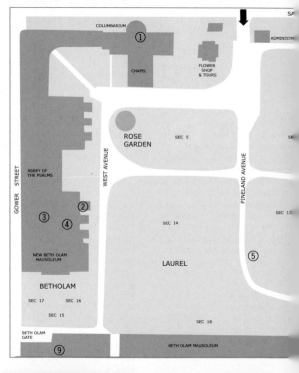

BELOVED FATHER
SON AND BROTHER
CARL "ALFALFA" SWITZER
AUG. 7, 1927   JAN. 21, 1959

Section 6, lot 26, grave 6 ⑧

IN LOVING
MEMORY
FROM THE FAMILY   BENJAMIN
SIEGEL
FEB. 28, 1906
JUNE 20, 1947

Beth Olam Mausoleum, corridor M-2, crypt 3087 ⑨

Section 11, sunken garden (Douglas Fairbanks) ⑫

Section 8 (Cecil B DeMille) ⑬

Section 2, grave 200 ⑯

Section 8 (Tyrone Power) ⑲

Section 8, lot 193 ⑭

Section 8, lot 193 ⑰

Section 8, Douras mausoleum (Marion Davies) ⑳

Section 8, lot 86 (Harry Cohn) ㉑

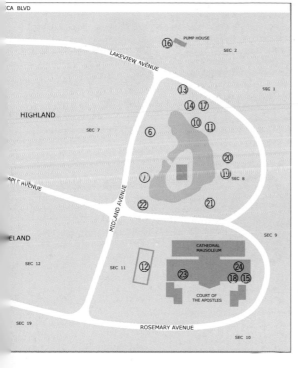

Section 8 ㉒

Peter Lorre
1904 – 1964

Cathedral Mausoleum, Alcove of Reverence, niche 5, tier 1 ㉓

Rodolfo Guglielmi Valentino
1895   1926

Cathedral Mausoleum, corridor A, crypt 1205 ⑮

Barbara La Marr
God In The Joy And Beauty Of

Cathedral Mausoleum, corridor A, crypt 1308 ⑱

Peter Finch
Distinguished Actor
Loving Husband And Father
SEPT 28 1916 – JAN 14 1977
Forever In Our Hearts

Cathedral Mausoleum, corridor A, crypt 1224 ㉔

Cathedral Mausoleum

Rudolph Valentino
(1895-1926)

It took him only six years and about a dozen movies to enter mythology. Hollywood's greatest screen lover, who caused women to faint in theaters worldwide, is laid to rest inside this unpretentious crypt. While on a national tour promoting his newest film, *The Son of the Sheik* (1926), Valentino died in New York of a perforated gastric ulcer and ruptured appendix. When his body was brought back to Hollywood, thousands of admirers piously stood at stations across the country as the train passed. A crowd of approximately 10,000 mourners gathered at the cemetery as Valentino's bronze coffin was carried into the mausoleum.

For many years a mysterious "Lady in Black," hidden behind a veil, brought flowers to Valentino's tomb on the anniversary of his death. Although she does not turn up any more, about hundred fans (mostly women and mostly octogenarian) gather every year at the Cathedral Mausoleum on August 23 for a memorial service at precisely 12:10pm, the exact moment of Valentino's passing.

Next to Valentino is the crypt of **June Mathis**, the screenwriter who wrote *The Four Horsemen of the Apocalypse* (1921) and insisted that Valentino play the lead role.

Body of Rudolph Valentino is viewed by a female mourner

Barbara La Marr
(1896-1926)

The "girl who was too beautiful" began her entertainment career at 14, when she was arrested for dancing in a burlesque theater as a minor. A judge supposedly told her she was "too beautiful to be in the big city, alone and unprotected." An exquisite beauty and talented actress, she reached stardom in *The Prisoner of Zenda* (1922) and *Thy Name Is Woman* (1924). La Marr became one of Hollywood's first stars, living a fast life ridden with scandals, alcoholism and drug abuse. After five unhappy marriages, she died of a heroin overdose, although causes of her sudden death were variously given as nervous exhaustion, tuberculosis and overdieting.

Peter Lorre (1904-1964)

This little man with a moon face and bulging, sad eyes created some of the most memorable screen personalities. Often portraying mysterious, cunning killers, spies and psychopaths, he is best remembered for his roles in *Casablanca* (1940) and *The Maltese Falcon* (1941).

Peter Finch (1916-1977)

The actor died of a heart attack in the lobby of the Beverly Hills Hotel and was posthumously awarded an Oscar for best actor for his role as a TV commentator in *Network* (1976). He is best remembered for his famous line from the film: "I'm mad as hell and I'm not going to take it anymore."

Beth Olam Mausoleum

Benjamin "Bugsy" Siegel
(1906-1947)

This gangster and Hollywood wannabe played a significant role in the development of Las Vegas. He was killed by fellow mobsters in his girlfriend's house in Beverly Hills (➔ p476), after the Flamingo casino he was building in Las Vegas went deeply into debt.

Abbey of the Psalms

Norma Talmadge
(1897-1957)

Norma was the oldest and most famous of the three glamorous Talmadge sisters and one of the most popular of silent screen actresses. She is best known for her title role in *Camille* (1927).

Norma's sisters **Constance** (1903-1973), a successful silent-film comedienne who appeared as the Mountain Girl in Griffith's *Intolerance* (1916), and **Natalie** (1900-1969), best known as the wife of Buster Keaton, are in the same alcove.

Jesse Lasky (1880-1958)

He was the producer of *The Squaw Man* (1914), the first feature-length motion picture made in Hollywood, and president of the Jesse L Lasky Feature Play Company that eventually became Paramount Pictures.

One of the better liked studio executives, Lasky died suddenly during a speech in the Beverly Hills Hotel. He is the father of screenwriter Jesse Lasky Jr.

Victor Fleming (1883-1949)

Fleming was a race car driver, cameraman and the director of two classics, *The Wizard of Oz* (1939) and *Gone With the Wind* (1939), for which he won an Academy Award as best director.

Columbarium

Bebe Daniels (1901-1971)

One of the silent screen's finest comediennes, Daniels appeared in over 200 comedy shorts before starring opposite Hollywood's leading men Rudolph Valentino and Douglas Fairbanks in such hits as *Monsieur Beaucaire* (1924) and *Reaching for the Moon* (1930).

Ben Lyon (1901-1979)

Next to Daniels's vault is a bronze urn shaped like a book that contains the remains of her husband, actor Ben Lyon. He starred in Howard Hughes's *Hell's Angels* (1930), in which he piloted his own aircraft and shot some of the dogfight scenes. As a casting director at 20th Century-Fox, Lyon arranged for a screen test of an unknown model. Before she signed the seven-year contract with the studio, Lyon changed her name to Marilyn Monroe.

Grounds

Douglas Fairbanks (1883-1939)

The most elaborate tomb in the cemetery, with a long reflecting pool, is the memorial to one of Hollywood's first great stars, whose popularity was rivaled only by his wife, Mary Pickford, and Charlie Chaplin. Athletic and good-looking, Fairbanks made a succession of swashbuckling adventures such as *The Three Musketeers* (1921), *Robin Hood* (1922) and *The Thief of Bagdad* (1924). He was one of the founders of the Academy of Motion Picture Arts and Sciences and its first president.

Douglas Fairbanks Jr (1909-2000)

Fairbanks' son from his first marriage, a handsome movie star of the 1930s and 1940s, is interred here beside his father.

Carl "Alfalfa" Switzer (1927-1959)

One of the stars of *Our Gang* comedy series, the freckle-faced Switzer appeared in the popular movie shorts between 1935 and 1940. He was killed during an argument over a lost hunting dog. It was suggested that the dog on the marker probably indicates Switzer's love of hunting, and not Petey, the popular dog that appeared in the series.

Mel Blanc (1908-1989)

The marker over the grave of Blanc, the voice of Speedy Gonzales, Tweety Pie, Bugs Bunny, Yosemite Sam, Daffy Duck and countless other cartoon characters, contains Porky Pig's unforgettable phrase, "That's All Folks."

Florence Lawrence (1890-1938)

Lawrence was one of the most popular stars during the early 1900s, who appeared in D W Griffith's films known only as "the Biograph Girl." Studios at the time did not promote their actors by name, fearing they would demand more money. It was Carl Laemmle, founder of Universal Pictures, who disclosed Lawrence's real name in 1910, when he lured her from Biograph (➔ p45). Although she appeared in more than 300 films, the first movie star was soon forgotten and committed suicide by eating ant paste.

Cecil Blount DeMille (1881-1959)

The twin sarcophagi of the legendary director, producer and screenwriter and his wife seem too modest for the filmmaker who made larger than life historic epics and religious spectacles. He probably did more than any other person to establish Hollywood as the movie center of the world. Among the 70 films he produced and directed are *The Squaw Man* (1914; also 1918 and 1931 versions), *The Ten Commandments* (1923 and 1956 remake), *The King of Kings* (1927), *The Sign of the Cross* (1932) and *The Crusades* (1935).

Jayne Mansfield (1933-1967)

More known for her 41-inch frontage than her film roles, Mansfield was nicknamed "Marilyn Monroe, King Size." With her Mr Universe husband, Mickey Hargitay, the "platinum bombshell" lived in the pink mansion with a heart-shaped pool. She also drove a pink (her favorite color) Cadillac. This pink granite memorial marker was placed by her fan club after the actress died in a tragic accident, when her car smashed into a parked 18-wheeler. Mansfield was killed instantly but was not decapitated, as was persistently rumored. Her body is actually buried in Pen Argyl, Pennsylvania, under a heart-shaped marker.

Virginia Rappe (1895-1921)

After a wild party at the St Francis Hotel in San Francisco, actress Virginia Rappe died of a ruptured bladder. In the first major Hollywood scandal, the famous silent screen comedian Roscoe "Fatty" Arbuckle was accused of raping and murdering her. After three trials, Arbuckle was acquitted of all charges, but his film career was over.

Janet Gaynor (1906-1984)

The petite beauty famous for her "sweetheart" roles, Gaynor won the first Academy Award ever given in the best actress category for her performances in three movies: *Sunrise* (1927), *Seventh Heaven* (1927) and *Street Angel* (1928). Gaynor was Hollywood's top box-office star in the early 1930s before she suddenly retired from films at the height of her career. She died following complications from an auto accident.

Adrian (1903-1959)

Next to Gaynor is buried her second husband, one of America's most innovative fashion designers. As the chief costume designer for MGM, where he worked on more than two hundred productions, Adrian created a glamorous image for Hollywood's leading stars including Greta Garbo, Jean Harlow, Joan Crawford and Katharine Hepburn.

John Huston (1906-1987)

The marker for director, screenwriter and actor John Huston was made of pink marble imported from Ireland. His most famous films include *The Maltese Falcon* (1941), *The African Queen* (1952) and *The Night of the Iguana* (1964). Huston won two Academy Awards for writing and directing *The Treasure of the Sierra Madre* (1948). His father, Walter, won the best supporting Oscar for the same film, and his daughter, Anjelica, won the Academy Award for best supporting actress in *Prizzi's Honor* (1985). Huston is the only director who cast both a parent and a child in Oscar-winning roles.

Marion Davies (1897-1961)

In this large, white-marble family mausoleum inscribed "DOVRAS" rests actress Marion Davies. She was best known as a lifelong mistress of newspaper magnate William Randolph Hearst, whose affair was the subject of ridicule in Orson Welles's *Citizen Kane* (1941). Born Marion Douras, she was a talented comedienne who did not reach her full potential due to Hearst's insistence on her taking serious roles.

Tyrone Power (1913-1958)

The memorial bench marks the grave of one of Hollywood's most romantic and popular leading men. Between bookends is a volume inscribed with lines from *Hamlet*. Power died of a heart attack while filming a fighting scene on location in Spain.

Harry Cohn (1891-1958)

Two marble sarcophagi mark the grave of co-founder of Columbia Pictures, the movie mogul who discovered Rita Hayworth, Kim Novak, Glenn Ford and William Holden (➔ p418). Buried next to his wife, this ruthless despot was the most feared and hated man in Hollywood. His funeral, attended by over 1,500 people, proved to be an occasion for memorable quotes: "Give the public what they want to see and there'll come out for it" and "You had to stand in line to hate him." A Jew who converted to Christianity under his wife's influence, Cohn's tomb bears both the star of David and a Christian cross.

The elder of Columbia's founding brothers, **Jack Cohn**, is buried in a grave in front of Harry's crypt.

Johnny Ramone (1948-2004)

Inspired by President Reagan's state funeral, the legendary guitarist of the seminal punk band, the Ramones, chose a monument for himself while battling cancer in his hospital bed.

The four-foot bronze statue, which shows the rocker in a leather jacket, with his signature bowl haircut playing his Mosrite guitar, bears the inscription: "If a man can judge success by how many great friends he has, then I have been very successful."

All members of the band, which was formed in 1974, adopted the surname Ramone, which they had heard Paul McCartney used as an alias when traveling.

Not far from Johnny, on the opposite side of the lake, is the grave of his former bandmate, bassist **Dee Dee Ramone** (1951-2002), who died of a drug overdose.

Hattie McDaniel (1895-1952)

McDaniel was the first black actress to receive an Academy Award. It was her wish to be buried in this memorial park, but at the time of her death, the cemetery did not accept blacks. Honoring her final request, the cemetery's new owner unveiled McDaniel's four-foot-tall granite memorial in 1999. Her remains still lie in Rosedale Cemetery (➔ p220).

Fay Wray (1907-2004)

Wray was an established actress who starred opposite such leading men as Ronald Colman, Gary Cooper and Fredric March before appearing in *King Kong* (1933). And it was the role of the near-naked beautiful girl, frightened and screaming in the hairy paw of the beast, which immortalized and made her a cult figure.

Paramount Pictures

Paramount traces its origins to 1912, when Adolph Zukor, a Jewish immigrant from Hungary and a furrier, founded a film production company called Famous Players. Zukor distributed his films through Paramount Pictures Corporation, a company formed in 1909 by exhibitor William W Hodkinson. Paramount also distributed the films of the Jesse L Lasky Feature Play Company, which was formed in 1913 by vaudeville musician Jesse Lasky, glove salesman Samuel Goldfish (later Goldwyn) and actor and playwright Cecil B DeMille. In 1916 Zukor and Lasky merged their two companies, resulting in a production giant called Famous Players-Lasky. Zukor quickly bought out Goldfish and managed to oust Hodkinson and take control of his company, together with its name.

In 1919 Paramount began a major movie theater acquisition campaign, eventually owning more than 2,000 outlets. During the Depression, it found itself in financial difficulties that led to bankruptcy in 1933, but recovered in the late 1930s. In 1966 Paramount was taken over by the giant conglomerate Gulf+Western, and in 1993 it became part of Viacom Inc, which merged with CBS in 1999.

Paramount was a pioneer in developing and utilizing the star system, beginning with its first top star, Mary Pickford, who was signed up in 1913. Legendary Rudolph Valentino was launched to stardom in *The Sheik* (1921). The studio's other early superstars were Gloria Swanson, Clara Bow, Pola Negri, Douglas Fairbanks and John Barrymore. In the 1930s, the Paramount roster included Marlene Dietrich, Gary Cooper, Cary Grant, Bing Crosby and box-office sensation Mae West.

Paramount has produced more than 3,000 films of all types over the years. The first film to win the Academy Award for best picture was Paramount's epic *Wings* (1927). The studio's other winners in the same category include *Going My Way* (1944), *The Lost Weekend* (1945), *The Greatest Show On Earth* (1952), *The Godfather* (1972), *The Godfather, Part II* (1974), *Ordinary People* (1980), *Terms of Endearment* (1983), *Forrest Gump* (1994), *Braveheart* (1995) and *Titanic* (1997).

Paramount's famous logo was sketched on a blotter by company head Hodkinson during a business conference. He took the name from an apartment building he saw in passing and the snow-capped peak reminded him of the Rockies at home in Utah. The halo of stars stood for the initial 22 stars under contract.

The four original partners in the newly formed Famous Players-Lasky Corporation in 1916, from left, Jesse Lasky, Adolph Zukor, Samuel Goldfish (later Goldwyn) and Cecil B DeMille. During the next two decades Zukor remained one of the most powerful moguls in the movie industry. Aggressive and ruthless, driven by a need for complete control, he built an empire that almost achieved a monopoly on American film production and distribution.

Wings (1927) was the first film to win the best picture Oscar

Marlene Dietrich was brought from Germany as Paramount's answer to MGM's Greta Garbo

Paramount Studios ⑥⑨

Paramount is the last major studio still located in Hollywood. The core of the present studio complex was built in 1918 by a company called Paralta Plays, and it was used as a rental lot by dozens of independent companies. The Paramount-Famous-Lasky Corp, which outgrew its original studio on Sunset and Vine (➔ p123), purchased the lot (then called United Studios) and moved here in 1926. In 1968, when Paramount bought its next-door neighbor, Desilu Productions, it also acquired the old RKO Studios lot,

Paramount Studios water tower

expanding its facilities to their present size of 63 acres (25 ha). Today, Paramount's 32 sound stages are used for film as well as television production, including such popular shows as *Entertainment Tonight* and *Frasier*.

The lot was featured in numerous films, including *Star Spangled Rhythm* (1942), *Variety Girl* (1947), *Sunset Boulevard* (1960) and *The Errand Boy* (1961), where it was disguised as the Paramutual studio, whose head dispatches an addled errand boy to monitor time-wasting employees.

5555 Melrose Ave.
☎(323) 956-1777.
⛟two-hour guided walking tour, departs hourly Mon-Fri 9am-2pm.
⑤ ⛏
Free tickets for tapings of the live-audience television shows are available August through March; for info call ☎(323) 956-5575.

"I've been to Paris, France and I've been to Paris, Paramount. Paris, Paramount is better."
— **Ernst Lubitsch, director**

The studio's trophy case displays Oscars, Emmys, Golden Globes and other awards won by Paramount over the years. Its star exhibit is the first Oscar in the best picture category, received for the 1927 film *Wings*.

Stages 30 and 31 were used for much of the shooting for both *The Godfather* and *The Godfathe, Part II* films. Stages 31 and 32 were the RKO stages used for many classic dance scenes in Fred Astaire and Ginger Rogers musicals, including *Top Hat* (1935). Stage 30 was the home of many scenes in *Forrest Gump* (1994), including the famous Oval Office scene.

The studio's new Main Gate at 5555 Melrose Ave. was constructed in the early 1980s. The double-gate entrance is modeled after the old Bronson Gate and retains the same arched look, together with the trademark script sign.

This is the bench Oscar-winner Tom Hanks sat on as the amiable simpleton in *Forrest Gump* (1994), while summarizing his life philosophy: "Life is like a box of chocolates—you never know what you're going to get."

All the interiors of the opulent mansion featured in *Sunset Boulevard* (1950) were built on Stage 18. Descending the stately staircase in the dramatic final scene, Gloria Swanson utters her unforgettable line: "All right, Mr DeMille, I'm ready for my close-up." This same line is repeated countless times by aspiring actors who, according to a Hollywood legend, have to hug the Bronson Gate's bars for good luck while quoting it. Unknown actor Charles Buchinsky even took up the gate's name as his own—he later became famous as Charles Bronson.

Fields Building
Howard Hughes had his nervous breakdown here. He refused to see anyone and received food under the door for several days.

The Administration Building was designed in Spanish Renaissance style by Ruth Morris and Milton Furdman in the late 1920s

Bronson Gate—the original studio gate at Bronson Ave and Marathon St is the prototype of all studio entrances and the symbol of the Hollywood system separating the dream factory from the real world. The wrought-iron Spanish Renaissance gate was built in 1926; the top filigree was added after Rudolph Valentino's death, to keep his adoring fans at bay. The gate was featured in a number of movies, including *The Day of the Locust* (1975), but its most famous appearance is in *Sunset Boulevard* (1950). In the memorable scene, a faded movie queen Norma Desmond (Gloria Swanson) returns to her former studio in her custom-built Isotta-Fraschini automobile, driven by her former husband Max, now butler, played by Erich von Stroheim. (Von Stroheim did not know how to drive, so the car had to be pulled by ropes.)

RKO Pictures

The famous RKO globe, once used as the base for a radio tower, today is painted over but still visible on top of Stage 21, at the corner of Gower St and Melrose Ave. The old front of the RKO Studios at 780 N Gower St is today used as Paramount's side entrance.

Radio-Keith-Orpheum (RKO) was a major film production company formed in 1928 after a merger between FBO Studio (owned by radio giant RCA) and the Keith-Albee-Orpheum theatre chain, followed by the takeover of Pathé Pictures. One of the figures in the merger was Joseph P Kennedy, father of the future president and former owner of FBO. During the Great Depression, RKO was on the verge of bankruptcy and never really achieved financial stability, despite several very successful movies.

Millionaire producer Howard Hughes bought the studio in 1948 and during his reign production dwindled and the studio's decline continued. Hughes sold the company in 1955 and two years later the new owner sold the entire RKO library of more than 700 features and 1,100 short films, together with all television rights.

The RKO lot (at 780 N Gower St) was purchased in 1958 by Desilu Productions, a company owned by former RKO star Lucille Ball and her husband, Desi Arnaz. It later became part of neighboring Paramount Pictures, which incorporated it into its facilities in 1968.

In its relatively short life RKO won only one Oscar in the best picture category, for the epic western *Cimarron* (1930-31). However, the studio produced a number of prestigious films that have become classics: *What Price Hollywood?* (1932), *The Hunchback of Notre Dame* (1939), Orson Welles's *Citizen Kane* (1941) and *The Magnificent Ambersons* (1942), John Ford's *The Informer* (1935) and Alfred Hitchcock's *Suspicion* (1941), along with nine Fred Astaire-Ginger Rogers musicals. It was RKO that introduced King Kong and Tarzan into popular mythology.

Katharine Hepburn was RKO's biggest discovery. The most honored performer in the history of the Academy Awards (with four wins in the best actress category), she received her first Oscar for *Morning Glory* (1933).

RKO never built up a roster of its own top stars. In its early years, the studio boasted such female stars as Bebe Daniels, Constance Bennett, Dolores Del Rio and Irene Dunne. Ginger Rogers stands out as the sole first-rate leading lady during the studio's most successful period. RKO's biggest discovery was Katharine Hepburn, who received her first Oscar here. Other stars who spent time at the studio were Cary Grant and Barbara Stanwyck. Among the big names who emerged during the 1940s and 1950s were Robert Mitchum, Robert Ryan, Jane Russell and Loretta Young.

The western *Cimarron* (1930-31) received RKO's only Oscar in the best picture category

Citizen Kane (1941) was RKO's greatest critical success, often ranked by film critics as No. 1 film in the history of cinema

View of the koi pond and the three-story northern wing of Garfield Court

Garfield Court ⑳

A J Waid, architect (1927)
1833-1839 Garfield Pl.
Private residences.

This imposing Spanish Colonial court is designed in a unique "J" shape and beautifully landscaped.

Chateau Elysée ㉑

Arthur F Harvey, architect (1928).
5930 Franklin Ave.
☎(323) 960-3100. ☛ Ⓢfree.

This French Renaissance Revival chateau was built by Eleanor Ince, widow of the famous pioneer movie producer, Thomas Ince. His death on board newspaper magnate William Randolph Hearst's yacht *Oneida* in 1924 is an enduring legend in Hollywood to this day. The popular belief is that he was mistakenly shot by Hearst, who mistook Ince for Charlie Chaplin. The wildly jealous Hearst thought that his girlfriend, actress Marion Davies, was having an affair with Chaplin. The official version was that Ince died of acute indigestion. The fact that his corpse was quickly cremated further added to controversy. It was rumored at the time that Hearst gave money for the château as a sign of redemption.

The seven-story residential hotel was the most prestigious address in Hollywood. During its hey day, in its 77 apartments lived Bette Davis,

Clark Gable, Carole Lombard, Edward G Robinson, Ginger Rogers, Errol Flynn, Cary Grant, Humphrey Bogart, Katharine Hepburn, George Gershwin and many others. It was the center of celebrity social life and the scene of countless glamorous parties.

Bought in 1973 and fully restored to its former glory, it is today the Celebrity Centre International of the Church of Scientology and serves as a hotel (for members only).

In *The Cat's Meow* (2001), starring Kirsten Dunst as Marion Davies, director Peter Bogdanovich tells the popular version of Ince's mysterious death.

Villa Carlotta ㉒

Arthur F Harvey, architect (1926)
5959 Franklin Ave.
Private residences.

Designed in the Spanish Churrigueresque style, this four-story brick building featured some of the most advanced amenities for its day, such as elaborate soundproofing, water filtration, a central refrigeration system and a ventilation system which changed the air in

each apartment every five minutes. It was originally a hotel built by Eleanor Ince, widow of Thomas Ince, who died on William Randolph Hearst's yacht under mysterious circumstances.

View of Villa Carlotta

Among Villa Carlotta's celebrity residents were director George Cukor, actors Marion Davies, Edward G Robinson and Adolphe Menjou, as well as the gossip columnist Louella Parsons, who was married in the lobby. She worked for the Hearst papers and was one of the most powerful journalists covering Hollywood. Parsons was reportedly on the Hearst's yacht at the time of Ince's death, and local rumor has it that she owed her carrier to the fact that she never talked about the incident.

Chateau Elysée was built as a luxury apartment hotel

Coffee Shop 101 ⑦

6145 Franklin Ave.
☎(323) 467-1175. ⚲

Known at the time as the Hollywood Hills Coffee Shop, this diner was the place where aspiring actors Vince Vaughn and Jon Favreau wrote *Swingers* (1996) over coffee. The famous scene in the movie, in which Vaughn, sitting in a red booth, matches goo-goo eyes with a woman, only to discover that she is making faces at her baby, was shot at this restaurant. The shop's famous guests include Johnny Depp, Gwyneth Paltrow, Brad Pitt, Jennifer Aniston and Quentin Tarantino. The original restaurant has since moved to Vermont Ave.

Vince Vaughn and Jon Favreau in *Swingers* (1996)

Alto Nido Apartments ⑦

1851 N Ivar Ave.
Private residences. ⚲

This is where Joe Gillis, the striving screenwriter played by William Holden in the classic *Sunset Boulevard*

Parva Sed-Apta Apartments

(1950), lived before he moved into the house of former silent film star Norma Desmond (Gloria Swanson).

Parva Sed-Apta Apartments ⑦

1817 N Ivar Ave.
Private residences. ⚫►

Author Nathanael West (➔ p75) lived in a seedy room in this apartment hotel while working on his famous novel *The Day of the Locust* in 1935. The hotel, whose Latin name means "small but suitable," served as the model for the lodging in which the book's main character, studio assistant art director Tod Hackett, lived.

El Cabrillo ⑦

Arthur and Nina Zwebell, architects (1928).
1832 Grace Ave.
Private residences.

Another charming example of the Zwebells' Andalusian design, this complex has

Montecito Apartments

been associated with the DeMille family and was at one time the home of one of the famous Talmadge sisters. The small central courtyard has the typical Zwebell features, including a round tower, wooden loggia and tiered fountain.

Montecito Apartments ⑦

Marcus Miller, architect (1931).
6650 Franklin Ave.
Private residences. ⚫► NRHP

Now converted to an apartment building for senior citizens, this Art Deco structure used to be a residential hotel and reportedly was Ronald Reagan's first Hollywood home. James Cagney, Mickey Rooney, Gene Hackman, George C Scott, as well as Elvis Presley and Bob Dylan, also lived here.

The building was used as the prototype for Chateau Bercy in Raymond Chandler's novel *The Little Sister*.

Alto Nido Apartments

View of El Cabrillo's central courtyard with fountain and tower

Las Palmas Hotel ⑦

1738 N Las Palmas Ave.
☎(323) 464-9236. ☞

Starring as a Hollywood streetwalker in *Pretty Woman* (1990), Julia Roberts lived in a humble apartment located at this hotel. In the movie's final scene, Richard Gere, playing a New York businessman who hires Roberts as an escort, rescues her from the hotel's fire escape.

KFAC Radio ⑦⑨

6735 Yucca St.

Formerly an Italian restaurant called the Villa Capri, this is where James Dean was a regular and where he spent the last evening of his life. After his death on September 30, 1955, his fans used to visit the place, sit at his table and order the same dishes he favored. It was a favorite watering hole of the "Rat Pack," whose members included Frank Sinatra, Dean Martin and Sammy Davis Jr.

First United Methodist Church

First United Methodist Church ⑧⓪

Thomas B Barber, architect (1929).
6817 Franklin Ave.
☎(323) 874-2104. ☞

Dedicated in 1929, this English Gothic Revival structure features a hammer-beam ceiling, reportedly a scaled-down replica of the one in Westminster Abbey. Wedding scenes from *What Price Hollywood?* (1932) were filmed

here, as well as Norman Maine's funeral in *A Star Is Born* (1937). It also appeared in the first two *Back to the Future* films, *Sister Act* (1992) and *That Thing You Do!* (1996).

The church is easily distinguished by the giant red ribbon, prominently displayed since 1992, which shows the church's commitment to its AIDS ministry.

Janis Joplin died at Highland Gardens of a drug overdose

Highland Gardens Hotel ⑧①

7047 Franklin Ave.
☎(323) 850-0536. ✋

On October 4, 1970, legendary rock singer of the 1960s, Janis Joplin, was found dead in room 105 of this hotel (the Landmark Hotel at the time). She died of a drug overdose, apparently mistaking pure heroin

Constance Bennett's wedding in *What Price Hollywood?* (1932) took place at the First United Methodist Church

for diluted (she injected the drug eight times more powerful than the dose she was used to). Her death at 27 was another shock to rock fans worldwide after Jimi Hendrix, also 27, died in London of a sleeping pills overdose three weeks earlier.

Magic Castle ⑧②

7001 Franklin Ave.
☎(323) 851-8946.
www.magiccastle.com.
🕐open for members only. ♠

This authentic Victorian mansion, built in 1908 and beautifully restored, now houses the world-famous club for magicians and lovers of magic. Visitors can see magic performances and stage shows in three main theaters, listen to invisible ghost Irma playing the piano and participate in a seance attempting to contact the great magician Houdini.

Magic Castle hosts magic performances and stage shows

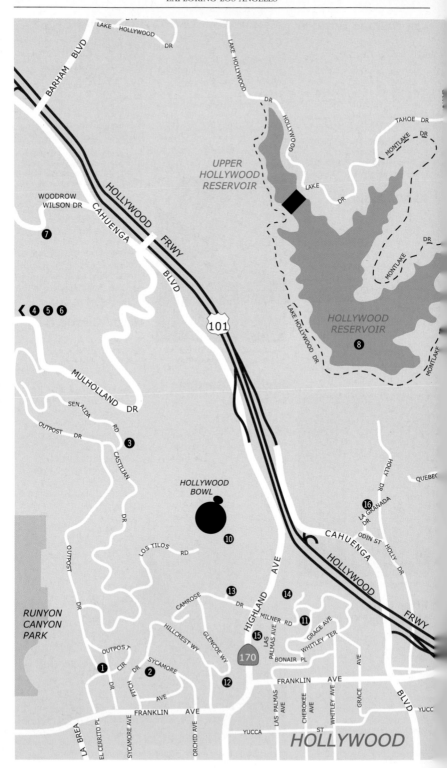

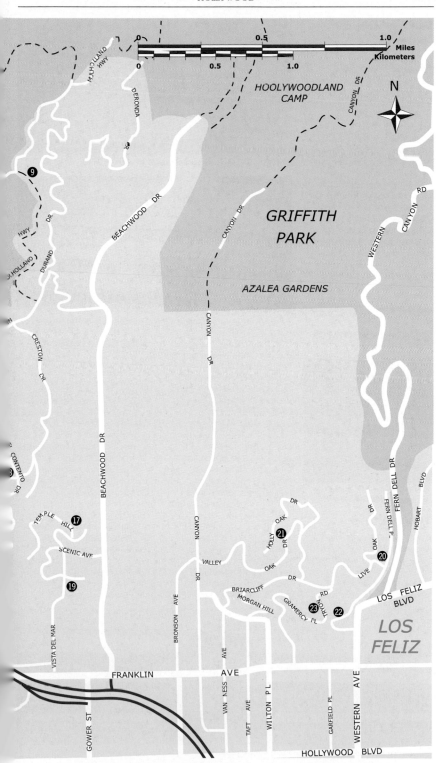

Dolores Del Rio Home ❶

1903 Outpost Dr.
Private residence.

This six-bedroom, Spanish-style home was built in 1927 for Dolores Del Rio, ravishing beauty of the silent screen and star of such hits as *What Price Glory?* (1926), *Bird of Paradise* (1932) and *Flying Down to Rio* (1933). Later in her career she appeared in supporting roles in John Ford's *Fugitive* (1947) and *Cheyenne Autumn* (1964).

The house was later the home of actress Maria Montez, another exotic beauty who starred in Hollywood adventures of the 1940s. She played Sheherazade in *Arabian Nights* (1942) and was a pinup girl during World War II. The house was also owned by fashion designer Richard Tyler.

This Spanish-style house belonged to actress Dolores Del Rio

Johnson House was designed with concrete-block ornaments

Yamashiro was the backdrop for *Sayonara* (1958)

Yamashiro ❷

Franklin M Small, Walter Webber, architects (1913).
1999 N Sycamore Ave.
☎(323) 466-5125. 📷

An authentic replica of a Japanese palace near Kyoto, (its name means Palace on the Hill), this opulent estate was constructed in 1914 as a residence for Adolph and Eugene Bernheimer, leading dealers in Oriental antiques. Built on the crest of a hill overlooking Hollywood, it features an original 600-year-old pagoda, Japanese gardens and a teahouse, but its most famous attraction is a stunning panoramic view of Los Angeles at sunset.

A Japanese restaurant since 1960, Yamashiro was seen on screen as the American Officers Club in a romantic drama *Sayonara* (1958), where Marlon Brando takes his girlfriend to dinner, and again in a romantic comedy/thriller *Man Trouble* (1992).

Johnson House ❸

Lloyd Wright, architect (1963).
7017 Senalda Dr.
Private residence.

This distinctive house was commissioned by a journalist who was impressed by the architect's studio while researching a newspaper article about him. Wright oriented the house toward back terraces and gardens, making it appear inaccessible from the street. Following the client's demand for the use of concrete-block ornaments, he designed chevrons that represent stylized pine tree needles. Wright used a quite unusual palette on the exterior: a lavender hue with mustard-green accents.

Yamashiro is a replica of a palace near Kyoto, Japan

John Lautner's landmark Garcia House

Sharon Stone's former home

Garcia House ❹

John Lautner, architect (1962).
7436 Mulholland Dr.
Private residence. 🔫

The giant arched roof of this landmark house allowed freedom in the configuration of the interior space, which has no retaining walls. Built on a steep hillside lot, the house rests on two V shaped steel supports. It is these supports that Mel Gibson tied to the axle of his pickup truck in *Lethal Weapon 2* (1989), and pulled the whole structure down the hill. The house, which in the movie was the residence of a South African diplomat and the leader of a drug smuggling ring is, of course, still standing, as Gibson actually destroyed the set replica.

Sharon Stone Home ❺

7809 Torreyson Dr.
Private residence.

When she moved to San Francisco after her marriage in 1998, Sharon Stone sold this house that she had owned since 1989, before her breakout role in *Basic Instinct* (1992).

Chemosphere ❻

John Lautner, architect (1960).
7776 Torreyson Dr.
Private residence. 🔫

The most famous in a series of architect John Lautner's experimental creations was the 1960 Malin House, better known as the Chemosphere. Resting on a tall concrete column, this single-story, octagonal structure was built on a steep, almost inaccessible hillside. Its occupants could reach the house either by a cable car or by climbing more than 100 steps from the street level.

Chemosphere appears in Brian DePalma's *Body Double* (1984) as a swinging single's hilltop pad

Called in 1961 by *Encyclopaedia Britannica* "the most modern house in the world," it resembles a giant saucer, especially at night, when its continuous glass surfaces reflect the lights of the valley below.

In Brian DePalma's thriller *Body Double* (1984), an unemployed actor spends time watching a striptease dance across the hill through the telescope and witnesses a bizarre murder with a power drill.

Chemosphere's present owner is book publisher Benedikt Taschen

Ehling House ❼

7110 Woodrow Wilson Dr.
Private residence.

Looking like an enchanted chateau from a fairy tale, this Mediterranean-style house built in the 1920s is the accomplishment of Hollywood studio craftsman and propmaker George Ehling. A fantasy appropriate for the movieland, the two-story building is entirely covered with countless tiles patiently laid over the years by Ehling. Even the gargoyles were cast from molds made of the prop figures used on the movie set.

Impressive tile decoration of the Ehling House

Jack Nicholson got his nose sliced in *Chinatown* (1974)

Hollywood Reservoir ❽

2460 Lake Hollywood Dr.
⊕the lake access road is generally open daily from 6:30am to 5pm. For info call DWP hotline ☎(323) 463-0830. ⏩

Nestled in the underdeveloped section of the Hollywood Hills, this scenic man-made lake is one of the city's most astonishing attractions. Lushly landscaped, this calm,

idyllic spot offers a superb view of the HOLLYWOOD sign. Runners, walkers and cyclists use a 3.1-mile (5-km) rustic jogging trail around the lake.

The monumental reservoir dam features concrete arches, buttresses and castings of the California brown bear heads built into the façade. It was designed and built in 1923 by William Mulholland, the head of the Los Angeles Water Department. The open reservoir, which remains filled, has not provided water for area residents since 2001. It was replaced by two gigantic tanks, each containing 30 million gallons of treated water.

In the classic *Chinatown* (1974), the reservoir is the site where water commissioner Hollis Mulwray, a character modeled after William Mulholland (➔ p34), was found dead. A famous scene where a thug played by Roman Polanski slices Jack Nicholson's nose also takes place here in the movie, but was actually shot at Stone Canyon Reservoir.

In the disaster epic *Earthquake* (1974), the lake's dam bursts and the wall of water floods the city below, destroying everything in its path.

Castillo del Lago

Castillo del Lago/ Madonna Home ❾

John de Lario, architect (1924).
6342 Mulholland Hwy.
Private residence. ♿

Built by an oil prospector above Lake Hollywood in 1924, this nine-story Spanish-style mansion was owned by mobster "Bugsy" Siegel in the 1930s. He operated a speakeasy and a gambling den in the castle until it was suddenly stormed by police from a neighbor's house.

When Madonna bought the estate in 1993 for $3 million, she had the property's retaining wall and the octagonal tower repainted in dark red and ocher stripes. It was here that the stalker, who claimed to be the Material Girl's husband, was shot and wounded by her guard as he scaled the wall in 1995. Madonna sold the castle in 1996.

View of the Hollywood Reservoir

Hollywood Bowl ⑩

Situated in a natural outdoor amphitheater, the world-famous Hollywood Bowl is one of Los Angeles' most recognizable attractions. The area, known then as Daisy Dell, was used by early filmmakers as a location for silent movies, mostly westerns. The property was purchased in 1919 for the purpose of presenting religious plays, and the first concert was held in 1921. The Bowl's first music shell was erected in 1922, and since then several acclaimed architects have been commissioned to design or remodel the shell and the amphitheater, including Myron Hunt and Lloyd Wright. In 1980, Frank O Gehry and Associates introduced the fiberglass spheres that hung from the shell's ceiling to improve the acoustic effects.

In 2004, new $25-million elliptical shell designed by Hodgetts + Fung replaced the deteriorating old shell. A steel-frame structure consists of a series of flat arches and an "acoustic canopy" hovering over the stage. Designed to improve the sound quality both for the performers and the audience, the canopy contains 20 translucent, computer-controlled louvers, which serve as acoustic reflectors whose movement controls the sound on the stage.

Home to the Hollywood Bowl Orchestra and summer venue for LA Philharmonic, the Hollywood Bowl has a capacity of 18,000. Although the Bowl became famous for its classical music performances, pop, jazz and rock concerts are held here as well. Among the luminaries who performed at the Bowl are Artur Rubinstein, Leonard Bernstein and Igor Stravinsky. After Vladimir Horowitz played Sergei Rachmaninoff's *Piano Concerto No. 3* in 1942, the composer walked to the stage and congratulated him for his performance. The Playboy Jazz Festival was inaugurated in 1979, since featuring artists such as Ella Fitzgerald, Ray Charles, Chick Corea and Miles Davis. The Beatles played here in 1964; other pop stars have included Bob Dylan, the Rolling Stones, the Doors, Jimi Hendrix and Elton John.

The Hollywood Bowl has appeared in a number of films, including *A Star Is Born* (1937), with Janet Gaynor and Fredric March; *Double Indemnity* (1944), with Fred MacMurray and Barbara Stanwyck; *Anchors Aweigh* (1945), with Gene Kelly and Frank Sinatra; and *Xanadu* (1980), with Olivia Newton-John.

Hodgetts + Fung, architects (2004)
2301 N Highland Ave.
☎(323) 850-2000. ⤴
www.hollywoodbowl.com.
⏰evening concerts from late June to mid September. ⑤
Box Office ⏰Tue-Sun 12 noon 6pm

A vintage post card shows a view of the Hollywood Bowl and nearby Whitley Heights in the 1920s. In its early days, the site was used to present religious plays. The Bowl's Easter Sunrise Services, first held in 1921, attracted tens of thousands of people. It's been a custom to come early and picnic on the grounds, or enjoy a dinner and a glass of wine in the stands. The box seats close to the stage are sold to subscribers only. Tickets start at $1 for seats at the top.

Drunken Fredric March is pursued by photographers at the Bowl in *A Star Is Born* (1937)

Edmund D Edelman Hollywood Bowl Museum

Located near the entrance to the Bowl
☎(323) 850-2058.
⏰ Tue-Sat 10am-8:30pm (Jul 2-Sep 19); Tue-Sat 10am-4:30pm (off-season). ⑤free.

The museum's permanent exhibition presents the history of the Hollywood Bowl and its role in the development of the performing arts in Los Angeles. Visitors can listen to recordings of outstanding Bowl performances.

The Hollywood Bowl's new elliptical shell was opened in 2004

Whitley Heights ⑪

North of Franklin Blvd, between Highland Ave and Cahuenga Blvd. Private residences. 🚏 ♿ NRHP

Nowhere else in Los Angeles can the look of Hollywood of the 1920s be better experienced than in this fashionable community. Retaining the charm and glamour of jazz-era Tinseltown, this is one of the oldest historic neighborhoods that has kept its architectural integrity mostly intact.

The hilltop enclave was laid out by Hobart J Whitley, an important land developer at the turn of the 20th century, who considered it his crowning achievement. Dubbed "the father of Hollywood," he modeled his development on Mediterranean hillside villages he remembered from his European trips. In order to achieve authenticity, he sent his chief architect, Arthur S Barnes, to Italy and Spain to tour and study local architecture and landscaping.

The original 1920s gas street lamp

Burgess Meredith sells his miracle medicine on Whitley Ave in *The Day of the Locust* (1975).

Between 1918 and 1928 Barnes designed the majority of the Mediterranean-style residences on the hill. They were mostly two- and three-level houses built downslope or upslope from narrow roads, each with unobstructed views. Perfectly suited for the Los Angeles climate and landscape, the houses contained red tile roofs, arched doorways, leaded glass windows, courtyards and fountains. Wrought iron was extensively used for lamps, balconies and balustrades. These features had not been seen in LA before, but quickly gained popularity and have been endlessly copied throughout the region ever since.

The seclusion and romantic appeal immediately attracted silent-screen stars to this posh neighborhood, which became Hollywood's first celebrity enclave. Whitley Heights was at one time or another home to such movie greats as Francis X Bushman, Tyrone Power, Bette Davis, Barbara Stanwyck, William Powell and his wife, Carole Lombard. Movie star home tours originated here in the 1920s, with sightseeing buses and drivers announcing star home locations over their megaphones.

Although no longer a preferred celebrity address, Whitley Heights and its 196 remaining homes still attract some notable names from the entertainment and art world, such as Oscar-winning filmmaker Sofia Coppola.

In the late 1940s, Whitley Heights was cut in two by the construction of the Hollywood Freeway, with about one-fifth of the original neighborhood now lying north of the freeway. Part of the hill was destroyed in the process and more than 40 homes were lost, including Rudolph Valentino's, Harold Lloyd's and Charlie Chaplin's.

Rudolph Valentino and Natacha Rambova in front of their Whitley Heights home

Rudolph Valentino House
(site)

6776 Wedgewood Pl.

This Spanish-style villa was the honeymoon house of legendary screen lover Rudolph Valentino and his second wife, Natasha Rambova, an American-born art director with an exotic Russian name. Rambova had a great influence on Valentino's career, nearly ruining it with a series of effeminate roles she wrote for him. The pair resided in this two-story, eight-room house from 1921 until 1925, when Valentino purchased a large mansion which he named "Falcon Lair" in fashionable Beverly Hills, a new celebrity enclave (➜ p466).

The Whitley Heights area had been featured in many films, including *Now, Voyager* (1942) and *The Day of the Locust* (1975).

A vintage post card shows Rudolph Valentino's home

Barbara La Marr House

Robert Vignola House

Willam Faulkner House

Barbara La Marr House

Arthur S Barnes, architect (1920).
6672 Whitley Ter.
Private residence.

One of the most exquisite silent-screen goddesses, Barbara La Marr lived scandalously in this partially hidden villa until her death of drug overdose at the age of 29. Built downslope, the three-story house, with its Oriental pagoda and colored glass Venetian window, is said to have had a secret passageway between the chauffeur's quarters and La Marr's bedroom.

Robert Vignola House

Nathan L Coleman, architect (1922).
6697 Whitley Ter.
Private residence.

This recently remodeled house was once the site of lavish parties thrown by director Robert Vignola. It was said that newspaper tycoon William Randolph Hearst built this large villa as a hideout for himself and his lover, actress Marion Davies.

Maurice Chevalier House

Lee and Scott, architects (1924).
6680 Whitley Ter.
Private residence.

When he came to Hollywood in 1929 sporting his signature boulevardier outfit of tilted straw hat and bow tie, the famous French enter-tainer moved to this three-story house. He starred in romantic classics such as *The Love Parade* (1929) and *The Merry Widow* (1934), living here until he left Hollywood in 1935.

Richard Barthelmess House

Arthur S Barnes, architect (1921).
6691 Whitley Ter.
Private residence.

A Hollywood leading man during the 1920s and early 1930s, Barthelmess was described by Lillian Gish, his co-star in *Broken Blossoms* (1919), as having "the most beautiful face of any man who ever went before the camera." This opinion was certainly shared by actress Norma Talmadge, who often visited Barthelmess in this house, though she was still married to producer Joseph Schenck at the time.

William Faulkner/ Gloria Swanson House

Harry McAfee, architect (1924).
2058 Watsonia Ter.
Private residence. ●◆

The Nobel Prize winner William Faulkner stayed here in the 1940s when he came to Hollywood to write screenplays for Warner Bros.
Actress Gloria Swanson rented the same villa with her mother between 1949 and 1950, during the filming of her comeback success, *Sunset Boulevard* (1950).

Villa Vallombrosa

Nathan L Coleman, architect (1928).
2074 Watsonia Ter.
Private residence.

With its concave façade and five-sided balcony, it is said that this neo-Venetian Gothic villa was modeled after a building on the Grand Canal in Venice. The three-story house was built by wealthy East Coast widow and socialite Eleanor DeWitt.

It was occupied at various times by actresses Ethel Barrymore and Dame Judith Anderson, screenwriter Ben Hecht, fashion photographer Baron Adolf Gayne de Meyer and conductor Leonard Bernstein. Legendary costume designer Gilbert Adrian lived here before moving to 6666 Whitley Terrace with his wife, actress Janet Gaynor.

Villa Vallombrosa

Hollywood Heritage Museum's building was a horse barn used as a set for the first feature-length film made in Hollywood

Freeman House ⑫

Frank Lloyd Wright, 1924).
1962 Glencoe Way.
Closed for restoration. **NRHP**

This remarkable little house was designed as the third of four Frank Lloyd Wright structures in Los Angeles built in his textile-block construction method. Commissioned by newlyweds Samuel and Harriet Freeman, members of LA's artistic circles, the house became the site of an avant-garde salon.

The building's most astonishing feature are the two-story mitered windows at each of the south corners, used here for the first time in residential architecture. The living room that extends to the balcony offers a spectacular view of Hollywood. It contains some original Wright furnishings, including floor lamps and a dining table.

Damaged during the Northridge 1994 earthquake, the house awaits restoration.

The High Tower ⑬

North end of Hightower Dr.
Private residences. 🎏

The five-story, Italian-style tower built in the early 1920s contains an elevator which services the houses on the hillside. The tower and the adjacent Moderne apartment to the right of it were featured in Robert Altman's *The Long Goodbye* (1973), starring Elliott Gould, and Kenneth Branagh's *Dead Again* (1991).

The High Tower

Hollywood Heritage Museum ⑭

2100 N Highland Ave.
☎(323) 463-6418. 🎏
🕐Sat-Sun 11:30am-3:30pm. ⑤

The museum building was originally a 1895 horse barn on Jacob Stern's citrus farm, located at Vine St and Selma Ave (➔ p123). It was used as a set during the filming of Cecil B DeMille's *The Squaw Man* (1914). The museum explores the early history of the movie industry in Hollywood through its displays of photographs, props, costumes and equipment.

Among the exhibits are Mary Pickford's make-up case, a camera used by Charlie Chaplin in *The Gold Rush* (1925) and a re-creation of Cecil B DeMille's 1913 office.

Roman Gardens ⑮

F Pierpont and Walter S Davis, architects (1926).
2000 N Highland Ave.
Private residences.

Drawing on Spanish, Italian and Moorish influences, this eclectic design is one of the most elaborate garden courts in Los Angeles. Hidden behind the lush landscaping of mature exotic trees, the only part visible from the street is the peculiar tower of North African origin. Hollywood lore has it that famous screen lover Rudolph Valentino used an apartment here for his amorous exploits shortly before his death in 1926.

The Roman Gardens' North African tower

View of the Freeman House from the terrace. Note patterned concrete blocks and the two-story corner windows.

Pola Negri and Rudolph Valentino House ⑯

2285 La Granada Dr.
Private residence.

This Mediterranean villa was built in 1923 by an opera singer, who later rented it to silent film star Pola Negri. The sultry Polish actress lived here for a while with her lover, legendary actor Rudolph Valentino, during the last year of his life. After Valentino's sudden death in 1926, Negri claimed that they had been engaged to be married.

Moorcrest/Charlie Chaplin House ⑰

Marie Russak Hotchener, architect (1921).
6147 Temple Hill Dr.
Private residence.

An example of early Hollywood exotic architecture, this Moorish-style house with a round tower and stained-glass windows was rented by Charlie Chaplin in the early 1920s. After the "photoplayer and motion-picture producer" built his own home on Summit Dr in Beverly Hills and moved out, the house was bought by the parents of actress Mary Astor. She reportedly made it the scene of her stormy love affair with actor John Barrymore.

Double Indemnity House ⑱

6301 Quebec Dr.
Private residence. ☞
"It was one of those California Spanish houses everyone was nuts about ten or fifteen years ago. This one must have cost somebody about thirty thousand bucks."
This monologue is said in flashback by Fred MacMurray as he navigates a winding street in the Hollywood Hills in the opening scenes of Billy Wilder's classic *noir* film *Double Indemnity* (1944). The Spanish-style mansion is owned in the movie by Bar-

Charlie Chaplin's Home, Hollywood, Calif.
A vintage post card depicts Charlie Chaplin house

bara Stanwyck and her oil-man husband, and serves as the location where Stanwyck and insurance salesman Mac-Murray plot to kill her husband and collect insurance money. The house was featured prominently in the film, notably in the scene where Stanwyck and her husband, who is on crutches, go down the stairs to the garage, where MacMurray awaits hidden in the car to strangle him. The house remains today virtually unchanged, except for a modern garage door.

Krotona Inn ⑲

Mead and Requa, architects (1912-13).
2130 Vista del Mar Ave.
Private residences.

Hollywood in the early 20th century was a fertile ground for numerous bizarre cults that thrived here when Albert Warrington arrived in 1911. He was president of the American branch of the Theosophical Society, a religious organization founded in New York in 1875 by Helena Blavatsky. A lawyer turned missionary, Warrington was looking all over the country for a suitable place to build a retreat for true believers. Luckily, he found it in the Hollywood Hills, which were "magnetically impregnated," as he ingeniously noticed. With throngs of faithful followers flocking to Krotona Colony, as it was called, an exotic complex of

buildings was constructed, including residences, a temple, a science building and a library. Most of these structures, though subsequently altered, still exist today.

Featuring Moorish domes, horseshoe arches and even a "psychic lotus pond" in the central courtyard, the Krotona Inn once contained apartments, dining and lecture rooms, and a space dedicated to meditation. It is now converted to residential use and called Goldwater Patio Villas.

It is said that Krishnamurti, one of the leading spiritual teachers of the 20th century, was a frequent visitor. After settling down in Ojai, he continued to make trips to Hollywood to give talks. During his visits he stayed at the Krotona Inn, since occasionally referred to as the "Home of Krishnamurti."

Entrance to the Krotona Inn

Taggart House ⓴

Lloyd Wright, architect (1924).
2158 N Live Oak Dr East.
Private residence.

This unique house was built for Martha Taggart, the mother of the actress Helen Taggart Pole who would became Wright's wife in 1926. With its white stucco walls and layered horizontal planks, the two-story building is often said to anticipate the forthcoming Art Deco style. Wright, who was trained as a landscape architect, sensibly integrates exterior and interior, connecting the house that descends a steep hillside with gardens and patios on different levels.

Taggart House

Samuel-Novarro House ⓴

Lloyd Wright, architect (1926-28).
5609 Valley Oak Dr.
Private residence.

Although it belonged to silent screen star Ramon Novarro, this astonishing house was originally built for his agent, Louis Samuel. It was designed only one year after the 1925 Paris Exposition that launched Art Deco style. The four-story, white stucco residence, trimmed with green copper panels, shows the influence the new style had on the architect, Lloyd Wright. Actresses Diane Keaton and later Christina Ricci owned the house.

Ramon Novarro, a lifelong bachelor, was beaten to death in his other home, on 3110 Laurel Canyon, on Halloween night of 1968 by two young men he picked up on Hollywood Blvd.

Nicolas Cage lived in this castle between 1991 and 2000

American Film Institute (AFI) ⓴

2021 N Western Ave.
☎(323) 856-7600.
www.afionline.org.

Founded in 1967, the American Film Institute is the nation's leading arts organization "dedicated to advancing and preserving the art of the moving image."

AFI trains the next generation of filmmakers through its Center for Advanced Film and Television Studies, which offers graduate programs in directing, cinematography, digital media, editing, producing, production design and screenwriting. Among AFI's famous alumni are directors David Lynch, Paul Schrader and Terrence Malick.

The AFI Fest, one of the major international film festivals in the country, is presented in October every year.

Nicolas Cage Castle ⓴

5647 Tryon Rd.
Private residence.

Cage, who won the best actor Oscar for his role in *Leaving Las Vegas* (1995), had bought this castle in 1991. Built in 1928, the three-story house is situated on a knoll overlooking the city and surrounded with high walls. The star sold the property in 2000 for $1.5 million.

Samuel-Novarro House

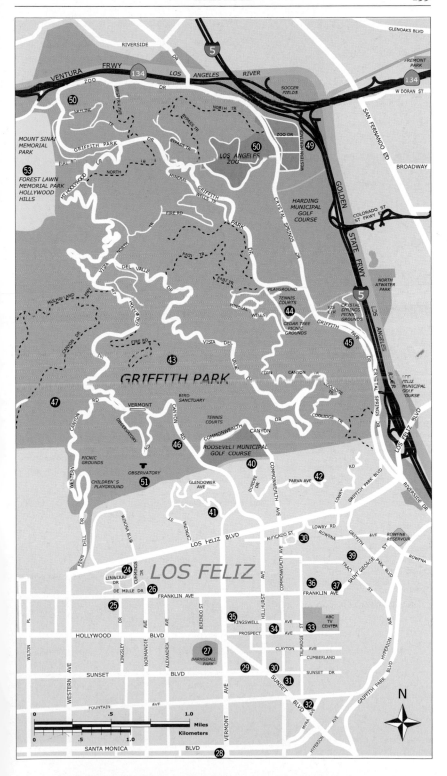

Director Cecil B DeMille in front of his palatial home

Laughlin Park ㉔

North of Franklin Ave to Los Feliz Blvd; between Lauglin Park Dr and Normandie Ave.

When this exclusive subdivision was developed in the late 1890s, its hills were covered with tropical gardens which grew all kinds of palms, water lilies and other exotic plants. In the late 1910s it attracted some prominent members of the burgeoning film community, who bought estates built by local land and oil barons. It is now a gated and secluded neighborhood with private streets closed to through traffic and only occasional public access.

Cecil B DeMille Mansion

2000 DeMille Dr.
Private residence.

The first palatial residence in Hollywood used by a member of the movie industry was built in 1914 in the semi-private area called Laughlin Park. In 1916, director Cecil B DeMille bought the 15-room Italianate Revival mansion for $27,893. The man whose street had been renamed after him lived here until his death in 1959.

DeMille used his backyard with its olive trees for the Garden of Gethsemane scenes in his spectacle *The King of Kings* (1927).

It is said that the house was maintained as it was when DeMille was alive, with fresh flowers on his desk every day, until it was sold in 1988.

Charlie Chaplin Home

2010 DeMille Dr.
Private residence.

Charlie Chaplin lived here with his first wife, 16-year-old Mildred Harris, between 1918 and 1919. DeMille later bought the Spanish Revival villa and connected the two properties by the breezeway. He used Chaplin's Gothic living room as an office and screening room.

W C Fields Home

2015 DeMille Dr.
Private residence. 🕭

The great comedian W C Fields lived in this house from 1938 until his death in 1946. It was said that the eccentric actor always kept a rifle handy, just in case a "hairy-nosed wombat" escaped from nearby Griffith Park Zoo. He fired a shot only once—in warning—when an unannounced guest showed up. This was his next door neighbor Cecil B DeMille, who got away unharmed, though somewhat shattered. In a tragic accident in 1942, Anthony Quinn's two-year-old son (DeMille's grandson) drowned in a pool on Field's front lawn.

Actress Lily Tomlin and writer-director Jane Wagner called this place a home between 1980 and 1999.

Carole Lombard Home

Lester Scherer, architect (1927).
5120 Linwood Dr.
Private residence.

One of the most glamorous Hollywood leading ladies lived at one time in this Art Deco palace at the end of Linwood Dr.

W C Fields Home

Charlie Chaplin Home

Casa Laguna courtyard

Entrance to Sowden House

Vermont/Santa Monica station

Casa Laguna ㉕

Arthur and Nina Zwebell (1928)
5200 Franklin Ave.
Private residences.

Painted in a deep yellow hue, the two-story Andalusian complex features a long balcony with stone columns and carved-wood capitals above the main entrance. In addition to the Zwebells' signature touches, such as the tiled fountain and an exterior fireplace, the architects applied colonnade with the upper balcony at the southern edge of the large square courtyard, adding to the sense of serenity.

Sowden House ㉖

Lloyd Wright, architect (1926).
5121 Franklin Ave.
Private residence. NRHP 🏳

One of the most famous of Lloyd Wright's buildings, this 1926 pink stucco house is constructed around the interior courtyard, which originally contained a fountain (now replaced with a pool). The cave-like entrance is under an impressive sculpture made of decorative concrete blocks. The house is featured in *The Aviator* (2004) as the stylish home of legendary actress Ava Gardner (played by Kate Beckinsale).

Hollyhock House ㉗

Frank Lloyd Wright, architect (1919)
4800 Hollywood Blvd.
☎(323) 644-6269. 🏳 NRHP
☛Wed-Sun 1:30-3:30pm. Ⓢ

This was Frank Lloyd Wright's first commission in Los Angeles, designed for oil heiress Aline Barnsdall and built between 1919 and 1921. It was planned as a complex of structures housing a dramatic arts community center, but never materialized as conceived and eventually only the Barnsdall home and two secondary residences were built. The house was named after a geometric motif based on the hollyhock, Barnsdall's favorite flower, which Wright incorporated into the roof eaves, walls, columns and furniture. The house's most notable feature is its transparency and the way it connects the interiors to the gardens, flowing freely, uninterrupted by thresholds.

The living room contains a prominent cast-stone fireplace featuring an abstract design. It is topped by a skylight and surrounded by a pool in front of the hearthstone. The room also contains replicas of two built-in sofas, tables, lamp units and footstools. The furniture and the original color scheme were reproduced using old photographs and original documents.

Vermont and Santa Monica subway station ㉘

Mehrdad Yazdani, architect/Robert Millar, artist (1999).

The astonishing design of this station features a huge, eye-shaped steel canopy hovering over the entrance. Descending to the underground platform, metro passengers face 10,000 questions embossed upon the concrete walls, relating to public art such as "Who will love this work?" "Who seeks beauty?" and "Who would want to live in a world without painting?"

Hollyhock House features stylized hollyhock ornamentation

The Babylon set built for the silent classic *Intolerance* (1916)

Babylon Site ㉙

Sunset Blvd at Hollywood Blvd.

This is the site of the Babylon set from D W Griffith's epic film *Intolerance* (1916). The colossal set was built in an open field on Sunset Blvd where it converged with Hollywood Blvd. After the film proved to be a financial failure, the 150 feet-high (50-m) structure remained standing for three years after the film was released; only then its removal could be financed.

Vista Theater ㉚

J H Woodhouse & Son (1923). 4473 Sunset Dr. ☎(323) 660-6639.

The Vista Theater, one of the last free-standing, single-screen theaters in Los Angeles, stands across the street from the site of D W Griffith's enormous Babylon set. Originally named Lou Bard's Hollywood Theatre after a local showman who built it, the Spanish-style structure was erected in 1923 as a neighborhood silent movie and vaudeville house. It was opened with a short subject *Tips*, starring child actress Baby Peggy. Today it shows first-run features and occasional re-releases.

The Vista's elaborate, Egyptian-style interior, popular in the 1920s, has been recently renovated, featuring pyramid-shaped lamps and

new gilding for the busts, eagles, serpents and sun discs. The lobby and women's restroom walls are covered with meticulous paintings of Egyptian gods and hieroglyphic inscriptions.

The new stucco ticket booth, designed as a shrine within a pharaoh's tomb, is painted gold and carved with Egyptian religious symbols, royal names and hieroglyphics. The exterior forecourt contains celebrity handprints in cement.

KCET Studios
(formerly **Lubin Studio**) ㉛

4401 Sunset Blvd. ☎(323) 666-6500. ☛ ☛free one-hour tour is available during business hours on weekdays.

This is claimed to be the oldest continuously producing movie lot in Hollywood.

Lubin Manufacturing Company was the first to take pictures on this site in 1912, producing educational films such as *An Alligator Farm*. Other film companies followed, including Essanay, Kalem, Charles Ray Productions, Monogram and Allied Artists. Among the films produced on this lot were *Invasion of the Body Snatchers* (1956), *El Cid* (1961) and *L.A. Story* (1991), in which the studio doubled as KYOY.

In 1970 the studio was purchased by KCET (TV channel 28), Community Television of Southern California, which produced several nationally acclaimed programs, including *Sesame Street* and Carl Sagan's *Cosmos*.

The red-brick exterior of the old studio and offices, built by Charles Ray in the early 1920s and still in use today, can be seen on the north side of the property (on Sunset Dr)

Auditorium of the Vista Theater

Triangle Scene Shop

This bungalow was Walt Disney's first Los Angeles home

Triangle Scene Shop ㉜

1215 Bates Ave.
☎(323) 662-8129. 🏳

In 1916 famous director and producer Mack Sennett built this triangle-shaped building as a private studio for Mabel Normand, brilliant silent film comedienne and his lover. The wooden structure originally had a muslin-topped roof designed to diffuse direct sunlight used to illuminate the set. The Mabel Normand Feature Film Company made only one film here, *Mickey* (1918), before the actress signed with Goldwyn. In 1917, western film star William S Hart leased the studio to make his own productions. Today it serves as a stage for commercials and feature films such as Barbra Streisand's Hollywood debut, *Funny Girl* (1968), and David Lynch's *Wild at Heart* (1990).

Prospect Studios ㉝
(formerly **Vitagraph Studio**)

4151 W Prospect Ave. 🏳

Prospect Avenue officially changed its name to Hollywood Boulevard in 1910, but the part of the street east of Vermont Ave still bears the old name. It was here, at Prospect Ave and Talmadge St, that Vitagraph, one of the pioneer film companies, built its studio in 1915. Vitagraph was an important early producer, whose films were the most popular among moviegoers in the early silent era.

Among its major stars were Florence Turner, the famous "Vitagraph Girl," Maurice Costello, Norma Talmadge and Rudolph Valentino. It was one of Hollywood's largest and most successful studios in the early 1920s.

Warner Bros purchased Vitagraph Company in 1926 and used its former studio as an annex. Parts of many famous Warner Bros pictures were filmed here, including the first talkie, *The Jazz Singer* (1927), *Public Enemy* (1931) and *Captain Blood* (1935).

In 1948 ABC bought the Warner Bros facility and remodeled it into what was then the largest television studio in the world. The lot, formerly known as ABC Television Center, was the home of local KABC-TV (channel 7) and such shows as *Family Feud*, and now is used for production of network shows and sitcom series.

The old Vitagraph studio gate (now a brick wall bearing the Prospect Studios sign) can still be seen at the corner of Prospect Ave and Talmadge St.

Walt Disney's First LA Home ㉞

4406 Kingswell Ave.
Private residence.

After the animation company he founded in Kansas City failed, Walt Disney came to Hollywood in 1923 to join his brother Roy. He stayed with his uncle Robert Disney in this unassuming Craftsman bungalow, paying $5 a week for room and board. Walt used the small garage in the back of the house as his first workshop, where he made a series of crude cartoons on a homemade animation stand.

The garage was moved from the site and now is on display in the Stanley Ranch Museum, 12174 Euclid St, Garden Grove, Orange County, ☎(714) 530-8871. ⏰3rd Sun of each month, at 1pm.

Vitagraph Studio was built in 1915

Disney Bros Studio

(site) ㉟

4649 Kingswell Ave.

Between 1923 and 1926 this was the location of the first Disney production studio. Brothers Walt and Roy Disney rented a small space in the rear of a real estate office at 4651 Kingswell Ave, but soon moved to the storefront next door, proudly displaying a sign reading Disney Bros Studio. They stayed here until a large facility was built on Hyperion Ave (➜ p171).

Shakespeare Bridge

Shakespeare Bridge ㊲

J C Wright, engineer (1924-26) Franklin Ave (between Myra Ave and St George St). 🚩

This elegant, 262-foot-long span, with its Gothic arches and pairs of turrets at each end, is one of the most picturesque bridges in the city. It was featured in Kenneth Branagh's psychological thriller *Dead Again* (1991).

Cedars/Norma Talmadge Home ㊳

4320 Cedarhurst Circle. Private residence. 🚩

This opulent hilltop villa that epitomizes Old Hollywood glamour is said to be a replica of the Duke of Alba's 17th-century palace in Florence. Called the Cedars, it was built for French film director Maurice Tourneur in 1926. Local lore has it that silent screen legend Norma Talmadge resided here at one time. Among its other tenants were Ralph Bellamy and Rod McKuen. During the 1960s,

Elliott House

Elliott House ㊱

Rudolf Schindler, architect (1930). 4237 Newdale Dr. Private residence.

With its pure geometric forms, the three-level house follows the contours of a hillside, partially concealed by the garden. Immediately visible from the street is a garage and entrance covered by pergolas. Initially intended for privacy, they correspond to the beautiful landscaping and contribute to the overall sense of openness.

Arthur Lee and his band Love lived here, as did famed rock guitarist Jimi Hendrix.

The house was used as a location for a number of television productions and such films as *Jane Eyre* (1944) and *Too Much, Too Soon* (1958).

John Marshall High School

John Marshall High School ㊴

3939 Tracy St. ☎(323) 660-1440. 🚩

Built in 1931, this Gothic structure was almost torn down after the 1971 Sylmar earthquake. It was saved through neighborhood effort and reinforced to meet earthquake standards.

The school has appeared as Dawson High School in *Rebel Without a Cause* (1955), Rydell High in *Grease* (1977) and Hemery High in *Buffy the Vampire Slayer*.

Among its famous alumni are actor Leonardo DiCaprio, Lance Ito, the judge in the O J Simpson case and the "Hollywood Madam," Heidi Fleiss.

The Cedars, former home of Norma Talmadge and Jimi Hendrix

The Lovell House with the Griffith Observatory in the background

Lovell Health House ⓐ

Richard Neutra, architect (1929).
4616 Dundee Dr.
Private residence. ↗ NRHP

Richard Neutra's Lovell House is the celebrated architect's first great success in America, widely regarded as one of the most significant monuments of International Style Modern. The house was included in the Museum of Modern Art's 1932 exhibition *Modern Architecture* as one of only a few American works. It was the first metal-framed house in the United States. Built on a steep hillside with prefabricated all-steel frame and concrete panels, it features large, unbroken expanses of glass, a cantilevered balcony and "open plan" interior. Designed for a health-conscious *Los Angeles Times* columnist, this residential icon drew 15,000 curious visitors within a few weeks

upon completion and brought the Vienna-born architect international acclaim.

The house was featured in *L.A. Confidential* (1997), a mystery thriller set in Los Angeles in the 1950s. It was the dwelling of pimp/black-mailer/corrupt developer Pierce Patchett (played by David Strathairn), who dies here in a Neutra chair with his wrists slashed.

Ennis House ⓐ

Frank Lloyd Wright, architect (1924)
2607 Glendower Ave.
☎(323) 668-0234.
Private residence. ↗ NRHP
☞ by appointment only. ♿

"You see, the final result is going to stand on that hill a hundred years or more. Long after we are all gone it will be pointed out as the Ennis House and pilgrimages will be made to it by lovers of the beautiful—from everywhere."
— Frank Lloyd Wright

Built in 1924, this is one of the most outstanding architectural landmarks in the city. The house, inspired by Pre-Columbian traditions, was constructed of 24 different forms of precast concrete blocks. It is the last, largest and most complex of Wright's four textile-block houses designed in the Los Angeles area.

A low, dark entrance hall on the ground floor leads up a marble stairway to the second level and all the principal rooms. They are unified by a 100-foot loggia, creating a space Wright called the great room. It features stained-glass windows and a glass-tile mosaic above the living room fireplace.

Harrison Ford's officer Deckard lives in the Ennis House in *Blade Runner* (1982)

The house has been the set for numerous movies and television productions. It is the art director Claude Estee's (played by Richard A Dysart) sleek mansion in *The Day of the Locust* (1975), Harrison Ford's home in *Blade Runner* (1982) and Steve Martin's house in *Grand Canyon* (1991).

Ennis House: the double-height living room features stained-glass clerestory windows and a glass-tile mosaic above the fireplace

Reminiscent of a Mayan temple, the Ennis House is dramatically located on a hill, commanding spectacular views of the city and the mountains

Walt Disney Home 42

F Scott Crowhurst, architect (1932).
4053 Woking Way.
Private residence.

Beyond reach on a high slope and partially hidden behind thick foliage, this fairy tale cottage with its round tower with a conical roof seems a proper dwelling for the creator of animated fantasies.

Griffith Park 43

Griffith Park Visitor's Center/Ranger Station, 4730 Crystal Springs Dr (1.5 miles north of Los Feliz and Riverside Dr intersection).
☎(323) 665-5188; 913-7390.
⏰daily 5:30am-10pm. ⑤ free.
Facilities: boys camp; girls camp; baseball; bicycle rentals; equestrian center; golf courses; picnic areas; pony ride; swimming pool; tennis courts; train ride.

With more than 4,000 acres (1.600 ha), this is the largest municipal park in the United States. It was named for its former owner, Colonel Griffith J Griffith (no relation to film director D W Griffith, although he used the park as a location). When Colonel Griffith, a wealthy mining speculator, donated the land in 1896 for public recreation, the city was more than happy to accept the gift. But when he offered $100,000 a few years later to build the observatory in the park, the city officials refused. That second offer came after Griffith was released from San Quentin prison, where he spent two years for attempted murder. Accusing his Catholic wife of conspiring with the Pope to deprive him of his money, a drunken Griffith shot her in the eye. It was not until his death in 1919 that the city finally accepted his money.
Many different theories existed as to the reason why Griffith donated his property to the city. Some insisted that he was trying to avoid taxes; others wondered if he could not sell the land owing to the

Merry-go-round beautiful, hand-carved horse

ancient curse. Whatever the reason, Angelenos and visitors can now enjoy its large undeveloped areas with hiking and horse trails in the mountainous portions of the park, as well as numerous amenities in the flatlands.

Merry-Go-Round 44

☎(323) 665-3051.
⏰daily mid-June to mid-Sept; Sat-Sun and LA public school holidays mid-Sept to mid-June. ⑤

Built by Spillman Engineering in 1926 for San Diego's Mission Beach pier, this merry-go-round was later moved to Balboa Park for the 1935 California Pacific International Exposition. The well-preserved machine finally settled at its present site in Griffith Park in 1937. The carousel has 68 jeweled, hand-carved horses with real horse-hair tails. Some of the horses were made by master carver-builder Charles Looff, who is credited with installing the first carousel at Coney Island, New York, in 1876. The custom-built Mighty Stinson organ, which is controlled by punched paper rolls, plays over 1,500 selections from its library, including Strauss waltzes and Sousa marches.
Hollywood legend has it that Walt Disney came up with the idea for Disneyland

Statue of Griffith J Griffith

here, while watching his daughters ride a carousel. "It started with my taking my two kids around to zoos and parks," Disney reportedly said. "While they were on the merry-go-round riding forty times or something, I'd be sitting there trying to figure out what you could do that would be more imaginative."

Holiday Light Festival 45

Crystal Springs Dr.
☎(323) 913-4688.
⏰daily 5-10pm. Nov 27-Dec 28, yearly. ⑤free.

This mile-long holiday attraction features hundreds of thousands of colorful lights depicting seasonal, historical and cultural images. The largest lighting display in Southern California can be enjoyed from the car or during a walk.

A colorful light display

Greek Theatre ㊻

2700 N Vermont Ave.
☎(323) 665-1927.
⏱ Jun through Oct. Ⓢ

Completed in 1930 and hidden behind a plain Doric façade, this open-air amphiteater is nestled in a natural bowl in the foothills. The 4,600-seat venue presents pop, rock, jazz, country and classical concerts as well as ballet and dance performances. Among the famous names who appeared on its stage are the Allman Brothers Band, Joni Mitchell, Crosby, Stills and Nash, Joe Cocker, Lionel Richie and Santana. Neil Diamond recorded his album *Hot August Night* (1972) here.

Bronson Caves ㊼

Brush Canyon (at the north end of Bronson Ave). ⚐

When Union Rock Company opened a quarry in what is now Griffith Park in 1903, it created caves that were later used countless times as a site for location filming. The foothill area doubled for an extraterrestrial landscape or passed for the Wild West in such movies as *Superman* (1949), *Invasion of the Body Snatchers* (1956), *The Legend of the Lone Ranger* (1981) and *Star Trek VI: The Undiscovered Country* (1991). The television shows that have been shot here include *Star Trek Voyager, Bonanza, Fantasy Island, Gunsmoke, The Virginian, Rawhide, Wild Wild West* and many others. But its most famous appearance was as the Batcave in both the television and movie versions of *Batman*.

Los Angeles Zoo ㊽

333 Zoo Dr.
☎(323) 667-4650. ⏱daily 10am-5pm. Closed: Christmas. Ⓢ

One of the ten largest zoos in the United States, this 80-acre (32-ha) compound houses approximately 1,600 mammals, birds, amphibians and

The 4,600-seat Greek Theatre presents a wide variety of concerts

reptiles. Of more than 400 different species represented, almost 70 are rare and threatened. Arranged according to the animals' native habitats, the zoo collection is divided into five geographical areas: Australia, Africa, Eurasia and South and North America.

Autry National Center, Museum of the American West ㊾

Windom, Wein and Cohen, architects (1988).
4700 Western Heritage Way.
☎(323) 667-2000. ⏱Tue-Sun 10am-5p; Thu 10am-8pm. Closed: Thanksgiving, Christmas. Ⓢ

Founded by the famous singing cowboy Gene Autry in 1987, this $54-million museum celebrates the people, cultures and events that have shaped the rich history of the American West from prehistoric times to the pres-

ent. The museum's permanent collection, which includes artifacts, artworks, posters, photographs and memorabilia, is displayed in seven thematic galleries.

Travel Town Transportation Museum ㊿

5200 Zoo Dr.
☎(323) 662-5874. ⏱Mon-Fri 10am-1pm; Sat-Sun 10am-5pm. Closed: Christmas. Ⓢfree.

This open-air museum exhibits railroad equipment from California and the Southwest, representing both short-line and main-line railroading with an emphasis on the steam era. Travel Town shows the impact of railroads on the development of the area. The collection is comprised of locomotives, freight and passenger cars and memorabilia.

The "Spirit of Cowboy" exhibit at the Autry National Center

F M Ashley and John C Austin,
architects (1931).
2800 E Observatory Rd.
☎(323) 664-1191 (recorded
information); (323) 663-8171 (sky
news, updated weekly).
🕐call for information. 🏃
www.griffithobservatory.com

Foucault pendulum

**Observatory archways form a
part of a backdrop for the
switchblade fight between
James Dean and Corey Allen in
Rebel Without a Cause (1955)**

Navigation (1934) by Hugo
Ballin, one of eight murals
depicting different scientific
and engineering disciplines. On
the left is a symbolic figure of
the Wind holding a sundial and
compass. To the right is Calm,
shown with a modern sextant.
The moon orbits around the
two figures, while an astrolabe,
an early astronomical instrument, sits at the top.

Griffith Observatory ⑤1

Griffith Observatory is one of LA's major attractions,
with nearly two million visitors each year. The Art Deco
building, with its three large copper domes, was completed in 1935. The observatory's main rotunda contains a
Foucault pendulum, its 240-lb (108 kg) brass ball suspended by a 50-foot-long (15-m) wire that swings in a
constant direction, demonstrating the earth's rotation. The
east rotunda features a 12-inch (31-cm) Zeiss refracting
telescope and the west rotunda houses a triple-beam
solar telescope. A major attraction is a Tesla coil, a step-
up transformer that increases voltage from 110 V to
500,000 V, with sparks that leap more than four feet (1,2 m).

The planetarium is a large theater that features live multimedia sky shows projected onto a 75-foot-diameter
dome with the aid of a one-ton Zeiss projector and more
than 100 special-effects projectors.

From the observatory terraces visitors can enjoy a spectacular panoramic view of the sprawling city, from the
mountains to the ocean and, on a clear day, all the way
to Catalina Island. Especially impressive is a night view,
with countless city lights sparkling in the distance.

The Observatory appeared in numerous films, including
take-off scenes in *The Rocketeer* (1991), as well as the
opening scenes in *The Terminator* (1984). But it was its
ample use as backdrop in Nicholas Ray's classic *Rebel
Without a Cause* (1955) that made this landmark world
famous. Among many remarkable scenes filmed here
were the sky show in the planetarium and Sal Mineo's
memorable death at the end of the film.

HOLLYWOOD Sign ⑤

One of the best-known landmarks in the world, the HOLLYWOOD sign was born as an advertising gimmick for real estate development. To attract attention to their 640-acre (260-ha) subdivision at the end of Beachwood Canyon, called "Hollywoodland," *Los Angeles Times* publisher Harry Chandler and other promoters erected the giant 13-letter billboard. At night, the sign illuminated with 4,000 bulbs was visible from many parts of the city, even from the harbor, 25 miles (40 km) away. It has stood on top of Mount Lee since 1923, although developers expected it would be there for only a year and a half—that's how long they hoped it would take to sell all the lots.

The sign, which became a world-famous symbol for the Hollywood film industry, was declared a Cultural-Historical Monument in 1973. It is 50 feet (15 m) tall and stretches 450 feet (137 m) along the mountainside. There is no access to the sign since all nearby trails have been fenced and the city is working to prevent vandalism and accidents.

Over the years the sign has gone through periods of neglect and has suffered damage by vandals, wind and rainstorms. In 1949 the first nine letters were repaired and the last four were removed. The restored sign has read HOLLYWOOD ever since, with a few exceptions. On several occasions it has been altered, as in 1987 during the Iran-Contra hearings, when it read OLLYWOOD; in 1976 it was modified to HOLLYWEED in connection to new state marijuana law, and in 1992 to PEROTWOOD during the presidential campaign.

Street signs

In 1978, celebrities joined the effort to restore the sign, donating $27,700 each to replace one of the letters. Rock singer Alice Cooper led the campaign, choosing the second "O" in honor of his friend Groucho Marx. *Playboy* magazine publisher Hugh Hefner hosted a fundraising party at his mansion and dedicated the "Y."

The sign became a part of Hollywood folklore after a tragic event. An aspiring movie actress Lillian Millicent "Peg" Entwistle came to Los Angeles after a successful stage career in New York, but her film career did not develop to her expectations. In desperation, she jumped off the letter "H" to her death on September 12, 1932.

Mount Lee, above Hollywood. Not on map. No direct access. ⚑ ⓦ

Hollywood welcomes the new millennium with a laser show on New Year's Eve 1999

The HOLLYWOODLAND sign was a scene of a tragic event in 1932, when aspiring actress Lillian Millicent "Peg" Entwistle committed suicide by jumping from the letter "H"

In *The Day of the Locust* (1975) Karen Black and William Atherton approach the HOLLYWOOD sign from an unusual direction

Forest Lawn Hollywood Hills ⑤

6300 Forest Lawn Dr.
☎(323) 254-7251; (800) 204-3131. ⏰daily 8am-5pm (6pm in summer).

After buying a 400-acre parcel adjacent to Griffith Park in 1944, Forest Lawn's owner Hubert Eaton asked the city for permission to open a cemetery. After being twice rejected by the LA City Planning Commission, Forest Lawn submitted a successful request to the Los Angeles City Council in 1948, which allowed the cemetery to open. Seizing the opportunity, Forest Lawn immediately buried six bodies on the site and pronounced the property legally a cemetery, based on the state's law that asserted that any site on which six bodies were lawfully buried would instantly and in perpetuity become a cemetery.

The grounds are filled with replicas of historic buildings, including a full-sized reproduction of Boston's Old North Church, immortalized in Longfellow's poem *Paul Revere's Ride*.

Billed as the largest historical mosaic in the world, *The Birth of Liberty* is composed of 25 famous scenes that depict the most important events in American history from 1619 to 1787. It is 162 feet long and 28 feet high (49,4 x 8,53 m) and contains more than 10 million pieces of Venetian glass.

D W Griffith filmed his Civil War epic *The Birth of a Nation* (1915) on a slope now occupied by Forest Lawn Hollywood Hills. Here he directs real Civil War veterans in one of the film's battle scenes.

Grounds

Buster Keaton (1895-1966)

One of the greatest comedians in the history of cinema, the "Great Stone-face" was famous for his trademark expressionless appearance in the portrayal of a restrained little man. Keaton started performing at age four in his parents' vaudeville act. His break into the movies began when Roscoe "Fatty" Arbuckle gave him roles in a series of short films in the late 1910s. Keaton's reputation quickly grew with movies such as *The Boat* (1921), *The Navigator* (1924), *Sherlock, Jr* (1924), *The General* (1927) and *The Cameraman* (1928), now considered classics. Keaton received a special Academy Award in 1959 "for his unique talents which brought immortal comedies to the screen." He died of lung cancer.

Stan Laurel (1890-1965)

The stone plaque on the wall marks the gravesite of the thin half of the famous Laurel and Hardy comedy team. Although he played the brainless one who always helplessly scratched his head and sobbed in their movies, Laurel is generally considered to be the creative force who conceived all the gags and wrote the stories. He received a special Oscar in 1960 for "his creative pioneering in the field of cinema comedy." Speaking of Hardy, Laurel said: "Babe and I had different hobbies. His was playing the horses. You know mine—I married them all." Laurel was married five times to four different women. He married one of them twice.

Marty Feldman (1934-1982)

A comedian with an unforgettable appearance emphasized by a prominent nose and bulging eyes is best remembered for such comedies as *Young Frankenstein* (1973) and *The Adventures of Sherlock Holmes' Smarter Brother* (1975). He died unexpectedly of a heart attack caused by food poisoning from eating tainted shellfish, reportedly while filming a death scene.

Gene Autry (1907-1998)

A popular singing cowboy, songwriter and producer, Autry made dozens of westerns with his comic sidekick Smiley Burnette and his horse Champion. He was also an extraordinary businessman, real-estate investor and owner of radio and television stations, as well as the California Angels baseball team. Autry is the only celebrity to have five stars on the Hollywood Walk of Fame, each for one of the five categories of recognition—film, radio, television, recording and live theater. He founded the Autry Museum of Western Heritage in 1988.

Telly Savalas (1922-1994)

The internationally popular actor is best known as the shaven-headed, lollipop-addicted star of the television detective series *Kojak*, which ran from 1973 to 1978. He played tough characters in war and action movies, including *The Dirty Dozen* (1967) and *Kelly's Heroes* (1970).

Fritz Lang (1890-1976)

A simple plaque marks the remains of one of the giants of world cinema. To escape the post of head of the German film industry offered to him by the Nazi minister of propaganda Goebbels, the Viennese-born director fled to Paris in 1932 and arrived in Hollywood two years later. Noted for his obsession with the psychology of violence, Lang's best-known films include *Metropolis* (1927), *M* (1931), *The Woman in the Window* (1944) and *The Ministry of Fear* (1944).

Dorothy Lamour (1914-1996)

One of Hollywood's most popular stars of the late 1930s and 1940s, she was typically cast as a seductive South Sea island heroine dressed only in a trademark sarong. Lamour is best remembered for her roles in the highly successful *Road* series, where she co-starred with Bob Hope and Bing Crosby.

Esther Phillips (1935-1984)

The great rhythm and blues singer had her biggest success and an international hit with the single *Release Me* (1962), which made it to the Top Ten on both the pop and country charts. Her other major hit was the single *What a Diff'rence a Day Makes* (1975), followed by the best-selling album of the same name. After years of drug and alcohol abuse, Phillips died of liver and kidney failure.

Ozzie (1906-1975) and Harriet (1909-1994) Nelson

This husband and wife team created one of the longest-running television series in history. *The Adventures of Ozzie and Harriet* premiered in 1944 and ran for eight years on radio and 14 more on television, from 1952 to 1966.

Ricky Nelson (1940-1985)

Two rows up from Ozzie and Harriet is the grave of their son, Eric Nelson, a popular actor and rock singer who died in a plane crash.

Courts of Remembrance

Bette Davis (1908-1989)

The white sarcophagus to the left of the entrance to the Courts of Remembrance is the final resting place of one of the most honored Hollywood actresses. Davis received 10 Academy Award nominations, winning twice, for her performances in *Dangerous* (1935) and *Jezebel* (1938). When she was not satisfied with the material she was offered, the strong-willed star sued Warner Bros studio for better roles and directors. Davis was the first woman to receive The American Film Institute's Lifetime Achievement Award. She died of cancer.

Liberace (1919-1987)

This large family sarcophagus contains the remains of one of the greatest concert performers of the 20th century. Liberace became the highest-paid pianist of all time when he received $138,000 for his single performance at Madison Square Garden in 1954. Famous for his flamboyant style and extravagant stage costumes, he has also been seen in hundreds of TV shows. He appeared in several films, including *The Loved One* (1965), a satirical view of the death culture inspired by Forest Lawn. Liberace died of AIDS, but the cause of death was kept secret; only an autopsy requested by a suspicious coroner revealed the truth.

Lucille Ball (1911-1989)

This small crypt inside the Columbarium of Radiant Dawn contained the cremated remains of a brilliant comedienne and studio executive (the first woman to run a Hollywood studio), before they were moved in 2002 to a family plot in New York. Lucille Ball gained enormous popularity as the redheaded star of the smash hit TV show *I Love Lucy*, which she created in 1951 with her husband, Desi Arnaz. It became one of the most successful comedy series in history.

Andy Gibb (1957-1988)

A pop singer who followed in the footsteps of his older brothers, the Bee Gees, Andy Gibb had two No. 1 singles, *I Just Want to be Your Everything* (1977) and *Shadow Dancing* (1978). After years of cocaine and alcohol abuse, he died of heart failure.

George Raft (1895-1980)

Tough guy of the gangster films, Raft counted such mobsters as "Bugsy" Siegel as his close friends. He is best-known for his role as the coin-tossing thug in *Scarface* (1932). Raft is also famous for the roles he turned down, including Sam Spade in *The Maltese Falcon*, which made Humphrey Bogart a major star.

Charles Laughton (1899-1962)

The large, thick-lipped actor with a plump face, Laughton played a wide range of roles. He is best remembered for the villains he played, such as Captain Bligh in *Mutiny on the Bounty* (1935). Laughton won an Oscar as best actor for *The Private Life of Henry VIII* (1933).

Forest Lawn Hollywood Hills

Gardens of Heritage, lot 1281 ①

Court of Valor, lot 5420 ②

Court of Valor, lot 5512 ③

Court of Liberty, lot 912 ④

Courts of Remembrance (Bette Davis) ⑤

Courts of Remembrance (Liberace) ⑥

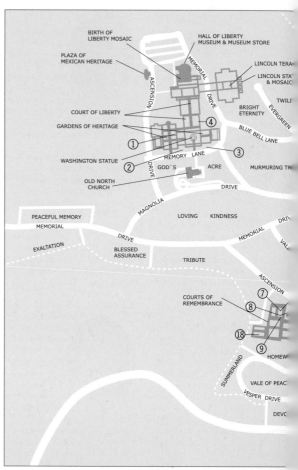

Courts of Remembrance, Sanctuary of Light, crypt 2355 ⑦

Courts of Remembrance, Sanctuary of Light, crypt 2356 ⑧

Courts of Remembrance, crypt 2534 ⑨

Revelation, lot 3538 ⑩

Revelation, lot 3540 ⑪

Revelation, lot 3540 ⑫

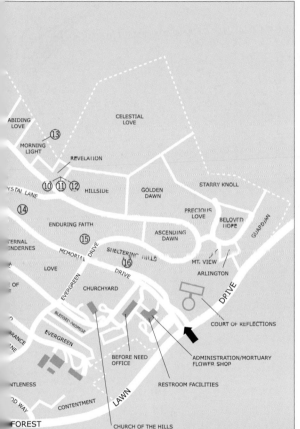

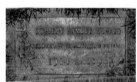

Morning Light, lot 2591 ⑬

Enduring Faith, lot 387 ⑭

Enduring Faith, lot 3818 ⑮

Courts of Remembrance, Columbarium of Radiant Dawn ⑱

Courts of Remembrance, crypt 310 ⑰

Sheltering Hills, lot 1048 ⑯

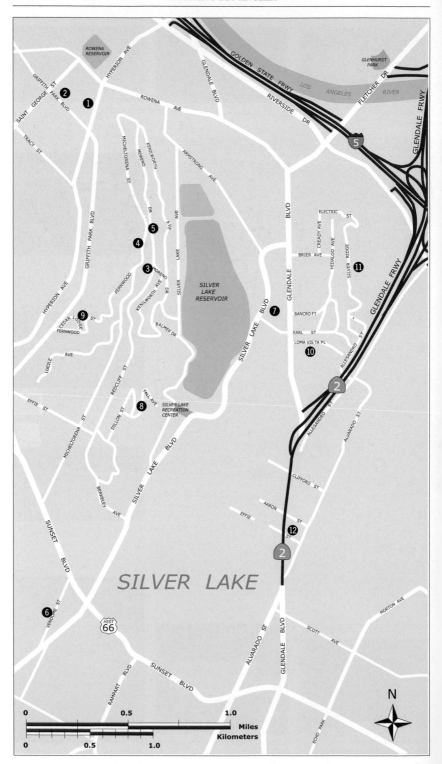

Walt Disney Studios (site) ❶

2719 Hyperion Ave.

This is the birthplace of an animation empire. On this site brothers Walt and Roy erected the buildings that housed the original Walt Disney Studios from 1926 to 1940. Here were created both the Mickey Mouse character (1928) and the first feature-length animated film, *Snow White and the Seven Dwarfs* (1937). The company eventually outgrew the facility and relocated to its current studios in Burbank (➔ p326). The old buildings were razed and on their place today stands a supermarket.

Walt Disney Studios on Hyperion Avenue (1930s)

This bungalow court was the inspiration for the Dwarfs' cottages in *Snow White and the Seven Dwarfs* (1937)

Norman Bungalow Court ❷

2906-2912 Griffith Park Blvd.
Private residences.

These eight miniature Norman cottages with a complementing little tower in the rear represent a popular housing concept in LA during the 1920s. Legend has it that this enchanted medieval forest fancy inspired Walt Disney for the Dwarfs' cottages in his animated film *Snow White and the Seven Dwarfs* (1937). Located just behind Disney's original studio on Hyperion Ave, it was said that the animators lived here while working on the film.

Daniel House ❸

Gregory Ain, architect (1939).
1856 Micheltorena St.
Private residence.

One of Ain's masterpieces, this yellow stucco box features such distinctive details as a narrow band of windows along the top. Above the entry, which is hidden behind a wall, the glass-filled hole forms a cover that shields the visitor.

Lautner House ❹

John Lautner, architect (1940).
2007 Micheltorena St.
Private residence.

Only the carport and a fenced terrace are visible of this low, concrete and redwood house Lautner designed for his family. This was the first structure built by the architect after he left training with Frank Lloyd Wright and moved to Los Angeles. A contemporary architectural critic called it the "best house by an architect under 30 in the US."

Silvertop ❺

John Lautner, architect (1957).
2138 Micheltorena St.
Private residence. ⚑

Sitting on a hilltop with unobstructed panoramic vistas and distinguished by its low-arched, sweeping concrete roof, this legendary house is not visible from the street and the best view is from across the reservoir.

Designed and constructed over a 10-year period with an unlimited budget, this was at the time one of the most expensive houses ever built. It included such details as a curved glass wall that moves at the push of the button and the first use in Los Angeles of thin glass panels suspended from above. Its most impressive feature is pool with water spilling over the edge, visually forming a continuous water surface with Silver Lake Reservoir below.

Now owned by director Kelly Lynch, the house had a cameo role in the movie *Less Than Zero* (1987).

View of Silvertop from acros Silver Lake Reservoir

The Music Box Stairs ❻

900 block of Vendome St.

Featured for the first time in *Hats Off* (1927), a comedy with Laurel and Hardy playing kitchen appliances deliverymen, these stairs became famous four years later when they appear in another film by the famed comedy team. In *The Music Box* (1932), the duo tries to move a piano up this long stairway to a house at the top. The film won producer/director Hal Roach an Oscar for best comedy short. It was a new category, inaugurated with the 1931-32 Awards. A memorial plaque marks the site.

Laurel and Hardy haul a piano in *The Music Box* (1932)

Neutra VDL Research House ❼

Richard and Dion Neutra, architects (1932, 1965-66).
2300 E Silver Lake Blvd.
🕐 by appointment only; call (909) 869-2667 to arrange a visit. ⑤

This experimental house was financed by a Dutch industrialist and patron of modern architecture C H Van der Leeuw, who met Neutra during his trip in Europe. Impressed by the architect's work, he visited Los Angeles in 1930 and offered to pay for the construction of Neutra's own home.

Neutra built this compact house/studio for his family as an experiment in space efficiency, demonstrating that high-density living does not necessarily sacrifice comfort. The house, which was named for its patron, was also tech-

View of the seminar room and the staircase from the interior courtyard of the Neutra VDL Research House

nologically advanced, as Neutra solicited the latest building materials from manufacturers and incorporated many custom details and new technical solutions.

The house was destroyed in a fire in 1963 and, after a decision had been made to rebuild on the footprint of the original, the architect's son, Dion, designed the new building. Although the first house was built as the characteristic International Style Modern silver box, the rebuilt was, essentially, California Modern, further developing the idea of interior/exterior living.

To shield the house from the strong western sun, two-story, electronically controlled vertical louvers were installed. Dion also introduced pools into each story. Especially effective is a two-

Front entrance of the Neutra VDL Research House

inch-deep rooftop infinity pool, designed to form a continuous line with Silver Lake when observed from the low seating in the glass penthouse.

The interior courtyard contains Neutra's ashes buried under the plaque by the small pool. The house is now owned and maintained by the School of Environmental Design at California Polytechnic University, Pomona.

The enchanting Mosque House

Mosque House ❽

1824 San Jacinto St.
Private residence.

Climbing four stories down the hill, this quintessential LA oddity features a brightly tiled dome and minaret, graceful arches and buttresses reminiscent of a miniature mosque. Enchanting details include wrought-iron grates, Moorish-style stained-glass windows and whimsical Islamic motifs.

CDLT 1, 2 House ❾

Michael Rotondi, architect (1987).
1955 Cedar Lodge Terrace.
Private residence.

Rotondi points out that he did not make any working drawings for his own house. He only made sketches for the contractor to work from each morning. As a result, the house emerged one piece at the time, each component added being influenced only by the previous decision. Nothing was ever subtracted as the architect decided not to question himself on this project.

Gaudiesque House ❿

2384 Loma Vista Pl.
Private residence.

Inspired by the work of the famous Barcelona architect, Antoni Gaudí, this Catalan fantasy is a remodeled version of a structure moved from another location. During the 1960s the owner applied concrete and tile fragments and added louvered windows to achieve a striking effect.

How House ⓫

Rudolf Schindler, architect (1925).
2422 Silver Ridge Ave.
Private residence.

Set on a steep slope over-looking the valley, this family home built for an eccentric owner is probably Schindler's

Mack Sennett's Keystone Studios (1910s)

most remarkable work. Here he used the "Schindler Frame," his signature design feature. The lower portion of the house, which is secluded from the street, is of solid concrete, while the upper portion is a transparent wooden box, as visible in this corner detail.

Keystone Studios
(site) ⓬

1712 Glendale Blvd. ☛

The area bordering Silver Lake from the east, formerly known as Edendale, was a thriving center of film production in the early twentieth century. Many pioneer motion picture companies opened their studios along Allesandro Ave (today Glendale Blvd), including the Selig Company, the Pathé

West Coast Studio and the Bison Company. All these early studios are long gone, and the only remaining one belonged to the New York Motion Picture Co, which turned it over to the Keystone Comedy Company, established here in 1913 with Mack Sennett as director.

The Keystone Studios was home to the hysterically incompetent Keystone Kops

Sennett produced the famous Keystone Kops and hundreds of silent comedies here, featuring such stars as Charlie Chaplin, Roscoe "Fatty" Arbuckle and Mabel Normand. Gloria Swanson started her Hollywood career here in a series of romantic comedies. Reportedly the first custard pie ever thrown in a movie was tossed here. The studio was a major production center until 1927, when Sennett moved to Studio City.

Much of the original complex has been torn down, except the enclosed stage that today serves as a public storage facility.

Gaudiesque House

How House

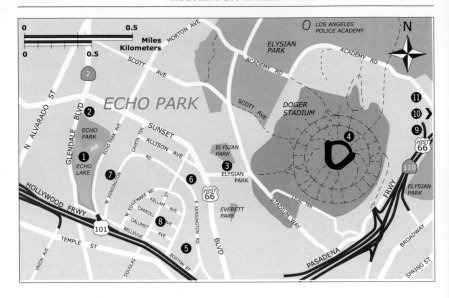

Echo Park ❶

Founded in 1891, this is one of the oldest public parks in Los Angeles. Its main attraction is a 15-acre (6-ha) lake edged by tall, century-old willow, eucalyptus and palm trees. It features a little island linked with a red arching footbridge and the largest lotus bed outside China, an impressive sight in early summer when in full bloom. The park is the setting of the Lotus Festival every July (➜ p66). A perfect way to explore this urban oasis is to take a ride in a rented paddleboat.

Many of the early Mack Sennett's Keystone Kops comedies were filmed in Echo Park. This is also where we see Jack Nicholson in a rowboat in the beginning of Roman Polanski's *Chinatown* (1974). It was used in director Allison Ander's film *Mi Vida Loca* (1994), a story about teenage gang girls set in Echo Park's Latino neighborhood.

Angelus Temple ❷

A F Leicht, architect (1923). 1100 Glendale Blvd. ☎(213) 484-1100. ⏱services Thu 7pm, Sun 10am. **NRHP**

This impressive circular domed structure with tall stained-glass windows was built and dedicated in 1923 by evangelist Aimee Semple McPherson. It can seat 5,500 people and was used as headquarters of the Foursquare Gospel Church, which she founded.

Charismatic and flamboyant, Sister Aimee became the most famous religionist of her time. She adopted a show-biz preaching style from a theater-like stage, and her words were broadcast nationwide from a church radio station.

As a pioneer media evangelist, McPherson acquired a massive following in the 1920s. Her fame, however, was tarnished in 1926 after a well publicized sexual scandal. She staged her disappearance, and then turned up a month later, claiming that she was kidnapped. Actually she was hiding with her lover in the Hollywood Hills. Mentally unstable, she suffered a nervous breakdown and died of a drug overdose in 1944.

Echo Park's lotus bed in bloom

Angelus Temple of the Foursquare Gospel Church

Elysian Park ❸

With more than 600 acres, this is the second largest park in the city. It occupies land set aside for the original Pueblo in 1781, but lost much of its initial acreage to the Los Angeles Police Academy, the Pasadena Fwy and Dodger Stadium. Elysian was laid out in 1886 as the first botanical garden in Southern California. It was planted over the next thirty years with hundreds of exotic trees and shrubs from all over the world. The Chavez Ravine Arboretum displays on its 10 acres (4 ha) the many remaining mature plantings. Angels Point, on the upper western edge of the park, offers great city views.

Dodger Stadium ❹

Emil Prager, architect (1959-62)
1000 Elysian Park Ave.
Tickets: ☎(323) 224-1400. Ⓢ

Dodger Stadium, one of the most beautiful ballparks in the US

When Brooklyn Dodgers owner Walter O'Malley was rebuffed by the city officials who refused to spend money for the new and improved field he requested, he made a surpassing and unprecedented move and brought his team to Los Angeles in 1958. The Dodgers played their first four seasons at the LA Coliseum, before the brand new, state of the art Dodger Stadium was completed in 1962. Designed by Emil Prager, the 56,000-seat arena features a unique cantilevered construction that eliminates columns and offers an unobstructed view of the game. Considered one of the most beautiful ballparks in the country, the stadium is nestled in Elysian Park within 300 acres of well-maintained landscaping and surrounded with one of the largest parking lots anywhere, with room for 16,000 cars.

Since their move to Los Angeles, the Dodgers repeatedly set attendance records, including 3.6 million in 1982, an all-time major league record.

The stadium's construction did not go without controversy. It was built in the heart of Chavez Ravine, the site of a once flourishing Latino community, whose residents were forced to leave after the city handed over the area to the Dodgers.

Angelino Heights ❺

On the hilltop site just east of Echo Lake, the area of Angelino Heights was developed by William W Stilson and Everett E Hall during the real estate boom of the 1880s as an upscale neighborhood of Victorian houses. The area's first residents were upper middle-class owners who wanted to live close to the city center but avoid its hustle. It was LA's first suburb, connected to downtown by a mile and a half-long streetcar line. In 1983, Angelino Heights was declared the city's first historic preservation overlay zone.

Gloria Swanson Home

Weller House ❻

824 E Kensington Rd.
Private residence.

Built by contractor Z H Weller in 1894, this residence was relocated from Bunker Hill in the early 1900s, when oil derricks began to dot the affluent neighborhood. The well-preserved structure is an excellent example of Queen Anne architecture with Eastlake ornaments and Moorish touches.

Weller House

Gloria Swanson Home ❼

1048 W Kensington Rd.
Private residence.

The most glamorous and highly paid actress of the silent screen, and later the memorable star of *Sunset Boulevard* (1950), Swanson reportedly lived here while making short comedies for Mack Sennett.

Carroll Avenue ⑧

☛for neighborhood tours, call LA Conservancy ☎(213) 623-2489. Private residences. NRHP 🎥

This was the main street of Angelino Heights, lined with houses representing many different styles, predominantly Queen Anne and Eastlake. When the real estate boom went bust in 1888 after only three years, the area gradually declined and its wooden Victorians began to deteriorate. During the 1960s, individual owners started refurbishing their homes, and now most of the houses are beautifully restored and well maintained. Today, the 1300 block of Carroll Ave contains the highest concentration of Victorian houses anywhere in Los Angeles, some of them moved from other parts of the city. The entire block has been placed on the NRHP. The street is the location of choice for film and television crews looking for Victorian settings.

Authentic, century-old streetlights

Innes House

1329 Carroll Ave. (ca. 1887)

Built for the councilman and shoe store magnate Daniel Innes of downtown's prosperous Innes Shoe Store, this house is typical Eastlake with its rectangular look and emphasized vertical lines. The two-story structure still has its original hardware, woodwork, fireplaces and stained-glass windows.

Sanders House

Sanders House

1345 Carroll Ave. (1887)

This sadly deteriorated building, with its red-brick foundation characteristic of the Queen Anne style, was featured in the establishing shots of Alfred Hitchcock's masterpiece of suspense, *Psycho* (1960). The building was also used in the 1982 music video *Thriller*, where Michael Jackson runs away from demons who chase him through a Victorian neighborhood.

Sessions House

Joseph Cather Newsom (1888). 1330 Carroll Ave.

Built for dairyman Charles Sessions by the prominent San Francisco architect, this Queen Anne house shows an Oriental influence in such details as the Chinese lion dogs guarding a large latticework arch. The second-floor porch contains moongate openings framed by unusual abacus spool screens.

Phillips House

Phillips House

1300 Carroll Ave. (1887)

This ornate, well-maintained house with stained-glass windows is a typical example of Queen Anne style, with touches of Eastlake decoration such as ornamental millwork, sunburst motifs and linear patterns that surround the windows.

Haskins House

1344 Carroll Ave. (ca. 1888)

Commissioned by developer Charles C Haskins, this pure Queen Anne style architecture was the last Victorian on Carroll Ave. The extraordinarily well-preserved and maintained house, with ornate spindlework and stained glass, has been featured in scores of movies.

Russell House

1316 Carroll Ave. (1887-88)

Note the brackets-and-shell-motif below the windows and over the porch steps in this Eastlake gem. The carriage house is in the back.

Innes House

Sessions House

Russell House

El Alisal ⑨

200 E Ave 43. Not on map.
☎(213) 222-0546. ⏰Fri-Sun 12
noon-4pm. ⑤free. NRHP

Charles Fletcher Lummis was a noted author, editor, photographer, historian and archaeologist. A city librarian and a champion of civil rights for Indians, he helped preserve four early Franciscan missions and founded the Southwest Museum. In 1898 Lummis began construction of his house on the east bank of the Arroyo Seco, a usually dry riverbed. He did most of the work himself and called the house El Alisal (Place of the Sycamore in Spanish). Today it is the headquarters of the Historical Society of Southern California and displays photographs, memorabilia, Indian baskets and other artifacts. A two-acre water-conserving garden features California native and other dry-climate plants.

Dining room of the Charles Lummis home (El Alisal)

Ford Residence (ca. 1887) at
Heritage Square Museum

Heritage Square Museum ⑩

3800 Homer St. Not on map.
☎(818) 796-2898.
⏰Sat-Sun noon-4pm.
☛ at 15 past the hour. ⑤

This open-air museum is actually a recreated Victorian village consisting of eight structures built in the late 19th century. They were saved from destruction and relocated here from various parts of Pasadena and Los Angeles. The museum aims to give a picture of everyday life in Los Angeles between the Civil War and World War I through its collections, programs and exhibits.

The most remarkable of the buildings is the fully restored Hale House (NRHP), a superb example of the Queen Anne-Eastlake style from 1887 (➔ p92).

The Valley Knudsen House, built in 1883, is one of only a few existing examples of 19th-century Mansard-style "Petite Château" architecture (➔ p92).

Southwest Museum ⑪

Sumner Hunt and Silas Burns,
architects (1914).
234 Museum Dr. Not on map.
☎(213) 221-2164.
⏰Tue-Sun 11am-5pm. ⑤

The Southwest Museum is the oldest museum in Los Angeles, founded in 1907 by Charles F Lummis and members of the Southwest Society. Designed in the Mission Revival style, the building was completed in 1914.

The museum houses one of the most important collections of Native American art works and artifacts in the United States. Although it documents various cultures from Alaska to Meso and South America, the collection is particularly rich in holdings from western North America, especially the Southwest and California.

Four permanent main exhibit halls concentrate on the native cultures of four main geographic areas: California, the Southwest, the Northwest Coast and the Great Plains. Each hall depicts cultural mores of Indian tribes, exploring daily life, social organization, art and religion.

Navajo blankets on display at the Southwest Museum

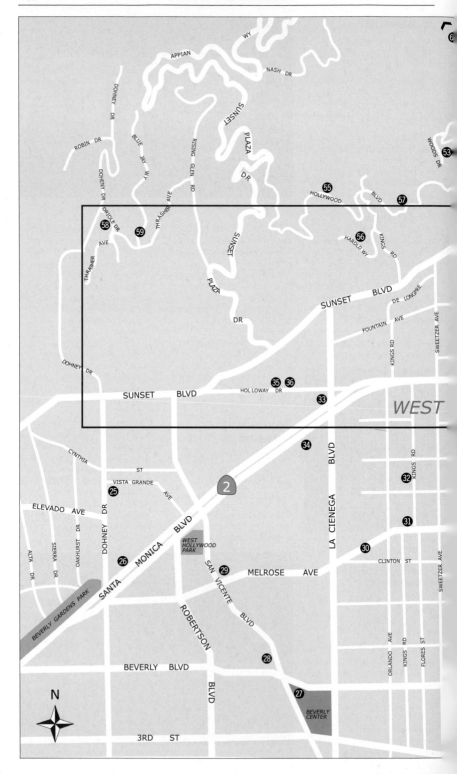

WEST

WATTLES
GARDEN
PARK

RUNYON
CANYON
PARK

WATTLES DR

NICHOLS CANYON RD

CURSON AVE

VISTA ST

CAMINO

PALMERO

45

43

44

FRANKLIN AVE

SYCAMORE AVE

LAUREL CANYON BLVD

54

CRESCENT HTS BLVD

HOLLYWOOD BLVD

SELMA AVE

OGDEN DR

COURTNEY AVE

STANLEY AVE

HAWTHORN AVE

HAWTHORN AVE

FORMOSA AVE

47

42

SUNSET BLVD

41

SUNSET STRIP, see pp 180-1

49 **50**

48

51

DE LONGPRE AVE

46

SIERRA BONITA AVE

MARTEL AVE

FULLER AVE

POINSETTIA PL

ALTA VISTA BLVD

DETROIT ST

FOUNTAIN AVE

GROVE AVE

FAIRFAX AVE

ORANGE

LAUREL AVE

HAYWORTH AVE

OGDEN DR

GENESEE AVE

SPAULDING AVE

CURSON AVE

GARDNER ST

VISTA ST

PLUMMER
PARK

POINSETTIA DR

POINSETTIA PL

FORMOSA AVE

LA BREA AVE

SYCAMORE AVE

NORTON AVE

NORTON AVE

HIST 66

SANTA MONICA BLVD

38

2

40

THE LOT

39

ROMAINE ST

HOLLYWOOD

ROMAINE ST

WILLOUGHBY AVE

GARDNER ST

POINSETTIA
REC CTR

WARING AVE

HAVENHURST DR

LAUREL AVE

CRESCENT HEIGHTS BLVD

MELROSE AVE

LA BREA AVE

CLINTON ST

FAIRFAX
HIGH
SCHOOL

CLINTON ST

ROSEWOOD AVE

SEWOOD AVE

KILKEA DR

OAKWOOD AVE

LAUREL AVE

EDINBURGH AVE

HAYWORTH AVE

FAIRFAX AVE

OGDEN DR

GENESEE AVE

SPAULDING AVE

STANLEY AVE

CURSON AVE

SIERRA BONITA AVE

VISTA ST

MARTEL AVE

FULLER AVE

POINSETTIA PL

ALTA VISTA BLVD

FORMOSA AVE

DETROIT ST

SYCAMORE AVE

LA BREA AVE

BEVERLY BLVD

PAN
PACIFIC
PARK

0   0.5

0   0.5

Miles
Kilometers

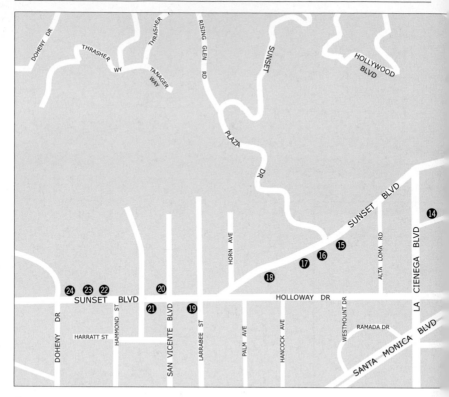

Sunset Strip

The 1.7-mile-long (2,7-km) stretch of Sunset Blvd between Crescent Heights and Doheny Dr became synonymous with glittering nightlife, packed with glamorous nightclubs, hotels and restaurants.

This is the most important showplace of the entertainment business, where new ideas are tested before being launched across the world. With its boundless energy and ever-changing social scene, the Sunset Strip sets the new trends—what is fashionable, what is chic— telling the young and hip how they should live and spend their free time (together with their dollars).

"The Strip," as it is always called, was once the playground of Hollywood. During the 1930s and 1940s, it was the glamorous hub of the city's nightlife, with illicit casinos, gorgeous call girls and posh night clubs such as Trocadero, Macombo and Ciro's. The reason for such concentration of nocturnal excitement was that this particular pocket was administered by the County of Los Angeles and not the city. The unincorporated area had tax advantages and was free of strict laws regulating alcohol, gambling and prostitution.

When during the 1950s all top entertainers flocked to Las Vegas, lured by astronomical salaries, the Sunset Strip clubs were unable to compete and closed their doors by 1960. In the following decade the alluring clientele were replaced with flower children.

The Strip became part of the city of West Hollywood in 1984 and today, with its flashy club scene, is the rock and popular music capital of the world.

Sunset Strip at night

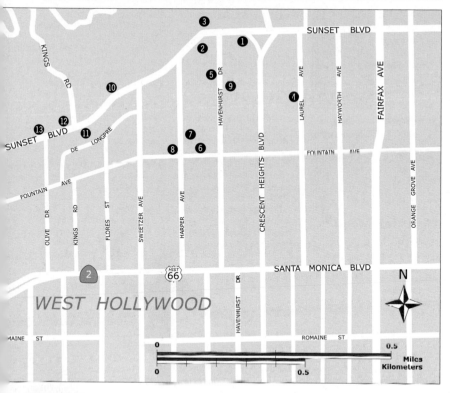

Billboards

The Sunset Strip Billboard Award gold statuette

Billboards on the Strip are generally oversized and custom made, featuring unique work by skilled artists and designers. Used to promote the entertainment industry's newest products, these giant signs are often technology marvels, executed in a variety of media, including glistening neon and video.

As one of the world's top locations for billboard advertising, the Sunset Strip rates range from $50,000 to $100,000 a month. More than 100 cutting-edge billboards,

murals, videotrons and "tall walls" dot the twists and turns of Sunset Blvd.

The first billboard on the Sunset Strip for a rock act was the advertising for the first Doors album in 1967. Once a status symbol and a common sight here, the rock billboards all but disappeared after the sharp decline of record sales in the 1970s.

To recognize the medium's iconic status and honor their creators, the City of West Hollywood created the Sunset Strip Billboard Awards in 2000. The winner in each of eight categories—automotive, beverage, consumer goods, fashion, movie, television, travel, celebrity tall wall—is presented with a curvaceous gold statuette.

Each of the state-of-the-art billboards is often one of its kind

West Hollywood street signs

West Hollywood

Motorists, beware! Notorious for its greed, this little city invented an infallible way to fill its public coffers by ripping off unsuspecting motorists with ludicrous traffic and parking violations. Among their moneymaking ploys are tickets for failure to turn the car's front wheels toward the curb on a street with no perceivable incline; citations for an expired parking meter even when the meter is broken and shows no time whatsoever; enforcement of the anti-cruising ordinance that bans passing through the same checkpoint more than twice within four hours.

Among the city's more serious (and unsolved) problems are illegal tree trimmers, who strip the trees in front of billboards of all the branches that block the view.

Garden of Allah

(site) **❶**

8152 Sunset Blvd.

The legendary Hollywood playground was once the home of the Russian-born silent film actress Alla Nazimova, former lover of Rudolph Valentino and one of the highest paid stars of her day. In 1927 her Spanish Revival mansion was converted into a hotel and 25 Spanish guest cottages were built around the pool. Shaped like the Black Sea, it was among the first pools in Hollywood with underwater lighting.

Initially named Garden of Alla, after Nazimova, the hotel opened with a lavish 18-hour party attended by many of the top Hollywood stars including Marlene Dietrich, Clara Bow and John Barrymore. It became Hollywood's favorite social center, attracting writers Robert Benchley, F Scott Fitzgerald and Dorothy Parker, who all lived here while writing film scripts for the studios. Movie stars such as Greta Garbo, Orson Welles, Errol Flynn, Gary Cooper, Frank Sinatra, Ava Gardner and hundreds of others also stayed in the Garden of Allah's bungalows. Humphrey Bogart and Lauren Bacall honeymooned here. Marlene Dietrich regularly swam nude in the pool. More

was written about this famous Hollywood landmark than any other hotel in the world. It was notorious for its hedonistic, unrestrained atmosphere, hard drinking and endless wild parties around the pool.

By the 1950s the Garden of Allah deteriorated and, in 1959, it was torn down, ending the same way it started—with a party. The next day all furniture was sold at public auction, Errol Flynn's bed being the most prized trophy. Today a bank and a minimall stand on its site, at the southwest corner of Sunset and Crescent Heights boulevards. The grand hotel was immortalized in a popular song *Big Yellow Taxi* (1970) by Joni Mitchell, who laments its destruction: "Don't it always seem to go/You don't know what you've got till it's gone/They paved paradise and put up a parking lot."

Bullwinkle and Rocky statue

Jay Ward Productions

(formerly) **❷**

8218 Sunset Blvd.

A 15-foot-tall fiberglass statue of Bullwinkle the Moose and Rocky the Flying Squirrel stands in front of the house that once was the headquarters of Jay Ward Productions, the animation company that originated them. It was erected as a parody of a giant showgirl statue placed in front of the Sahara Hotel in Las Vegas. Among the company's other creations were such memorable cartoon characters as Boris and Natasha, Sherman and Peabody, George of the Jungle, and Crusader Rabbit and Rags, popular television stars of the 1960s. The property is now occupied by Hollywood Hounds, a celebrity dog-watching service.

A vintage post card depicts the Garden of Allah

Château Marmont ❸

Dominating the Sunset Strip since 1929, this eclectic building became a symbol of the movie capital's glitter and still is one of the rare places in the city where you can experience the old Hollywood charm. The Loire Valley château with Gothic Revival hints, elegant suites, cottages and bungalows, it has become a favorite hideout for the rich and famous. Almost every movie star has either stayed or lived in this landmark hotel, adding countless stories, scandals and gossip to its colorful history.

Its seclusive and relaxed atmosphere lured such celebrities as Errol Flynn, Clark Gable, Bette Davis, Jean Harlow, Hedy Lamarr and Grace Kelly. It is said that Greta Garbo never stayed anywhere but the Château. Long term residents were Boris Karloff, Howard Hughes and director Billy Wilder, who said when he found the hotel was fully booked: "I would rather sleep in a bathroom than in another hotel." (He actually did, spending a few nights in the ladies toilet ante-room around Christmas 1935.) Wilder liked his Château suite so much that he actually used it as a model for Fred MacMurray's apartment in *Double Indemnity* (1944).

Regarded "the greatest womanizer in Hollywood history," Hughes orchestrated an endless flow of Hollywood beauties through his hotel suite. Besides unknown young starlets, his list of conquests included such stars as Jean Harlow, Katharine Hepburn, Ginger Rogers, Lana Turner, Ava Gardner, Linda Darnell and Rita Hayworth.

The hotel was the stage of secret rendezvous between the most desirable men and women in movieland. In 1939, Columbia mogul Harry Cohn rented a small penthouse here for his stars William Holden and Glenn Ford with a warning: "If you must get in trouble, do it at the Château Marmont." Among the famous romances that started here were those between Paul Newman and Joanne Woodward, and Jessica Lange and Sam Shepard. Director Nicholas Ray stayed in the hotel's Bungalow No. 2 while having an affair with his young star Natalie Wood in 1955, the same one in which comedian John Belushi died from an overdose of a "speedball"—a mix of cocaine and heroin—on March 5, 1982.

Hotel sign

Today's regulars are Robert De Niro, Dustin Hoffman, Sean Penn, Keanu Reeves, Winona Ryder and Matt Dillon. At the Château's suites Helmut Newton, Annie Leibovitz, Ellen Von Unwerth and other celebrity photographers captured many of their glamorous photos of the stars, models and musicians. Helmut Newton spent every winter of the last 25 years of his life living at the Marmont. He was killed in January 2004 while leaving the hotel, when he lost control of his Cadillac which careened and crashed into the retaining wall across the street.

Among the rockers who stayed here were Bob Dylan, Iggy Pop, Mick Jagger, John Lennon and Yoko Ono. Jefferson Airplane and the Eagles were also guests; Led Zeppelin rented bungalows here for their infamous orgies. Red Hot Chili Peppers wrote and recorded most of the songs for their 2002 album *By the Way* while living at the hotel.

View of Château Marmont

Arnold Weitzman, architect (1928); Craig Ellwood, bungalows (1956). 8221 Sunset Blvd. ☎(323) 656-1010. ⓑ ⚐

Château Marmont's side entrance arcade, with a courtyard featuring Gothic archways and painted ceilings

In Oliver Stone's film *The Doors* (1991), Val Kilmer, playing drunken rock singer Jim Morrison, tumbles from the hotel's balcony.

Façade of the Andalusia with its paved forecourt

The Andalusia's inner court and flower garden

Courtyard Apartments

Based on the bungalow court, a new housing type immediately identifiable with LA blossomed in the city during the 1920s and 1930s. In an attempt to transplant Mediterranean lifestyles, the two- and three-story apartments were arranged around a lushly landscaped central courtyard containing pools and mosaic fountains. Built predominantly in the Spanish Colonial Revival style, these buildings featured white plaster walls and red-tiled roofs, together with such charming details as colorful tiles and wrought-iron balconies.

Some of the most beautiful courtyard apartment complexes in Los Angeles were built by the husband and wife team of Arthur and Nina Zwebell. Although they did not have formal training or a license to practice architecture, they designed eight extraordinary buildings that remain part of LA's distinctive heritage. The North Harper Ave Historic District, with several courtyard apartments, is listed on the **NRHP**.

Villa d'Este ❹

F Pierpont and Walter S Davis, architects (1928).
1355 N Laurel Ave.
Private residences. 🐾

The work of the distinguished Davis brothers design team, this is one of the most elegant courtyard apartment buildings in LA. Inspired by its 16th-century namesake in Italy, this ele-

gant, two-story Italian Renaissance villa features such details as a high archway and an exclusive lion pond in the forecourt.

A central courtyard, lushly landscaped with tropical vegetation, contains a tiled, tiered water fountain and a unique design of waterways. At the back is a lion fountain, a copy from a palazzo in Bologna, Italy.

Villa d'Este was once home to silent screen star Pola Negri. It was used as an apartment building where a young couple resided in the film *Under the Yum Yum Tree* (1963), disturbed by the amorous landlord played by Jack Lemmon.

Andalusia ❺

Arthur and Nina Zwebell, architects (1926).
1471-75 Havenhurst Dr.
Private residences.

Designed in 1926 in Spanish Colonial Revival style, the

Andalusia is the Zwebells' top achievement. Modeled after pure Andalusian prototypes, the building has a symmetrical façade with a wood-rail balcony above the entrance archway and tiled stairs leading to second-story dwellings. The complex is approached through a paved forecourt with a pair of garage pavilions on each side.

The two-story building is wrapped around an inner court, with a round tower, an outdoor fireplace and a meticulously maintained flower garden. Its most striking feature is the central fountain decorated with hand-painted glazed tiles, said to be a copy of the original in Seville.

The Andalusia attracted many members of the thriving movie colony, counting Clara Bow, Claire Bloom, Jean Hagen, Caesar Romero, John Payne and Teresa Wright among its celebrity residents.

The entrance to Villa d'Este with a pond filled with water flowing from a lion's mouth

A brightly-colored, vaulted corridor connects a forecourt with a landscaped main courtyard

Patio del Moro ❻

Arthur and Nina Zwebell, architects
(1925).
8225-8237 Fountain Ave.
Private residences. **NRHP**.

Responding to a request by
their client, an avid traveler
who toured North Africa and
Spain, the Zwebells used various Arab elements in this
design, such as arabesque
patterns, pointed and horseshoe arches, and even
included a small Moorish
tower. The enclosed courtyard contains an exterior fireplace and a reflecting pool.
The building's extraordinary
façade features an ornamented arched entrance with flat
grillwork and garage doors
with quatrefoil pattern.

The Patio del Moro's façade with its impressive arched front gate

**View of the Villa Primavera's
fountain and elaborately landscaped, enclosed courtyard**

Villa Primavera ❼

Arthur and Nina Zwebell, architects
(1923).
1300-1308 N Harper Ave.
Private residences. ⚲

This one-story complex
(except for the two-story east
wing) is the Zwebells' first
Spanish Colonial Revival
design, and became their
own residence.

It is said that James Dean
and Katharine Hepburn were
tenants here. The building
appeared in the film *noir*
thriller *In a Lonely Place*
(1950), starring Humphrey
Bogart as a Hollywood
screenwriter suspected of
murdering a young woman.

Romanesque Villa ❽

Leland A Bryant, architect (1928).
1301-1309 N Harper Ave.
Private residences.

Built in the Spanish Churrigueresque style, this courtyard apartment building was
the first Hollywood home of
actress Marlene Dietrich
upon her arrival from Germany in 1930. In the same
complex lived her mentor,
director Josef von Sternberg,
who had cast her as the sexy
vamp Lola Lola in her first
major role in *The Blue Angel*
(1930). This prompted
rumors of their romantic
involvement, later sustained
by a lawsuit filed by Sternberg's wife. Three decades
later, another sensuous star,
Zsa Zsa Gabor, lived here for
a while after her Beverly
Hills home burned down.
Marilyn Monroe shared an
apartment here with her acting teacher, Natasha Lyttes.

**Decorative tile work details of
the Ronda's façade**

Ronda ❾

Arthur and Nina Zwebell, architects
(1927).
1400-1414 Havenhurst Dr.
Private residences. ⚲ NRHP

A beautiful façade stepping
from four to two stories is
decorated with wrought iron,
hand-painted tiles and sculpted fountains. Instead of a
single central court, this
building has two paved and
tiled garden courtyards that
resemble Andalusian streets,
which makes it unique
among the Zwebells' designs.

**From the tiled roof of the
Ronda, Jack Nicholson, playing private eye Jake Gittes in
Chinatown (1974), takes pictures of Hollis Mulwray and a
girl in the courtyard**

Among its former celebrity
residents, the Ronda (now
called Mi Casa) counts actress
Louise Brooks, a famous flapper of the 1920s. Actor Cary
Grant lived here in 1934 with
his wife, actress Virginia
Cherrill, better known as the
blind flower girl in Chaplin's
City Lights (1931).

Cabo Cantina
(formerly **the Source**) ⑩

8301 Sunset Blvd.
☎(323) 656-6388. ⚑

Formerly a health food restaurant the Source, this was the place where Diane Keaton dumped Woody Allen in *Annie Hall* (1977). Allen plays a Manhattanite who tells his girlfriend Keaton, who clearly prefers LA to New York: "I don't want to live in a city where the only cultural advantage is that you can make a right turn on a red light."

Sunset Tower ⑪

Leland A Bryant, architect (1931).
8358 Sunset Blvd.
☎(323) 654-7100. ⚑ NRHP

Once touted "Hollywood's Most Distinguished Address" and formerly known as the St James Club and the Argyle Hotel, this remarkable building is one of the greatest Art Deco masterpieces in Los Angeles. It features rounded corner windows typical of the style and is elaborately decorated by a series of friezes containing stylized floral and animal motifs.

Completed between 1929 and 1931, it once provided luxurious homes for Hollywood stars such as Marilyn Monroe, Errol Flynn, Jean Harlow, Clark Gable, Howard Hughes, Roger Moore, the Gabor sisters and even gangster "Bugsy" Siegel. Director Peter Bogdanovich lived for about two years in the 7th-floor apartment with actress

The Sunset Tower's pool is the setting where Tim Robbins listens to a story pitch in *The Player* (1992)

Cybill Shepherd. Legend has it that John Wayne kept a pet steer on the balcony while living in the 12th-floor penthouse.

The building was featured as the exterior of the Voltaire Restaurant in *Pretty Woman* (1990) and John Travolta's hotel room in *Get Shorty* (1995). In the same movie we see Dennis Farina exiting the building after he received the key for the locker at the airport containing a bag with cash. Dick Powell was held captive in one of the hotel's suites in *Murder, My Sweet* (1944). The hotel's lobby, the bar and the pool appeared in *The Player* (1992).

The building was featured on the cover of Don Everly's *Sunset Towers* (1976) album.

Sunset Tower

Hyatt West Hollywood ⑫

8401 Sunset Blvd.
☎(323) 656-1234. ⚑

Known as the "Riot House" during the 1970s, the hotel was a favorite haunt for visiting rock bands who turned it into the stage for their wild antics. Led Zeppelin drummer John Bonham threw furniture over a balcony and smashed a car. Keith Richards tossed a television out a window. Axl Rose reportedly had barbecue on a balcony

Hyatt West Hollywood

and threw steaks on the curious crowd below. Mötley Crüe bassist Nikki Sixx allegedly was in the room of Guns N' Roses guitarist Slash when he overdosed.

The hotel (formerly the Continental Hyatt House) has attracted hordes of teenage groupies trying to get to upper floors where corridors were packed and room doors were always left open. Led Zeppelin rented six floors for their orgies and roared motorcycles down the hotel's hallways. They used to cause such devastation to hotel rooms that their entourage eventually included an accountant who kept track of the damage they left behind.

The hotel was featured in the movie *This Is Spinal Tap* (1984). In *Almost Famous* (2000), its lobby is used in a mob scene.

Comedy Store
(formerly **Ciro's**) ⑬

8433 Sunset Blvd.
☎(323) 656-6225. ♠

On this site in 1940 opened the world-famous Ciro's, Hollywood's hottest hangout during the 1940s and 1950s. Ciro's was the place to see and be seen, frequented by almost every Hollywood celebrity. Entertainment was provided by such stars as Josephine Baker, Mae West, Dean Martin, Jerry Lewis, Maurice Chevalier, Sammy Davis Jr, Nat "King" Cole, Billie Holliday, Liberace and many others. Hollywood legend has it that actress

Paulette Goddard crawled under the table to show her admiration to director Anatole Litvak. During her semi-nude performance at Ciro's, classy stripper Lili St Cyr was arrested in 1951 for indecent exposure. It was also here that screen Tarzan Johnny Weismuller tipped a table filled with food onto the lap of his wife, Mexican actress Lupe Velez, during one of their public brawls.

Ciro's closed its doors in 1957 when its owner went bankrupt facing charges for unpaid taxes. During the 1960s, the reopened club featured Sonny and Cher, Tom Jones and the Byrds, who debuted at Ciro's and played as the resident band in 1965, attracting a huge following.

The building now houses the Comedy Store, one of the most important showcases for standup comedy. When they first played here, Roseanne Barr, Jim Carrey, Billy Crystal, David Letterman and Robin Williams were all unknowns waiting to be discovered.

El Palacio Apartments

Dorothy Dandridge Death Site ⑭

El Palacio Apartments
8491-8499 Fountain Ave.
Private residences. ⓜ

This Spanish-style courtyard complex was Marilyn Monroe's home from 1947 to 1948. It was also here that the 41-years-old actress Dorothy Dandridge died in her apartment in 1965. She was found lying naked on the bathroom floor, covered only with her scarf. She died allegedly from an overdose of barbiturates, but her death remains a mystery.

Ciro's was one of Hollywood's most famous hotspots

Mocambo

(site) ⑮

8588 Sunset Blvd.

Following its star-studded opening night on January 3, 1941, when it outraged the public with an astronomical $10 cover charge, the Mocambo established itself as Hollywood's favorite celebrity nightspot. With its Mexican-themed décor, complete with an aviary of 30 live birds, including cockatoos, macaws, lovebirds and parakeets, it was the setting of choice for Hollywood's extravagant parties, including Lana Turner's $40,000-birthday-bash for one of her husbands.

Among the stars who packed "the nightclub's nightspot" every night were Marlene Dietrich, Myrna Loy, Henry Fonda, Judy Garland, Hedy Lamarr, Cary Grant, Carole Lombard and Clark Gable. Humphrey Bogart and Lauren Bacall were greeted

with *That Old Black Magic* whenever they arrived.

The guests were entertained by some of the world's greatest performers, including Edith Piaf, Jacques Brel, Billy Daniels and Lena

Mocambo's matchbox

Horne. Frank Sinatra first became known in Hollywood here. The Mocambo closed in 1958.

The Comedy Store's exterior walls are inscribed with the names of famous headliners who performed at the club

Café Trocadero

(site) **16**

8610 Sunset Blvd. 🏳

This glitz and glamour hub of Hollywood was opened in 1934 by the publisher of the trade paper *Hollywood Reporter*, W R Wilkerson, who also started the famous Ciro's. Wilkerson's name ensured that everybody who was somebody frequented the Troc. Among its most prominent patrons were Clark Gable, Fred Astaire, Cary Grant, Tyrone Power, Jean Harlow and Lana Turner. Entertainment was provided by some of the greatest performers of the day, such as Nat "King" Cole and Count Basie. Countless premiere parties were hosted here, including one for *Gone With the Wind* in 1939.

Every Saturday night, in a back room filled with cigar smoke, studio moguls Irving Thalberg, Samuel Goldwyn, Joseph Schenck, Darryl F Zanuck, and others played high stakes poker.

The Trocadero was immortalized in the film *A Star Is Born* (1937), where both its exterior and French-themed interior were featured.

A vintage post card depicts the Trocadero in the 1930s

Sunset Plaza **17**

Sunset Blvd at Sunset Plaza Dr.

One of the few areas where Angelenos actually walk (thus resembling Beverly Hills), the two-block Plaza is the commercial center of the Strip. This cluster of one-story, fashionable shops, outdoor cafes and beauty salons was built in the 1930s and still retains the elegance of its original façades. It is the perfect place for people-watching in a relaxed, open-air atmosphere.

To help an AIDS fund-rising campaign, Elizabeth Taylor and her dog Sugar left their footprints in wet cement in front of the Kenneth Cole store

Kenneth Cole Walk of Fame (site) **18**

8752 Sunset Blvd.

To help raise research funds for an AIDS cure, several stars voluntarily stepped barefoot into wet cement in front of this trendy shoe store. Liz Taylor poured her signature White Diamonds perfume as her dog Sugar left its tiny footprints alongside hers. Rosie O'Donnell made a deep impression. Among other "Supporting Soles" are footprints of Richard Gere, Matthew Modine and Patricia Arquette.

Until a cure is found, Kenneth Cole has pledged to donate a portion of daily sales on each of the participating stars' birthdays.

Viper Room **19**

8852 Sunset Blvd.
☎(310) 358-1880. ✊ 🏳

Co-owned by actor Johnny Depp between 1993 and 2004, this nightclub was previously known as the Melody Room, Filthy McNasty's (the name of one of two bank robbers in W C Fields' movie *The Bank Dick*) and the Central. The place was used as the London Fog in Oliver Stone's movie *The Doors* (1991), although the actual location of that club was further west on the boulevard.

Tommy Lee attacked here a paparazzo who tried to take a picture of he and his wife, Pamela Anderson.

The Viper Room gained international fame when young actor River Phoenix was brought outside on the sidewalk in front of its Sunset exit and died of a drug overdose on Halloween, October 31, 1993.

View of Sunset Plaza

Entrance to the Viper Room

Whisky à Go Go ⑳

8901 Sunset Blvd.
☎(310) 652-4202.

Known simply as "the Whisky," this is perhaps the most famous club in the history of rock music. Go-go dancing was born here when the audience enthusiastically responded to a girl DJ spinning records in a glass-walled cage suspended over them. Since its opening in 1964, almost every important rock act played here, including the Byrds, Buffalo Springfield and Jimi Hendrix, along with British invaders Cream, the Kinks, Led Zeppelin and the Who. In the summer of 1966, the Doors were the house band here before they rose to world fame. Otis Redding recorded his *In Person at the Whisky à Go Go* album on this stage in 1967, shortly before his premature death.

The club was once more in the spotlight in the late 1970s, featuring such punk bands as X, the Germs and the Weirdos, and again in the 1980s, with Guns N' Roses and Mötley Crüe.

The legendary Whisky à Go Go invented go-go dancing

Handprints of the porn star

Hustler Porn Walk of Fame ㉑

8920 Sunset Blvd.
☎(310) 860-9009.

On the sidewalk in front of this erotic shop some of the most renowned porn stars left their handprints in wet cement: Jenna Jameson, Ron Jeremy, Seka, Ginger Lynn, along with the *Hustler* publisher Larry Flynt. To the disappointment of many, no other body parts were immortalized for posterity.

Roxy ㉒

9009 Sunset Blvd.
☎(310) 278-9457.

Another legendary rock club on the Strip, the Roxy opened in 1973 and has since featured some of the biggest names in rock and pop music. Bob Marley & the Wailers introduced reggae to America during their appearance at the club in 1975. The Bee Gees, Chuck Berry, David Bowie, Linda Ronstadt, Bruce Springsteen, Neil Young and Frank Zappa all played here at one time or another.

At the upstairs private club, On the Rox, John Belushi reportedly had his last dinner while partying with pals Robert De Niro and Robert Williams. (The nearby Rainbow club claims the same, stating that the owner took Belushi's last meal—lentil soup—off the menu.)

Rainbow Bar and Grill ㉓

9015 Sunset Blvd.
☎(310) 278-4232.

Formerly the Villa Nova Restaurant, this was the place where Vincente Minnelli proposed to Judy Garland in 1945. It was also here that baseball star Joe DiMaggio met his future wife, Marilyn Monroe, on a blind date in 1953. The place reopened in 1973 as the Rainbow Bar and Grill, and immediately became a favorite rock-and-roll hangout, frequented by such legendary bands as Led Zeppelin and Guns N' Roses. It is still popular with rockers and rock fans.

Key Club ㉔

9039 Sunset.
☎(310) 274-5800.

Two huge video screens glow on the façade of this landmark rock club, part of the Strip music scene since the mid 1960s. Then known as Gazzarri's, it hosted many famous acts who played here early in their careers, including the Doors, the Byrds, and Buffalo Springfield, as well as Van Halen and Guns N' Roses. It was renamed Billboard Live in 1986 and now is the high-tech Key Club.

Entrance to Key Club

Lloyd Wright's home-studio

Lloyd Wright Home 25

Lloyd Wright, architect (1927). 858 N Doheny Dr. Private residence. **NRHP**

Inspired by his father's Mayan-themed houses, Lloyd Wright built his own home-studio on this small corner lot. The two-story rectangular structure, with its plain-colored plaster walls and concrete block decoration, is possibly his best residential design. Pre-cast blocks feature stylized Joshua trees, the decorative motif that became Wright's personal symbol. The house is almost hidden behind two huge Italian pines and thick foliage that covers large wall surfaces.

Troubadour 26

9081 Santa Monica Blvd. ☎(310) 276-1158; (310) 276-6168 (recorded info).

This legendary club gained notoriety in 1962 when the controversial comedian Lenny Bruce was arrested for obscenity after his performances here. On this stage appeared some of the greatest rock names of the 1960s and early 1970s, when it became one of the most famous nightclubs in the world. Jackson Browne, Van Morrison, Carole King, Linda Ronstadt, John Denver, Willie Nelson, Neil Diamond, Janis Joplin and Miles Davis all played here. In 1970, Elton John's sensational engagement at the Troubadour launched him to stardom.

After harassing performers on stage while wearing a Kotex on his forehead, a drunken John Lennon was kicked out onto the pavement in a well-know incident in 1974. Guns N' Roses exploded on the LA rock scene while playing here as a resident band in 1985.

Hard Rock Café

(formerly) 27

8600 Beverly Boulevard. 📍

Located on the ground floor of the Beverly Center shopping mall, this was the first in America and second in the world (after London) of what is now a popular restaurant chain. The walls of the rock-and-roll-themed establishment, which opened in 1983 (and closed in 2006), were covered with photos, posters, clothes, gold records and other memorabilia. Guitars once owned by Jerry Garcia, John Lennon and

Hard Rock Café

Eddie Van Halen, as well as Elvis Presley's Harley Davidson, were also on display.

The Hard Rock Café, with its signature tilted Cadillac on the roof, was prominently featured in *L.A. Story* (1991).

Tail o' the Pup 28

329 N San Vicente Blvd. ☎(310) 652-4517. 📍

Built in 1938 and threatened many times by developers' bulldozers, this survivor was moved from its original location on 311 N La Cienega Blvd. A hot dog stand shaped like a hot dog in a bun, it is one of the last remaining examples of the city's programmatic structures (➔ p98). These buildings, whose function is made obvious through their forms, proliferated in Los Angeles during the 1920s and 1930s.

The stand was featured in *Body Double* (1984) and *L.A. Story* (1991), where its mock-up is seen flying over the city in the opening scenes.

The Troubadour

Tail o' the Pup, one of the last programmatic structures in LA

Façade of the Pacific Design Center

Pacific Design Center's escalator stairwell

Pacific Design Center ㉙

Cesar Pelli, architect (1975-88).
8687 Melrose Ave.
☎(310) 657-0800. 🎥
www.pacificdesigncenter.com.

With its peculiar form and signature cobalt-blue spandrel glass, this gigantic structure became an instant LA landmark. Dubbed the "Blue Whale" at its opening, the seven-story structure raised controversy because of its size, which stands in disparity to neighboring small shops and houses. A nine-story addition was built in 1988, clad in similar green glass. Serving as a marketplace for interior designers, the center contains almost 200 showrooms of furniture, fabric and antiques, the largest of its kind in the West.

Two monumental stainless steel sculptures by designer Robin Perkins, *Seat of Design* and *Illuminating Design*, were unveiled in 2002.

The MOCA satellite gallery, located on the plaza level, presents exhibitions on architecture and design, as well as new work by emerging and established artists.

The building appeared in the action comedy *Demolition Man* (1993). Its escalators and glassy, barrel-vaulted gallery roof were used in the chase sequence in the film *Lipstick* (1976).

Melrose Avenue ㉚

Melrose had been LA's hippest street since the mid-1980s, when it captured everybody's attention with its intense cool, cutting-edge trendiness and anti-establishment spirit.

One of the rare places to stroll outdoors in LA, this authentic pedestrian neighborhood offers block after block of eclectic little boutiques selling everything imaginable: trendy clothes and accessories, rocks and crystals, memorabilia, glass pipes, knickknacks, nostalgia items, comic books, wind-up toys and games, and custom-made neon signs. It is also perfect for people-watching: an endless stream of eccentric characters, including fluorescent-haired punkers, kids with facial piercings and leather-clad skinhead bikers.

The area's flashiest section is the nine-block stroll between Alta Vista Blvd and Spaulding Ave. The western stretch (between La Cienega Blvd and Doheny Dr) features upscale galleries, antique stores and interior design shops.

Gemini Gel Studios

Gemini GEL Studios ㉛

Frank O Gehry and Associates, architect (1976).
8365 Melrose Ave.
☎(323) 651-0513.

In 1976 Frank Gehry designed an addition to an old building that houses a fine arts gallery and an internationally renowned lithography workshop. The new structure features two of Gehry's signature touches—forced perspective, created by an unfinished plywood staircase, and clashing volumes, indicated by tilting skylights.

Extravagant storefronts and outlandish window displays on Melrose. Some of the wilder interiors need to be seen to be believed.

Schindler House, view from the east patio. Note sliding doors connecting patios and studios.

Schindler Studio House ㉜

Rudolf Schindler, architect (1921)
835 N Kings Rd.
☎(323) 651-1510
⊕Wed-Sun 11am-6pm. NRHP

Hidden behind a densely planted garden stands the first house built in Los Angeles by architect Rudolf Schindler. Born and educated in Vienna, he moved to the US in 1914 to work as a draftsman in Chicago. After joining the office of Frank Lloyd Wright in 1918, he came to LA to superwise the construction of Hollyhock House.

The unconventional design of the house manifests both Schindler's European and American experiences. The integration of the building and the landscape makes it one of the most innovative residences in modern architecture.

Alta Cienega Motel ㉝

1005 N La Cienega Blvd.
☎(310) 652-5797.

Room 32 on the upper level of this motel was Jim Morrison's temporary home in 1969, conveniently located across the street from the Doors' business office. The walls of the corner room are inscribed with messages from the popular singer's fans.

Benvenuto Café ㉞

8.512 Santa Monica Blvd.
☎(310) 659-8635.

The Doors' business office was located in this building, which is now an Italian restaurant. In the recording studio downstairs the Doors rehearsed and recorded their album *L.A. Woman* (1971).

Sal Mineo Death Site ㉟

8563 Holloway Dr.
Private residences. ⓦ

An apparently random robbery gone wrong grabbed national headlines when actor Sal Mineo, who had just returned from a play rehearsal on the evening of February 12, 1976, was stabbed in the carport of this apartment building. The 37-year old actor, who gained fame when he received an Oscar nomination for his supporting role in *Rebel Without a Cause*

(1955), died on the spot. The killer escaped the scene but was caught two years later, when his wife told the police that he confessed the crime to her. Four actors from the *Rebel* died premature and tragic deaths: James Dean, Nick Adams, Mineo and Natalie Wood.

Marilyn Monroe Apartment ㊱

8573 Holloway Dr.
Private residence.

In this courtyard apartment building Marilyn Monroe and Shelley Winters shared a two-bedroom upstairs unit in 1951. The actresses reportedly on one occasion made up lists of the world's most desirable bachelors. On Marilyn's list appeared both Arthur Miller, her future husband, and Yves Montand, her later lover.

Alta Cienega Motel

Marilyn Monroe Apartment

Barney's Beanery ㊲

8447 Santa Monica Blvd.
☎(323) 654-2287. ☛

Looking like a roadhouse ever since its opening in the 1920s, Barney's Beanery was a place for slumming popular with movie people in the 1930s. Stars such as Jean Harlow, Clara Bow, John Barrymore, Errol Flynn and director Howard Hawks were frequently seen here. During the 1960s it became a favorite rocker hangout, with guests like the Doors leader Jim Morrison and singer Janis Joplin, who had their famous fights and often drank each other under the table. Janis reportedly partied here the night she died, downing shots of her drink of choice, Southern Comfort.

The place was immortalized in 1965 by sculptor Edward Kienholz, who created a life-size assemblage of the bar (➔ p87).

The Beanery's interior has appeared in numerous films, including *Body Double* (1984) and *The Doors* (1991).

Hand- and footprints of Linda Lovelace, the star of porn hit *Deep Throat* (1972)

Porn Walk of Fame ㊳

Tomkat Theatre
7734 Santa Monica Blvd.
☎(323) 650-9551.

Following the Hollywood tradition, porn legends left their mark in wet cement right outside the all-gay Tomkat movie theater. However, don't expect any prints of performers' trademark body parts here. All you can

Barney's Beanery was a favorite rocker hangout during the 1960s and 1970s

find are the usual hands and feet, along with signatures, of such porn stars as Marilyn Chambers and John Holmes, as well as Harry Reems and Linda Lovelace, whose cult porn movie *Deep Throat* had a long run here in what was then called the Pussycat Theatre. A sensation at the time, *Deep Throat* played in Los Angeles for more than 10 years and became the top grossing movie during the 1972-73 season. Made in 1972 for only $22,000, it was the first porn film to draw mass audiences from all walks of life, grossing several hundred million dollars worldwide.

Formosa Café ㊴

7156 Santa Monica Blvd.
☎(323) 850-9050. ☛

The restaurant was built from an abandoned red car of the city's dismantled electric trolley system. The walls of the dark, low-ceiling For-

mosa rooms are covered top to bottom with movie memorabilia and photographs signed by famous guests. A favorite industry hangout since 1945, this Chinese/American restaurant was popular with celebrities such as Clark Gable, John Wayne, Humphrey Bogart and Marilyn Monroe. Gangsters Benjamin "Bugsy" Siegel and Mickey Cohen, who were friends with owner Jimmy Bernstein, had their headquarters in the rear office in the 1940s. They kept a small safe in the floor; when it was opened with much fanfare a few years ago, nothing was found inside. One of Elvis Presley's favorite haunts, the Formosa still has the middle booth decorated with a collection of statuettes of "the King" and Elvis memorabilia.

In a famous scene in *L.A. Confidential* (1997), detective Ed Exley investigates Lana Turner's mobster boyfriend Johnny Stompanato. When he mistakes Turner for a hooker, he gets a drink thrown in his face. The scene was filmed in booth #7 at the Formosa.

Colorful Formosa Café was built from an old railroad car

In this 1922 publicity shot for a fan magazine, Mary Pickford and Douglas Fairbanks pretend to nail up the sign of their newly purchased studio

The Lot

(formerly **Pickford-Fairbanks Studios**) ㊵

1041 N Formosa Ave.
☎(323) 850-3180. ☛

Mary Pickford and Douglas Fairbanks bought this small studio from producer Jesse D Hampton in 1922 and renamed it the Pickford-Fairbanks Studios. It was here that Fairbanks made his swashbuckling hits *Robin Hood* (1922) and *The Thief of Bagdad* (1924). The facility changed its name in 1928 to United Artists Studios, and in 1939 it became Samuel Goldwyn Studios. Classics such as *Wuthering Heights* (1939) and *The Best Years of Our Lives* (1946) were produced here by Samuel Goldwyn.

Poster for *The Thief of Bagdad* (1924), which was filmed at the Pickford-Fairbanks Studios

The studio was sold to Warner Bros in 1980 and since has been used for both television and movie production. The popular series *Dynasty* and *Love Boat*, as well as the features *Volcano* (1997), *Basic Instinct* (1992) and *Species* (1995) were all filmed here. In 2000 Warner Bros sold the lot to BA Studios. A small vintage photo exhibit is on display at the receptionist's office.

Hollywood's Rock-Walk ㊶

7425 Sunset Blvd.
☎(323) 874-1060.
www.rockwalk.com

Located at the former site of the Oriental movie theater, the Guitar Center Hollywood displays an enormous collection of musical instruments, though primarily focusing on guitars. Customers with various degrees of talent, here called "wankers," testing the equipment frequently produce a hell of a noise.

John Lennon's bronze plaque

Outside the shop, under the big red awning, immortalized in concrete are the handprints and signatures of dozens of rock 'n' roll legends, including the Doobie Brothers, Steely Dan, Emerson, Lake and Palmer, ZZ Top, Black Sabbath, ACDC, Kiss, Van Halen, Animals, Los Lobos, the Yardbirds, Herbie Hancock, Aerosmith and X.

Founded on November 13, 1985 by then-Guitar Center Chairman Ray Scherr, Hollywood's RockWalk honors famous musicians and innovators whose enduring creative contributions helped establish rock and roll as a legitimate art form. All inductees are chosen exclusively by past honorees through secret ballot.

Just to the left of the shop's entrance, a small museum features rock and roll memorabilia, including clothes, signed photographs, record covers and guitars of such stars as Jimmy Page, Bob Dylan, Paul McCartney and Johnny Cash.

Hugh Grant Arrest Site ㊷

Pickup site: Sunset Blvd and Courtney Ave. Arrest site: Curson Ave and Hawthorn Ave. ☝

On June 27, 1995, actor Hugh Grant picked up streetwalker Divine Brown in his BMW on the northeast corner of Sunset Blvd and Courtney Ave. He drove a few blocks north to the intersection of Curson and Hawthorn avenues, where he was arrested for lewd conduct with an alleged prostitute.

Grant got probation and a small fine; his mug shot on front pages everywhere apparently did not hurt his career, which got a boost after the incident. Divine reportedly ended up modeling lingerie in Brazil.

Anita Stewart House ㊸

7425 Franklin Ave.
Private residence.

This palatial house was once the home of Anita Stewart, a major star at Vitagraph Studios during the 1910s. Louis B Mayer signed Stewart in 1917, offering her $3,000 a week—an unprecedented salary at the time, together with the additional incentive of a car—although her contract with Vitagraph had not yet expired. In a landmark lawsuit Vitagraph won, enforcing the contract system that maintained the studios' total dominance over actors for years to come.

Here Freddy Krueger terrorized a girl in her dreams in *A Nightmare on Elm Street* (1984)

In her film debut, Jamie Lee Curtis played a babysitter in this house in *Halloween* (1978)

Samuel Goldwyn Estate ㊹

Arthur Heineman, architect (1916).
1800 Camino Palmero.
Private residence.

Samuel Goldwyn bought this six-bedroom Neo-Classical mansion around 1925, after he married actress Frances Howard. The most successful independent producer in Hollywood, who won an Oscar for *The Best Years of Our Lives* (1946), Goldwyn hosted nearly every celebrity of Hollywood's Golden Age. Clark Gable reportedly used to play cards with the host in the pool house cabana, young Judy Garland lounged by the water and drunken Errol Flynn often ended up in a guestroom upstairs.

Actress Katharine Hepburn was quoted as saying: "You always knew where your career stood by where you were seated at the Goldwyn table."

Ozzie and Harriet House ㊺

1822 Camino Palmero Dr.
Private residence. ♠ 🐾

This is the house which was used for the exterior shots in the popular ABC family sitcoms *The Adventures of Ozzie and Harriet* (1952-66). The real Nelson family—Ozzie, Harriet, David and Ricky—actually lived in the house while portraying the middle class American family in this long-running hit. Harriet sold the house, which is reportedly haunted by Ozzie's ghost, several years after his death in 1975.

A Nightmare on Elm Street House ㊻

1428 N Genesee Ave.
Private residence. 🐾

Familiar to all the fans of the Freddy Krueger horror movies, this two-story house in a quiet residential neigh-

borhood was used as the abode where he terrorized the Elm Street kids in the original 1984 film.

Halloween Houses ㊼

Orange Grove Ave.
Private residences. 🐾

Lacking the usual omnipresent palm trees, this Midwestern-looking street was used for exterior shots in the *Halloween* horror movies. The Colonial-style house at 1530 Orange Grove Ave is the place where Jamie Lee Curtis was baby-sitting in the John Carpenter's 1978 original. At 1537, just across the street, her best friend was murdered. Scenes from *Halloween 3: Season of the Witch* (1983) were filmed at 1536.

Directors Guild ㊽

7920 Sunset Blvd.
☎(323) 289-2000. For programs open to the public call ☎(323) 461-9622. www.dga.org

This six-story bronze and glass tower is the headquarters of the professional association which represents more than 12,000 directors.

In 1948 the Guild began an Awards program to honor their members' achievements, presenting Joseph Mankiewicz with the first Annual Award for Directorial Excellence for his *A Letter to Three Wives*. Besides theatrical direction for film, the Awards today include television, documentaries, commercials and Special Awards.

Samuel Goldwyn Estate

Schwab's Pharmacy

(site) **49**

8024 Sunset Blvd. 🎥

Contrary to popular belief, this is not the place where Lana Turner was discovered (➔ p127), but it remained a part of Hollywood mythology as a gathering point for out-of-work actors, writers and other film folk. Schwab's used the Turner story as a publicity tool, attracting countless wannabes to its coffee shop. Although no one was ever discovered here, the legendary pharmacy was the birthplace of Harold Arlen's memorable hit *Over the Rainbow*.

Schwab's pharmacy was a meeting location for celebrities

Schwab's interior is featured in *Sunset Boulevard* (1950)

Writer F Scott Fitzgerald suffered a heart attack while buying cigarettes at Schwab's in 1940. Among the drugstore's regulars were Clark Gable, Judy Garland, the Marx Brothers, Orson Welles and Shelley Winters. Charlie Chaplin and Harold Lloyd played pinball in the back room. Chaplin was allowed to make his own milkshakes behind the soda fountain.

Gloria Swanson bought her makeup here. Schwab's closed its doors in 1983 and the building was demolished in 1988 to make way for a shopping complex.

In the classic *Sunset Boulevard* (1950), William Holden's character, screenwriter Joe Gillis, refers to Schwab's by its common name: "After that, I drove down to headquarters. That's the way a lot of us think about Schwab's. Kind of a combination office, coffee klatsch and waiting room. Waiting, waiting for the gravy train."

Sunset 8000 **50**

The site of the famous Schwab's drugstore is now occupied by a shopping complex dominated by the Virgin Megastore, the giant record warehouse that stocks over 150,000 titles. The mall also houses the Sunset 5 movie theaters which screen independent and foreign films.

F Scott Fitzgerald Apartment **51**

1401 N Laurel Ave, Apt 6. Private residence. ➔ 🎥

This château-style apartment house was the last residence of F Scott Fitzgerald, author who epitomized the Jazz Age. He lived in apartment #6 while writing his Hollywood novel, *The Last Tycoon*. The novel remained unfinished as Fitzgerald died

Author F Scott Fitzgerald lived in this apartment building

of a heart attack in December, 1940. It was published posthumously in 1941 and filmed by Elia Kazan in 1976.

The building was featured in the film *Beloved Infidel* (1959), an adaptation of the book by Fitzgerald's lover, journalist Sheilah Graham, about their affair and the great novelist's last days in Hollywood. Gregory Peck and Deborah Kerr star as Fitzgerald and Graham.

Sunset 8000 shopping complex

Neighborhood store on Laurel Canyon Blvd immortalized in the Doors' song *Love Street*: "I see you live on Love Street/There's this store where the creatures meet"

Laurel Canyon 52

This non-glamorous serpentine street that connects Hollywood to the San Fernando Valley gained fame in the late 1960s as a bohemian refuge. Amid its rustic surroundings many musicians, writers, and movie people found a home. Among the canyon's residents, or the "creatures" as Jim Morrison referred to them, were such music legends as Jackson Browne, Joe Cocker, Leonard Cohen, David Crosby, John Densmore, Micky Dolenz, Tim Hardin, Carole King, Stephen Stills, Cass Elliott, and John and Michelle Phillips. Members of the Beatles, Eagles, Rolling Stones, Yardbirds and Led Zeppelin occassionally stopped by.

The northwest corner of Laurel Canyon Blvd and Lookout Mountain Rd was once occupied by a log cabin owned in the 1920s by legendary cowboy star Tom Mix. Frank Zappa, the bandleader of the Mothers of Invention, lived in the house from 1966 to 1968. Across the street, at 2398 (now 2400) Laurel Canyon Blvd, once stood a 1920s Italianate, 40-room mansion where the magician Harry Houdini is believed to have lived at one time. Today, only the steps and the servant quarters remain on the grounds, which are reportedly haunted. Both the Mix and Houdini houses burned down.

John Mayall's home on Grandview Dr also ended up in flames, but it was rebuilt on the same spot. It was here the British blues great wrote his album *Blues From Laurel Canyon* in 1968, featuring the song *Laurel Canyon Home*.

A bungalow on Lookout Mountain Rd was the home of singer-songwriter Joni Mitchell when she wrote her albums *Clouds* (1969) and *Ladies of the Canyon* (1970). She reportedly sketched the *Ladies* album cover drawing inspired by the view through the kitchen window. Her lover Graham Nash wrote the song *Our House* about this "very, very, very fine house" while sharing the bungalow with Joni.

Over a five-week period in 1991, Red Hot Chili Peppers recorded their album *Blood Sugar Sex Magik* in the man-

sion at 2451 Laurel Canyon Blvd.

Porn star John Holmes was accused of going on a drug-related killing spree that left four people dead in this house at 8763 Wonderland Ave on July 1, 1981. He was later acquitted. The 2003 movie *Wonderland*, starring Val Kilmer as John C Holmes, tells the story of the murders and Holmes's downfall. The same events inspired a sequence with Mark Wahlberg and Alfred Molina in *Boogie Nights* (1997), another film about a star in the hardcore industry.

The site of the infamous cocaine murders in 1981

The movie *Laurel Canyon* (2003) recreates the early 1970s-era mindset of the Los Angeles music world and the neighborhood known as the rock hotbed. Frances McDormand plays a record producer and a freewheeling mother who lives with her lover in the canyon pad she is suddenly forced to share with her son and his fiancée.

Joni Mitchell's album *Ladies of the Canyon* (1970)

The famous Hollywood Hills neighborhood was the setting for *Laurel Canyon* (2003)

Hollywood Hills

Comprising several distinct neighborhoods, the eastern portion of the Santa Monica Mountains (extending from Griffith Park to Beverly Hills) contains some of the city's finest parks and outdoor recreational areas. Its canyons and steep hillsides offer their affluent residents tranquility and privacy, along with stunning city views. Narrow, winding roads that are difficult to navigate lead to secluded exclusive homes, hidden behind lush landscaping. The Hollywood Hills is a repository of notable residential buildings, featuring works of such acclaimed architects as Wright, Neutra, Schindler and Lautner.

From the 1920s to the early 1950s, movie stars of Hollywood's Golden Age made these reclusive hills their home. Today, the area is a big draw for young Hollywood again, with such residents as Leonardo DiCaprio, Ben Affleck, George Clooney, Halle Berry, Brad Pitt, Tobey Maguire and Winona Ryder.

Wright's Storer House is faced with pre-cast concrete blocks

Valentino's advertising campaign featured Case Study House No. 22

Case Study House No. 22 ⑤③

Pierre Koenig, architect (1960).
1635 Woods Dr.
Private residence. 🏃

Probably the most famous building developed for *Arts & Architecture* magazine's Case Study House program (➔ p97), this L-shaped marvel represents a full realization of Koenig's radical experiments with new building materials. The use of steel columns allowed the architect to clad all sides of the house in glass, except for a walled-off side facing the street. The transparent cantilevered living room extending over the edge of a precipice offers a breathtaking panoramic view of the whole Los Angeles basin, made world-famous in a celebrated Julius Shulman photograph (➔ p97).

CSH No. 22 is one of the most photographed houses in the world. It is used as a location for more than 50 photo shoots each year, including campaigns for Armani, Gucci, Miu Miu and Valentino. It has been the backdrop for such movies as *Galaxy Quest* (1999) and *Nurse Betty* (2000).

Storer House ⑤④

Frank Lloyd Wright, architect (1923).
8161 Hollywood Blvd.
Private residence. **NRHP**

Built in 1923 for a retired surgeon from the Midwest, this was the second in the series of Frank Lloyd Wright's concrete block houses in Los Angeles. The relatively small, five-bedroom house fits perfectly into the steep, terraced hillside. With colonnaded façade, floor-to-ceiling windows and vertically extended walls, Wright made the house look larger than it really is. After it was bought in 1984 by movie producer and Wright devotee Joel Silver (*Lethal Weapon, Die Hard* and the *Matrix* series), the house was completely restored with the help of architect Eric Wright, Frank Lloyd Wright's grandson.

Orson Welles Home ⑤⑤

8545 Franklin Ave.
Private residence.

This home was long owned by the celebrated director, producer, screenwriter and actor. Welles is best remembered for his masterpiece *Citizen Kane* (1941), for which he won an Oscar for best original screenplay.

Façade of Case Study House No. 22, seldom shown in photographs

Ricardo Montalbán Home was inspired by colonial haciendas

Liberace Estate ⑤⑥

8433 Harold Way.
Private residence.

This seven-bedroom Spanish Mission Revival estate was the home of one of the most popular concert entertainers of the 20th century. Famous for his extravagant performances, Liberace set still unsurpassed attendance records. The late showman, who died of AIDS in 1987, lived here from the early 1960s until the early 1980s.

Lenny Bruce Death Site ⑤⑦

8825 Hollywood Blvd.
Private residence. Ⓤ

A standup comedian who was repeatedly arrested for narcotics violations and lewd speech, died in his hilltop house above Sunset Strip on August 3, 1966 of an accidental overdose of heroin. When he was found on a toilet in his bathroom, he still had a hypodermic needle in his right arm.

Ricardo Montalbán Home ⑤⑧

Ricardo Legorreta, architect (1985).
1423 Oriole Dr.
Private residence.

This house was the first commission outside his home country for the famous Mexican architect, Ricardo Legorreta, and was designed for another Mexican native, actor Ricardo Montalbán.

Following the client's request for a modern interpretation of Mexican architectural heritage, Legorreta designed this residence as a contemporary version of the colonial hacienda. With its massive walls in earth colors, the windowless entrance façade resembles an ancient monument and provides privacy for a public figure.

Street sign

Blue Jay Way ⑤⑨

One of the glamorous "bird streets" in the Hollywood Hills, Blue Jay Way was immortalized by George Harrison, who rented a house here in 1968. One night, as the story goes, he was expecting a publicist who lost his way in the narrow roads winding up the hill. While waiting, George wrote the song *Blue Jay Way*, which appeared on the Beatles' album *Magical Mystery Tour*. The street sign was reportedly stolen by souvenir hunters so many times that it now bears the warning: "Property of the City of Los Angeles."

Case Study House No. 21 ⑥⓪

Pierre Koenig, architect (1958)
9038 Wonderland Park Ave.
Not on map. Private residence.

This exquisite but simple steel-and-glass building consists of a series of prefabricated steel frames which were assembled on the site. The architect's idea was to develop a prototype for the affordable house as the ideal machine for modern living, adapted for mass production from basic industrial materials. "I was trying to develop 1,300 square feet in an efficient, social, and exciting plan that people could afford"—Koenig remarked.

He uses natural ventilation to cool the interior of the houses he designed. Constructed according to a complex design technique, his buildings do not need air conditioning despite all glass walls.

To soften the boxlike design and make a smooth transition between the interior and exterior, Koenig surrounded the structure with a series of reflecting pools.

The architect restored the house in 1998.

Pierre Koenig's Case Study House No. 21

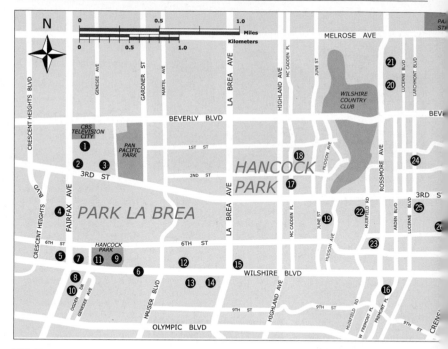

Midtown

Encompassing many distinct neighborhoods, the precinct between downtown and Beverly Hills is one of the ethnically, socially and architecturally most diverse areas in the city.

The area's main thoroughfare, Wilshire Blvd, was named after eccentric local entrepreneur, millionaire and Marxist, Henry Gaylord Wilshire. It was just a dusty country road running across the open bean fields when he decided to develop it in the 1880s. Reaching westward 16 miles (26 km) from downtown to the sea, the corridor (especially its stretch between downtown and Fairfax Ave) is a showcase of architectural treasures from the 1920s and 1930s. Home to the city's most opulent shops and department stores, Wilshire Blvd was for several decades Los Angeles' major commercial center.

Miracle Mile neon sign

Not yet touched by commercial development, the intersection of Wilshire Blvd and Fairfax Ave was the site of two airfields in 1920. Pictured here is an air show held at the airport maintained by Charlie Chaplin's brother Syd. Right across from it was another field, operated by famous director and aviator Cecil B

Aerial view of the airfield during air show in 1920

DeMille. In the first decade of the 20th century the area was dotted by oil derricks (visible in the background), but the fields soon dried up. It is often said that Wilshire Blvd was the world's first shopping street conceived with the automobile in mind. The boulevard also pioneered synchronized traffic lights, parking time limits and Christmas street decorations.

Although the drive-in phenomenon did not originate in Los Angeles, it was here this roadside establishment was perfected. The first Simon's

Simon's drive-in was designed with an automobile in mind

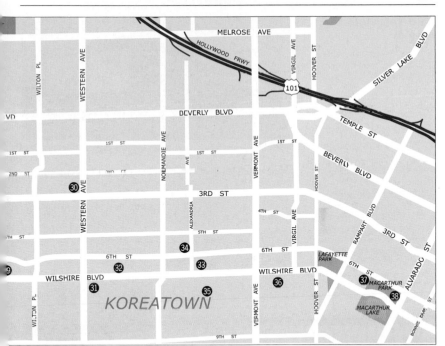

La Brea Tar Pits

drive-in (now demolished) was designed by Wayne McAllister in 1935, on the northwest corner of Wilshire Blvd and Fairfax Ave. In this completely automobile-oriented design, the circular plan enabled cars to park at an equal distance from the kitchen, easily accessible to the carhops.

Designed in the Spanish Baroque style, with its signature multicolor circular dome, rooftop neon sign and marquee, the Carthay Circle Theatre once stood at Carillo Dr and San Vicente Blvd. The legendary movie palace opened in 1926 with the world premiere of Cecil B DeMille's *The Volga Boatman*. It also hosted the world premiere of Disney's *Snow White and the Seven Dwarfs* (1937), with Marlene Dietrich, Charles Laughton and Judy Garland in attendance, as well as the Hollywood premiere of *Gone With the Wind* (1939). The landmark theater, which was one of Hollywood's most famous venues for more than 40 years, was demolished in 1969 for an office complex.

The La Brea Tar Pits in Hancock Park is one of the world's richest Ice Age fossil sites. The tar (*brea* means tar in Spanish) is actually asphalt in which unwary prehistoric animals, many of them extinct species, were trapped. The fossils were preserved by asphalt impregnation over thousands of years, making them possibly the most perfect in the world. Excavated fossils are on display at the George C Page Museum. Local Indians used tar from these pits for centuries to caulk and waterproof their homes.

A vintage post card depicts premiere at the Carthay Circle Theatre

CBS Television City ❶

Pereira and Luckman, architects
(1952); addition Gin Wong Associates (1976).
7800 Beverly Blvd.
☎(323) 852-2624. ☞
www.cbs.com. Closed to the public.
For free tickets for a sitcom or game
show taping call (323) 575-2345
or stop by a ticket window, Mon-Fri
9am-5pm. Tours are not available.

CBS Television offers free trickets to shows currently being filmed

With its modern boxes that
contain offices and studios,
this 25-acre studio complex
was one of the first built
exclusively for television production. Among the famous
shows that originated here
were *All in the Family, The
Carol Burnett Show, Sonny
and Cher, Family Feud, Politically Incorrect, The Price is
Right*, and *Hollywood Square*.

Farmer's Market ❷

6333 W Third St.
☎(323) 933-9211.
www.farmersmarketla.com.
🕑Mon-Sat 9am-6:30pm; Sun
10am-5pm.

A long time favorite with
Angelenos and visitors alike,
the Farmer's Market was
established in 1934 as an
informal outdoor market-
place. During the Depression
era local farmers used to sell
fresh produce off their trucks
directly to the public. The
property has been owned by
the Gilmore family since
1880, and was the site of a
dairy farm, the city's first self-
service gas station, a baseball
field, a stadium featuring

midget car races and a drive-
in theater.

Today, the market has more
than 160 stands and stalls
offering a variety of fresh
produce, flowers, specialty
foods and gift items. The
many restaurants and cafés
offer an array of international
food. This is a great place for
a hearty meal. People-watching while having an open-air
breakfast under an umbrella
or awning is one of the quintessential LA experiences.
Celebrities also enjoy the
casual atmosphere, making
this one of the best spots for
stargazing in the city.

Farmer's Market fame made
"Meet Me at Third and Fairfax" a local catch phrase.

The Grove ❸

Adjacent to the Farmer's
Market and opened in March
2002, this glitzy, open-air
retail complex features high-
end stores and outdoor cafés
designed in a blend of architectural styles. Inspired by
the Bellagio's dancing waters
display in Las Vegas, the
Grove's huge fountain shoots

jets of water 70 feet (21 m)
in the air.

The atmosphere of a small-
town main street is enhanced
by a double-decker trolley
that uses clean inductive
power technology, the first
such use for transit in the
United States.

A trolley in the Grove

Silent Movie Theatre ❹

611 N Fairfax Ave.
☎(323) 655-2520. 🕭

When it was opened by
silent film collector John
Hampton in 1942, the theater
attracted a wide audience,
both fans of the classic films
and the stars who created
them (Charlie Chaplin was a
regular here during the
screenings of his early films).
The theater was restored and
reopened in 1999, two years
after its second owner was
shot and killed in the lobby
by a hired gunman. It now
screens classic films with
musical accompaniment.

Thomas Jane proposed to
Patricia Arquette here by having the message "Will you
marry me, Patricia?" inserted
into the storyboards at a
screening he had arranged.
(She said yes.)

Farmers Market at Fairfax and Third

Johnie's Coffee Shop Restaurant ❺

Louis Armet and Eldon Davis, architects (1955).
6101 Wilshire Blvd
🕐closed to the public. 🚩

Originally called Romeo's Times Square, this neighborhood diner was one of the few remaining classic examples of "Googie" or "coffee shop modern" architecture before it closed its doors in 2000. The locale has been used in a number of movie productions, including *Volcano* (1997), *Reservoir Dogs* (1992), *City of Angels* (1998), *American History X* (1999) and *Gone in 60 Seconds* (2000). With its vinyl booths and dark wood paneling, Johnie's was the setting for the scene where Lily Tomlin waitressed her husband Tom Waits in Robert Altman's *Short Cuts* (1993). In the thriller *Miracle Mile* (1989), musician Anthony Edwards learns of the imminent nuclear attack on Los Angeles when he picks up a ringing pay phone outside the restaurant. In *The Big Lebowski* (1998), a comedy about mistaken identity, Johnie's can be recognized in the scene in which John Goodman tells Jeff Bridges that he can get him a tow by 3pm.

Johnie's Coffee Shop has been the backdrop for numerous films

Miracle Mile ❻

When in the early 1920s visionary realtor A W Ross recognized the automobile would change the way people shop, he bought empty land along Wilshire Blvd with the idea of developing it into a shopping district. Everyone laughed at the time, calling his idea Ross's Folly, but by the end of the decade his concept became a surprising success, attracting many famous retailers who opened upscale stores here. Dubbed "Miracle Mile," the commercial strip between Fairfax and La Brea avenues tended to appeal to passing motorists rather than pedestrians. The buildings were designed with wide ground-floor windows to catch the attention of driving shoppers in an instant. Although the area has been in decline since the 1960s, losing its trade to shopping malls, it is still a showcase of Streamline Moderne and Art Deco buildings, many with their original façades.

The district was the setting for the apocalyptic black comedy of Los Angeles facing nuclear annihilation in *Miracle Mile* (1989),

Former May Company Store

May Company Department Store (formerly) ❼

Albert C Martin and Samuel Marx, architects (1940).
6767 Wilshire Blvd.
🕐➜ LACMA, p205.

Designed in the popular Streamline Moderne style of the 1940s, this was one of the grandest department stores in Los Angeles. The building's impressive gold mosaic corner tower, framed with a concave surface of black granite, served as a signpost visible to motorists from afar. Resembling a perfume bottle, the tower also marked an undistinguished street entrance. Like other department stores along the Mile, its main entrance was from the parking lot at the back of the building.

It was here that glamorous star Hedy Lamarr, famous for rejecting the Ingrid Bergman parts in *Gaslight* and *Casablanca*, was arrested in 1966 for allegedly shoplifting $86 in retail goods. She was later acquitted and unsuccessfully sued the store for $5 million in damages.

After May Company left the building, LACMA took it over in 1998 and, after spending three million dollars for renovation and adaptation, opened it as LACMA West. The annex now serves as the museum's venue for changing exhibitions.

Johnie's interior is featured in *Short Cuts* (1993) with Lily Tomlin and Tom Waits

LA Autotude exhibit at the Petersen Automotive Museum depicts bizarre and eccentric cars seen on the streets of Los Angeles

Petersen Automotive Museum ⑧

6060 Wilshire Blvd.
☎(323) 930-CARS.
🕐Tue-Sun 10am-6pm. Closed:
Thanksgiving, Christmas and New Year's Day. ⑤

Opened in 1994, this is the largest and most innovative automotive museum in the world. It is named after Robert E Petersen, whose company is a leading publisher of specialized magazines such as *Hot Rod* and *Motor Trend*.

The museum recounts the history of the automobile and its link to Los Angeles, the only major city in the world to be almost entirely shaped by the automobile. Through its multitheme exhibits, it traces the evolution of the car culture through the 20th century and its influence on the city, the country and the rest of the world. The museum also exhibits vintage cars

(there are more than 200 vehicles on display at any given time) as well as cars owned by celebrities and cars featured in movies and television.

Notorious B.I.G. Murder Site ⑨

It was here just outside the Petersen Museum that the Brooklyn rap star Notorious B.I.G. (born Christopher Wallace) was gunned down after leaving a Soul Train Awards party on March 9, 1997.

Six months after the rapper Tupac Shakur's death in Las Vegas, Wallace was killed by a drive-by shooter while he was waiting in his SUV at a red light. It was rumored that Wallace put a $1-million bounty on Shakur's head and supplied the gun used in his arch-rival's killing.

Although both the Shakur and Wallace murders remain unsolved, many believe Wallace was killed in retaliation for Shakur's death.

George C Page Museum ⑨

Willis Fagan and Frank Thornton, architects (1977).
5801 Wilshire Blvd.
☎(323) 857-6311.
🕐Tue-Sun 10am-5pm. Closed:
Thanksgiving, Christmas and New Year's Day. ⑤

Through its vivid exhibits, the museum illustrates life during the Ice Age, some 4,000 to 40,000 years ago. It houses over one million prehistoric specimens recovered from the asphalt deposits in the Rancho La Brea tar pits. Among the fossils on display are skeletons of many extinct species including the saber-toothed cat, Harlan's ground sloth, American lion, western horse and long-horned bison.

12-foot-tall skeleton of imperial mammoth at the Page Museum. It was the largest of the elephants that lived in North America during the Ice Age.

Buck House ⑩

Rudolf Schindler, architect (1934).
805 S Genesee Ave.
Private residence.

Influenced by the International Style, this beautiful house is considered one of Schindler's best works. Its private front elevation, with plain white stucco walls and narrow band of windows, only enhances the house's orientation to the rear, where it opens to the garden through large glass surfaces.

Buck House is one of Rudolf Schindler's best works

Los Angeles County Museum of Art (LACMA) ⑪

5905 Wilshire Blvd.
☎(323) 857-6000.
🕐Mon, Tue, Thu noon-8pm; Fri noon-9pm; Sat, Sun 11-8pm. Ⓢ; admission free to all on second Tue of every month. 🚶

Considered the largest encyclopedic art museum west of Chicago, LACMA was founded in 1910 and opened at this location in 1965. Its notable holdings of 250,000 works cover the entire range of the history of art.

The collections are organized into ten curatorial departments: the American Art Collection covers the early 18th through late 19th centuries); the Ancient and Islamic Art Collection contains examples of Egyptian, Near Eastern, Greek and Roman, Islamic and pre-Columbian art; the Textiles and Costumes Collection, one of the largest in the United States, is made up of antique and modern textiles and period costumes representing ancient Egypt, Persia, the Far East and Europe; the Decorative Arts Collection includes European and American pieces from medieval times to the present; the European Painting and Sculpture Collection ranges from the early 14th through the late 19th centuries; the Far Eastern Collections span 3,000 years

View of LACMA's Anderson Building

and comprise works from China, Korea, Japan and Central Asia; the Collection of Indian and Southeast Asian Art is considered the finest in the Western World; the Photographs Collection and the Prints and Drawings Collection include works by both European and American masters; the Collection of 20th-Century Art includes examples of every major movement in modern and contemporary art.

The museum occupies three buildings designed in 1964 by Pereira and Associates. The complex was enlarged by the addition of the Anderson Building in 1986 (designed by Hardy Holzman Pfeiffer) and the Japanese Pavilion in 1988 (Bruce Goff and Bart Prince). The former May Company Store is now used as the museum's venue for changing exhibitions. Plans are underway for expansion, which will include the Broad Art Museum, a new building to house LACMA's contemporary art collection, designed by Pritzker Prize-winning architect Renzo Piano.

The Ahmanson Building features objects from a wide range of cultures as well as the permanent collection of paintings, sculpture, graphic arts, costumes, textiles and decorative arts. The Hammer Building contains the print, drawing and photography collections. The Robert O Anderson Building houses 20th-century paintings and sculpture, along with special loan exhibitions.

LACMA's Japanese Pavilion. Its interior space is a marvel with winding ramps and diffused lighting from fiberglass wall panels.

Los Angeles County Museum of Art (LACMA)

Altar Frontal for the Cathedral of St John the Baptist (ca. 1600)

Studies of the Virgin, Drapery and the Hand of Saint John the Baptist Holding a Shell (ca. 1628) by Tanzio da Varallo

Young Woman of the People (1918) by Amedeo Modigliani

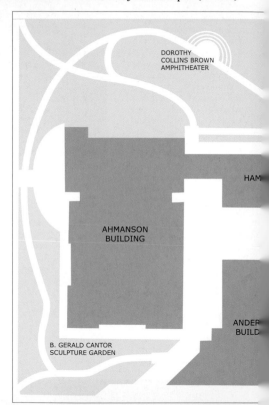

DOROTHY COLLINS BROWN AMPHITHEATER

HAM

AHMANSON BUILDING

ANDER BUILD

B. GERALD CANTOR SCULPTURE GARDEN

South Wind, Clear Dawn (1831) by Hokusai

Soap Bubbles (1739) by Jean-Baptiste Chardin

Tile (15th c), Greater Iran

Ibis (712-332 BC), Egypt

Pepper No. 4 (1930) by
Edward Weston

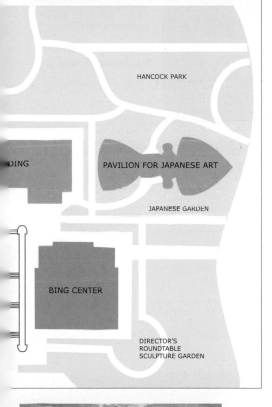

Flower Day (1925) by Diego
Rivera

Bouquet of Flowers in an Urn
(1724) by Jan Van Huysum

The Swineherd (1888) by Paul Gauguin   *The Cotton Pickers* (1876) by Winslow Homer

El Rey Theater

El Rey Theater ⑫

Clifford Balch, architect (1936).
5519 Wilshire.
☎(323) 936-4790. ⑤

With its smooth stucco
façade featuring inset panels
of floral and geometric ornaments, the El Rey Theater is
a superb example of the Art
Deco style. Opened in 1936
as a movie house, the small
building retains such original
details as a neon marquee
and signage, a remarkable
box office and terrazzo flooring. This is the place where
Bob Dylan and Blondie
launched their comebacks.
Once a thriving venue for
rock concerts, today it is an
active nightclub.

Desmond's ⑬

Gilbert Stanley Underwood, architect (1928).
5514 Wilshire Blvd.

This was the first significant
structure to be built on
Wilshire Blvd, in what was
then vast farmland. The
building was anchored by
Desmond's, a popular men's
clothing store, whose owner
was persuaded by developer
A W Ross to open a branch
here. Its name is still embedded in the façade and around
the top of the tower. The
store helped establish the
Miracle Mile shopping district, with some of the most
remarkable examples of Art
Deco architecture in LA.
  The Desmond's was built in
the Streamline Moderne style,
with an eight-story office

tower rising from a two-story
commercial base. It features
such popular elements of the
style as streamlined, rounded
corners, marquees and flamboyant ornamentation. The
terazzo flooring extends from
the entryway on to the sidewalk. The building pioneered
the back entranceway from
the parking lot to accommodate customers who arrived
by automobile.

The Darkroom

The Darkroom ⑭

Marcus Miller, architect (1938).
5370 Wilshire Blvd.

To advertise cameras and
photographic supplies
offered within the store, the
owner built this unusual programmatic storefront
designed in the Streamline
Moderne style. The building's
façade is a giant Argus 35mm
camera made of black vitro-
lite, a material invented in
the 1930s. The tenants have
changed in the meantime,
but the display window still
advertises whatever is going
on behind the glass.

**Former Desmond's Depart-
ment Store Building**

Security First
National Bank ⑮

Morgan, Walls and Clements,
architects (1929).
5209 Wilshire Blvd.

Sheathed in glazed black-
and-gold terra-cotta tiles, this
one-story gem is a miniature
version of the downtown
Richfield Building, a famous
landmark designed by the
same architectural firm, which
was demolished in 1968.

Fremont Place ⑯

Hidden behind the pair of
imposing entrance gates off
Wishire Blvd, Fremont Place
is one of Los Angeles' most
exclusive private streets. At
one time or another within
this enclave lived Mary Pickford (at 56 Fremont Pl), Cliff
Robertson (97), Muhammad
Ali (55) and Angela Bassett
(69).

Former Security First National Bank of Los Angeles Building

Hancock Park ⓱

Once part of old Rancho La Brea, this area was purchased in 1860 by Henry Hancock, who discovered oil here and tapped it for 30 years before his son subdivided the property in 1919.

Developed as an exclusive suburb, this elegant neighborhood have changed little over the years. Its opulent mansions were home to some of the most prominent families in Los Angeles, including Doheny, Banning and Huntington. Built on large lots in a variety of historic revival styles with lavish landscaping, these houses still retain their original charm.

El Royale Apartments

What Ever Happened to Baby Jane? (1962) was filmed here

What Ever Happened to Baby Jane? House ⓲

172 S McCadden Pl.
Private residence. 🏴

This decaying mansion was used in exterior scenes in the 1962 movie about sibling rivalry and the bitterness of broken Hollywood dreams.

Bette Davis plays an aging vaudeville star Jane who tortures her crippled sister and former matinee idol Blanche (played by Joan Crawford), confined to a wheelchair after a bizarre accident.

Francis Ford Coppola Home ⓳

340 N June St.
Private residence.

This magnificent two-story Tudor was once home to Lindsey Buckingham, singer/guitarist of the famed rock band Fleetwood Mac. After he joined them in 1974, the group released several No. 1 hits, including *Rumors*

(1977), at the time the best-selling album in rock history.

This was also the home of celebrated director Francis Ford Coppola, who won Academy Awards as co-writer for *Patton* (1970) and *The Godfather* (1972). In 1974 he won three Academy Awards (as producer, director and co author of the screenplay) for *The Godfather Part II*.

El Royale Apartments ⓴

William Douglas Lee, architect (1929).
450 N Rossmore Ave.
Private residences. 🏴

Dominating the Hancock Park vicinity, this 12-story structure designed in the Spanish Renaissance Revival style was called home over the years by a number of celebrities. Harry Cohn, founder and former president of Columbia Pictures lived here, as well as actors George Raft, Loretta Young and Clark Gable.

The building was used in several film and television productions, including the comedy *Switch* (1991) and *Other People's Money* (1991), as the location of Penelope Ann Miller's apartment.

Francis Ford Coppola Home

Ravenswood Apartments ㉑

570 N Rossmore Ave.
Private residences.

This seven-story 1928 Art Deco Moderne apartment building was for 48 years the home of Mae West, at one point the highest-paid woman in America and one of the cinema's greatest sex goddesses. A successful vaudeville performer who introduced the shimmy on stage, West was noted for her guilt-free attitude to sex, and was once jailed for obscenity. Her popularity reached such proportions that sailors and pilots named their inflatable life vests after her. She was famous for her wit and lines such as "Why don't you come up sometime and see me" passed into common usage. The star of sensational hits *Night After Night* (1932), *She Done Him Wrong* (1933) and *Everyday's a Holiday* (1938) lived in the same penthouse from 1932, when she came to Hollywood, until her death in 1980. Among the building's other famous tenants were Judy Garland, Clark Gable and Ava Gardner.

Ravenswood Apartments

Mae West lived at Ravenswood Apartments for 48 years

Mae West's luxuriant apartment No. 611 had her signature white-on-white décor, featuring white French furniture with an occasional gold accent and a lot of mirrors. Concerned about her looks, the star kept her windows shut and her blinds drawn, fearing that direct sunlight and fresh air might damage her alabaster skin.

Nat "King" Cole Home ㉒

401 S Muirfield Rd.
Private residence.

This elegant Tudor mansion was the home of the famous black pianist and singer while he was at the peak of his career. Noted for his warm, relaxed singing, Cole recorded over 700 songs for Capitol Records, including such top hits as *Route 66*, *Mona Lisa* and *Unforgettable*.

Cole and his wife were the first black residents to live in the exclusive white neighborhood of Hancock Park in the 1950s. Enraged nearby home owners harassed them for years, threw racial epithets and poisoned a family dog. When angered residents petitioned against "undesirables," he coolly responded that if he saw any, he would let them know. Cole was the first black performer with his own network variety series.

Harry M Warner House ㉓

A Burnside Sturges, architect (1923).
501 S Rossmore Ave.
Private residence.

This authentic "Old Hollywood" residence was built in 1923, the same year Warner Bros, one of the leading Hollywood film studios, was incorporated. It was the first home of Harry Warner, the company's president and one of the four Warner brothers who founded the studio.

Nat "King" Cole Home

Larchmont Village

Situated on a stretch of Larchmont Blvd between First St and Beverly Blvd, this is a neighborhood shopping district with small-town charm. Established in the 1920s, with many period buildings still standing, Larchmont Blvd was once a busy thoroughfare with a streetcar line. Today, it is a true pleasure to stroll past a variety of stores, antique shops and outdoor cafés and restaurants in its unhurried atmosphere.

John Malkovich Home

346 S Lucerne Blvd.
Private residence.

Between 1991 and 2001 this was the home of famous screen and stage actor John Malkovich, star of such hits as *The Killing Fields* (1984), *Empire of the Sun* (1987) and *Dangerous Liaisons* (1988). He was twice nominated for an Academy Award for best supporting actor—for his role as a blind man in *Places in the Heart* (1984) and for playing the assassin in *In the Line of Fire* (1993).

John Malkovich Home

Los Tiempos/ Chandler House

J Martyn Haenke and W J Dodd, architects (1913).
455 S Lorraine Blvd.
Private residence.

With its classical columns, wide stone steps and impressive black iron gate, this stately Beaux-Arts mansion is one of the city's landmarks.

Getty House is the residence of the Mayor of Los Angeles

Known as Los Tiempos (the Times in Spanish), the historic residence was designed by partners of architect Julia Morgan, the designer of Hearst Castle in San Simeon. The house was built in the heart of Hancock Park's Windsor Square by Dr Peter Janss, well-known land baron of the real estate family that developed Westwood Village and Holmby Hills.

Since the mid-1950s, it had been home of Norman Chandler, publisher of the *Los Angeles Times*, and his wife, Dorothy, who led the fund rising drive to build the Music Center in downtown. She lived here until her death in 1997 (he died in 1973).

Over the years the grand estate was scene of many cultural and historic events, hosting numerous notables, including Presidents Eisenhower, Kennedy, Johnson and Nixon. Its unique treasure is the paneled music room, originally built as a rehearsal space for Mozart and imported by Chandlers from a castle near Munich.

Getty House

605 S Irving Blvd.
☎(323) 930-6430.
www.gettyhouse.org. ☛occasional free tours; call for reservations.

Built in 1920, this mock English Tudor house has been the official residence of the Mayor of Los Angeles since 1975. Among the house's famous tenants were actress Dolores Costello, who lived here in the 1930s after her separation from movie star John Barrymore, and Lee Strassberg, artistic director of the Actor's Studio and head of the Lee Strassberg Institute of the Theater, who resided here in the 1970s.

The property of Getty Oil since the 1940s, the house was offered to the city in November 1975 in memory of George F Getty, the eldest son of J Paul Getty—hence its name. The first mayor to reside in the house was Tom Bradley, who lived here from 1977 until 1993. Today, the house is used for official city functions and various community programs.

Los Tiempos/Chandler House

Sunset Boulevard Mansion (site) ㉘

4201 Wilshire Blvd. 🎥

Los Altos Apartments

"I had landed myself in the driveway of some big mansion that looked rundown and deserted," narrates hapless screenwriter Joe Gillis (played by William Holden), whose dead body floats in the swimming pool behind the imposing structure.

The site of the palatial residence where Gillis was killed and where silent movie star Norma Desmond (played by Gloria Swanson) lived in the movie *Sunset Boulevard* (1950) was at the northwest corner of Wilshire and Irving boulevards. The house was built in 1924 for William Jenkins, a United States consul in Mexico, and later was purchased by oilman J Paul Getty, whose wife conducted a school for acting in the 25-room mansion. The mansion was demolished in 1957 and replaced with a high-rise.

The two-story Italianate house lacked the swimming pool needed for the opening scene, so Paramount built a fake one, without any plumbing.

The mansion was the setting for scenes in both *Sunset Boulevard* (above) and *Rebel Without a Cause* (below)

The driveway scene at the beginning of the movie was filmed at the entrance to the first home of Vincente Minnelli and Judy Garland in Brentwood.

The mansion was later used in another Hollywood classic, *Rebel Without a Cause* (1955), where it appeared as the deserted house where James Dean, Natalie Wood and Sal Mineo retreated. Near the end of the movie, they mocked their parents by the same pool constructed for *Sunset Boulevard*. The scenes with Sal Mineo fighting the intruders at the bottom of the empty pool were also filmed here.

Los Altos Apartments ㉙

Edward B Rust, architect (1925).
4121 Wilshire Blvd.
Private residences. **NRHP**

Built in the Spanish Colonial Revival style with Italian-influenced ornamentation, the Los Altos was one of the first co-op houses on the West Coast. It was once a prestigious address, with a tennis court behind the building, its own beauty parlor and a high-ceiling lobby that hosted glamorous balls.

In its heyday it was home to such Hollywood celebrities as silent-screen sex symbol Clara Bow, Douglas Fairbanks Jr and Ava Gardner.

Newspaper magnate William Randolph Hearst bought a two-story apartment here for his mistress, actress Marion Davies. Their ten-room unit boasted a marble entrance, a screening room, vaulted ceilings and wood paneling and gold leafing throughout.

Dilapidated and abandoned in the early 1990s, the building was painstakingly restored to its former glory and re-opened in 1999.

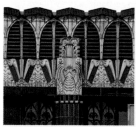

The elaborate ornament in gold glazed tile is strikingly contrasted to a shiny black background of the Selig Store

Selig Retail Store ㉚
(formerly **Crocker Bank**)

Arthur E Harvey, architect (1931).
273 S Western Ave.

Though only one story high, this is one of the best examples in Los Angeles of an Art Deco building sheathed in glazed terra-cotta tiles. Originally built for a posh clothier/couturier, the building was later used as a bank and now houses retail stores.

Wiltern Theatre ③

Originally known as the Pellissier Building, this landmark Zigzag Moderne complex consists of an office tower, two-story flanking wings intended for retail space, and a theater. It was built by real estate developer Henry de Roulet on the land owned by his grandfather, Germain Pellissier, which was used to raise Merino sheep in the early 1880s. In 1929 that parcel of land comprised the southeast corner of Wilshire Blvd and Western Ave, described at the time as the busiest intersection in the world. The Wiltern was on the verge of destruction in 1979, but was rescued at the last moment by developer Wayne Ratkovich, whose real estate company bought the complex and completely restored it in 1985. Another revamping came in 2002, when the floor seating was removed to allow a live concert audience to move freely.

Designed by famed architect Stiles O Clements, whose works included the now-demolished Richfield Building and the Samson Tire Company, the building reached the city-imposed 150-foot height limit. Clad in signature blue-green terra-cotta tile, the stately corner tower looks taller than its actual twelve stories, due to the bands of narrow, recessed windows that lead the eye upward.

The theater's grand opening, complete with klieg lights and a brass band, took place on October 7, 1931, with the premiere of the movie *Alexander Hamilton*, starring George Arliss. Thousands watched as celebrities arrived across a specially constructed wooden "Bridge of Stars" that spanned Wilshire Blvd. Called Warner Bros Western Theatre, it was the most glamorous venue in the Warner Bros' theater chain.

The ornate interior of the theater was the work of G Albert Lansburgh, who also designed the Warner Bros Theater in Hollywood and the Orpheum downtown. It has been restored to its former splendor and features murals, elaborate tile work, decorative plaster reliefs, metallic leaf designs and original light fixtures. Originally a 2,300-seat movie house, the theater today serves as a performing arts center.

Façade of the Wiltern Theatre

Morgan, Walls and Clements, architects (1931).
3790 Wilshire Blvd.
☎(323) 380-5005.
www.thewiltern.com. ⚑ NRHP

The lobby rotunda with original chandelier and Anthony B Heinsbergen mural in the dome. The restoration of the murals was supervised by Anthony T Heinsbergen, the late designer's son.

The renovated starburst ceiling decoration and the original fire-curtain from 1931 adorn the Wiltern's auditorium

The Wiltern's exterior foyer ceiling features cast plaster ornaments

Façade of Wilshire Boulevard Temple

The temple's opulent interior

Wilshire Boulevard Temple ③②

A M Edelman, S Tilden Norton and David C Allison, architects (1928).
3663 Wilshire Blvd.
☎(213) 388-2401. NRHP

This stately, Byzantine-inspired synagogue was built in 1929 for the oldest and largest Jewish congregation of Los Angeles (founded as Congregation B'nai Brith in 1862). The temple's imposing dome is 100 feet (30 m) in diameter and raises to the height of 125 feet (38 m).

The opulent sanctuary features a coffered ceiling, Byzantine columns, Italian marble, rare woods, and lustrous mosaics and stained glass windows.

The temple's interior is adorned with famed murals by Hugo Ballin, depicting episodes from 3,000 years of Jewish history.

The Brown Derby (site) ③③

3377 Wilshire Blvd. ☛

This internationally renowned tourist attraction was opened in 1926 by Herbert Somborn, the second of actress Gloria Swanson's six husbands. Designed in the unlikely shape of a hat, it was created on a bet with a friend, who challenged Somborn saying, "If you know anything about food, you can sell it out of a hat." It soon became part of a famous restaurant chain, although only the original was built in the shape of a hat (the other three eateries bearing the same name were in Los Feliz, Beverly Hills and Hollywood).

The famous Cobb salad was invented here when manager Bob Cobb prepared himself a quick dinner of chopped leftover chicken and fresh vegetables.

The landmark restaurant closed in 1980 and was

saved from demolition by a group of preservationists. Today, the remodeled dome is incorporated into a small shopping mall.

While working at the Brown Derby, Constance Bennett was "discovered" in *What Price Hollywood?* (1932).

Chapman Park Market ③④

Morgan, Walls and Clements, architects (1929); restored by Levin & Associates (1988).
3465 W Sixth St.

This Spanish Colonial Revival structure, with rich Churrigueresque decorations and plaster, cast stone and wrought iron details, is a remarkable example of the early "drive-in" market (➜ p55). Occupying the entire city block, the Chapman shopping center consists of retail stores grouped around an auto courtyard to offer the convenience of one-stop shopping.

The Brown Derby served as a location for many films, including the quintessential Los Angeles movie, *Chinatown* (1974). This is the restaurant where private eye Jake Gittes (Jack Nicholson) and Evelyn Mulwray (Faye Dunaway) have lunch after the murder of her husband, city official Hollis Mulwray.

A vintage post card depicts the original Brown Derby

Ambassador Hotel (site) ㉟

Myron Hunt, architect (1921).
3400 Wilshire Blvd.

Designed by famous architect Myron Hunt, who also built the Rose Bowl and Huntington Art Gallery, the Ambassador was Los Angeles' first grand resort hotel. The six-story, 500-room Mediterranean structure had a flared H-shape and was painted in its signature, salmon-colored shade. The 23.5-acre (9,4 ha) landscaped grounds contained lawns, fountains, tennis courts, putting green and a swimming pool with a sandy beach. Opened with great pomp on New Year's Day in 1921, the hotel immediately became a magnet for international luminaries, Hollywood celebrities and star-gazers.

After its closure in 1989, the hotel was involved in a 11-year-long legal battle over ownership between the investment group once led by Donald Trump and the Los Angeles Unified School District. The LAUSD eventually took control of the 24-acre property and, despite the objections of local preservation groups, razed the building in 2005 to replace it with a multi-school campus.

Entrance to the Ambassador Hotel. The landmark building was demolished in 2005 to make room for a school.

Among the hotel's star guests and long-time residents were Rudolph Valentino, Gloria Swanson, Al Jolson, Jean Harlow, Howard Hughes, Omar Sharif, John Wayne and Elizabeth Taylor. It was here that Pola Negri walked her pet cheetah on a leash; John Barrymore lived with a monkey in his bungalow; F Scott and Zelda Fitzgerald set their room ablaze and escaped without paying their bill; heavyweight boxing champion Jack Dempsey threw his wife out of the window. During a costume party in the 1920s, actress Marion Davies rode a horse through the hotel's lobby and into the nightclub. A favorite with politicians, the hotel hosted every American president from Hoover to Nixon. When Soviet Premier Nikita Khrushchev stayed here in 1959, Mickey Mouse came all the way from Disneyland to visit him.

Senator Robert F Kennedy was shot and killed in the hotel pantry on June 5, 1968, shortly after he announced his victory in the California presidential primary. Although assassin Sirhan Sirhan, a Palestinian immigrant, was arrested at the scene, theories still circulate that Sirhan did not act alone and that a second gun was fired from a close distance.

During the trial of Charles Manson and his followers in 1969-70, the jury was sequestered at the Ambasador for nine months.

Shirley Temple and James Stewart at the fabled Cocoanut Grove. It was billed as the nightclub "where stars of the motion picture and theatrical world mingle with Southern California's smart set nightly."

A vintage post card depicts the 500-room Ambassador Hotel

Scenes in *Catch Me If You Can* (2002) with Jennifer Garner, playing high-class hooker Cheryl Ann, and Leonardo DiCaprio as con artist Frank W Abagnale, who pays for her entire-night services with a fake check, were shot at the Ambassador

The third Academy Awards ceremony was held in the Fiesta Room of the Ambassador Hotel on November 5, 1930 (above).

The Academy of Motion Picture Arts and Sciences was officially founded on January 11, 1927 at the Ambassador Hotel, during a dinner attended by 36 leaders of the film industry (→ p461).

The Academy Awards presentations were held at the hotel six times between 1930 and 1943. Among the stars who received their Oscars during the banquets held at the Ambassador were Mary Pickford, Norma Shearer and Vivien Leigh.

The Cocoanut Grove was the most glamorous night-club in Los Angeles. Called "the Playground of the Stars," it quickly achieved legendary status amongst the glitzy nightspots of Hollywood. According to legend, it was decorated with life-size papier-mâché palm trees—props bought from the production of Rudolph Valentino's hit film *The Sheik* (1921). For several decades, virtually every Hollywood celebrity was a regular at the Grove.

All the big bands played here. Bing Crosby and Merv Griffin started their careers at the Grove; Frank Sinatra and Sammy Davis Jr performed regularly and Barbra Streisand made her West Coast debut at the nightclub. Stars such as Joan Crawford, Loretta Young and Barbara Stanwyck were discovered while dancing at the Grove.

The fabled hangout was only a shadow of its former glory when it closed its doors in 1988, but it is hard to believe that any other nightspot will ever take its place in the social life of Los Angeles.

Over the years the hotel served as a location for numerous movie and television productions, including *Murder, She Wrote* and *Beverly Hills 90210*, as well as *Pretty Woman* (1989), *L.A. Story* (1991), *True Lies* (1994), *The Mask* (1994), *Forrest Gump* (1994) and *Blow* (2001). For the nightclub scenes in *The Aviator* (2004), the Cocoanut Grove was recreated on a soundstage in Montreal. *Bobby* (2006) was filmed in the hotel's hallway corridors and coffee shop shortly before its demolition.

Greer Garson, who won the best actress Oscar for her role in *Mrs. Miniver* (1942), gave the longest acceptance speech in the Academy's history, thanking everyone who had ever helped her. At the banquet held at the Cocoanut Grove on March 4, 1943, her address reportedly lasted nearly an hour, or so it looked to the impatient guests, causing Academy officials to put a time limit on all acceptance speeches thereafter.

A vintage post card depicts the Ambassador's Cocoanut Grove

Bullocks Wilshire (formerly) ㊱

The most remarkable monument of the Art Deco era in Los Angeles, Bullocks Wilshire was influenced by new ideas that the Parkinson architects (father and son) brought from the 1925 Paris Exposition. The building's centerpiece is a 241-foot (73-m) tower, with its 50-foot (15-m) top intended as a giant advertising sign and built entirely of metal. The whole structure is sheathed in light tan terra-cotta and trimmed with dark copper panels.

Bullocks Wilshire was totally dedicated to its customer's satisfaction and with such impeccable service it quickly became the shopping destination of choice for the city's fashionable elite. On the second-floor salons, live models, called "mannequins," exhibited for patrons creations of the world's most famous designers.

The store was frequented by many Hollywood stars, including Greta Garbo, who bought her signature suits in the men's boutique, and Marlene Dietrich, who made it her only emporium and kept it open late until she finished her shopping. Mae West never set foot in the store. She preferred to sit in her car while salesclerks brought the merchandise from the store to her black limo parked on Wilshire Blvd. Wearing a trenchcoat, Garbo once entered the fitting room to try a swimsuit. When she removed the coat, the stunned clerk realized that she was not wearing anything else!

Among the celebrities who worked at the store as young sales clerks were former First Lady Pat Nixon and actress Angela Lansbury.

The landmark building was used as a location in numerous films, including *Topper* (1937), *Sunset Boulevard* (1950) and *Bugsy* (1991). Alfred Hitchcock used the grand foyer and the lingerie department as backdrops in his last movie, *Family Plot* (1976).

Due to sagging sales and the rapidly declining neighborhood, the store closed in 1993. The building was later bought by Southwestern University School of Law, and underwent an extensive and award-winning restoration and adaptation for contemporary use as a law library.

View of Bullocks Wilshire

John and Donald Parkinson, architects (1928).
3050 Wilshire Blvd.
☎(213) 738-6825.
Southwestern University School of Law 🚇 ➡ NRHP
Closed to the public. 🚶occasional tours or by appointment only

View of the Cactus Lounge and the fifth-floor elevator lobby

An elaborate light fixture. Built in 1929, the legendary Bullocks was considered the ultimate in style and elegance. It was the first department store built in the suburbs and the first that catered to the automobile (➔ p54).

High-domed Central Hall with walls of taupe-colored stone cut from St Genevieve marble, accentuated by ribbed glass and metal light fittings. This was formerly the magnificent Perfume Hall, once called by admiring critic "a great marble basilica."

Park Plaza Hotel
(formerly **Elks Club**) ㊲

Curlett and Beelman, architects
(1927).
607 S Park View St.
☎(213) 384-5281.
www.parkplazaevents.com

With its monumental façade of stuccoed concrete, this imposing 12-story structure was built for the Elks Club Lodge and served as a meeting place for the Club's members and guests, including Bing Crosby, Jack Dempsey and Eleanor Roosevelt. After a recent renovation it has become a boutique-style hotel. Though essentially Romanesque, the structure shows the influence of Bertram Goodhue's Central Library. Especially noteworthy is the three-story bronze arched entry flanked by Corinthian columns.

The building's most impressive feature are large sculptured figures that rise up from the tower and upper corners of each of the wings.

The impressive façade of the Park Plaza Hotel

Elk Club's matchbox

Decorated by the famous interior designer Anthony B Heinsbergen, the impressive 50-foot-high (15-m), marble-floored lobby features a massive stairway, a wooden barrel-vaulted, hand-painted ceiling and huge chandeliers.

The lobby and the grand ballroom were used as a set for numerous movie and TV productions, including *New York New York* (1977), *Bugsy* (1991), *Hook* (1991), *Chaplin* (1992), *What's Love Got to Do With It* (1993); and *Nixon* (1995). The building's exterior can also be seen in *The Body Guard* (1992). In the brutal opening scenes of *Wild At Heart* (1990), Nicolas Cage and Laura Dern are ambushed on the hotel's lobby staircase.

MacArthur Park ㊳

Wilshire Blvd, between Alvarado and Park View streets.

This area was originally developed in the 1880s, when the city cleaned up the swamp, planted rare trees and shrubs, and created an artificial lake by filling a ravine with water. The Westlake Park, as it was known, looked more like a Victorian garden, and became a favorite leisure spot for suburban families living nearby.

It was a fashionable area at the time, and some of its single-family houses are still standing today, providing a rare glimpse of the middle-class neighborhood of the 1890s and early 1900s.

The park was renamed after World War II for General Douglas MacArthur. After a long decline, the area is now a center of immigration, mostly from Central America, and plagued by crime.

In 1968 Richard Harris immortalized the neighborhood with Jimmy Webb's hit song *MacArthur Park*, where "someone left the cake out in the rain." In 1970, Donna Summer hit the charts with her disco version of the same song.

View of Westlake Park before Wilshire Blvd traversed the area

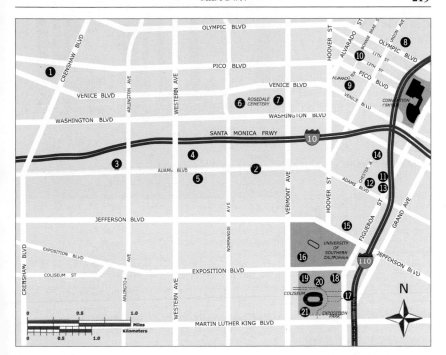

Paul Williams Home ❶

Paul Williams, architect (1952).
1690 S. Victoria Ave.
Private residence.

Designed by noted architect Paul Williams for his own family, this International Moderne house features cantilevered balconies, flat roofs and semicircular bay.

West Adams Blvd ❷

☛for architecture guided tour, call West Adams Heritage Association at ☎(323) 732-2774.

In the early 1900s West Adams Blvd was one of Los Angeles' most fashionable residential areas. Its posh neighborhoods such as West Adams Heights, Berkeley Square and Chester Place featured elegant Tudor, Victorian and Craftsman mansions. Some of these precincts did not survive, ultimately giving way to the construction of the Santa Monica Freeway.

West Adams was also the first residential area sought by the newly rich of Hollywood. Actors Theda Bara,

"Fatty" Arbuckle, Leo Carrillo and director Busby Berkeley were among the celebrities who lived here. After World War II, West Adams played a significant role in the fight for integrated housing.

Fitzgerald House ❸

Joseph Cather Newsom, architect (1903).
3115 W Adams Blvd.
Private residence.

Designated Italian Gothic, one of the most imaginative designs in the neighborhood features an elaborate brick chimney pierced with an arched window.

Hattie McDaniel Home ❹

2203 S Harvard Blvd.
Private residence.

Hattie McDaniel was the first African American nominated for an Academy Award. She was also the first to win, receiving an Oscar as best supporting actress for her portrayal of the black servant Mammy in *Gone With the Wind* (1939). McDaniel lived in this house in the exclusive West Adams area, but only after winning a fight against restrictions that excluded non-whites from homeownership.

Fitzgerald House is representative of the district's creative designs

Greater Page Temple ❺

2610 La Salle Ave.

This church was used as a backdrop for chase scenes in Buster Keaton's comedy *Seven Chances* (1925). After discovering that he must acquire a wife by 7pm in order to inherit seven million dollars, Buster places an ad in the newspaper seeking a lucky bride. Carrying newspaper ads with his picture, hundreds of applicants eager to marry him and share his fortune arrive at the designated church. When an irked preacher disperses their hopes telling them that they were the victims of a joke, scorned and angry would-be-brides chase Buster from this church through the streets of Los Angeles.

Angelus-Rosedale, one of the oldest cemeteries in Los Angeles

Greater Page Temple is seen in Buster Keaton's comedy *Seven Chances* (1925)

Angelus-Rosedale Cemetery ❻

1831 W Washington Blvd.
☎(323) 734-3155.
🕐daily 8am-5pm.

Established in 1884, this was the first cemetery in LA to adopt the memorial park concept. Set among curving rows of mature palm trees, it has some remarkable examples of funerary architecture, including the Grigsby Mausoleum, shaped like a miniature Egyptian pyramid and faced in black slate.

Among the cemetery's notable permanent residents are Frederick Hastings Rindge, the owner of the

Malibu land grant; Phineas Banning, Los Angeles Harbor developer; jazz pianist Art Tatum; and Arthur "Dooley" Wilson, best known as Sam, Humphrey Bogart's pianist in *Casablanca* (1942).

Maria Rasputin (1900-1997)

Maria was the daughter of Russian peasant and mystic Grigory Rasputin, whose ability to temporary halt the bleeding of the hemophiliac Prince Aleksey won him the trust of Russian Emperor Nicholas II. Rasputin had a significant influence over the Russian court before he was killed in a plot.

Anna May Wong (1905-1961)

Wong was the first Asian actress to reach stardom in the West. During the fad for Oriental exotica in the 1920s, her enigmatic, slender good looks brought her mostly stereotyped roles, often as a mysterious villainess. She gained international fame playing the slave girl/Mongol spy in Douglas Fairbanks's *The Thief of Bagdad* (1924). Her most famous role was of the Chinese woman who shares a train compartment with Marlene Dietrich in *Shanghai Express* (1932). Wong died in her sleep of a heart attack.

Hattie McDaniel (1895-1952)

Starting her professional career as a singer, McDaniel was among the first black women to sing on American radio, eventually playing the lead in the popular radio and later television series, *Beulah*. She appeared in over 300 films during her career. McDaniel made history as the first black performer to win an Oscar. She died of breast cancer.

Chapel of the Pines ❼

Just around the corner, at 1605 Catalina St, is Chapel of the Pines, a round, domed building of classical proportions. It contains the remains of glamorous actress Ann Sheridan (1915-1967), known as "the Oomph Girl" and the star of such films as *The Man Who Came to Dinner* (1941) and *King's Row* (1942). Also cremated here were Walter Huston (1884-1950), who won an Academy Award as best supporting actor for his role in *The Treasure of the Sierra Madre* (1948), and Hal Ashby (1929-1988), who won an Oscar for editing for *In the Heat of the Night* (1967) and also directed such hits as *Harold and Maude* (1973) and *Shampoo* (1976).

Loyola Law School ❽

Frank O Gehry and Associates,
architect (1982-91).
1441 W Olympic Blvd.
☎(323) 736-1000.

One of Gehry's most
important works, the Loyola
Law School campus resem
bles a small village, designed
to create a more humane
architectural program on an
indistinctive urban site. The
architect arranged individual
buildings around an open
space resembling the Roman
Forum. With its free-standing
columns and landscaping elements, the public area
encourages casual meetings
and discussions.

Pictured here is the Burns
Building, with its striking
twisting stairway that connects the plaza to a gabled
roof greenhouse.

Alvarado Terrace ❾

Laid out in the first decade
of the 20th century, this curving, affluent residential street
became one of the most fan-
cied addresses in Los Angeles. The prestigious neighborhood was developed by
Pomeroy Powers (president
of LA City Council at the
time), on the grounds of the
former LA Country Club. It is
said that most of the structures were built by and lived
in by Powers before being
sold to their final owners.
The seven remaining stately
houses indicate a variety of
architectural styles—Queen
Anne, Tudor, Shingle and
Mission Revival. NRHP

The bright yellow stucco façade of the Loyola's Burns Building

Powers House

A L Haley, architect (1903).
1345 Alvarado Terrace.
Private residence.

This lavish Mission Revival
house was the last structure
built on Alvarado Terrace by
real estate developer
Pomeroy Powers, the one
that he, not surprisingly, kept
for himself.

House (ca. 1896)

Bonnie Brae Street ❿

At the end of the 19th century Bonnie Brae Street was
one of several fashionable
streets in Westlake, one of
Los Angeles' first suburbs.
The 800 and 1000 blocks of S
Bonnie Brae St today remain
home to some of the finest
Victorian houses in the city.
This affluent residential
neighborhood was built during the 1890s and its mansions represent the variety of
architectural styles that were
in vogue at the period.
NRHP

House (ca. 1896)

1036-38 S Bonnie Brae St.
Private residence.

With its corner turrets and
intricate wooden detailing,
this lively painted French
Chateauesque house is one
of the most picturesque
buildings on the street.

Wright-Mooers House

818 S Bonnie Brae St.
Private residence.
NRHP

Built in 1894 by contractor
Frank Wright, this remarkable
house was later purchased by
Frederick Mitchell Mooers,
one of the discoverers of the
Yellow Aster gold mine in
Kern County.

The well-preserved Queen
Anne residence, with its
ornate decorative woodwork,
features three-story tower
with elongated dome and
onion dormers above the
windows. Its most striking
feature is a veranda framed
with an unusual asymmetrical
curve.

Powers House

Wright-Mooers House

Stimson House ⑪

Carroll H Brown, architect (1891).
2421 S Figueroa St.
Private residence. NRHP

Clad in solid reddish sandstone, with a crenellated, four-story octagonal tower, this elaborate house is one of the rare examples of the Richardsonian Romanesque structures in Los Angeles (➔ p92). Built as a retirement home for Chicago lumberman Thomas D Stimson, the building is now owned by the nuns of Mount St Mary's College and serves as a convent.

Theda Bara in *Cleopatra* (1917). Advertised as a "vamp," she decorated her home with all sorts of vampire paraphernalia.

Theda Bara House ⑫

649 W Adams Blvd.
Private residence.

Between 1915 and 1925, this historic Tudor-style mansion was home to several silent screen legends. Its earliest celebrity resident was the first film *femme fatale*, Theda Bara. Living up to her advertised image of the man-eating vamp, Bara surrounded herself with ravens and snakes, and decorated the house with symbols of death and mystery, such as animal skins, human skulls, crystal balls and other gothic paraphernalia.

The house's next occupant was famous slapstick comedian Roscoe "Fatty" Arbuckle, whose trial for the murder of a starlet in 1921 cut short his residence here. Other celebrity tenants include director Raoul Walsh and his actress wife Miriam Cooper, as well

Theda Bara, Roscoe "Fatty" Arbuckle and Norma Talmadge House

as producer Joseph Schenck and his wife, the great silent star Norma Talmadge. It was rumored that she kept her expensive jewelry collection hidden all around the house, diamonds reportedly in an ice box and colored gems in shoes of matching colors.

The house is now owned by the Vincentian fathers and brothers and serves as a residence for seminarians.

St Vincent de Paul Church ⑬

Albert C Martin, architect (1924).
621 W Adams Blvd.

With its entrance façade intricately carved with statues of saints and the colorfully tiled 45-foot (15-m) dome, this church is an extraordinary example of the Churrigueresque Revival style. It was inspired by California Building designed by Bertram Goodhue for the 1915 Panama-California Exposition in San Diego. The richly decorated interior ceiling is the work of renowned artist John B Smeraldi. The church was a gift of oilman Edward L Doheny, one of the richest Americans of his time, whose family lived nearby at Chester Place and was renowned for their charitable commitments.

St Vincent de Paul Roman Catholic Church

Chester Place ⑭

Built around the turn of the 20th century, the exclusive Chester Place was one of the most luxurious enclaves in Los Angeles. Encompassing 20 acres of lushly landscaped grounds, this residential park originally contained 13 remarkable mansions built in a variety of styles.

Edward L Doheny, then called the richest man in Los Angeles, bought the entire area in 1901 and occupied its largest and most elegant house. After his involvement in a bribery scandal (he was later acquitted), Doheny hired an armed guard, bought up all the houses on the block and fenced off the estate to discourage gawkers, creating the city's first gated enclave. Following the death of Doheny's second wife, Estelle, in 1958, the enclave was bequeathed to Mount St Mary's College and became home to its downtown campus in 1962.

Doheny Mansion

Theodore Eisen and Sumner Hunt, architects (1899).
8 Chester Pl.
Closed to the public.
☞ for occasional tours call
☎ (213) 477-2761; for information about concerts, call ☎ (213) 477-2957. ☞

Today called Doheny Hall, this stately three-story mansion was originally built for a mining company's general manager Oliver P Posey, who lived here shortly before selling it to oil magnate Edward L Doheny. Built in the Spanish Gothic Revival style, the

Doheny Mansion's stately Pompeian room

house boasts gabled tiled roofs with copper Gothic detail and a 12-sided tower topped with a heavily ornamented pavilion. Initially it had 22 rooms, and later additions included a new dining room which could accommodate more than one hundred guests, as well as a giant indoor swimming pool and tennis courts.

The Dohenys enclosed the open palm court in 1906, calling the new space, the Pompeian room, after the ancient city buried in the eruption of Mount Vesuvius in 76 BC. The room's name and design reflect a 19th-century fascination with archeological discoveries and exploration. The radiating star mosaic floor is made of marble from Italy, Spain and Africa. The gold leaf and antique bronze walls are lined with wedgewood medallions. The room is furnished with pieces copied from ancient Pompeian designs. The focal point is the 40-foot (12-m) dome, one

of just a few such examples in the world, created by Louis Comfort Tiffany out of shell-shaped favrile glass. It is supported by eleven Corinthian columns of Siena marble and encircled by stained-glass skylights.

The Dohenys here entertained some of the greatest notables of their day, including future king Edward VIII, famous tenor John McCormack and Cardinal Pacelli (later Pope Pius XII). Their lavish dinners were rumored to equal those at the White House. To bring the splendor of the ceiling to their guests, the hosts arranged them around a mirror-topped table which reflected the dome and glass panels above them, so they did not have to crane their necks.

The house has appeared in numerous movies, television productions and music videos, including Mel Gibson's *Payback* (1998). In *The Godfather Part II* (1974), it was used as the New York City house of 1917.

Doheny Mansion's Great Hall

Doheny Mansion

Shrine Auditorium ⓯

Murals above the proscenium arch feature bedouins on camels set in an exotic Near Eastern landscape. The work of an unknown artist, they reflect the building's overall Islamic theme.

John C Austin, A M Edelman, G Albert Lansburgh, architects (1926).
665 W Jefferson Blvd.
☎(213) 748-0173. ⚑ NRHP

Shrine Auditorium

The Shrine doubled as the New York theater in the original *King Kong* (1933), where the gigantic gorilla was chained to the stage and displayed to the curious audience

The ceiling, which appears to the audience below as the billowing cloth of a richly decorated emir's tent, is actually made of poured concrete with painted plaster details. From its center hangs a magnificent, four-ton crystal chandelier, featuring more than 500 colored lightbulbs.

Also known as the Al-Malaikah Temple, this landmark structure features such common Islamic architectural motifs as twin domed cupolas topped with crescent moons and huge horseshoe arches. It is the headquarters of the Masonic organization the Ancient Arabic Order of the Nobles of the Mystic Shrine, popularly known as the Shriners. Members of this fraternity are noted for their signature red fezes and inclination towards play.

Since the foundation of the Los Angeles chapter in 1888, the Shriners' rosters have included such famous names as Harold Lloyd, Tom Mix, Roy Rogers, John Wayne, Gene Autry, Glenn Ford and Ernst Borgnine.

With a seating capacity of 6,300, the Shrine was the largest theater in the world when it opened in 1926; it is still the largest in the nation. It was frequently used as a venue for opera, concerts, ballet and other public events. USC and UCLA used to play their basketball games on its huge stage. The auditorium was also booked for many famous rock and roll shows. Among performers who made legendary appearances here were Elvis Presley (1956), the Grateful Dead (1967) and Jimi Hendrix (1968). Frank Sinatra celebrated his 80th birthday here (1995).

It was here during the filming of a Pepsi commercial in 1984 that Michael Jackson's hair caught on fire in a pyrotechnic accident, after which the singed star was hospitalized. Val Kilmer performed on the same stage as the rock idol Jim Morrison in *The Doors* (1991).

In the opening scenes of the 1954 remake of the classic *A Star Is Born*, the Shrine is seen during the celebrity arrivals. Its stage is also the site of the first encounter of Esther Blodgett (Judy Garland) and drunken Norman Maine (James Mason) during the "Night of the Stars" benefit. *Naked Gun 33 1/3* (1994) was also filmed here.

The Shrine is best known for hosting the well-publicized award shows, including the Grammys, the Emmys, the American Music Awards, MTV Awards and the Screen Actors Guild Awards. Since 1947, when the Academy Awards ceremony was hosted here for the first time, the hall has often been used for the popular event. The last such show was held here in 2001, before the Oscars were moved to the new Kodak Theatre in Hollywood.

University of Southern California (USC) ⑯

University Park
☎(213) 740-2311 (general info).
☛Trojan Hall, Mon-Fri 10am-3pm,
☎(213) 740-6605 (reservations).
Maps are available at the entrance gates. www.usc.edu. ☛

USC is the oldest and largest private research university in the western United States, founded by the members of the Methodist Episcopal Church in 1880. It is also one of the most expensive places to study in the country, called by some "University of Spoiled Children." The university is so highly regarded for its outstanding academic programs that *Time* magazine named it the "College of the Year 2000." Among its professors, USC boasts a Nobel Prize winner. The 150-acre (60-ha) campus features fine northern Italian Romanesque buildings from the 1920s and 1930s, but since 1945 many unremarkable structures have been built on almost every remaining piece of open space. The campus enrollment has grown from 53 in 1880 to more than 28,000 today. Among its celebrated alumni are filmmakers George Lucas, Ron Howard and Robert Zemeckis, actor John Wayne, astronaut Neil Armstrong, architects Pierre Koenig and Frank Gehry, General Norman Schwarzkopf and athlete O J Simpson.

Tommy Trojan statue, the USC mascot, was created by sculptor Roger Noble Burnham in 1930. The nickname Trojans was first used in 1912, when *The Times* reported that the USC track team "fought like Trojans."

USC upholds a long tradition in athletic excellence and its highly successful teams can be seen competing in a variety of sports.

Cloisters of the Mudd Hall complex (left). The second floor houses the double-height Hoose Library of Philosophy (right).

Visitors may attend a variety of cultural events on campus, including art exhibitions, concerts, film programs and stage performances.

Widney Alumni House
Ezra F Kysor and Octavius Morgan, architects (1880).

Opened on October 6, 1880, this Colonial Revival structure was the first USC building. It was originally an Italianate house before being remodeled in the 1930s by Lawrence Test, who painted it white and added green shutters.

Tommy Trojan

Mudd Hall of Philosophy
Ralph C Flewelling, architect (1929)

The Lombardy Romanesque complex, with narrow red brick facing and a prominent 146-foot-high (44-m) cam-

panile, was modeled after a medieval Tuscan monastery. The exceptional design features stained-glass windows, decorative tiles, statuary and especially attractive cloisters.

The Italian Romanesque-style Student Union Building, richly decorated with cast-stone ornaments and relief plaques

Bovard Administration Building
John and Donald Parkinson, architects (1921).

Built in the northern Italian Romanesque-style, the building's 116-foot-tall (35-m) tower is surrounded by eight statues of statesmen and philosophers, including Abraham Lincoln, Theodore Roosevelt, Cicero and Plato. The building contains the large Gothic-style Norris Auditorium, one of the oldest facilities of its kind still operating in Los Angeles.

Bovard Administartion Building

Doheny Memorial Library
Cram and Ferguson, architects (1932). ☛

Called the crown jewel of the university when it was built in 1932, the Doheny Library was constructed from a grant offered by oil baron Edward L Doheny in memory of his only son. Built in the northern Italian Romanesque style, the lavish structure features a soaring entrance hall with stained-glass windows and huge reading rooms with painted vaulted ceilings.

The Doheny Library's Treasure Room is decorated with nine panels painted by Samuel Armstrong depicting a history of the printed word. Originally intended as a space to display rare books, the room is used today for changing exhibitions.

Doheny Memorial Library was once called the crown jewel of USC

In *The Graduate* (1967), Dustin Hoffman is seen sitting on this fountain in front of the Doheny Library

The USC campus has been featured in a number of films, including *Marathon Man* (1976), *Escape from New York* (1981), *Ghostbusters* (1984) and *Legally Blonde* (2001). In *Forrest Gump* (1993), the campus stood in for the University of Alabama. In the movie *The Graduate* (1967), it doubled for UC Berkeley.

School of Cinematic Arts
A Quincy Jones and Associates, architect (1983).
☛days and times vary, for info call ☎(213) 740-2892.

USC's cinema and television program is ranked first in the country and its alumni receive an Academy Awards nomination almost every year. It is also the nation's oldest, established in 1929 with a course called "Introduction to Photoplay" and inaugurated by Douglas Fairbanks. The new five-building complex was opened in 1983 and each of the structures bears the name of one of the prominent entertainment industry professionals, including George Lucas, Steven Spielberg and Johnny Carson, who provided the funds necessary for opening and maintaining the state-of-the-art facilities.

Arnold Schoenberg Institute
Adrian Wilson Associates (1977).

Named for the revolutionary Austrian-born composer who taught at USC in the 1930s, this research, study and performance center houses his archives and the study from his Brentwood home. The building's geometric forms and cantilevered planes echo Schoenberg's experiments with atonal sounds and his innovative concepts of musical composition, many of them based on a 12-tone scale.

Leavey Library
Shepley, Bulfinch, Richardson and Abbott Architects, (1994).

This technologically advanced facility was intended as a campuswide teaching and studying library, designed to synthesize information from diverse sources and deliver it on demand to students at individual computer work stations.

One of nine panels in the Doheny Library's Treasure Room depicting a history of writing

Leavey Library serves as a resource for innovative teaching in the information age

Exposition Park Rose Garden

California Science Center

Exposition Park ⑰

Between Exposition and Martin Luther King blvds, and Vermont Ave and Figueroa St.

Between 1872 and 1910, this site served as an agricultural fairground and horse track, as well as home to automobile and bicycle races. It was dedicated as a public park in 1913, after a successful drive spearheaded by a judge to expel soliciting prostitutes and close local salons. He hoped to establish an educational and recreational center and today Exposition Park contains a number of major museums, sport facilities and a formal garden.

Rose Garden ⑱

701 State Dr.
☎(213) 748-4772.
⏰daily 8:30am-sunset. NRHP

This is one of the largest and most significant public rose gardens in California. It contains over 19,000 rose bushes representing about 200 cultivars, including grandifloras, hybrid teas, climbers and miniatures. As a display garden, it provides visitors the opportunity to see many rose varieties, and it offers various activities, such as educational pruning demonstrations. The garden is the recipient of new hybrids, especially the annual All-America rose selections, many of them developed locally. The flowering period occurs from the end of April to early November, but the peak time is between June and September.

Natural History Museum ⑲

900 Exposition Blvd.
☎(213) 744-3414.
⏰Tue-Sun 10am-5pm. Closed: Thanksgiving, Christmas and New Year's Day. ⑤ NRHP

Established in 1913, this is the third largest natural history museum in the US. Its collections encompass over 33 million specimens and artifacts covering more than 600 million years of the earth's history. The museum is divided into three departments: Life Sciences, Earth Sciences and History. Among its highlights are dinosaur exhibits, including one of the finest T rex skulls on display anywhere (featured in the movie *Jurassic Park*), a Megamouth, the world's rarest shark, the Schreiber Hall of Birds, the Insect Zoo, more than 2,000 specimens of gems and minerals and the Hall of Native American Cultures.

California Science Center ⑳

700 State Dr.
☎(213) 744-7446.
⏰daily 10am-5pm. Closed: Thanksgiving, Christmas and New Year's Day. ⑤free.

The California Science Center is dedicated to stimulating and nurturing interest in science, mathematics and technology. Through its lively, hands-on exhibits visitors can explore how science, math and technology relate to everyday life. The museum's Aerospace building, designed by Frank Gehry, houses real aircraft and spacecraft, as well as replicas and models of satellites.

One of the greatest attractions is the new IMAX 3D Theater. It uses film frames 10 times bigger than the standard 35-mm film format, projected on a 7-story high screen with Surround Sound (call ☎744-2014 for info).

Tyrannosaurus rex and Triceratops, two fierce dinosaurs from the Cretaceous period (between 65 and 70 million years ago) are locked in mortal combat in front of the Natural History Museum

Los Angeles Memorial Coliseum ㉑

John and Donald Parkinson, architects (1921-23).
3911 S Figueroa St.
☎(213) 748-6131.
⑤ticket prices vary for different events. ⌁ NRHP

Opened in June 1923 and named in honor of those who lost their lives in World War I, the 93,000-seat Coliseum was the world's largest sports stadium at the time. It has been the site of numerous historic events, including both the 1932 and 1984 Summer Olympics, two Super Bowl games (I and VII), and the 1959 baseball World Series. JFK delivered his acceptance speech here during the 1960 Democratic Convention.

Olympic Gateway (1984), a bronze sculpture by Robert Graham, stands in front of the Los Angeles Memorial Coliseum

Los Angeles Coliseum appears in *Escape from L.A.* (1996), starring Kurt Russell

In John Carpenter's sci-fi adventure *Escape from L.A.* (1996), Los Angeles is turned into a prison island after it is broken off the mainland in a catastrophic earthquake. Captured by gangsters, the legendary outlaw Snake Plissken (Kurt Russell) is taken to the Coliseum, where he is forced to play a game of basketball for his life in an updated gladiator-style contest.

The Coliseum was home to the Rams (1946-79) and the LA Raiders (1982-94) of the NFL, the Dodgers (1958-61), and the Lakers (1960-68). Today, it hosts football and soccer games, track and field competitions, concerts and a variety of other outdoor events. It is the home of the USC Trojan football team.

Adjacent to the Coliseum, at 3939 S Figueroa St, the 16,000-seat Sports Arena hosts basketball games, boxing matches and other indoor events.

Olympic Gateway (1984) by Robert Graham

Erected to commemorate the 1984 Olympic Games, Robert Graham's Olympic Arch is topped by two bronze headless nudes—male and female. The sculpture that symbolically represents all athletes caused an upheaval at the time when it was dedicated.

Watts Towers ㉒

Simon Rodia, creator/builder (1921-1954).
1765 E 107th St. Not on map.
☎(213) 847-4646.
☛Fri 11am-2pm; Sat 10am-2pm; Sun noon-3pm. ⑤ NRHP

Los Angeles' most notable work of folk art, the Watts Towers, is the accomplishment of one man, Italian immigrant Simon Rodia. He erected the towers between 1921 and 1954 without any outside help, buying material out of his wages as a construction laborer and working on them every moment of his free time during the 33-year period. Having no general plan and building without sketches or blueprints, Rodia improvised every stage of the construction. He had no power equipment and used only a tile setter's tools and a window washer's belt and buckle.

The monument consists of nine major structures built of steel rods, pipes and wire mesh covered with cement. The tallest of Rodia's three towers is 99 feet (30-m) high.

Watts Towers, embellished with glass, pottery, tile and seashells

Downtown Los Angeles

Downtown's distinct skyline, dominated by skyscrapers displaying the corporate logos of major financial institutions and law firms, began to develop its tall profile only since the 1960s. Before that, city ordinances limited building heights to 150 feet (45 m). The only exception was the 28-story City Hall, built in 1928.

Seal of the city of Los Angeles

The prime motive behind the building code restriction was the wish to keep the human scale of downtown architecture and avoid the grim look of Manhattan streets. The height limitation (13 stories) was repealed in 1957 when new construction techniques allowed increased earthquake safety for high-rises.

Beginning in the 1960s, the city's efforts to revitalize downtown resulted in many office towers being built in the new business district of Bunker Hill. Today, the streets are packed with thousands of commuters who work here during the day, but leave in the evening. Deserted streets at night (save the homeless) prompted developers to start converting dilapidated buildings into artists' lofts and residential apartments. Downtown and the neighboring areas remain a vivid multicultural scene with their dynamic ethnic enclaves. The district boasts a rich historical and architectural legacy and is home to a number of major cultural institutions.

Alarmed by the rapid rate of demolition of the city's architectural landmarks, a group of concerned citizens formed the Los Angeles Conservancy in 1978. Today, it is the largest organization dedicated

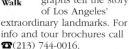

Marker along Angels Walk

to the recognition, preservation and revitalization of the historic architectural and cultural resources in Southern California. Led by knowledgeable docents, the Conservancy conducts twelve regular Saturday morning walking tours, focusing on historic buildings and areas in downtown. For schedule, fees and reservations call ☎(213) 623-2489 or log on to www.laconservancy.org.

Designed as a self guided walking tour of downtown Los Angeles, Angels Walk pays homage to the area's rich historic and cultural heritage. Important architectural and historic sites are indicated by 12-foot-high metallic markers, which through text and photographs tell the story of Los Angeles' extraordinary landmarks. For info and tour brochures call ☎(213) 744-0016.

Easily recognizable with their purple T-shirts and

safari hats, the downtown Purple Ambassadors patrol the streets of the district central area on foot or bicycles, providing visitors with maps, directions and other useful information. For more details call ☎(213) 624-2425 or visit their Service Center at 801 S Hill St.

Seal of the City of Los Angeles

The lion of León and the castle of Castile derive from the Arms of Spain and represent Spanish rule from 1542 to 1821. The eagle holding a serpent originates with the Arms of Mexico and suggests the period of Mexican control from 1822 to 1846. The bear flag indicates the brief California Republic of 1846. The Stars and Stripes stand for the American conquest and the present status of Los Angeles as an American city. The sprays of olive, grape and orange signify the location of LA as a city set in a garden. The rosary surrounding the shield represents the Franciscan mission period, when the city was founded.

Downtown Los Angeles skyline

Downtown Beginnings

The area encompassed today by downtown is where Los Angeles began, founded in 1781 as a supply outpost for Spanish garrisons in Alta California (➔ p16). For about one hundred years, the city's life was centered around the Plaza, but during the 1870s, the commercial focus began moving southward. By the 1920s, downtown was already established as a centralized city, with government offices,

Manhole in downtown Los Angeles

financial institutions, retail stores and theaters. With the advent of the automobile, LA lost its central core by the end of the 1920s, as people dispersed to outlying suburbs, creating essentially a multicentered urban sprawl. The Depression marked the beginning of the slow decline of the area that once was the heart of the city, opening the way for the gradual influx of a low-income immigrant population.

The first official map of Los Angeles, drawn by Lt Ord of the US Army in 1849

In the first few decades of its existence the pueblo of Los Angeles grew slowly. It was a small, dusty, agricultural town, consisting of a handful of one-story adobe houses with flat roofs covered with tar. They were surrounded with corn fields, vineyards and grazing lands. Upon visiting the area in 1836, a traveler from the East

Coast, Richard Henry Dana, wrote in his classic *Two Years Before the Mast* (1836) that he had been "in the remote parts of the earth, on an almost deserted coast, in a country where there is neither law nor gospel."

The streets were laid out at random with no particular plan, and the houses stood at different angles to the streets. This irregular layout was subject to change after the American annexation in 1848. With the influx of newcomers from northern California and Midwest, a sleepy Mexican pueblo was slowly transformed into an American frontier town.

Lieutenant Edward O C Ord of the US Army made the first official map of the city. Completed on August 29, 1849, it was called *Plan de la Ciudad de Los Angeles*. Ord was paid $3,000 to "survey the city . . . from the church to the last house before reaching the vineyard

of Señor Celis, and from the vineyards to the hills." The main door of the Plaza Church designated the center of the city. Street names were given in both Spanish and English: *Calle Principal*—Main Street; *Calle Loma*—Hill Street; *Calle Primavera*—Spring Street.

It is said that the lieutenant named Spring St for his sweetheart, Trinidad Ortega, one of Governor Pío Pico's nieces (➔ p.23), whom he nicknamed *mi primavera*—my springtime.

The first known photograph of the Plaza was taken in 1867 (below). The brick structure at the center is the city's first water reservoir. Behind it is the Vicente Lugo House, the first two-story building in Los Angeles. To the right is the Del Valle House and to the far right the Carrillo Adobe, site of the later Pico House. The Plaza Church is in the lower left-hand corner.

The 1867 photograph of the Plaza is the earliest known view of Los Angeles

Movies in Downtown

Perhaps the most photographed city in the world, Los Angeles has been used as a backdrop for countless movies and television productions. In one of the most published stills in the history of film, Harold Lloyd dangles over downtown Los Angeles in *Safety Last* (1923), while the life goes along on the busy street below. The comedian hangs from the hands of a giant clock in an attempt to climb up a side of a skyscraper at the corner of Sixth St and Broadway. "And all for the love of a maid!," of course. Lloyd was reportedly forced to take this climb after his stuntman broke a leg.

Thomas Tally brought the first motion picture to Los Angeles

The man who brought movies to Los Angeles was exhibitor Thomas Tally, who opened his Phonograph and Kinetoscope Parlor in 1896 at 311 S Spring St. Known as a peep show, his open-front store contained six viewing machines for patrons who were afraid to go into a dark room during the day. They could instead stay outside and peak at the screen through an eye hole.

Tally opened the city's first (some say the country's first) real movie house in 1902. His Electric Theater at 262 S Main St had 200 seats and solely showed moving pictures. It was very successful, but when the ground-breaking western *The Great Train Robbery* arrived in 1903, Tally sold his establishment and took the film on the road.

In 1906 Tally opened the New Broadway Theater, the Los Angeles' first custom-designed cinema. The Tally's theater sign is visible under a clock in the classic scene in *Safety Last* (1923).

Lobby card for *Safety Last* (1923) shows Harold Lloyd high above downtown street

The first movie set ever built in Los Angeles was a makeshift open stage assembled in 1907 on the rooftop of a downtown building at Olive and Eighth streets. Here director Francis Boggs of the Selig Polyscope Company from Chicago shot a short film version of the opera *Carmen* and several scenes from *The Count of Monte Christo*. After the filming was interrupted in Chicago by winter, the director and film crew came to Los Angeles lured by a promotional brochure promising 350 days a year of sunshine.

The first permanent movie studio in Los Angeles was also established in downtown (➔ p43).

Tally's New Broadway Theater, the city's first custom-designed cinema, opened in 1906

The Selig Company from Chicago built the first movie set in LA

Los Angeles River

The city's chief water engineer William Mulholland may have called it "a beautiful, limpid little stream with willows on its banks," but to rein in the volatile river, which recurrently flooded a wide area, the city imbedded it in cement for most of its 58-mile-long course. Once lined with vegetation, the stream was turned into a concrete spillway, which is usually dry most of the year. Today, the river is fenced off and not accessible, but can be observed from several

The Los Angeles River's channel was set in concrete in 1938

The giant radioactive desert ants poured into Los Angeles out of the bridge-tunnel in the science-fiction film *Them!* (1954)

This action scene with Samuel L Jackson and Colin Farrell from *S.W.A.T.* (2003) was filmed on the Sixth Street Bridge

bridges on the eastern border of downtown.

Although LA does not have many bridges, the few it has are often recognized for their distinguished architecture and considered important historic monuments.

Built in 1930, the Fourth St Viaduct Bridge is one of several bridges that cross the Los Angeles River east of downtown. Designed in the loose Gothic Revival style, this double-arch bridge was once crossed by electric trolley cars, and its four balconies were used by pedestrians and transit passengers as rest areas. Other important bridges include the First St Viaduct Bridge, the Sixth St Viaduct Bridge and Macy St Viaduct Bridge.

The Los Angeles River has been used as a location in numerous films, including *To Live and Die in L.A.* (1985) and *Terminator 2* (1991), as well as in the television series *Twilight Zone*.

In the science-fiction film *Them!* (1954), mutated monster ants swarmed into Los Angeles out of the tunnel under the Sixth Street Bridge Viaduct. It was on the stretch of concrete-lined riverbed between the Sixth St and the Fourth St Viaduct bridges that high school student John Travolta took part in the wild drag race in *Grease* (1978). In this section of the river, the neurotic bank clerk played by Jim Carrey found an ancient mask that gave him mind-boggling magical powers and turned him into a green-faced superhero in *The Mask* (1994).

In the action thriller *S.W.A.T.* (2003), members of an elite Los Angeles police team, played by Samuel L Jackson and Colin Farrell, take cover behind a Learjet which has landed on the Sixth St Bridge. During the filming of the scene, in a life-imitates-art scenario typical of Los Angeles, a real-life car chase took place, with 15 police cars pursuing a stolen car, which had to squeeze between the plane and the curb.

First Street Viaduct Bridge

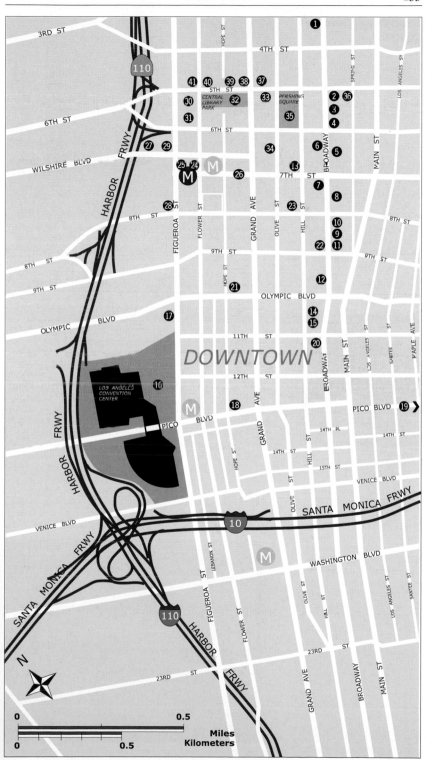

Broadway Theater District

"When you enter these portals you stray magically from the dull world of confusion and cares into a fairy palace whose presiding genius entertains you royally."
— Program note, Capitol Theatre, New York, 1921

By the early 1930s, Los Angeles was established as the nation's entertainment capital with more than 1,500 movie theaters in operation. The city's (and some say the world's) largest concentration of movie palaces was on the stretch of South Broadway between Third St and Olympic Blvd, offering seating for 17,000 people. Built

Broadway, with the Loew's State Theatre (right) and the Morosco Theatre (left), as seen in Buster Keaton's movie *Go West* (1925)

A vintage post card depicts the Philharmonic Auditorium Building (demolished in 1985)

between 1910 and 1931, these twelve theaters comprise the first and largest Historic Theater District in the United States listed in the National Register of Historic Places. Containing a variety of theaters—nickelodeons, vaudeville houses, movie palaces and legitimate theaters—this area presents a vivid history of entertainment in LA during the first decades of the 20th century.

Built by some of the greatest showmen and designed by major architects of the time, the opulent theaters were exotic palaces in a true sense. Designed to provide spectacular escapist environment, these architectural fantasies fed the popular imagination and carried the ordinary viewer into the enchanted world of motion pictures.

Today, the Broadway theaters survive in different states of preservation. Some of them remain in their original condition and occasionally show films or stage music performances. Many have been converted into swapmeet malls, night clubs or serve as churches catering to the neighborhood Latino population.
☛The interiors of most of these theaters are accessible during the guided walking tours conducted by LA Conservancy every Saturday at 10am; for reservations call (213) 623-2489. Every summer, the Conservancy also organizes a popular series of classic movies held in three of these movie palaces, called *Last Remaining Seats*.

The streets around Broadway still contain some important early theaters, although several landmark downtown palaces have been demolished over the years. Of these, the Philharmonic Auditorium Building was the grandest, built in 1906 in the Moorish Revival style. D W Griffith's landmark film *The Birth of a Nation* (1915) had its world premiere at its 2,300-seat auditorium. The Paramount Theater (opened in 1923 as the Metropolitan Theater), was a blend of various exotic architectural styles, including Hindu, Islamic, Moorish and Spanish. Its 3,500-seat auditorium, the largest in Los Angeles at the time, was built to resemble an ancient temple.

The auditorium of the Paramount Theater (demolished in 1963)

Million Dollar Theatre ❶

Legendary showman Sid Grauman began his career in Los Angeles with this opulent theater, one of the first true movie palaces in America. Originally called Grauman's, it was soon renamed in honor of the reported cost of its construction. This was the first major structure in Los Angeles built in the Spanish Baroque style known as Churrigueresque, which became fashionable after the San Diego Panama Pacific Exposition of 1915. The oversize marquee is a later addition.

The building's fascinating exterior is lavishly decorated with Churrigueresque ornament, blending traditional Spanish with whimsical American. Inspired by silent movies, elaborate terra-cotta sculptures by Joseph Morra abandoned customary religious themes for Hollywood fantasies. They include fanciful Wild West images such as bison heads and longhorn cattle skulls with bronze horns, as well as a series of figures representing the fine arts.

The theater's Third Street side entrance is decorated with the elaborate terra-cotta ornamentation inspired by Wild West

Albert C Martin, architect (1918); William L Woollett, interior.
307 S Broadway.
Not open to the public. Now used for special events and as a film location. **NRHP**

The 2,200-seat Baroque auditorium is designed to appear like the interior of a Spanish Colonial cathedral. Its stage is flanked by two enormous, purely decorative Corinthian columns, while a winged figure representing the West Wind tops the proscenium arch.

The Million Dollar opened on February 1, 1918 with a premiere of the western *The Silent Man*, starring William S Hart. Among the celebrities in attendance were Mary Pickford, Lillian Gish, Charlie Chaplin, Mabel Normand, D W Griffith, Mack Sennett and Cecil B DeMille.

To enhance the movie-going experience, Sid Grauman introduced a new kind of stage show, called the *prologue*. These glamorous performances followed the theme of the feature picture and were so elaborate they sometimes lasted half an hour and engaged 90 people in the act.

For more than three decades, the Million Dollar was a popular venue for Mexican movies and stage shows called *variedades*. The sidewalk in front of the theater once honored notable Latino performers, including Pedro Infante, Jorge Negrete, Dolores Del Rio and Maria Felix.

The theater appeared in the sci-fi classic *Blade Runner* (1982), its marquee glowing behind Harrison Ford as he entered the Bradbury Building across the street for a final showdown with the androids.

The Million Dollar was a first-run house which premiered top films of the day, including Rudolph Valentino's *The Son of the Sheik* (1926)

Auditorium of the Million Dollar Theatre. Its decoration includes ornately carved organ screens, niches, cornices and statues.

The auditorium has a splendid coffered ceiling

Roxie Theater ❷

John M Cooper, architect (1932).
518 S Broadway.
The lobby has been converted to retail use.

The Roxie was the last picture palace built in downtown before Hollywood emerged as LA's principal entertainment district. With its long, narrow auditorium, the 1,600-seat theater was designed specifically for sound films. Its Art Deco façade features a stepped roofline with a central metal tower, open grilles and zigzag cast concrete ornaments. The only Art Deco theater on Broadway, the Roxie marked a departure from the trend of opulent and excessively decorated movie houses toward a more modest design that reflected the harshness of the Depression era. An elaborate terrazzo sidewalk with a sunburst design graces the entrance to the Roxie.

Cameo Theater ❸

Alfred F Rosenheim, architect (1910).
528 S Broadway.
The lobby has been converted into commercial space.

When it opened as Clune's Broadway in 1910, this "picture playhouse" was one of the first theaters in LA to be built exclusively for motion picture showings. It was operated by William Clune, a real estate developer, theater owner and film production pioneer who produced movies to exhibit in his theaters. He helped finance D W Griffith's *The Birth of a Nation* (1915) and owned Clune Studio (today known as Raleigh Studios).

Clune's Broadway Theater as it looked in 1919

The simple two-story structure originally featured an electric sign with a clock above the roof. The sign was later replaced with the present billboard that once displayed 24-sheet movie posters.

Enduring virtually intact for 80 years, the Cameo remained an excellent example of a nickelodeon (a silent movie theater named for its 5 cents admission). When it closed its doors in 1991, it was the oldest continuously running movie theater in California.

Arcade Theatre ❹

Morgan and Walls, architects (1910).
534 S Broadway.
Now converted to retail space.

Opened as the Pantages on September 26, 1910, this was the first of three theaters operated in Los Angeles by the famous vaudeville producer, Alexander Pantages. His decision to locate his theater on Broadway marked the beginning of the thriving theater district.

The 1,400-seat theater was designed to resemble a Beaux-Arts English music hall. The opening night attraction was sensational Sophie Tucker, later labeled "the last of the red-hot mamas." Some of vaudeville's most popular acts appeared on the Pantages stage, including Stan Laurel of Laurel and Hardy fame, who played here in 1919.

The seven-story structure was built with a classic Beaux-Arts façade, but it has undergone several remodels which added Streamline Moderne touches. The name PANTAGES is still visible above the marquee. Its present name refers to the Arcade Building next door.

The lobby was converted into small stores and the auditorium, with its cast plaster ceiling and proscenium intact, is now used as a storage space for retailers.

Roxie Theater, Cameo Theater and Arcade Theater occupy the same block of Broadway

Palace Theatre ❺

Built as the third LA home of the famous Orpheum, one of the nation's largest traveling vaudeville circuits, the Palace is today the oldest remaining original Orpheum theater in the country. For 15 years, until its conversion to a movie theater in 1926 when the new Orpheum opened down the street, it showcased the greatest vaudeville stars of the era. The preeminent comedians, singers, dancers, acrobats and animal acts filled the eight-act programs twice a day. Charlie Chaplin, Sarah Bernhardt, the Marx Brothers, Fred Astaire, W C Fields, Will Rogers, Al Jolson and Mae West all performed on its stage. Magician Harry Houdini caused a sensation here when he sawed a lady in half while an ambulance waited outside, just in case. The Palace has been the scene of shootings and killings and reportedly has 22 ghosts in residence.

Designed by one of the most prominent theater designers in the West, this 6-story theater and office building was reportedly modeled after the Casino Municipale in Venice, Italy. Its exterior, styled after a Renaissance palazzo, is noted for the first use of polychrome terra cotta in Los Angeles. Featuring double arcaded windows and cornice finishings, the façade is richly decorated with terracotta ornaments that include theatrical masks, floral friezes, swags and gremlins. Four figures, sculpted by Spanish artist Domingo Mora, represent the muses of vaudeville—song, dance, music and drama.

The Palace's steep, 2,200-seat auditorium features two balconies that ensure that nobody in the audience was farther than 85 feet (26 m) from the stage. The second balcony, which is accessible only from exterior stairs, was designated "Negroes only" until the 1930s.

Designed for live performances, the curved plaster ceiling with cast ornaments and softly lit lunettes amplifies sound naturally. Painted in pastel tones, the elaborately detailed French-influenced interior has garlanded columns and originally featured two rows of stair-step boxes. Regarded obsolete for the movie theater, they were removed in the late 1920s and the area was later plastered and painted over by the artist Anthony B Heinsbergen with murals depicting pastoral scenes.

The opening scenes of Michael Jackson's music video *Thriller* were shot at the Palace in 1982.

A new marquee replaced the original wrought-iron canopy over the entrance in the 1930s

G Albert Lansburgh, architect
(1911)
630 S Broadway
Closed to the public. Now a performance and special events venue.
♠ ⓦ ☛ ☛(→ p234)

The theater's exterior foyer features gold columns, gold-framed wall display cases, mirrors and a frescoed ceiling with chandeliers. The "island" ticket booth was added in the 1940s. Behind the drapes above the entrance is the ladies lounge with an observation window overlooking the foyer, once used for viewing entering crowds.

French-inspired auditorium of the Palace Theatre

Murals adorn the side walls

Los Angeles Theatre ❻

The crowning achievement of S Charles Lee, one of the most distinguished theater architects of his time, the Los Angeles was the last of the grand movie palaces built on Broadway. Designed in the French Baroque style, it was modeled after legendary Fox Theater in San Francisco (demolished in 1962). Besides its opulent décor, the Los Angeles featured a number of technological innovations never before seen in a movie theater.

Built in 1931 for independent film exhibitor H L Gumbiner at a cost of nearly $2 million, the Los Angeles soon got into financial trouble despite its grandeur. Because the owner was not affiliated with any major studio, he could not get first-run movies and quickly went bankrupt, losing his theater to the Fox Film Corporation. It was said that the ruined Gumbiner ended as a suit salesman at Brooks Brothers.

The grand opening on January 30, 1931 angered Angelenos standing in a Depression breadline nearby, who booed glamorously dressed stars and other wealthy guests arriving in limos. When a crowd of 25,000 people smashed the windows next door, police were called to intervene and disperse the unruly mob.

In the rare example of a recent downtown premiere, *Chaplin* was opened here in 1992 with the film's star Robert Downey Jr and director Richard Attenborough in attendance, along with Chaplin's daughter and co-star Geraldine, Steven Spielberg, Charlton Heston and Chaplin's second wife, Lita Grey.

The Los Angeles has been used as a location for countless films, including *The Last Tycoon* (1976), *Funny Lady* (1975) and *W C Fields and Me* (1976). Its ballroom was made up to be the lobby of a grand hotel in *New York, New York* (1977). It was briefly seen in *Chaplin* (1992) as the site of the *Limelight* 1952 premiere. The opening sequence of *Alex in Wonderland* (1970) was also filmed here. The theater appeared as the world's most lavish strip club in *Armageddon* (1998).

The theater's massive terra-cotta exterior features twin elaborately decorated Corinthian columns on either side of the ribbed niche. The 80-foot-high (38-m) façade is topped with broken pediment, urns and other sculptured forms. The terrazzo sidewalk and the original marble box office under the marquee date from the late 1930s.

The Los Angeles' two-story lobby features immense Corinthian columns, ornate bronze banisters, gilt ornaments and 14-foot-tall (4-m) crystal chandeliers. The walls of great tinted mirrors, specially designed and divided by curved mullions, visually enhance the space. Every seat in the theater was wired and connected to an electric light board in the lobby, which indicated vacant seats, making the ushers' job much easier.

A grand central stairway leads to a 20-foot-tall (6-m) fountain on the mezzanine level. Simulating the flow of water, strings of crystal beads cascade down four tiers into a black onyx base adorned with sculpted dolphins. A mosaic basin is embellished with two white marble sea serpents. Painted in the style of the French artist Jean Fragonard, an intricate Heinsbergen mural serves as a backdrop.

The Los Angeles Theatre opened on January 30, 1931 with the world premiere of Charlie Chaplin's silent film *City Lights*. Among the dignitaries in attendance were Albert Einstein, who was Chaplin's special guest, and Hollywood big names, including Gloria Swanson, John Barrymore, Marion Davies, Cecil B DeMille, King Vidor, Jack Warner and Darryl F Zanuck.

S Charles Lee, architect (1931).
615 S Broadway.
Closed to the public. Now available as a film location and special events venue. ▶ NRHP

The Los Angeles' majestic two-story lobby was fashioned after the Hall of Mirrors at Versailles. Over the doorway, a large sunburst motif hints at Louis XIV, the France's Sun King.

The Los Angeles' auditorium features a coffered ceiling and the original hand-embroidered curtain

With a seating capacity of 1,400, the main auditorium's plush and easily accessible seating was originally designed with only six seats across in any row, putting an end to the nuisance caused by latecomers. Two balconies and opera boxes had 600 additional seats. To further assist the customers getting to their seats in the dark, blue neon lighting was installed in the floor along the aisles. Behind the balcony were two soundproof crying rooms, equipped with earphones and loudspeakers, where mothers with wailing babies could retreat and watch the film behind double glass panels without disturbing other patrons.

An ornately coffered ceiling features lunettes painted with Anthony B Heinsbergen's trompe l'oeil murals. The original hand-embroidered curtain was made of a special rayon silk material into which has been woven a metal thread, achieving an extraordinary shimmering effect; it was one of the two most expensive theater curtains ever made in America. Following the theater's French Renaissance theme, the curtain depicts the pomp and splendor of the court of Louis XIV and the king's military conquests. The life-sized padded figures wear clothes of real silk and velvet and wigs of real hair; the horses have real horse hair tails.

Downstairs, the oval ballroom was paneled in carved walnut and softly lit through 112 sand-blasted glass panels, each one of different design. Elegant amenities included a men's room which featured a barber shop and a marble shoe-shine stand. A ladies' lounge contained 16 individual rooms, each finished in a different shade of Italian marble and each with matching color of porcelain fittings. In the French cosmetic room, ladies could sit at individual dressing tables and primp themselves in front of triplicate mirrors, while enjoying novelties such as individual electric cigarette lighters. An expert full-time cosmetician was always available, together with a manicurist, to offer a helping hand.

Viewers with children could leave their kids in a playroom, where matrons on duty would take care of them in a space decorated like a circus tent, with animal toys, a small merry-go-round and even a miniature washroom and toilet

For those patrons who were late, in the lower lounge was installed a small viewing screen which, through an elaborate system of prisms, simultaneously showed the film being projected on the main screen upstairs

Weeks and Day, architects (1921).
703 S Broadway.
Now operating as a church. 🖝

State Theatre Building

This was the first theater on Broadway to feature a mobile refrigerated concession stand, later transformed into a permanent snack bar

The metal filigree chandelier

The original fire curtain was titled *LA in the 21st Century*

The State's auditorium with its elaborate Spanish Rococo ceiling

State Theatre ❼

Built in 1921 by New York exhibitor Marcus Loew, this 13-story Spanish Renaissance building is the largest brick-clad structure in Los Angeles. Patterned to simulate rusticated stone, its terra-cotta sculpted decoration features faces, cherubim, satyrs, eagles, garlands and urns.

Loew owned some 400 motion picture theaters when he formed Metro-Goldwyn-Mayer in 1924. Now providing his own films to his nationwide cinema chain, he made the State the MGM's downtown showcase. Because of its prominent location at a busy intersection and the fact that it premiered MGM and 20th Century-Fox movies, the Loew's State was the most popular and successful Broadway theater for decades. As was customary with other Loew's theaters, the State offered both films and vaudeville acts, featuring its own orchestra and chorus line.

The popular Fanchon and Marco vaudeville troupe performed their *ideas*, or stage productions developed around a particular theme. Among its chorines were future stars Janet Gaynor and Myrna Loy. In contrast to Sid Grauman's *prologues*, these revues were rarely related to the film being shown.

In 1929, a singing act called the Gumm Sisters made their debut on the State's stage. The youngest singer, six-year-old Frances, would several years later become known around the world as Judy Garland.

The current marquee was installed in the 1950s

Designed to resemble a Spanish Renaissance castle, the theater's interior features Spanish, medieval and classical details. In the 2,450-seat auditorium, the intricate plaster ceiling is painted to look like carved wood and plaster walls are deliberately aged to give the impression of timeworn stonework.

The original asbestos fire curtain features a futuristic vision of Los Angeles, with onion-domed palaces and towering minarets against the planetary system in the background.

The State has been frequently used as a film location, from Buster Keaton's *Go West* (1925) to the Tina Turner biopic, *What's Love Got to Do With It* (1993).

Globe Theater ❽

When the famous theatrical producer Oliver Morosco opened it in 1913, this was the first legitimate theater on Broadway, surrounded by vaudeville houses and nickelodeons. Originally named Morosco (the name still stands on the façade over the marquee), the theater housed live dramatic productions with such stars as Leo Carrillo and Edward Everett Horton. Morosco's plays, which originated in Los Angeles, were smash hits both here and in New York. The Morosco was hailed as the finest theater in the country, boasting such amenities as a fat-man section, with special seats accomodating patrons who weighed more than 200 pounds.

During the Depression it became the first theater in Los Angeles to feature an all-newsreel program. Over the next 25 years it was the theater's exclusive policy.

The 11-story building is a typical Beaux-Arts design, with glazed brick façade and terra cotta ornaments.

Although the seats and stage were removed and the 1,300-seat auditorium leveled, two balconies, marble staircases and a suspended plaster coffered ceiling survive relatively unchanged. Note the rectangular gilded proscenium with cove lighting and partially visible original asbestos curtain.

The upper balcony with its lowest priced wooden seats has a small side door leading to the fire escape. It was originally used as the required entrance for minorities.

Morgan and Walls, architects (1913)
744 S Broadway.
Now converted into a swap meet and nightclub. ☛(➔ p234)

The entrance to the Globe

The Globe's marquee advertises newsreels (ca. 1945)

The rectangular proscenium of the Globe Theater's auditorium

Rialto's program from 1921

Rialto Theater ❾

Built as a nickelodeon in 1917, the Rialto was leased in 1919 by showman Sid Grauman, who featured his famous pre-film *prologues*. Grauman hired William Lee Woollett to redesign the interior.

Over the years, the exterior has been extensively remodeled and no portion of the original façade survives; the interior was completely destroyed. The theater's only remaining significant feature is its striking neon marquee, the longest on Broadway. Though not original (it was installed in the 1930s), the elaborate rectangular marquee with its sunburst pattern and a variety of other neon elements has been preserved in remarkably good condition. Note the Art Deco box office and marble entry floor.

Oliver P Dennis, architect (1917).
812 S Broadway.
Now converted to retail space.

The Rialto's marquee, the oldest on Broadway, has survived almost intact from the 1930s

Tower Theatre ❿

Featuring both Movietone and Vitaphone sound systems, the Tower was the first theater in Los Angeles to be equipped for sound films; it was also the first to be air-conditioned or, as it was called then, "mechanically refrigerated." The Tower was the site of the West Coast premiere of the first talkie, *The Jazz Singer* (1927). The landmark film caused such a sensation that it sold out houses for months, with ticket lines stretching continuously around the block.

This was the first theater designed by S Charles Lee, one of the most prominent and innovative American theater architects, who designed 400 picture palaces during his long and prolific career. One of the most imposing structures on Broadway, the Tower is a Spanish Baroque building with Moorish and Romanesque details, clad in glazed, buff-colored terra-cotta tiles.

The asymmetrical Broadway façade features a row of blind arches, a richly decorated niche and a Romanesque arch over the entrance. It contains a stained-glass window depicting film as an art form. At the top of the Eighth St façade is a row of billboards that once displayed 24-sheet ads; bellow is a long Romanesque arcade. On the second floor, above storefronts, is a symmetrical grouping of blind windows. The façades are tied together by a striking corner tower with a clock, designed to increase visibility and attract passers-by. The tower top was removed after the 1971 earthquake.

Reclining on the blind window pediments are two figures: one is a male movie director holding a camera and a megaphone, the other is a nude actress with beads and a mirror. The windows were once illuminated by lights concealed by scallops.

Inside the theater, the architect recreated the scaled-down Paris Opera lobby using opulent details such as painted plaster decorations, Corinthian columns, a glittering chandelier and a sweeping staircase with ornate bronze railings.

The theater's small corner lot limited the architect to a long, narrow 900-seat auditorium. Designed in the French Renaissance style, its walls and ceiling are lavishly decorated with cast plaster ornament and moldings. Mural paintings by Anthony B Heinsbergen adorn the dome.

Façade of the impressive Tower Theatre is clad in glazed tiles

S Charles Lee, architect (1927).
802 S Broadway.
Currently serves as a church.
☛(➔ p234)

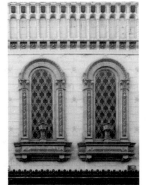

The windows were once illuminated by lights concealed by scallops

In the theater's lobby marble was used as a wall covering only to the patrons' height; above this the walls were painted to simulate marble

The Tower Theatre's auditorium

The Orpheum's auditorium has a gold-leaf coffered ceiling

G Albert Lansburgh, architect (1926)
842 S Broadway.
Closed to the public; available as a
film location and performance and
special events venue. ☛(→ p234)

Orpheum Theatre ⑪

Probably the best preserved movie palace in Los Ange-les, this spectacular theater was designed in 1926 by G Albert Lansburgh as the fourth and final house of the famous Orpheum vaudeville circuit in LA. The $1.9-mil-lion Orpheum is considered the famous architect's most successful design. The façade of the 12-story theater and office building is Beaux-Arts with Spanish Revival orna-ments and cornice; still standing is the huge original rooftop electric sign. Note the fine neon marquee which was added in 1936, the original bronze ticket booth and polished brass doors.

The 2,300-seat auditorium was designed in the French Renaissance style which the architect called "François Pre-mièr," after the style popular during the reign of Francis I, the 16th-century King of France. The 90-foot-high (27-m) auditorium has the original ceiling intricately decorated with gold leaf and stenciling. Two massive, 12-foot (6-m) wrought iron and crystal chandeliers, rimmed with blue glasswork, illuminate the space.

Orpheum Circuit News and Program, October 8, 1917

The elaborate décor includes wall panels of expensive Scalamandre silk, luxurious brocade drapery and bronze light fixtures. Other details, such as Gothic arches, marble pilasters and scalloped cornices, along with round stained-glass panels that light the area under the balcony, further contribute to the overall sense of grandeur.

In a brush of extravagance, in the theater's heyday the patrons were refreshed by rose water which was sprayed through the ventilation system during the performance.

The Orpheum was a favorite venue for the greatest entertainers of the day, such as Will Rogers, Eddie Cantor, Sophie Tucker, Jack Benny and the Marx Brothers. Musicians, including Count Basie, Duke Elling-ton, Aretha Franklin, the Everly Brothers and Nat "King" Cole, were also presented on its stage. Offering the best vaudeville shows anywhere, the Orpheum attracted star patrons too. Famous film cowboy Tom Mix always reserved two seats: one for himself, the other for his enormous white hat.

The Orpheum's original Wurlitzer, the last great theater organ remaining on Broadway, is still in use. Installed in 1928, this 13-rank, three-manual wonder can simulate over 14,000 orchestral sounds.

The Orpheum's opulent lobby, done entirely in white marble, recreates the ambience of a Euro-pean grand hotel. It is illuminated by five ornate bronze and gold glass chandeliers, featur-ing semi-nude Nubian female figures holding clusters of lights (above). Rich detailing includes bronze railings, newel posts shaped like sala-mander dragons and bronze figures of bare-breasted female angels holding flambeaux lights (left).

The entrance to the theater

The Spanish Gothic auditorium of the United Artists Theater

Walker and Eisen, architects;
C Howard Crane, interior (1927).
929 S Broadway.
Used by TV preacher Dr Gene
Scott as the University Cathedral
from 1986 until his death in 2005.

**The auditorium ceiling's dome
is imbedded with hundreds of
circular gold mirrors of vary-
ing sizes which, together with
hanging crystal pendants,
reflected the soft lighting and
created a glittering lightshow**

**The richly ornamented plaster
walls of the lobby are textured
to imitate travertine, while
huge gold-edged and gold-
backed mirrors are designed
to visually widen the space**

United Artists Theater ⑫

This was the first theater commissioned by United
Artists, the only major studio that had its flagship house
(preview theater) in Los Angeles instead of New York.
The theater's style was chosen by Mary Pickford and
Douglas Fairbanks after their return from a grand European tour. Impressed by cathedrals and castles of Europe,
they built this Spanish Gothic fantasy with its pointed
arches, intricate tracery and details such as grotesques
holding movie cameras and musical instruments.

The 12-story office and theater building is faced with
cast stone and two shades of terra cotta, textured to produce an effect of the weather-worn surfaces of medieval
Spain. With its square lacey tower, the building exceeded
the city's 150-foot height limit. Using a technicality to cir-
cumvent the building code, the fake tower was declared
a sign post on stilts and so was exempt from the city's
regulation.

The auditorium's most spectacular feature is the ceiling,
made in the form of a colossal sunburst. Over the proscenium arch is an elaborate plaster canopy, behind which
an asbestos curtain bears the motto *The Picture's the
Thing* (a parody on Shakespeare's *The Play's the Thing*,
since Mary Pickford did not believe in live theater). Large
decorative drops of ornamented plasterwork and plaster
organ screens and grilles are all finished in dull gold.

On both balcony walls are two large murals on canvas
painted by Anthony B Heinsbergen, depicting famous
stars of the day in their popular film roles. The mural on
the right side features Mary Pickford, Douglas Fairbanks,
Gloria Swanson and, above them, four youthful riders on
horseback with faces of the United Artists Board of Directors. On the left side are depicted Rudolph Valentino,
Charlie Chaplin and again Douglas Fairbanks. Hovering
above them, with devilish looks, are heads of competing
Hollywood studios.

The theater lobby is modeled after the nave of a Spanish Cathedral, with vaulted ceilings featuring frescoes by
Anthony B Heinsbergen. The richly ornamented plaster
walls of the lobby are textured to imitate travertine, while
huge gold-edged and gold-backed mirrors are designed
to visually widen the narrow space. Two double-deck
bridges connect balconies with lobby staircases.

Pantages Theater (Warner Bros Downtown) ⑬

Ten years after he opened his first vaudeville house in Los Angeles on Broadway (now known as the Arcade), variety show producer Alexander Pantages opened his second theater, which presented both movies and live acts. He managed his 80-theater empire from his second floor office, which became an alleged scene of statutory assault in 1929. A 17-year-old vaudeville dancer caused a sensational scandal when she accused Pantages of raping her. Behind the plot was Boston banker and political patriarch Joseph P Kennedy (the father of President JFK), who masterminded a hostile takeover of the Pantages theaters The dancer later confessed that she was paid by Kennedy to frame her boss. Pantages was initially sentenced to 50 years in prison, but was finally acquitted after two years and $250,000 in legal fees. Kennedy, who had spent several years doing business in Hollywood, eventually succeeded in taking over the Pantages's theater chain.

A Greek immigrant, Alexander Pantages was only 18 when he landed in Alaska in 1889, trying his luck in the Yukon gold fields. He invested his $24 grubstake to open a honky-tonk dance hall and with $4,000 in profits bought his first theater in Seattle. He would later expand to Los Angeles and ultimately build the largest privately owned vaudeville circuit in the world. Pantages sold his theater chain in 1929 for a reported $24 million. Ruined by the Depression and exhausted by a long lawsuit, he died of a heart attack in 1936.

The impressive, nine-story Beaux-Arts building is clad in white terra cotta. Lavishly decorated with such classical elements as fluted columns, garlands, floral patterns, scrolls, busts and faces, it has one of the most ornate façades in downtown.

Although it has been converted into a jewelry mart, part of the interior, including the splendid gilded ceiling of the lobby, is still intact. The balcony seats remain in place, together with the gilded proscenium and Corinthian columns flanking the stage. Magnificent hanging lights drop from a central starburst design, surrounded by a mural featuring Egyptian, Oriental, Greek and Roman figures.

The Pantages's focal point is a rounded corner tower topped by a Baroque Revival dome ringed with large cartouches. A rounded marquee still bears a trademark Warner Bros shield, although the inscription "WB" has been replaced with a diamond sign.

B Marcus Priteca, architect (1920). 655 S Hill St. Now open as a retail jewelry center. (→ p234) ⚫ ⚐

The Warner Bros' marquee in 1932. It is one of the earliest electric marquees in LA.

The 2,000-seat Pantages's auditorium in the 1920s

The fine cast plasterwork of the Baroque ceiling is still intact. Side boxes were removed after Warner Bros took over the theater in 1929.

Mayan Theatre ⑭

Financed by oil magnate Edward L Doheny, who wanted to complement the Belasco Theatre next door, the Mayan initially housed live musical comedy presentations. It operated under the direction of Edward Belasco and opened on August 15, 1927 with a live stage production of the George Gershwin musical *Oh, Kay*.

The Mayan was one of only three theaters in America built in the Pre-Columbian Revival style. The elaborate ornamentation was designed by Mexican artist Francisco Cornejo, who paid special attention to authenticity. All design elements were based on motifs found on the remains of ancient Mayan and Aztec temples and palaces in Mexico and Guatemala.

Originally painted in a shade of gray, the façade was later repainted in bright colors

Morgan, Walls and Clements, architects (1927).
1040 S Hill St.
Now operates as a nightclub. ↗

The fantastic façade features cast-concrete decorations comprising human and animal heads, serpents and Mayan glyphs, and includes an impressive row of seven giant figures of the Mayan god Huitsilopochtli seated on a symbolic earth monster.

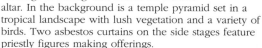

The stage is divided into three parts, the main stage and two tableau stages. The proscenium arch incorporates stone monuments found in the ancient city of Quirigua, Guatemala. The main asbestos curtain represents a procession of officials presenting offerings to a king who stands on a stone altar. In the background is a temple pyramid set in a tropical landscape with lush vegetation and a variety of birds. Two asbestos curtains on the side stages feature priestly figures making offerings.

Entwining serpent flanks the stairway

Detail in the mezzanine

One of the most striking features of the theater is the auditorium ceiling, with a colossal Aztec calendar at the center. From its center hangs a massive, multi-layered light fixture in the form of a sunburst, inlaid with precious and semiprecious stones such as turquoise, emeralds and black obsidian glass. Brightly colored ceiling panels depict ceremonial music and dance, as well as priests making offerings to the Sun God.

The Mayan was an X-rated theater when Jack Lemmon visited it in his Oscar-winning role as an LA garment manufacturer in *Save the Tiger* (1973). The interior was also seen in the romantic thriller *The Bodyguard* (1992).

The auditorium's three-tiered chandelier was patterned after a famous Aztec calendar stone

The lobby's coffered ceiling with exquisite light fixtures

The proscenium arch with the curtain representing a tropical scene. The refurbished theater now operates as a nightclub.

A large dome ceiling towers above the Belasco's auditorium

Façade of the Belasco Theatre

Belasco Theatre ⑮

Commissioned by oil millionaire Edward L Doheny, the theater was the second in Los Angeles named after the prominent theatrical family from the East Coast. David Belasco was a famous theatrical producer/playwright in New York, noted for his spectacular staging and sight and sound effects. Edward Belasco was a local stage producer who brought Belasco's Broadway productions to the West and secured the appearance of major New York actors on Los Angeles stages. The building was designed to complement the adjacent Mayan Theatre, designed by the same architectural firm, and form the core of a planned legitimate theater district.

The six-story structure was built in the Spanish-Moorish Revival style. Although the ground level has been remodeled, the upper portion of the façade retains its elaborate cast stone ornamentation, including conquistador figures above the second story. The Belasco's four-story façade is considered the most important example of the Spanish Churrigueresque style in Los Angeles.

The theater opened on November 1, 1926 with the Los Angeles premiere of *Gentlemen Prefer Blondes*, the great comedy success by Anita Loos. Among the luminaries who attended the gala opening were Charlie Chaplin, Buster Keaton, Harold Lloyd, Constance Talmadge, John Barrymore, Ramon Novarro, Pola Negri, Norma Shearer and Lillian Gish.

Especially designed for legitimate drama in a pre-amplified age, the 1,100-seat auditorium is noted for its acoustics and excellent sight lines. The ornate oval plaster ceiling, with its rich old gold finish, is illuminated by concealed lighting. Both the ceiling and the asbestos curtain were painted by Anthony B Heinsbergen. Stained glass windows were originally backlit with artificial light and are unique to this theater.

The theater's flamboyant and opulent interior is decorated with an eclectic mix of Churrigueresque, Italianate, Moorish and Gothic cast stone details. Note the exceptionally abundant and intricate tile work throughout the lobby and lounge.

The Belasco's auditorium was featured in the film *Swordfish* (2001), starring John Travolta and Halle Berry.

Morgan, Walls and Clements, architects (1926).
1050 S Hill St.
Closed to the public; available as a film and video location. ⚑

The ceiling with finely detailed plaster ornamentation

Tiled drinking fountain

Los Angeles Convention Center ⑯

Charles Luckman Associates (1972);
Pei Cobb Freed & Partners; Gruen
Associates, architects (1993).
1201 S Figueroa St.
☎(213) 741-1151.

The newest expansion, completed in 1993, tripled the facility's original size to 810,000 sq ft (73,000 m²) of floor space. On the structure's freeway-facing side is a huge curved, canopied wall of blue-green glass. Its most striking feature are two soaring, 155-foot-high (48-m) steel-and-glass entrance lobbies. Comprising three huge exhibit halls, theaters and other amenities, the modernized center is intended to attract major conventions and trade and industry shows.

Artist Alexis Smith's two terrazzo floor designs adorn the lobbies, one of the night sky, the other of a world map.

Los Angeles Convention Center's entrance lobby

Staples Center ⑰

NBBJ Architects (1999).
1111 S Figueroa St.
☎(213) 742-7100.
www.staplescenter.com.

Built at a cost of $375 million, the state-of-the-art Staples Center is LA's newest sports and entertainment complex. Staples Inc paid $116 million for the naming rights for the next 20 years.

Staples Center, home to five professional sports teams

Designed in a non-customary elliptical shape, the venue is wrapped in sloping walls of transparent glass that allow views into expansive concourses. Inside, illuminated with a specialty lighting package, the arena has an eight-sided center display, 1,200 television monitors and a specially designed sound system with 675 speakers, so fans never miss any part of the action.

Officially opened with Bruce Springsteen and the E Street Band's concert on October 17, 1999, the facility offers the finest entertainment experience imaginable. Audiences have seen performances by such icons as Madonna, Ray Charles, Cher, Eric Clapton, Tina Turner, Janet Jackson and Barbra Streisand, who performed the final concert tour of her career here.

The huge arena is home to five professional sports franchises—the NBA's Lakers and Clippers, the NHL's Kings, the AFL's Avengers and the WNBA's Sparks. Besides sports, the facility hosts live concerts, entertainment shows and other special events, including the annual Grammy Awards presentations.

Among the 20,000 fans who watch basketball games at the Staples Center, the most privileged are those seated courtside. Fetching $1,750 a game, the 130 most visible and prestigious floor seats are occupied by die-hard Laker fans, including Hollywood celebrities Denzel Washington, Dyan Cannon, Dustin Hoffman and Steven Spielberg. For more than 20 years, the Lakers' most famous regular, Jack Nicholson, has been cheering from his front-row seat (he prefers to sit near the visitors' bench).

Entrance to the Morrison Hotel

Morrison Hotel
(formerly) ⑱

1246 S Hope St.

In spite of the owner's alleged objection, the Doors were photographed in front of this downtown hotel for the cover of their aptly named album *Morrison Hotel* (1970).

***Morrison Hotel* album cover**

Coca-Cola Bottling Plant ⑲

Robert V Derrah, architect (1936).
1334 S Central Ave.

Coca-Cola Bottling Plant resembles an ocean liner

Wrapped around existing industrial structures, this remodeled bottling plant in the form of a sleek ocean liner is one of the most photographed buildings in LA. The Streamline Moderne landmark features rounded corners and variety of nautical details such as portholes, pipe railings, ship's doors, promenade deck and a giant sign in the form of a flying bridge.

The building's smooth white walls and flowing lines suggested an image of cleanliness which the company was seeking in an era when the purity of bottled drinks was not taken for granted. The nautical motif is also said to reflect the company president's enthusiasm for boating.

Colorfully tiled dome

Herald-Examiner Building ⑳

Julia Morgan, architect (1912).
1111 S Broadway.
Closed to the public. 🏴

This exuberant, Mission Revival-style edifice was built by newspaper magnate William Randolph Hearst as the headquarters for his *Los Angeles Examiner*. Founded in 1903, the paper later merged with another Hearst daily, creating the *Los Angeles Herald-Examiner*, which for decades remained the most influential newspaper in the city.

The block-long structure was designed by architect Julia Morgan, who was inspired by the California Building at the 1893 World Columbian Exposition in Chicago. She was the first woman to graduate from the École des Beaux-Arts in Paris, and was later commissioned to design the Hearst Castle in San Simeon.

The building features a Mission-style ground level arcade, a large parapet wall, bell towers with colorfully tiled domes, loggias, ornamental ironwork and a red-tiled roof. The property remains virtually unchanged, except for the arched windows on the ground floor, which were filled in during the World War II blackouts.

Since 1989, when the *Herald-Examiner* closed, the building has occasionally been used as a location site. Films such as *The Rookie* (1990), *The Usual Suspects* (1995), *The Cable Guy* (1996) and *End of Days* (1999) were all shot here.

Museum of Neon Art (MONA) ㉑

501 W Olympic Blvd.
☎(213) 489-9918.
🕐Wed-Sat 1-5pm; Sun noon-5pm.
💲 🚌 bus tours.

Founded in 1981, MONA aims to exhibit fine art in electric and kinetic media and to document and preserve outstanding examples of neon signs, billboards and marquees. Besides contemporary neon art, its permanent collection contains more than 50 vintage signs. It is the only permanent institution of its kind in the world. MONA conducts nighttime bus tours of neon signs and installations of contemporary electric fine art in the city.

Mission Revival-style Herald-Examiner Building

Eastern Columbia's tiled façade

Eastern Columbia Building ㉒

Claude Beelman, architect (1929).
849 S Broadway.
Closed to the public. ⏎

This magnificent landmark is the best remaining example of Art Deco (Zigzag Moderne) architecture in Los Angeles. Opened in 1930, it was originally a department store, owned by one of the largest local retailers, Adolf Sieroty. The building housed his two retail businesses: Eastern Outfitting sold furniture and Columbia Outfitting sold clothing and accessories.

With vertical, deeply recessed bands of windows and a stepped-back design, this 13-story building is a distinctive LA skyscraper. It was one of just a few buildings that exceeded the city's 150-

foot height limit for its day. The architect innovatively circumvented the city building code restriction—the two-story clock-tower technically was not part of the building; it was considered a billboard, separate from the structure itself.

The building's most distinguished feature is its stately façade, clad in highly glazed turquoise, steel-blue and gold terra-cotta tiles. Gold leafing for the tiles was made with real gold dust. The architect used a variety of motifs in the decoration, including stylized plant forms and geometric patterns such as chevrons, zigzags and sunbursts.

The main entrance features a stunning gold terra-cotta sunburst pattern. The entrance originally led to an interior shopping arcade which separated the two retail stores.

At the top of the building is a huge, four-faced clock tower, emblazoned with the department store's name. The building was noted for its innovative use of the tower to hold utilities. The clock was originally neon-lighted and its chimes were designed to sound every quarter hour.

The building was prominently featured in *Predator 2* (1990), a movie set in futuristic Los Angeles, where an alien with camouflage abilities lands amid the war between the police and powerful drug dealers.

Garfield's elevator lobby

Garfield Building ㉓

Claude Beelman, architect (1930).
403 W 8th St.
Closed to the public. NRHP

Clad in cream terra-cotta, the exterior of this 12-story Art Deco building is embellished with reliefs of palm leaves, grape clusters and solar motifs. The stylized floral patterns are repeated on the intricate wrought-iron grillwork above the entrance. The canopy ceiling is decorated with a striking sunburst design of radiant inlaid marble.

The Garfield Building's real thrill is the opulent two-story elevator lobby with its gold-leaf plaster cornices, black and red marble walls, ornate display cases framed in German silver and gold-toned Gothic-style chandeliers.

Eastern Columbia Building's entrance vestibule

Garfield Building's wrought-iron canopy

Fine Arts Building ㉔

Walker and Eisen, architects (1925)
811 W Seventh St.
☞(➔ p234) 🏃

Designed in the Romanesque style, this remarkable 12-story brick and terra-cotta building was originally intended as a complex of artists' studios and workshops. Tenants could display their artwork in the showcases in the lobby, readily available for purchase to shoppers entering from the busy commercial street. Although the building has been converted to office space, art exhibits are still displayed in the lobby in 17 elaborate bronze showcases.

The building's façade, said to be modeled after a 12th-century cathedral in Lucca, Italy, is lavishly decorated with twisted columns and arched windows, featuring arcaded galleries at the top and a recessed, ornate entrance. Rich terra-cotta detailing includes flowers, masks, musicians and an array of real and fantastic bestiary—fish, birds, gargoyles, griffins. Giant reclining figures of Sculpture and Architecture rest above the third floor windows.

The building's most remarkable feature is a magnificent, two-story arcaded entrance lobby. Its walls are covered with terra-cotta blocks and colored tiles designed by famous Ernest Batchelder of Pasadena, who also designed sculptured figures on the mezzanine level. An elaborately painted beamed ceiling and fanciful murals were created by Anthony B Heinsbergen. The central section is occupied by a fountain and decorated with bronze sculptures by Burt Johnson representing Architecture, Painting, Textile Arts and Ceramics.

The building has often been used as a film location, including the high-tech action movie *True Lies* (1994), with Arnold Schwarzenegger as a top special agent.

The Fine Arts Building's splendid two-story lobby

Home Savings Tower ㉕

Albert C Martin & Associates, architect (1989).
660 S Figueroa St.
☞(➔ p234)

Inspired by the French Chateauesque style, this 24-story structure bears strong historical reference to the neighboring buildings with its base richly detailed in different shades of marble and steeply pitched copper roof with triangular gables. The tower's most distinctive space is the two-story sky lobby, located on the 6th floor, with its central fountain, marble floors and walls, and 30-foot-high arches opening onto balconies. The lobby is decorated with the mural *Latitude 34, Longitude 118, A Southern California Panorama* by Richard Harris, depicting a fictitious aerial view of LA.

Façade of the impressive Home Savings Tower

The Home Savings' soaring two-story sky lobby

Seventh Street ㉖

Once described by the *Daily Times* as "Los Angeles' counterpart of New York's Fifth Avenue," Seventh St (together with Broadway) was the city's main shopping and entertainment corridor. When its flagship Robinson Department Store opened in 1915, the newspapers' headlines boasted every possible convenience for clientele, "including a lighting system that provides the closest imitation of daylight ever devised by science."

Robinson Department Store provided "every conceivable convenience for the examination of merchandise"

Many commercial buildings along the street were designed with large display windows on the second floor, featuring live models standing still—20 minutes without moving—so merchandise could be viewed by shoppers from double-decker public transport.

777 Tower

A glass-walled, three-story lobby of the 777 Tower

Coast Savings Building ㉗

Kohn Pedersen Fox & Associates, architects (1987).
1000 Wilshire Blvd.

Located at the edge of the central city overlooking the Harbor Fwy, this 21-story building is one of downtown's most distinguished Post Modern structures. Sitting on a podium which serves as a pedestrian plaza, the facility is uniquely shaped with its curved front and gabled ends. Its façade displays an intricate pattern of two shades of granite and two shades of glass, featuring contrasting horizontal banding and windows visually enlarged with wide framing.

777 Tower ㉘

Cesar Pelli and Associates, architect (1991).
777 S Figueroa St.

Clad in white enameled metal and glass, this 725-foot-high (221-m) building has one of the most distinctive silhouettes in downtown. The 53-story tower of telescoping cylinders has its front and back bowed out, while the sides remain flat. To invigorate the façade and visually reduce the building's mass, the architects made the piers to be wider in the middle than at the corners.

Designed to capture the bright Southern California light, the building features sculpted metal surfaces that create bold highlights and deep shadows. Particular attention was paid to details, including indented corners and metal panels that crown the setbacks and the top of the building.

Screened by an aluminum-clad arcade, the magnificent three-story lobby features window walls on the east and south. Its highly veined Italian marble floor is composed of pieces which were individually selected and marked at the quarry to achieve desired pattern.

Corporate Head **(1992) by Terry Allen and Philip Levine**

Set against Citicorp Plaza at the southwest corner of Seventh and Figueroa streets is a life-sized bronze figure of a man in a three-piece suit with a briefcase, who is inserting his head into the wall. It is a monument to an unknown businessman who lost his head to the corporation.

Entrance to Sanwa Bank Plaza

Sanwa Bank Plaza ㉙

A C Martin & Associates (1991).
601 S Figueroa St.

This 52-story, 760-foot (232 m) office tower, clad in glass and rose granite, achieves an elegant and dynamic appearance with its slight setbacks and clipped corners. The building is rotated 45 degrees to the street grid, creating a triangular outdoor space, well connected with the dramatic, 75-foot high (23-m) lobby. Comprising the top three stories, the tower's green glass crown is illuminated at night, setting it apart on the LA skyline. This was the site of Saint Paul's Episcopal Cathedral, a major LA landmark razed to make way for the high-rise.

L.A. Prime Matter (1991), a large sculpture-fountain by Eric Orr is located at the cor-

ner of Figueroa St and Wilshire Blvd. Water slowly slithers down a bronze rectangular column and stone base, surprising observers with sporadic bursts of fire from its top.

ARCO Plaza ㉚

A C Martin & Associates, architect (1972).
505-555 S Flower St.

Smooth, simple and restrained, these twin, 52-story, 699-feet (213-m) monoliths are sheathed in polished forest green granite and panels of solar bronze glass. The south tower houses Bank of America and the north once housed ARCO until the oil giant was acquired and moved out. Once the most recognizable name in downtown, ARCO Tower was renamed in 2002 after its new tenant, the law firm Paul Hastings.

Formerly on this site was the famous Art Deco Richfield Building. Razed in 1972, the only remnants of this masterpiece are two 20-foot-high (6-m) bronze doors, now displayed near the entrance to the north tower.

Between the towers is a wide plaza with an impressive red fountain-sculpture by Herbert Bayer entitled *Double Ascension* (1973). Below the plaza and underground garage is a completely enclosed, two-level shopping mall.

Richfield Oil Building

Richfield Building (site) ㉛

Morgan, Walls and Clements, architects (1928).

In its modernization frenzy Los Angeles did not show much respect for its rich architectural legacy. One of the most distinguished landmarks not to survive the wrecking ball was the magnificent Richfield Oil Company Building. This 12-story Art Deco masterpiece was sheathed in black and gold terra cotta, reportedly representing the company's "black gold." The building was surmounted by a 130-foot-high (40-m) beacon tower with the name RICHFIELD spelled in neon letters. It was replaced in 1972 by the twin ARCO Towers.

The building is seen on screen in *Zabriskie Point* (1970).

A sculpture *Double Ascension* (1973) by Herbert Bayer looms over the fountain at ARCO Plaza

Bronze doors from the old Richfield Building

Bertram Goodhue and Carleton M Winslow, architects (1922-26); addition: Hardy Holzman Pfeiffer Associates (1993).
630 W Fifth St.
☎(213) 228-7000. www.lapl.org
⏰Mon, Thu-Sat 10am-5:30pm; Tue, Wed 10am-8pm; Sun 1-5pm.
Ⓢfree. ⟲ NRHP
☛free guided library tours run weekdays at 12:30pm, Sat at 11am and 2pm, and Sun at 2pm; call ☎(213) 228-7168 for info.

View of Los Angeles Central Library

From the rotunda's center hangs a one-ton bronze chandelier, modeled after the solar system, with planets and crescent moon in the chains. In the middle is a translucent, illuminated blue glass globe, surrounded with the signs of the zodiac.

A soaring, eight-story atrium was designed to bring natural light through its glass roof. Its three massive chandeliers of painted fiberglass and aluminum, created by Therman Statom in 1993, represent natural, technological and ethereal worlds.

Richard J Riordan Central Library ㉜

One of the most distinctive buildings in the city, the Central Library blends various exotic styles with modern themes, marking a unique transition towards Art Deco in Los Angeles. The structure incorporates Egyptian, Roman, Byzantine and Spanish architectural elements with plain concrete surfaces and the clean lines of modern geometric forms. Its most striking feature is a central square tower, topped by a tiled pyramid with brightly colored sunbursts. It is surmounted by a hand-held torch, symbolizing the Light of Learning.

The building is adorned with relief sculptures by artist Lee Lawrie, famous for his work on the main entrance to the RCA Building in New York's Rockefeller Center. Throughout the exterior walls are busts of prominent historical figures, personifications of various disciplines and allegories of learning, along with inscribed aphorisms and quotations on the theme of knowledge.

The library's new Maguire Gardens feature a series of stepped pools that incorporate sculptures and fountains, together with inscriptions in many of the world's scripts and languages. Called *Spine*, the work is designed by Jud Fine and refers to the pursuit of knowledge, emphasizing ideas of evolution and language.

The library's second-floor rotunda is located beneath the pyramid, its dome painted in a stylized sunburst pattern, reflecting the pattern on the tiled dome outside. The rotunda walls are covered with four large, elaborate murals, 19' x 38' (5,8 x 11,6 m), painted in 1932 by Dean Cornwell. They represent a romanticized version of four eras in California history—*Discovery* (north wall), *Mission Building* (east), *Founding of Los Angeles* (west) and *Americanization* (south). Twelve smaller panels on piers depict American Arts and Industries in California.

In 1986 two devastating arson fires seriously damaged the library, destroying a third of its collection. The damaged building was facing demolition, and was saved when its unused air rights were sold to the development across the street, thus providing money necessary for renovation. After seven years of planning and construction, the original building was carefully restored and the new wing was added. It doubled the facility size, making it the third largest public library in the nation.

Biltmore Hotel ㉝

When it opened to much fanfare on October 2, 1923, the $10-million Biltmore was the largest and most luxurious hotel west of Chicago. Named for George Vanderbilt's extravagant estate in Asheville, North Carolina, the building was designed by the same architectural firm responsible for the Waldorf Astoria in New York. The landmark 11-story structure is essentially Beaux-Arts architecture, with Italian and Spanish Renaissance detailing. It is easily distinguished by its three massive towers on the Olive St façade, with their reddish brickwork, cream-colored stone and terra-cotta roof tiles.

With its 1,000 lavishly decorated rooms, the hotel attracted a glamorous clientele from around the world, including countless heads of state, royalty and celebrities. Every American president since Franklin D Roosevelt has stayed here, as did Winston Churchill, Princess Margaret and the Duke of Kent. The Biltmore hosted significant social events and was Hollywood society's focal point for socializing. During the 1930s and 1940s, the Biltmore Bowl was a showcase for all big bands of the era. The hotel's Music Room (now lobby) served as JFK's headquarters during the 1960 Democratic National Convention. The Beatles were dropped by helicopter on the hotel roof and hid out for a few days during their first US tour in 1964.

The Biltmore's interiors are a rich mixture of different styles, with Spanish and Italian Renaissance dominating. Sparing no expense with the décor, the hotel was renowned for its rich tapestries, carved marble and ornately painted and gilded walls and ceilings. Most of the interior was decorated and hand-painted by Italian artist Giovanni Smeraldi, who also worked on New York's Grand Central Station and the Blue Room of the White House.

The banquet held at the Biltmore on May 11, 1927 marked the official founding of the Academy of Motion Picture Arts and Sciences. It is widely believed that the Oscar statuette took shape that night (→ p48). The hotel also hosted several Academy Awards ceremonies—in 1931, 1935-39, 1941 and 1942.

The Biltmore has been used as a location in countless films and television productions. Among the best known are *Chinatown* (1974), *Farewell, My Lovely* (1975), *Beverly Hills Cop* (1984) and *The Nutty Professor* (1996).

Schultze & Weaver, architects (1923).
515 S Olive St.
☎(213) 624-1011.
☛(→ p234) ⚑

One of the hotel's most remarkable rooms, the four-story Rendezvous Court (until 1984 the main lobby) is entered through a grand portal on Olive St. Its vaulted, richly painted Moorish ceiling of plaster with wood beams features the opulent detailing and original bronze chandeliers. A Spanish Baroque double staircase, topped with a cast-iron grille decorated with plaster and bronze ornaments, leads to the Churrigueresque-style doorway.

As notorious mobster Benjamin "Bugsy" Siegel, Warren Beatty relaxed in the hotel's health club in the film *Bugsy* (1991). The Biltmore's Crystal Ballroom served as the fight arena for Sylvester Stallone in *Rocky III* (1981) and the stage where Michelle Pfeiffer performed in *The Fabulous Baker Boys* (1989). In *The Sting* (1973), the Gold Room was used as a setting for the bookie joint. The lobby was seen in *The Poseidon Adventure* (1972) and *Ghostbusters* (1984).

A vintage post card depicts the Biltmore Hotel

Façade of the Oviatt Building

Walker and Eisen, architects
(1928).
617 S Olive St.
Lobby open to the public.
🏁 NRHP

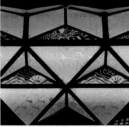

The marquee features colored panels of frosted glass

The Oviatt Building's mail box was designed by René Lalique

Oviatt Building ㉞

After attending the Paris *Exposition Internationale des Arts Décoratifs* in 1925, haberdasher James Oviatt became so fascinated with the new style of Art Deco that he chose it for an office building that also housed a retail store and his private penthouse apartment. Although featuring the Italian Romanesque style on the exterior, with arched windows, tiled roof and tower, this 13-story landmark is internationally renowned for its Art Deco details.

The building's open-air lobby is visible from the street through ornate wrought-iron gates. To decorate the lobby, Oviatt commissioned famed French jeweler and art glass designer René Lalique, who designed all the fixtures and furnishings. It was said that over 30 tons of Lalique glass were manufactured in France and shipped to LA, the artist's largest commercial commission ever.

Lalique used a new alloy known as maillechort to design such details as mailboxes, directories and lighting fixtures. The elevators contain hand-carved oak paneling and the elevator doors are faced with opalescent glass depicting stylized California oranges.

The spectacular marquee features colored panels of frosted glass (much of the original glass in the lobby was removed and has been replaced with modern replicas).

The building's first three floors were occupied by the elegant Alexander & Oviatt Haberdashery, the most exclusive and expensive men's clothier in the city. Among his clientele James Oviatt counted Clark Gable, John Barrymore, Errol Flynn, Gary Cooper and other impeccably dressed Hollywood stars. The actor Adolphe Menjou, considered the best dressed man in Hollywood, was also a customer.

A former clothing shop on the ground floor now houses an upscale restaurant that retains some of the original store décor. The old oak display cases and drawers that once housed shirts and ties now hold tablecloths and silverware. It has been a favorite film location and can be seen in a memorable scene in *Pretty Woman* (1990). While having dinner with her companion, businessman Richard Gere, the hooker played by Julia Roberts grapples with escargot tongs and accidentally sends a snail flying across the room.

The Oviatt Building's open-air lobby originally contained decorative glass designed by French designer René Lalique

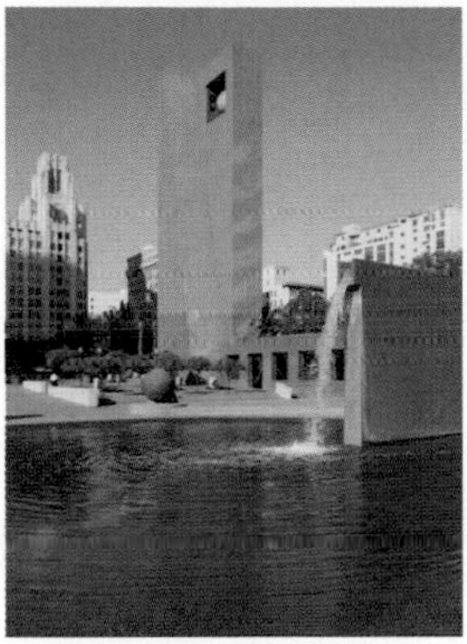

View of Pershing Square

Pershing Square ㉟

Ricardo Legorreta, architect; Laurie Olin, landscaping (1993).

The oldest public park in Los Angeles, this site was part of the original Spanish land grant which was given to the early Pueblo in 1781. It got its present name in 1918 in honor of General John Pershing, commander of the American Expeditionary Force during World War I. The five-acre square was declared a public park in 1866 and once was a jungle-like sanctuary with birds-of-paradise and giant palm and banana trees. In 1950, the park was stripped of its specimen vegetation to make way for a multilevel underground parking garage. Most of the removed trees eventually ended up at Disneyland's Jungle Cruise ride. During the 1960s and 1970s, the place gradually disintegrated, becoming home to drug dealers, the homeless and prostitutes.

The park was redesigned in 1993 by Mexican architect Ricardo Legorreta. Borrowing from Mexican tradition, he used exuberant colors to paint his concrete structures, attempting to bring two bordering downtown cultures, Latino and Anglo, together. The park is dominated by a 120-foot-high (36-m) purple campanile, topped by a large pink ball. A circular reflective pool is supplied with water by an aqueduct connected to the tower. To the north, a landscaped terraced area is used as an amphitheater for outdoor performances.

Public artworks, created by Barbara McCarren, are incor porated throughout the square and include an earthquake fault line, vintage ceramic postcards embedded in benches and telescopes that provide historic views of old Pershing Square. A colorful quote by historian Carey McWilliams is inscribed on a concrete wall by the pool.

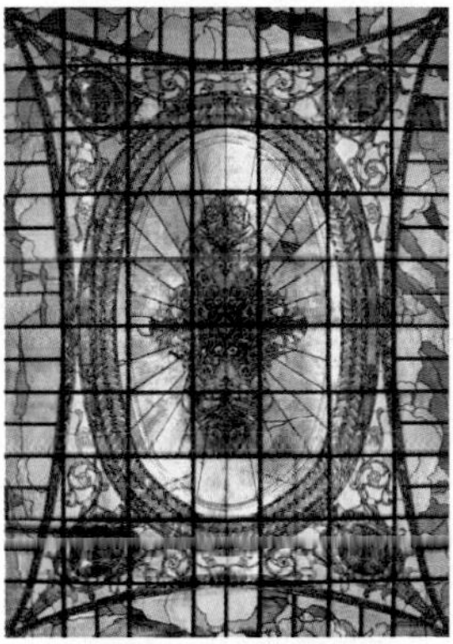

Stained-glass ceiling of the Alexandria's Palm Court

Alexandria Hotel ㊱

John Parkinson, architect (1906).
210 W 5th St/501 S Spring St.

With its 500 luxurious rooms, this was the glory of LA's hospitality and the city's most prestigious hotel when opened in 1906. It was home away from home for Presidents Theodore Roosevelt, William H Taft and Woodrow Wilson. King Edward VIII and Winston Churchill stayed here, as well as countless celebrities including Enrico Caruso, Sarah Bernhardt and literally every silent film star.

For almost two decades it was the center of the city's social life; it was here that the power lunch and networking were born. The hotel lobby reportedly was the scene of a fistfight,

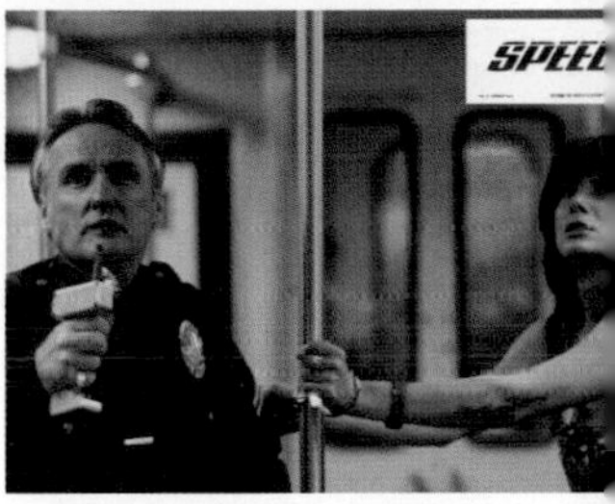

Pershing Square is the location where Dennis Hopper kidnaps Sandra Bullock in *Speed* (1994)

when film mogul Louis B Mayer knocked-down Charlie Chaplin after an argument. It was here that Gloria Swanson met Herbert Somborn, her future husband and founder of the Brown Derby restaurant.

Charlie Chaplin, D W Griffith, Mary Pickford and Douglas Fairbanks announced the formation of their independent company, United Artists, in the Alexandria's main dining room in 1919.

In his autobiography, Chaplin called the Alexandria "the swankiest hotel in town ... marble columns and crystal chandeliers adorned the lobby, in the center of which was the fabulous 'million dol lar carpet'—the mecca of big movie deals."

By the late 1920s, most of its celebrity clientele had left for the newly opened Biltmore Hotel, and the Alexan dria never recovered. Today, the dilapidated building provides housing for welfare families. Refurbished true to its original décor, the Palm Court features the magnificent stained-glass ceiling that extends across the 196-foot (60-m) former dining room.

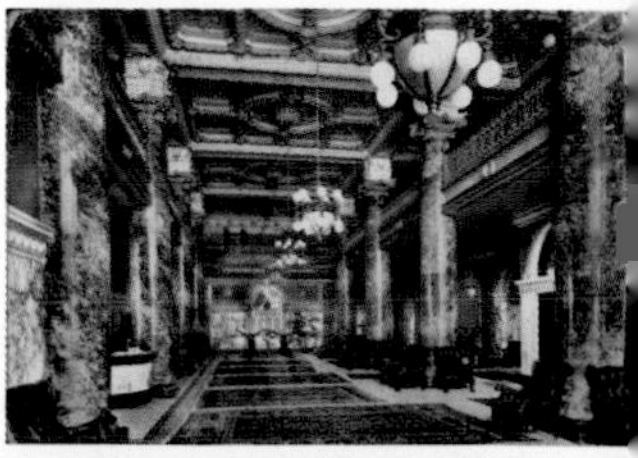

A vintage post card depicts the Alexandria's marble lobby

Library Tower was destroyed by a massive alien spaceship in *Independence Day* (1996)

Gas Company Tower ③⑦

Skidmore, Owings and Merrill, architects (1991).
555 W Fifth St. ⌲

A setback at the top of this 55-floor, 733-foot (223-m) tower of blue-gray granite reveals an elliptical core of reflective blue glass, shaped like a flame of the Gas Company logo. The building's imposing three-story lobby, reached by ground-floor escalators, faces an outdoor water garden. Integrating interior and exterior, ten rows of glass-covered water fountains run through the lobby granite floor to the garden, where they spurt forth from the ground.

An apparently seamless lobby glass wall showcases a 300-foot-high (91-m) mural, *Dusk* (1991), by Frank Stella. Painted on the adjacent Pacific Bell/AT&T Building, it is said to be the largest abstract mural in the world.

The building's main lobby, with four limestone-clad elevator banks, was featured in the opening scenes of *Speed* (1994). Keanu Reeves, as a LAPD SWAT cop, descends the high-rise's elevator shaft and rescues passengers trapped in a bombed elevator, just before it plunges into the abyss below.

One Bunker Hill ③⑧

James and David Allison, architects (1931).
601 W Fifth St. ⌲(➔ p234)

This was in its time on the cutting-edge of technology as one of the first all-electrically heated and cooled buildings in the western United States and one of the first earth-quake-proof structures in LA.

Designed in Art Deco style, the 14-story limestone and terra-cotta office tower was originally the home of the Southern California Edison Company. In order to make a public statement about the owner, three stone reliefs by Merrell Gage, with allegorical representations of Hydroelectric Energy, Light and Power, were placed above the octagonal corner entrance.

Inside, the intricate Art Deco patterns of the lobby floor are composed of 17 varieties of marble, while the 30-foot high coffered ceiling is etched in gold. A mural by Hugo Ballin, *The Apotheosis of Power* (1930), celebrates electric energy. The two prominent figures at the right are Benjamin Franklin and Dr William Gilbert, an English doctor who made important discoveries about static electricity in the 16th century.

Library Tower ③⑨

I M Pei & Partners, architects (1992).
633 W Fifth St. ⌲

Lobby of the One Bunker Hill

Formerly known as the First Interstate World Center, this magnificent white tower is located across the street from the Central Library. The 75-story skyscraper, the tallest on the West Coast, was made possible when its developer purchased air rights from the city, which allowed the high-rise to exceed the normal zoning limits. In return, the library was provided with funds necessary for the restoration and expansion of its building damaged in the arson fires of 1986.

Standing 1,018 feet (310 m) tall, the cylindrical skyscraper is seismically reinforced with an innovative dual frame.

Citigroup Center, Library Tower and Gas Company Tower

The building is based on an interaction of circular and orthogonal geometries, which essentially creates a squared circle as its floor plan. Its diameter decreases toward the top through a series of setbacks, ending up with a splendid circular crown of glass and faceted stone.

On the first weekend in October, the annual "Stair Climb to the Top" takes place in the Library Tower's staircase, intended for the rest of the year as an emergency exit. The fund-rising event attracts more than 1,000 climbers, who pay $25 each for an opportunity to jump, run or crawl up the highrise's 1,500 stairs, from the sidewalk to the rooftop.

Unity (1993), a lobby relief by Vitaly Komar and Alexander Melamid, adorns the Library Tower's lobby. Three large figures of angels are the artists' interpretation of a 13th-century fresco painted in a chapel in Assisi, Italy.

In the blockbuster hit *Independence Day* (1996), a fire beam blast by a gigantic alien spaceship blows up the Library Tower, together with a group of Angelenos gathered on the rooftop to greet the invaders.

Citigroup Center ④⓪

A C Martin & Associates, architect (1979).
444 S Flower St. ⌨

Formerly known as the Wells Fargo Tower, this 48-story-high, stepped-back rectangular building features recognizable horizontal bands of stainless steel and mirrored insulating glass windows. Set back from the street corner, the skyscraper is surrounded with a spacious, palm-shaded plaza, connected via escalators to the upper Hope St and a small garden with a waterfall. A remarkable collection of sculptures by Mark DiSuvero, Michael Heizer, Bruce Nauman, Robert Rauschenberg and Frank Stella is displayed throughout its outdoor areas.

The building served as a location for a number of movies, including *Gotcha!* (1985), *Baby Boom* (1987), *Beverly Hills Cop II* (1987) and *Black Rain* (1989). It was also the bank Robert De Niro and Val Kilmer robbed in *Heat* (1995). While exiting the building with their loot, they were ambushed by Al Pacino and the LAPD, followed by an astounding chase and shootout on the streets of downtown LA.

However, the building's most famous role was as the home of the McKenzie Brackman law firm in the television hit series *L.A. Law* (1986-1994).

Futuristic-looking Westin Bonaventure Hotel

Westin Bonaventure Hotel ④①

John Portman, architect (1976).
404 S Figueroa St.
☎(213) 624-1000. ⌨

Consisting of five cylindrical towers sheathed in bronze mirror-glass, this flashy futuristic structure is one of the most distinctive on the city's skyline. Twelve external glass-bubble elevators slide up 35 floors to the rooftop, where a revolving cocktail lounge offers panoramic views across the city.

The Bonaventure's sci-fi inspired design has qualified it as a particularly suitable site of futuristic or action films such as *Buck Rogers in the 25th Century* (1979), *Blade Runner* (1982), *Blue Thunder* (1983) and *Lethal Weapon 2* (1989). A scene in

Citigroup Center was used as the exterior of the bank robbed in *Heat* (1995)

Rain Man (1988), in which Tom Cruise refused an offer of $250,000 to return his autistic older brother (Dustin Hoffman) to the mental institution from which he was kidnapped, was filmed by the Bonaventure's pool. In the suspense thriller *In the Line of Fire* (1993), veteran Secret Service Agent Clint Eastwood, while trying to foil an assassination attempt on the president, was held hostage in the hotel's glass elevator by psycho killer John Malkovich. In the thriller *Nick of Time* (1995), which is set almost entirely within the Bonaventure, Johnny Depp rides the same elevators. He plays a blackmailed father who must kill the governor of California in order to save his kidnapped young daughter.

But the hotel's most memorable appearance was in *True Lies* (1994). In this action movie Arnold Schwarzenegger, playing a top spy Harry Tasker, chases a terrorist suspect galloping on a horse through the hotel lobby, kitchen and finally into the Bonaventure's glass elevator.

Arnold Schwarzenegger rode in the Westin Bonaventure's elevator in *True Lies* (1994)

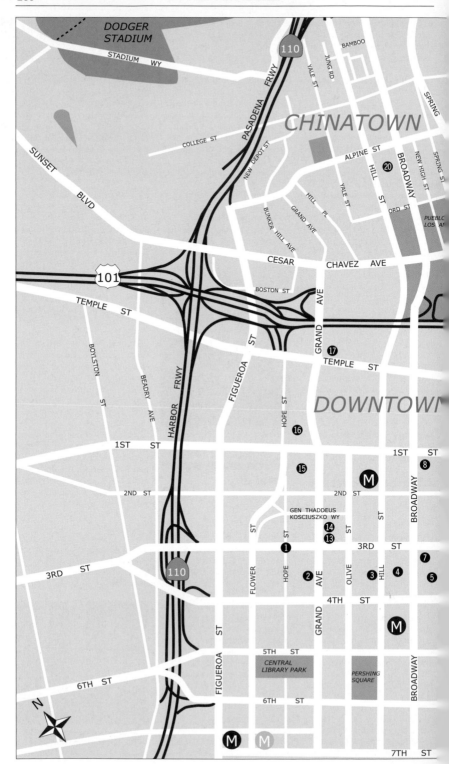

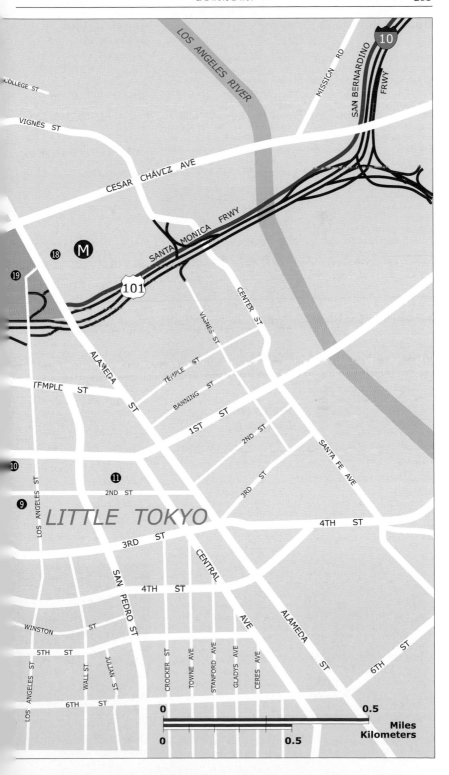

Bunker Hill (site) ❶

" . . . the top of Bunker Hill . . . you could find anything from down-at-heels ex-Greenwich-villagers to crooks on the lam, from ladies of anybody's evening to County Relief clients brawling with haggard landladies in grand old houses with scrolled porches . . . It had been a nice place once . . . "
—Raymond Chandler, *The King in Yellow* (1938)

Developed in the 1870s, Bunker Hill was an upscale neighborhood of lavish Victorian mansions, which attracted many of Los Angeles' leading families, including the Crockers and Bradburys. When its wealthy class started departing westward after World War I, Bunker Hill entered a slow decline, and in the following decades the once exclusive area deteriorated into a collection of crumbling old structures. To rid itself of this eyesore, the city introduced a plan for radical "urban renewal." In the early 1960s, all existing buildings in the area were bulldozed away and the hilltop leveled off, making way for gleaming office towers and cultural attractions that now form the nucleus of modern downtown.

Bunker Hill's decaying urban landscape, with its crumbling manors and dilapidated rooming houses, was

Bunker Hill mansions and Angels Flight Railway in 1903

the perfect setting for the Dark City stories of film *noir* of the 1940s and 1950s. In the 1948 thriller *The Night Has a Thousand Eyes*, the clairvoyant played by Edward G Robinson descends a long flight of stairs paralleling Angels Flight, which connected Bunker Hill to the streets below. Portraying a famous jazz musician, James Stewart climbs the same stairs in *The Glenn Miller Story* (1954).

Wells Fargo Center

Wells Fargo Center ❷

Skidmore, Owings and Merrill, architects (1983).
333-355 S Grand Ave.

With its striking profile rising from the top of Bunker Hill, this development was originally known as Crocker Center before Wells Fargo Bank acquired the Crocker Bank in 1986. The project is comprised of two trapezoidal high-rises of 54 and 45 stories, linked by a three-story pavilion. The angled office towers are sheathed in polished red granite and copper-bronze insulating glass.

Between the towers, a glass-walled atrium features a water garden designed by Lawrence Halprin and sculptures by Robert Graham, Jean Dubuffet, Nancy Graves, Juan Miró and Louise Nevelson.

The Wells Fargo History Museum traces the history of the company.

Angels Flight Railway ❸

351 S Hill St.
☎(213) 626-1901. ⌐ NRHP

When it first opened on New Year's Eve in 1901, this inclined funicular railway was billed as "the Shortest Paying Railway in the World." Funicular means that the system's twin cars, one ascending and one descending, were counterbalanced and drawn by the same cable. Two orange-and-black cars, Olivet and Sinai, named for two hills in the Holy Land, quickly became a favorite mode of transportation to residents and visitors alike. The line carried riders up and down a steep incline of 315 ft (96 m), between the fashionable Bunker Hill neighborhood and the commercial district on the streets below.

The railway was dismantled in 1969 to make way for the California Plaza development, and the old wooden cars were put into storage. In 1996, after a careful restoration, the beloved landmark was reinstalled a half-block south from its original location. Following a fatal crash in February 2001, when one car plummeted back down track and rammed into the other, the line has been closed for repairs.

When it opened in 1901, Angels Flight was called "the one-cent line" for the penny fare. The cost of a ride soon

Angels Flight Railway

Countless varieties of dried hot chiles are offered for sale at the Grand Central Market

Biddy Mason Monument features a timeline wall that chronicles the former slave's life

was raised to a nickel and remained unchanged until 1969, when the railway ceased operation. When it reopened in 1996, passengers paid 25 cents for a ride that takes about a minute.

While riding Angels Flight Railway in *The Turning Point*, (1952), an investigative reporter played by William Holden witnesses a shooting. The railway also appears in the musical biopic *The Glenn Miller Story* (1954), in a scene where James Stewart looks in a store window.

Grand Central Market ④

317 S Broadway.
☎(213) 624-2378.
🕐Mon-Sat 9am-6pm and Sun 10am-5:30pm.

The focal point of downtown's Historic District and the heart of Los Angeles' Latino community, this block-long enclosed market is fashioned after traditional Mexican marketplaces. The building, formerly known as the Homer Laughlin Building, was designed in 1897 as a department store and was the first steel-reinforced structure in the city. Since its ground floor was remodeled into a market in 1917, waves of immigrants and generations of Angelenos have flocked to this huge food hall.

The market is one of the busiest places in downtown, with 25,000 daily visitors attracted by an unforgettable blend of vivid colors, crisp

aromas and loud peddling. Its 50 individual food stalls offer an incredible variety of exotic products from Latin American countries. Here can be found such rare delicacies as fresh chicken feet, necks and gizzards, lamb heads, pork tails and beef feet. Also present are mounds of inexpensive fresh fruits and vegetables, including cactus and jicama, all types of beans and chiles, along with spices and healing herbs. Fast-food counters sell all kinds of Latin American and Asian specialties.

Biddy Mason Monument ⑤

Sheila Levrant de Bretteville (1991)
333 S Spring St.

Born a slave, Biddy Mason *walked* behind her owner's wagon for seven months, all the way from Mississippi to Utah. Mason followed the wagon train again to California, a free state, where she won her freedom in a landmark court victory in 1856.

Working as a midwife and nurse, she saved enough to buy a small lot at 331 S Spring St, where she built a house. Out of her home she operated the city's first orphanage and helped found the city's first black congregation, the First African Methodist Episcopal Church. One of LA's first philanthropists, she sent food baskets to prisoners in local jail and paid for food given to homeless flood victims.

Commemorating Biddy Mason's life with a timeline wall, this small urban park is a tribute to a remarkable African-American woman.

Spring Street Financial District ⑥

As the site of the major financial institutions in the first decades of the 20th century, Spring St earned the reputation as the "Wall Street of the West." Following the area's slow decline, the city's business district relocated to the new Bunker Hill development beginning in the 1960s. The structures that remain comprise a remarkably homogenous collection of Beaux-Arts and Art Deco buildings. Designated as a National Register Historic District, efforts are underway to preserve and renovate these treasures.

A vintage post card of Spring St

Entrance to the Bradbury Building. The façade is generally regarded unremarkable compared to its imposing sky-lighted interior.

George Wyman, architect (1893).
304 S Broadway.
☎(213) 626-1893.
⏰lobby open to the public Mon-Fri 9am-6pm; Sat, Sun 9am-5pm.
🏛 NRHP

Elaborate cast-iron and wood-encrusted balustrades

In *Blade Runner* (1982), the Bradbury Building was used as the bizarre residence of the character J F Sebastian, the genetic designer. Here special police officer Deckard (played by Harrison Ford) "retires" replicant Pris (Daryl Hannah) and then faces Roy (Rutger Hauer) in a climactic duel.

Bradbury Building ❼

When mining millionaire and real estate tycoon Lewis Bradbury decided to leave a legacy by erecting a unique office building, he approached the famous local architect Sumner Hunt. Dissatisfied with the architect's proposals, he asked Hunt's draftsman, George Wyman, for a new plan. It is still a mystery why Bradbury offered a job to an inexperienced apprentice. Wyman, who didn't have any formal architectural training, was initially reluctant to accept an assignment. He allegedly consulted his dead brother via Ouija board, who advised him to take the Bradbury commission because it would make him famous. Wyman's design was influenced by an 1887 book *Looking Forward* by Edward Bellamy, which described an utopian society in the year 2000. The book depicted a futuristic commercial building with a "vast hall full of light, received not alone from the windows on all sides, but from the dome, the point of which was a hundred feet above." Bradbury didn't live to see his building completed; he died a few months before its opening. Wyman later signed up for a correspondence course in architecture, but never again designed anything significant.

The plain exterior of the Bradbury Building does not warn the unprepared visitor of the architectural marvels waiting inside. One of the most fascinating spaces in the country, the building's interior is bathed in diffused sunlight entering through a glass roof. Five stories high, the central court is surrounded with two open-cage elevators, balconies and open stairways, and covered with intricately designed ironwork balustrades. It combines walls of glazed yellow bricks, tiled floors, marble stairs and rich oak paneling for a startling effect.

The Bradbury Building has long been a popular Hollywood location. It was the setting where dying Edmund O'Brien tracks down and kills his own murderer in the first version of *D.O.A.* (1950). It served as a New York publishing house where Jack Nicholson had his office in *Wolf* (1994). But the building's most prominent appearance was in sci-fi thriller *Blade Runner* (1982).

Ross Cutlery. For those still interested, this shop at the front of the Bradbury Building was mentioned during the O J Simpson murder trial as the place where the actor allegedly bought that infamous 15-inch (38-cm) knife.

The magnificent interior court of the Bradbury Building

Los Angeles Times Building ⑧

Gordon B Kaufmann, architect
(1935)
202 W 1st St.
☎(213) 237-5000.
☞free guided 45-minute tour,
Mon-Fri; call for reservations a week
in advance: ☎(213) 237-5757.

This stately building is the headquarters for the *Los Angeles Times*, the nation's third largest daily newspaper. Founded in 1881, the newspaper was controlled by the influential Chandler family for more than a century, until it was taken over by the Chicago-based Tribune Corporation in 2000. Built in PWA Moderne style with Streamline touches, the monumental 10-story structure was designed to house both editorial offices and printing facilities

The first two floors of the exterior are sheathed in pink granite, while cream-colored limestone clads the upper stories. The façade, with its linear detailing, concrete grilles and decorative sculpture, is dominated by an imposing clock tower. Sculpted eagles, a popular motif at the time, were repeatedly used.

The original building, which no longer accommodates printing presses, was expanded with two later additions. The newspaper's Globe Lobby features a revolving Art Deco planet Earth and a small display of the history of *The Times*. Two large murals by Hugo Ballin, entitled *Newspaper* (1935), depict different stages in the production of the newspaper and the history of LA.

St Vibiana's Cathedral ⑨

Ezra F Kysor, architect (1876).
114 E 2nd.
Closed to the public.

Easily recognized by its 83-foot (25-m) bell tower, this landmark church was built in the Spanish Baroque style in

The Caltans District 7 headquarters was dubbed the "Death Star"

1876 by Ezra F Kysor, who is considered the city's first professional architect. In 1922 architect John C Austin expanded and remodeled the building in the Italianate style. The former seat of the Archbishop of Los Angeles, the cathedral was supposedly inspired by a church in Barcelona, Spain, and features a barrel-vaulted, coffered ceiling supported by rows of Corinthian columns The relics of St Vibiana, a third-century Christian martyr whose remains were discovered near Rome in 1853, were preserved in a marble sarcophagus inside the church (➔ p272).

Devastated by the 1994 Northridge earthquake, the building will undergo a costly seismic retrofit and will house a public library and host cultural events.

St Vibiana's Cathedral

Caltrans Building ⑩

Thom Mayne/Morphosis (2004)
100 S Main St.

This 13-story monumental building was designed by Thom Mayne for the California Department of Transportation (Caltrans).

On the east and west façades, the modernist structure is sheathed in perforated blue-gray aluminum panels that reduce the heat gain by 50 percent. More than 1,000 mechanized louvered screens automatically open and close depending on the time of day, controlling light and allowing air circulation. Hiding windows, the panels seem nontransparent from the street, while they are easy to look through from offices. The south façade incorporates solar panels that shield the interior and generate approximately 5% of the building's energy.

The building's most striking feature is a 120-foot (36-m) light well. Cut through 12 stories, it brings natural light down and forms an entryway from the courtyard.

The four-story, open-air lobby is lined with stripes of neon and argon tubes designed by artist Keith Sonnier. With its shifting patterns of red and blue fluorescent lights, the striking installation mimics cars passing on a freeway at night. Titled *Motordom*, it is the largest public art installation in LA.

Little Tokyo ⓫

An area bounded by First, Third, Main and Alameda streets.
☛guided 90-minute group tours are offered by Little Tokyo Business Association on weekdays; call ☎(213) 628-8268 for reservations. Ⓢ ⬚ NRHP ☛(→ p234)

The first Japanese immigrants settled in this neighborhood in the 1880s, and the small community thrived until the outbreak of World War II. In February 1942, under Executive Order 9066, the army forcibly removed the entire population of Japanese ancestry from the Pacific Coast to government internment camps inland. Detained for the war's duration, these Japanese Americans, most of them US citizens, lost everything they had—their land, homes and businesses. After the war, they received only a small fraction of their wealth in compensation from the federal government.

Ceremonial entrance of the Nishi Hongwanji Temple

Little Tokyo recovered slowly until the 1970s, when both local and Japanese investments started redevelopment of the area. The project transformed the traditional town into a busting modern city with office buildings, plazas, hotels and shopping centers. Today, Little Tokyo serves as an economic, social, cultural and spiritual center to Southern California's more than 200,000 Japanese Americans.

Yagura, a fire watchtower

The Japanese Village Plaza

David Hyun and Associates, architect (1979).
335 E Second St.
☎(213) 620-8861.

This is the community's focal point, an open-air mall designed in the style of a small Japanese village. It features one- and two-story shops and restaurants with white stucco walls and blue tile roofs, lined along a winding landscaped path. Its most distinctive symbol is *yagura*, a traditional fire watchtower, used to alert villagers to fires in medieval times.

Historic Little Tokyo

This row of thirteen buildings on the north side of First St between Central Ave and San Pedro St is the only unchanged block of Little Tokyo that survived the

recent redevelopment. Dating back to the early 1900s, these two-story buildings with narrow storefronts were placed on the National Register of Historic Places in 1986.

Fugetsu Do

315 E First St.

Opened in 1903 and still owned by the same family, this confectionery shop is the oldest continually operated store in Little Tokyo. It is said that the Chinese fortune cookie was invented here by the store founder Seiichi Kito, although similar claims were made by a Japanese American gardener in San Francisco and a local noodle manufacturer in downtown LA.

Fortune cookies contain slips of paper with encouraging messages or predictions

Remembering Old Little Tokyo (1996)

Representing the history of the area, this art project runs along the north part of First St. Embedded in brass letters in the sidewalk are inscriptions about historic events related to Little Tokyo and quotations by people who lived on First St from 1890 to 1941.

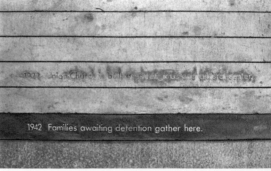

1922 Union Church built as a religious and cultural center

1942 Families awaiting detention gather here.

***Remembering Old Little Tokyo* by Sheila Levrant de Bretteville**

Higashi Hongwanji Buddhist Temple

Gold altar of the Higashi Hongwanji Temple

Nishi Hongwanji Buddhist Temple

Edgar Cline, architect (1924).
355-369 E First St.
Closed to the public.

This splendidly restored building was designed in a mix of styles, including Oriental, Italian and Egyptian. Its First St façade is an unremarkable brick commercial block, while the ceremonial entrance on Central Ave features an elaborate concrete canopy styled after the gateway to a temple in Kyoto, Japan. Interestingly enough, four brick pilasters of this former Buddhist temple have Egyptian papyrus capitals made of colored terra-cotta. Now a Historic Building, the structure is part of the Japanese American Museum.

Japanese American National Museum

Gyo Obata, architect (1999).
369 E First St,
☎(213) 625-0414.
www.janm.org.
⏱Tue-Sun 10am-5pm; Thu 10am-8pm. Closed major holidays. Ⓢ

This is the only museum in the country dedicated to the Japanese-American experience. Designed by the famous architect, the new pavilion symbolizes a melding of East and West, old and new. The building's two curved façades, one glass, the other red sandstone, intersect at the entry suggesting a blend of two cultures. The museum's stone and water garden, with its waterfall and reflecting pool, provides a serene contemplative environment.

Higashi Hongwanji Buddhist Temple

Kajima Associates, architect (1976)
505 E Third St.
☎(213) 626-4200.
⏱services are conducted on Sundays at 10am with sermons in both English and Japanese.

Belonging to the Jodo Shinshu Sect and established on another site in 1904, this was the first Japanese Buddhist temple in Los Angeles. Inspired by the Todaiji Temple in Nara, Japan, the present temple was built in concrete rather than customary wood. Traditionally shaped, its blue-tiled roof (*kawara*) is symbolically protected from fire by two gold-leafed stylized fish.

Inside the sanctuary, the traditional lanterns decorate a stunning lattice ceiling, masterfully constructed without a single nail. Imported from Japan, a magnificent gold altar displays a statue of Amida Buddha, small shrines and many ritual objects.

James Irvine Garden

244 S San Pedro St. Adjacent to the Japanese American Cultural and Community Center.

The garden's 170-foot (50-m) stream with small waterfalls symbolizes the experiences of several generations of Japanese in America. This winding stream gives the garden its Japanese name, *Seiryuen* (Garden of the Clear Stream). The garden contains several bamboo species, including a grove of rare *matake*, Japanese black pine, Japanese maple and Japanese flowering cherry,

To the Issei (1983)

Dominating the round plaza, this monumental rock sculpture is dedicated to the Issei, the first generation of Japanese immigrants to America. It is the work of the world-famous Japanese-American artist, Isamu Noguchi, who was born in the Boyle Heights neighborhood of East Los Angeles.

Japanese American National Museum

The City Hall's tower is prominently featured on police badges and official seals and documents

John C Austin, John Parkinson, Albert C Martin, architects (1928). 200 N Spring St.
☞free 45-minute tours: Mon-Wed 9am-1pm; for reservations call ☎(213) 978-1995. Visit the observation deck for panoramic views. ☛

The rotunda's tiled dome with the bronze chandelier

City Hall was dramatically demolished by Martian death rays in the sci-fi film *War of the Worlds* (1953)

City Hall ⑫

One of the city's most recognizable landmarks, this imposing building blends many different architectural styles. It combines a classical temple base with a skyscraper tower, incorporating Spanish Colonial and Moderne elements. The structure bears many references to local history and the builders made every effort to use materials originating in California. The building's sleek tower, capped with a ziggurat-like stepped pyramid, is the most distinctive visual symbol of the city.

Completed in 1928, this was LA's fourth modern City Hall. At 28 stories and 454 feet (138 m), it was for three decades the tallest building in the city, the only structure allowed to exceed the 150-foot (45-m) height limit. Damaged during the 1994 Northridge earthquake, the building underwent a three-year, $299-million seismic reinforcement and renovation. It is now considered the tallest retrofitted structure in America to use base isolators, devices that absorb shock during major earthquakes and allow buildings to move independently from the ground.

The interior's main feature is the 135-foot-wide (41-m) central rotunda. Rising four stories from the floor, the rotunda's tiled dome is decorated with eight figures symbolizing primary functions of the municipal government. Hanging from the dome, the completely restored 2,000-pound (900-kg), bronze-and-glass chandelier again dominates the rotunda after nearly 70 years. Considered a public hazard, it had been removed after the 1933 Long Beach earthquake and stored in the basement. The figures on the chandelier depict prominent individuals who shaped California history.

Over the years, City Hall has been the location of countless movies and television shows. It doubled as police headquarters and was featured in the opening shot in the popular 1950s series *Dragnet*. During the 1950s and 1960s, it housed the Daily Planet building in the original *Superman* television series, starring George Reeves. The building also appeared in such hits as *Mildred Pierce* (1945), *D.O.A.* (1950), *Chinatown* (1974), *48 Hours* (1982), *Another 48 Hours* (1990), *Die Hard II* (1990), *Speed* (1994), *L.A. Confidential* (1997) and *A Civil Action* (1998).

The rotunda's elaborate floor is covered with 4,000 pieces of colored marble, inlaid in intricate mosaic patterns. At its center is a cast bronze insert of a Spanish caravel in full sail.

Museum of Contemporary Art (MOCA) ⑬

Arata Isozaki, architect (1986).
250 S Grand Ave.
152 N Central Ave. (The Geffen)
☎(213) 626 6222.
www.moca.org
🕒Mon 11am-5pm; Thu 11am-8pm; Fri 11am-5pm; Sat-Sun 11am-6pm. Ⓢ

Since its opening in 1986, MOCA's permanent facility at California Plaza received accolades from both critics and the general public. In 1991 the American Institute of Architects named the building one of the ten best works of American architecture completed since 1980.

Museum of Contemporary Art (MOCA) was named one of the ten best works of American architecture completed since 1980

Architect Arata Isozaki said that a sinuous curve of the wall above the sunken courtyard was inspired by Marilyn Monroe's curvaceous figure

This was the first major building in the United States by internationally renowned Japanese architect Arata Isozaki, who prepared 30 different designs before the final solution was accepted. Isozaki combined cube, pyramid and cylinder shapes with the textures of sandstone, granite, aluminum and crystallized glass to achieve a stunning blend of Western form and Japanese tradition. From the street, visitors can see only the separate north and south wings; all galleries are on the entry level and surround a sunken courtyard.

MOCA is the only museum in Los Angeles devoted exclusively to collecting and presenting art from 1940 to the present. Founded in 1979, MOCA is the result of a partnership between the City of Los Angeles and major local collectors and artists.

The museum is located in two internationally acclaimed facilities, MOCA Grand Avenue and The Geffen Contemporary.

MOCA's remarkable permanent collection comprises more than 5,000 works in all visual media created from 1940 to the present by established as well as emerging artists.

Colburn School of Performing Arts ⑭

Hardy Holzman Pfeiffer Associates, architects (1998)
200 S Grand St.
☎(213) 621-2200.

With its masonry patterns and sloping, zinc-coated shingled roof, the Colburn School of Performing Arts echoes MOCA's limestone cladding and pyramidal skylights next door. The three-story complex houses offices, rehearsal rooms, teaching studios, a 100-seat recital hall and the 420-seat Zipper Concert Hall. With its variety of music, dance and drama programs, the school attracts more than 1,000 students per semester, ranging in age from three to eighteen.

Located at the upper level lobby is a reconstructed studio of the famous violinist Jascha Heifetz. Designed by Lloyd Wright in 1946, the hexagonal room was moved from the artist's house in West Los Angeles and now serves as a unique teaching space.

Colburn School of Performing Arts

The Disney Hall's sculptural exterior is sheathed in more than 6,400 stainless steel panels and 3,000 smaller "shingles" of polished steel

Frank O Gehry and Associates, architect (1988-2003).
111 S Grand Ave.
☎(323) 850-2000.
www.disneyhall.com.
☛self-guided audio tours and guided group tours daily; call
☎(213) 972-4339. ⑤
Concert tickets: box office open Tue-Sat noon-6pm; Sun noon-4pm.

The Hall's interior balconies

Walt Disney Concert Hall ⑮

More than 15 years in the making, this long-awaited new home of the LA Philharmonic opened in October 2003 and immediately emerged as Los Angeles' cultural landmark and the city's international symbol. It started in 1987 with a donation of $50 million by Walt Disney's widow, Lillian, who wished to build a new concert hall in memory of her late husband. In 1988, LA-based architect Frank Gehry won an international competition with his unconventional sculptural design, which immediately became a subject of intense public debate and criticism. The building's complex shape stirred controversy, forcing Gehry to go through more than 60 changes and revisions, which hampered construction for a decade.

The galleon-like, $274 million-structure occupies an entire square block. Its pulsating exterior consists of a series of folding and curving surfaces, resembling a sail at full mast. For its cladding, Gehry chose stainless steel over initially considered limestone for budgetary reasons, but also looking for a material reflective enough in the California daylight to "go almost white, like white sails."

The 2,265-seat main auditorium was designed by Gehry in collaboration with acoustician Yasuhisa Toyota specifically for classical music. Its "vineyard" shape seating arrangement retains the acoustical characteristic of a traditional "shoe box" style concert hall. The idea behind this unique concert space was to design the floor on different levels, thus dividing the seating area into several segments, with the audience surrounding the orchestra platform on all sides for an intimate experience.

Backlit after dark, pinholes in the stainless steel wall that flanks the main entrance stairway spell the hall's name in four-foot-tall (1,2-m) letters. The typeface, which is also used on signs throughout the hall, was custom-designed and named Gehry in honor of the architect.

Designed by Melinda Taylor and landscape architect Lawrence Reed Moline, the expansive garden features six species of flowering trees and more than 30 varieties of shrubs, perennials and ornamental grasses. They flower throughout the year, their ever-changing seasonal colors reflecting on the building's stainless steel surfaces.

Filtered down through skylights, natural light bathes five levels of lobby space

With its billowing ceiling and curved hardwood walls made of Douglas fir, the main auditorium is shaped to resemble a ship's hull and achieve the warmest possible natural sound

Music Center ⑯

Welton Becket and Associates, architect (1969).
135 N Grand Ave.
☎(213) 972-7211.
www.musiccenter.org
☛free guided one-hour tours: Tue-Fri 10am-1:30pm; Sat 10am-12 noon. Tour schedules are subject to change; call (213) 972-7483 to check availability and make reservations (necessary for groups only).

View of the Mark Taper Forum and the Dorothy Chandler Pavilion

Perched on what remained of Bunker Hill after its hilltop was leveled off, the imposing Music Center complex comprises three separate theaters. Sitting on the seven-acre plaza above the multi-level parking garage, three elegant white marble buildings are connected by mosaic pavements, a central reflective pool and fountains. Until the Music Center's opening, Los Angeles' performing companies were dispersed at different venues around town. Recognizing the need to concentrate performing arts at one location, Dorothy Buffum Chandler spearheaded the fund drive for construction during the 1960s. The wife of *Los Angeles Times* publisher Norman Chandler, she was legendary for her brazenness and was called "the greatest fund-raiser since Al Capone." When an affluent man once presented her with a $20,000 check for the Center, "Buff" tore it up in front of him saying that he could do much better. After campaigning for nine years, she eventually succeeded in raising more than $20 million in private donations.

Dorothy Chandler Pavilion
LA Opera: ☎(213) 972-7219; (213) 972-8001,
www.losangelesopera.com
Box office ⊕ Mon-Sat 10am-6pm.

The largest of the three theaters, named for the philanthropist civic leader, opened with fanfare in December 1964 with a gala concert of the Los Angeles Philharmonic conducted by Zubin Mehta. The 3200-seat auditorium has one of the largest stages in the country and is the main

venue for the Los Angeles Opera. It was also the home of the Los Angeles Philharmonic and the Los Angeles Master Chorale until the opening of Walt Disney Concert Hall across the street in 2003. The lavish interior boasts a stunning marble lobby furnished with gigantic crystal chandeliers, tapestries and sculptures.

In 1969, the Academy Awards moved to the new pavilion and stayed here until 1986, when they returned to the Shrine Auditorium. The Awards alternated between the Shrine and the Music Center until 2002, when the Oscar's permanent home at Kodak Theatre in Hollywood was inaugurated.

Mark Taper Forum
Box office ⊕ Tue-Sun noon-8pm.
Tickets: ☎(213) 628-2772.

Opened in 1967, this low, circular structure in the center of the complex is enclosed by a reflecting pool. Surrounded by a lofty colonnade, the theater's exterior walls are covered by an abstract, concrete bas-relief. Its intimate, 760-seat auditorium with an open stage is used for a variety of innovative and experimental productions, including *Zoot Suit* and *Children of a Lesser God*. Under the artistic direction of Gordon Davidson, the theater received every major theatrical award and many of its plays ended up as hits on Broadway.

Ahmanson Theatre
Box office ⊕Tue-Sun noon-8pm.
Tickets: ☎(213) 628-2772.

On the north end of the complex is the Ahmanson Theatre. Opened in 1967, it was recently completely renovated. Seating an audience of up to 2,100, with movable walls that configure the size of the auditorium, this theater brings productions that have broader appeal. It features mainly touring shows, including musicals, plays, dance and concerts. Among its best known musicals are *Phantom of the Opera* and *Miss Saigon*. If you don't get seats in the front half of the theatre, bring binoculars to see the star performers.

A bronze sculpture entitled *Pacem et Terris* (Peace on Earth) by Jacques Lipchitz (1969) is surrounded by a computer-controlled fountain that shoots plumes of water from ground level.

Peace on Earth (1969) by Jacques Lipchitz

José Rafael Moneo, architect
(2002).
555 W Temple St.
☎(213) 680-5200.
🕐 Mon-Fri 6:30am-7pm; Sat 9am-
5pm; Sun 7am-5pm.
☛ Mon-Fri at 1pm; free recitals on
the pipe organ most Wed at
12:45pm.

Suspended over an upturned crescent moon, Robert Graham's 8-foot (2,4-m) statue of Mary, the Mother of God, spreads her arms in welcome. An astonishing effect is achieved with a conic cut in the golden wall behind her head that creates a halo of blue sky.

Gregory Peck (1916-2003)
The legendary actor and a leading star of such memorable films as *Gentleman's Agreement* (1947), *Roman Holiday* (1953) and *The Omen* (1976) is interred in a crypt below the cathedral. He is best remembered for his portrayal of the heroic lawyer Atticus Finch in *To Kill a Mockingbird* (1962), for which he won the best actor Academy Award.

Cathedral of Our Lady of the Angels ⑰

Designed by Spanish architect José Rafael Moneo, the winner of the prestigious Pritzker Prize for architecture in 1996, this monumental complex was influenced by the cathedrals of Spain and South America. Built to endure for three centuries, the imposing modern structure with its sharp-angled, sand-colored concrete walls sits majestically on a hilltop site, encouraging visitors to embark on an introspective journey that starts inside.

Opened in 2002 to critical acclaim, the $200-million edifice was surrounded by controversy from the project's very beginning. Its critics denounce the building as a cover-up for the child sex-abuse scandal. They maintain that the church would better have spent the money on services to the poor and homeless.

Standing 30 feet (10 m) tall, the cathedral's front bronze doors weigh 25 tons and operate on a hydraulic system. Designed by sculptor Robert Graham, they depict in relief multicultural religious symbols and diverse ethnic representations of the Virgin Mary.

The interior is accessed through a long, narrowing ambulatory that leads past chapels alongside the nave, then abruptly turns right, revealing the soaring sanctuary in all its splendor. The 3,000-seat worship space is illuminated by 60-foot-high (18-m) clerestory windows of translucent alabaster stone, which filter natural light into golden hues. Particularly effective is a patterned wood ceiling, but the fussy bronze chandeliers, which were installed despite the architect's objections, only clutter the magnificent, light-filled space.

Two facing walls of the nave display 36 banner-like tapestries created by artist John Nava and produced by Belgian weavers. Depicting the Communion of Saints, the tapestries show 135 portraits of canonized saints and figures of common people from around the world.

In the Mausoleum beneath the Cathedral, in the Chapel bearing her name, lies the marble sarcophagus with the remains of St Vibiana, the third-century martyr and patron saint of the Archdiocese of Los Angeles (➔ p265).

The cathedral's interior is illuminated by clerestory windows of translucent alabaster, which filter natural light into golden hues

The 52-feet-high waiting room features original furnishings, including massive wood chairs and wrought-iron chandeliers

Arched front entrance to the Union Station

Union Station ⑱

John and Donald Parkinson, architects (1939).
800 N Alameda St.
☎(213) 683-6979.
🕐open 24 hours. ⌖ NRHP
📷(➜ p234)

When it was completed on May 3, 1939, over half a million people showed up to see the parade and opening day festivities for this distinguished building. The last of the nation's grand railway passenger terminals to be built, Union Station was jointly constructed by three major railroad companies—Southern Pacific, Santa Fe and Union Pacific. It was erected on the site of Los Angeles' original Chinatown, which was demolished and its inhabitants evicted to make way for the new station.

Its architecture is Spanish Colonial Revival, with Streamline Moderne and Moorish details. Reflecting the romantic heritage of the American Southwest, this low stucco structure features tiled roofs, huge rounded arches and a 135-foot (41-m) observation and clock tower.

During World War II, the station met the huge demand for passenger train traffic, bringing thousands of soldiers and workers to the area. After the war, train use steadily declined due to increased competition from automobile and air travel.

The building was revived in the 1990s with the arrival of the subway and now serves as the hub for a public transit system, in addition to the inter-city rail. The station's new wing, the Gateway Transit Center, houses a large collection of public art.

Colorful ceramic tiles, inspired by Native American patterns, edge the walls of the waiting room

The magnificent four-story-tall waiting room is graced with inlaid marble floors and multicolored tiled walls inspired by Native American designs. From its elaborate walnut-beamed ceiling hang 3,000-pound (1.350-kg) wrought-iron chandeliers. The mainly Spanish motifs of the interior are combined with elements of the Streamline Moderne and Art Deco, such as original wood-and-leather armchairs, light fixtures and glass signs.

The station's interior has often been used as a movie location. It provided the nostalgic World War II setting in the melodrama *The Way We Were* (1973). In *Blade Runner* (1982), it appeared as a police station of the future. In the sci-fi thriller *Species* (1995), the alien played by Natasha Henstridge arrives in Los Angeles at this station. It was also featured in *Gable and Lombard* (1975), *To Live and Die in L.A.* (1985), *Bugsy* (1991), *Grand Canyon* (1991) and *Nutty Professor 2* (2000).

The station appeared in the aptly named classic *Union Station* (1950), starring William Holden. In the movie the building served as a busy railway terminal set in Chicago.

El Pueblo de Los Angeles Historic Monument ⑲

An area bounded by Spring and Alameda streets, and Sunset Blvd and Arcadia St.
☎(213) 680-2525.
☛two-hour docent-led walking tour, Tue-Sat hourly between 10am and 1pm; call ☎(213) 628-1274 for info. Visitors' center is located at the Sepulveda House (➔ p275). A free 18-minute film on LA history, *Pueblo of Promise*, is shown here Mon-Sat at 11am and 2pm. ☛

Church of Our Lady the Queen of the Angels (Old Plaza Church)

This is the oldest surviving section of the city, comprising 27 historic buildings in a 44-acre state historic park. Although the monument is celebrated as the original site where, by order of King Carlos III of Spain, the city was founded on September 4, 1781 (➔ p16), the actual birthplace of Los Angeles was located just a short distance to the northeast from the present plaza. None of the original structures remain, being washed away by the flood of 1815, which forced settlers to move their pueblo to its present location.

With the growth of the town, its historic core was neglected and buildings steadily deteriorated until 1926, when civic activist Christine Sterling launched a campaign to preserve the entire area. Today, restored El Pueblo is the center of the Latino community and the site of fiestas and festivals year round, as well as a major tourist attraction with two million visitors per year.

Plaza de Los Angeles

An area between Main and Los Angeles streets. NRHP

Surrounded by public buildings and adobes of the rancheros, the square public plaza was the core of the pueblo until the 1870s, when the city's commercial center moved south. The plaza we know today was established in 1825, though its present circular layout and topiary landscaping, including four huge Moreton bay fig trees,

date from the 1870s. Around the plaza are statues of the founders of the pueblo, King Carlos III of Spain and Governor Felipe de Neve, and a plaque with a list of the first 44 settlers. In its middle is the hexagonal, wrought-iron bandstand known as the *kiosko*, which serves as the setting for annual fiestas and celebrations that revive the spirit of the Mexican era.

Plaza de Los Angeles is the stage of an armed car robbery in the opening scenes of *Lethal Weapon 3* (1992).

The Plaza's *kiosko* is the setting for numerous festivals

Church of Our Lady the Queen of the Angels

535 N Main Street.
☎(213) 629-3101.

Popularly known as the Old Plaza Church, this modest structure was completed in 1822 and is the oldest religious building in the city. It was designed by José Antonio Ramírez and built by Indian laborers supervised by

Joseph Chapman, the first US citizen to arrive in Los Angeles. To help bring in cash and complete the church, San Gabriel Mission padres donated seven barrels of brandy to be sold at auction. In an excess of moral zeal, God-fearing townsmen, on their own, helped the common cause by quickly emptying the barrels. The simple adobe structure originally had a flat roof covered with *brea* (tar) and a pounded earthen floor, which were subsequently replaced with red brick façade, a pitched roof and a Mission-style *campanario* (bell tower).

The Annunciation (1981) by Isabel Piczek.

This mosaic on the church façade is a replica of a detail from a mural painted in the Porziuncola Chapel in the Italian town of Assisi, the cradle of the St Francis's order. Spanish explorer Gaspar de Portolá gave the name Porciúncula to the river his expedition crossed in the Los Angeles basin in 1769 (today the Los Angeles River).

América Tropical (1932) by David Alfaro Siqueiros.

Italian Hall, 650 N Main St.
Closed to the public. (➔ p82)

Pico House

Ezra F Kysor, architect (1870).
430 N Main Street.
Closed to the public.

When it was opened in 1870 at the cost of $50,000 for the building and $30,000 for the furnishings, the Pico House was considered the most luxurious hotel in Southern California. Built by Pío Pico, the last governor of Mexican California, the 80-room hotel boasted such extravagancies as indoor plumbing, gas lighting fixtures and even two zinc bathtubs.

The Italianate building, with its elegant façade featuring incised arched openings, was the first three-story masonry structure in LA. The hotel was recently thoroughly restored, its gray and maroon shades selected after a careful study of old photographs.

LA-19 TYPICAL OF EARLY LOS ANGELES—OLVERA STREET, LOS ANGELES, CALIFORNIA

A vintage post card of Olvera Street shows a typical market scene

Olvera Street

125 Paseo de la Plaza.
☎(213) 628-1274.
🕐shops open daily 10am-7pm.
www.olvera-street.com.

Before it was opened as a colorful Mexican *mercado* in 1930, Olvera St was a filthy, dilapidated alley filled with machine shops and crumbling adobe and brick buildings. In a widespread effort to save the city's birthplace, Christine Sterling, called the "Mother of Olvera Street," used even the help of prison laborers, who graded and bricked the street.

Originally called Wine St, because of its proximity to vineyards and a winery, the street was renamed in 1877 in honor of the first county judge, Agustín Olvera, who once lived there.

The restored brick-paved block is lined with gift shops and *puestos* (stalls), selling Mexican handcrafted items including pottery, *piñatas* (clay or papier-mâché animals), hand-woven clothing and leather goods such as belts, bags and *huaraches* (sandals). Restaurants and sidewalk cafés offer authentic Mexican food, while street vendors sell all kind of confections, including *churros* (cinnamon bread sticks) and candied cones with tropical fruit flavors. Usual weekend entertainment includes singers, dancers and *mariachis*.

Avila Adobe

E-11 Olvera St.
🕐daily 10am-5pm. ⑤free.

This is the oldest existing residence in Los Angeles, constructed in 1818 as a town house for the Avila ranching family. Its first

owner, affluent cattle rancher Don Francisco Avila, became *alcade* (mayor) of the pueblo in 1810.

Originally built of adobe bricks, with walls three feet thick and floors of packed earth, the house was damaged by the 1870 and 1971 earthquakes and thoroughly restored in 1977. Today it is decorated to recall the atmosphere of a prosperous ranching family home in the late 1840s. Six rooms are furnished with period reproductions or antiques, including several pieces that belonged to the Avila family.

Sepulveda House

George F Costerisian and William O Merithew, architects (1887).
624 N Main St; W-12 Olvera St.
☎(213) 628-1274. ⑤free.
🕐Mon-Sat 10am-3pm. NRHP

The two-story combination business and residential building was constructed in the Eastlake style and today is one of only a few such structures still existing in the city.

The visitors' center is located on the first floor, in a room decorated in Victorian style, and features exhibits on the history of the pueblo. Two exhibits depict the lifestyle of the late 19th century: the kitchen has been restored to represent a boardinghouse kitchen of the 1890s and the bedroom reflects the cultural changes in Los Angeles, from Mexican traditions to a more American style.

Señora Sepulveda's bedroom (ca. 1890s) in the Sepulveda House

The West Gate was built in 1938 for New Chinatown's opening

Chinatown ⑳

An area bounded approximately by Alameda, Ord, Yale and Bernard streets.
☛ guided waking tours are offered by Chinese Historical Society by appointment; for reservations call ☎ (323) 222-0856. ➤ www.chinatown.com

The first Chinatown in Los Angeles was established in the 1870s, on a dilapidated street known as Calle de los Negros or Nigger Alley (➜ p25). The first Chinese who arrived in California during the Gold Rush were laborers working in mines and building railroads. In the LA area, Chinese worked as house servants, cooks, food peddlers or farm hands. They competed with whites for scant jobs and endured widely spread discrimination and open hatred. Racial tensions culminated in the "Chinese Massacre" of 1871, which left 19 Chinese men and boys dead at the hands of a white mob.

The maze of narrow streets and alleys belonging to the original Chinese settlement was demolished in 1933 to make way for the construction of Union Station. Displaced Chinese families relocated several blocks to the north, creating a new Chinatown in 1938.

Although the Chinese have moved out in large numbers to the suburbs of Monterey Park and Alhambra in recent years, Chinatown is still the cultural and commercial center of their community.

Authentic markets with their colorful and fragrant offerings sell a variety of traditional medicines, clothing, art and antiques. Food stores carry fresh produce and such dried culinary oddities as exotic mushrooms, sea snails, shark's fins, sea cucumbers, squid and shellfish. Many of the animals are sold alive, including frogs, turtles, poultry, rabbits, fish, crabs and lobster. Medicinal shops feature open bins of ginseng, ginger and other roots, dried bark, antler chips, herbs and tea.

The area's main attraction is, however, a variety of restaurants offering all kinds of Chinese food. Especially popular are *dim sum* parlors, which serve their delicacies from rolling steam carts.

Wishing Well
Gin Ling Way.

One of the most popular tourist attractions is this fanciful fountain, a copy of one in China, with its miniature mountain, tiny paths with bridges, and small shrines and statues.

Pagoda-shaped Hop Louie

Hop Louie Restaurant
950 Mei Ling Way.
☎ (213) 628-4244. ➤

Featuring exaggerated ornaments and trimmed in neon for additional effect, this easily recognizable place is the only pagoda-shaped structure in Los Angeles. Opened in 1940 as Golden Pagoda Restaurant, the famous five-tiered building has been featured in several Hollywood movies, including *Lethal Weapon* and *Rush Hour* (1998), in a scene where Jackie Chan jumps from the restaurant.

The Wishing Well is modeled on the Seven Star Caverns in China

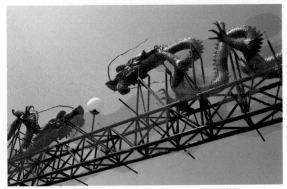

The Dragon Gateway symbolizes luck, prosperity and longevity

Gateway to Chinatown Monument
N Broadway, just north of Cesar E Chavez Ave.

This ornate gateway was designed by artist Rupert Mok in 2001 and features two dragons, male and female, facing each other on the metal framework. Painted in gold, with red flames at the elbows, the 3,000-pound (1.350-kg) fiberglass creatures appear engaged in some mythical fight. An opaque pearl, symbolizing longevity and prosperity, floats between them.

Elaborate visual effects are created by artificial lights and a nozzle system hidden under the fighting dragons. A fine spray of water creates a mist that, together with clouds made of aluminum mesh, suggest an illusion of the dragons descending from the sky.

East Gate
900 block of N Broadway.

Chinatown's central plaza is marked by an ornately decorated entrance gate (*pai lou*) dedicated to all mothers. Just behind the gate is the statue of Sun Yat-Sen, called the father of modern China.

The first planned urban Chinatown in the US, it was originally meant to attract tourists as much as locals. Its tiny pedestrian alleys are lined with brightly painted highly ornamented theme buildings spiced up with lanterns and neon strips. Tiled roofs, featuring animals that are supposed to give protection from evil, have their corners curved up to avert bad spirits.

Thien Hau Temple
750 N Yale St.
☎(213) 680-1860.
🕐daily 7am-6pm.

Housed in a former Italian Church purchased in 1990 by a Chinese-Vietnamese group, this small Buddhist chapel is dedicated to Thien Hau, goddess of heaven and protector of seafarers.

The narrow room, decorated with red and gold banners and lanterns, is filled with the sweet odor of burning incense. Fruit offerings lie in front of the carved altar shipped from China, adorned with statues of the temple's patron goddess and other deities.

Plans are underway to build a much larger temple on an empty lot next door.

The last scene in *Chinatown* (1974) was filmed on Spring St

In Roman Polanski's classic *Chinatown* (1974), the last utterance of the movie, "It's Chinatown, Jake," brings out LA's dismissive attitude toward the Chinese, so prevalent among many Angelenos during the Depression era. The film's final sequence, in which Evelyn (played by Faye Dunaway) is shot to death by a detective, was set in Chinatown's Spring St.

Bruce Lee Studio
628 W College St.

Formerly a martial arts academy, this is the place once frequented by Bruce Lee, who arrived in California from Hong Kong after being expelled from school for frequent fistfights. Lee was the pioneer of the *kung fu* genre and the internationally popular star of such cult action films as *Fists of Fury* (1971), *Enter the Dragon* (1973) and *Return of the Dragon* (1973).

The red and guilt altar with offerings in Thien Hau Temple

Calvary Cemetery

Mausoleum, block 56, crypt E-19 ④

Mausoleum, block 353, crypt E-4 ⑤

Mausoleum, block 352, crypt F-4 ①②

Mausoleum, block 354, crypt B-1 (Lou Costello) ③

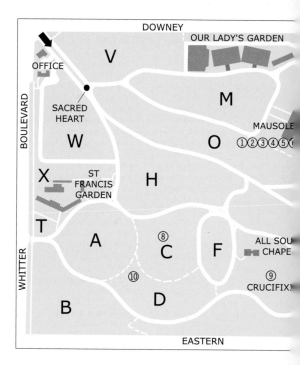

Angels on the facade of the Mausoleum of the Golden West

Egyptian-style monument

Mausoleum, block 60, crypt 3-F ⑥

Mausoleum, block 303, crypt D-7 ⑦

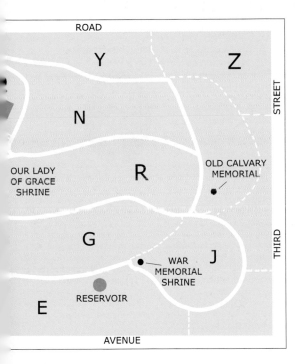

Grounds, section C, lot 586, grave 5 ⑧

Grounds, section F, lot 1693, grave 14 ⑨

Grounds, section D, lot 877, family plot ⑩

Gothic-style monument

Interior of the Mausoleum of the Golden West

Calvary Cemetery ㉑

4201 E Whittier Blvd. (Not on map; 6 miles east of downtown.)
☎(323) 261-3106.
🕐daily 8am-6pm.

This large Catholic cemetery was consecrated in 1896. The fourteen Stations of the Cross, represented by hand-painted plaster figures displayed in glass boxes, are placed throughout the cemetery. Most of the luminaries interred here are on the second floor of the main mausoleum.

Mausoleum of the Golden West, with ten-foot-tall statues of angels

Mausoleum of the Golden West

Ross Montgomery, architect (1927)

Designed by the leading architect of the Catholic Church of the period, the large, three-level concrete structure is one of the best examples of Art Deco Moderne style in Los Angeles. This remarkable building is a successful blend of the dominant style of the late 1920s and references to antiquity, including one of the reconstructions of the tomb of Mausolus at Halicarnassus. Ten Corinthian columns flank a wide stone courtyard, each carrying the statue of a ten-foot-tall angel heralding the Second Coming.

Inside, there are marble floors and walls, murals of California scenes and fine examples of stained-glass windows manufactured by the local Judson Studios.

John Barrymore
(1882-1942)

Although a marble crypt bearing his name and the Shakespearean epitaph "Good Night, Sweet Prince" is still here, the cremated remains of the youngest of the "Fabulous Barrymores" are buried in the family plot in Philadelphia. He was interred here for 38 years before his body was

removed to be cremated, honoring his last will (at the time of his passing in 1942, the Catholic Church did not allow cremation).

Considered to be the greatest Shakespearean actor to ever work on the American stage, Barrymore played on screen roles of great lovers. He was a top box-office attraction, starring with Mary Astor in *Don Juan* (1926), Joan Bennett in *Moby Dick* (1930), Greta Garbo in *Grand Hotel* (1932) and Carole Lombard in *Twentieth Century* (1934). *Rasputin and the Empress* (1932) was the only film in which John, Lionel and Ethel Barrymore appeared together.

His hard drinking and years of wild lifestyle took its toll, and toward the end of his life he appeared in B movie roles that were parodies of himself.

According to a Hollywood legend, after Barrymore's death, director Raoul Walsh and a few of his grieving pals bribed a guard and borrowed Barrymore's body from the mortuary. They took it to Errol Flynn's house and propped it into a chair, together with a drink. When Flynn returned home and saw his dead friend in front of the fireplace, he ran out screaming.

Actress Drew Barrymore is the granddaughter of John Barrymore and actress Dolores Costello (see below).

Lionel Barrymore
(1878-1954)

The elder brother of John and Ethel, Lionel was an accomplished stage actor when he joined Biograph Company in 1909, appearing in many of D W Griffith's two-reelers. He was a Hollywood leading man in the 1920s and later appeared in character roles, winning an Academy Award for best actor for his performance in *A Free Soul* (1931). During his career he appeared in some 250 films; he was also a director, writer, painter and a composer of orchestral music.

Ethel Barrymore Colt
(1879-1959)

Known as "the first lady of the American theater," Ethel appeared in several silent films in the 1910s before returning to the stage for the next 25 years. She made a triumphant Hollywood comeback in 1944, winning an Oscar for best supporting actress for her performance in *None But the Lonely Heart* (1944). A Broadway theater in New York was named after her.

Pola Negri (1899-1987)

The Polish-born dancer and stage actress became a German film star under the direction of Ernst Lubitsch. Upon her arrival in Hollywood, the dark-haired, green-eyed vamp became an immediate attraction for her exotic beauty and the aura of mystery she deliberately cultivated.

Noted for her rivalry with Gloria Swanson and romantic links with Rudolph Valentino, Charlie Chaplin and Howard Hughes, her career effectively ended with the advent of sound. It is said that Adolf Hitler was a great fan and watched her German-made film *Mazurka* (1935) weekly. She died of a brain tumor.

Mabel Normand (1894-1930)

She began modeling at thirteen and went to work for Biograph at sixteen, where director Mack Sennett made her a star. She was credited with throwing the first custard pie in the movies. The dark-haired beauty was considered the most talented comedienne of the silent screen. In the early 1920s, Normand's cocaine addiction was revealed and she was

Interior of the mausoleum

involved in several scandals, including the unsolved murder of director William Desmond Morris. Her career ended soon after and she died of a combination of pneumonia and tuberculosis.

Lou Costello (1906-1959)

Lou Costello and his partner, Bud Abbott, made one of the most successful comedy teams in cinema history. Abbott was the tall, lean, streetwise guy, while Costello played the short, chubby, slow-witted fellow.

Their comedy routines in smash hits such as *Buck Privates* (1941) and *Abbott and Costello Meet Frankenstein* (1948) made them the top box office attraction during the 1940s—they ranked number one in 1942. Costello died of a heart attack.

Irene Dunne (1901-1990)

Although she aspired to be a singer and auditioned for the Metropolitan Opera, Dunne ended up in Hollywood and received an Academy Award nomination for best actress for her first role in *Cimarron* (1931). She was nominated for an Oscar four more times before retiring from movies in the early 1950s. Dunne later became involved in politics and charitable work. On her crypt are the emblems of a Knight of Malta and a Knight of the Order of the Holy Sepulchre.

Grounds

Ted Healy (1896-1937)

A successful vaudeville comedian in the early 1920s, Healy first brought his boyhood friend Moe, and later his brother, Shemp Howard, to the act, which was known

as "Ted Healy and His Stooges." They appeared in several Broadway revues before arriving in Hollywood, where they made ten two-reel comedies together. After the Stooges left the act in 1934, Healy continued his film career, playing mostly supporting roles.

Ramon Novarro (1899-1968)

Mexican-born Novarro was a romantic idol of Hollywood silent films and the star of such hits as *The Prisoner of Zenda* (1922) and *Ben-Hur* (1925), in which he played the title role. He was often compared to Rudolph Valentino as the next Latin lover, but never reached Valentino's popularity.

Novarro was beaten to death on Halloween night by two hired male prostitutes. The murderers searched in vain for $5,000 in cash, reportedly hidden in the house.

Dolores Costello Barrymore (1903-1979)

She started her acting career at age eight, appearing in Vitagraph films with her famous father, Broadway matinee idol Maurice Costello. Dolores attained stardom with her role in *The Sea Beast* (1926), opposite legendary John Barrymore, whom she married two years later. Their son John Barrymore Jr is the father of actress Drew Barrymore.

A gorgeous, exquisite blonde, Dolores was known as the "Goddess of the Silent Screen." One of her last roles was Isabel Amberson in Orson Welles's *The Magnificent Ambersons* (1942). Next to her are buried her mother and father, **Maurice Costello**.

Front entrance of the mausoleum in Home of Peace Memorial Park

Mausoleum, Corridor of Love, family room ①

Mausoleum, Corridor of Immortality, crypt SW-405 ②

Mausoleum, Corridor of Eternal Life, crypt 215 ③

Home of Peac

GARDEN OF MAIM

ADDITION 4

FOUNTA

MAUSOLEUM AND CHAPEL ① ② ③

TALMUD TORAH EAST

EASTERN AVE

EAST

ADDITION X2

⑤

④

SECTION "D"

ADDITION 2

BENEVOLENT

SECTION "B"

ADDITION 1

REGULAR

FOUNTA

NORTHEAST

GARDEN OF DEBORAH

WHITTIER B

Warner Family Mausoleum I, Section D ④

emorial Park

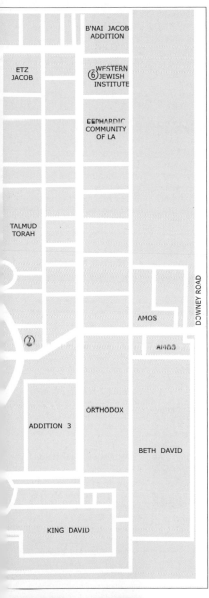

The mausoleum's interior features a dramatic dome with ornate chandelier, horseshoe arches for doorways and stained glass windows

Western Jewish Institute Section, row 5, grave 1 ⑥

Warner Family Mausoleum II, Section D ⑤

Joshua Section ⑦

Home of Peace Memorial Park ㉒

4334 Whittier Blvd. (Not on map; 6 miles east of downtown.)
☎(323) 261-6135.
🕒Sun-Fri 9am-4pm; closed Sat.

The oldest Jewish cemetery in Los Angeles originally opened in 1855 in another location and moved to its present site in 1902. The mausoleum, which was dedicated in 1934, has a Near Eastern appearance, with its Islamic dome and two turrets resembling minarets.

Mausoleum

Carl Laemmle (1867-1939)
Behind the brass doors is the crypt of Carl Laemmle, one of the first film moguls, inventor of the idea of a movie star, founder of Universal Pictures and its president for 25 years (➜ p333). He was notorious for his nepotism—besides his son, who became the studio's head of production on his 21st birthday, Laemmle at one point hired 70 relatives. This prompted poet and humorist Ogden Nash to write a famous rhyme, "Uncle Carl Laemmle has a very large faemmle." A number of the family members are interred in the same room here, including his son, producer **Carl Laemmle Jr** (1908-1979), known for high quality of his filmss.

Louis B Mayer (1885-1957)
In charge of Metro-Goldwyn-Mayer for 27 years, tyrannical film mogul Louis B Mayer ruled his fiefdom with an iron fist (➜ p414). He built MGM into an entertainment giant, controlling every aspect of production and often interfering with the personal lives of his greatest stars. He died of leukemia. At Mayer's funeral, producer Samuel Goldwyn reportedly commented, "The reason so many people showed up at his funeral was because they wanted to make sure he was dead."

The Three Stooges were a hugely popular comedy team whose specialty was crude slapstick, consisting of such vulgarities and physical abuses as hitting each other on the head with sledgehammers, poking each others' eyes, grabbing each others' noses or kicking shins. Original members were brothers Moe and Shemp Howard, who appeared in 1923 with vaudevillian Ted Healy in an act called "Ted Healy and His Stooges." They were joined in 1928 by violinist Larry Fine and moved to Hollywood, where Shemp was replaced by his brother, Curly (Jerome Howard). In 1946 Curly left the Stooges after suffering a stroke, and Shemp rejoined the team. After Shemp's death in 1955, Joe Besser joined the act, and he was replaced by Joe DeRita (Curly-Joe) in 1959. The Stooges were among the most profitable performers of the period, appearing in some 200 shorts between 1934 and 1958. Two of the brothers, Shemp and Jerome "Curly" Howard, are interred at the Home of Peace Memorial Park.

The Three Stooges—Larry, Moe and Curly

Shemp Howard (1901-1955)
An original member of the Three Stooges, Shemp died of a heart attack while on his way home from a boxing match.

Fanny Brice (1891-1951)
The ashes of the famous singer and comedienne were moved from the niche in the Corridor of Benevolence to the new Memorial Gardens area at Westwood Memorial Park in 1999.

Grounds

Jack Warner (1892-1978)
Best known of the four Warner brothers, Jack was the driving force of Warner Bros Studio (➜ p329). Because of his harsh treatment of the employees, even major stars, the studio earned title "Buchenwald of Burbank." In 1957 Jack talked his brothers Harry and Albert into selling their stock in the company to a group of investors. When they did, Jack bought his shares back, thus remaining the largest shareholder of Warner Bros. When he heard about his brother's deception, Harry refused to talk to him again. Jack died of pulmonary edema.

Warner Mausoleum I

The larger of two Warner family mausoleums contains the remains of Benjamin Warner and his wife Pearl Leah, the parents of twelve children, including the four founders of the Warner Bros Studio. Their three daughters and two sons are also interred here, including **Samuel L Warner** (1885-1927), the most enthusiastic of the four Warner brothers about the "talking pictures" novelty.

Warner Mausoleum II

The smaller Warner family mausoleum contains the remains of **Harry Morris Warner** (1881-1958), president of Warner Bros. Here also rest his wife, son, and daughter and her husband, director **Charles Vidor** (1900-1959). Vidor was a Hungarian-born director, best known for *Gilda* (1946), a masterpiece of screen erotica. He died during the filming of *Song Without End* (1960).

Jerome Howard (1903-1952)
The most popular of the Three Stooges, "Curly" was a regular victim of screen abuse by his older brother, Moe Howard. He died of a stroke.

Pasadena

The first American community was established here in 1873 by farmers from Indiana, who bought the land that was part of the former Rancho San Pasqual. They named their settlement Pasadena, which reportedly means "crown of the valley" in the Chippewa Indian language. Located at the base of the San Gabriel Mountains, Pasadena featured gentle Mediterranean climate, clean air, proximity of the sea and snow-capped peaks.

Seal of the city of Pasadena

capped peaks.

When the Southern Pacific and Santa Fe railroads connected Pasadena to the East in 1885, the small town flourished overnight. An influx of visitors who sought refuge from the harsh winters at home turned Pasadena into a fashionable winter resort. Fancy hotels, such as Hotel Green, were quickly constructed to accommodate wealthy tourists.

The Mt Lowe Scenic Railway, or "Railway to the Clouds," as it was popularly known, was once Southern California's main tourist attraction. Opened in 1893, the 3,200-foot-long (975-m) cable line reached a height of 1,325 feet (400 m) in an almost perpendicular ascent of the mountainside. During the four decades it was in operation, it carried more than 3.1 million passengers, offering unsurpassed panoramic views of the entire Los Angeles basin along the way.

An open car of the Mt Lowe Railway offered top scenic views

In this idyllic 1904 photo, a group of trolley line passengers picks poppies in the Altadena foothills

Some of the wealthy visitors, including chewing gum magnate William Wrigley, Jr and David Gamble of Procter & Gamble, decided to become permanent residents. They built elaborate mansions on "Millionaire's Row" on Orange Grove Ave, such as the lavish estate of beer magnate Adolphus Busch, surrounded with 30 acres of exotic gardens.

Around the turn of the 20th century Pasadena attracted numerous artists, writers, craftsmen and especially architects, becoming a center of the aesthetic movement known as the "Arroyo Culture." Pasadena's impressive cultural legacy can today be seen in its world-class art collections and unequaled architectural heritage. It is one of the nation's largest repositories of the Craftsman-style architecture, which reached its peak in the works of local architects, brothers Charles and Henry Greene (→ p303). The city also boasts one of the finest groups of Spanish Colonial Revival houses, with the works of such masters as George Washington Smith and Bertram Goodhue, as well as Pasadena residents—architects Roland Coate, Gordon B Kaufmann and Wallace Neff.

A vintage post card depicts Busch's lavish sunken gardens

El Molino Viejo (The Old Mill) ❶

1120 Old Mill Rd. San Marino.
☎(626) 449-5458.
www.old-mill.org
🕐Thu-Sun 1-4pm. ⓢfree. NRHP

This well-preserved building is one of the last examples of Spanish Mission-style architecture in southern California. Built about 1816 by converted Gabrieliño Indians under the supervision of the Franciscan padres at San Gabriel Mission, it was the first water-powered gristmill in southern California.

In 1823 another mill was built adjacent to the mission and the old mill was gradually abandoned. Following the secularization of the missions, Pío Pico, the last Mexican Governor of California, sold 16,000 acres (6,400 ha) of the mission lands in 1846.

Since then the Old Mill has gone through several different hands. Among its more prominent owners were James S White, the editor of Los Angeles' first newspaper, *The Star*, and Henry Huntington, who used the building as a clubhouse for his hotel's golf course.

The Old Mill is the southern California headquarters of the California Historical Society. The museum features changing exhibitions covering the history of the state and displays the water wheel and several pieces of old Spanish furniture. The wheel chamber contains a cross-sectioned working model, which demonstrates how the building functioned as a gristmill.

El Molino Viejo (The Old Mill)

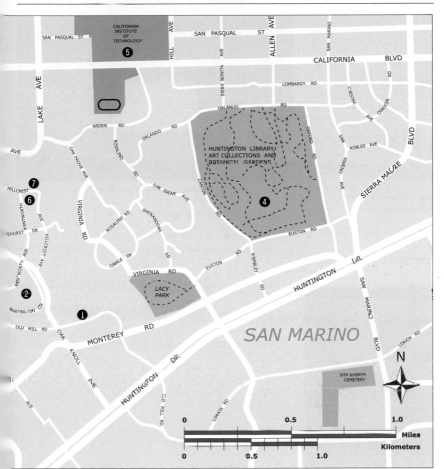

The Ritz-Carlton Huntington Hotel ❷

Charles Whittlesey, Hunt and Grey, architects (1907, 1914).
1401 S Oak Knoll Av, San Marino.
☎ (626) 568-3900. 🔫

Named for its original owner, Civil War General Marshall C Wentworth, the Hotel Wentworth opened in 1907 as the grand resort for wealthy Easterners and Mid-westerners. It was acquired in 1913 by railroad tycoon Henry Huntington, who renamed it and redesigned the main building and grounds. Among the famous visitors who stayed here were Theodore Roosevelt, Albert Einstein, the Dalai Lama, and Prince Philip and Princess Anne of England.

With its 23 acres of exquisitely landscaped Horseshoe and Japanese gardens, the imposing six-story structure exudes the grandeur of Pasadena's golden age. The California's first Olympic-size swimming pool was built here. The Ritz-Carlton received a complete renovation in 1991, when its central observation tower was razed and rebuilt in the Mission Revival style.

The hotel's main attraction is the Picture Bridge, a covered redwood footbridge spanning the arroyo, which features 39 triangular panels of California scenes painted by artist Frank Moore in 1932.

The hotel is featured in the films *Nixon* (1995) and *The Parent Trap* (1998), as well as the television series *Murder, She Wrote* and *West Wing*.

The Ritz-Carlton Huntington Hotel

Although defaced, the Rialto's façade still bears Spanish Baroque touches

The Rialto's richly flamboyant Egyptian interior is almost intact

Rialto Theatre ❸

L A Smith, architect (1925).
1023 Fair Oaks Ave, South Pasadena.
☎(626) 388-2122. 🐾 NRHP

Designed by foremost California theater architect, L A Smith, who also designed the Beverly Theatre in Beverly Hills, the Rialto originally included the theater, retail shops and an apartment. The Rialto opened on October 17, 1925 with the world premiere of the film *What Happened to Jones?* Klieg lights, brought from Hollywood especially for this occasion, criss-crossed the sky throughout the evening.

With its multicolored plaster ornaments and vivid stenciling, the dazzling interior is mostly unaltered. Harpies (half woman, half vulture) bear up Moorish organ screens (the theatre organ was removed and sold after a fire in 1968). An Egyptian proscenium arch features the central head of a mythological monster gazing at the auditorium with its frightful red eyes.

A picture tile by Ernest Batchelder graces the drinking fountain in the lobby

Originally designed for both vaudeville and film entertainment, the Rialto was equipped with ten dressing rooms, orchestra pit, scenery loft, a green room and a deep stage. After a backstage fire in the 1930s, both the vaudeville and live theater left for good.

It was in the Rialto that Robert Altman staged the fateful meeting between the movie executive (played by Tim Robbins) and the scriptwriter (Vincent D'Onofrio) in *The Player* (1992). After confronting the writer Robbins (wrongfully) suspected was sending him anonymous postcards with death threats, he kills him in the nearby parking lot.

To lure patrons during the Depression era, the theater offered various gimmicks in the form of raffles or giveaways with paid admission. There was a free pass to a local miniature golf course; Dish Night had as a bonus a free piece of china or glassware; the Bank Night raffle offered a cash prize.

The auditorium features colorful stenciling and elaborate fixtures

Huntington Library, Art Collections and Botanical Gardens ❶

Myron Hunt and H C Chambers, architects—Library (1920); Myron Hunt and Elmer Grey, architects—Art Gallery (1910); Warner and Gray, architects—Virginia Steele Scott Gallery (1984).
1151 Oxford Rd, San Marino.
☎(626) 405-2100.
www.huntington.org ⊕winter: Mon, Wed-Fri noon-4:30pm; Sat-Sun 10:30am-4:30pm. summer: Wed-Mon 10:30am-4:30 pm. Ⓢ 🏴

The imposing façade of the Huntington Art Gallery

Created by Henry Huntington in 1919, this splendid estate is one of the greatest attractions in California and one of the nation's foremost cultural, research and educational centers, attracted by 500,000 visitors annually. It consists of a library, art collections and botanical gardens, with an emphasis on Anglo-American history, art and literature.

Huntington was one of the most successful businessmen of his day (➔ p30). He retired in 1910 and devoted all his time to art and book collecting and the landscaping of his 600-acre (240-ha) ranch. In 1913 he married Arabella Duval Huntington, the widow of his uncle and railroad magnate, Collis P Huntington. She was a renowned art collector and had great influence over the development of the Huntington art collection.

The Huntington Library houses one of the world's finest collections of rare books and one of the largest and most complete collections in the US of British and American history and literature. Many rare books are rotated on display in the exhibit hall. The library possesses an unrivaled collection of Shakespeare's quartos and folios and early editions of all the major British writers. The library's west wing houses the Arabella Huntington Memorial Collection, consisting of 18th-century Sèvres porcelain and French furniture, French sculpture and Renaissance paintings.

The Huntington Art Gallery, formerly the Huntington residence, houses primarily British and French art of the 18th and early 19th centuries. The Main Room displays the finest group of full-length British portraits anywhere in the world. Besides British and French paintings and sculpture, the fascinating collection contains tapestries, furniture, porcelain, silver, drawings and watercolors. The collection of 18th-century French furniture and decorative arts is one of the finest of its kind in the US.

The Virginia Steele Scott Gallery of American Art displays American paintings, sculpture, drawings, prints, photographs and furniture from the 1730s to the 1930s. The north wing is devoted to the Arts and Crafts movement, featuring decorative arts and furniture designed by Charles and Henry Greene.

Development of the Botanical Gardens began in 1904, under the direction of German landscape designer William Hertrich. Today, the majestically maintained gardens span 150 of the 207-acre (80-ha) estate, with almost 150,000 kinds of plants from all over the world, presented in fifteen specialized gardens. Among the most impressive are two Camellia Gardens, which display 1,700 camellia cultivars, one of the nation's largest collections. The Desert Garden, one of the largest research and display collections of cacti and other succulents in the world, includes over 2,500 species of desert plants.

Main Portrait Room at the Huntington Art Gallery

Huntington Library, Art Collections and Botanical Gardens

The Ellesmere manuscript of Geoffrey Chaucer's *Canterbury Tales* (ca. 1410)

Blue Boy (ca. 1770) by Thomas Gainsborough is the most famous painting in the Huntington

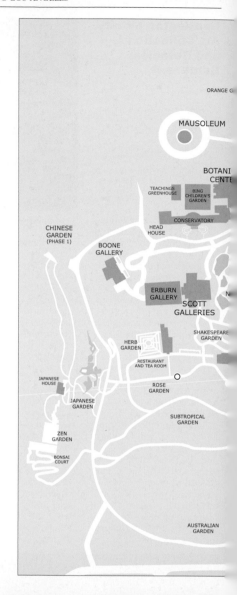

ORANGE G

MAUSOLEUM

BOTANI CENTE

TEACHINGS GREENHOUSE
BING CHILDREN'S GARDEN

CHINESE GARDEN (PHASE 1)

CONSERVATORY

HEAD HOUSE

BOONE GALLERY

ERBURN GALLERY

SCOTT GALLERIES

SHAKESPEARE GARDEN

HERB GARDEN

RESTAURANT AND TEA ROOM

JAPANESE HOUSE

ROSE GARDEN

JAPANESE GARDEN

SUBTROPICAL GARDEN

ZEN GARDEN

BONSAI COURT

AUSTRALIAN GARDEN

Breakfast in Bed (1897) by Mary Cassatt

French furniture in the Large Library Room

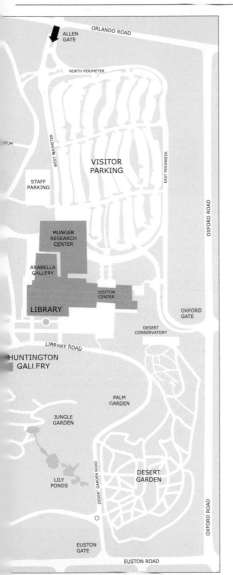

Sarah Siddons as the Tragic Muse (1784) by Joshua Reynolds is one of the artist's finest works

Madonna and Child (ca. 1460) by the Flemish master Rogier van der Weyden is one of the most important paintings in the Huntington's collection

Japanese Garden

Desert Garden

Ornamented façade of the West Kerckhoff Building

California Institute of Technology (Caltech) ❺

551 S Hill Ave.
☎(626) 395-6811.
www.caltech.edu
☛architectural tours: fourth Thu at
11am; call (626) 395-6327 for
reservations; general campus tours:
Mon-Fri 2pm. Ⓢ free. 🚩

This distinguished private institution traces its beginnings to Throop University, a local vocational and teacher training school founded in 1891. A relatively small university, with only 900 undergraduate and 1,100 graduate students, Caltech is one of the world's leading research centers. Its faculty and alumni have received a total of 28 Nobel Prizes. Among its major accomplishments are the development of aeronau-

Contributing to the Spanish theme, drinking fountains are set in colorful glazed tile throughout the campus

tical principles; the creation of a logarithmic scale for measuring the magnitude of earthquakes (the Richter scale); the discovery of the nature of quasars; the theory of quarks and anti-quarks; the discovery of the nature of the chemical bond. Caltech also operates Palomar Observatory and the Jet Propulsion Laboratory, which developed the Mars Polar Lander.

Caltech's campus comprises an interesting collection of Spanish and Italian Renaissance-style buildings. The first campus plan was designed by Myron Hunt and Elmer Grey; their work was continued by Bertram Goodhue and his architectural firm. Two buildings were designed by Gordon B Kaufmann. The Modern Movement buildings which were added after World War II (a few of them replacing older structures) destroyed the stylistic unity of the original campus.

West Kerckhoff Building
Goodhue Associates, architect
(1928).

Rising above the long arcade, the plain plastered walls of this three-story laboratory building are ornamented with Churrigueresque decorative panels. Its west façade features an abundance of plants and animals, suggesting a wide spectrum of biological research. Marking the entrance of the original campus are blue-tiled domed porticos.

Athenaeum
Gordon Kaufmann, architect
(1930).

Modeled after faculty clubs at Oxford and Cambridge, the U-shaped Athenaeum was formally opened with a dinner honoring Albert Einstein. During his stint as a visiting professor in 1932-33, the famous physicist stayed with his wife in one of the Athenaeum's suites. The other suite was occupied by Madame Curie. The Italian Renaissance-style structure is built around an inner courtyard and features a grand porte cochère on the south side.

The Athenaeum's exterior (called Harrow in the film) can be seen in *Beverly Hills Cop* (1984). Its magnificent main dining hall, with its painted beamed ceiling, was the backdrop for a fight scene in which Eddie Murphy throws a villain's bodyguard on the buffet table.

Broad Center for the Biological Sciences
Pei Cobb Freed and Partners, architects (2002).

The 120,000-square foot building, consisting of three floors above ground and two below, houses 13 research groups from a wide range of disciplines. The Center's façade is clad in travertine marble, glass and Japanese stainless-steel panels.

An interior dome of the Gates Annex Library, decorated with gold tiles and eight circular stained-glass windows

Robert R Blacker House ❻

Greene & Greene, architects
(1907-9).
1177 Hillcrest Ave.
Private residence. NRHP

Built as a retirement home for a Michigan lumber magnate, this is the largest and most elaborate of the Greenes' bungalow masterpieces. The house was constructed on the corner of a 5 1/2-acre estate, which allowed an expansive view of the once magnificent Japanese gardens and the lily pond (subdivided in the late 1940s).

The exterior's most striking feature is the massive, timbered porte cochère, set at an angle to the north façade. It is balanced by the second-story balcony that covers the living room terrace. The overhangs of the roof protect the house from the sun and rain.

Batchelder House

Cordelia Culbertson House ❼

Greene & Greene, architects
(1911-13).
1188 Hillcrest Ave.
Private residence. NRHP

Commissioned by the three maiden sisters of a former client, this was the last large Pasadena residence designed by the Greenes. The modest frontal elevation hides a two-story structure in the rear, as the U-shaped house follows the slope that drops down from the street into a ravine. Resembling a Chinese temple, the simple gable roofs are covered with dark and

Robert R Blacker House

light green glazed tiles, accented with occasional burnt red pieces. In a departure from the brothers' earlier designs, the entire house is clad in ocher-colored Gunite.

Batchelder House ❽

Ernest Batchelder, architect
(1909-13).
626 S Arroyo Blvd.
Private residence. NRHP

Overlooking Arroyo Seco, this celebrated Craftsman bungalow was built in an area inhabited by artists and intellectuals at the turn of the 20th century. Set under tall trees and discretely landscaped, the house is covered with dark, redwood shingles and features a second-story bedroom and a sleeping porch. The tiled walkway and a small tiled panel on an arroyo boulder chimney offer a hint of its original owner.

The house was built by Ernest Batchelder, the famous designer and manufacturer of decorative Arts and Crafts tiles. A former instructor in Pasadena's Throop Polytechnic Institute (now Caltech), he set up a design school in this house

in 1910. The original kiln, where he produced tiles with his students, still stands in the backyard.

Perkins House

Perkins House ❾

Richard Neutra, architect (1955).
1540 Poppy Peak Dr. Not on map
Private residence.

One of the well-known examples of post-and-beam architecture of the 1950s, this 1,300-square-foot (520 m²) house was built for an Occidental College art professor Constance Perkins. Although the rather small house appears closed from the street, it actually opens up to the outdoors in the rear.

Cordelia Culbertson House

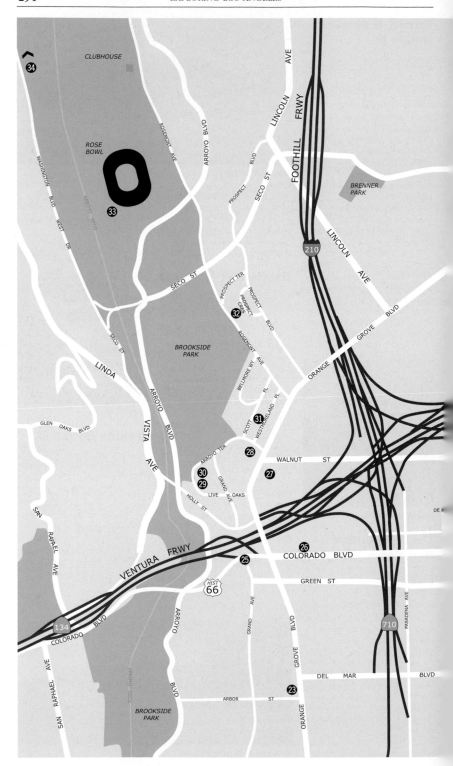

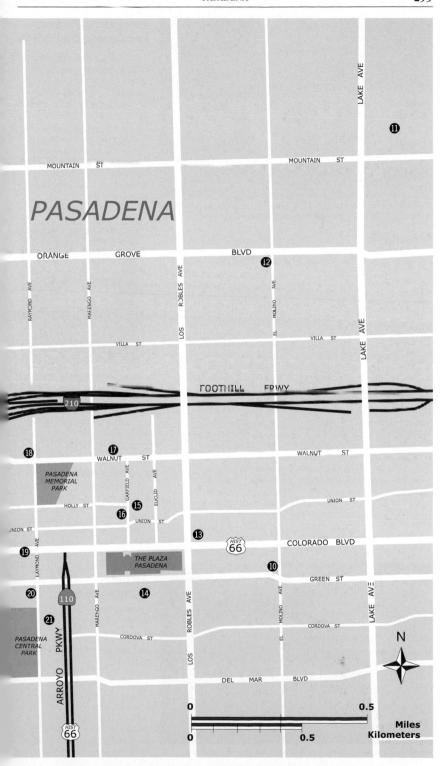

Opened in 1925, the Pasadena Playhouse building is an excellent example of Spanish Colonial Revival architecture

Pasadena Playhouse ⑩

Elmer Grey, architect (1925).
39 S El Molino Ave.
☎(626) 356-7529.
☛behind-the-scenes tours, by appointment only. NRHP

Founded in 1917, the acclaimed Pasadena Playhouse became nationally renowned for its innovative productions under the leadership of its founder and long-time director Gilmore Brown. Housed in the beautiful Spanish Revival-style building since 1925, it was declared the State Theatre of California in 1937.

In 1966, the Playhouse closed its doors because of financial difficulties; when reopened in 1986, it re-established itself as one of the premier theatres in the country.

The Playhouse's famous actor training program began in 1928, coinciding with the advent of talkies. When Hollywood suddenly realized that its stars did not know how to speak, they were quickly dispatched to Pasadena to learn. Between the 1930s and 1950s, the School of Theatre Arts, also known as the Hollywood star factory, launched the careers of such leading actors as William Holden, Charles Bronson, Dustin Hoffman and Gene Hackman.

The main 700-seat auditorium still has the original asbestos curtain featuring a Spanish galleon under full sail. On this stage have been presented hundreds of world premieres, including plays by Tennessee Williams, Eugene O'Neill and Arthur Miller. The Playhouse was the first American theatre to produce Shakespeare's complete works.

Bungalow Heaven Landmark District ⑪

Pasadena's first residential historic landmark district boasts one of the largest concentrations of intact Craftsman bungalows in the country. The six-block neighborhood between Lake and Chester avenues, bordered on the north by Washington Blvd and on the south by Orange Grove Blvd, features several hundred homes built for middle-class families between the 1900s and 1930s.

Bungalow Heaven street sign

Bungalow Heaven annual neighborhood tour of selected homes is held on the last Sunday in April.
☎(626) 585-2172.
www.bungalowheaven.org. ⑤

Craftsman Weekend annual event takes place on the third week in October and includes lectures, restoration seminars, workshops and a drive-yourself tour of private homes. ☎(626) 441-6333.
www.pasadenaheritage.org. ⑤

Airplane Bungalow ⑫

677 N El Molino Ave.
Private residence.

With a pavilion added on its low-pitched roof and a huge wingspan of spreading eaves, this 1914 structure is a good example of the "airplane bungalow." Requiring a large lot to be built on, this type of building is typical of Southern California, which had an abundance of cheap land in the early 1900s.

Airplane bungalow is a typical Southern California building

Façade of the Pacific Asia Museum

Pacific Asia Museum ⑬

Marston, van Pelt and Maybury, architects (1929).
46 N Los Robles Ave.
☎(626) 449-2742.
⏲Wed-Sun 10am-5pm. NRHP

The museum is housed in a Chinese Imperial Palace Courtyard-style building, the only example of this kind of architecture in southern California. Its permanent collection consists of more than 17,000 art and ethnographic objects spanning more than 5,000 years. The museum's garden is one of only two authentic Chinese courtyard gardens in the United States.

Pasadena Civic Auditorium ⑭

Edwin Bergstrom, architect (1932).
300 E Green St.
☎(626) 449-7360. NRHP

This Italian Renaissance palace is the home of the Pasadena Symphony and various ballet, music and theater events. Since its dedication in 1932, the impressive list of performers who appeared on its stage has included Eric Clapton, Bob Dylan, Stevie Wonder, Bob Hope, Ella Fitzgerald, Arthur Rubinstein and Luciano Pavarotti. The Civic Auditorium gained national fame with live radio broadcasts of big band dances in the 1940s. The annual Emmy Awards were held here consecutively for more than two decades.

It was in this hall that Michael Jackson first demonstrated his signature "Moonwalking" on March 25, 1983. Following the tune of *Billie Jean*, he seemed to effortlessly float above the stage, provoking a frantic response from the audience.

The elegant 3,000-seat auditorium, with its hand painted walls and ceilings, was decorated by Giovanni Smeraldi.

Pasadena City Hall ⑮

John Bakewell and Arthur Brown, Jr, architects (1927).
100 N Garfield Ave.
☎(626) 774-4000. ☏ NRHP

This imposing structure was designed by the same architectural firm that designed San Francisco City Hall. It was influenced by three famous domed structures: the church of Santa Maria della Salute in Venice, the Hôtel des Invalides in Paris and St Paul's Cathedral in London.

The building's massive, six-story-high tower is capped by the Spanish Baroque dome, covered with fish-scale tile. The three-winged building surrounds a large, airy courtyard landscaped with trees and flowers, and a central cast stone fountain.

Pasadena City Hall

Among its numerous appearances in movies and television productions, Pasadena City Hall doubled as Beverly Hills City Hall in both *Beverly Hills Cop* films (1984, 1987) and as a French castle in *Patton* (1970). In Charlie Chaplin's *The Great Dictator* (1940), the building was depicted as the palace where dictator Adenoid Hynkel lived and was also viewed in scenes where Hynkel delivers public speeches. However, Chaplin did not shoot on location in Pasadena; a matte shot of the structure served as a backdrop instead.

Interior of the Pasadena Civic Auditorium

Robinson Memorial

Robinson Memorial ⑯

Ralph Helmick, Stuart Schecter, John Outterbridge, artists (1997). Centennial Square (across from Pasadena City Hall). ☎(626) 584-6648.

These two monumental bronze sculptures pay homage to brothers Jackie and Mack Robinson, sports legends who grew up in Pasadena. Two years after he signed with the Brooklyn Dodgers in 1945, Jackie became the first black professional player to play major league baseball. Mack won a silver medal in the 200 meter sprint at the 1936 Olympics.

Pasadena Public Library ⑰

Myron Hunt and H C Chambers, architects (1927). 285 E Walnut St. ☎(626) 744-4052. ➤

The entrance courtyard of the library's Spanish Colonial Revival building features a splashing central fountain.

The three-story-high central block of the U-shaped building features five distinctive arched windows, Corinthian columns and intricate cast-concrete ornamentation including books, scrolls, urns and acanthus leaves.

The building's interior can be glimpsed in the library scenes in *Legally Blonde* (2001). It was also here that Jeff Daniels, playing Dr Ross Jenning, conducted his insect research in *Arachnophobia* (1990).

Pasadena Public Library

Raymond Theatre ⑱

J Cyril Bennett, architect (1921). 129 N Raymond Ave. Closed to the public. ➤

Opened in 1921 as an elegant live theater, the Jensen's Raymond Theatre continued as a showcase for vaudeville, silent and talking pictures and even porn films. The 1,800-seat venue has been host to such acts as Blondie, Bruce Springsteen, Fleetwood Mac, Mötley Crüe and Van Halen. With its Beaux-Arts façade and Georgian-style interior featuring elaborate ceiling and opulent fittings, this landmark has been closed for more than ten years, facing an uncertain future.

The theater is briefly seen in *Pulp Fiction* (1994) as Bruce Willis passes by in a taxi.

Old Pasadena ⑲

A district centered on Colorado Blvd and bounded by De Lacey Ave and Arroyo Pkwy, and Holly and Green streets. ☎(626) 666-4156. ➤ NRHP

This historic 20-block area of vintage brick buildings dates back to the 1880s and 1890s, when it was the commercial center of the city. By the 1970s it had fallen into disrepair; during the 1990s it was restored and reborn as Old Pasadena, a main shopping and entertainment center. Its streets and alleys are lined with hundreds of cafés and restaurants, nightclubs and movie theaters, bookstores, art galleries, antique stores, stylish boutiques and upscale clothing stores.

The area's trendy street scene attracts thousands of visitors, especially over the weekend evenings, when it becomes almost impossible to navigate its sidewalks.

Old Pasadena's Kendall Alley was featured in both *Paper Moon* (1973) and *Pulp Fiction* (1994).

Centered on Colorado Blvd, Old Pasadena comprises a historic area of century-old brick buildings

The Hotel Green (ca. 1901) viewed from the corner of Raymond Ave and Green St

Castle Green ⑳

Frederick Roehrig, architect (1898, 1903).
99 S Raymond Ave.
Private residences.
☛special events and open house tours are conducted throughout the year. Call ☎(626) 793-0359 and (626) 577-6765 for info. Ⓢ
☛ NRHP

This was once one of America's premier resort hotels, attracting numerous wealthy vacationers from the East who enjoyed the mild Southern California winters. Among its famous guests were tycoon John D Rockefeller and several American presidents, including William H Taft and Theodore Roosevelt.

The main building (left), originally known as the Webster Hotel, opened in 1890 and was promptly acquired by patent medicine magnate, Colonel G G Green. He amassed a fortune selling popular cure-all oils such as Green's August Flower and Green's Ague Conqueror. Responding to the enormous demand created by tourists, Green opened the extensive hotel annex in 1898.

The buildings were connected by the covered pedestrian bridge, which featured a miniature trolley car to shuttle guests and luggage. The older building was demolished in 1934 and the "Bridge of Sighs" promenade, which was a favorite spot for viewing the Rose Parade, was cut in half at the sidewalk.

The former hotel annex, now called Castle Green, was converted into apartments and condominiums. The six-story structure is a blend of Moorish, Spanish Colonial and Classical styles. The ochre building features pairs of squat and round towers, red tiled roofs and domed turrets, arched windows, romantic loggias and wrought-iron balconies.

Although the building is closed to the public, open house tours are conducted twice a year, when visitors can glimpse the downstairs public rooms and several private apartments. Its exotic public rooms retain much of their original look, with authentic furnishings and decorative arts.

Because of its historic look and peculiar architecture, Castle Green is a popular filming location. It was used in David Lynch's *Wild at Heart* (1990) and was the setting for "the sting" in *The Sting* (1973). Its exterior doubled as the Hotel Nacional de Cuba in *Bugsy* (1991).

Pasadena Railroad Station ㉑

H L Gilman, architect (1935).
222 S Raymond Ave. ☛

Before Union Station in downtown Los Angeles was built in 1939, the former Santa Fe Railroad depot was the main terminus for transcontinental travelers, the last stop for the famed Super Chief trains.

During the 1930s and 1940s, this small station was the preferred place for departures or arrivals for celebrities such as Mae West, Jean Harlow, Clark Gable and Gary Cooper. Movie stars preferred to take off anonymously at the Pasadena stop and take a car ride to Los Angeles. The alternative station allowed them to avoid the press and enthusiastic fans waiting for them at Union Station.

The Spanish Colonial Revival depot features splendid tiles by Ernest Batchelder in the waiting room.

The Pasadena station figured prominently in a number of movies. Buster Keaton arrives here on a train with a cow for the film *Go West* (1925). Harold Lloyd arrives at this depot in *The Freshman* (1925). Legendary star Errol Flynn stepped off the train here to start his conquest of Hollywood, a moment described in his book *My Wicked, Wicked Ways*.

In his best and commercially most successful silent comedy, *The Freshman* (1925), Harold Lloyd introduces himself to a group of fellow college students upon his arrival at the Pasadena Railroad Station

A 5.5-mile (8,8-km) route along Colorado Blvd.
☎(626) 449-4100.
www.tournamentofroses.com.
⑤for grandstand tickets, call ☎(626) 795-4171; viewing from the street is free (no seating). Floats are available for viewing before the parade at several float-decorating sites. After the parade, floats are displayed for public viewing close-up for two days at Victory Park, 2575 Paloma St. ⑤

The Tournament of Roses Parade features spectacular floral floats

A vintage post card depicts the Tournament of Roses ca. 1909. Horse-drawn carriages later evolved into elaborate floats.

Each float is decorated with an average of 100,000 blossoms

Shirley Temple posing as 1939 Rose Parade Grand Marshal

Tournament of Roses ㉒

Every New Year's Day Pasadena becomes the stage of a world-famous spectacle. With its elaborate floats, marching bands and prancing equestrian units, the Rose Parade attracts about 1 million spectators along its 5.5-mile (8,8 km) route. To ensure the best spot, many of these fans camp out on the sidewalks the night before. As many as half a billion television viewers from more than 100 countries watch the event worldwide.

The first Tournament of Roses was held in 1890, modeled after similar events in Europe. It began as a marketing ploy, a way to showcase the region's mild winters to the people on the East Coast, and so increase local real estate sales.

Initially, it consisted of a parade of flower-decked, horse-drawn carriages, followed by foot and bicycle races, tug-of-war matches and a game known as the tourney of rings. In subsequent years other events were added, including chariot races (inspired by the then-popular book *Ben-Hur*), ostrich races and, only in 1913, an elephant-camel race (if you must know, the elephant won). The parade's first queen was crowned in 1905.

The parade's major attraction are more than 50 colorful floats, constructed of steel, foam and plastic screens, weighing about 25 tons and costing up to $400,000 each. Each float is propelled by a V-8 engine and equipped with a powerful sound system and hydraulics that move animated parts and lower pieces of the structure as it passes under the freeway bridge on its route.

Only organic materials can be used to decorate the floats—leaves, dried seeds, bark, corn husks, fruit rinds, beans, rice, vegetables, spices, etc. Fresh flowers are added during the last few days before the parade and cover every inch of each float. About 20 million blossoms, including half a million roses, are used every year. On the photograph to the left, a decorator puts the finishing touches to a bird, covered with coconut slices and seaweed, attached with glue to the base.

In 1933 Mary Pickford was the first movie celebrity (and the first woman) to become grand marshal. Since then, many Hollywood luminaries have received this honor, including Shirley Temple, who held the title of grand marshal four times—in 1935, 1939, 1989 and 1999.

Tournament House and Wrigley Gardens ㉓

391 S Orange Grove Blvd.
☎(626) 449-4100.
⏰grounds open daily.
🏠house tours Thu 2-4pm. ⑤free.

The house was once owned by chewing gum magnate William Wrigley Jr. In 1958 it was donated to the city to became the permanent base of operations for the Tournament of Roses. With its impressive woodwork and extensive use of marble, this remarkable house exemplifies the type of mansion once located on Pasadena's historic Millionaires' Row. Today only the formal dining room is furnished with original furniture, while throughout the house are displays of Tournament of Roses artifacts, photographs and historical mementos.

Tournament House

Pasadena Doo Dah Parade ㉔

Colorado Blvd, Old Town.
☎(626) 440-7379.
www.pasadenadoodahparade.com
⏰Sunday before Thanksgiving.

What started as a joke in Pasadena Chromo's Saloon in 1978, eventually became an irreverent and offbeat alternative to the mainstream Rose Parade. With no official rules (except "no damn roses"), the Doo Dah Parade attracts thousands of spectators with its absurd, quirky and sometimes wild style.

Among the more than 100 participating groups are the Briefs Brigade, a bunch of men and women who march in underwear and brush their teeth, getting ready for their daily routine; the Horny Band, a band of musicians

Colorado Street Bridge

playing horns and "flashing" spectators at the same time. Other attractions include World Famous Couch Potatoes and Pregnant Nuns.

The Parade's all-time favorite is the Synchronized Briefcase Drill Team, a parody on straight-faced corporate executives, who snap their Samsonites with military-style precision. They appeared in the 1983 video of Jackson Browne's song *Lawyers in Love*.

Colorado Street Bridge ㉕

Waddell and Harrington, architects (1913).
Colorado Blvd at Arroyo Seco.
⚑ NRHP

When it opened in 1913, this 1,468-foot-long (447-m) and 150-foot-high (46-m) bridge became an instant attraction with its elegant double arches, ornamental balustrade and 48 lamp clusters that illuminated its two-

lane road. A local and national landmark, it was the longest and highest bridge of its time. Spanning Arroyo Seco (the dry riverbed), it played a significant role in Pasadena's growth, connecting the town with surrounding communities.

It also gained notoriety as "Suicide Bridge" because more than 100 people jumped from its span to their death, most of them in the 1930s, after the stock market crash left many investors desperate. Today, the bridge is secured with a new steel fence that prevents suicide attempts.

When it reopened after extensive restoration in 1994, the bridge became a favorite gathering place for preservationists, who throw their annual party on it each July.

The bridge was featured in a comedy *Roman Scandals* (1933), with Eddie Cantor as the Roman Emperor's food taster who raced his horse-drawn chariot across it.

The Synchronized Briefcase Drill Team on the Doo Dah Parade

Norton Simon Museum with Rodin's *Burghers of Calais*

Norton Simon Museum ㉖

Ladd & Kelsey, architects (1969).
411 W Colorado Blvd.
☎(626) 796-4978.
www.nortonsimon.org.
🕘Wed-Mon noon-6pm; Fri till 9pm. Ⓢ

This is one of America's most remarkable art collections and one of the largest in the world amassed by an individual. Over the course of 25 years, Norton Simon created an outstanding collection of European art from the Renaissance to the 20th century and superb examples of Asian sculpture spanning a period of 2,000 years.

Simon was a 24-year-old businessman when he bought a bankrupt orange juice bottling plant in Fullerton. The plant later became the giant Hunt Foods and Industries empire. The multinational corporation, Norton

***Portrait of a Peasant* (1888) by Vincent van Gogh**

Simon Inc, was ultimately formed through mergers with McCall Publishing, the *Saturday Review of Literature* and Canada Dry Corporation.

The museum was founded in 1924 as the Pasadena Art Institute. The present building was constructed in 1969 and dedicated as the Pasadena Art Museum. In 1974 the museum was reorganized, renamed and established as the home for Norton Simon's collection.

The earliest works from the European collection include Pre-Renaissance and Renaissance masterpieces. There are splendid examples of 17th- and 18th-century painting. Impressionism, Post-Impressionism and 20th-century collections also feature numerous masterpieces.

There is a permanent exhibit of over 100 paintings, pastels, drawings and prints by Edgar Degas. A highlight of the collection is a group of 71 bronze models cast from the artist's wax originals.

The museum's outstanding Asian collection consists of religious sculpture from all parts of India and Southeast Asia. It is particularly rich in works from the Gandaran period (2nd-5th centuries BC), Gupta dynasty (4th-6th centuries AD) and Chola dynasty (10-12th centuries AD). Another section features Buddhist, Hindu and Jain bronze and stone sculpture from the Himalayas, Cambodia, Laos and Pakistan.

Pasadena Museum of History (Fenyes Mansion) ㉗

Robert Farquhar, architect (1905).
470 W Walnut St.
☎(626) 577-1660.
www.pasadenahistory.org
☛Wed-Sun 1;30 and 3 pm. Ⓢ
NRHP

The 18-room Beaux-Arts Fenyes Mansion is one of the few remaining examples of the grand residences that represented a particular lifestyle prevalent at the turn of the 20th century when Orange Grove Ave was known as "Millionaires' Row." It was commissioned by Pasadena's leading citizens, Dr Adalbert and Eva S Fenyes. Their home was a center for frequent social gatherings.

The house is furnished with original antique furniture from all over the world, Oriental rugs, tapestries and decorative arts gathered across generations. There is a fine collection of American Impressionist paintings.

The beautiful gardens are planted with redwoods, fruit trees, camellias, ferns and bamboo, and feature frormal terraces, ponds and a stream.

Finnish Folk Art Museum
Adjacent to the Fenyes Mansion, the museum is a replica of a 19th-century Finnish farmhouse. The Finnish folk art exhibits, handmade furniture, *ryijy* rags, utensils and folk costumes are displayed in three rooms..

Fenyes Mansion epitomizes affluent life in Pasadena

Greene and Greene

I seek till I find what is truly useful, then I try to make it beautiful.
—Charles Sumner Greene

Brothers Charles and Henry Greene, whose more than 40 houses are still standing in Pasadena, created an unequalled legacy of highly refined design and extraordinary craftsmanship. Their meticulous attention to materials and sophisticated detail is visible in their furniture, which was specifically designed for particular rooms, as well as in joinery, fireplaces, light fixtures and art glass. The Greenes' elegant and charming residences, built of stone, brick and timber, are well-suited to the warm California climate, while terraces, covered porches and pergolas create soft boundaries between house and garden.

Charles and Henry Greene

Mary L Ranney House ㉘

Greene and Greene, architects (1907).
440 Arroyo Ter.
Private residence.

Mary Ranney was a talented draftsman in the brothers' firm and the only designer ever to receive the credit in the Greenes' office. She was allowed to design her own home, a modest, two-story house (later altered with the addition of a northwest wing). Situated on the corner lot, the house maintains a close relationship with the outdoors through a clinker brick entrance wall, patterned brick walkway and short flight of steps.

Theodore Irwin Jr House shows a Japanese influence

Theodore Irwin Jr House ㉙

Greene and Greene, architects (1901-6).
240 N Grand Ave.
Private residence.

Positioned on a magnificent site overlooking the Arroyo Seco, this large house was originally a small, one-story cottage built in 1901 for Pasadena dressmaker Katherine Duncan. In 1906 the house was remodeled and significantly expanded with a complete second floor for Theodore Irwin, the son of a wealthy industrialist from New York.

With its exposed timber elements, overhanging roofs and smooth flow between inside and outside, the house shows a Japanese influence, as reflected in the stone lantern on the west entrance walkway.

Charles Sumner Greene House ㉚

Greene and Greene, architects (1902-15).
368 Arroyo Ter.
Private residence.

Charles Greene's family home began as a simple, one-story, two-bedroom house, placed under the enormous oak tree (hence its name "Oakholm"). It is set on a hillside overlooking Arroyo Seco and behind an imposing cobblestone and clinker brick retaining wall.

The structure has undergone numerous additions over the years to accommodate Charles's growing family, eventually rising up four levels. This is the place where he perfected many of the famous Greene and Greene designs over the 15 years, before moving to Carmel.

Mary L Ranney House

The Gamble House represents the finest and best-preserved example of the Greene brothers' work

Gamble House ㉛

Greene and Greene, architects (1908).
4 Westmoreland Pl.
☎(626) 793-3334.
www.gamblehouse.org
☛docent-led, one-hour tours Thu-Sun 12 noon-3pm. Tours leave every 20 minutes. ($) NRHP

Often described as an "ultimate bungalow," this internationally renowned landmark is a widely recognized masterpiece of the American Arts and Crafts movement. Designed by the famous architectural team of brothers Charles and Henry Greene, it represents the finest and best-preserved example of their work. The house was commissioned by David and Mary Gamble of the Procter & Gamble Company of Cincinnati, as a retreat from the cold Midwestern winters.

Partially influenced by Japanese and Swiss traditions, the Greenes' notably articulated design elevated the Craftsman bungalow to high architecture, making the entire house a giant work of art. Every extraordinary detail, either of woodwork, furniture or accessory, was not an end in itself, but part of the whole design.

The interior décor is entirely custom designed and original to the house, including furniture, built-in cabinets, paneling, wood carving and fixtures. The house was built with over twenty types of wood, including teak, mahogany, ebony, Port Orford cedar, maple and oak. Here the Greenes' obsession with the natural qualities of wood, its color and texture, reached its peak. Each detail,

A magnificent ceiling fixture hangs over the dining table, which can be stretched out to seat fourteen by means of its unique extension mechanism

The inglenook in the living room is softly illuminated by a pair of leaded-glass lanterns suspended by leather straps. The rich tone of Burmese teak panels, massive trusses and beams dominates the room. All the rugs were designed and rendered in watercolor by Charles Greene, then hand-woven in Austria. They feature a stylized tree-of-life design, a fashionable motif at the time.

The focal point of the living room is the inglenook fireplace

Extraordinary stained-glass fixtures bring a luminous beauty throughout the house. Windows in the dining room depicting a blossoming vine are surrounded by built-in sideboard drawers and cabinets

however small, was painstakingly crafted, hand polished to a glossy finish and elegantly joined. The Greene brothers designed every piece of furniture specifically for each room.

Well integrated with its surroundings, the house appears to grow from the land, blending man-made and natural materials—boulders and stones are mixed with bricks; the stepping stones of the rolling lawn lead to curving brick stairs and a vine covered retaining wall.

The house was well adapted to the Southern California climate with its novel concept of indoor-outdoor living. It features large terraces and open sleeping porches, while a covering of redwood shingles and overhanging eaves protects it from the direct, mid-day sun.

The house remained in the Gamble family for some 60 years, until it was presented in 1966 to the city of Pasadena in a joint agreement with the University of Southern California. It is remarkably well-preserved—it was never remodeled, the woodwork was never painted over and the walls retain their original colors. It is the only Greene and Greene house that contains all of its original furniture.

In the *Back to the Future* movies, the Gamble House served as the laboratory and home of Doc Brown.

The central staircase, with its cascading handrail wrapped around a built-in bench, is a marvel of polished joinery

Separated bath and water closet in the guest area

The wide teak door at the front entrance has the stained and leaded glass inspired by a California oak tree. Note the beautiful hanging lantern with the emblazoned number 4.

Entrance to the Rose Bowl stadium

Millard House ("La Miniatura") ㉜

Frank Lloyd Wright, architect (1923).
645 Prospect Crescent.
Private residence. NRHP.

Designed for Alice Millard, this was the first of Wright's concrete block houses to be built on the West Coast. It is generally considered his best work employing this structural system. Resembling a small Mayan tower (hence the name "La Miniatura"), it was constructed of pre-cast concrete blocks that were plain-faced, patterned or perforated with cruciform shapes. Set in a ravine, the building's most striking feature is a two-story living room that overlooks a small pool and exuberant garden.

The house is today almost completely obscured by dense overgrowth. The best vantage point from which to glimpse the house is through the gate on Rosemont Ave.

Rose Bowl ㉝

Myron Hunt, architect (1922).
1001 Rose Bowl Dr.
☎(626) 577-3100.
www.rosebowlstadium.com.
No public tours. NRHP

Since 1922, this famous Pasadena icon has been the site of the annual New Year's Day Rose Bowl football game matching two of the country's top college football teams. The 104,000-seat stadium has hosted a variety of sporting events, including many Super Bowl Games, the 1994 Men's World Cup Final and the 1999 Women's World Cup Final. It is also the home of the UCLA Bruins football team and the Los Angeles Galaxy soccer team.

During the game between the University of California Bears and Georgia Tech in 1929, Roy Riegels of the Bears caught the ball and ran with it a full 64 yards—in the wrong direction. When a teammate finally stopped him, it was too late. Georgia Tech players gang-tackled him at the one-yard line.

The arena was originally open-ended and horseshoe-shaped, but over the years has undergone many remodellings and modifications.

The Rose Bowl is also the site of a huge flea market, held the second Sunday of each month. For information call ☎(323) 560-7469.

Art Center College of Design ㉞

Craig Ellwood Associates, architect (1976).
1700 Lida St.
☎(626) 396-2200.
www.artcenter.edu.
Williamson Gallery open Tue-Sun 12 noon-5pm; Thu til 9pm.
free campus tours are offered Mon-Fri at 2pm.

Established in 1930, this famous international school has a reputation as one of the world's leading educational institutions in the field of design and visual arts. It offers a bachelor degree in nine majors—advertising, environmental design, film, fine art, graphic design, illustration, photography, product design and transportation. The work of Art Center graduates is widely recognized and over the years has shaped the lifestyles of millions of consumers worldwide with such celebrated designs as the Chevrolet Corvette, Cadillac Eldorado, Mazda Miata, the new Volkswagen Beetle and the 2004 Rolls-Royce Phantom.

Inspired by the work of Mies van der Rohe, the impressive 627-foot-long (191-m) steel and glass box spans a ravine in its bucolic setting. Sited on a chaparral-covered hillside, the campus was designed with clear respect for the environment.

The College's sculpture garden displays large-scale artworks, while its galleries feature rotating exhibitions of works by students as well as established and emerging artists and designers.

Art Center College of Design

San Gabriel Valley

Extending northeast from downtown Los Angeles, this loosely defined area at the foot of the San Gabriel Mountains was the site of the first European settlement in the LA basin. On 8 September 1771, Mission San Gabriel Arcángel was established here. After the enormous Mexican ranchos were broken into smaller tracts, the whole area was converted into a giant garden paradise, with citrus orchards, vineyards and walnut groves.

El Camino Real mission-bell guidepost

Occasional exotic enterprises, such as ostrich, pigeon, lion or crocodile farms, also thrived. The region was a hotbed for early 20th-century art and architecture, with a large concentration of Craftsman style palatial houses. After World War II, huge population growth caused a merger of the Valley's series of small towns, creating a continuous, 30-mile-long (54-km) suburban sprawl.

Arboretum of Los Angeles County ㉟

301 N Baldwin Ave, Arcadia.
Not on map.
☎(626) 821-3222.
www.lacountybotanicgarden.org
⊕daily 9am-4:30pm. Closed:
Christmas. ⑤ 🚩

The 127-acre arboretum contains more than 30,000 plants adapted to the mild California climate, representing 4,000 species and varieties from all over the world. Among the major collections are 175 species of cycads, 27 species of coral trees, 79 species of ficus and 17 varieties of magnolias. The Arboretum's highlights include the tropical greenhouse, which contains anthuriums, bromeliads, staghorn ferns, Spanish moss and one of the largest displays of orchids in the country, with over 1,500 species and varieties.

With its jungle and 4-acre Baldwin lake, the Arboretum was the location of more than 200 film and television productions which required exotic locales. Here were

filmed eight Tarzan movies, including *Tarzan Escapes* (1936), *Tarzan and the Amazons* (1945) and *Tarzan and the Leopard Woman* (1946), all starring Johnny Weissmuller. The leech scene in *The African Queen* (1951), with Humphrey Bogart and Katharine Hepburn, was also filmed here. More productions include *Terminator 2* (1991) and *Wayne's World* (1992).

According to a local newspaper, Johnny Weismuller set an unofficial Olympic swim record trying to escape the crocodiles who shared Baldwin Lake with him during the filming of *Tarzan and the Huntress* (1947).

The Queen Anne Cottage

The Cottage has been a popular filming location, and its most famous appearance is in the hit television series *Fantasy Island* (1977-84), where it served as Mr Rourke's house and appeared in the opening sequence of a seaplane landing on the lake. NRHP

Cary Grant and Ingrid Bergman, the stars of Alfred Hitchcock's *Notorious* (1946), are sitting by the lake next to the Arboretum's Cottage

Aztec Hotel ㊱

Robert Stacy-Judd, architect (1925)
311 W Foothill Blvd, Monrovia.
Not on map.
☎(626) 358-3231. NRHP

The exuberance of the Mayan decoration applied over a simple stucco box is the work of Robert Stacy-Judd, the notable proponent of the pre-Columbian Revival style, which he regarded as a true American architecture. He chose the name "Aztec" for the exotic hotel because it sounded better than "Mayan."

Arboretum of Los Angeles County

Aztec Hotel

Santa Anita Racetrack ㊲

Grandstands designed by Gordon B Kaufmann (1935).
285 W Huntington Dr, Arcadia.
Not on map.
☎(626) 574-7223.
www.santaanita.com
Horse racing: Dec 26-late Apr; the Oak Tree Meeting: Oct-Nov. ($)
☛free morning workout every racing day at 7:30am. A free tram tour of the grounds Sat-Sun 7:30-9:30am during the racing season. Saturday morning Seabiscuit-themed tour.

Santa Anita Racetrack

With its imposing grandstands decorated with friezes featuring horseracing themes and the stunning backdrop of the snow-capped San Gabriel Mountains, Santa Anita is one of the most alluring racetracks in the country. It hosted the first horse race on grass in the West and pioneered the development of the automated starting gate, photo finish camera and electrical timer. During World War II, thousands of Americans of Japanese ancestry were housed in the stable compound before being transferred to a Manzanar detention camp.

Santa Anita has been known as "the Home of Seabiscuit," honoring the fabled racehorse who won many of his legendary victories at the racetrack here and retired in 1940 as the leading money winner of all time. A life-size bronze statues of Seabiscuit and his jockey George "Iceman" Woolf stand in the Paddock Garden near the walking ring.

Since opening day on December 25, 1934, Santa Anita's thoroughbred horse racing has attracted the glamorous Hollywood crowd. One of the track's founders and its president was director and producer Hal Roach. Some of the celebrities came to the course to be seen, but many others were horse owners, including movie moguls Louis B Mayer and Harry M Warner, as well as actors Errol Flynn, Zeppo Marx, Robert Taylor, Barbara Stanwyck and Spencer Tracy.

Among many movies made on location here were the Marx Brothers' *A Day at the Races* (1937), *A Star Is Born* (both the 1937 and 1954 versions), *Nixon* (1995) and *Seabiscuit* (2003).

San Gabriel Mission ㊳

537 W Mission Dr, San Gabriel.
Not on map.
☎(626) 457-3035.
www.sangabrielmission.org
🕘daily 9am-4:30pm. Closed Thanksgiving, Christmas, New Year's Day, Easter. ($) NRHP

Named for the archangel Gabriel, the 4th of 21 California missions was founded in 1771 by Franciscan fathers Pedro Cambron and Angel Somera. It was originally established four miles to the south, but floods forced it to move to its present site five years later. In 1779 a new church was started, architecturally unlike any other in the California mission chain. The fortress-like structure was designed by Father Antonio Cruzado, who was influenced by the cathedral in his native Cordoba, Spain. Built by local Indians of stone, brick and mortar, it features Moorish elements such as buttressed walls, narrow windows and a vaulted roof.

The mission's holdings once encompassed all of what today are Los Angeles, San Bernardino, Orange and Riverside counties (→ p19). On the grounds is the Campo Santo, the oldest cemetery in Los Angeles County. It was first consecrated in 1778 and features a memorial to 6,000 Indians buried there.

San Gabriel Mission Museum houses a magnificent collection of embroidered and hand-painted vestments, some of them dating back to the 17th century, that were used by the mission fathers.

A vintage post card depicts San Gabriel Mission

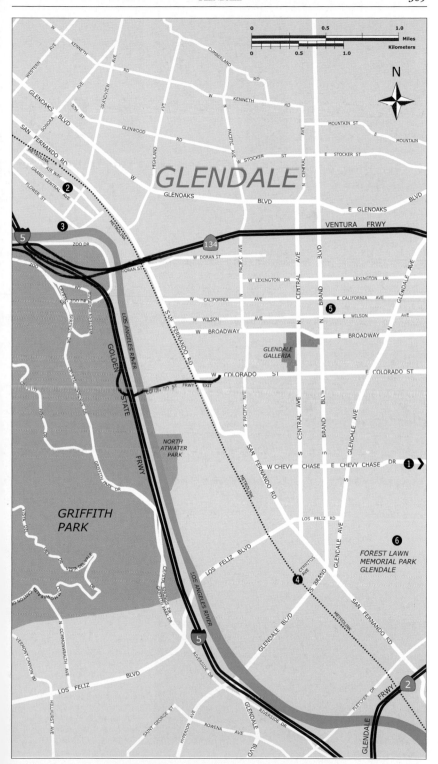

Derby House

Glendale Airport

Glendale Amtrak Station

Derby House ❶

Lloyd Wright, architect (1926).
2535 Chevy Chase Dr.
Private residence. NRHP

Built for local businessman John Derby and his wife, this is an outstanding example of Lloyd Wright's textured concrete block structures. Clearly visible from the street, a three-story concrete block, wood and stucco box is crosscut diagonally by a rectangular stucco wing. Perforated screens projecting from the square box use zigzag motifs inspired by American Indian textiles found throughout Southwest.

Glendale Airport ❷

(formerly)

1310 Air Way.

This facility offered the first transcontinental airline service in the region, with the inaugural flight to New York piloted by Charles Lindbergh. Among notables on board were Mary Pickford and Douglas Fairbanks. The first airport with a paved runway in Los Angeles, the Glendale Airport was an instant hit with celebrities such as Jean Harlow, Shirley Temple and

Gary Cooper. William Randolph Hearst and Marion Davies kept a plane on the field ready for their frequent trips to San Simeon.

The airport also attracted such aviation legends as Howard Hughes and Amelia Earhart. It was here that Douglas "Wrong Way" Corrigan built the plane used for his famous, although unauthorized, Atlantic flight in 1938.

Officially opened in 1929, the Mission Revival-style Grand Central Air Terminal and its Art Deco observation tower were abandoned when the runway was declared too short for jet planes. The airport was closed for air traffic in 1955 and converted into an industrial park. Disney Imagineering now occupies many of the buildings.

DreamWorks SKG Studios ❸

Steven Ehrlich Architects (1998).
1000 Flower St.
☎(818) 695-5000.
Not open to the public.

Founded in 1994, DreamWorks was Hollywood's first successful new studio in more than 50 years. The multimedia entertainment compa-

ny is the brainchild of celebrated director Steven Spielberg, former record company mogul David Geffen and former Walt Disney Studios chairman Jeffrey Katzenberg. The studio was very successful in its first decade, winning the best picture Oscar for *American Beauty* (1999), *Gladiator* (2000) and *A Beautiful Mind* (2001).

DreamWorks' tranquil, Tuscan-style fourteen acre campus houses the company's animation department, whose hit *Shrek* (2001) won the first-ever Academy Award for an animated feature.

Glendale Amtrak Station ❹

Mac Donald and Cuchot, architects (1924).
400 W Cerritos Ave.
🏛 NRHP

Built in 1924 for the Southern Pacific Railroad on the site of the original 1883 depot, this Mission Revival-style station has been frequently featured in movies, television series and commercials. Its most famous appearance was in Billy Wilder's thriller *Double Indemnity* (1944), where it doubled as the Pasadena Train Station. When Wilder was refused permission to shoot on location in Pasadena, he filmed Fred MacMurray boarding the "10:15 from Glendale" here, posing as Barbara Stanwyck's husband. In the complex setup, designed to collect on a life insurance policy, MacMurray and Stanwyck kill her husband and leave his body on the railway tracks.

DreamWorks SKG Studios

Alex Theatre ❺

This famous landmark is a splendid example of the grand vaudeville and movie palaces of the second decade of the 20th century. The theatre was designed by local architects and featured an unusual combination of Greek and Egyptian motifs. It was built when the frenzy for exotic movie palaces was at its peak and was inspired by Sid Grauman's Egyptian Theatre in Hollywood.

The venue was named Alexander after a three-year-old son of the theater mogul Claude L Langley, who commissioned it for West Coast Theatres, Inc. The Alexander opened on September 4, 1925 with the world premiere of John Ford's film *Lightnin'*.

In 1940, renowned theater architect S Charles Lee added a 100-foot-tall (30-m), neon-lit Art Deco pylon, topped with a spiked starburst. The marquee, box office and the ornate terrazzo flooring were also added, and the theatre name was shortened to "Alex". It was renovated in 1993 and today is used as a performing arts venue.

Although changed from the original design, the theater's open forecourt is still impressive. The façade is dominated by two giant Doric columns and an entablature of the classical temple, together with a coffered ceiling and a sunburst above the front doors.

A large golden sunburst above the proscenium arch dominates the theater's interior. The auditorium was originally designed as an "atmospherium." An illusion of an open air theater was created with its domed ceiling, two pairs of Doric columns flanking the stage and murals on the side walls depicting garden scenes. It is one of rare surviving examples of this kind of theater in California.

Along with the best in film entertainment, the theater featured Orpheum Vaudeville acts and popular live stage shows of the famous brother-sister dance team of Fanchon and Marco.

Its proximity to the major Hollywood studios and its typical, middle-class suburban clientele made the Alexander a perfect preview house. Here studio executives tested their new films before general release, often changing endings based on audience reaction.

Sneak previews became regular in the 1930s. They were shown unannounced following the advertised movie, with studio bosses and actors taking their seats after the lights went off.

The fluted Art Deco pylon, marquee and outdoor ticketing kiosk were added in 1940

Arthur Lindley and Charles Selkirk, architects (1925); pylon and new façade, S Charles Lee (1940). 216 N Brand Blvd. ☎(818) 243-2539. ☛occasionally offers a public backstage tour, call ☎(818) 243-7700 x216 for info. NRHP

The Alex's forecourt with a large sunburst above the theater's doors

The proscenium arch of the Alex Theatre's auditorium

After screenings, the autograph-seeking crowds often swarmed the celebrities, as shown on this 1936 photo of stars Robert Taylor and Barbara Stanwyck, taken in the theater's forecourt at the preview of their movie *His Brother's Wife*

Forest Lawn Memorial Park-Glendale ❻

Frederick A Hansen, landscape architect (1917).
1712 S Glendale Ave.
☎(818) 254-3131; (818) 241-4151.
🕐daily 8am-5pm (6pm in summer)
Maps of the grounds are available at the entrance gates.

Forest Lawn Memorial Park pioneered flat grave markers

The brain child of Hubert L Eaton, a mining engineer from Missouri, Forest Lawn was created in 1917 as a memorial park dedicated to the celebration of life. Instead of dreary traditional burial grounds, Eaton envisioned a parklike setting, with fountains, sweeping lawns, gardens and courts. Upright tombstones were eliminated and replaced with simple flat markers. Eaton invented the way to make death a big business, pioneering the "before need" sales concept and offering cradle-to-grave services, with baptisms, weddings and funerals.

With its museums, art replicas, sculpture gardens, historic artifacts, live shows and musical performances, 300-acre (120-ha) Forest Lawn, which has been called a country club for the dead, attracts one million visitors annually.

Beautifully landscaped, Forest Lawn is also the ultimate celebrity cemetery—the list of stars interred here resembles a *Who's Who* of Hollywood luminaries. Grave-hoppers are, however, discouraged; the cemetery staff will not point to their prominent guests' final resting places.

Among the artworks on display are two of the world's largest religious paintings: *The Crucifixion* by Jan Styka is displayed every hour on the hour in the Hall of Crucifixion-Resurrection. It measures 195 feet by 45 feet (59,4 x 13,7 m). *The Resurrection* by Robert Clark (70 by 51 feet—21,3 x 15,5 m) is revealed every hour on the half-hour in the same hall.

There are also full-scale recreations of famous churches. The Church of the Recessional was inspired by Rudyard Kipling's home church of St Margaret in Rottingdean, England, dating back to the 10th century. Funeral services for Carole Lombard and Clark Gable were held here in 1942 and 1960, respectively. Wee Kirk o' the Heather is modeled after a 14th-century church in Glencairn, Scotland. It was the scene of Ronald Reagan and June Wyman's wedding in 1940.

Jean Harlow's spectacular funeral services, with more than 250 Hollywood celebrities in attendance, were held at Wee Kirk in 1932. Not particularly concerned about the dignity of the occasion, the usual mob of the curious and autograph bookies gathered in large numbers. To exclude those who hold nothing sacred, Hollywood figures decided to limit attendance at the funerals of movie stars in the future.

British expatriate authors Aldous Huxley and Evelyn Waugh caricatured Southern Californian lifestyle and customs formalizing death. In his novel *After Many a Summer Dies a Swan* (1939), Huxley ridiculed a "personality cemetery" named Beverly Pantheon, with its replicas of old churches and statuary of voluptuous female nudes.

The story of Waugh's scathing novel *The Loved One* (1948), inspired by Forest Lawn and set at what he calls Whispering Glades, satirizes the cemetery as a kind of amusement park. The book was followed by a movie in 1965, which was billed as "the film with something to offend anyone."

Jean Harlow's funeral services in 1937 attracted a large crowd

Great Mausoleum

The massive Great Mausoleum contains some of the park's most distinguished names. Large portions of it are roped, locked or otherwise inaccessible to the public. Unless you have any dear departed ones buried inside to whom you are paying respect, the best way to get past the guard at the entrance is to ask to see a stained-glass version of Leonardo da Vinci's *The Last Supper*, located in the Memorial Court of Honor. This room also contains exact recreations of Michelangelo's *La Pieta*, *Moses*, *Medici Madonna and Child*, and other of his well-known sculptures.

A vintage post card depicts the Memorial Court of Honor in the Great Mausoleum

SANCTUARY OF BENEDICTION

Sid Grauman (1874-1950)
Grauman opened several opulent motion picture palaces in Los Angeles, the most famous being the Chinese and the Egyptian in Hollywood. He was credited for inventing klieg-light movie premieres, but his best-known legacy is a large collection of celebrities' handprints and footprints in the cement forecourt of the Chinese Theatre.

Alexander Pantages
(1867-1936)
A theater magnate who started his career as a variety show producer and eventual-

ly built an empire of 80 theaters, including the Hollywood Pantages, the largest movie palace in LA. In 1929, he was framed for statutory rape by one of his usherettes. Pantages was initially sentenced to 50 years in prison, but was acquitted in 1931.

Jean Harlow (1911-1937)
Called the "Blonde Bombshell," Harlow was the most sensational film star and America's hottest sex symbol of the 1930s. The public's enthusiastic response to her provocative sexuality was further fueled by some details from her personal life which were made public—she posed nude in public parks, never wore underwear and bleached her pubic hair. Harlow made her break when Howard Hughes cast her in *Hell's Angels* (1930), and shocked the audience with her famous line, "Do you mind if I slip into something more comfortable?"
She collapsed on the set during filming and was sent home to rest. As her mother, a Christian Scientist, refused to get a medical help, she died of uremic poisoning at age 26. Her fiancé, actor William Powell, is said to have spent $25,000 on her alcove lined with imported marble.

Irving Thalberg (1899-1936)

At age 20, Hollywood's "boy wonder" was appointed head of production at Universal Studios. Later, as supervisor of production at MGM, Thalberg was responsible for the glamorous extravagance for which MGM's films became famous. Constantly in frail health since childhood, he died of pneumonia at 37. He was

immortalized as Monroe Stahr in F Scott Fitzgerald's unfinished novel *The Last Tycoon* (1940). The Academy instituted the Irving G Thalberg Memorial Award in his honor, presented for high levels of production achievement.

Norma Shearer (1900-1983)

Buried with Thalberg is his widow, actress Norma Shearer, who reportedly spent $50,000 for her husband's private mausoleum. One of MGM's leading ladies, Shearer starred in such hits as *Romeo and Juliet* (1936) and *Marie Antoinette* (1938). She was nominated six times as best actress, and won an Oscar for her performance in *The Divorcee* (1930).

Marie Dressler (1869-1934)

Dressler made her screen debut as Charlie Chaplin's co-star in *Tillie's Punctured Romance* (1914). Although an unlikely star—she was large and homely—Dressler remained for years the top box-office attraction. She won the best actress Oscar for *Min and Bill* (1930).

COLUMBARIUM OF MEMORY

Theda Bara (1890-1955)

Theda Bara was the first sex symbol of the silent screen (➔ p45). She became an instant sensation when the famous line, "Kiss me, you fool!" from a subtitle card of her first big film, *A Fool There Was* (1915), became the slogan of the day. Bara played vamp roles in such hits as *Carmen* (1915), *Cleopatra* (1917) and *Salome* (1918).

COLUMBARIUM OF PRAYER
SANCTUARY OF TRUST

Clark Gable (1901-1960)

Voted "the King" of Hollywood by screen audiences, Gable was the top moneymaking star in the 1930s.
He won an Academy Award for best actor in *It Happened One Night* (1934), and made film history as unforgettable Rhett Butler in *Gone With the Wind* (1939), a role that perfectly fitted his tough and arrogant style. His best role was probably in *The Misfits* (1961), with Marilyn Monroe, but Gable did not live to see it. The national idol died of a heart attack in his bed while reading a magazine.

Carole Lombard
(1908-1942)

Interred next to Gable is his third wife, Hollywood's top comedienne of the 1930s and a star of such films as *Twentieth Century* (1934) and *My Man Godfrey* (1936). The glamorous star died in 1942 in a plane crash while returning from a War Bond drive. Lombard requested in her will to be buried in a white gown designed by Irene.

David O Selznick
(1902-1965)

An alcove at the end of the hallway contains the crypt of the independent Hollywood producer, personally responsible for one of the top box-office hits of all time, *Gone With the Wind* (1939). Selznick also launched the careers of director George Cukor and actress Katharine Hepburn. He brought to Hollywood Swedish actress Ingrid Bergman and English director Alfred Hitchcock, whose US debut, *Rebecca* (1940), he closely supervised.

HALL OF INSPIRATION
COLUMBARIUM OF NATIVITY

W C Fields (1879-1946)

One of the greatest Hollywood comedians, who excelled in roles of drunkards, cynics and misanthropes.
His private and screen personalities were almost indistinguishable and his viewpoint was best summed up in the line, "Any man who hates small dogs and children can't be all bad." His distrust of authority went to such an extreme that he deposited his money in 700 separate savings accounts all over the world, most under invented names. His most famous film is *David Copperfield* (1935).

BEGONIA CORRIDOR

Harold Lloyd (1893-1971)

At one time the most successful of the silent screen comedy triumvirate that included Charlie Chaplin and Buster Keaton. Lloyd created a wildly popular character of an average young man, serious and with trademark horn-rimmed spectacles, that made him the highest-paid actor in Hollywood. Among his most famous films are *Safety Last* (1923) and *The Freshman* (1925). In 1952 he received a special Oscar as a "master comedian and good citizen."

SANCTUARY OF MEDITATION

Lon Chaney (1883-1930)

Chaney was called "The Man of a Thousand Faces" for the makeup artistry that enabled him to transform on screen in myriad ways. In one of the most remarkable careers in film history, he

appeared in a wide range of roles in more than 150 films, including *The Phantom of the Opera* (1925).

SANCTUARY OF GOLDEN SLUMBER

Paramahansa Yogananda
(1893-1952)

One of great spiritual leaders of the 20th century, Indian-born Yogananda introduced thousands of followers around the world to the science and philosophy of yoga and meditation techniques. He spent 30 years in America, devoting his life to helping others on their spiritual search. Newspapers at the time widely reported that his body did not show any sign of decay for three weeks after his death.

Freedom Mausoleum

SANCTUARY OF HERITAGE

Clara Bow (1905-1965)

Clara Bow was the most famous flapper of the jazz age, the popular "It" girl who possessed that particular magnetism and unique sex appeal. Her first major hit was *Mantrap* (1926), and she reached legendary status in *It* (1927), becoming the greatest sex symbol of the Roaring Twenties. Her image of an energetic, liberated girl with bobbed hair, bow lips and sparkling glances inspired women everywhere to imitate her style. She was declared America's most popular female star by a national poll in 1928.

Bow's wild private life became exposed when her former secretary sold stories of her sexual exploits to the press. Amid scandals involving drinking, drugs, gambling and adultery, her career ended by 1930. Mentally fragile, she suffered several nervous breakdowns and spent years in sanatoriums. She is buried with her husband, actor **Rex Bell** (1903-1962).

Nat "King" Cole (1919-1965)

The legendary singer and jazz pianist was the first black performer to host his own television show. During his career Cole sold more than 50 million records, including a No. 1 hit *Mona Lisa, Sweet Lorraine, That Ain't Right, Sweet Georgia Brown* and *Tenderly*. He also appeared in several films, including the title role in *St Louis Blues* (1958). Cole died of smoking-related lung cancer. He is the father of Grammy-winning singer Natalie Cole.

Alan Ladd (1913-1964)

Although short in stature and lacking the prerequisites of a major star, his handsome face devoid of expression and deep, resonant voice made him a phenomenon. Ladd gained fame as a cold-blooded killer in *This Gun for Hire* (1942). His most successful role was that of a mysterious gunfighter in the western *Shane* (1953). He suffered injuries from a self-inflicted gunshot wound and died of an overdose of sedatives combined with alcohol. A bronze bust of Ladd stands in front of his crypt.

Gracie Allen (1902-1964)
George Burns (1896-1996)

The crypt of this popular comedian team and couple bears the inscription "Together Again." In 1925 they formed the famous comedy team of Burns and Allen, where George was a straight man and Gracie his scatter-brained partner. They were the top act in vaudeville, appeared in a number of short and feature films and later had a successful radio career. Their television hit series, *The Burns and Allen Show*, was enormously popular during the 1950s. For his portrayal of an ex-vaudeville star in *The Sunshine Boys* (1975), Burns won a best supporting actor Oscar.

COLUMBARIUM OF VICTORY

Dorothy Dandridge
(1922-1965)

The famous actress, singer and dancer started as a professional performer at the age of four. Dandridge had a successful career on radio and television, as well as a nightclub entertainer. During the 1950s, she became a major movie star and was the first African American to be nominated for an Academy Award as best actress, for her performance in *Carmen Jones* (1954). She was also the first black woman to appear on the cover of *Life* magazine. Unhappy in her personal life, she died under mysterious circumstances in her apartment.

The Marx Brothers—Zeppo, Groucho, Chico and Harpo

The Marx Brothers

One of the funniest comedy teams in the history of the movies, the Marx Brothers started in vaudeville at an early age. Developing immediately recognizable personal characteristics, they made a series of greatly successful comedies in the 1930s, noted for their anarchic humor. After they stopped making movies together in 1950, the brothers returned to Broadway and later frequently appeared on television.

SANCTUARY OF WORSHIP

Chico Marx (1886-1961)

He was the Marx brother with the Tyrolean hat who played the piano in his eccentric, "finger-pointing" style. Chico translated Harpo's visual expressions into his broken English with the pseudo-Italian accent. In his private life he was a womanizer (hence his nickname) and a compulsive gambler who spent a vast fortune made in motion pictures and died penniless.

SANCTUARY OF BROTHERHOOD

Gummo Marx (1893-1977)

Gummo got his nickname because he wore gum-soled shoes. He was a prominent performer with his brothers during their vaudeville days, but left the act to pursue a career as a theatrical agent.

SANCTUARY OF GRATITUDE

Francis X Bushman
(1883-1966)

The inscription on the crypt identifies Bushman as "King of the Movies." During the 1910s, the former sculptor's model was billed as "the Handsomest Man in the World" and enjoyed unequalled popularity, especially among female audiences. Bushman's fame plummeted when it was discovered that he was secretly married and had five children. His best-known role is that of Messala, opposing Ramon Novarro in *Ben-Hur* (1925).

SANCTUARY OF LIBERATION

Larry Fine (1902-1975)

The wild-haired member of the popular comedy team the Three Stooges, Fine joined brothers Moe and Shemp Howard in 1928 to make more than 200 two-reelers.

Forest Lawn Memorial Park-Glendale

Gardens of Remembrance ①

Wee Kirk Churchyard, lot 8 ②

Cathedral Slope, lot 1675 ③

Whispering Pines, lot 986 (Tom Mix) ④

Whispering Pines, lot 1132 ⑤

Whispering Pines, lot 1689 ⑥

Gardens of Memory, Little Garden of Eternal Love (Mary Pickford) ⑦

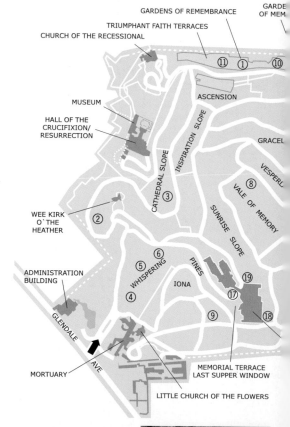

Vale of Memory, lot 2086 ⑧

Section G ⑨

Gardens of Memory,
Columbarium of Eternal Light,
niche 647G ⑩

Triumphant Faith Terraces,
Garden of Enduring Faith,
space A ⑪

Garden right of entrance to
Garden of Everlasting Peace ⑫

Garden right of entrance to
Garden of Everlasting Peace ⑬

Garden of Everlasting Peace ⑭

Eventide Section, lot 2998,
space 2 ⑮

Across from the entrance to
the Great Mausoleum ⑰

Eventide Section, lot 2896,
space 2 ⑯

Sunrise Slope (Joe E Brown) ⑱

Sunrise Slope (Aimee Semple McPherson) ⑲

Grounds

Walt Disney (1901-1966)

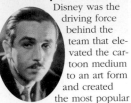

Disney was the driving force behind the team that elevated the cartoon medium to an art form and created the most popular animation character in history—Mickey Mouse. One of the most recognized names of the 20th century, Disney built an entertainment empire that is a household name around the world. He died of lung cancer.

Errol Flynn (1909-1959)

As a fearless swashbuckler in a series of costume adventure films, athletic and charming Flynn achieved enormous popularity during the 1930s and 1940s. His private life consisted of a series of scandals—his heavy drinking, drug abuse and charges of statutory rape all contributed to his downfall. When Flynn died of a heart attack at age 50, it was rumored that he was buried with six bottles of whiskey at his side.

Spencer Tracy (1900-1967)

Playing roles of sturdy, unpretentious average Americans, he was admired for his straightforward and natural acting style. Although he was seldom used as a typical leading man, Tracy won two Academy Awards in succession for best actor—for *Captains Courageous* (1937) and *Boys Town* (1938). His heavy drinking took a toll on his health and he died of a heart attack at the home of Katharine Hepburn, his long time companion.

GARDENS OF HONOR

The gates of this private garden are locked and accessible only to those possessing the "Golden Key of Memory."

Sammy Davis Jr (1925-1990)

One of America's top entertainers, Davis was a highly versatile singer, dancer and actor. A man of boundless energy, he recorded 40 albums and appeared in countless films, television programs and Las Vegas shows. Upon the news of his death, the lights on the Vegas Strip went dark for ten minutes as a special tribute to a member of Frank Sinatra's "Rat Pack." A heavy smoker, Davis died of cancer.

Robert Taylor (1911-1969)

Billed as "the Man With the Perfect Profile," Robert Taylor was Clark Gable's great rival as Hollywood's top romantic lead. Taylor played opposite some of the screen's most glamorous female stars, including Greta Garbo, Jean Harlow, Joan Crawford, Ava Gardner and Barbara Stanwyck (his first wife). He died of lung cancer attributed to smoking.

Dick Powell (1904-1963)

Powell started his film career in musicals and later switched to roles of tough guys and private detectives. During the 1950s Powell began producing and directing films and headed a TV production company. He was the popular host of television's *Dick Powell Show*. His second wife was actress Joan Blondell.

Joan Blondell (1909-1979)

One of Hollywood's most popular comediennes and musical stars, Blondell usually played gold-diggers with a heart of gold. Although she appeared in more than 80 films, she never reached her full potential due to dull roles or insignificant movies.

Mervyn LeRoy (1900-1987)

The famous director's Hollywood career began with a letter of recommendation from his nephew, producer Jesse L Lasky. LeRoy's breakthrough came with *Little Caesar* (1931), the movie that started Warner Bros' gangster series and launched Edward G Robinson's career. Besides social dramas, LeRoy directed musicals and comedies.

George Cukor (1899-1983)

Cukor came to Hollywood as an established Broadway director. He quickly gained a reputation as a "woman's director" for his ability to bring forth stellar performances from the screen's most glamorous female stars. He discovered Katharine Hepburn and their successful collaboration continued for decades. Cukor received an Oscar for his direction of *My Fair Lady* (1964).

Samuel Goldwyn (1882-1974)

Called the greatest independent producer in Hollywood, Goldwyn (born Goldfish) was part of two historic mergers that shaped the American cinema: first Paramount and then MGM. He was, however, edged out from both companies and in 1923 formed Samuel Goldwyn Productions. His company made many popular movies, including *The Best Years of Our Lives* (1946), for which he got his best picture Academy Award.

GARDENS OF MEMORY

Humphrey Bogart
(1899-1957)

A cult hero of American film with a huge international following, Bogart's fame reached its peak with such classics as *The Maltese Falcon* (1941), *Casablanca* (1942) and *The Treasure of the Sierra Madre* (1948). He won an Oscar for best actor for his performance in *The African Queen* (1951).

"Bogey" died shortly after an operation for cancer of the esophagus. He was cremated with the gold whistle his wife Lauren Bacall gave him to commemorate her line from the movie they both starred in, *To Have and Have Not* (1944): "You know how to whistle, don't you, Steve? You just put your lips together and blow."

Mary Pickford (1893-1979)

Popularly known as "America's Sweetheart" for her typical juvenile roles, Pickford was a crucial figure in developing the motion picture industry. She was the nation's biggest box-office draw and Hollywood's first international superstar. To millions of fans, Pickford and her husband, Douglas Fairbanks, represented Hollywood royalty.

A shrewd businesswoman who expertly handled her career and business affairs, she was also the first woman to own her own production company. In 1919 Pickford joined Chaplin, Griffith and Fairbanks in founding United Artists. She was also one of the founders of the Academy of Motion Picture Arts and Sciences in 1927. Pickford won the best actress Oscar for her performance in *Coquette* (1929).

TRIUMPHANT FAITH TERRACES

Vincente Minnelli
(1910-1986)

Besides being the husband of Judy Garland and father of Liza Minnelli, Vincente Minnelli established himself as a prominent director of musicals, some of which are considered classics of the genre. He was noted for his discriminating use of color and smooth integration of musical numbers with action. Among the most famous of his films are *An American in Paris* (1950) and *Gigi* (1958), for which he won an Oscar for best director.

GARDENS OF REMEMBRANCE

Merle Oberon (1917-1979)

Her regal appearance and exotic beauty secured her starring roles in numerous productions in Hollywood and Britain, most notably *The Dark Angel* (1935) and *Wuthering Heights* (1939). Throughout her career she played glamorous upper-class women and her private life as a member of the international jet set matched her on-screen image.

EVENTIDE

William Wyler (1902-1981)

The German-born director was a distant cousin of Universal's founder Carl Laemmle, who brought him to the United States. An outstanding craftsman and perfectionist, he was called "90-take Wyler" for the number of takes he filmed of each shot until he was pleased with the result. He won an Oscar for best director three times—for *Mrs Miniver* (1942), *The Best Years of Our Lives* (1946) and *Ben-Hur* (1959).

Ernst Lubitsch (1892-1947)

The German-born director came to Hollywood in 1922 to direct one of Mary Pickford's films. His long list of hits includes sex comedies, political satires and musicals, distinguished by his famous "Lubitsch touch." The director of *Ninotchka* (1939) was buried in a glass-topped coffin, holding a cigar.

WEE KIRK CHURCHYARD

James Stewart (1908-1997)

With his endearing drawl and relaxed manner, Jimmy Stewart was one of the most beloved of Hollywood leading men, epitomizing the sincere, honorable guy next door. Early in his career he often portrayed shy, country-boy types but later played a wide range of characters. He starred in such classics as *You Can't Take It With You* (1938), *It's a Wonderful World* (1939) and *Mr Smith Goes to Washington* (1939). Stewart received an Oscar for his role in *The Philadelphia Story* (1940).

CATHEDRAL SLOPE

Edith Head (1907-1981)

Head was Hollywood's most celebrated and most successful costume designer, with more than 1,100 screen credits. With eight Academy Awards, she is also the most awarded designer and the most honored woman in the history of cinema. Head's Oscar-winning films include *All About Eve* (1950), *Roman Holiday* (1953), *Sabrina* (1954) and *The Sting* (1973).

VALE OF MEMORY

Wallace Beery (1886-1949)

With his rough looks and gravel voice Beery was an unlikely leading star, but he was one of the most popular actors of his time, not to mention the first husband of Gloria Swanson. He shared the best actor Oscar with Fredric March for his work in *The Champ* (1931).

Aimee Semple McPherson
(1890-1944)

An elaborate stone memorial with two kneeling angels marks the grave of this wildly popular Canadian-born evangelist. "Born again" at the age of eighteen, McPherson arrived in Los Angeles penniless and soon established the Foursquare Gospel Church with a large following. She preached from the altar of her Angelus Temple and broadcast nationally from her own radio station, KFSG. In 1926 she staged her own kidnapping, while she actually spent a few weeks with her lover in hiding. This caused a huge scandal and Sister Aimee barely escaped prosecution. After a nervous breakdown, she died of an accidental drug overdose.

Joe E Brown (1892-1973)

The family monument marks the grave of a comedian famous for his elastic face and wide mouth, imprinted for posterity in the cement in front of the Chinese Theatre. He is best remembered for his role in *Some Like It Hot* (1959), where he plays the confused millionaire who pursues Jack Lemmon masquerading in drag. Upon Lemmon's confession that she is actually a he, Brown utters one of the greatest curtain lines in history, "Well, nobody's perfect."

L Frank Baum (1856-1919)

A large gravestone marks the final resting place of the author and playwright famous for his fantasies for children. Baum wrote fourteen books about the imaginary land of Oz. The best-known in the series, *The Wonderful Wizard of Oz* (1900), was made into an extremely popular film starring Judy Garland in 1939.

The Great Mausoleum at Forest Lawn-Glendale Memorial Park

Jean Hersholt (1886-1956)

The grave of the Danish-born actor and humanitarian is marked by an unusual monument. Inspired by the Hans Christian Andersen tale, it shows a boy riding a goat and waving a dead bird over his head. Hersholt appeared in over one hundred films, being often typecast in doctor parts. He is best remembered for the character of Dr Paul Christian, which he portrayed in the radio series and several films in the 1940s. Upon his death from cancer, the Academy of Motion Picture Arts and Sciences instituted the Jean Hersholt Humanitarian Award in his honor.

Tom Mix (1880-1940)

Perhaps the top western star of the 1920s, Tom Mix appeared in four hundred action-packed movies. Despite the fact that his films were utterly simplistic, he remained for years the highest paid actor and an extremely popular showman. In an eternal conflict of good and evil, Tom Mix was always on the right side, playing good guys and wearing a white hat to distinguish himself from the bad guys who, naturally, wore black hats. He died in a car crash and reportedly was buried in a silver coffin, wearing a belt buckle that spelled his name in diamonds.

Theodore Dreiser
(1871-1945)

A famous novelist and editor, Dreiser was a pioneer of naturalism in American literature, noted for his scrutiny of social issues and his contempt for conventional morality. He is best-known for *Sister Carrie* (1900) and *An American Tragedy* (1925), a novel based on an actual murder case.

Alla Nazimova (1879-1945)

Russian-born motion-picture actress and producer, an accomplished violinist and dancer, Nazimova was one of the leading stars on Broadway. She toured with Rudolph Valentino on stage before coming to Hollywood, where she appeared in a series of silent films. In 1921 she opened the Garden of Allah, a famous hotel and watering place on Sunset Blvd, and for years was the head of a lesbian cult. Nazimova was the godmother of First Lady Nancy Reagan. She died of coronary thrombosis.

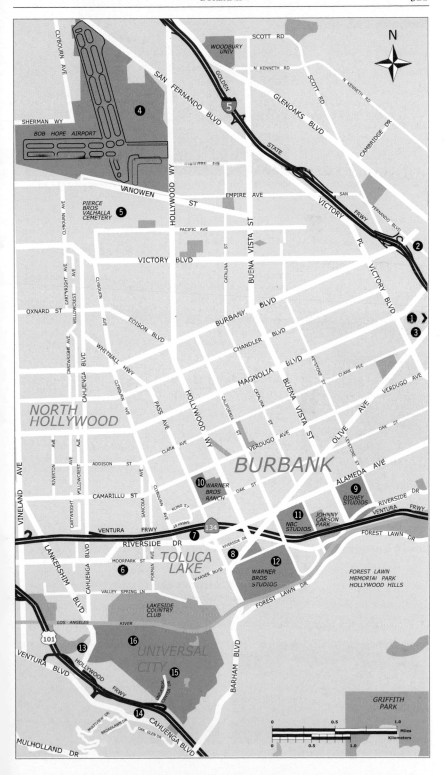

Burbank City Hall ❶

William Allen and George W Lutzi,
architects (1941).
275 E Olive Ave. Not on map.
☎(818) 238-5850. ⚑ NRHP

This PWA Moderne building
is characterized by a dominating five-story tower with
tall windows covered by
large cast-concrete Art Deco
screen, and a turquoise fountain in the central courtyard.
The two-story lobby fea-
tures refined ornaments and
decorative detailing, including brass stair railings, a balcony balustrade and a grand
chandelier. Above the mezzanine landing, a large mural
by Hugo Ballin depicts Burbank commerce of the 1940s,
dominated by the aircraft,
film-making, oil and con-
struction industries.

Burbank Airport during the opening day ceremonies (1930)

**The beautifully lit, two-story
lobby of the Burbank City Hall**

Looff Carousel ❷

Media City Center, Magnolia at
San Fernando boulevards.
NRHP

This remarkable merry-go-
round was created by Charles
I D Looff, one of the earliest

and most influential American carousel carvers. It traveled a long way from Fair-
park, Texas, where it was
originally placed in 1895.
During the 1950s, the carousel operated at Pacific Park in
Santa Monica. The beautifully
restored carousel, with its
finely carved horses and
menagerie of other creatures,
including a dragon, bear,
dog, goat and giraffe, was
placed here in 1997.

Nickelodeon ❸

231 W Olive Ave.
☎(818) 736-3000.
www.nick.com

This unconventional building is home to the critically
acclaimed and wildly popular
children's animated television
programs. Fans of all ages
will find on the studio's roof
their three-dimensional cartoon heroes, including
SpongeBob SquarePants,
Arnold, The Angry Beavers
(Daggett and Norbert) and
The Fairly OddParents.

Bob Hope Airport ❹
(formerly **Burbank Airport**)

2627 Hollywood Way.
☎(818) 840-8847.

What started in 1930 as the
nation's first privately-owned
"million dollar airport," by
1934 became the busiest air
terminal in Los Angeles.
Known as the United Air Terminal, this is the airport
movie stars and other affluent passengers used for their
transcontinental flights in the
1930s. The airport's Hangar
14 housed the planes of
Amelia Earhart, transatlantic
hero Charles Lindbergh, and
aviator and motion picture
producer Howard Hughes,
who built and flew some of
his planes here. On January
19, 1937, taking off from Burbank Airport, Hughes set a
transcontinental speed record
of 7 hours and 28 minutes,
flying an airplane of his own
design. During World War II,
many critical aircraft were
built here, including B-17,
Hudson bombers and P-38
fighters. At this time it was
the only commercial airport
serving the greater LA area.
Today it is one of several
local alternatives to LAX,
serving over three million
passengers annually. In
December of 2003, the old
Burbank Airport was
renamed Bob Hope Airport,
honoring the late entertainer.

Historic Looff Carousel at the Media City Center

Cat-Dog on the roof of the Nickelodeon building

Pierce Bros Valhalla Memorial Park ❺

10621 Victory Blvd, North Hollywood.
☎(818) 763 9121.
🕐daily 8am-7pm. ⚑
The map of celebrities' graves is available at the office.

The mammoth Heritage Fountain was featured in one of the last episodes of the long-running television series *Dallas*, in which Valhalla stood for the Dallas cemetery where the Susan Lucci character was interred.

The ornate Heritage Fountain at Valhalla Memorial Park

Portal of the Folded Wings

Portal of the Folded Wings
🕐daily 9am-4pm. NRHP

This lavish open-domed structure was built in 1924 by architect Kenneth MacDonald and sculptor Federico Giorgi. With its ornate cast concrete ornamentation and colorful tiled dome, it was originally known as Valhalla Memorial Rotunda and was intended as an entrance to the park. In 1953, on the 50th anniversary of the first powered flight by the Wright brothers, the shrine was renamed Portal of the Folded Wings and was dedicated to the pioneers of aviation. Beneath the bronze tablets on the floor are the remains of the thirteen early fliers, including Charles Taylor, who helped design and build the engine the Wright brothers used on their legendary plane. Memorial plaques on the walls honor famous aviators such as Amelia Earhart, the Wright brothers, Admiral Richard Byrd and General William Mitchell.

Oliver Hardy (1892-1957)

A bronze memorial plaque on the small wall marks the final resting place of Oliver Hardy, the heavyset member of the most famous comedy duo in the history of cinema. After they were teamed up in 1926 in the Hal Roach Studios, Laurel and Hardy worked together for 25 years and made more than 100 films. Among their best shorts are *Busybodies* (1933) and *The Music Box* (1932), which won an Academy Award for best comedy short. Hardy died of complications resulting from a paralytic stroke.

Mae Murray (1885-1965)

One of silent film's most glamorous blondes, Mae Murray started as a dancer in New York, where she was known as "the Toast of Broadway." Billed as "the Girl with the Bee-Stung Lips," she was the screen partner of such leading men as Rudolph Valentino and John Gilbert. Her best performance was the starring role in *The Merry Widow* (1925), directed by Erich von Stroheim.

Curly-Joe DeRita (1909-1993)

After he joined the Three Stooges in 1958, the actor appeared in eight feature films with the popular comedy team. He debuted with the Stooges in *Have Rocket, Will Travel* (1959), their first feature-length film.

Garden of Hope, enclosing wall, Lot 48

Adoration, Lot 6, Section 6328, Block G

Prayer, Lot 48, Section 338, Block D

Famous signboard and mascot

Interior of Bob's Big Boy, an icon of midcentury design

Bob Hope Home ⑥

10346 Moorpark St.
Private residence.

This traditional white-brick, 34-room mansion was the home of the legendary comedian from 1940 to 2004. Hope, who was one of the world's wealthiest entertainers, established his name in radio in the 1930s and later ventured into film and television. His regular annual trips overseas to entertain troops were widely publicized.

Bob's Big Boy ⑦

Wayne McAllister, architect (1949)
4211 Riverside Dr.
☎(818) 843-9334. 🚩

This is the third Bob's ever built and the oldest still in existence in the famous chain of family restaurants. The structure, which is considered an icon to the mid-century car culture, was designed by Wayne McAllister, one of the most prominent representatives of the Googie architectural style (➔ p98). With its 1940s Streamline Moderne features such as large curved windows and canopies, incorporated with elements of freeform coffee shop architecture of the 1950s, including imposing signage, cantilevers and an open kitchen, it is an excellent example of a transitional design. The building's most striking feature, the 35-foot-high (12-m) rectangular signboard is designed to

counterbalance the length of the roof and vast expanses of windows. Although freestanding, it is an essential part of the design.

The famous Bob's Big Boy fast-food restaurant chain started as a small hamburger joint in Glendale in 1936. It was the birthplace of a fast-food American icon—the "double-decker" cheeseburger—which was originated there by owner Bob Wian and served by popular car hops. Maintaining the tradition, patrons with custom cars and hot rods gather in the parking lot Friday nights and cruise around in true LA fashion. On Saturday and Sunday nights, from 5 to 10pm, nostalgic car-hop service is offered, with orders delivered on window trays.

The famous Big Boy trademark was modeled after a chubby six-year-old boy who used to clean counters in exchange for double-decker hamburgers. The mascot was

first sketched on a napkin by Ben Washam, a Looney Tunes animator. It was later developed into a familiar fiberglass statue which welcomed patrons to Wian's restaurants.

The red-checker-wearing Big Boy mascot was featured in the first two *Austin Powers* movies (1997, 1999), as the rocket in which Dr Evil escaped into outer space.

Warner Bros Office Building ⑧

Charles Luckman Partnership (1979)
3903 W Olive Ave.

With its smooth walls and rounded edges, this imposing Post-Modern building was obviously inspired by the Streamline Moderne. Its unique interior, featuring movable walls designed to meet the specific needs of a film production company, is mirrored in the flowing surfaces and curved balconies of the structure's façade.

Curving surfaces of the Warner Bros Office Building's façade

Walt Disney Company

Walt Disney began his career as a commercial artist, but soon switched to animation, although initially without much success. Upon his arrival in Hollywood in 1923, Walt joined forces with his brother Roy and with the help of friend/animator Ub Iwerks, started making a series of cartoons. During the 1920s and 1930s, Disney produced short animated cartoon series such as the *Alice Comedies* and *Silly Symphonies*. The breakthrough came in 1928 with the creation of Mickey Mouse, the most popular of all Disney characters. Mickey's sensational reception gave rise to a whole menagerie of other animal characters, including Donald Duck, Goofy and Pluto. Walt Disney and his creative team had elevated the humble cartoon medium to a respected and widely popular art form.

Disney's next triumphs arrived with feature-length animated cartoons in the 1930s and 1940s. In 1934, the company began production of the first-ever feature-length animated film, *Snow White and the Seven Dwarfs*. Widely regarded as an industry milestone, the 83-minute film premiered on 21 December 1937 and proved a tremendous success at the box office. Other animated classics followed, including *Pinocchio* (1940), *Fantasia* (1940), *Cinderella* (1950) and *Alice in Wonderland* (1951).

The next step was a series of documentaries and live-action films, including *Treasure Island* (1950), *20,000 Leagues Under the Sea* (1954) and *Mary Poppins* (1964).

Walt Disney also pioneered the concept of the theme park, and the opening of Disneyland in 1955 fundamentally changed the leisure industry (→ p489). The company made an early transition to television, using it to introduce the public to its movies. Its purchase of TV distributor Capital Cities/ABC Inc in 1995 created an international giant producing entertainment for the family market.

Walt Disney is the most honored individual in the history of motion pictures, winning 26 Academy Awards, including the Irving G Thalberg Memorial Award and two Special Awards. Setting another precedent in 1991, Disney's animated feature *Beauty and the Beast* achieved the unthinkable—a nomination as best picture of the year.

Although he started as an animator, Walt Disney was far more successful as a visionary producer and executive, whose unique style and innovative techniques set the standard for the whole industry. Gambling everything each time, Disney produced the first cartoon with synchronized sound, the first cartoon in full color and the first feature-length animated film, all of which were triumphs. His name, recognized by millions all over the world, became a synonym with family entertainment and the company he founded is still the dominant force in the field.

The most famous mouse in the world was born in 1928 on a train ride back from New York. Walt initially wanted to call his character "Mortimer," but his wife objected and suggested "Mickey" instead. Mickey Mouse was the first cartoon character to talk, appearing in the landmark synchronized sound cartoon, *Steamboat Willie*. Referring to the source of his fortune, Walt used to remark to his employees, "I hope we never lose sight of one fact . . . that this was all started by a Mouse."

Lobby card for *Snow White and the Seven Dwarfs* (1937), the first feature-length animated film in history

Walt Disney Studios ❾

When their operations had overgrown the modest lot on Hyperion Ave (➔ p171), the Disney brothers decided to move their studio to Burbank. They purchased a 50-acre (20-ha) site for $100,000 using the profits from their first major success, *Snow White and the Seven Dwarfs*. Built in 1940, the brand new studio was specifically designed for the needs of animation, with most rooms allowing the maximum available daylight preferred by artists. The original buildings were created by one of

Walt Disney Studios water tower

the leading industrial designers of his time, Kem Weber, and represent a mix between Streamline Moderne and industrial architecture. Weber also designed the interiors and much of the furnishings. The small lot features only four sound stages, used for the production of live action adventures and television programming. All of the studio's classic animated films from *Fantasia* (1940) on, including such recent hits as *Beauty and the Beast* (1991), *Aladdin* (1992) and *The Lion King* (1994), were made here.

Kem Weber, architect (1939-40); numerous later additions.
500 S Buena Vista St.
☎(818) 560-1000.
⏱closed to the public. Usually open third Sat in November, 10am-3pm. For info, call ☎(818) 560-1000. ⑤ 🏳
To get free tickets for live TV shows filming on the lot, call ☎(818) 753-3470 or (818) 506-0043, or visit **www**.tvtickets.com.

"I hope we never lose sight of one fact . . . that this was all started by a Mouse."
—Walt Disney

The fence surrounding the studio incorporates little Mickey Mouse heads

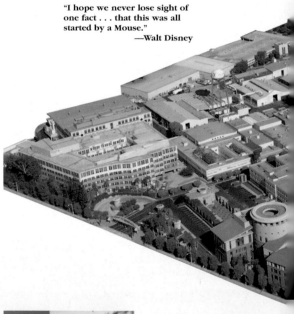

Tours of Walt Disney Studios are not available. However, once a year, during a Christmas Craft Fair, part of the lot is open to the public. Visitors can stroll among the buildings, shop in the Disney Store and the commissary, and take pictures with costumed Disney characters.

The 3-story Animation Building was constructed in 1939 with eight wings designed to provide maximum daylight for the animators. Windows featured mechanized shutters controlled by wire, which enabled the artists to adjust the amount of incoming natural light in every room. Among the classic Disney animated features produced here are *Dumbo* (1941), *Cinderella* (1950), *Peter Pan* (1953) and *Lady and the Trump* (1955).

Administration Building (Michael Graves, 1991). This distinctive postmodern structure, with its red sandstone cladding on lower levels and yellow stucco facing on higher levels, is clearly visible from the street. Its classically inspired façade features six of the seven dwarfs from *Snow White*, each 19 feet (5,7 m) tall, which serve as caryatids supporting the roof. The seventh dwarf, little Dopey, stands under the gable.

One of the largest stages on the West Coast, Stage 2 was completed in 1949 and used for the filming of the television series *Dragnet*. Disney features *Mary Poppins* (1964) and *The Princess Diaries* (2001) were also filmed here. During the construction of Disneyland in the 1950s, much of the work was done on the stage, including the giant *Mark Twain* paddleboat, which was built here and then dismantled, transported and reassembled at the theme park.

Amusing street signs incorporate one or two Disney characters, such as Mickey and Dopey, shown here

Animation Building (Robert Stern, 1995). The headquarters of the animation department that houses more than 700 artists features a striped red and white exterior resembling a streamlined train and 14-foot-high (4,3-m) letters spelling the structure's purpose. Its focal point is the 85-foot-high (30-m) conical tower, painted blue with stars and a crescent moon, and placed over the CEO's office. It is similar to the wizard's magic hat worn by Mickey Mouse as the sorcerer's apprentice in *Fantasia* (1940).

Numerous films and TV series were filmed at Warner Bros Ranch

Warner Bros Ranch ⑩

3701 W Oak St.
Not open to the public. 🚩

Behind the high fence of this little-known back lot can be glimpsed movie sets and props used in many famous movies and television series. Originally founded as the King Features Ranch, it was known as the Columbia Ranch beginning in the late 1920s. It was used for filming of outdoor scenes in such classics as *Lost Horizon* (1937), *You Can't Take It with You* (1938), *Mr Smith Goes to Washington* (1939) and *High Noon* (1952). The townhouse from the *Murphy Brown* television series, Danny Glover's house in *Lethal Weapon 2* (1989) and Kevin Spacey and Annette Bening's house in *American Beauty* (1999) were all built on the lot.

Since Columbia created its Screen Gems division in 1949, many popular television series were also shot here, including *Bewitched, Leave It to Beaver, The Donna Reed Show, The Partridge Family*, and *Dennis the Menace*.

NBC TV Studios ⑪

3000 W Alameda Ave.
☎(818) 840-4444.
🖙this is the only commercial network to offer a public studio tour; for info call ☎(818) 840–3537.
🕐Mon-Fri 9am-3pm. Open weekends and extended hours during summer and holiday seasons. Closed Easter, Thanksgiving, Christmas Day and New Year's Day. Ⓢ

Founded as a radio network in 1926, the National Broadcasting Company (NBC) became a television broadcaster in the 1940s. An industry pioneer in technology and programming since its inception, NBC's numerous "firsts" include: the first permanent broadcasting network in the nation; the first US coast-to-coast broadcast (1927); the revolutionary first color telecast (1953) and the first made-for-TV movie (1964).

NBC opened the present 43-acre studio lot in 1952, and moved its LA headquarters here when its old studio at Sunset and Vine was demolished in 1964. This is the place where many of the Bob Hope specials were created; Rowan and Martin's *Laugh-In*, the show that introduced the "Beautiful Downtown Burbank" tagline, was also taped here. But the studio's greatest fame came from *The Tonight Show*, first hosted with Johnny Carson for 30 years, and from 1992 starring Jay Leno.

If you want to be part of the audience during the recording of *The Tonight Show*, there are two ways to obtain free tickets: 1. In person—at the NBC ticket counter on a first come first serve basis, starting at 8am

on the day of the taping. Tickets are also available at the Chinese Theatre (TV tickets booth) and Universal CityWalk at the NBC ticket booth. 2. By mail—send your requests to NBC Tickets (address above) several weeks in advance. Taping starts at 5pm, but you must be in line at least by 4pm. However, bear in mind that the studio gives out more tickets than there are seats and even ticketholders are regularly turned away.

During the 70-minute studio tour visitors can view a video about NBC's history and see demonstrations of special effects ("chroma key") and sound effects (the laughing machine). Guests do not see the actual make-up and wardrobe departments; instead, they can examine mannequins and props exhibited in display cases, such as *Mission Impossible* effects masks.

The highlight of the visit is a behind-the-scenes look at *The Tonight Show* set, where tour guests can sit inside the 320-seat theater in the same seats as the live studio audience will during recording. They can also see Jay Leno's car on the reserved spot No. 1 on the star parking lot in front of Studio 3. Leno, an avid car collector who keeps his spectacular car collection in an airport hangar, drives a different car to work every day.

Waiting for *The Tonight Show* tickets

Warner Bros Pictures

The four Warner brothers who founded the famous studio—Harry, Albert, Sam and Jack—first entered the movie business as nickelodeon operators. In 1903 the family bought a projector and showed a print of *The Great Train Robbery* in a rented store. Soon after they ventured into film distribution and production, and in 1919 owned their own studio in Hollywood on Sunset Blvd. In 1925 the Warners acquired Vitagraph and in 1928 First National Pictures, complete with studio facilities and a large number of theaters. Known during its modest beginnings as "the working man's studio," Warner Bros was elevated to the status of a major Hollywood player with the release of *The Jazz Singer* in 1927.

Upon his retirement in 1967, Jack Warner sold his interest in the studio to the Canadian-based Seven Arts Productions. After another take-over in 1969, the company changed its name to Warner Communications Inc. In 1989, Time-Life merged with Warner Bros, creating the huge Time Warner Inc conglomerate. In 2001, it was acquired by Internet service provider America Online.

Warner Bros invested heavily in experiments involving a synchronous sound-on-disc process called Vitaphone in the 1920s, although it had been rejected by other major studios. The gamble paid off with *The Jazz Singer* (1927), and Warners established a lead in the production of talking pictures. During the 1930s and 1940s, the studio developed its characteristic look with social dramas and gangster films such as *Little Caesar* (1930) and *Public Enemy* (1931). Lavish musicals, including *42nd Street* (1933) and *Gold Diggers of 1933* (1934) directed by Busby Berkeley, were unmatched by any other studio.

Warner Bros' famous contract players in the 1930s were James Cagney, Edward G Robinson, Errol Flynn, Joan Blondell, Olivia de Havilland and Loretta Young. The studio's top star in the 1940s was Humphrey Bogart, and in the 1950s new talents included Burt Lancaster, Marlon Brando, James Dean and Doris Day.

The Warners' films that carried off Oscars in the best picture category were *The Life of Emile Zola* (1937), *Casablanca* (1942), *My Fair Lady* (1964), *Chariots of Fire* (1981), *Driving Miss Daisy* (1989) and *Unforgiven* (1992).

Warner Bros Pictures logo

The youngest of 12 children of a poor Jewish cobbler who immigrated from Poland, Jack Warner served as head of the famous studio for more than 30 years. He ruled with a dictatorial and frugal hand and had frequent disputes with his stars and other creative personnel over salaries. Jack was notorious for his rough sense of humor and undiplomatic bursts. On one occasion, when he was introduced to Mme Chiang Kai-shek, he mumbled that he had forgotten his laundry.

Lobby card for *Casablanca* (1942), the best picture Oscar winner

Bette Davis was the queen of the Warner Bros lot and one of the studio's top money-makers. She won two Academy Awards in the best actress category—for *Dangerous* (1935) and *Jezebel* (1938).

Warner Bros Studios ⑫

The studio was originally built for First National, an early film company formed in 1917, whose stars included Charlie Chaplin and Mary Pickford. The lot was purchased by Warner Bros in 1929, two years after the release of *The Jazz Singer* started the sound era. That same year the studio turned out 86 features on its new lot. In 1972, Warner Bros and Columbia Pictures made an agreement to jointly use the facility, renamed the Burbank Studios. When Columbia was acquired by Sony in 1990, it moved to the former MGM lot in Culver City.

Warner Bros Studios water tower

The 110- acre Warner Bros lot features 34 soundstages and 9 exterior sets, used for both movie and TV productions. The tour offers a behind-the-scenes look at the actual working studio, emphasizing the technical aspect of production, with visits to such areas as the crafts mill where sets are constructed, the prop shop and the scenic art department. The tour starts with a 15-minute film collage featuring some of the studio's most famous stars, as well as some hilarious outtakes and blunders.

Memorial plaques list the best-known films and TV productions filmed in the Warner Bros Studios' sound stages

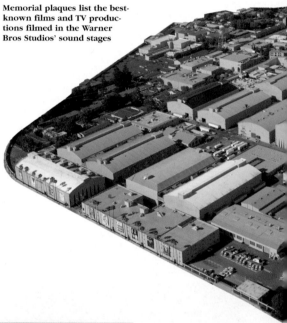

4000 Warner Blvd.
☎(818) 954-6000.
🚌 a 2 1/4-hour tram Studio Tour. For info call ☎(818) 972-TOUR, or visit **www.wbstudiotour.com**.
🕐Mon-Fri 8:30am-4:30pm on the hour; in the summer every half hour. Closed weekends and major holidays. 💲 📷 📍
To get free tickets for live TV shows filming on the lot, call ☎(818) 753-3470 or (818) 506-0043, or visit **www.tvtickets.com**.

Simulating New York tenements of the early 20th century, Annie Street is the oldest section of the backlot, constructed for the studio's signature gangster movies of the 1930s. It was used as the front side of the orphanage in *Annie* (1981) and was the site of Jim Carrey's apartment in *The Mask* (1994). Trimmed in neon, this fake city block posed as the city of the future in *Blade Runner* (1982) and served as Gotham City in *Batman Returns* (1992).

Featuring the studio's animated heroes painted on its façade, Stage 1 served as the set for such memorable movies as *The Life of Emile Zola* (1937), *Mildred Pierce* (1945), *The Treasure of the Sierra Madre* (1948), *A Star Is Born* (1954), *Bonnie and Clyde* (1967) and *Lethal Weapon 2* (1989)

Since the 1950s, when it became the first major studio to use its facilities for television output, Warner Bros has maintained its position as the top producer of television series in Hollywood. It was home to some of the biggest prime-time shows such as *West Wing*, *ER* and *Friends*. A special outdoor set with the emergency room entrance to the Chicago county hospital, together with a piece of mock elevated train track, is used in the hit television series *ER*.

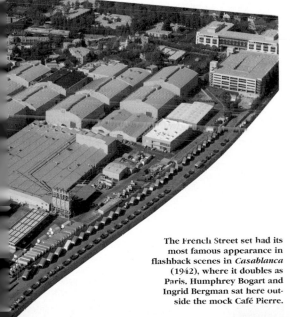

The French Street set had its most famous appearance in flashback scenes in *Casablanca* (1942), where it doubles as Paris. Humphrey Bogart and Ingrid Bergman sat here outside the mock Café Pierre.

With its height of 95 feet (29 m), Stage 16 is the tallest such structure on this continent. It houses a two million-gallon capacity water tank, used for maritime scenes in *The Old Man and the Sea* (1958). A jungle and a waterfall were built inside this stage for a scene in *Jurassic Park* (1993). Special effects in *The Perfect Storm* (2000) were also filmed here. They included computer-generated images of large bodies of water, a boat "Andrea Gail," operated with hydraulics, and the replica of a helicopter mounted at the end of a crane.

Hanna-Barbera Studio, former home of Tom and Jerry

Campo de Cahuenga ⑬

3919 Lankershim Blvd.
☎(818) 623-4166.
⏱Sat 11am-3pm. $free.

This is the site where the Treaty of Cahuenga was signed on January 13, 1847, by Lt Col John C Frémont and General Andrés Pico. The treaty ended the war between the United States and Mexico in California (➜ p22).

The existing building is a replica of the six-room Feliz Adobe, built in 1845 on the Rancho Cahuenga, where the signing took place. It features exhibits related to the history of the treaty, including copies of documents and artifacts.

Hanna-Barbera Studio (formerly) ⑭

Arthur Froehlich, architect (1962).
3400 Cahuenga Blvd.
Closed to the public.

This cultural landmark was for 35 years one of the busiest animation studios in the world. It was the founding site of television animation, the cartoon factory where Hanna-Barbera Productions utilized their "limited animation" technique to cut down the cost of animation production.

Opened in 1963, six years after Oscar-winning animators William Hanna and Joseph Barbera founded their production company, this

was the birthplace of countless cartoon stars that influenced popular culture around the world. This building was home to such classic animated characters as Tom and Jerry, Yogi Bear, Huckleberry Hound, Augie Doggie, Wally Gator, Scooby-Doo, The Flintstones, Quick Draw McGraw and Baba Looey.

The building's futuristic design evokes a sense of the space-age related to the popular animated series, *The Jetsons*, which was created here in the 1960s. It was a functional, state-of-the-art facility, perfectly adapted for every aspect of animation production. With its cantilevered concrete construction, distinctive porthole-pierced awnings and concrete screens, the three-story edifice is an excellent example of mid-20th-century modernism.

Universal CityWalk ⑮

The Jerde Partnership, Inc, architects (1992, expanded 2000)
Adjacent to Universal Studios.
☎(818) 622-4455.
www.citywalkhollywood.com.
⏱daily 11am-11pm. $free.

Designed by famous shopping mall architect Jon Jerde, this open-air dining, shopping and entertainment complex offers an idealized version of a real city. Opened in 1992, the two-block-long pedestrian mall is a reflection of contemporary pop culture dominated by mass-consumption and aggressive marketing.

Simulating Main Street in a city without one, CityWalk's mis-matched mix of brightly colored façades mirrors the notorious lack of a dominant architectural theme in Los Angeles. Here you'll find a store selling beachwear with a roof in the form of a huge surfboard. Atop an ice cream shop is an upside-down pink Chevy convertible bursting through a freeway sign. Giant frames mark the entrance to the sunglasses store. There is a science-fiction comics store with a spacecraft that has crashed into its façade.

CityWalk features the newest in interactive technology and special effects, including a video board, huge screens and animated graphics, while the vintage neon signs nostalgically evoke a bygone era.

Two-block-long Universal CityWalk is lined with fanciful façades

Universal Pictures

This giant among the film production companies and one of the oldest continuously operating movie studios was founded by film pioneer Carl Laemmle in 1909 as the Independent Motion Picture Company. In 1912 IMP became Universal Pictures after a merger with several smaller film companies, including Bison, Nestor and Powers. The story goes that, while looking for a suitable name for his company, Laemmle saw through the window of his New York office a wagon bearing words "Universal Pipe Fittings." The name instantly appealed to him and so Universal was born.

Universal Pictures logo

In the early 1930s, Universal established its reputation with the critically acclaimed film *All Quiet on the Western Front* (1930). Box office success came with its cycle of horror films which immediately became classics of the genre: *Dracula* (1931), *Frankenstein* (1931), *The Mummy* (1932), *The Invisible Man* (1933) and *The Wolf Man* (1935). During the Depression Era, a series of musicals starring Deanna Durbin kept the studio afloat. In the 1950s, comedies starring Abbott and Costello and bedroom farces with Doris Day were especially popular. Labeled as one of the "Little Two" studios (together with Columbia) during the Hollywood Golden Era, Universal was elevated to the top position in the industry with a series of sensational hits: *The Sting* (1973), *American Graffiti* (1973), *Jaws* (1975) and *E.T. The Extra Terrestrial* (1982), which count among the biggest money grossers of all time.

Despite the fact that its head, Carl Laemmle, invented the star system (→ p45), Universal did not have many major stars of its own; most of the studio's top actors were often on loan from elsewhere. Among the stars of the silent era who have made their films here were Rudolph Valentino, W C Fields, Lon Chaney and later Bela Lugosi and Boris Karloff. During the 1950s, the Universal roster included James Stewart, Tony Curtis, Cary Grant and the studio's top-billing male star, Rock Hudson.

Universal films that won the Academy Award for best picture were *All Quiet on the Western Front* (1930), *The Sting* (1973), *Out of Africa* (1985), *Schindler's List* (1993), *Gladiator* (2000) and *A Beautiful Mind* (2001).

Carl Laemmle was born in Germany as the tenth of 13 children in a Jewish family of modest means. He arrived in America at age 17 and held a variety of jobs before opening his first nickelodeon in 1906. The former clothes salesman soon became one of the leading American distributors. Founder and president of Universal for quarter century, Laemmle was forced to sell his interest in the studio to his creditors in 1936 for a mere $4.5 million—a fraction of its worth. A branch of the family today owns the Laemmle movie theater chain.

Lobby card for the horror classic *Dracula* (1931)

Universal's star Boris Karloff became a household name as the *Frankenstein* monster

Universal Studios—Lower Lot ⑯

When film pioneer Carl Laemmle decided to consolidate several production facilities on one site, he bought a 230-acre (92-ha) chicken ranch in the foothills of the Santa Monica Mountains, where he moved the operations of his Universal Film and Manufacturing Company. He ran ads in local newspapers for several months, announcing the launch of the new studio, equipped for both interior and exterior shooting. In March 1915, the company opened with much fanfare Universal City, an independent municipality in the San Fernando Valley, attracting a crowd of 20,000.

Univeral Studios neon sign

The Universal Studios complex comprises three areas: the Entertainment Center (where visitors see live performances and stroll and shop in recreated streets of the world), the Studio Center (featuring film-related rides), and the Backlot Tour, a 45-minute narrated tram ride that takes visitors around the studio's famed backlot. Despite the ride behind the scenes of a working studio, it is unlikely that the public will see any actual filming. The studio features 35 soundstages, over 500 outdoor sets and façades depicting diverse locations, recognizable from hundreds of Universal movies.

100 Universal Plaza.
☎(818) 622-3801.
www.universalstudios.com.
🕐summer: Mon-Fri 9am-9pm, Sat-Sun 9am-10pm; winter: 9am-6pm daily. Closed Thanksgiving and Christmas. ⑤ ♠ ⛳
🚌a 45-minute tram Studio Tour. To get free tickets for live TV shows filming on the lot, call ☎(818) 753-3470 or (818) 506-0043, or visit www.tvtickets.com.

Featured in *Psycho* (1960), this is the infamous Bates House where Anthony Perkins's character, hotel proprietor Norman Bates, keeps his mother's skeleton

Universal was the first studio to open its doors to sightseers. Carl Laemmle charged visitors 25 cents a head (which included a box lunch) to see how motion pictures were made. "Uncle" Carl didn't miss a chance to augment his income by selling the audiences fresh eggs from the chicken ranch on their way out. In this photograph spectators watch from bleachers the shooting of a scene from the western *Love's Lariat* (1916), starring famous screen cowboy Harry Carey.

Stage 27 housed the Houston mission control room for the epic *Apollo 13* (1995). Some key scenes with scientists and the flight director, played by Ed Harris, were filmed here.
Also filmed here was a famous scene in *Jurassic Park* (1993), in which a giant brontosaurus sneezes on children hiding in a tree.

Stage 28 was built to house the magnificent Paris Grand Opera House set in the classic *The Phantom of the Opera* (1925). The stage still contains the spectacular set, which is haunted by the mysterious man in the black cape, reportedly spotted on the catwalks. Legend has it that it is the Phantom himself, the immortal Lon Chaney.

The classic shower scene in Alfred Hitchcock's masterpiece *Psycho*, in which Anthony Perkins brutally murders the motel guest played by Janet Leigh, was shot on Stage 18. It was filmed 70 times before the director was satisfied.

Cartoon backdrops such as this snow-covered street of Whoville are part of the lavish movie set specially built for the fable *How the Grinch Stole Christmas* (2000)

Standing 30 feet (9 m) tall, weighing nearly seven tons and covered with 660 pounds (300 kg) of synthetic fur, King Kong is the world's largest animated figure. It is also one of the most sophisticated movie creatures—his facial movements are controlled by computers.

Universal Studios—Upper Lot

Spreading across 420 acres (170 ha), Universal is the world's largest working movie and TV studio. Since 1915, it has produced more than 8,000 films and more television programs than any other studio in the world. With its five million annual visitors, it is also one of the most popular attractions in the US, and Southern California's second most visited theme park (after Disneyland). The modern Universal tour was reestablished in 1964, when the studio offered tram rides of

Universal Studios globe

its back lot. The modest tour gradually expanded and became more elaborate with the constant addition of new attractions inspired by the studio's most spectacular movies and TV programs. The tour now includes shows and rides featuring astonishing special effects and cutting edge video and audio technology. This is an overwhelming experience and visitors should dedicate the whole day and arrive early to derive the most from the complex.

Jurassic Park-The Ride
Called the most technically advanced attraction ever designed, this interactive ride utilizes the most sophisticated state-of-the-art computer and robotic technology to create impossibly real animatronic figures. Visitors ride in a 25-seat float through the recreation of a prehistoric jungle, encountering friendly, five-story-high herbivorous dinosaurs. They soon discover that their runaway raft becomes the prey of blood-thirsty Spitters, Raptors and the ultimate terror—a giant Tyrannosaurus Rex, before plunging 84 feet (25 m) to safety.

Terminator 2: 3D
This multi-sensory virtual adventure blends live stunt action, including a Harley Davidson motorcycle roaring on the stage, with the most sophisticated digital imaging technology ever created. Projected on the world's largest 3-D screen and surrounding visitors, it produces the spectacular illusion of depth.
To save the human race from annihilation, our heroes from the original movie must destroy the dreadful T-1000 cyborg, shown here with his tentacles protruding into the audience.

Backdraft
A recreation of breathtaking scenes from this fire-fighting movie puts the audience in the center of a blazing inferno at a temperature of several thousand degrees. Tremendous explosions of fuel drums, overhead pipes and ruptured fuel lines create an immense firestorm that consumes the roof and causes the collapse of the supporting structure.

Shrek 4-D
Universal's newest, multi-sensory, state-of-the-art attraction combines 3-dimensional animation with in-theater effects for a sensational fantasy experience. Visitors, equipped with special OgreVision glasses, follow Shrek and his bride, Princess Fiona, on their honeymoon, while the ghost of Lord Farquaad tries to take his revenge.

Revenge of the Mummy-The Ride combines elaborate special effects inspired by the *Mummy* movies with cutting-edge roller coaster engineering to produce a thrilling ride experience

WaterWorld
Universal's No. 1 rated show, this thrilling water extravaganza combines high-tech special effects, pyrotechnics and human stunt work culminating in wild battle scenes between warriors defending the atoll and roving pirates on jet skis. Highlights include giant fireballs shooting 50 feet (15 m) in the air and a spectacular seaplane crash landing just a few feet from amazed spectators.

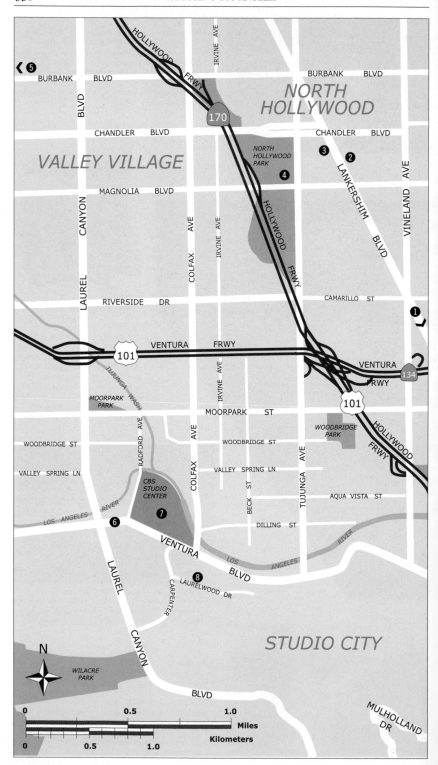

Barris-designed Batmobile IV

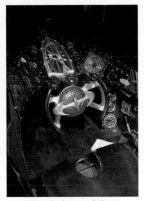

Dashboard of Batmobile IV

Academy of Television Arts and Sciences (ATAS) ❷

5230 Lankershim Blvd, North Hollywood.
☎(818) 754-2885.
www.cmmys.com
🕒only the library and theater are open to the public. Plaza open at all times.

A 27-foot (8-m) Emmy statue flies over fountain in front of the Academy's new headquarters, opened in the summer of 1991. Founded in 1946, one month after network television came into being, the Academy is devoted to the advancement of telecommunications arts and sciences. Its greatest fame, however, comes from its presentation of the annual Emmy Awards.

Since the Hall of Fame was initiated in 1984, more than 80 of the industry greats have been honored. The Academy's Hall of Fame Plaza features bronze busts, life-size statues and bas-reliefs of such inductees as Lucille Ball, Jack Benny, Milton Berle, Sid Caesar, Johnny Carson, Bill Cosby and Bob Hope.

Barris Kustom Industries ❶

10811 Riverside Dr, North Hollywood.
☎(818) 984-1314.
www.barris.com.
🕒by appointment only.

This legendary body shop turned out unforgettable vehicles featured in hundreds of movies and television series such as *American Graffiti* (1973), *Blade Runner* (1982), *The Beverly Hillbillies* (1993), *Jurassic Park* (1993), and *Gone in 60 Seconds* (2000). The cars were styled by George Barris, a pioneer and a mythical figure in the colorful world of car body modifications. Among his most famous creations are the original bubble-domed Batmobile seen in the 1960s *Batman* television series; the chopped Mercury driven by James Dean in *Rebel Without a Cause* (1955); Christopher Lloyd's DeLorean time machine from the *Back to the Future* movies and the foot-powered Flintmobile driven by John Goodman in *The Flintstones* (1994). Some of the cars are displayed in the showroom, whose walls are covered with posters of movies that featured vehicles Barris customized.

Barris's services were in high demand by countless show business celebrities. He customized Zsa Zsa Gabor's gold Rolls Royce with retractable bar, complete with sterling-silver wine goblets. David Carradine wanted the seats of his new BMW taken out, a Pakistani carpet installed, together with a backrest, so he can sit on the carpet while driving. For the color sample of the paintjob he wanted, he brought a fresh peach. Elvis Presley was big on gold; for his 1960 Fleetwood Cadillac, the singer requested a yacht interior with portholes, as well as a gold-plated bar, gold-plated record player and gold plated TV; the roof liner was studded with gold records.

The Academy of Television Arts and Sciences' Emmy statue

Façade of El Portal Theatre

El Portal ❸

L A Smith, architect (1926).
5267 N Lankershim Blvd, North
Hollywood.
☎(818) 508-4200.
www.elportaltheatre.com

Designed by prominent
Southern California architect
L A Smith, this landmark
Spanish Colonial Revival the-
ater building also included
retail and office space.

Opened as a vaudeville
house in 1926, it later served
as a silent movie theater and,
during the sound era, a sec-
ond-run theater. During World
War II, the Army maintained
a recruiting station in the
lobby. Sustaining significant
damage in the 1994 North-
ridge earthquake, the theater
was restored and re-opened
in 2000. The original proscenium arch is preserved,
together with the theater's
most distinguished feature,
the 1926 fire curtain. Made of
asbestos fabric and splendidly painted, it depicts a Spanish galleon setting sail.

The once 1,132-seat palace
now houses three theaters
and is devoted to professional theater productions.

Amelia Earhart
Memorial Statue ❹

North Hollywood Park.
Magnolia Blvd and
Tujunga Ave
(NW corner).

This eight-foot-
tall bronze statue
by sculptor Ernest
Shelton is a memori-
al to Amelia Earhart,
one of the most
famous aviators in
history. Flying a Bur-
bank-built Lockheed
Vega on May 20-21,
1932, she became the
first woman to make a
solo flight over the
Atlantic Ocean. She
was also the first per-
son to flight solo
from Hawaii to Cali-
fornia (a longer dis-
tance than the

transcontinental flight). While
attempting to fly around the
globe with navigator Fred
Noonan in a twin-engine
Lockheed Electra, Earhart
vanished in the Pacific Ocean
on July 2, 1937. Her disappearance is still surrounded
with mystery.

A Toluca Lake resident,
Earhart lived at 10042 Valley
Spring Lane with her hus-
band, publisher George Put-
nam.

Great Wall of Los
Angeles ❺

Designed by Judith Baca, painted
by various artists (1976-83).
Coldwater Canyon Ave between
Burbank Blvd and Oxnard St.

Occupying a half-mile
stretch of Tujunga Wash and
consisting of a series of panels, this is the world's
longest mural. Painted
on the west concrete
wall of the flood
control channel, the
mural depicts land-
mark events in the
ethnic history of
California, from pre-
historic times to the
present. Judith Baca
was commissioned to
sketch out plans,
which then were exe-
cuted by multi-cultural
neighborhood youth,
many of them mem-
bers of street gangs.
Trained artists
oversaw the project
and added finish-
ing touches.

**Amelia Earhart
statue**

Great Wall of Los Angeles: *Zoot Suit Riots LA 1943*

Studio City Walk of Fame ⑥

Ventura Blvd, between Rhodes Ave and Carpenter Ave, Studio City.

Inspired by its Hollywood Blvd namesake, the Studio City Walk of Fame acknowledges the city's contribution to popular culture with the countless movies and TV shows produced here. About 300 granite tiles installed on the sidewalks along the boulevard immortalize such popular shows as *Leave It to Beaver*, *Gilligan's Island*, *Hill Street Blues*, *Seinfeld* and *Will and Grace*, and honor the people who made them.

Granite tiles celebrate popular movies and television shows produced in Studio City

CBS Studio Center ⑦

4024 Radford Ave, Studio City
☎(818) 655-5000.
www.cbs.com.
Closed to the public. Tours are not available.
To get free tickets for live TV shows filming on the lot, call ☎(818) 753-3470 or (818) 506-0043, or visit www.tvtickets.com.
The studio's walk-up ticket booth is open 9am-5pm. ⫯

The studio was built in 1928 when Mack Sennett, the legendary "King of Comedy," moved his operation here from Silver Lake. When the advent of sound signaled an end to Sennett's career, the lot was leased by Mascot Pictures in 1933. It later became the home of Republic Pictures when the company was formed in 1935 as a result of a merger of four

Laurelwood Apartment Building was called an outstanding work by a major architect at the time it was built

smaller studios. A profitable movie factory during the 1930s and 1940s, Republic was a major producer of B movies, mostly westerns. Among its major stars were John Wayne, Gene Autry and Roy Rogers. When the demand for B pictures waned in the 1950s, Republic switched to television production, but eventually went out of business in 1959.

CBS leased the lot in 1963 and purchased it in 1967. It was used for the production of many long-running television shows and sitcoms, including *Rawhide*, *Gunsmoke*, *Gilligan's Island*, *Wild Wild West*, *Get Smart*, *Hill St. Blues*, *The Mary Tyler Moore Show*, *Roseanne*, *Cybill*, *Seinfeld* and *The Larry Sanders Show*.

Remaining parts of the studio's back lot (Western Street and the old soundstages) can be glimpsed at from Colfax St.

Laurelwood Apartment Building ⑧

Rudolf Schindler, architect (1948).
11833-11837 Laurelwood Dr, Studio City.
Private residences.

Sited on a narrow, long lot, this plain stucco box was the last apartment complex designed by iconic modern architect Rudolf Schindler. He skillfully arranged 22 apartments in two terraced structures along a central walkway, which climbs up a gentle incline. Each unit has either a private garden or a roof terrace.

Isolated from the street by garages concealed by a front wall, the buildings are now largely screened from view by mature landscaping.

Many private residences designed by Shindler dot the hills in the neighborhood.

CBS Studio Center, home to many memorable television shows

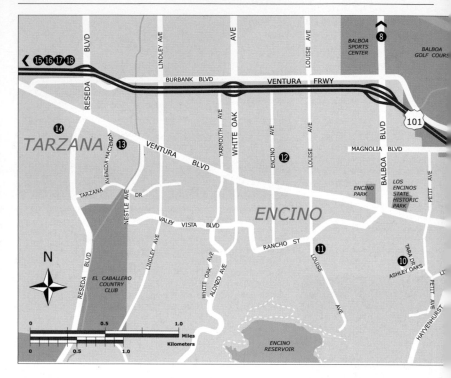

San Fernando Valley

Like Alicia Silverstone's character in *Clueless* (1995), who would not be caught dead in this sprawling bedroom community, most Angelenos express a certain note of derision when they refer to it simply as "the Valley." With its dull, middle-class housing tracts, endless shopping centers and commercial strips, and a seemingly boundless asphalt grid of streets and boulevards, it became widely known as the epitome of boring modern suburbia.

Although separated from the city by the Santa Monica Mountains, this vast, flat region of 220 square miles (570 km²) is legally part of the city of Los Angeles, containing half of its land area. With more than 1.7 million residents, the Valley is home to one-third of the city's population. Framed by mountain ranges, it is more smoggy and 10 to 20 degrees Fahren-

heit hotter in the summer than the basin over the hill.

The first recorded mention of the area occurred in 1769, when the diarist of Father Juan Crespi's expedition referred to it as "a very pleasant and spacious valley." The Valley was named after the Mission San Fernando Rey de España, which was established here in 1797 in the name of the king of Spain. After Mexico gained independence from Spain in

1822, all California missions were secularized. The enormous land holdings of the San Fernando Mission passed into private hands when Pío Pico, the last Mexican Governor of California, sold parts of it to raise desperately needed funds to fight the American military invasion. The Mexican-American War in California ended with the Treaty of Cahuenga in 1847.

In the late 19th century, vast expanses of sparsely

A vintage post card depicts Lankershim and Van Nuys ranchos

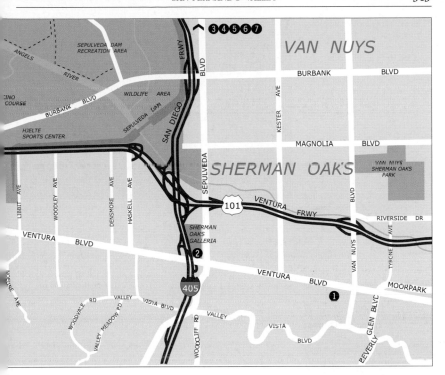

Rush hour in the San Fernando Valley in 1890. Before the advent of water, it was one great pasture.

populated and non-irrigated valley were used for ranching and extensive wheat farming. The largest landholders were Isaac Lankershim and Isaac Newton Van Nuys, who cultivated grain in the southern part of the valley on their 60,000-acre (24.000-ha) ranch.

Anticipating the completion of the Owens River Aqueduct (→ p34), speculators, organized in a syndicate, bought up large chunks of the Valley land. When water finally came in 1913, property values skyrocketed and the speculators cashed in after subdividing tens of thousands of acres. The arrival of water had an enormous effect on the area. Tens of thousands of acres were irrigated, opening the Valley to endless farms, orchards, vineyards and citrus groves.

The Valley was a locale for a number of books, the most famous being written by resident, James M Cain (→ p73). His bestselling novel, *The Postman Always Rings Twice* (1934), was set in Agoura.

Jack Nicholson and Jessica Lange are compelled to murder by a passion in *The Postman Always Rings Twice* (1981)

Here, the bored wife of a gas station-café owner and her lover murder the husband and then unsuccessfully try to cover up the crime on a mountain road. The novel was twice made into a movie, first in 1946 with Lana Turner and John Garfield, and again in 1981, starring Jack Nicholson and Jessica Lange.

When early movie studios left Hollywood looking for cheap land in which to expand, they came to the Valley. Today, it is home to Universal, Warner Bros, The Walt Disney Company, Dream-Works SKG, CBS and NBC. The Valley is so packed with movie and TV studios that two of its towns are named Studio City and Universal City. From the early 1910s on, this area was also the site of numerous movie ranches, used for location shooting for thousands of motion pictures. A plaque at 12841 Foothill Boulevard marks the site of one of the oldest, the D W Griffith ranch, since converted into an industrial park.

Edward Fickett's house design with a tennis court on the roof

Spectacular flight scenes in *Hell's Angels* (1930) were filmed in the Valley

The Valley has a long tradition as a film locale, starting with such classics as *The Squaw Man* (1914), *The Birth of a Nation* (1915) and *Hell's Angels* (1930). Its suburban way of life was featured in *Foxes* (1980), *Valley Girl* (1983), *2 Days in the Valley* (1996), *Go* (1999) and *Magnolia* (1999).

After World War II, the Valley experienced a huge population boom, when thousands of GIs flocked into the region. Between 1940 and 1960 the number of residents tripled, reaching nearly one million. In 1950 Lloyds of London declared the Valley the fastest growing area in the world. The remaining agricultural land was quickly subdivided and affordable tract homes, with pools and front lawns, emerged as the prototype of modern suburban housing.

Award-winning architect Edward Fickett, who was called "the Father of the Valley" for his pioneering design of modular, prefabricated units for affordable housing developments, brought Modernism to the masses. He built tens of thousands of low-cost tract homes.

The Valley's rapid development provided a fertile ground for mid-century Modern architecture, with numerous works by such renowned architects as Richard Neutra, Rudolf Schindler, A Quincy Jones and John Lautner emerging across the Valley.

Pornography

If you suck a woman's breast, it's rated X. If you cut it off, it gets an R.
— Jack Nicholson, actor

Often called the porn capital of the world, San Fernando Valley produces more than 80% of America's XXX-rated movies and 90% of its sex toys. Americans pay between $10 billion and $15 billion every year for a variety of sex-related products, spending more money annually for porn than they do on movie tickets, all major professional sports combined, or all the performing arts combined.

It is not unusual to see scantily-clad actresses in six-inch heels hanging around rented houses in nondescript residential areas, where location shooting commonly takes place. The proximity of mainstream Hollywood, availability of film crews with equipment and no shortage of unemployed or hopeful actors makes this unhurried, typical suburbia home to most of the leading porn production companies. The San Fernando Valley-based adult entertainment industry churns out more than 11,000 new porn titles each year.

The Valley porn movie community of the 1970s was featured in *Boogie Nights* (1997), which follows the rise and fall of a young porn star, played by Mark Wahlberg.

A Sunset Blvd billboard promotes Vivid Video's top female stars

Restored interior of San Fernando Mission church

San Fernando Mission ❸

15151 San Fernando Mission Blvd, Mission Hills. Not on map. ☎(818) 361-0186. ⊕daily 9am-5pm. Closed Thanksgiving and Christmas. Ⓢ NRHP

Mission San Fernando Rey de España was founded in 1797 by father Fermin Francisco De Lausen, who was president of all the California missions at the time. The mission was named after the cannonized 13th-century king of Spain, Ferdinad III. It was the 17th in a chain of outposts along El Camino Real (the King's Road), between the Ventura and San Gabriel missions. The mission played a significant role in the economic life of Los Angeles, containing granaries, stables and workshops, and supplying the growing community with large quantities of food.

La Reina Theatre ❶

S Charles Lee, architect (1939). 14626 Ventura Blvd, Sherman Oaks.

Designed by eminent LA architect for the Fox West Coast Theatres, the one-story Streamline Moderne building was considered one of the finest theaters in the country. Sadly, it was converted into a mini mall in 1987, and only its facade and a three-sided neon and fluorescent marquee were preserved.

Sherman Oaks Galleria ❷

15301 Ventura Blvd, Sherman Oaks.
☎(818) 382-4100. ☛

Opened in 1980, this legendary mall became the favorite hangout of the suburban teens immortalized in the satirical hit song *Valley Girl*, written by Frank Zappa and his teenage daughter,

Moon Unit. In the 1982 song, Moon Unit imitates her classmates stretching their vowels and their extensive use of the terms "like," "fer sure," "awesome" and "totally." The song popularized local "mallspeak" and phrases such as "Gag me with a spoon," establishing a reputation of shallowness and rampant materialism for the Valley Girl.

The mall culture rapidly spread across the country, and the Valley Girl style launched here (with mini skirts, headbands, anklets and feathered haircuts) set an international trend.

The Galleria was featured prominently in a number of movies including *Valley Girl* (1983) and *Weird Science* (1985), but its top billing in *Fast Times at Ridgemont High* (1982), most of which was filmed here, propelled it to national fame, making it an icon of teenage mall culture across America.

Fast Times at Ridgemont High **(1982) was filmed at Sherman Oaks Galleria. The movie helped establish stereotypes about suburban culture and the Valley Girl.**

During its history the mission suffered substantial damage from earthquakes, was periodically vandalized and fell into disrepair before it was extensively restored in 1923. The present church is the fourth on the grounds, rebuilt as an exact replica of the earlier structure erected in 1806 and demolished after the devastating Sylmar earthquake in 1971. The most remarkable building on the mission complex is the 1822 *convento*, featuring four-foot adobe walls and a corridor with 21 Roman arches.

La Reina Theatre

Entrance to the Mission Hills Cemetery. Nearby Campo Santo cemetery contains the remains of 2,425 Native Americans who were interred here between 1797 and 1852.

Bob Hope (1904-2004)

The English-born actor came to America at the age of four and tried his hand at vaudeville and Broadway shows, before gaining notoriety as a radio comedian. His popularity brought him to Hollywood, where he was the top office draw of the 1940s and early 1950s. He is best remembered for the series of seven enormously popular "road" films with Bing Crosby and Dorothy Lamour.

Hope, who has four stars on the Hollywood Walk of Fame, won five special Academy Awards for his humanitarian work and contribution to the industry.

The Bob Hope Memorial Garden is attached to the San Fernando Mission Church

Section C, lot 248, grave 2

Mission Hills Cemetery ❹

11160 Stranwood Ave, Mission Hills. Not on map.
☎(818) 361-7387.
🕐daily 8am-5pm.

Ritchie Valens (1941-1959)

Valens was an unknown teenager living in the San Fernando Valley when his first hit single *Come On, Let's Go* tapped the record charts in early 1958. Later that year, his career skyrocketed with his double-sided record *Donna/La Bamba*, which reached No. 2 on the charts. He was on tour with rock stars Buddy Holly and J P "the Big Bopper" Richardson when their plane crashed during a snow storm on February 3, 1959, killing all on board. This tragic event was described by Don McLean as "the day the music died" in his hit *American Pie* (1972).

The story of Valens's short life was told in the biopic film *La Bamba* (1987), and the title song, played by Los Lobos, became a hit again.

Eden Memorial Park ❺

11500 Sepulveda Blvd, Mission Hills. Not on map.
☎(818) 361-7161.
🕐Sun-Fri 9am-5pm.

Mount Nebo Section

Lenny Bruce (1925-1966)

For some a social satirist, for others just a "sick comic," the controversial comedian gained fame when he appeared naked as an emcee at a burlesque show. Notorious for shocking his audiences with his social commentaries and rough humor, he was often arrested for obscenity and drug possession. He died of an overdose of heroin in his Hollywood home. Bob Fosse's film *Lenny* (1974), starring Dustin Hoffman in the title role, gives an account of Lenny's complex and troubled life.

Groucho Marx (1890-1977)

The most recognizable of the Marx Brothers (➔ p315), Groucho's trademark props included a greasepaint moustache and highlighted eyebrows, glasses, cigar and a crouched walk. He was best known for timeless wisecracks such as "I don't wish to belong to any organization that will accept me as a member." During the 1960s, Groucho developed a successful television career as the host of a comedy-quiz show, *You Bet Your Life*. He received an honorary Oscar in 1973 in recognition of his brilliant creativity.

In an unexplained incident in 1982, Groucho's ashes were stolen from the mausoleum and then mysteriously appeared the same day at the gates of Mount Sinai Memorial Park.

Court of Tribes Mausoleum

Nethercutt Museum/ San Sylmar ❻

15151/15200 Bledsoe St, Sylmar. Not on map.
☎(818) 364-6464; (818) 367-2251.
www.nethercuttcollection.org
☛two-hour guided tours only, Tue-Sat, 10am and 1:30pm. Reservations required. Children under 12 not permitted. ⑤free.

1930 Rolls-Royce Phantom II once belonged to Constance Bennett

This is one of the world's finest collections of "functional fine art," consisting of custom-bodied vintage cars and antique mechanical musical instruments. The collection was assembled by J B Nethercutt, chairman of the board, chief executive officer and co-founder of Merle Norman Cosmetics. The collection is displayed in the original building, called San Sylmar, and in the new facility, called the Nethercutt Museum, which is across the street and houses about 200 cars.

Among the collection's highlights are examples of the Bugatti, Duesenberg, Hispano-Suiza, Isotta Fraschini, Packard, Pierce-Arrow and Rolls-Royce, including all models of the latter's Phantom series.

The celebrity-owned vehicles in the collection include Rudolph Valentino's 1923 Avions Voisin C5 Sporting Victoria (➔ p59), the 1930 Cord L-29 Town Car that belonged to actress Dolores Del Rio and the 1923 TV McFarlan Model 154 Knickerbocker Cabriolet owned by comedian Roscoe "Fatty" Arbuckle.

Another of the star exhibits is the 1930 Rolls-Royce Phantom II Brewster Town Car. This remarkably engineered car, with a one-of-a-kind-body and unique Art Deco coachwork, is widely regarded as the most beautiful town car ever built. It belonged to film star Constance Bennett and appeared in many Hollywood films, including *The King and the Chorus Girl* (1937). Bennett owned the Phantom for 12 years and earned significant

sums by renting it to movie studios. She had to part from the car when her husband lost it in a poker game.

With its marble floor and columns, mirrored walls and crystal chandeliers, the museum's Grand Salon evokes luxurious car showrooms of the 1920s and 1930s. It displays 30 impeccably restored antique and classic automobiles. Oil is changed regularly, tires inflated, batteries charged. These cars are in perfect driving condition and are even occasionally driven on the freeway. There is a large collection of hood ornaments, many of them in Lalique crystal, and automobile mascots.

Also housed in San Sylmar is one of the world's largest collection of mechanical musical instruments, including musical pocketwatches, music boxes and nickelodeons. The main attractions are the reproducing pianos, enormous electropneumatic "orchestrians" and the mighty Wurlitzer theatre pipe organ.

Vasquez Rocks Park ❼

10700 W Escondido Rd, Agua Dulce. Not on map.
☎(661) 268-0840.
🕐8am to a half hour before sunset ❧ NRHP

These surreal jagged rocks were named after Southern California's most notorious bandit, Tiburcio Vásquez (➔ p24), who used to hide from posses in this rough terrain. He was wounded here in a shootout and captured shortly afterwards in his friend's cabin in what is today West Hollywood.

The picturesque sandstone slabs have appeared in countless television productions, including *The Lone Ranger*, *Bonanza* and the original *Star Trek*. They have been seen in western and science fiction features such as *Star Wars* (1977), *The Legend of the Lone Ranger* (1981), *Star Trek IV* (1986), *The Flintstones* (1994), *Starship Troopers* (1997) and *Wild Wild West* (1999).

The surreal sandstone formations of Vasquez Rocks Park

Van Nuys Airport ⑧

16700 Roscoe Blvd, Van Nuys.
Not on map.
☞available Mon-Fri at 9:30 and
11am. For reservations call
☎(818) 785-8838. ⑤free. ↗

Opened in 1928 as Metropolitan Airport amid walnut and peach groves, the field became a favorite location for private flying, air races and film production. Amelia Earhart set a new world speed record during a race hosted by the airport in 1929. Hollywood celebrities such as Howard Hughes, Wallace Beery, Cecil B DeMille and Gene Autry kept their aircraft here. Today, with 500,000 takeoffs and landings every year, it is the world's busiest general aviation airport.

Marilyn Monroe was discovered here in 1945, when army photographer David Conover came to the airport to take "morale boosting" pictures of women working on the assembly line. In the Radio Plane Munitions Factory, a beautiful redhead named Norma Jean Dougherty caught his eye, and his color shots of her marked the beginning of her modeling career.

A vintage post card shows Clark Gable and Carole Lombard's home

The arrival of Conrad Veidt in *Casablanca* (1942) was filmed at Van Nuys Airport

The airport was a popular location for Hollywood production companies. Among countless movies and TV shows filmed here over time were *Lost Horizon* (1937), *Men With Wings* (1938), *The Flying Deuces* (1939), *Dante's Peak* (1997), *Air Force One* (1997) and *Pearl Harbor* (2001).

But the airport's most famous appearance was in *Casablanca* (1942). Airport hangars seen in the scene of the arrival of Nazi Major Strasser, played by Conrad Veidt, are still standing, but are no longer a part of the airport complex. The hangars can be seen in the adjacent alleys of Waterman Dr and Lindbergh St. Contrary to popular belief, the legendary tearful farewell between Humphrey Bogart and Ingrid Bergman was not filmed here, but on the Warner Bros Studios lot in Burbank.

The Van Nuys Airport Aviation Expo is organized every June, when more than 300,000 spectators view displays of rare World War II and modern military aircraft during free weekend air shows. Highlights include fly-overs by fighter planes, sky diving, sky sailing in a glider with pyrotechnics and aerial demonstrations (➔ p65).

Michael Jackson Home ⑨

4641 Hayvenhurst Ave, Encino Lake.
Private residence.

Hidden behind the gate is the 20-room compound where the King of Pop resided with his family and his private menagerie until 1988, when he moved to the 27,000-acre (10.800-ha) Neverland ranch in Santa Ynez Valley, north of Santa Bar-

bara. Jackson was under criminal investigation in 1993, when the LA Police Department raided the house, looking for evidence in child molestation allegations. Criminal charges against the star were never filed, and he settled a civil case for a sum reported to be between $15 million and $24 million.

Clark Gable Home ⑩

4543 Tara Dr, Encino.
Private residence.

Hollywood's legendary couple Clark Gable and his third wife, Carole Lombard, lived on their 30-acre Encino ranch estate between 1939 and 1942. In order to show their "normal" lifestyle to the public, they used to stage a show for curious reporters, with Gable milking a cow and Lombard collecting eggs in the henhouse.

After Lombard was killed in an airplane accident in 1942, Gable lived in the house with his fourth and fifth wives, Lady Sylvia Ashley and Kay Williams Spreckles, until his death in 1960. His widow sold the ranch in 1973, and the house was bought in 1977 by financier Michael R Milken. The house still stands today and can be glimpsed through the iron gate, partially hidden behind a wall, but the ranch has been subdivided into an expensive tract-housing development called "Clark Gable Estates."

Legendary western star John Wayne's ranch

Former home of actor Samuel L Jackson

John Wayne Home ⑪

4750 Louise Ave, Encino.
Private residence.

A Hollywood legend and a tough, hard-drinking leading man both on- and off-screen, "Duke" lived on this five-acre ranch between 1951 and 1965 with his second wife, Esperanza Bauer, and his third wife, Pilar Palette. After he was diagnosed with lung cancer, the actor moved to Newport Beach.

The star of such memorable movies as *Stagecoach* (1939), *The Searchers* (1956), *The Longest Day* (1962) and *The Man Who Shot Liberty Walance* (1962), Wayne won the best actor Oscar for his performance as a one-eyed marshall in *True Grit* (1969).

Samuel L Jackson Home ⑫

5128 Encino Ave, Encino.
Private residence.

Between 1995 and 2002 this stately Tudor residence was the home of actor Samuel L Jackson and his actress wife LaTanya Richardson. Jackson received an Oscar nomination for his portrayal of Jules Winnfield, the scripture-quoting gunman in *Pulp Fiction* (1994). He had a title role in the remake of *Shaft* (2000) and played Jedi Knight Mace Windu in *Star Wars: Episode I-The Phantom Menace* (1999), *Star Wars: Episode II-Attack of the Clones* (2002) and *Star Wars: Episode III-Revenge of the Sith* (2005). Richardson appeared in such movies as *Malcolm X* (1992) and *Sleepless in Seattle* (1993).

Edgar Rice Burroughs Burial Site ⑬

18354 Ventura Blvd, Tarzana.
Private residence

This is the final resting place of Edgar Rice Burroughs (1875-1950), the best-selling writer and creator of Tarzan. His ashes were buried beside those of his mother under the "big, black walnut tree" in the front yard of his office. Burroughs died in bed, in his home at 5565 Zelzah Ave in Encino (now demolished), reportedly while reading the Sunday comics.

Tarzana ⑭

Today one of numerous communities in the San Fernando Valley, Tarzana was named by famous author and resident Edgar Rice Burroughs after his fictional character. Burroughs already had sold two million copies of his *Tarzan* books when he moved from Chicago to Los Angeles in 1919. He bought the 550-acre (220-ha) ranch called Mil Flores, established by the *Los Angeles Times* publisher Harrison Gray Otis, and renamed it Tarzana. He later applied the name to the subdivision, when he offered lots for sale to the public in 1922.

Fleetwood Center ⑮

Matlin Dvoretzky and Partners, architects (1987).
19611 Ventura Blvd, Woodland Hills.

Another example of Programmatic architecture and a fitting tribute to the city's primary mode of transportation, this stucco office building is designed to resemble the front of a pink 1970 Fleetwood Cadillac.

Author Edgar Rice Burroughs is buried here

Programmatic façade of Fleetwood Center

The Fight, **sculpture by John Ehn (1951-1981)**

Old Trapper's Lodge Sculptures ⑯

Pierce College. Not on map.
6201 Winnetka Ave, Woodland Hills. (entrance on Stadium Way)
☎(818) 347-0551.

This is one of the remarkable California folk art monuments. It was designed over a period of 30 years by John Ehn, a self-taught artist who learned how to make sculptures from a Knott's Berry Farm's sculptor he hired for three days. Ehn recreated "Boot Hill" with such tombstones as "Able Grook. 1831-1871. Used loaded dice on Stella Steel. She used loaded gun on Able."

Based on personal experiences, Mormon mythology and tall tales of the Old West, Ehn's luridly painted concrete statuary was constructed on the site of his Old Trapper Lodge motel in Sun Valley. When it was threatened with demolition to make way for the expansion of Burbank Airport in the late 1980s, preservationists moved some of the sculptures to the Pierce College campus, an appropriate setting with its livestock and horticultural fields.

Los Angeles Pet Memorial Park ⑰

5068 N Old Scandia Lane, Calabasas. Not on map.
☎(818) 591-7037.
⏲daily 8:30am-4:30pm.

The first pet cemetery in Los Angeles, the park has served since 1928 as the final resting place for more than 40,000 dearly departed best friends. Besides the usual dogs and cats, there are interred horses, rabbits, birds, monkeys and even one African lion.

Some of the permanent residents reached notoriety through their celebrity owners or had successful Hollywood careers themselves. Buried in this pet cemetery are Petey, the speckled canine star of the *Our Gang* comedies; Spot, the dog from *The Little Rascals*; one of the Lassies; Hopalong Cassidy's horse Topper; Tonto's steed Scout from *The Lone Ranger*;

Marker in Los Angeles Pet Memorial Park

Rudolph Valentino's black doberman Kabar; Humphrey Bogart's cocker spaniel Droopy; Charlie Chaplin's cat Boots and Mae West's monkey (name unknown).

The ten-acre interment park was described as "the Happier Hunting Ground" in Evelyn Waugh's satirical novel *The Loved One*. Some of the owners spare no expense in order to preserve memories of their beloved pets. They erect eccentric monuments or have marble markers embossed with animal likeness, sentimental epitaphs, even Christian crosses or Stars of David.

Oakwood Memorial Park ⑱

22601 Lassen St, Chatsworth. Not on map.
☎(818) 341-0344.
⏲daily 8:30am-5pm.

Ginger Rogers (1911-1995)

Although she appeared in nearly one hundred films and won the best actress Oscar for her dramatic performance in *Kitty Foyle* (1940), Rogers is still best known as Fred Astaire's dancing partner in a string of wildly popular musicals in the 1930s. After she was paired with Astaire in *Flying Down to Rio* (1933), the couple made ten films together, including *Top Hat* (1935), their quintessential musical.

Fred Astaire (1899-1987)

Hollywood legend has it that the report of Astaire's first screen test read: "Can't act. Can't sing. Balding. Can dance a little." Proving the studio wrong, an elegant and perfectionist professional who choreographed most of his numbers, Astaire became the greatest dancer in the history of cinema. After his dancing partnership with Ginger Rogers split up, he continued to dominate Hollywood musicals with such stars as Rita Hayworth, Cyd Charisse, Eleanor Powell and Judy Garland.

Section E, lot 303, space 1

Section G, lot 82, space 4

Beach Cities

Although to most tourists Los Angeles is now synonymous with its long, sandy beaches, the coastal area was long used as ranch land and was "discovered" by visitors relatively late. During the 1860s, Angelenos wishing to escape the stifling summer heat of the city began camping in canvas tents in Santa Monica Canyon. These first tourists had to endure a half-day ride from downtown by horse-drawn wagons or stagecoach to enjoy the surf

Beach umbrella

and cool ocean breezes. The first auction of lots in what is today Santa Monica took place in 1875. The auctioneer announcing the sale solemnly proclaimed: "The title to the land will be guaranteed by the owner. The title to the ocean and the sunset, the hills and the clouds, the breath of life-giving ozone and the song of the birds is guaranteed by the beneficent God who bestowed them in all their beauty."

At the turn of the 20th century, beach fashion meant long, bulky bathing suits that covered almost the bather's entire body, as seen in this photograph taken in Long Beach ca. 1900

Called by newspapers a "terrestrial paradise where life was pleasant, languid and carefree," Santa Monica drew thousands of wealthy newcomers from the East and Midwest. The elaborate second homes they built were soon followed by grand hotels, along with resort facilities such as North Beach Bathhouse. Built in 1894, it was for years the city's largest and most popular bathing facility, containing a huge plunge, about a hundred porcelain-lined tubs for

hot salt and freshwater baths and modern amenities such as a ballroom, roof garden and bowling pavilion with eight alleys.

In the Ocean Park Bath House (below left), spectators on side bleachers used to view the bathers enjoying the plunge filled with saltwater heated to 80 degrees F (27 degrees C).

Throughout the nation Santa Monica was considered the quintessential "California beach resort." Drawn by its allure and excitement, the

beach was overrun by thousands of locals and visitors alike.

In its ceaseless effort to promote Los Angeles across the country, the Chamber of Commerce organized promotional events, published fliers and advertised the beauties of the city and benefits of its Mediterranean climate. Photographs like the one below right were used in the early 1920s, a period of intense migration to Southern California, to entice East Coast businesses to come West.

The Ocean Park Bath House as it appeared on a vintage postcard, ca. 1909

Business on the beach in the early 1920s, a photo by Los Angeles Chamber of Commerce

Ocean Park California Pageant 1926. Miss Los Angeles is entrant number 21 from the left.

One of the most popular events in beach cities were bathing beauty contests, which began as newspaper promotional stunts in the early 1910s. They always attracted large crowds and, in the early days, winners were chosen by the amount of noise coming from the cheering audience. Among the hundreds of competing young women were aspiring silent screen actresses or starlets hoping for publicity for their films.

Jane Fonda and Michael Sarrazin in the marathon dance sequence of *They Shoot Horses, Don't They?* (1969)

During the 1920s, dance marathons emerged as another popular attraction. Some of contestants competing for prize money danced continually for 260 hours. Marathon dancing was banned in Los Angeles in 1928, when the city decided that the endurance contests posed a health risk to the participants.

The most spectacular of the dance palaces that housed marathons, the La Monica Ballroom on Santa Monica Pier, was billed as the largest in the world. Opened every night of the year, its dance floor could accommodate 5,000 dancers, with an additional 5,000 spectators.

In Sidney Pollack's film *They Shoot Horses, Don't They?* (1969), Jane Fonda and Michael Sarrazin portray two desperate contestants competing for the big jackpot. In his adaptation of Horace McCoy's book, Pollack depicts the degraded world of marathon dancers in their grueling struggle for survival.

The first film crew that came to the coastal area was Chicago's Selig Polyscope Company. In 1907 they shot scenes on the beach for *The Count of Monte Christo*. Others quickly followed, including Vitagraph, Kalem and Essanay, who built studios in Santa Monica. In 1913 director/producer Thomas Ince established a studio in Santa Ynez Canyon, at the foot of what is today Sunset Blvd and PCH. Known as Inceville, this was the location of many silent films starring William S Hart, Dustin Farnum and Douglas Fairbanks. D W Griffith's masterpiece, *The Birth of a Nation* (1915), was largely made here. Inceville was destroyed by fire in the early 1920s.

Inceville was founded by producer/director Thomas Ince in 1919

Pageants like this one were common throughout Southern California in the early 20th century.

The beaches of Santa Monica and Venice were also frequently used as locations for Mack Sennett's famous *Bathing Beauties* comedies.

World-famous Muscle Beach, just south of Santa Monica Pier, was the place where America's physical fitness movement was born. From 1954 until 1958, when it moved to Venice (→ p390), this small beachfront spot was a favorite place for gymnasts and bodybuilders to practice and show their muscles to the appreciative public. At Sunday afternoons a large crowd might gather to admire exhibitions of strength and skill. Among the colorful characters who worked out here were bodybuilders and health-fad entrepreneurs Joe Gold, Vic Tanny, Jack LaLanne and actor Steve "Hercules" Reeves.

Bodybuilder Steve Reeves playing the title role in *Hercules Unchained* (1960)

Between the late 1950s and mid 1960s, a number of bodybuilders from Muscle Beach appeared in Italian or Spanish productions of Greco-Roman epics. Actors such as Mickey Hargitay and Gordon Mitchell achieved enormous popularity as action figures in hundreds of these low-cost costume spectaculars. Steve Reeves, who won the title of Mr America in 1947, Mr World in 1948 and Mr Universe in 1950, became a major international star overnight playing a legendary Greek hero in such films as *Hercules* (1959) and *Hercules Unchained* (1960). He was considered at the time to be the most famous derring-do performer of the world cinema since Errol Flynn.

A photograph taken during the filming of *Bathing Beauties*

Weekend exhibition of strength at Muscle Beach in 1942

Panoramic shot of crowd jamming Ocean Park in 1926, with Lick Pier in the background.

Visitors stroll or sit along Ocean Front Walk, watching bathers lucky enough to find their place under the sun (or beach umbrella) in this beach scene at Ocean Park in 1926. Located just south of Santa Monica, Ocean Park was founded in 1892 as a prime seaside resort. It became a great attraction at the turn of the 20th century, featuring a pleasure pier, an auditorium, a racetrack and a beachfront promenade of small hotels, cafés, casinos, curio shops and game parlors.

With its scenic railroad, fun house and two carousels, Ocean Park Pier was a huge draw for funseekers. Its popular Bon Ton Ballroom inspired Horace McCoy in his *noir* novel *They Shoot Horses, Don't They?* (1935).

Abbot Kinney (1850-1920)

When thirty-year-old Abbot Kinney settled in Los Angeles in 1880, he already was the wealthy heir to a family fortune derived from the manufacturing of Sweet Caporal cigarettes. Widely traveled and well educated, he possessed a rare combination of courage and vision. One of the founders of Ocean Park resort, he dreamed of an even more ambitious project: the creation of a new development in the marshlands south of Ocean Park, to be called Venice of America. "To see Venice Is To Live," Kinney advertised.

Kinney acquired the land for his Venice by chance, winning a coin flip when he broke away from his partners. He drained the marshlands and built a network of cemented canals, spanned by high-arching foot bridges. Singing Italian gondoliers navigated seven canal waterways in imported Venetian gondolas.

The arcaded buildings along Windward Ave in 1906

Modeled after Venice, Italy, Kinney's dream city opened on July 4, 1905 to a crowd of 40,000 people. Its flamboyant, faux Venetian architecture featured colonnaded façades, ornate arcades, porticos and balustrades. Especially extravagant was Windward Ave, lined with elegant, three-story hotels such as St Marks, a one time favorite of silent movie stars.

Resembling an Arabian palace, elaborate Ocean Park Bath House became a major beach attraction at its opening in 1905

With their numerous attractions, ocean pleasure piers were extremely popular beach amusements.

However, the canals were hastily constructed and made too shallow, making natural water circulation difficult. After state health officials declared the canal system a menace to public health, the original lagoon and most of the canals were filled in and paved over in the late 1920s.

Kinney envisioned Venice as a cultural center with world renowned performers such as Sarah Bernhardt and the Chicago Symphony. After residents failed to support his idea, Kinney was forced to replace high culture with entertainment for less exalted tastes. He added side shows, fun zones, a miniature railway, camel rides, cotton candy and carnival-type concessions that turned Venice into an amusement park,

The Venice Pier midway as it looked in 1925

similar to New York's Coney Island. The Venice Pier was the major attraction, featuring the first racing roller coaster built on the West Coast—Race Thru the Clouds—which attracted 25,000 spec-

tators on opening day in 1911. Another draw was a hot nightspot, the Ship Café, a replica of Spanish explorer Juan Cabrillo's galleon.

Other attractions included the mammoth Bath House, which could accommodate 2,000 bathers in its heated saltwater plunge, the largest on the West Coast, and the Venice Ballroom, a favorite dancing spot where sidemen Benny Goodman and Glenn Miller launched their careers.

The silent screen comic Buster Keaton sits on the hot-water fountain in the Venice Plunge in *The Cameraman* (1928)

In the comedy *The Cameraman* (1928), Buster Keaton plays a tintype photographer turned inept newsreel cameraman who cannot do anything right. His stupidity gets him into all sorts of troubles, including loosing his oversized bathing suit while swimming in pool surrounded with girls.

Venice of America: view of Grand Lagoon and Midway Plaisance

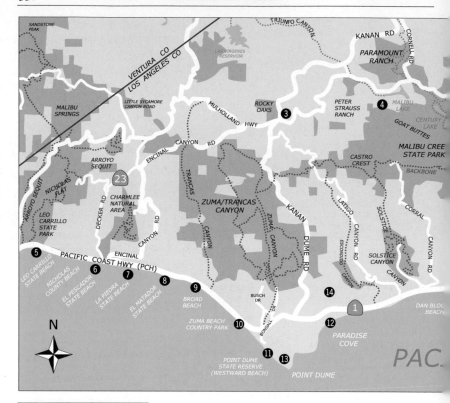

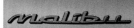

The Chevrolet Malibu was introduced in 1964 as the Chevelle Malibu SS 327 and since has gone through numerous iterations

Malibu

. . . "For these and other reasons Malibu tends to astonish and disappoint those who have never before seen it, and its very name remains, in the imagination of people all over the world, a kind of shorthand for the easy life. I had not before 1971 and will probably not again live in a place with a Chevrolet named after it."

— Joan Didion,
Quiet Days in Malibu

Malibu derives its name from the Chumash Indian word *Humaliwu* (place where surf crushes loudly). Part of a Spanish land grant,

Rancho Malibu was acquired by Frederick H Rindge in 1887, when he and his young bride arrived from the East Coast. After her husband's death in 1905, May Rindge spent a fortune defending holdings that comprised 25 miles (40 km) of coast, considered the finest real estate in the nation. She built fences and hired armed horsemen to warn tres-

passers—to no avail. The "Queen of Malibu," as May Rindge was called by newspapers, fought and lost the grandest and longest battle in California history to hold a large real estate empire intact. The Supreme Court decision that gave the state right-of-way was announced in 1925 and three years later the present Pacific Coast Highway (PCH) was opened to traffic.

A lone car struggling on a narrow beach road north of Santa Monica ca. 1910 anticipates the future congestion on PCH

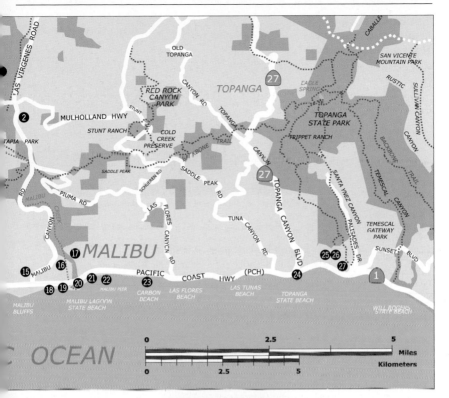

To pay her mounting legal expenses, May Rindge was forced to lease part of Malibu Beach in the spring of 1926, and then to sell lots in the 1930s. Among the first who rushed to lease beach frontage and built homes were film luminaries Jack Warner, Clara Bow, Barbara Stanwyck and Dolores Del Rio. Many others followed. This was the beginning of the Malibu Movie Colony, a world-famous hideaway for stars and executives of the motion picture industry.

Since the late 1920s, when the first members of the motion picture industry flocked to its beaches, Malibu has remained a world-famous playground of the movie stars. Stretching some 20 miles (32 km) from Topanga Canyon to the Ventura County line, this beach community has the highest concentration of entertainment industry celebrities anywhere. However, the multi-million dollar

Malibu Movie Colony ca. 1940. A vintage post card depicts aerial view of the beachfront homes belonging to many of Hollywood's celebrities.

shorefront homes are not the most fashionable property in the enclave today. They were recently replaced by huge compounds in the canyons above Malibu. Despite the constant danger of summer

wildfires, winter storms, floods and mudslides, Malibu is so desirable that it encompasses some of the priciest real estate in the world.

Among those who owned multi-million dollar homes in Malibu at one time or another are Pamela Anderson and Tommy Lee, Jon Bon Jovi, Pierce Brosnan, Nicolas Cage, Jim Carrey, Johnny Carson, Cher, Cindy Crawford, Jackie Collins, Leonardo DiCaprio, Bob Dylan, Richard Gere, Mel Gibson, Whoopi Goldberg, Tom Hanks and Rita Wilson, Anthony Hopkins, Michael Jackson, Madonna, Olivia Newton-John, Robert Redford, Sting, Steven Spielberg and Kate Capshaw.

Beachfront enclaves are often walled-off from the outside world. Some of the multi-million dollar shorefront homes are hidden from the casual observer's view by tall walls or disguised by shabby backsides looking at Pacific Coast Highway.

Santa Monica Mountains National Recreation Area ❶

Visitor Center: 30401 Agoura Rd, Suite 100, Agoura Hills.
☎(805) 370-2301.
www.nps.gov/samo.
🕐daily, 9am-5pm. Closed Thanksgiving, Christmas, New Year's Day. Office publishes maps, books, guides, and *Outdoors*, a quarterly calendar of events.
⑤general access to the area is free, although various parks and beaches may require permits or charge fees.

Whipple's yucca, laurel sumac and other plants along the trails

Comprising some 150,000 acres (60.000 ha) of hills and seashore, the Santa Monica Mountains protected zone spans 55 miles (88 km), from Griffith Park in LA County to Point Mugu in Ventura County. Large parts of the area, consisting of mountains, plains and canyons are undeveloped and crisscrossed with miles of trails and hiking paths.

The Mountains boast a variety of plant life, with more than 800 species of wildflowers, shrubs and trees in environments such as grassy hillsides, oak woodlands, riparian or chaparral. They provide habitat for hundreds of animal species, some of them endangered, including mountain lions, deers, coyotes and golden eagles. Visitors can enjoy various recreational activities including hiking, horseback riding, mountain biking, bird watching, picknicking and camping, or can take part in interpretive and

ranger-led programs and festivals. Mostly undiscovered by tourists, the area is well worth exploring in all seasons. Repeat visits are recommended to fully enjoy its vast and diverse resources.

Mulholland Highway
from the Hollywood Fwy to Leo Carrillo State Beach (just east of the Ventura County line).

Winding 50 miles (80 km) along the crest of the Santa Monica Mountains, Mulholland Highway offers some of the finest vistas of the city and the ocean. It was built in the 1920s to promote the sale and development of huge tracts of land and named after the engineer who brought water from the Owens Valley (➔ p34). A 7-mile-long portion westward from 405 Fwy is unpaved and closed to vehicles, while the most scenic is the section between Las Virgenes and Kanan Dume roads.

Charmlee Nature Preserve
2577 Encinal Canyon.
☎(310) 457-7247. ⑤free.
🕐Nature Study Center Sun 1-5pm.
Activities: docent-led fool-moon hikes; picnicking; hiking; summer camps for children.

Charmlee preserve is noted for its displays of spring wildflowers. Some endangered native plants can be seen here, including the Santa Susana tar plant and the Catalina Mariposa lily. Here also can be found a full range of mammals and over 240 bird species, including rare and endangered black-shouldered kites and golden eagles. There are ranger-led full moon hikes beginning at 7pm every month. A small nature study center has displays of natural history artifacts, as well as static and live animal exhibits.

Paramount Ranch
2813 Cornell Rd.
☎(805) 370-2301. ⑤free.
Activities: picnicking; hiking; equestrian trails; rangers lead history walks at 9:30am on first and third Sat of every month.

Since 1927, Paramount Pictures filmed on this "movie ranch" its early westerns and epics such as *The Adventures of Marco Polo* (1938). Visitors can walk through the old Western Town set, built in the 1950s, which was used in numerous films and television series, including *The Virginian*; *The Cisco Kid*; *Have Gun, Will Travel* and *Dr. Quinn, Medicine Woman*.

View of the mountains and the ocean from Mulholland Highway

Malibu Creek State Park
1925 Las Virgenes Rd.
☎(818) 880-0367.
🕐Visitors Center open weekends noon-4pm. ⑤free. Parking fee.
Activities: camping; fishing; hiking; mountain biking; equestrian trails; naturalist walks.

The 5,000-acre park offers excellent hiking on its 15 miles of trails. Fishing for trout, catfish and bass is popular on Century Lake. Naturalist walks and group programs are regularly scheduled. Call for reservations.

Hiking trails meander around sandstone rocks in Castro Crest

Castro Crest
end of Corral Canyon Rd.
☎(805) 370-2301. ⑤free.
Activities: hiking; equestrian trails; mountain biking.

Reddish sandstone rocks distinguish the Castro Crest area. Its 800 acres (320 ha) include excellent hiking trails with stunning views. Especially interesting are night hikes on the ridge. Call (818) 880-0350 for information.

Topanga State Park
20825 Entrada Rd.
☎(310) 455-2465.
⑤ free; parking fee.
🕐Nature Center open Sun noon-4pm, Jan-Jun.
Activities: camping; hiking; mountain biking; equestrian trails; naturalist walks; docent-led walks.

Featuring 10,000 acres of meadows, chaparral, streams and woodlands, this large park offers 35 miles (56 km) of hiking and riding trails, including a self-guided nature trail. Trails begin from the old Trippet Ranch (enter from Entrada Rd). Visitors can explore the park's earthquake faults, marine fossils and sedimentary formations, while its peaks offer splendid vistas of the ocean and San Fernando Valley. Docent led Sunday hikes depart at 1pm from the Nature Center.

20th Century-Fox Ranch
(formerly)
20th Century-Fox owned part of the Malibu Creek State Park called the Century Ranch until 1974 and used it as the location for many of its film and television productions. *Viva Zapata!* (1952), *Love Me Tender* (1959), the original *Planet of the Apes* (1968), as well as *M*A*S*H* (1970) and its enduring television version were all filmed here. The *M*A*S*H* sets have been moved to the Smithsonian, but the Goat Buttes that appear in the opening credits can still be seen here.

The 19th-century Welsh coal mining village, as seen in John Ford's *How Green Was My Valley* (1941), was created at the Fox movie ranch by the art director Nathan Juran, for which he won an Academy Award.

Paul Newman and Robert Redford escaped a posse jumping off the cliff in Century Lake in *Butch Cassidy and the Sundance Kid* (1969). The lake was also used as a backdrop in *Cleopatra* (1963), with myri-

A 19th-century Welsh coal mining village was built at the Fox Ranch for *How Green Was My Valley* (1941)

ad model boats engaged in the decisive sea battle. *Tora! Tora! Tora!* (1970) and *The Poseidon Adventure* (1972) were also filmed here.

Topanga Canyon
The Chumash Indians, who lived here some 8,000 years ago, gave Topanga its name, which means "Mountains that Run Into the Sea." There are scores of Chumash sites throughout the canyon, along with a few simple, faded rock paintings. Topanga's current residents are predominantly creative types, who maintain an alternative, eccentric lifestyle, influenced by New Age philosophy. The area retains a hippie aura which arose during the 1960s, when Neil Young, the Byrds and other rockers lived and played here. Nearby Red Rock Rd was the home of such rock bands as Buffalo Springfield, Taj Mahal and Cream.

Malibu Creek State Park

Leo Carrillo State Beach

Sri Venkateswara-swamy Temple ❷

S M Ganapathi (1982-88).
1600 Las Virgenes Canyon Rd,
Calabasas.
☎(818) 880-5552. ☞
🕐weekdays 9am-noon; 5-7pm;
weekends and holidays: 8am-7pm.

This is the biggest Hindu temple on the West Coast, a sanctuary to more than 120,000 devoted Hindus who came here to worship annually. It was built in the Chola style of architecture in the southern India tradition by craftsmen brought from India. The temple was originally dedicated to the god Vishnu, but a Shiva temple was later added. The temple's ornate, stepped towers are covered with friezes of dancing female figures, elephants, lions, lotus flowers and countless other images. It was the setting for scenes in *Beverly Hills Ninja* (1997).

Sri Venkateswaraswamy Temple

Tommy Lee, Pamela Anderson Home ❸

31341 Mulholland Hwy, Malibu.
Private residence. 🖐 ☞

Partially hidden behind lush exotic landscaping, this Moorish-style house was featured in an episode of MTV's show *Cribs*. It was the home of the former Mötley Crüe drummer Tommy Lee and his wife, former *Baywatch* star Pamela Anderson. The house made news in 2001 when a child accidentally drowned in the pool during a birthday party. Lee sold the estate in 2003 for $3 million.

Charlie Sheen's bachelor pad

Charlie Sheen Home ❹

1845 Olivera Dr, Agoura Hills.
Private residence.

Described as "the ultimate bachelor pad," this 6,000-square-foot house overlooking Malibu Lake was the scene of actor Charlie Sheen's wild parties. The star of the ABC sitcom *Spin City* and such movies as *Platoon* (1986), *Wall Street* (1987) and

The Three Musketeers (1993), Sheen spent 10 years remodeling the home. Its most unusual feature is a firehouse pole that connects a closet in the master suite with the front entrance for a quick escape in case of fire. After he married actress Denise Richards in June 2002, Sheen sold the 2.5-acre compound for reported $3.6 million.

Leo Carrillo State Beach ❺

36000 block of PCH.
☎(805) 488-5223.

Named after the actor who played Pancho in the famous television series *The Cisco Kid*, this spectacular mile-long beach is popular with surfers and divers. A small bluff, called Sequit Point, divides the beach into a western section, popular with sunbathers and fishermen, and an eastern part, used by surfers. The beach features a natural tunnel, sea caves and secret coves, and is ideal for exploring at low tide. Join a ranger or examine on your own the animal and plant life of the kelp forest, tidepools and coastal bluffs.

Call ranger for reservations:
☎(805) 986-8591.

El Matador, La Piedra and El Pescador State Beaches ❻❼❽

32900, 32700 and 32350 PCH.

These three separate and picturesque beaches are all part of Robert H Meyer State Beach. They are widely regarded as the most beautiful and romantic in LA County. With their coves and huge, unusual rocks and arches, these secluded hideaways are quite rewarding for those willing to drive all the way from Los Angeles. These beaches can be easily missed, however, as they are marked only by small signs on the highway. To get to the beaches, you have to use a steep trail or stairway.

Ali MacGraw Home

Dustin Hoffman Home

Frank Sinatra Home

Broad Beach ❶

Access: stairways at 31346 and 31200 block of PCH.

Considered by many the best beach in Southern California, this fashionable mile-and-a-half stretch of sand has probably a higher concentration of celebrities than any other place in the world. Among the stars who owned the beachfront houses here at one time or another are Steven Spielberg, Goldie Hawn, Pierce Brosnan, Jon Bon Jovi, Robert Redford and Eddie Van Halen. Before their deaths, Carroll O'Connor, Jack Lemmon and Walter Matthau also called this beach home.

Ali MacGraw Home
31108 Broad Beach Rd.
Private residence.

This tranquil beach home is owned by Ali MacGraw, the star of the phenomenally popular cult movies of the seventies, *Love Story* (1970) and *The Getaway* (1972). Married twice—to producer Robert Evans and actor Steve McQueen—MacGraw was

chosen by *People* magazine as one of the 50 most beautiful people in the world.

Dustin Hoffman Home
31054 Broad Beach Rd.
Private residence.

The legendary actor Dustin Hoffman, who starred in *Midnight Cowboy* (1969), *Papillion* (1973) and *Tootsie* (1982), owns this contemporary, two-story beach house. He won the best actor Oscar twice—for *Kramer vs Kramer* (1979) and *Rain Man* (1988).

Danny DeVito Home

Danny DeVito Home
31020 Broad Beach Rd.
Private residence.

The actor and director Danny DeVito, who starred in *Throw Momma From the*

Train (1987), *Batman Returns* (1992), *Get Shorty* (1995) and *L.A. Confidential* (1997), is the owner of this beachfront house.

Frank Sinatra Home
30966 Broad Beach Rd.
Private residence.

This five-bedroom residence is the former beach home of the legendary balladeer and actor who was named entertainer of the century in 2000. Sinatra starred in such films as *Tony Rome* (1967), *The Manchurian Candidate* (1962) and *From Here to Eternity* (1953), for which he won an Oscar for best supporting actor. He had a number of No. 1 albums but only two No. 1 singles, *Strangers in the Night* and *Somethin' Stupid*, the latter with his daughter, Nancy.

Sylvester Stallone Home

Sylvester Stallone Home
30900 Broad Beach Rd.
Private residence.

One of the highest-paid Hollywood actors purchased this 16-room beach home in 1995. Sly's big break came with *Rocky* (1976), a huge hit followed by equally popular sequels. The success continued with his action-hero roles in *First Blood* (1982) and its two sequels, and *Cliffhanger* (1993).

El Matador State Beach

Zuma Beach ↗

Street sign pointing to world-famous Zuma Beach

Zuma Beach County Park ⑩

30000 block of PCH.
☎(310) 457-9891. ⚑

With over 100 acres (40 ha) of white sand, Zuma is the largest beach in the Malibu area. This two-mile long, breezy sand strand is great for socializing and all sorts of beach fun. It is popular with families and teenagers alike and can be jam-packed on summer weekends. Large waves make it especially attractive for surfing, though rip tides could be dangerous.

Zuma was a location for cult movies of the 1950s and the early 60s, including *Beach Blanket Bingo* (1965) and its sequel, *Back to the Beach* (1987). It was featured on the cover of Neil Young's album *Zuma*, which added to the beach's fame after it was released in 1975.

Westward Beach and Point Dume State Beach ⑪

End of Westward Beach Rd.
☎(310) 457-9891. ⚑

Immediately to the south of Zuma Beach is the half-mile, sandy Westward Beach, which was the location of Madonna's *Cherish* music video.

Point Dume, the 200-foot-high (60-m) lava bluff, provides stunning views of the entire Santa Monica Bay. It is a rewarding challenge to rock climbers and an excellent spot for dolphin and whale watching, especially popular during the midwinter migrating season of gray whales, (→ p61).

To reach an (unofficial) nude beach, follow the trail from Westward Beach which leads to the top of the bluff, then go down the stairway to small and secluded Pirate's Cove.

Paradise Cove ⑫

28128 PCH.
☎(310) 457-2511. ⚑

If you are ready to pay high parking charges, you can enjoy this small, secluded (but open to the public) beach. For those who like fishing, this is the place to cast their lines.

Paradise Cove has been a set for beach movies such as *Gidget* (1959), *Beach Blanket Bingo* (1965), *Beach Party* (1963), *Muscle Beach Party* (1964) and *Back to the Beach* (1987). Woody Harrelson proposed to Demi Moore on the pier on Paradise Cove Rd in *Indecent Proposal* (1993).

The private investigator played by James Garner parked his trailer at the edge of Sand Castle Restaurant's parking lot in the television series *The Rockford Files* (1974-80).

Pristine Paradise Cove is an ideal spot for tidepool exploration. Wake up at dawn, though, for low tide comes early during the summer and it is the only time of the day to observe the underwater life forms (→ p60).

Paradise Cove is seen on the cover of the Beach Boys' debut album, *Surfin' Safari*, which was released in the United States on October 1, 1962

Point Dume ⑬

Some of the most famous and expensive Malibu homes are situated in this area, where palatial residences are hidden behind tall gates and protected by tight security.

Perched on the edge of the bluff is Johnny Carson's spectacular home, purchased for $8.9 million in 1985. Next to it is the former Unger Estate, where Sean Penn married Madonna in 1985. A well-publicized incident took place here, when Penn ran down to the beach irritated by paparazzi who had laid siege to the compound. A furious groom inscribed FUCK OFF in large letters on the sand and fired shots at helicopters flying over. Another neighbor is Barbra Streisand, whose compound comprises three homes. She sued an environmental activist who posted an aerial photograph of her clifftop mansion on the Internet, claiming invasion of privacy. Her suit was dismissed as frivolous.

Other famous residents who lived or still live nearby are Bob Dylan, Michael Jackson, Cher, Martin Sheen, and David Duchovny and Tea Leoni.

Point Dume State Beach

On July 16, 1996, Malibu made headlines as the site of a bizarre incident: after walking into a bedroom, a man tidily folded his clothes over a chair and went to bed. Unfortunately, he was in the wrong house—the place he actually leased was 17 houses away. After panicked residents found a stranger asleep in their child's bed, they called the police, who arrested him for trespassing. The intruder turned out to be actor Robert Downey, Jr, who had stumbled into a neighbor's house under the influence of drugs and passed out in a bed. He later claimed that his limo driver dropped him off at the wrong address.

Ramirez Canyon Park ⑭

5750 Ramirez Canyon Rd.
☎(310) 589-2850.
☛Wed 1pm. Two-hour, guided walking tours (by reservation only). The compound could be rented for weddings, photo shoots and movies. ⑤

Formerly known as the Streisand Center for Conservancy Studies, this 22-acre complex comprising five houses, gardens and sports facilities was once the private playground of actress, singer and movie producer Barbra Streisand. When she could not find a buyer for the astronomical sum she requested, Streisand donated the rustic estate in 1993 to the Santa Monica Mountains Conservancy and took a $15-million tax write-off. The guided tour of the property, which includes houses and extensive gardens, concludes with an informal tea served on the patio.

Famous for her eccentricity, Barbra replanted redwoods and other non-native species and even had the stream, which ran through the middle of the property, moved 100 yards so she could enjoy a bigger lawn. It was here that she hosted huge fundraisers for several hundred guests. Streisand erected

Hodges Castle dominates the hill

bizarre buildings, including the Barwood, a Craftsman bungalow transformed into a semi-treehouse that once was the base of her production company, and the strangely shaped Barn, which was the entertainer's actual residence. The most remarkable is the Art Deco house, with its red and-black color scheme and interior decorated with geometric motifs. Streisand never lived here—it was built solely to house her Art Deco collection.

Pepperdine University ⑮

24255 Pacific Coast Hwy.
☎(310) 456-4000.

Dubbed "Surfers U" for its proximity to the beaches, Pepperdine University was founded in 1937 by George Pepperdine, a rich car supplies salesman. Rising above sloping lawns on a hill overlooking the ocean, the beautiful residential campus was designed by architect William Pereira in 1973.

Hodges Castle ⑯

23800 Malibu Crest Dr.
Private residence. ⚑

Sitting on a hilltop overlooking the Pacific coast (and guarding the canyons from the imaginary enemy), this replica of a 13th-century Scottish castle features real towers and battlements. Built in 1979 by dentist Dr Thomas Hodges, it was used as the location for a number of film and television productions.

Serra Retreat ⑰

3401 Serra Rd.
☎(310) 456-6631.
🕘9am-4:30pm, daily. ⑤free

Named after the founder of the California missions, father Junípero Serra, this Franciscan spiritual retreat has provided a serene getaway in the Malibu hills since 1943. With its stillness, flowering gardens and quiet natural beauty, it offers a perfect setting to people of all faiths to spend some time away from the distractions of everyday life.

Red-and-black interior of Barbra Streisand's Art Deco home

Malibu Colony is a world-famous entertainment industry enclave

Malibu Colony ⑱

Along Malibu Colony Dr (junction of PCH and Webb Way). 🏴

Silent film luminaries were the first residents in the early days of the "Malibu Motion Picture Colony." Since 1926, when the first beachfront homes were built here, it has been an internationally famous celebrity playground. Now known just as "The Colony," it is still a snobbish and private community of the rich and famous.

Extending for over a mile along the coast, the ultra-exclusive and heavily guarded enclave has been home over the years to Gloria Swanson, Lana Turner, James Stewart, Michael Landon, Barbra Streisand, Tom Hanks, Goldie Hawn, Linda Ronstadt, John McEnroe, Paul Newman and Joanne Wood-ward, Burt Reynolds, Sting, Ted Danson and many other celebrities. (Leonardo DiCaprio lives just outside the Colony gates.) In recent years the Colony lost many of its star residents to the more fashionable Carbon and Broad beaches.

The owners of this extravagant row of beachfront homes fiercely guard their privacy by barrier reefs, gates and armed security. Guarded entrance to Malibu Colony Dr is as far as you can get without an invitation. Although there is no direct walkway, the beach is public and accessible by boat or foot (nearest public access is a stairway at the 24300 block of Malibu Rd and walkways at 19900, 20300, 22700 and 25100).

The colony appears in Robert Altman's adaptation of Raymond Chandler's novel *The Long Goodbye* (1973).

Elliott Gould, portraying private detective Philip Marlowe, tries to protect a friend suspected of murder, only to find himself framed.

Stevens House

John Lautner, architect (1968). 23524 Malibu Colony Rd. Private residence.

Ingeniously solving the problems imposed by an impossibly narrow lot, Lautner used two opposite half-catenary curved shells, one behind the other, which open up to the sea at the front and mountain at the back. The catenary curve was chosen for structural reasons, as well as for its resemblance to an ocean wave. Concrete was the best answer to the concerns about the effects of salt air in the beach environment. The beachfront home's most remarkable feature is a lap pool, built under the concrete roof and illuminated by diffused light coming through translucent glass leaves.

The John Lautner-designed Stevens House is a marvel of glass and concrete

Malibu Lagoon ⑲

23200 Pacific Coast Hwy. ☎(310) 456-8432.

This is one of only a few remaining coastal wetlands in Los Angeles area. The estuary and small marsh is the natural fish nursery which supports a variety of animal and plant wildlife. It is also a home to about 200 species of native and migratory birds.

Malibu Lagoon wetlands area supports a variety of bird life

Adamson House ⑳

Stiles O Clements, architect (1929)
23200 Pacific Coast Hwy.
☎(310) 456-8432.
☞Wed-Sat 11am-3pm (last house tour at 2pm). ⑤free. NRHP

This splendid example of Moorish-Spanish Colonial Revival Style was designed by the famous architect Stiles O Clements. The 10-room house was built in 1929 as a beach residence for Rhoda Rindge Adamson and her husband, Merritt Huntley Adamson. She was the daughter of Frederick and May Rindge, the last owners of the 17,000-acre (6.800-ha) Rancho Malibu (➜ p94).

Adamson House is renowned for its lavish use of decorative ceramic tiles

Each room in the house is embellished with ceramic tiles of different patterns, produced at the Malibu Potteries Tile Company. The company was owned by the Rindge family and during its short life from 1926 to 1932, it developed a wide range of world-famous glazed tiles. The Spanish-style furniture was designed especially for the house, which also contains magnificent examples of elaborate iron-work. The 13 acres of landscaped grounds, restored to their former beauty, feature well-kept gardens.

Adjacent to the Adamson House is the **Malibu Lagoon Museum**, which provides an account of life in Malibu from before the Spanish conquest to the present. It features exhibits on the Chumash Indians, Rancho Malibu, the history of local surfing and the movie colony.

Adamson House kitchen features tiles of Native American motifs

Malibu Lagoon State Beach and Surfrider Beach ㉑

23200 block of PCH.
☎(818) 880-0350. ☞

The most celebrated of all Southland beaches, this is the place where California surfing was born in 1926. Locals boasted that the surfboard riding here was even better than on Waikiki Beach. This "paradise for surfriders" was popularized by many beach movies filmed here in the 1950s and 1960s, including *Gidget* (1959) and *Beach Blanket Bingo* (1965). These waters are off-limits for beginners and swimmers—this is a beach for serious surfers, offering great, orderly waves year-round, although the best surf is in August and September.

Unfortunately, the lagoon is often unsafe for swimming, especially after rainstorms when urban runoff raises the bacteria counts in water to dangerous levels. The beach frequently gets an "F" rating for pollution from the Heal the Bay organization.

Malibu Pier ㉒

23000 Pacific Coast Hwy. ☞

The original pier was built in 1903 by Frederick Rindge as the sole landing point for supplies for his 17,000-acre Malibu Rancho and for his private, 20-mile-long Rindge Railroad. It suffered severe storm damage several times in its history and went through major restorations in 1944 and 2001. The pier is a popular observation point for watching surfers on the nearby Surfrider Beach.

In the movie *California Suite* (1978), divorced couple Jane Fonda and Alan Alda compare the strong points of Los Angeles and New York in the now defunct Alice's Restaurant, located at the foot of the Malibu Pier.

Surfers crowd the breakers at Surfrider Beach near Malibu Pier

Bruce Willis and Demi Moore Home

David Geffen Home

Carbon Beach ㉓

Today Malibu's prime real estate, Carbon Beach is frequently referred to as "Deal Beach" for the number of entertainment industry executives who own homes on this deep, long and secluded strip of sand. They do not actually live on the beach—they only spend their weekends or a few weeks in summer here.

Among Carbon's famous residents are co-founders of DreamWorks SKG studio Jeffrey Katzenberg and David Geffen; producers Aaron Spelling and Jerry Bruckheimer; Terry Semmel, former co-chief executive of Warner Bros and chairman of Yahoo!; Richard Riordan, former Los Angeles mayor, Lou Adler, veteran music producer and billionaires Eli Broad and Haim Saban.

Bruce Willis and Demi Moore Home
22470 Pacific Coast Hwy.
Private residence.

This beach house was purchased in 1987, when Willis's star was on the rise with his Emmy-winning role in the ABC comedy series *Moonlighting*. The leading man in such hits as *Pulp Fiction* (1994), *The Fifth Element* (1997) and *The Sixth Sense*

(1999) sold the property in 2000, after his divorce from actress Demi Moore.

Ackerburg Residence
Richard Meier, architect (1986, addition 1994).
22466 Pacific Coast Hwy.
Private residence.

Richard Meier's first residential commission in LA, this oceanside house features the architect's signature white cubic forms and curving screen walls, with expanses of glass on the beach façade. Other frequently used elements include square windows, glass blocks, ramps and pipe railings. The house has an ample courtyard, hidden behind a wall of trees—something seldom seen on the Malibu beachfront.

Segel Residence
John Lautner, architect (1979).
22426 Pacific Coast Hwy.
Private residence.

The famous architect chose a protective, cave-like concept for this wood and concrete house. All its glass is frameless and designed to withstand strong winds. With its flowing forms which mimic the ocean waves, the house is noted for its curved glass front that allows stunning beach and ocean views. It was the home of actors

Courtney Cox and David Arquette from 2001 to 2007.

David Geffen Estate
22126 Pacific Coast Hwy.
Private residence.

Music producer and DreamWorks SKG co-founder, billionaire David Geffen, pierced together four neighboring lots into the property with the most beach frontage in Malibu—285 feet (87 m). The estimated value of the estate, which comprises a main house, guest house, pool, complete with poolhouse and gym, all handsomely landscaped and protected by a sea wall, is about $80 million.

Janet Jackson Home
21822 Pacific Coast Hwy.
Private residence.

Grammy-winning singer and the youngest of the nine children in the Jackson musical family, Janet made headlines when she signed a $80-million deal with Virgin Records in 1997. She caused a scandal during the 2004 Super Bowl, when her right breast was very briefly exposed during the halftime show duet with singer Justin Timberlake. The pop diva bought this beachfront home in 1991 for $4.5 million and sold it in 2004 for $9 million.

Ackerburg Residence

Segel Residence

Steady winds power a board rider's kite at Topanga Beach

Topanga State Beach 24

18500 block of PCH.
☎(310) 394-3266; 451-2906.

This narrow, mile-long rocky beach is popular for swimming and surfing; you'll also see many windsurfers and sailboats. Sometimes dolphins can be spotted frolicking just offshore.

J Paul Getty Museum at the Getty Villa 25

17985 Pacific Coast Hwy.
☎(310) 440-7300.
🕐Thu-Mon 10am-5pm; Closed Tue, Wed and major holidays.
💲free. Parking fee.

The building is a reconstruction and adaptation of the ancient Roman Villa dei Papiri, built outside the walls of the city of Herculaneum on the Bay of Naples. The city and the villa were buried in a catastrophic eruption of Mt Vesuvius in AD 79.

The Villa is North America's only cultural resource dedicated entirely to the display, conservation and interpretation of ancient art. The collection of Greek and Roman antiquities is the third most important of its kind in the United States. It consists of Greek vases and sculpture, Cycladic figures and vessels, Roman portraits, Hellenistic metalwork and Egyptian portrait paintings.

Villa de Leon 26

Kenneth MacDonald, architect (1927).
17948 Porto Marina Way.
Private residence.

Situated dangerously close to the edge of a cliff eroded by continuous landslides, this remarkable Mediterranean villa overlooks the coastal highway and the entrance to the Getty Museum. Built by the Russian immigrant and wool magnate Leon Kauffman in 1927, the towering 35-room house has intrigued passing motorists on PCH ever since. Rumors were spread (unfounded) that it was the home of actress Rita Hayworth and her third husband, Prince Aly Khan.

Main Peristyle Garden and the Getty Villa façade

Thelma Todd's Sidewalk Café
(formerly) 27

17575 Pacific Coast Hwy. 🚻
During the 1930s, this Spanish-style building housed a glamorous restaurant and popular celebrity hideaway. It was co-owned by Thelma

Villa de Leon

Todd, the beautiful actress who played wisecracking characters in comedies such as *Monkey Business* (1931) with the Marx Brothers and *Fra Diavolo/The Devil's Brother* (1933) with Laurel and Hardy.

On December 16, 1935, the body of "The Ice Cream Blonde" was discovered by her maid in the garage of her apartment above the café, at 17531 Posetano Rd. She was seated behind the wheel of her Lincoln Phaeton, with her mink coat and $20,000 worth of jewelry. Although there was blood on her face, the coroner ruled her death as accident caused by carbon monoxide poisoning. A theory circulated that mobster Lucky Luciano wanted to establish a gambling operation at the café. When Todd refused the mafia plan, she was brutally murdered. Others suspected that she was killed by her business partner and lover, film director Roland West. However, her death remains a mystery.

Thelma Todd's Sidewalk Café was housed here in the 1930s

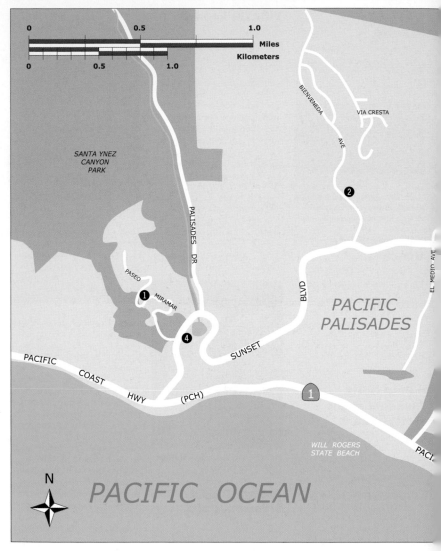

Pacific Palisades

Initially a summer beach colony, this community was founded in 1922 by the Methodist Episcopal Church as a place for cultural, educational and religious gatherings. Pacific Palisades is today one of the most desirable sections of Los Angeles, an upscale neighborhood bursting with celebrities. Among the stars who, at one time or another, owned homes or still live here, are: Deborah Kerr, David Niven, Anthony Quinn, Robert Taylor, Ronald and Nancy Reagan (two homes), Michelle Pfeiffer and David Kelley, Tom Hanks and Rita Wilson, Tom Cruise and Nicole Kidman, Goldie Hawn and Kurt Russell, as well as Bill Cosby, Billy Crystal, Whoopi Goldberg, Anthony Hopkins, Michael Keaton, Sydney Pollack and Sylvester Stallone.

The area contains some important Modernist buildings, as well as significant examples of contemporary Los Angeles architecture.

Villa Aurora ❶

Mark Daniels, architect (1927, restored 1993).
520 Paseo Miramar.
☎(310) 454-4231.
By appointment only.

The house, whose design was reportedly based on a Spanish castle in Sevilla, was the home of German-Jewish novelist Lion Feuchtwanger, who fled the Nazis and lived in Los Angeles from 1941 until his death in 1958. His widow deeded the Villa to the University of Southern

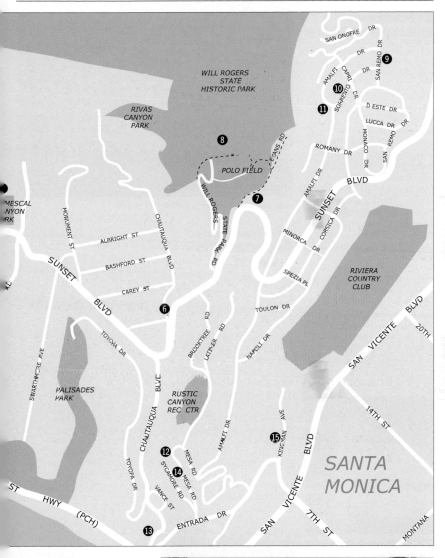

California and it was later purchased by a German consortium, which restored it to its original splendor. It is now a study center and home to the California Institute for European-American Relations.

The Villa was famous for the literary salons hosted by Feuchtwanger and his wife, Martha. Among the German émigrés and local artists who frequented here were Bertolt Brecht, Heinrich and Thomas Mann, Ludwig Marcuse, Franz Werfel, Marlene Dietrich and Charlie Chaplin.

Villa Aurora played host to many prominent German exiles

St Matthew's Episcopal Church ❷

Moore Ruble Yudell, architects (1982-83).
1031 Bienveneda Ave.
☎(310) 454-1358.

When architect Charles Moore signed a contract to design the replacement for a sanctuary destroyed in a hillside fire, there was a condition stipulating that construction would not begin until two-thirds of the congregation had approved the design. After four years of workshops, planning and building, the architects and parishioners arrived at a solution that satisfied both traditionalists and modernists among the church members.

The result is a church with a cruciform plan, noted for its extensive use of wood in the internal space and exposed beams under a ceiling. Skylights provide soft natural light for intimate amphitheater seating, while inset windows offer views of the landscaped grounds.

Interior of St Matthew's Episcopal Church

Eric Owen Moss Home

Moss House ❸

Eric Owen Moss, architect (1979).
708 El Medio Ave.
Private residence.

Architect Eric Owen Moss extensively remodeled a former 1940s ranch house for his family, turning it into one of his signature creations. He added a flying buttress and a false gable, and combined an inordinate color scheme with decorative elements such as giant numerals for street number to create a startling effect.

Self-Realization Fellowship Lake Shrine ❹

17190 Sunset Blvd.
☎(310) 454-4114.
🕑gardens Tue-Sat 9am-4:45pm; museum 11am-4pm. Ⓢ free.

Lake Shrine was opened to the public in 1950 by Paramahansa Yogananda, one of the most influential spiritual leaders of the 20th century, who spent many years in Los Angeles introducing thousands of followers to yoga and meditation. Highlights of the grounds include the Golden Lotus Archway, a "wall-less temple," and the Gandhi World Peace Memorial, containing a portion of Mahatma Gandhi's ashes.

The grounds are beautifully maintained and visitors can take a scenic walk along a path meandering around the lake, enjoying the picturesque beauty of this peaceful environment. The museum offers exhibits on the life and work of Sri Yogananda.

Temescal Gateway Park ❺

Temescal Canyon Rd.
☎(310) 455-2465.
🕑open daily. Ⓢfree. Parking fee.
Activities: hiking, picnicking; docent-led hikes.

This is one of the more popular, easy climbs for beginning hikers. Following scenic paths among oaks and sycamores, visitors cross wooden footbridges, pass a small waterfall and enjoy splendid panoramic views from the ridge crest. Join the Temescal Canyon Association docents for 3-4-mile hikes on the park's trails. Call ☎(310) 459-5931 for more info.

The Golden Lotus Archway

Waterfall in Temescal Park

Bridges House

Bridges House ❻

Robert Bridges, architect (1989).
820 Chautauqua Blvd
Private residence.

Sitting on massive concrete piers on a high bluff, this three-level residence/office provides stunning canyon views and overlooks Sunset Blvd 70 feet (21 m) below.

Arnold Schwarzenegger Estate ❼

Evans Rd (private).
Private residence.

An Austrian-born bodybuilder turned one of the highest-paid Hollywood stars, Arnold Schwarzenegger won a record number of bodybuilding titles, including seven Mr Olympia titles and five Mr Universe titles. His film breakthrough came with *Conan the Barbarian* (1982), followed by such major successes as *Total Recall* (1990), *True Lies* (1994) and three *Terminator* films (1984, 1991 and 2003).

After they were married in 1986, Schwarzenegger and his journalist wife, Maria Shriver, bought a home at 14209 Sunset Blvd. They later added to the property, buying neighboring houses from actor John Forsythe (who played the patriarch-tycoon Blake Carrington in the television series *Dynasty;* actor Daniel J Travanti (star of the television series *Hill Street Blues*) and developer Jay Lustig, part owner of the Pittsburgh Pirates. The newly formed compound, hidden behind a gate on private Evans Rd, is comprised of four mansions on 5.5 acres (2,2 ha).

The wealthy couple and their four children moved in 2002 to a newly built home in a gated Brentwood community, bought for $11.9 million. The Pacific Palisades compound, which was divided into three parcels, was sold in 2004 for around $16 million. After being elected Governor of California in 2003, Schwarzenegger lives most of the week at the Hyatt in Sacramento, and spends weekends in Brentwood.

Will Rogers State Historic Park ❽

1501 Will Rogers State Park Rd.
☎(310) 454-8212.
🕐park grounds open 8am to sunset; the house and visitors' center 10am 5pm.
🎫 free. Parking fee.

This 186-acre ranch was once owned by Will Rogers (1879-1935), famous cowboy, trick roper, rodeo performer, comedian, actor, newspaper columnist, radio commentator, author and humorist, who set all the box office records of his day.

The living room of the ranch house features a swing porch and a mounted calf, given to Rogers to rope instead of roping his friends. On exhibit are also Indian

Fireplace in the living room of the Will Rogers's ranch house

rugs, baskets, costumes and numerous drawings, watercolors, paintings and bronzes.

The visitors' center displays photographs and memorabilia and shows a short film featuring highlights of Rogers's career. Among the most beloved Americans of his time, famous for his wit and humor, Will Rogers will be best remembered for his saying: "I have never met a man I didn't like."

Visitors can stroll on picnic grounds or trek the two-mile loop trail to Inspiration Point and enjoy an impressive view of Santa Monica Bay. On summer weekends, between April and September, occasional polo matches are held on the field (check with the ranger for times). Built in the 1930s, this is where Rogers played with celebrity friends such as Spencer Tracy and Walt Disney.

Arnold Schwarzenegger compound comprised four mansions

Thomas Mann Home ⑨

J R Davidson, architect (1941).
1550 San Remo Dr.
Private residence. ●◆

Designed for the famous novelist Thomas Mann and his daughter Erika, this two-story Modern glass-and-stucco house is almost invisible from the street. The German émigré and Nobel Prize laureate for literature in 1929 lived here from 1942 until 1952, when he moved to Switzerland in protest over government policies during the McCarthy period. While living in Los Angeles, Mann conceived and wrote his masterpiece *Doctor Faustus* (1947) and *The Holy Sinner* (1951).

Tom Cruise Home ⑩

1525 Sorrento Dr.
Private residence.

Hollywood leading man and one of the most bankable actors in history, Tom Cruise starred in such mega hits as *Top Gun* (1986), *Rain Man* (1988), *Mission Impossible* (1996) and *Minority Report* (2002). He was chosen as *People* magazine's Sexiest Man Alive in 1990.

Cruise bought this 1940s gated house for about $4.7 million shortly before his marriage to actress Nicole Kidman in 1990. The couple co-starred in *Days of Thunder* (1990), *Far and Away* (1992) and *Eyes Wide Shut* (1999).

David O Selznick, Cary Grant and Steven Spielberg lived here

A tall, strawberry blonde beauty from Australia, Kidman has played lead roles in such movies as *To Die For* (1995), *Moulin Rouge* (2001), *Cold Mountain* (2003) and *Stepford Wives* (2004). She won a best actress Oscar for her portrayal of Virginia Woolf in *The Hours* (2002).

The couple shared this home until they were divorced in 2001. Kidman got the house through the divorce and sold it in 2002 for close to $11 million.

Steven Spielberg Home ⑪

1515 Amalfi Dr.
Private residence.

Hidden behind tall gates, this fabled mansion was home to a number of Hollywood celebrities, the last one being Steven Spielberg. He has directed some of the biggest grossing films in history, including *Jaws* (1975), *Raiders of the Lost Ark* (1981), *E.T. The Extra-Terrestrial* (1982) and *Jurassic Park* (1993). Spielberg won Academy Awards for directing *Schindler's List* (1993) and *Saving Private Ryan* (1998).

When he purchased the mansion in 1985, Spielberg was intrigued by the fact that its first owner was legendary producer David O Selznick, who lived here while making *Gone With the Wind* (1939). Other famous tenants included actors Douglas Fairbanks, Jr, Cary Grant and his wife, Woolworth heiress Barbara Hutton, and teen idol, singer Bobby Vinton.

Entenza House ⑫

Harwell H Harris, architect (1937); restored 1998.
475 Mesa Rd.
Private residence.

Built for John Entenza, editor of the influential *Arts & Architecture* magazine (➜ p97), this house is the architect's only work demonstrating the influence of the International Style. With its curved carport and spiral staircase it blends Streamline Moderne and the International Style, though it lacks some of the elements, such as post-and-beam, that later became typical of Entenza's Case Study House program.

Entenza House

The steel-and-glass Eames House was built of mass-produced parts | Schwartz House

Eames House ⑬

Charles and Ray Eames, architects
(1949).
Private residence.
☛available for tours Mon-Fri
between 9 30am and 5pm by
appointment only and under certain
conditions. Call ☎(310) 459-
9663 for the house rules, address
and directions. ⑤free.
www.eamesoffice.com

Completed in 1949, this
was one of the first houses to
be designed as part of the
landmark Case Study Pro-
gram (➔ p97). It was built
by Charles and Ray Eames as
their own home and studio
and consists of two box-
shaped buildings, connected
by a small garden. Conceived
as a model of inexpensive
housing after World War II,
the steel-and-glass house was
constructed entirely of prefabricated building materials.
Many of the standardized
industrial components used
here were readily available
from parts catalogues.

Case Study House No. 8, as
it is also known, is famous
for its simplicity, large transparent surfaces and unusual
use of color. Charles Eames's
design achieved international
significance and still attracts
the attention of architects and
architecture buffs around the
world.

The house now serves as
headquarters for the Eames
Office, whose "mission is to
communicate, preserve and
extend" the legacy of the
famous designer couple.

Schwartz House ⑭

Pierre Koenig, architect (1995).
444 Sycamore Rd.
Private residence.

The famous architect essentially reduced the structure to
a solid cube, which he rotated inside a steel frame to
avoid direct afternoon sun.
The house is wrapped in corrugated metal sheets, with
large surfaces of clear glass
which offer the canyon and
street views, while sunblasted
glass panes add privacy.

Dolores Del Rio and Cedric Gibbons Home ⑮

Douglas Honnold and Cedric Gibbons, architects (1929).
757 Kingman Ave.
Private residence.

An extraordinary blend of
Art Deco and International
Style Modern, this house was
designed by art director

Cedric Gibbons for his bride,
Mexican actress Dolores Del
Rio. A star of the silent
screen, she was often called
the most beautiful woman in
the world.

Behind a blank, white-stuc-
co façade and unpretentious
entrance, Gibbons created a
stylish streamlined interior
with built-in mirrors in tribute
to his wife's stunning beauty.

In 1928 Gibbons designed
the gilded Academy Award
statuette, now known as
Oscar (➔ p48). As MGM's art
director from 1924 until 1960,
he himself won 11 Oscars for
the design of such movies as
Pride and Prejudice (1940),
Gaslight (1944), *An American
in Paris* (1951) and *Julius
Caesar* (1953). He was the
most famous and probably
the most important production designer in American
film, influencing the taste of
millions of movie goers
around the world.

Dolores Del Rio and Cedric Gibbons Home

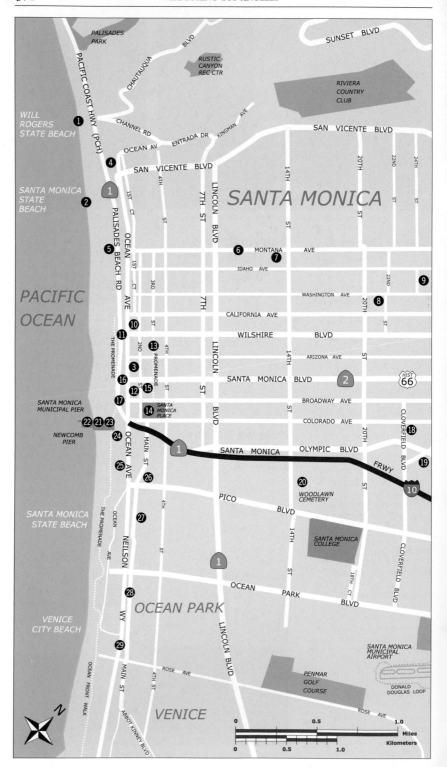

Santa Monica

With its clean air, cool ocean breezes and year-round sunshine, Santa Monica epitomizes the Southern California beach community. Its image as a seaside heaven has been popularized by countless films, television series and songs that depicted casual life by the beach. The city is the home of liberal activism, noted for tolerance toward homeless, rent control

Seal of the city of Santa Monica

(a policy now abandoned) and concern about environmental issues. Santa Monica is an elegant, friendly town with an unpretentious atmosphere and a vivid art scene that attracts an eclectic crowd. One of the relatively safest areas in Los Angeles, it is ideal for exploring on foot, with its main attractions, shopping and dining located near the coast.

Will Rogers State Beach ❶

16000 block of PCH.
☎(310) 394-3266. ⚑

Named after the famous movie cowboy and humorist, this wide, two-mile long beach is a favorite with swimmers and beginning surfers. The beach was a frequent filming site for the popular television series *Baywatch*. Its fans will recognize lifeguard station 18, where the show's episodes were often filmed. The scenic bike trail that winds 22 miles (35 km) south along the coast starts here.

Santa Monica State Beach ❷

PCH at California incline.
☎(310) 394-3266.

Easily accessible, this is the busiest beach on the bay, especially on summer weekends when it becomes jampacked. It is the widest stretch of sand on the Pacific Coast, largely due to a man-

Situated atop steep sandstone bluffs overlooking the Santa Monica Bay, Palisades Park provides panoramic ocean views from Palos Verdes to Malibu

made breakwater which has caused white sand to accumulate over time. The famed boardwalk starts here. The beach offers full facilities and is popular for family outings, as well as for sunbathing and socializing. Swimming can be dangerous due to possible pollution after rains. To avoid expensive beach parking lots,

park in municipal garages on Second and Fourth streets.

Palisades Park ❸

Ocean Ave (between Colorado Ave and Adelaide Dr).

This 2-mile (3.2-km) stretch of parkland on a cliff's edge is one of Los Angeles' most scenic and popular parks. Lushly landscaped with palm, eucalyptus and other trees and semi tropical plants, the park is a great place to walk, jog or enjoy spectacular sunsets. Steps opposite Montana Ave lead down to the beach.

David Hasselhoff and his pack of beauties in red swimsuits. The internationally renowned television series *Baywatch* was partially filmed at Will Rogers State Beach.

Alaskan Totem Pole ❹

Palisades Park.

Specially ordered and made in 1925, this authentic, 34-foot (10 m) totem pole was erected at Inspiration Point, at the park's north end. It was carved by the Chilkat Thlinger Indian tribe of Sitka, Alaska.

A nice stretch of sand south of the Santa Monica Pier

View of the Gold Coast from Palisades Park. Former celebrity beach houses line the mile-long stretch of sand north of the pier

Gold Coast ❺

As the wealthiest motion picture personalities flocked to the shore during the 1920s and 1930s, this section of Santa Monica became a fabled playground of the stars and Hollywood's first beach-resort community. Almost every home that stands here belonged to some of the biggest names in the film industry. Initially built as "beach cottages" intended for use as summer or weekend retreats, several Gold Coast homes reached palatial proportions.

Among the notables who lived along Palisades Beach Rd were silent screen actress Bebe Daniels (at 964 and 972); head of production at MGM Irving Thalberg and his wife, film star Norma Shearer (at 707); Harry Warner, head of Warner Bros (at 605); legendary producer Samuel Goldwyn (at 602); 20th Century-Fox co-founder and chief of production Darryl F

Zanuck (at 546); screenwriter Anita Loos (at 506); famous comedian Harold Lloyd (at 443); the richest man in the world, oilman J Paul Getty (at 270).

Although some of the early Gold Coast star homes have been demolished, many of the original buildings are still standing, even if remodeled or walled in.

Norma Talmadge/ Cary Grant Home
Paul Roe Crawley, architect (1929)
1038 Palisades Beach Rd.
Private residence.

Standing between two public parking lots, this distinct French Norman-style residence was built in 1929 by silent screen idol Norma Talmadge. She was the wife of producer Joseph Schenck, the co-founder and president of 20th Century-Fox.

After her divorce in 1930, Talmadge, one of the most popular of silent screen actresses, retired from movies, unable to make a

successful transition to sound. She sold the house in the mid-1930s to actor Cary Grant, who lived here first with his friend, actor Randolph Scott (they were reportedly more than just friends), and later with his second wife, Barbara Hutton. Among its other tenants were producer Howard Hughes, actress Grace Kelly, as well as director Roman Polanski and his wife, actress Sharon Tate.

Louis B Mayer Home
625 Palisades Beach Rd.
Private residence.

Designed by MGM art director Cedric Gibbons, this 20-room Mediterranean-style villa was built in 1936 for Louis B Mayer, head of MGM and the most powerful of the Hollywood moguls.

When Mayer hosted lavish parties at the house, his living room served as a small theater, equipped with a soundproof projection booth and a stage under the floorboards that could be raised by hydraulic lifts. Here he staged screenings of his studio's latest films, including one of the first previews of *Gone With the Wind* (1939).

The house was later owned by actor and "Rat Pack" member Peter Lawford and his wife Patricia Kennedy, whose famous brothers were frequent guests here. It is rumored that President JFK and Senator Robert Kennedy entertained Marilyn Monroe and other Hollywood starlets in this opulent beach house. Marilyn visited Lawford here on the day of her death.

Norma Talmadge/Cary Grant Home

Louis B Mayer Home

Silent film celebrities gather for a regular weekend party at Norma Talmadge's beach house on Santa Monica's Gold Coast (ca. 1926). Among the guests are Roscoe "Fatty" Arbuckle, Mae Murray, Rudolph Valentino, Pola Negri, Howard Hughes, Richard Barthelmess, Constance Talmadge and Natalie Talmadge.

many as 2,000 guests at a time. No expense was too high for the hosts when it came to entertaining: the large orchestras from several Hollywood hotels were brought here, even a carousel was installed during their legendary costume parties.

The only remains of the Marion Davies's palatial estate are the former servants' quarters. After Hearst and Davies moved in 1946 to Beverly Hills, they sold the beach house for the mere sum of $600,000. It later became a posh hotel, but most of it was eventually demolished in the 1950s. The Sand and Sea Club occupied what was left

Douglas Fairbanks Home
705 Palisades Beach Rd.
Private residence.

The silent screen's most famous swashbuckler kept this beach house in a settlement after his divorce from actress Mary Pickford in 1936. He lived here with his third wife, Lady Sylvia Ashley, who later became the fourth Mrs Clark Gable. A skilled athlete who performed his own stunts in countless adventure movies, Fairbanks died here of a massive heart attack in 1939.

Marion Davies Estate (site)
Julia Morgan, architect (1928).
415 Palisades Beach Rd.

Designed by architect Julia Morgan (who also designed the Hearst Castle in San Simeon), this fabulous Georgian Colonial estate was the largest and most extravagant beach house on the whole West Coast. It comprised a

three-story main house, three guest houses, servants' quarters, two heated swimming pools with a thousand lockers for guests, tennis courts, garages and dog kennels.

The magnificent compound was built in 1928 at a cost of over $3.5 million by newspaper magnate William Randolph Hearst for his mistress, actress Marion Davies. The 110-room residence featured 55 bathrooms, 37 antique fireplaces, a private theatre, a ballroom and 750 feet (230 m) of beach frontage. An original Elizabethan pub was imported from England and installed as a basement bar. Hearst even imported whole paneled rooms, some dating back four centuries, from European castles and palaces and reassembled them here.

Ocean House, as it was called, was the scene of the most lavish parties in Hollywood history, attended by as

Joan Crawford and Douglas Fairbanks, Jr arrive at the Baby Party, one of the inventively themed costume parties thrown by Marion Davies at her beach estate

of the mansion until the structure was damaged in the 1994 Northridge earthquake. Today vacated, the remnants of the former Gold Coast glory were used as a location for the television series *Beverly Hills 90210* and *Baywatch*.

Douglas Fairbanks and Mary Pickford Home

Marion Davies palatial beach house

Montana Avenue ❻

Commercial area between 7th and 17th streets.

Transformed in the 1970s from a nondescript business street into a flashy and upscale commercial area, Montana is ideal for walking and shopping. Since it attracts neighbors from the surrounding affluent residential areas of north Santa Monica and Brentwood, it is not unusual to come across a celebrity here. This friendly strip of specialty stores offers designer wear, vintage jewelry, folk art, gifts and furnishings, along with casual dining in many outdoor cafés.

Aero Theater was built as a venue for aircraft industry workers

Aero Theater ❼

P M Woolpert, architect (1939).
1328 Montana Ave.
☎(310) 395-4990. ⌖

Designed in French Norman Style with touches of Art Deco, this independent theater features a striking neon-lit marquee and a tiny box-office. The 550-seat Aero was built in 1939 by aircraft manufacturer Donald Douglas as a neighborhood movie house. It operated around the clock so wartime employees from his local plant could watch movies at all hours of the day as they finished their shifts. Robert Redford, who saw his first movie here as a child, planned at one point to turn the Aero into a venue for independent films.

The single-screen theater was refurbished in 2003 and is now operated by American Cinematheque, which screens the same range of films here as at the Egyptian Theatre in Hollywood.

The picturesque Aero was featured in the film *Get Shorty* (1995) as the theater where John Travolta and Rene Russo watch a movie together.

Gehry House ❽

Frank O Gehry, architect (1978; extended 1993).
1002 22nd St.
Private residence.

Frank Gehry's own house announced in 1978 a new movement in architecture

and so outraged his neighbors that some threatened to sue. The architect partially dismantled the existing bungalow situated on a corner lot, revealing its wood framing behind the glass. He then wrapped it with a new shell using inexpensive materials such as corrugated metal sheets, chain-link fencing and raw plywood, leaving the impression of construction still in progress.

Shirley Temple Home ❾

948 24th St.
Private residence.

This Spanish-style house is the former home of Shirley Temple, famous child performer and one of the greatest money-makers in cinema history. Born in Santa Monica in 1928, Shirley began her film career at the age of four, starring in the series of shorts. Her first major success was *Stand Up and Cheer* (1934), followed by such hits as *Bright Eyes* (1934) and *Rebecca of Sunnybrook Farm* (1938). She received a special Academy Award for her contribution to screen entertainment. She was a member of the US delegation to the UN General Assembly and served as US ambassador to Ghana.

Frank Gehry House

The enormous Moreton Bay fig in the Miramar Hotel's courtyard

Fairmont Miramar Hotel ⑩

101 Wilshire Blvd.
☎(310) 394-3731. ⚑

On this site was originally the stately mansion of Senator John P Jones, founder of the seaside community of Santa Monica. Today, in the hotel's center courtyard is the only remainder of his estate a massive Moreton Bay fig tree, planted in 1889.

Upon her arrival from Europe in September 1925, twenty-year old actress Greta Garbo stayed at a suite in the hotel's historic, six-story brick building. She resided here while working for MGM on *The Torrent* (1926) and *Flesh and Devil* (1927), the films that started the Garbo myth.

At that time the Miramar offered entertainment that equaled that of the Hollywood nightclubs. Betty Grable was discovered here while performing for a short time as a singer. Lana Turner even got married at the hotel. The hotel's pool area is seen in the romantic comedy *That Touch of Mink* (1962), with Cary Grant and Doris Day.

Santa Monica Statue ⑪

Ocean Ave at Wilshire Blvd.

The statue of the city's patron and namesake watches over Santa Monica. Legend has it that the first mention of the future city's name

occurred during the Spanish military expedition in 1769. Franciscan Father Juan Crespi, who accompanied the soldiers, called the springs in the area Santa Monica, after its waters reminded him of the tears she shed for her son, Saint Augustine.

Vitagraph Studio building

Vitagraph Studio
(formerly) ⑫

1438 Second St.

Built in 1875, this is believed to be the oldest brick structure in Santa Monica. Over the years, it served as a saloon, jail and the first City Hall. Today it is a part of an international hostel. In 1911 the building was used for the offices of the Vitagraph Company of America, the leading motion picture producer at the turn of the 20th century. Just to the north stood a larger building which Vitagraph used as a studio until 1915, when it moved production to a lot in East Hollywood (➔ p159).

Third Street Promenade ⑬

Third St between Broadway and Wilshire Blvd.

Just three blocks from the ocean, this outdoor pedestrian mall opened in 1989 after undergoing a major revitalization. One of the most popular shopping and entertainment areas in Los Angeles, it features a diverse array of sidewalk cafés and restaurants, street vendors, movie theaters, nightclubs, specialty boutiques and bookstores.

Widely acclaimed for its design, the three-block Promenade is lined with palm and jackaranda trees and decorated with metal and topiary dinosaur fountains. This pedestrian-only area attracts a lively mix of musicians, minstrels, bohemian poets and performers. They provide appreciative audiences with free entertainment including music, dance, shows and tricks.

A decorative fountain on the Third Street Promenade

The elaborate façade of the Mayfair Music Hall

Camera Obscura

Santa Monica Place

Frank O Gehry and Associates, architect (1979-81).
300 block of Broadway.

Architect Frank Gehry's three-level indoor shopping mall is the home to major department stores, chain and boutique shops and a large food court. Santa Monica Place's parking structure features the architect's signature chain link screen. Together with lettering and palm trees, it creates an interesting visual effect on the south façade.

Several fight scenes from *Terminator 2: Judgement Day* (1991), starring Arnold Schwarzenegger, were filmed at Santa Monica Place

The mall was used as a location for the television series *Beverly Hills 90210* and the film *Internal Affairs* (1990), with Richard Gere and Andy Garcia. This is also the mall where several scenes from *Terminator 2: Judgement Day* (1991) were filmed, including the fight between Schwarzenegger and his technologically more advanced opponent, and a scene in which he is thrown through a store window.

Mayfair Music Hall

214 Santa Monica Blvd.
Closed to the public.

Built in 1911 as the Majestic Theater and restored in 1973, it was called the oldest legitimate theater operating in Los Angeles. This small, cozy venue featured popular shows and musicals. It was damaged during the Northridge earthquake and has been closed since 1994.

Route 66 Western Terminus

Palisades Park. Ocean Ave at Santa Monica Blvd.

A memorial plaque erected in 1952 marks the western end of the original Route 66. Also known as the "Main Street of America," the famous interstate was renamed Will Rogers Hwy to

Santa Monica Place's skylit atrium with pools, fountains and palm trees

pay tribute to the famous actor and humorist.

Rising above its basic transportation role, this narrow, two-lane road connecting the Midwest and California became an American cultural icon. Millions of motoring visitors poured in via Route 66, making Santa Monica one of the most popular tourist destinations.

A plaque marks the Route 66 western terminus

Camera Obscura

Palisades Park.
1450 Ocean Ave (at Broadway).
☎(310) 458-8644.
Mon-Fri 9am-4pm, Sat-Sun 11am-4pm. free.

A forerunner of the modern camera, this 1899 device projects outside scenes onto a white circular surface indoors. It is composed of a revolving turret with a mirror that bounces sunlight through a convex lens into a completely darkened room. Viewers can rotate the turret and change the scene on the table by turning what looks like an old ship's wheel.

The camera is a long-time local attraction, located in an upstairs room at the Senior Recreation Center (ask for the key at the desk).

Sony Music ⑱

Steven Ehrlich Architects (1992).
2100 Colorado Ave.
☎(310) 449-2100.

This huge complex houses the Sony Music corporate services and its two main labels—Columbia and Epic Records. Arranged around a courtyard, the three separate buildings are the architect's interpretation of the Streamline Moderne architecture of the 1930s. The central point of the street façades, clad in red Arizona sandstone and green translucent glass, is the striking contrast between the curve of one building and the triangular wedge of another, said to symbolize the meeting of East and West.

The Sony Music complex houses Columbia and Epic Records

A visitor views artworks at Bergamot Station during the LA International Biennial

Bergamot Station ⑲

2525 Michigan Ave.
☎(310) 829-5854 or 453-7535.
⏰most galleries are open Tue-Sat 11am-5pm. ⑤free.

Named for the old Red Car trolley station that stood on this site until the 1950s, this compound comprises more than 30 prestigious art galleries. The area was an abandoned industrial site before the warehouses were converted into an arts complex in 1994. The galleries exhibit photography and contemporary art in a wide range of mediums.

Woodlawn Cemetery ⑳

1847 14th St
☎(310) 450-0781.
⏰daily 8am-5pm.

Woodlawn Cemetery was originally established in 1876 as the final resting place for the pioneer Carrillo family on part of what once was their ranch. The Carrillos were one of the oldest and most prominent Southern California families, established by a soldier in the Portolá expedition in 1769. Members of the Carrillo family were respected land owners, governors, judges and attorneys.

Today the cemetery is owned by the City of Santa Monica. It is dominated by an elaborate mausoleum located in the central section. There is also a Civil War Monument, erected in 1917.

Leo Carrillo (1880-1961)

The descendant of Spanish settlers, Leo Carrillo started his acting career in vaudeville and on the legitimate stage before entering films in the 1920s. During the 1930s and 1940s he became one of Hollywood's leading character actors, starring in such films as *Viva Villa!* (1934), *Love Me Forever* (1935) and *The Gay Desperado* (1936). During the 1950s, he played Pancho, Duncan Renaldo's sidekick, in the popular television series *The Cisco Kid*.

Paul Henreid (1908-1992)

Austrian-born actor Henreid was discovered by Otto Preminger and began his acting career on the Vienna stage. He later moved to England, where he appeared in such films as *Goodbye Mr Chips* (1939). In the US since 1940, he was cast as a sophisticated Continental leading man during the war. Henreid starred opposite Bette Davis in *Now, Voyager* (1942), but is best remembered as the Resistance hero Victor Laszlo in *Casablanca* (1942).

Section 2, grave 7-B

Section 3

Santa Monica Pier ㉑

At the foot of Colorado Ave.
☎(310) 458-8900.
www.santamonicapier.org
🕐open 365 days a year; operating hours vary by season. Ⓢfree.
Parking: fee. 🏴

A popular tourist attraction that hosts 3 million visitors a year, this landmark structure is the oldest pleasure pier on the West Coast still standing. Constructed between 1909 and 1916, it was originally built as two adjacent boardwalks—a long and narrow strolling and fishing municipal pier, and a short and wide privately owned amusement pier. Expanded and rebuilt several times, it is now the last of several pleasure piers that dotted the area early in the 20th century. In its heyday it was an internationally renowned entertainment center, boasting famous carousel, a giant roller coaster and fascinating La Monica Ballroom (➔ p352).

An arched neon sign at the Santa Monica pier's entryway is a widely recognized symbol of the city. It was featured in *Forrest Gump* (1993) as the end of Tom Hanks's run across the country.

The pier offers a variety of entertainment, including live music, dancing, dining, karaoke and night clubs. Free concerts with dancing, called the Twilight Dance Series, are held here every Thursday evening during the summer.
Santa Monica Pier was a popular location featured in countless movies and television productions. The pier, which once featured a magnificent ballroom, was used

Santa Monica Pier during the 90th anniversary celebration (2000)

as a setting in *The Glenn Miller Story* (1954). The home Natalie Wood lived in as a teenage girl before becoming a star in *Inside Daisy Clover* (1965) was located on the pier. Barbra Streisand and Omar Sharif rambled along it in the musical biography *Funny Girl* (1968). In the action thriller *Cellular* (2004), the final showdown between a policeman (played by William H Macy) and kidnapper (Jason Statham) takes place at the Santa Monica Pier. Among the television shows which were shot at the pier were *Charlie's Angels*, *Three's Company*, *Fresh Prince Of Bel Air* and *Baywatch*.
When Tom Hanks started running across the country in *Forrest Gump* (1993), he went all the way to the Pacific Ocean. When he reached the end of the Santa Monica Pier, he turned around and "just kept on goin'."

Pacific Park ㉒

Santa Monica Pier.
☎(310) 260-8744.
www.pacpark.com.
🕐daily 10am-10pm in summer; shorter hours in winter. Ⓢfree (there is a charge for various attractions).

Opened in June 1996, this amusement park is Santa Monica's newest draw, offering a West Coaster roller coaster, a flying submarine and similar rides, as well as typical attractions such as video arcades, fairground games, bumper cars and several features just for kids. Recently introduced are virtual reality motion simulator theaters. Visitors can enjoy great ocean and shoreline views from a nine-story Pacific Wheel, the largest Ferris wheel on the West Coast.
Near the end of the pier fishermen can rent a pole and cast their line (no permit is necessary).

Pacific Park

Santa Monica Pier Carousel dates back to 1922

Santa Monica Pier Carousel ㉓

Santa Monica Pier.
☎(310) 458-8867.
⊕Tue-Fri 11am-9pm; Sat-Sun 10am-9pm; open only on weekends in winter. Ⓢ ➤ NRHP

This vintage merry-go-round, manufactured at Philadelphia Toboggan Co in 1922, was originally located in Nashville, Tennessee. At one time it was on Venice Pier, and was brought to its present home in 1947, where it was lovingly restored. The carousel features 44 intricately hand-carved and cheerfully painted horses, each one unique. Some 200,000 annual riders take a spin here, accompanied by the old tunes played by the original 1922 Wurlitzer band organ. This is one of only 140 old wooden carousels still operating in the US and Canada (between 5,000 and 7,000 carousels were in use during the 1920s).

Wind Harp (1987), a sculpture by Douglas Hollis

The two-story Moorish-Byzantine building that houses the carousel, originally called Hippodrome, was erected in 1916 and was recently restored. The most distinguishable structure on the pier, it was designated a National Historic Landmark.

The carousel has been the backdrop for many films, including George Roy Hill's classic *The Sting* (1973). Starring Robert Redford and Paul Newman as a pair of con artists, the comedy was set in Depression-era Chicago.

Carousel Park ㉔

Moore Ruble Yudell, architects (1988).
At Colorado and Ocean Ave.

Designed as a stepped gateway to the pier, this area is a prime spot for beach sports. A children's playground features carnival rides designed for the kids, including stone sculptures suitable for climbing, such as a dragon made of river-washed boulders that snorts water mist.

To the south, the three-mile stretch of beach became the Natural Elements Sculpture Park. Among the examples of public art installed here are *Santa Monica Art Tool* (a miniature metropolis imprinted in wet sand) by Carl Cheng and *Wind Harp* (singing chairs) by Douglas Hollis. A delightful example of functional art, these oversize lifeguard chairs make soothing music on a breezy day.

Muscle Beach
(site) ㉕

South of the Santa Monica Pier (at the foot of Arcadia Ter).

A sign posted just north of the Loews Santa Monica Beach Hotel marks the location of the original Muscle Beach. During the 1930s, this world-famous stretch of beachfront ignited a national fitness boom. Such noted musclemen as Jack LaLanne and Vic Tanny, as well as actor Steve "Hercules"

In *The Sting* (1973), Paul Newman operates the carousel and masterminds an elaborately set-up gambling operation

Reeves, worked out and performed on the beach platform. Their public shows became increasingly popular with onlookers—on some Sundays crowd of 10,000 assembled to watch buffed athletes practice and exhibit their strength. In 1958 Muscle Beach closed and later moved to Venice Beach (➔ p390), although there are efforts underway to restore it at the primary location.

Carousel Park is a favorite children's playground

Santa Monica Civic Auditorium

Santa Monica Civic Auditorium ㉖

Welton Becket, architect (1958).
1855 Main St.
☎(310) 458-8551; 393-9961.

Designed by the same architect who built the Los Angeles Music Center, this 3,500-seat auditorium hosts art exhibitions, trade shows and rock and jazz concerts. Almost every great name has played here, including such stars as David Bowie, Bob Dylan, Elton John, Bruce Springsteen, Rod Stewart, Prince, Jefferson Airplane, the Doors, Santana and many others.

On October 29, 1964, director Steve Binder filmed a legendary concert film *The T.A.M.I. Show* (Teenage Awards Music International), which set standard for future rock-and-roll documentaries. Among the performers were Chuck Berry, James Brown, Marvin Gaye, the Beach Boys, the Rolling Stones and the Supremes.

The Civic's most glorious period was from 1961 to 1968, when it was also the site of the Academy Awards ceremonies.

Next to the Civic Auditorium stands *Chain Reaction* (1991), a sculpture by Pulitzer-winning political cartoonist Paul Conrad. Its 26-foot-tall (8-m) atomic mushroom cloud, made of steel and copper chain, is a strong statement against nuclear arms.

Chain Reaction

Edgemar Development ㉗

Frank O Gehry and Associates, architect (1989).
2401 Main St.

In 1989 Frank Gehry transformed this former dairy and egg processing plant into a shopping complex containing a restaurant and small retail stores. He arranged a group of five low buildings around a central court and added three towers topped with angular forms. He also retained a portion of the old plant's wall on the street front and covered it with green tiles.

Main Street ㉘

Between Pico Blvd and Rose Ave.

At the turn of the 20th century this district, called Ocean Park, consisted of a seaside resort and a large amusement area (➔ p354). The attrac-

tions are long gone, and today this refurbished street is a popular shopping and dining district. Its relaxed, small town atmosphere attracts both visitors and locals, who find it pleasant for browsing, strolling or shopping. The street boasts a dynamic mix of mainstream and stylish stores, art galleries, antique shops and hip cafés and restaurants.

Parkhurst Building

Parkhurst Building ㉙

Norman F Marsh, architect (1927).
2940 Main St. **NRHP**

One of the most prominent city landmarks, this remarkable Spanish Colonial Revival building features an octagonal turret with ornate upper façade and intricate brickwork. Built in 1927 by realtor and former Venice mayor, C Gordon Parkhurst, this commercial building has been beautifully restored.

The Edgemar complex is organized around an open courtyard

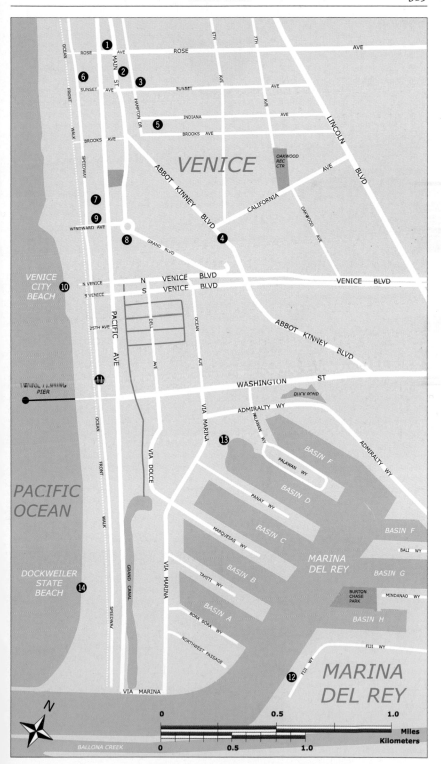

VENICE

OAKWOOD REC CTR

VENICE CITY BEACH

PACIFIC OCEAN

TENICE FISHING PIER

DOCKWEILER STATE BEACH

MARINA DEL REY

BASIN F
BASIN D
BASIN C
BASIN B
BASIN A
BASIN F
BASIN G
BASIN H

BURTON CHASE PARK

DUCK POND

BALLONA CREEK

N

0   0.5   1.0
Miles
Kilometers
0   0.5   1.0

Venice

One of the most diverse areas of Los Angeles, Venice is multiethnic and multicultural, noted for its creative, easy-going and free-wheeling residents. By the 1950s, the community's low rents attracted poets, actors, musicians and other members of the beatnik counterculture. During the 1960s, hippies and flower children appeared—among others,

Venice capital

Jim Morrison and the Doors lived here. The 1970s and 1980s were marked by the arrival of the New Agers. At the same time, Venice emerged as an important art scene, with many working artists opening their studios here. The area also became home to some of the most acclaimed contemporary architecture in Los Angeles.

Orson Welles's _Touch of Evil_ (1958) was filmed in Venice

The long decline of Venice reached its lowest point during the 1950s, when its seedy urban landscapes induced Orson Welles to use it as a location in his film _Touch of Evil_ (1958). A deteriorated neighborhood stood for a backwater Mexican border town, where the ruthless cop played by Welles ends up floating in a canal. While on honeymoon with her husband Charlton Heston (portraying a Mexican government official), Janet Leigh has some tough moments with a gang of drug racketeers.

fellow," as Chaplin often called him, was wearing his signature costume, including baggy trousers, tight coat, large shoes, derby and cane, topped off with a little moustache. In this 7-minute movie produced by Mack Sennett's Keystone Studio, the grimacing Chaplin wanders around during a children's car race, disrupting things and interfering with a newsreel shot.

Venice Canals

Of the original 16 miles (25,6 km) of canals that Abbot Kinney built in the early 1900s (➜ p354), only two miles remain today. The six surviving canals and four original bridges were restored in 1993 as a reminder of the area's colorful past. Only the Grand Canal has road access, and from the corner of Venice Blvd and Pacific Ave you can launch a boat and row along the hidden, serene waterways. Venice canals were used as a location for _Hollywood Homicide_ (2003), starring Harrison Ford.

Movie Star Homes

During the 1910s and 1920s, the Venice coastal community became a favorite playground for movie stars, who flocked to its attractions to relax and have fun. Some of the celebrities stayed at local hotels, such as the Waldorf Astoria, which was Chaplin's favorite, or St Marks, where Rudolph Valentino and Douglas Fairbanks were frequent guests. Other stars owned weekend retreats here, including Mary Pickford, Clara Bow, Norma Shearer, Janet Gaynor and Harold Lloyd.

The house of silent screen comedian Roscoe "Fatty" Arbuckle is still standing on 39 Thornton Ave, while Olivia de Havilland's former residence can be found on 17 Park Ave.

With its flamboyant and cosmopolitan atmosphere, today's Venice is still attractive to celebrities. At one point its residents included actors Nicolas Cage, Jane Fonda, Julia Roberts, Maria Bello and John Cusack.

Charlie Chaplin's character, the Tramp, was born in Venice

Kid Auto Races at Venice, California (1914) was the first film in which Charlie Chaplin appeared as the Tramp, his most famous screen character. "The little

The Venice canal scene, with small houses lining the waterways. The six canals and four original bridges were restored in 1993.

Ballerina Clown ❶

Northwest corner of Main St and Rose Ave.

This controversial 34-foot-high (10-m) sculpture, perched on the façade of the Venice Renaissance Building, is a well-known local landmark. It is a bizarre combination of a ballerina's body, appropriately clad in a tutu, and a huge male head with a sad clown's face.

The building's arcades and the column capitals are apparent references to the colonnades of the early Venice sidewalks on Windward Ave.

Ballerina Clown (1989) by Jonathan Borofsky

Chiat/Day Agency Building ❷

Frank O Gehry and Associates, architect (1991).
340 Main St.

Frank Gehry designed this building as a headquarters for Chiat/Day Advertising, a creative force behind the famous drum-beating Energizer bunny. Its Apple Macintosh 1984 television commercial caused a sensation when first aired during the Super Bowl.

The structure consists of three distinctive sections: to the left is a white, boat-shaped wing that houses staff offices, and to the right is a copper-clad executive building with a forest of abstract tree forms. The façade's central feature is a giant pair of

Frank Gehry's Chiat/Day Building with its signature binoculars

black binoculars by Claes Oldenburg and Coosje van Bruggen. Below this four-story sculpture, which became a well-known logo for the agency, is an entrance to the underground parking garage.

Gold's Gym ❸

360 Hampton Dr.
☎(310) 392-6004.
🕐 Mon-Fri 4am-midnight; Sat-Sun 5pm-11pm. Members only.
www.goldsgym.com/veniceca.

Also known as "the Mecca of Bodybuilding," this is the world-famous gym which produced generations of champion bodybuilders. It was founded in 1965 by Joe Gold, legendary bodybuilder and designer of workout machines. He sold it in 1969 and founded World Gym in 1977, now an international chain of about 650 clubs worldwide.

Gold's Gym was the site of numerous bodybuilding competitions, including the 1977 Mr America contest, where 85-years-old screen legend Mae West presented the trophies to the winners. Over the years, the gym's stellar membership included Kareem Abdul-Jabbar, Muhammad Ali, Wilt Chamberlain, Faye Dunaway, Jane Fonda, George Foreman, Mel Gibson, Magic Johnson, Dennis Rodman and Sylvester Stallone.

A street crossing sign near Gold's Gym on Hampton Dr

Gold's Gym
sign

at Sunset Ave warns drivers of passing hardbodies.

When Arnold Schwarzenegger arrived in Los Angeles in 1968, he started training at Gold's Gym under Joe Gold's supervision. Gold's Gym (at its original location on Pacific Ave) was the backdrop for the 1977 cult bodybuilding film *Pumping Iron*. The low-budget documentary was Schwarzenegger's film debut and shows him as he works out in an attempt to win the Mr Olympia title.

Abbot Kinney Blvd ❹

Named after the city's founder, Venice's main shopping street is perfect for outdoor browsing and shopping in a relaxed atmosphere. It features an eclectic blend of art galleries, design stores, antique and crafts shops, as well as casual cafés and coffee houses.

Arnold Schwarzenegger shows his muscles in bodybuilding classic *Pumping Iron* (1977)

Dennis Hopper Home

Eric Clapton Home

Spiller House

Dennis Hopper Home ❺

BAM, architects (1990).
330 Indiana Ave.
Private residence.

This stunning building belongs to Dennis Hopper—rebel, director, photographer and artist, as well as star of such cult movies as *Easy Rider* (1969), *Apocalypse Now* (1979) and *Blue Velvet* (1986). Situated in a gritty Venice neighborhood, the house stands like a metal fortress behind a white picket fence in front and razor wire in back. Architect Brian Murphy sheathed the exterior walls in unpainted corrugated steel with few windows, creating uninterrupted surfaces for displaying the actor's art collection.

Eric Clapton Home ❻

16 Paloma Ave.
Private residence.

The legendary British rock and blues guitarist and singer, member of such semi-

nal bands as the Yardbirds and Cream, Eric Clapton won multiple Grammys for his songwriting and also wrote scores for films, including the *Lethal Weapon* trilogy. He owned this house close to the beach for four years before he sold it in 2004.

Spiller House ❼

Frank O Gehry and Associates, architect (1980).
39 Horizon Ave.
Private residence.

Gehry's design called for cheap materials to achieve the rough, unfinished appearance of this three-level duplex. Built on a narrow lot, the house is wrapped in unpainted corrugated metal sheaths, with exposed timber framing the skylight.

Race Through the Clouds ❽

Steven Ehrlich Architects (1990).
77 Windward Circle.

What is now a paved traffic circle, between 1905 and 1929 was the Grand Lagoon,

around which were located the main Venice attractions. Of the three stucco buildings which architect Steven Ehrlich designed on the west side of today's Windward Circle, the most interesting is Race Through the Clouds. Its square façade and cylindrical volume are connected by metal gridwork and a neon loop, echoing the structure's namesake, once the world's largest roller coaster, that stood nearby.

Anjelica Huston and Robert Graham Home ❾

Robert Graham, architect.
Windward Ave.
Private residence.

Robert Graham is today one of the best known figurative sculptors in America, whose recent works include the new cathedral's great bronze doors and the statue of the Virgin Mary in downtown Los Angeles. Noted for his anatomically correct female bronzes, Graham here tried his hand in architecture, designing this house for his actress wife, Anjelica Huston. Daughter of the legendary director John Huston, Anjelica starred in such films as *The Adams Family* (1991) and *Prizzi's Honor* (1985), for which she won an Oscar for best supporting actress.

The house is separated from the sidewalk by a high terra-cotta-colored masonry wall which ensures privacy on one of the beach town's busiest streets.

Anjelica Huston and Robert Graham Home

Venice City Beach ⑩

Ocean Front Walk.
☎(310) 394-3266.

This beautiful, wide, sandy beach is especially good for swimming and surfing. The palm-lined shore is amazingly uncrowded, with all the attention (and people) going to the colorful Venice Boardwalk fronting the beach. The Boardwalk's winding path, which runs for miles, features an endless flow of scantily-clad joggers, bicyclists and rollerbladers.

Under the watchful eye: LA mounted police patrolling the beach

A musician performing on Venice Beach

Ocean Front Walk

A variety of bizarre characters wander past tarot tables and palm readers, tattoo parlors, sand sculptors, massage stands and hundreds of sidewalk vendors selling cheap goods. One of LA's wackiest shows, it features all kinds of street performers, including acrobats, chain saw jugglers, magicians, stand-up comedians and one-man bands.

Amid the ever-changing eccentric scene consisting of people-watchers, musicians, clowns and jugglers, there are several perennial street favorites: the turbanned, in-line skating guitarist Harry Parry; metallic-painted humanoid, fire eater Tony the Fireman (who breathes and rubs fire onto his body) and dancing husband and wife team Elton and Betty White (who offer a photo opportunity in exchange for a tip).

A hidden camera on the roof of Venice's Sidewalk Café enables internet users around the world to view the live carnival-like show of Ocean Front Walk. Check www.westland.net/beachcam.

This street circus was showcased in several movies, including *The Doors* (1991) and *L.A. Story* (1991), as well as television shows such as *Three's Company*.

Venice Beach Drum Circle
www.venicebeachdrumcircle.com.

A good vibe flows as drummers, percussion players,

A pantomimist entertains the curious on Ocean Front Walk

dancers and spectators assemble for lively concerts that often last well past sundown. Drum Circle has been a microcosm of Venice Beach culture for forty years, as the drummers, whose numbers reach into the hundreds, gather on weekend afternoons to dance to the beat. The circle's loud throbbing brings angry complaints from neighbors, who once circulated a petition requesting its relocation.

Venice Beach Drum Circle has been a major attraction for forty years, despite continuous objections from nearby residents

Workout at Muscle Beach

***Morning Shot* by Rip Cronk**

Muscle Beach
Ocean Front Walk, between 18th and 19th avenues.

This legendary outdoor gym, where muscle people pump iron under the watchful eye of the curious spectators, is the world-famous weightlifters spot. Since the late 1950s, when bodybuilders moved from Santa Monica to Venice Beach, this workout area was called "the pit."

Adjacent to Muscle Beach are the pickup basketball courts where Woody Harrelson and Wesley Snipes played in *White Man Can't Jump* (1992).

The Doors' birthplace
The large 1991 mural of Jim Morrison, lead singer of the rock group the Doors, is painted on a wall facing the beach where the legendary group was formed.

During the summer of 1965, recent UCLA graduate Ray Manzarek was out at the beach in Venice when he met his old friend Jim Morrison. As Manzarek remembers, "Jim said he had been writing some songs. So we sat down on the beach and I asked him to sing some of them. He sang *Moonlight Drive*. I said, 'That's it.'"

Art in Venice

With its multitude of studios and galleries, Venice is a dynamic artistic community without equal in Los Angeles. Many renowned LA artists have worked and lived in the area for years, including Ed Moses, Charles Arnoldi and Billy Al Bengston.

Venice Art Walk
More than 60 artists' studios can be explored on this charitable annual event that began in 1979 to aid the Venice Family Clinic, which provides free medical care to the homeless. It is a self-guided walking tour of the private working studios and homes of acclaimed Venice artists that takes place on the fourth Sunday each May. For info call ☎(310) 392-8630.

Venice Murals
Venice has scores of street murals, which can be viewed on a guided tour organized by the Social and Public Art Resource Center (SPARC). For information call ☎(310) 822-9560.

Venice and its murals were strikingly featured in the 1983 remake of *Breathless*, starring Richard Gere. In 1980, French director and local resident Agnès Varda made *Murs, Murs,* a full-length documentary about Venice's murals.

Norton House

Norton House ⑪
Frank O Gehry and Associates, architect (1984).
2509 Ocean Front Walk.
Private residence.

The building's most remarkable feature is a front tower inspired by nearby lifeguard stations, with raised wood panels that shield the small study from direct sunlight. It overlooks the beach and the crowded boardwalk, acting simultaneously as a screen to increase residents' privacy. Gehry used a variety of building materials—notice the *torii* behind the gate made of wooden logs.

At the time he designed this three-story beach house for a screenwriter and his artist wife, Gehry's office was on the Venice Boardwalk, just minutes away.

Venice mural *Homage to a Starry Knight* (1990) by Rip Cronk

With 10,000 moorings, Marina del Rey is the world's largest artificial small-craft harbor

Flying model aircraft at Dockweiler State Beach, one of the least crowded beaches in LA County

Marina del Rey

The marshlands of La Ballona were a haven for duck hunters before they were transformed into a recreational harbor. The development was dedicated in 1965, boasting the world's largest manmade small-boat harbor. The Marina's giant residential towers and apartment complexes seem to attract mostly young, single professionals, offering them a variety of recreational attractions.

This lively painted lifeguard tower at Mother's Beach is the work of local artist Rip Cronk

Fisherman's Village ⑫

13755 Fiji Way.
☎(310) 823 5411.

This is Marina del Rey's sole tourist attraction, a replica of a New England fishing town, engulfed by South-Seas foliage. Located at the south end of Fiji Way, it offers a great view of the harbor, featuring gift shops, restaurants and cafés. Lighthouse Plaza is

the site of free, year-round live jazz concerts (every Sunday 2pm to 5pm, weather permitting).

Marina del Rey has been the setting for many television series, including *Charlie's Angels, Mission Impossible, Melrose Place* and *Beverly Hills 90210*. The widely popular beach drama *Baywatch* was inspired by the County Lifeguard Baywatch patrol, whose real boats are docked south of Fisherman's Village. Among the movies filmed here are the political thriller *Enemy of the State* (1998), starring Will Smith, and *The Parent Trap*, Disney's 1998 remake of its famous comedy.

Mother's Beach ⑬

Admiralty Way at Via Marina.
☎(310) 821-0555.

A favorite with families, this beach was so named because it is perfect for small children. This is the only county

beach with no waves. Its calm waters are safe for handicapped people as well, who can ride a ramp into the water on their wheelchairs. Swimmers, however, should check the water condition because of harbor pollution; call ☎(800) 432-5229 for info.

Dockweiler State Beach ⑭

Vista del Mar.
☎(310) 322-5008; 372-2166.

If you are looking for solitude, this is the place to go. Jets taking off from LAX fly overhead every few minutes—the reason this clean, white-sand beach is not swamped with people. It is one of the widest and cleanest beaches in Los Angeles County, and the only one with fire rings for those who like to cook on the sand. Nude sunbathers gather at the southern portion of the beach, although nudity was recently officially banned.

Fisherman's Village in Marina del Rey is a replica of a New England fishing town

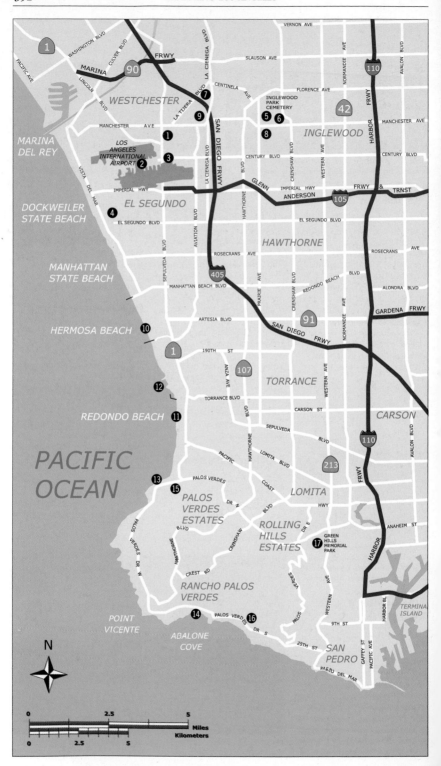

LAX Illuminated Columns

Old Town Music Hall

Loyola Theater ❶

Clarence J Smale, architect (1946).
8610 S Sepulveda Blvd.

Often described as Baroque-Streamline Moderne, this remarkable movie house served as a preview theater for 20th Century-Fox. Designed to attract attention of the passing motorists, the building's façade is dominated by a 60-foot-tall (18-m) swan's-neck tower. This neon-decked sign, the triangular marquee, ticket booth and etched glass doors are the only remnants of the theater's glory days, since the luxurious auditorium has been converted into offices.

LAX Theme Building ❷

Paul Williams, architect (1961).
LA International Airport.
☎(310) 215-5151.
🕐daily 11am-10pm. 🚩

Soaring 70 feet (21 m) above the runways, a flying-saucer structure houses an intergalactic Encounter Restaurant, with many "futuristic" dishes and cocktails on the menu. Its observation desk offers exciting views of aircraft takeoff and landing and is also a great place for stargazing. The building was prominently featured in the opening scenes of *California Suite* (1978).

The world's fifth busiest airport is used as the backdrop for NBC's *LAX* television series, starring Heather Locklear and Blair Underwood. In the action thriller *Speed* (1994), Sandra Bullock drives a public bus in circles at the

Los Angeles International Airport before it hits an airplane on the runway, creating a huge explosion. The airport scenes in *Collateral* (2004), staring Tom Cruise, were shot here at Bradley International terminal.

LAX Illuminated Columns ❸

Along W Century Blvd.

Designed by architect Ted Tokio Tanaka in 2000 and called an "Electronic Stonehenge," these 30 illuminated pylons provide a pathway to Los Angeles International Airport (LAX). At the airport entrance, they form a towering ring of frosted glass surfaces. The pylons' height gradually raises from 25 feet to 100 feet (8 to 25 m), suggesting an airplane takeoff. In a light program that quickly became popular with Angelenos, the glass columns continually change colors, controlled by a computer program.

Old Town Music Hall ❹

140 Richmond St, El Segundo.
☎(310) 322-2592.

Built in 1922 and formerly known as the State Theater, this 188-seat movie house is the only theater in LA where you can hear old-fashioned live organ sound. It comes from a 1925 Mighty Wurlitzer pipe organ, which contains 26 ranks, 2,000 pipes and 244 keys on four keyboards. Beside mimicking 268 musical instruments such as bells, drums, cymbals, clarinet and trumpet, it can also create more unusal sound effects, including a genuine ambulance siren, machine guns, horses' hooves, surf and smashing pottery. It is used either as accompaniment to a silent movie or before the screening of old-time Hollywood films, mostly musicals from the 1920s to 1950s.

The California Assembly declared the theater a living museum for classic films and music of the silent era.

Night view of the landmark Theme Building, with its distinctive four spidery legs, illuminated by a gradually changing light show

Inglewood Park Cemetery ❺

720 E Florence Ave.
☎(310) 412-6500.
🕐Mon-Fri 8:30am-5pm; Sat
8:30am-4pm. 🦽

Founded in 1905, this is one of the largest cemeteries in the LA area. With its tall palm trees and Mission-style buildings, it has a typical Southern California look.

The cemetery's most imposing structure is the Art Deco-style Mausoleum of the Golden West, designed by Walter E Erkes in the 1930s. Its interior is immersed in soft light coming from the colored glass roof and stained-glass windows located at the end of each hall. Designed by the Judson Studios, the colorful windows depict scenes from early California history.

The interior of the Mausoleum of the Golden West was used in the fight scene between Karen Black and William Atherton in *The Day of the Locust* (1974)

Sunset Misson Mausoleum

Ella Fitzgerald (1917-1996)

Legendary jazz singer, known as the "first lady of song," Ella Fitzgerald was one of the best-selling vocalists in history. The wide range of her voice and broad repertoire earned her 13 Grammy Awards and brought international fame. Her famous "scat" singing, where she improvised as a musical instrument and used nonsense syllables, was much imitated.

Mausoleum of the Golden West

Betty Grable (1916-1973)

During World War II, actress Betty Grable was voted the number one pin-up girl by American servicemen. Her famous 1943 photograph, in a white bathing suit, looking over her shoulder with a smile, made her the new Hollywood sex symbol. Her big break came with the lead in *Million Dollar Legs* (1939), a film that gave Grable her nickname (although the film's title refers to a race horse). Fox insured her shapely legs with Lloyds of London for $1 million. Grable made a string of popular Technicolor musicals in the 1940s, and was ranked the country's top box-office attraction and the highest-paid woman in America. A heavy smoker, Grable died of lung cancer at 56.

Ray Charles (1930-2004)

Billed as "the Genius," singer, pianist and composer Ray Charles profoundly influenced and transformed American pop music. With his early recordings, which blended rhythm and blues with gospel, he laid the groundwork for rock 'n' roll and soul music. Among his major hits are *Georgia on My Mind* (1960), *Hit the Road Jack* (1961) and *I Can't Stop Loving You*, the biggest selling single of 1962. Charles had 12 singles in the Top 10 and won 12 Grammy Awards.

Born Ray Charles Robinson, he dropped his last name to avoid confusion with boxer Sugar Ray Robinson (who is buried at the same cemetery). Charles contracted glaucoma at the age of five and com-

pletely lost his sight at seven. Throughout his life he wore signature dark glasses, which contributed to his mystique. His life story is told in a biopic *Ray* (2004), starring Jamie Foxx in a title role.

Grounds

Sugar Ray Robinson (1921-1989)

Voted "Fighter of the Century" by boxing authorities, Robinson was six times a world champion, once as a welterweight and five times as a middleweight. Born Walker Smith Jr, he was too young to legally fight so he used the amateur certificate of another boxer, named Ray Robinson. Under his new name, which he kept throughout his 25-year career, Robinson won 175 of 202 bouts, 109 by knockout.

Gypsy Rose Lee (1914-1970)

One of the best-known strippers of all time, Lee performed refined striptease acts in burlesque houses across the country, becoming a national celebrity. Once she was accused of performing without clothes. "I wasn't naked," Lee defended herself, "I was completely covered by a blue spotlight." She wrote a best-selling autobiography *Gypsy* (1957), which was made into a Broadway musical hit in 1959 and has been revived several times. Hollywood made two movies based on the book, in 1962 and 1994.

Norman Spencer Chaplin (July 7-July 10, 1919)

The infant son of actor Charlie Chaplin and his first wife, Mildred Harris, was born deformed and lived only three days. The child's marker, which is one of the most moving in the cemetery, identifies him simply as The Little Mouse.

Mausoleum of the Golden West

Mausoleum interior

Monument in the cemetery

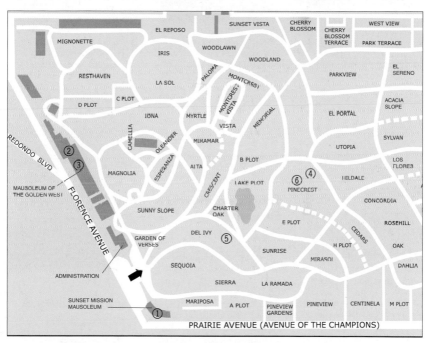

Sanctuary of Bells, crypt 1063
①

Sanctuary of Dawn, crypt A-78
②

Sanctuary of Eternal Love, crypt A-32 ③

Pinecrest Section, lot 1087, grave 8 ④

Del Ivy Section, lot 496, Grave 3 ⑤

Pinecrest Section, Lot 24, Grave 1 ⑥

Marquee and tower of the Academy Theater   **The Great Western Forum**

Academy Theater ❻

S Charles Lee, architect (1939).
3141 Manchester Blvd.

Considered the greatest Streamline Moderne achievement of prolific theater designer S Charles Lee, the Academy features many hallmarks of the style, including glass bricks and interlocking, stucco-sheathed cylinders. It is dominated by a 125-foot-high (38-m), spiral-finned tower, topped with a neon globe. The landmark building is now used as a church.

Pann's ❼

Armét and Davis, architects (1958).
6710 La Tijera Blvd.
☎(310) 670-1441.
🕑daily 7am-11pm. 🏃

This is one of the few remaining (and the only one left mostly intact) of the countless examples of Coffee Shop Modern designs built in LA in the decade immediately after World War II. All the details of the futuristic style, called "Googie" (➜ p98), such as glass walls, geometric accents, multicolored uphol-

stery and open kitchen are present here.

Lovingly restored in 1991 by the same family that has owned and operated it since 1958, Pann's retains the angled gravel roof, animated neon sign, space-age light fixtures and exotic plantings. Even the menu racks and the napkin holders are preserved, tracing back to the days when Marilyn Monroe was a regular here.

In the opening scenes of *Bewitched* (2005), Nicole Kidman and Michael Caine are having lunch at Pann's.

The Great Western Forum ❽

3900 Manchester Blvd.

Until the opening of Staples Center in downtown LA in 1999, the 17,000-seat Forum was home to the LA Lakers basketball team and LA Kings hockey team. The Lakers won six NBA championships while playing here. During the 1984 Olympic Games, the basketball competition was held at the Forum. The stadi-

um also hosted concerts by some of the most famous rock and pop stars. The Rolling Stones, Led Zeppelin, Elvis Presley, David Bowie, Bruce Springsteen and Prince all performed here.

The arena was acquired in 2000 by a church and today is one of the largest places of worship in the country.

Randy's Donuts

Randy's Donuts ❾

805 W Manchester Blvd.
☎(310) 645-4707.
🕑open 24 hours. 🏃

This programmatic architectural (➜ p98) landmark was once part of the Big Donut Drive-In chain, founded in the 1950s by the small doughnut shop owner Russ Wendell. By placing a giant doughnut on the roofs of his establishments, Wendell hoped to ensure the attention of the passing motorists. Today known as Randy's, this LA icon has been seen in countless music videos, television productions and movies, including *The Golden Child* (1986), *Earth Girls Are Easy* (1988), *Mars Attacks!* (1996) and *Volcano* (1997).

Pann's is the best remaining example of the "Googie" architecture

South Bay

The area called the South Bay is comprised of a string of beach towns that runs south from Los Angeles International Airport (LAX) to Palos Verdes Peninsula. Characterized by an unpretentious, easygoing atmosphere, these communities are the prototype of the outdoorsy Southern California lifestyle as perceived by the rest of the world. Although it does not offer much in terms of art and architecture, the area attracts visitors who enjoy a variety of beach activities.

South Bay beach scene

Firmly embedded in California surf culture, the South Bay was immortalized during the 1960s by the Beach Boys' song *Surfin' USA*:

All over Manhattan
and down Doheny Way,
Everybody's gone surfin', surfin' USA.
. . .
Haggerties and Swamies, Pacific Palisades,
San Onofre and Sunset, Redondo Beach, LA,
All over La Jolla, at Waimia Bay,
Everybody's gone surfin', surfin' USA

Manhattan Beach

Anchored by its pier, downtown Manhattan Beach is the commercial center of this casual beachtown, lined with shops selling beach wares, as well as cozy restaurants, pubs and cafés. The city's main draw and a favorite site for people-watching is the Strand, a popular two-lane strip open to skaters, bicyclists and pedestrians. At the end of the 900 foot (300 m) pier is the Roundhouse Aquarium, which features tanks filled with marine creatures common to Southern California.

This is the beach where the Beach Boys used to hang out in the 1960s. (They did not surf the only surfer among them was Dennis Wilson; the group's leader, Brian, was scared to death of the water and never even tried to surf.) Manhattan Beach, with its gorgeous beach town scenery and stunning views of the ocean, is the backdrop for the romantic thriller *Tequila Sunrise* (1988), starring Mel Gibson and Michelle Pfeiffer.

Hermosa Beach

Rollerblade and skateboard traffic is allowed at Hermosa Beach's newly renovated pedestrian area at the end of Pier Ave. Lined with palm trees, this rollicking strip is brimming with non-stop activity at its equipment rental shops and packed outdoor bars and eateries.

The Surfers Walk of Fame, consisting of bronze plaques cemented into the Hermosa

View of Manhattan State Beach with the 900-foot (300-m) pier

Beach Pier, honors local surfing history.

Redondo Beach

Redondo's main attraction is Seaport Village, a double-tiered, U-shaped pier that features a variety of shops, galleries and restaurants. One of the oldest piers in Southern California, it was built in 1889 and went through various reincarnations, the last one after a big storm and fire caused substantial damage in 1988. You can rent fishing gear and buy live bait here if you wish to join the scores of others who fish off the pier.

Surfing was introduced to California at Redondo Beach in 1907, when George Freeth, a native of Hawaii, demonstrated the ancient Polynesian sport of kings. A bronze bust, located at the pier, commemorates this pioneer surfer (➔ p62).

The renovated, pedestrian-friendly area in Hermosa Beach

Fishing off the pier at Redondo Beach

Hermosa City Beach ⑩

☎(310) 372-2166.

This wide, white-sand beach is good for surfing and all kinds of beach sports. It is the beach-volleyball capital of the coast, packed with a predominantly young crowd, mostly partying college kids.

Redondo State Beach ⑪

☎(310) 372-2166.

Stretching two miles south from the King Harbor Pier, this narrow, sandy beach is popular with families. It is also busy with surfers, joggers and volleyball players.

Seaside Lagoon ⑫

200 Portofino Way, King Harbor, Redondo Beach.
☎(310) 318-0681.
🕐10am-5:45pm. Ⓢ
www.redondo.org/seasidelagoon

This is a popular attraction between Memorial Day and Labor Day. The open swimming pool with heated ocean water and sandy bottom features a large sand area for sunbathing, children's play equipment, volleyball courts, barbecues and picnic tables.

Palos Verdes Peninsula

Featuring large Spanish-style villas and exuberant gardens, Palos Verdes Peninsula is an exclusive hillside community with some of the most expensive real estate in Los Angeles. The area was bare hills when a group of developers envisioned it as a "Millionaire's Colony" in the 1920s, with large estates, parks, clubs and three model villages. Noisy wild peacock flocks, which roam the neighborhood parks since the 1920s, became the area's distinguished attraction.

This is one of the best places to experience nature in Los Angeles, with sea cliffs, secluded coves, tide pools, as well as sprawling hills, rugged canyons and hiking trails. Palos Verdes Peninsula also offers stunning panoramic views of the coastline and some of the most spectacular scenic drives in Southern California.

Malaga Cove ⑬

Path to the beach at Flat Rock Point, 600 block of Paseo del Mar, Palos Verdes Estates.
☎(310) 372-2166.

The only sandy beach on the Palos Verdes peninsula is easily accessible from Paseo del Mar, with a paved path leading down to the beach. A favorite with surfers and scuba divers, it is also a popular spot to explore tide pools.

Abalone Cove Beach ⑭

5970 Palos Verdes Dr S, Rancho Palos Verdes.
☎(310) 377-1222.
🕐weekdays 12 noon-4pm; weekends 9am-5pm. Parking fee.

This secluded, narrow rocky beach, easily accessible from the parking lot, is great for swimming, surfing and snorkeling. An ecological reserve boasting large tide pools, it is an excellent spot for sea life exploration.

Serene rocky shoreline of Abalone Cove Beach

Malaga Cove Plaza ⑮

Webber, Staunton and Spaulding, architects (1924).
Palos Verdes Dr W (between Via Corta and Via Chico), Palos Verdes Estates.

This picturesque two-story colonnaded building and semicircular brick arch over Via Chico were completed in 1925. Of the four commercial centers planned for the area, this Spanish Colonial Revival structure was the only one built. Note the color and pattern variations of decoratively painted beams in the ceiling of the arcade. In the plaza's center is Neptune Fountain, a two-thirds scale replica of Giambologna's 1563 original of the same name in Bologna, Italy.

Neptune Fountain in the Malaga Cove Plaza

Wayfarers Chapel ⑯

Lloyd Wright, architect (1949-51).
5755 Palos Verdes Dr South, Rancho Palos Verdes.
☎(310) 377-1650.
www.wayfarerschapel.org.
⏰daily 7am-5pm. 🐾

Commissioned by the Swedenborgian Church of New Jerusalem, Wayfarer's Chapel is Lloyd Wright's most recognized and critically acclaimed work. Sitting on a cliff near Portuguese Bend and now almost completely covered by trees, it embodies the architect's affinity for integrating buildings with landscapes. Wright, who was a son of America's greatest architect, created a web-like

Glass-enclosed Wayfarers Chapel is surrounded by redwoods

interior using geometric forms that resemble tree branches, honeycombs and snowflakes. Built of Y-shaped redwood frames, glass panels and Palos Verdes stone, the transparent chapel provides views of the ocean and surrounding wooded hills, linking the outer and inner spaces.

The chapel is a popular tourist site, attracting half a million visitors annually. Almost 800 wedding ceremonies take place here every year, 300 of them performed for couples from Japan.

In the 1987 movie *Innerspace*, Dennis Quaid and Meg Ryan's wedding took place here. The actors were married four years later in real life, although not in the chapel. Among other celebrities who were married here are Jayne Mansfield, Dennis Hopper and Brian Wilson.

Green Hills Memorial Park ⑰

27501 S Western Ave, Rancho Palos Verdes.
☎(310) 831-0311.
⏰daily 6am-6pm.

Charles Bukowski
(1920-1994)

A writer-poet of international fame, Charles Bukowski was the hard-drinking, hard-smoking laureate of underground Los Angeles. His autobiographical novel *Post Office* (1971) and other works inspired the films *Tales of Ordinary Madness* (1981) and *Barfly* (1987).

Daniel Boon (1958-1985)

Legendary frontman of the hardcore band the Minutemen, Daniel Boon left an enduring legacy with his speed, energy and passion. Formed in San Pedro in 1980, the seminal punk band remained close to their hometown and often mentioned it in their songs. Boon's death in a van accident while on tour in Arizona marked the end of the group.

Ocean View Section, plot 875, space I

Lake View Lawn, plot 365, space B

San Pedro

San Pedro is an old seaport community with a long maritime tradition that goes back to the days when it was a major trade center for hides and beef tallow. It became LA's main port of entry after it defeated Santa Monica in the political battle to be the "free harbor." With federal funding secured, work began in 1899 on construction of a huge breakwater and a port that is now the busiest in the United States and the third largest in the world (Hong Kong and Shanghai are the largest). San Pedro retains the Mediterranean flavor of the old port town, many of its mariners and fishermen being of Greek and Yugoslav descent.

Korean Friendship Bell ❶

Angels Gate Park.
3601 S Gaffey St.
☎(310) 548-7705. ⚐

The Korean Friendship Bell, a Bicentennial gift to the United States presented by South Korea in 1976, is the largest bell in the United States. Inscribed with Korean characters, the 17-ton cast bronze giant is a replica of an 8th-century original. Since it does not have a clapper, the bell is rung by a heavy log—but only three times a year: on New Year's Day, Independence Day and Korean Liberation Day, August 15.

The Bell is housed in a pagoda-like structure, standing on a hilltop in Angels Gate Park. The area was formerly a military reservation where the harbor's defense artillery was installed until 1944. Many of the huge gun emplacements can still be seen; one of the batteries houses the Fort MacArthur Military Museum.

The Bell can be seen in a number of movies and television productions, including *Dragnet* (1987), *A Few Good Men* (1992) and *The Usual Suspects* (1995).

Korean Friendship Bell

Point Fermin Lighthouse ❷

807 W Paseo Del Mar.
☎(310) 241-0684.
⏱Tue-Sun 1-4pm. ⓢfree. NRHP

Sitting on a cliff overlooking the ocean, this scenic park offers stunning views of the coast and Santa Catalina Island. The point was named in 1793 by British explorer George Vancouver in honor of Father Fermin Francisco de Lausen, who was president of all the California missions. It is the site of one of California's oldest lighthouses, an Eastlake structure with a four-sided tower. The lighthouse was built in 1874 from bricks and lumber shipped around Cape Horn. Its navigational light remained lit until December 7th, 1941. The building is now restored and open to the public. Access to the lighthouse tower is by tour only.

Point Fermin Lighthouse

Cabrillo Beach ❸

40th St and Stephen M White Dr, San Pedro.
☎(310) 372-2166.

Popular with families for its calm waters, this beach is also great at low tide when its tide pools are teeming with marine life. This is one of the best places around to see the grunion running (➜ p61). You can watch them on your own or can join a docent for a lecture at the Cabrillo Marine Aquarium and then walk to the beach to see the little fish spawning. For info call ☎(310) 548-7562.

Cabrillo Marine Aquarium ❹

Frank O Gehry and Associates, architect (1981).
3720 Stephen M White Dr.
☎(310) 548-7562.
⏱Tue-Fri 12 noon-5pm, Sat-Sun 10am-5pm. ⓢfree.

The aquarium's exhibits are organized around three major environments: rocky shores, sandy beaches and mud flats, and open ocean. They emphasize the diversity, adaptations and ecological relationships of local marine life. Each section shows common animals and plants, most of them live and displayed in 35 large aquariums. On display in the whale room are a 28-foot (8,5-m) whale baby and the skeleton of a one-year-old Pacific gray whale.

The Warner Grand's lavish interior retains original decorations

The theater's façade is modestly decorated with geometric patterns and stylized floral motifs. The lavish marquee and a Moderne neon sign have been recently restored.

Warner Grand Theatre ❺

Billed by movie mogul Jack Warner as "the castle of your dreams," this lovely movie palace opened on January 20, 1931 with a screening of *Going Wild*, attended by stars Barbara Stanwyck and Joan Blondell. Architect B Marcus Priteca and designer Anthony B Heinsbergen intended this modestly-sized neighborhood theater to be a flagship example of Art Deco Moderne.

The theater's exuberant lobby, adorned with decorative stenciling and plaster ornaments, features an ornate ceiling, etched-glass chandeliers and tiled fountains. An elegant double staircase leads to lavish mezzanine lounges.

The opulent 1,500-seat auditorium, still with its original decoration and furnishings, is very well preserved. The theater contains a vaudeville stage house and an orchestra pit designed for up to 14 musicians, although it never presented the live acts with the movies. The 30-by-50-foot (10 x 15 m) screen is set back behind the rich drapes to allow for an open, unobstructed stage.

The theater's most spectacular feature is the intricate auditorium ceiling. Made of molded and carved plaster and painted to resemble wood, its dazzling appearance is achieved by elaborate blue and green stenciling, and gold, silver, bronze and copper leafing.

Purchased by the city in 1995 and restored, the theater now shows live performances, concerts and classic films.

B Marcus Priteca, architect (1931).
478 W 6th St, San Pedro.
☎(310) 548-7672.
NRHP

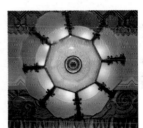

Flamboyant, etched-glass light fixtures with opulent Art Deco detailing adorn the theater

The ornate organ screens and rectangular proscenium arch are finished in metallic shades of gold, silver and copper

Soaring 45 feet (13,5 m) above the audience, the Warner Grand's immense ceiling is a magnificent sunburst extravaganza

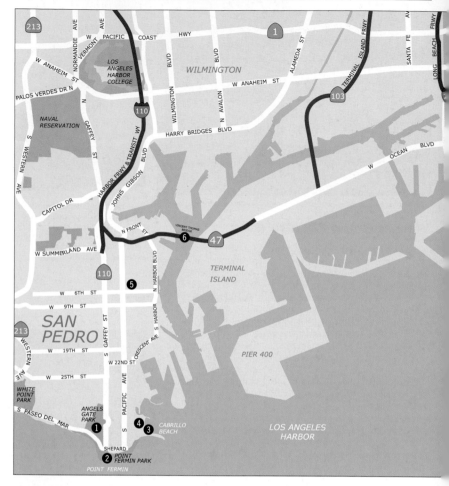

Vincent Thomas Bridge

Vincent Thomas Bridge ❻

This 6,050-foot (1.844-m) bridge, which connects San Pedro to the Terminal Island industrial zone, rises 35 stories above the nation's largest and the third-busiest port in the world. It was opened in 1963 and today is the fourth-longest suspension span in California. The landmark structure is covered with several coats of specially designed sea-green paint. The final coat is flecked with silver, giving the bridge its unique iridescent glow. It takes a crew of nine workers 12 years to completely paint the bridge.

Long Beach

Long Beach is the second largest city in LA County and the fifth largest in the state. Named for its 5.5-mile (9-km) stretch of white sand, it was founded in the 1880s as a seaside resort. Its famous Pike Amusement Park, called Walk of a Thousand Lights, with a roller coaster and other draws, became one of the most popular attractions in Southern California. The city's population was so dominated by Midwestern transplants that it gained the nickname "Iowa by the Sea." Long Beach thrived with a growing harbor and the oil boom of the 1920s. Petroleum is still a major industry

here, with several hundred wells in operation. Some of the oil drilling platforms are visible from the shore, carefully guised in pastel garb.

In 1933 Long Beach was devastated by a 6.3-magnitude earthquake, which killed 120 people and caused extensive damage. The subsequent building activity in downtown resulted in a number of Art Deco buildings—the prevalent style of the era.

Architect Edward H Fickett designed the Los Angeles Harbor (Cargo and Passenger Terminals), for which he received the AIA Outstanding Aesthetic Design Award. Port of Los Angeles is the busiest in the nation and the third largest in the world.

Aquarium of the Pacific is home to more than 12,000 ocean animals representing 550 species

Rancho Los Alamitos ❼

6400 Bixby Hill Rd.
☎(562) 431-3541.
🕐Wed-Sun 1-5pm (last tour at 4pm). ⑤free. NRHP

Rancho Los Alamitos (Ranch of the Little Cottonwoods) dates back to 1790, when Manuel Nieto, a Spanish foot soldier, received the area as part of a 300,000-acre (120.000-ha) land grant for his retirement. The original adobe was built in 1806 as a shelter for *vaqueros* of the Nieto family. The structure was changed by later additions and enlarged many times through its history. It is considered the oldest domestic structure in the state.

With its historic buildings and grounds, Rancho Los Alamitos recounts the history of the early days of ranching and farming in Southern California. The grounds contain a working blacksmith shop and six early 20th-century barns featuring original farm tools and equipment. There are exhibits of old spurs, bridles, harnesses and veterinary instruments, dating from the 18th and 19th centuries.

Long Beach Aquarium of the Pacific ❽

100 Aquarium Way.
☎(562) 590-3100.
www.aquariumofpacific.org.
🕐daily 10am-6pm. ⑤

Opened in 1998, this $117-million attraction is one of the largest and technologically most advanced aquariums ever designed. Its 17 major habitats and 30 smaller tanks are filled with over a million gallons of salt water. More than 12,000 live marine animals representing 550 species inhabit the Aquarium.

As they enter the building, visitors encounter a life-size model of the blue whale, the largest living creature on the planet, which hangs from the ceiling. The marine life exhibits focus on the three major regions of the Pacific Ocean.

The Southern California and Baja Gallery features a kelp forest, sea lions, seals and endangered turtles. Its three-story high *Predator* exhibit features leopard sharks, barracuda, giant sea bass and other predators.

The ice cold waters of the Northern Pacific Gallery are home to giant Pacific octopus, sea stars, sea otters and giant Japanese spider crabs, as well as puffins, murres and other diving birds, which nest overhead.

The most fascinating is the Tropical Pacific Gallery, with its warm water, coral lagoons and deep reefs bursting with colorful sea creatures, including blue-spotted stingray, guineafowl puffer and yellow cardinalfish.

West Coast sea nettle in *Jellies: Phantoms of the Deep* exhibit

Planet Ocean ❾

Long Beach Arena.
300 E Ocean Ave.

Called by *Guinness Book of Records* the largest mural in the world, artist Wyland's *Planet Ocean* covers 116,000 sq ft (11.000 m²) of the Long Beach Arena's curving walls.

It features life-size images of marine creatures indigenous to Southern California, including gray and blue whales, orcas, bottlenose dolphins, sea lions and numerous fish species.

Planet Ocean (Whaling Wall Number 33) by Wyland (1992)

Skinny House ⑩

708 Gladys Ave.
Private residence.

Ripley's Believe It or Not!
calls this three-story, 860-
square-foot (77-m²) house the
thinnest in the nation. Constructed by Nelson Rummond
in 1932 as the result of a bet,
this English Tudor-style cottage is squeezed on a tiny lot
measuring only 10 by 50 feet
(3 x 17 m).

Cruising along Naples' canals on an authentic Venetian gondola

Skinny House is only 10 ft wide

St Anthony's Church ⑪

Emmet Martin and Laurence Weller,
architects; remodel by Barker and
Ott (1952).
600 Olive Ave

This modest, gable-roofed
church was remodeled in
1952 with the addition of two
extravagant towers. The
church's most remarkable
feature is a large mosaic

depicting the Virgin Mary's
assumption into heaven,
observed by Pope Pius XII
and two local church officials. Designed in Rome, the
mosaic took nine months to
assemble and three months
to install on the façade.

Villa Riviera ⑫

Richard D King, architect (1928).
800 E Ocean Blvd.
Private residences. NRHP

Curving along Ocean Blvd,
this impressive Tudor Gothic
structure was erected in 1929
as a luxury oceanfront apartment building. During the
1930s, it was briefly owned
by silent film star Norma Talmadge. The villa's signature
elements—dormed, pitched
copper roof and pointy
octagonal tower—became
distinguishing features of the
city's skyline. Restored and
seismically strengthened in

1989, the 16-story landmark
was the tallest building in
Long Beach until the 1980s.

Naples ⑬

Consisting of three islands
in the middle of man made
Alamitos Bay, Naples is a
charming residential neighborhood of eclectic architecture, both traditional and
modern. Developed on
marshlands between 1903
and 1905, this upscale water-
side community was intended to front on a series of
canals, although they cannot
be found in its namesake in
Italy. You can take a ride in
one of 10 custom built Venetian gondolas, but the best
way to explore the canals
and marinas is strolling
around on the Italian-named
streets. To book a cruise, call
Gondola Gateway, ☎(562)
433-9595.

The large mosaic on St Anthony's Church façade

Villa Riviera is one of Long Beach's landmarks

1126 Queens Highway.
☎(562) 435-3511.
www.queenmary.com.
🕐daily 10am–6pm; extended
hours in summer. ⑤ ♠ 🏴 NRHP
☛Royal Historic guided tour; self-
guided shipwalk tour.

Queen Mary ⑭

Spanning more than 1,000 feet (311 m) in length, weighing more than 81,000 gross tons and boasting 12 decks,
the *Queen Mary* is the largest, fastest and most luxurious
ocean liner ever built. Named after the wife of the British
King George V, it is the last survivor from the era of the
great super liners. After completing 1,001 Atlantic crossings, she was retired from regular passenger service in
1967. The ship was purchased by the city of Long Beach
and, after a three-year renovation, converted into a major
tourist attraction. It features the luxury 365-room hotel,
situated in the original staterooms, and a variety of
restaurants and salons. More than 1.5 million visitors each
year stroll the decks and explore the ship's many facets.

Built for Cunard, the preeminent steamship company of
its time, the *Queen Mary* was a marvel of technology,
craftsmanship and luxury. When the ship embarked on
her maiden voyage from Southampton to New York City
on May 27, 1936, she was filled with more than 3,000
passengers and crew members.

During World War II the *Queen
Mary* was transformed into a
troopship, camouflaged with
gray paint and nicknamed
"The Gray Ghost" for her
astonishing speed. Hitler
offered the equivalent of
$250,000 and Germany's high-
est military honor to the U-
boat captain who could sink
her. By the end of the war, the
Queen Mary had carried more
than 800,000 servicemen and
set a still standing record for
the most passengers carried in
one crossing—over 16,000.

Among the celebrities and dignitaries who traveled on
her were Charlie Chaplin, Mary Pickford, Douglas Fairbanks, Alfred Hitchcock, Clark Gable, Marlene Dietrich,
Joan Crawford, Fred Astaire, newlyweds Elizabeth Taylor
and Nicky Hilton, and the Duke and Duchess of Windsor.

The Art of the RMS Queen Mary permanent exhibit features original works of art from the 1930s, including
paintings and sculptures, as well as representative examples of decorative glass panels, ornamental woodwork,
textiles and other furnishings.

The *Queen Mary* has been featured in countless films
since she docked here in 1967. Her interiors stood in for
SS *Poseidon* on its fateful voyage chronicled by *The Poseidon Adventure* (1972). The liner is also seen in *Someone
to Watch Over Me* (1987), *L.A. Confidential* (1997), *Titanic*
(1997) and *Pearl Harbor* (2001). Among hundreds of television productions filmed on board are *Charlie's Angels,
The Love Boat III, Winds of War, X-Files* and *Melrose Place*.

Numerous visitors and staff members have reported
mysterious happening aboard the ship, including voices,
rattling, knocking, drifting lights, moving objects and
even the presence of full-bodied apparitions. Because of
hundreds of these incidents, the *Queen Mary* has been
called the world's "best-known and best-documented
haunted ship." Included in the price of general admission, guests can see a "Ghosts and Legends" show.

Once the lounge area for First
Class passengers, the Queen's
Salon still features its original
decorations, including the
mural *Unicorns in Battle*, pictured here. Considered by
many of the wealthiest passengers as the *only* civilized way to
travel, the majestic liner featured lavishly decorated Art
Deco lounges and cabins, now
carefully restored to evoke the
charm and elegance of a
bygone era. Many artworks
from its extensive art collection are permanently displayed
in the Promenade Gallery.

The *Queen Mary* is one of the most famous ships in history

Catalina Island

ⓘ 1 Green Pleasure Pier.
Not on map.
☎(310) 510-1520, or call Catalina Island Conservancy, ☎(310) 510-2595. www.catalina.com.

Before the first vacationers came in the 1880s, Catalina Island was inhabited by Indians, sheltered Russian sea otter hunters, became a haven for Yankee smugglers and served as a camping ground for Union soldiers. In 1919, most of the island was purchased by chewing-gum baron William Wrigley, Jr. In order to develop a unique tourist resort, Wrigley planted palm trees, founded fishing clubs and started glass-bottom boat tours. He even brought out his baseball team, the Chicago Cubs, and made the island their spring training camp. Wrigley's publicity efforts paid off: during the 1930s, the island's main city, Avalon, became a fashionable tourist spot, and has remained a popular destination ever since.

Just 22 miles (35 km) from the mainland, Catalina's coastline, mountains and canyons remain largely unspoiled, with crystal-clear water and miles of hiking trails. Today, most of the 8-by-28-mile (13 by 45 km) island is owned by the Santa Catalina Island Conservancy, which purchased 88% of Catalina in 1975 in order to preserve and protect the land and its natural beauty.

Catalina's unique ecosystem is inhabited by some 400 plant species, including eight endemic ones, as well as over 100 bird types and a variety of animals, notably the small gray Catalina fox and the Beechey ground squirrel.

Since private cars are restricted, the best way to explore Avalon and environs is on foot, or by rented bicycles or golf carts. Shuttle or tram tours of Avalon and bus trips outside the city are also available.

The island is a paradise for outdoor activities such as hiking, bicycling, horseback riding, hunting, camping, jet skiing, fishing, swimming, diving, snorkeling, parasailing, boating and water-skiing.

A vintage post card depicts Catalina Island's Avalon Bay

Wrigley Memorial

Bennett, Parsons and Frost, architects (1934).
Wrigley Botanical Garden.

Built by the Wrigley family as the resting place for chewing-gum magnate William Wrigley, Jr, the monument was never used as intended. Situated within the botanical garden, the imposing memorial is 232 feet wide and 130 feet high (70 x 40 m). Its main tower is reached by a grand spiral staircase leading to the mausoleum, built of blue Catalina flagstone and inlaid with decorative handmade tiles, made by the now defunct Catalina Pottery production plant.

Wrigley Botanical Garden

1400 Avalon Canyon Rd.
☎(310) 510-2288.
⏰ daily 8am-5pm. ⓢ

The garden was founded in the 1920s, when the collection of cacti and succulents was established. Today, the 37-acre (15-ha) garden has expanded to include plants native to California, including Torrey pine, California laurel and mountain mahogany. Among the species native to California islands are Catalina cherry, lemonade berry and Catalina currant. Of particular interest are eight endemic plants that grow naturally only on Catalina Island, including St Catherine's lace, wild tomato, Yerba Santa, Catalina bedstraw, Catalina ironwood, Catalina live-forever, Catalina mahogany and Catalina manzanita.

Cactus and Succulent areas in the Wrigley Botanical Garden

The 12-story-high Casino is Catalina Island's most famous landmark

Webber and Spaulding, architects (1928).
1 Casino Way. Not on map
☎ (310) 510-8687.
➤ daytime guided tours. ⑤
Catalina Island Museum
☎ (310) 510-2414.
🕐 daily 10am-4pm. ⑤
Avalon Theatre
☎ (310) 510-0179.
🕐 first-run films shown nightly. ⑤

The elaborate chandelier in the Casino's ballroom

A mermaid swimming in an underwater garden is depicted on one of nine Art Deco panels on the entrance pavilion's 40-foot-high (12-m) loggia. The muralist was inspired by Catalina's colorful sealife observed through a glass-bottomed boat.

Casino

The island's signature building, the white circular Casino, is an unusual blend of Spanish, Moorish and Art Deco (Zigzag) Moderne styles. Despite the association its name might evoke (casino means "gathering place" in Italian), the building was never used for gambling. Built by William Wrigley, Jr in 1929 and refurbished in 1987, the Casino houses several attractions, including ballroom, theater and the Catalina Island Museum. Located in the lower level, the museum is devoted to the archaeology and natural history of the island.

The magnificent ballroom on the top floor, which is 180 feet (55 m) in diameter, is covered with a clear span dome (built without supporting columns). Its dance floor, laid with strips of maple, white oak and rosewood, was during its heyday packed with more than 6,000 people on weekend nights. This was an enormously popular dance venue during the Big Band era of the 1930s and 1940s. Kay Kyser, Benny Goodman, Jimmy Dorsey and other top bands were broadcast live from the Casino, making it famous across the nation.

The 1,200-seat Avalon Theatre on the Casino's main floor was one of the first movie palaces acoustically designed for the showing of sound motion pictures. It was opened on May 29, 1929 with a Douglas Fairbanks production *The Iron Mask*. The theater was used by Cecil B DeMille, Louis B Mayer, Samuel Goldwyn and other movie moguls to preview new talkies. It was said that the theater's sound system was so well designed that engineers working on Radio City Music Hall in New York came to study its acoustics. Today, a demonstration of the theater's classic 1929 Page pipe organ includes such sound effects as bird whistles and automobile horn stops.

Since there is no center chandelier, the circular auditorium is illuminated with colorful indirect lighting from the perimeter. Star-shaped openings in the silver-leafed dome ceiling provide additional twinkling lights effect.

One of the finest movie theaters in America, this Art Deco masterpiece is lavishly decorated with still intact murals depicting regional historical imagery, underwater scenes and abstract motifs. They were painted in 1929 by John Gabriel Beckman, who also took part in decorating Grauman's Chinese Theatre in Hollywood.

The Art Deco murals of the Avalon Theatre were painted by John Beckman, who was at one point art director for Columbia

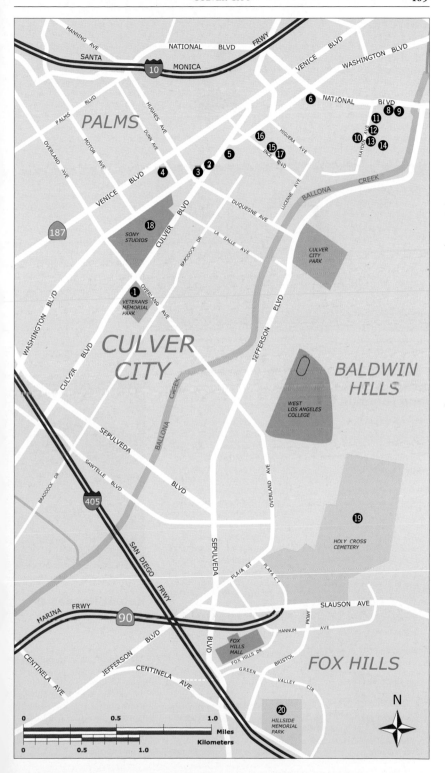

Culver City

Once part of a 134,000-acre land grant, the area now comprising Culver City was a grain field before real estate developer Harry Culver bought and subdivided the former Rancho La Ballona. Named for its founder in 1914, the city soon began attracting movie studios, which relocated here fleeing high rents in Hollywood. The first to come was producer Thomas Ince, who founded his Triangle Studios

Culver City street marker

on land donated by Culver in 1915. At one time, three studios were located here: MGM, Selznick International and Hal Roach. Silent film buffs can still spot many locations on city streets used by Hal Roach for his early comedies. Although it has now lost much of its movie glamour, this town produced half of the films released in America during the 1930s and 1940s.

Rich in movie history and lore, Culver City proudly proclaims itself "The Heart of Screenland"

and tower, and is occasionally utilized as a location for filming. The theater was later split up into a multiplex and was vacant for 15 years before being rehabilitated as a live performance playhouse. The theater exterior has been preserved and restored, while the old interior was demolished and a new, more intimate interior with 300 seats was built. The venue was renamed Kirk Douglas Theatre, for the actor whose donation fueled the fundraising efforts.

Film Strip USA/ Heart of Screenland Fountain ❶

Natalie Krol (1981).
Corner of Culver Blvd and Overland Ave.

Standing in front of the Veterans Memorial Building, these giant strips of stainless-steel film pay homage to the city's crucial role in the history of motion pictures. A plaque proudly proclaims: "Dedicated by the citizens of Culver City—the Motion Picture Capital of the World."

The Culver Hotel ❷

9400 Culver Blvd.
☎(310) 838-7963. ⚑ NRHP

The hotel was built in 1924 on the site of Culver City's first movie theater. The flat-iron building served as a part-time residence for such Hollywood stars as Clark Gable, Joan Crawford, Greta Garbo and Ronald Reagan. It is best remembered for hosting the actors who played the Munchkins during the filming of *The Wizard of Oz* (1939). Recently restored, the hotel itself has been featured in several movies, including *The Last Action Hero* (1993).

Culver Theater ❸

James Zerbe and Gus Kalionzes, architects (1947).
9820 W Washington Blvd.

Originally built as a 1,600-seat, single-screen theater in 1947, the Culver was frequently used by neighboring MGM for sneak previews. This landmark movie house is best known for its huge Streamline Moderne façade

Storybook-style Hobbit Houses

Hobbit Houses ❹

3819 Dunn Dr.
Private residence.

This remarkable Storybook-style creation was built from 1946 to 1970 by Lawrence Joseph, an artist who had worked for Walt Disney Co. Known locally as the Hobbit Houses, the whimsical buildings look like Bilbo Baginns's home transported straight from Middleearth.

Culver Theater

Many unforgettable movies were filmed on the Culver Studios lot

Culver Studios ➎

9336 Washington Blvd.
Not open to the public. ♠ 🚩

This was the second major studio built in Culver City. Called the Thomas H Ince Studios, it was opened in 1919 by the silent film director/producer who made many successful movies here, mostly westerns. After Ince's premature death in 1924, the studio changed owners several times, becoming known as DeMille Studios, RKO, RKO-Pathé, Selznick, Desilu, Culver City Studios, Laird International and, most recently, the Culver Studios. It is now part of Sony Pictures Entertainment.

Among the productions filmed on this lot over the years were *What Price Hollywood?* (1932), the Astaire/Rogers musicals *The Gay Divorcee* (1934) and *Top Hat* (1935), *A Star is Born* (1937), *Rebecca* (1940), *Citizen Kane* (1941), *Airplane* (1980), *E.T.* (1982), *City Slickers* (1991), *A Few Good Men* (1992) and *Bewitched* (2005), as well as

television's *Lassie*, *The Untouchables* and the pilot for the original *Star Trek* series.

The distinctive Colonial Revival Southern house was built as a set for one of Thomas Ince's films in 1924. It is said to be a replica of George Washington's home, Mt Vernon. It was later converted into an administration building and was sometimes confused with Tara, Scarlett O'Hara's plantation home. When producer David O Selznick leased the studio in 1935, the mansion became a logo of his company, Selznick International, appearing in the opening credits of all his films.

The building is reportedly haunted by Ince's spirit, which has been spotted by workers on stages and in the screening room.

The spectacular scene of the burning of the Atlanta munitions depot in *Gone With the Wind* (1939) was filmed on the studio's back lot, which is now an industrial tract. Selznick, however, did not build new sets;

instead, he torched the remaining sets of *The King of Kings* (1927) and *King Kong* (1933), which were furnished with false fronts to simulate the burning warehouses. After the old sets burned down, the real ones for *Gone With the Wind* could be built on the cleared ground.

The street just east of the lot was named for the studio's founder, Thomas Ince. He is credited with the introduction of detailed shooting scripts. Ince insisted that directors stick closely to the scenarios, demanding, "Shoot it as it is written." Before his time films were mostly improvised.

The burning of the Atlanta munitions warehouses in *Gone With the Wind* (1939)

Hal Roach Studios

(site) ➏

SW corner of Washington and National boulevards. 🚩

Opened in 1919, this was the third major studio in Culver City. Known as the "Laugh Factory to the World," it was here that Hal Roach produced and frequently directed countless Harold Lloyd, Laurel and Hardy and *Our Gang* comedies.

During World War II the studio, also called "Fort Roach," made training and propaganda films for the US military, featuring many famous names including Lt Ronald Reagan. The Hal Roach company closed in the late 1950s and the studio was demolished in 1963, making way for a car dealership and a small park. Today a simple plaque marks the site of the famous studio.

A vintage post card depicts Hal Roach Studios in Culver City

Moss in Culver City

Since the mid-1980s, a remarkable development has transformed the character of northeast Culver City. An impressive series of unconventional rebuilding projects came as the result of close collaboration between developers Frederick Norton Smith and Laurie Samitaur Smith and architect Eric Owen Moss. This partnership turned a fragmented and depressed neighborhood into a showplace of ultramodern architecture and an international tourist magnet. Moss converted mostly abandoned warehouses into "creative space," occupied by new firms in the thriving multimedia and entertainment industries.

To see the interiors of the Moss-designed buildings, call ☎(310) 204-4464.

The Box and the Beehive

Samitaur

Samitaur ❼
Eric Owen Moss Architects (1997). 3457 La Cienega.

Constructed over a privately owned road, the new block is supported on 15-foot-high circular steel columns, allowing uninterrupted truck traffic.

The Box ❽
Eric Owen Moss Architects (1994). 8520 National Blvd.

Sitting atop a simple box-shaped building, the black cement plaster Box projects from the roof at an unusual angle. The windows, which are boxes themselves, open the opposite corners of the Box. Originally designed as a private room for a restaurant, it now serves as a conference space.

The Beehive ❾
Eric Owen Moss Architects (2000). 8522 National Blvd.

A paneled skin which is alternately transparent, translucent and opaque encompasses the irregular and collapsed curvatures of the building.

Pittard-Sullivan Building ❿
Eric Owen Moss Architects (1997). 3535 Hayden Ave.

Housing a multimedia digital communications firm, the four-story building uses the double bowstring truss system of the old warehouse, now demolished. The exposed wooden bowstrings extending beyond the south wall had to be cut to make room for cars.

Trivida ⓫
Eric Owen Moss Architects (1998). 3524 Hayden Ave.

Three steel windows pierce this undulating wall constructed from one thousand pieces of concrete blocks, each of them individually cut and wired into a supporting structure.

Trivida

IRS Building ⓬
Eric Owen Moss Architects (1994). 3520 Hayden Ave.

The entrance area to the IRS Building is an assemblage of old steel elements from the existing structure and a new stairway and steel pyramid at the top. Moss unveils this sculpture to the viewer by cutting the originally solid wall by a window and covering it with pieces of acrylic.

Pittard-Sullivan Building

IRS Building

Lindblade Tower

The Stealth

The Stealth ⓭
Eric Owen Moss Architects (2000).
3528 Hayden Ave.

The 325-foot long, 60-foot-high (100 x 18 m) building serves as headquarters for an international advertising firm. Angular, dark surfaces enfold the structure which continuously changes its shape, from the three sided north end to the four-sided south end. Inside the old warehouse a new performance stage faces a large sunken courtyard. It can hold six hundred seats and was constructed in the area where petrochemical waste was once removed.

The Umbrella ⓮
Eric Owen Moss Architects (1999).
3542 Hayden Ave.

Named after the LA Philharmonic's experimental music series called the Green Umbrella, the building was intended as a stage for both indoor and outdoor concerts. Outlined by a curved steel pipe, the umbrella structure cuts the roof at the corner of the building, cantilevering over the ramp. A canopy made of slumped glass panels is mounted over the concentric stairway.

Lindblade Tower ⓯
Eric Owen Moss Architects (1989).
3958 Ince Blvd.

The tower, which provides the entrance to the remodeled building, is constructed of red concrete blocks. Its pyramidal metal roof is slightly rotated and cut off on three sides, but extends over the front wall. The vitrified clay pipes supporting the canopy are cut away to expose their concrete filling.

Gary Group Building ⓰
Eric Owen Moss Architects (1990).
9046 Lindblade St.

Designated by sheared red signage, this thoroughly renovated warehouse is home to an advertising and promotion agency. At the top of the inclined concrete block wall of Lindblade Street elevation are ornamental steel components, including a clock and a ladder leading to nowhere. The wall facing the parking lot is adorned with jutting stone blocks, chains, wheels and re-bar, along with a series of windows and square acrylic panels.

Paramount Laundry

Paramount Laundry ⓱
Eric Owen Moss Architects (1989).
3960 Ince Blvd.

Moss inventively used sewer pipes which serve as columns supporting the entry canopy. One of the columns is displaced and bent in accordance with its "conventional duties, because in the vocabulary of vitrified clay pipes are pieces that go around corners."

Gary Group Building

The Umbrella

A roaring lion, encircled with the motto "Arts Gratia Artis" (roughly, "Art for Art's Sake"), became one of the most famous trademarks in the world

Metro-Goldwyn-Mayer (MGM)

The biggest and most famous Hollywood studio was formed in 1924 in a merger of the Metro Pictures Corporation, the Goldwyn Pictures Corporation and Louis B Mayer Productions, under the corporate control of Loew's Inc. Its president was theater-chain magnate Marcus Loew, a son of Jewish immigrants from Austria. He started as a furrier but eventually became one of the main exhibitors, owning more than 400 theaters. Louis B Mayer was named head of the new studio, and its chief of production became Irving Thalberg. Under their leadership MGM was established as the supreme motion picture company, with a standard of production that no other Hollywood studio could equal.

As most other studios, MGM was affected by dwindling audiences caused by competition from television in the 1950s and 1960s. A huge blow came in 1952, when Loew's was forced by government antitrust laws to split, and MGM became a separate corporation. The studio was taken over in 1969 by financier Kirk Kerkorian. In a series of transactions that followed, MGM changed hands several times. Kerkorian bought it for the third time in 1996 and finally sold it to Sony for $4.9 billion in 2005.

First used in 1926, the studio slogan "More stars than there are in the heavens" underscores the importance MGM placed on developing and maintaining its stars. The impressive roster included Greta Garbo, Clark Gable, Jean Harlow, Katharine Hepburn, Judy Garland, Ava Gardner, Cary Grant, Gene Kelly, Lana Turner and Elizabeth Taylor.

MGM's preeminence during the heyday of the film industry was based on technical excellence and the unsurpassed quality of its productions. "If it is an MGM film, it has to look like an MGM film," Louis B Mayer said to one of his cameramen. During the 1930s and 1940s, the studio produced a number of glittering movies such as *The Wizard of Oz* (1939). Musicals, including *Singin' in the Rain* (1952), continued MGM's prestige in the 1950s.

MGM's winners in best picture category include *The Broadway Melody* (1928-29); *Grand Hotel* (1931-32); *The Great Ziegfeld* (1936); *Gone With the Wind* (1939); *Mrs Miniver* (1942); *An American in Paris* (1951), *Gigi* (1958) and *Ben-Hur* (1959).

Louis B Mayer was head of MGM from 1924 until his ousting in 1951. The son of Jewish immigrants from Russia, he was a scrap-metal dealer, theater owner and producer before becoming the most powerful of the Hollywood moguls. In 1927 he became the highest paid business executive in the nation, with an annual salary of $1,296,000. Dictatorial and ruthless, this power-driven egomaniac was the master of sensing popular taste and hand-picked many of Hollywood's greatest stars.

Through a carefully organized campaign MGM launched Joan Crawford toward stardom. From its beginning, MGM put an emphasis on stars. It had more major names under contract than any other studio.

The golden age of MGM began with an epic production of *Ben-Hur* (1925). Ironically, it ended with the film's 1959 version, which set a new record for most Oscars won by one film, winning 11 Academy Awards out of 12 nominations.

United Artists (UA)

So, the inmates have taken over the asylum.
— Richard Rowland, President of Metro Pictures,
on the creation of United Artists in 1919

United Artists logo

Unique among the Hollywood studios, United Artists was not founded by movie moguls but by the most famous artists of the silent screen—Mary Pickford, "America's Sweetheart," Douglas Fairbanks, the cinema's ultimate swashbuckler, Charlie Chaplin, the world's premiere comedian, and D W Griffith, the celebrated director. It was formed in 1919 as a distribution company, with the idea of giving independent producers greater artistic freedom in the production of their pictures, while retaining control of marketing and profits. UA was able to attract the most famous of Hollywood's actors, directors and producers, gaining prestige for its well-crafted productions.

The company went public in 1957 and was bought by insurance giant Transamerica Corporation in 1967. Following the disaster of Michael Cimino's *Heavens Gate* (1980), which lost more than $40 million, UA was bought by financier Kirk Kerkorian and MGM in 1981 for $380 million. In 1985 TV and media mogul Ted Turner acquired MGM/UA Entertainment Company and later sold it back to Kerkorian, while keeping the huge film libraries.

Founders of United Artists: Douglas Fairbanks, Mary Pickford, Charlie Chaplin and D W Griffith

Although United Artists was not a production company and was limited to distributing a relatively small number of films from independent producers, its reputation for the outstanding quality of its features was established early. Among its memorable releases are *The Gold Rush* (1925), *The Son of the Sheik* (1926), *Stagecoach* (1939), *High Noon* (1953), *Some Like It Hot* (1959), *The Magnificent Seven* (1960) and *Apocalypse Now* (1979).

UA has done remarkably well with the Oscars, a tribute to its high standards, winning the best picture Academy Award 12 times: *Rebecca* (1940), *Marty* (1955), *Around the World in 80 Days* (1956), *The Apartment* (1960), *West Side Story* (1961), *Tom Jones* (1963), *In the Heat of the Night* (1967), *Midnight Cowboy* (1969), *One Flew Over the Cuckoo's Nest* (1975), *Rocky* (1976), *Annie Hall* (1977) and *Rain Man* (1988).

Buster Keaton remained only two years with UA, starring in such hits as *The General* (1926), *College* (1927) and *Steamboat Bill, Jr* (1928). Apart from the three legends of the silent era and its co-founders (Pickford, Fairbanks and Chaplin), UA did not have stars of its own. Being essentially a distribution company, its producers had to borrow stars from the major studios. Among the top names who appeared in UA films but did not stay for long were Alla Nazimova, Norma Talmadge, Rudolph Valentino, William S Hart, Gloria Swanson, Janet Gaynor, Fredric March and Merle Oberon.

Among the company's greatest money-making triumphs are the James Bond movies, one of the most successful series of all time

Sony Pictures Studios ⑱

One of the most famous studio lots in the history of motion pictures was founded in 1915 by legendary film pioneer Thomas Ince. Together with fellow producers/directors Mack Sennett and D W Griffith, he built Triangle Studios, the most prestigious cinema facility at the time. Triangle, however, ceased to exist in 1918 after the financial disaster caused by Griffith's *Intolerance*, and the following year the property was purchased by Goldwyn Pictures. In 1924, after a three-way merger, MGM acquired ownership of

Sony Pictures water tower

the lot and for over half a century this was the site where many unforgettable movies were made. Financial woes forced MGM to sell the studio to Ted Turner in 1986. Sony Pictures (which owns Columbia Pictures and TriStar Pictures) took over the lot in 1990, and Columbia moved here from Burbank. After a $100-million face-lift in 1994, the modernized and refurbished studio is now used for the production of both motion pictures and television programs.

10202 W Washington Blvd.
☎(310) 244-4000.
www.sonypicturesstudios.com
Closed to the public.
☞studio offers a two-hour walking tour for visitors over the age of 12. ⏰Mon-Fri at 9:30 and 11am, 12 noon, 3pm (by reservation only). For reservations call ☎(323) 520-8687. Ⓢ ⚑
To get free tickets for live TV shows filming on the lot, call ☎(818) 753-3470 or (818) 506-0043, or visit www.tvtickets.com.
This is a working studio, so visitors may encounter actors from many movies and TV series filmed here.

MGM's backlot sets once included a lake and harbor, a jungle, a park, a railway station, city streets and whole neighborhoods. At its peak in the 1940s, the studio boasted five lots on 187 acres (75 ha). In 1969, most of it was demolished and sold off to developers. The following year, even the studio props and costumes were auctioned off, including Dorothy's ruby slippers from *The Wizard of Oz*. Sony Pictures today operates on a more compact lot comprising 44 acres (18 ha).

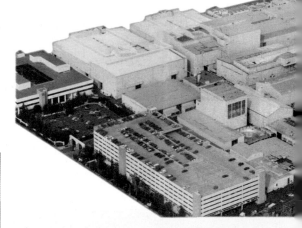

Stage 30: This water tank stage was built originally with Tarzan films on mind. Here were filmed *Tarzan's Secret Treasure* (1942), *Mutiny on the Bounty* (1959), *Shaft* (1971), *Poltergeist* (1982) and *Hook* (1991). The asteroid sets in *Armageddon* (1998) were also built on this stage. Elaborate swimming scenes in Esther Williams's musical extravaganzas, such as *Million Dollar Mermaid* (1952), were staged in this water tank.

The original studio gate on Washington Blvd is no longer in use, but its elaborate ironwork has been restored. The structure behind the imposing classical colonnade was Triangle Studio's office building in 1916.

Built in 1937, this impressive Moderne building was named for Irving Thalberg, MGM's celebrated head of production. Originally used as MGM's administrative building (Louis B Mayer's office was here), it now houses offices for Columbia Pictures. In the lobby are displays of the Oscar statuettes that Columbia won for best picture.

The building's entrance is seen in the movie *Mommie Dearest* (1901), which starred Faye Dunaway as Joan Crawford.

Stage 15: When it was built in the early 1930s, this was the largest sound stage in the world. *The Wizard of Oz* (1939)—complete with the Yellow Brick Road, Munchkinland and cornfield—was shot here. Other movies include *Rocky* (1976) and *Rocky II* (1979), *Dracula* (1992), *Men in Black* (1996) and *Spider-Man* (2002).

Crawford Building: This is the old school building where MGM's underage stars—Mickey Rooney, Judy Garland and Elizabeth Taylor—convened to school for three hours a day, as required by law. "The only thing I learned was to smoke cigars and chase women," Rooney later recalled.

Included in the studio tour is the wardrobe department, which provides custom-made clothing for various productions shot on the lot. Here were made the 350 different pirate costumes seen in the movie *Hook* (1991). On exhibit in the lobby are outfits from Columbia's recent movies.

Stage 11: Visitors can join the studio audience of one of the many long-running sitcoms or shows taped here, including, *Jeopardy* and *Wheel of Fortune*. Five gameshows are taped daily, two days a week.

Columbia Pictures

Columbia Pictures' famous torch-lady logo

In 1920 brothers Jack and Harry Cohn and Joe Brandt, all former employees of Universal's founder Carl Laemmle, formed a tiny company called CBC Film Sales. Because it rented studio space on Hollywood's Poverty Row and operated on a shoestring budget, its acronym soon became known as "Corned Beef and Cabbage." Renamed Columbia Pictures in 1924, the company steadily increased its film output until it was able to purchase its own studio on Gower St in 1926 (➔ p125). Gradually expanding from its modest beginnings, Columbia rose to the rank of a major studio during the 1930s with its successful screwball comedies.

Columbia Pictures continued its string of hit movies into the 1940s and 1950s, being the only Hollywood studio that never operated in the red. During the industry restructuring in the 1970s, the company was purchased by investment banker Allen & Company Inc, which sold it to Coca-Cola Corporation in 1982. After Columbia's merger with TriStar Pictures in 1987, Sony Pictures Entertainment bought the company in 1990 and moved the studio to the former MGM lot in Culver City.

Because it did not have many stars of its own, Columbia frequently borrowed major talent from other studios. One of the few Columbia's discoveries was Rita Hayworth, the *femme fatale* of the film *noir* and one of the greatest sex symbols of Hollywood. Other stars included Barbara Stanwyck, Rosalind Russell, Kim Novak, Barbra Streisand, Glenn Ford and William Holden.

A former vaudeville singer, Harry Cohn was co-founder of Columbia and its head until his death in 1958. The son of a Jewish tailor who immigrated from Germany, he was a vulgar and brutal ruler, ill-famed for alienating his top stars and directors. Cohn was quoted as saying, "I don't have ulcers, I give them!" He was also notorious for giving a lot of freedom to those writers and directors whom he trusted. His remarkable ability to spot talent and sense a profitable movie was acknowledged even by his enemies.

It Happened One Night (1934) won Columbia its first Oscar for best picture, and also for the two leads, director and screenplay, being the first ever to "sweep the board" in all five major categories. Columbia was very successful with the Oscars, winning an Academy Award for best picture for the following films: *You Can't Take It with You* (1938); *All the King's Men* (1949); *From Here To Eternity* (1953); *On the Waterfront* (1954); *The Bridge On the River Kwai* (1957); *Lawrence of Arabia* (1962); *A Man For All Seasons* (1966); *Oliver!* (1968); *Kramer vs Kramer* (1979); *Gandhi* (1982) and *The Last Emperor* (1987).

Screen goddess Rita Hayworth, Columbia's greatest discovery

Lobby card for Frank Capra's *It Happened One Night* (1934)

Holy Cross Cemetery ⑲

5835 W Slauson Ave.
☎(310) 670-7697.
(J)mausoleum: Mon-Sat 8am-5pm, Sun and holidays 11am-5pm; cemetery grounds: daily 8am-6pm ☞ a list with exact locations of celebrity graves can be obtained from the cemetery office.

Set on a hillside in the area known as Baldwin Hills, this huge Catholic cemetery contains the remains of some of the most prominent Hollywood stars. The tract is dominated by a large white mausoleum building set at the top of the hill. Above the entrance is a white sculpture of the Crucifixion, set against a glittering gold background.

The cemetery's most distinct feature is the Grotto, an artificial, cave-like structure, situated up the hill and to the left of the main entrance. In this area is the highest concentration of the cemetery's famous names.

Front entrance of the Mausoleum is dominated by a crucifixion

Grotto

Bing Crosby (1904-1977)

Probably the greatest star interred at Holy Cross, singer and actor Bing Crosby was one of the most significant and successful American entertainers of all time. He starred in a series of musicals during the 1930s and 1940s and won an Academy Award for best actor for his portrayal of a priest in *Going My Way* (1944).

Bela Lugosi (1882-1956)

Buried in his signature black cape, Hungarian-born actor Bela Blasko gained world fame after playing a title role in the 1931 movie *Dracula*. He became the personi-fication of evil after creating a character that no other screen Dracula was ever able to match. He died during the filming of *Plan 9 From Outer Space* (1958), regarded by most critics to be the worst film ever made.

Rita Hayworth (1918-1987)

Called the Great American Love Goddess by *Life* magazine, Rita Hayworth became the favorite of millions of servicemen during World War II. Her pinup picture even adorned the atomic test bomb dropped on the Bikini atoll in 1946. The redheaded sex symbol (born Margarita Carmen Cansino) starred in *Gilda* (1946) and *The Lady From Shanghai* (1949). She died at 68 after a long battle with Alzheimer's disease.

Sharon Tate Polanski (1943-1969)

Actress Sharon Tate, the wife of famous director Roman Polanski, is buried here with her unborn son, Paul Richard, her mother and her sister. Sharon was eight and a half months pregnant when brutally murdered by four members of the Charles Manson gang in a crime that shocked the world. She appeared in *The Fearless Vampire Killers* (1967) and *Valley of the Dolls* (1967) before her promising career was abruptly ended.

Charles Boyer (1897-1978)

This famous matinee idol was an established stage and film actor in his native France before he moved to Hollywood in 1929. Here he cultivated his legendary image of a sophisticated, charming continental seducer. Boyer starred opposite some of Hollywood's most glamorous leading ladies, including Marlene Dietrich (*The Garden of Allah*, 1936), Greta Garbo (*Conquest*, 1937), Hedy Lamarr (*Algiers*, 1938), Bette Davis (*All This and Heaven, Too*, 1940) and Ingrid Bergman (*Gaslight*, 1944).

He took his life with an overdose of Seconal tablets two days after his wife died of cancer. Their only son killed himself at 21.

Holy Cross Cemetery

St Anne's, lot 186, grave 5 ①

St Anne's, tier 55, grave 47 ②

Grotto, lot 119, grave 1 ③

Grotto, lot 120, grave 1 ④

St Anne's, lot 152, grave 6 ⑤

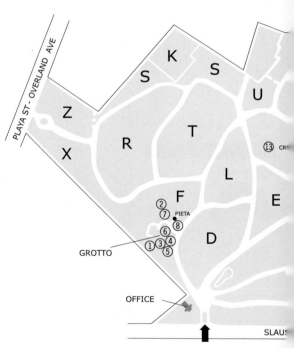

Grotto, lot 196, grave 6 ⑥

Section F, tier 56, grave 62 ⑦

Section F, tier 96, grave 6 ⑧

Mausoleum, block 84, room 7L, crypt D1 ⑨

Mausoleum, block 46, crypt D2 ⑩

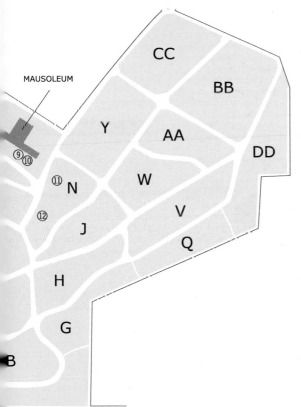

Section N, lot 523, grave 5 ⑪

Section N, lot 490, grave 1 ⑫

Section M, lot 304, grave 5 ⑬

Rosalind Russell Brisson
November 28, 1976

Section M, lot 536, grave 2 (at the foot of the large crucifix) ⑭

Grounds

Rosalind Russell
(1908-1976)

One of the easiest to spot, the grave of Rosalind Russell is located under a large white crucifix in section M. Russell was a great humanitarian and a funny lady who referred to her parish in Beverly Hills as "Our Lady of the Cadillacs." Best known for her roles as career women in numerous comedies of the 1940s, she gave unforgettable performances in *His Girl Friday* (1940) and *Auntie Mame* (1958).

John Ford (1895-1973)

Born Sean O'Feeney, Admiral John Ford was one of the most admired American film directors. He won four Academy Awards, for the direction of *The Informer* (1935), *The Grapes of Wrath* (1940), *How Green Was My Valley* (1941) and *The Quiet Man* (1952). His other memorable films include *Stagecoach* (1939), *My Darling Clementine* (1946) and *The Searchers* (1956).

Mary Astor (1906-1987)

This delicate beauty, who often played elegant, bitchy women, was launched to stardom at eighteen, as John Barrymore's leading lady in *Beau Brummel* (1924). Their off-screen love affair was well publicized, and over the years Astor remained a popular subject of Hollywood gossip for her independence, alcoholism and four failed marriages. During a divorce and custody battle with her second husband in 1936, Astor's private diary was made public, including graphic details of her love affair with playwright George Kaufman. Her most memorable part was the *femme fatale* in *The Maltese Falcon* (1941). Astor won a best supporting actress Oscar for her performance in *The Great Lie* (1941).

Mack Sennett (1880-1960)

Son of Irish immigrants (born Mikall Sinnott), actor, director and producer Mack Sennett was the founder of Keystone—the silent screen's leading studio in the comedy field. The legendary father of slapstick comedy, Sennett was also credited as the inventor of the casting couch, where many of his scantily clad Bathing Beauties were "discovered." Among the stars who started their film careers with Sennett were Charlie Chaplin, Gloria Swanson and Carole Lombard.

Jackie Coogan (1914-1984)

His film debut was at 18 months old and at four he caught the eye of Charlie Chaplin, who made him the co-star of *The Kid* (1921), Chaplin's first feature-length film. With his spontaneity, bright eyes, tattered cap and oversized throusers, Coogan instantly became an international attraction. The silent screen's first child star, Coogan made astronomical sums of money, most of which was spent by his mother and stepfather. To prevent future abuses to child actors, California passed the Child Actors bill, popularly known as the Coogan Act.

Jimmy Durante (1893-1980)

A comedian, actor and songwriter, Durante started his long show-biz career playing piano in nightclubs. He appeared in 29 movies, but achieved the greatest popularity on radio and television. A beloved entertainer, who charmed audiences with his trademark raucous voice and large, bulbous nose, is best remembered for his signature song, *Inka, Dinka Doo.*

Pat O'Brien (1899-1983)

O'Brien played tough guys in many of the Warner Bros crime and social-justice films of the 1930s and 1940s, usually portraying forces of good—either cops, priests or soldiers. His best known films are *Angels With Dirty Faces* (1938), where he co-starred with James Cagney, and *Knute Rockne—All American* (1940).

Mausoleum

Mario Lanza (1921-1959)

Lanza was an extremely popular actor and singer who sold tens of millions of records. His greatest film success was the title role in the huge hit *The Great Caruso* (1951), in which he portrayed the celebrated tenor. An associate of gangster Lucky Luciano, Lanza died under mysterious circumstances at a clinic in Rome.

Fred MacMurray
(1908-1991)

While touring California with a band as a saxophonist, MacMurray made his first film appearance as an extra in the late 1920s. After Paramount signed him in 1934, he appeared in lead roles, mostly as a comedian, opposite such female stars as Claudette Colbert, Katharine Hepburn and Carole Lombard. He is best remembered as insurance agent Walter Neff in *Double Indemnity* (1944). During the 1960s, he appeared in the long-running television series *My Three Sons* and in a string of popular family films for Disney.

Al Jolson Memorial

Hillside Memorial Park ⑳

6001 Centinela Ave.
☎(310) 641-0707.
🕐Sun-Fri 8am-5pm. Closed Sat and Jewish religious holidays.

The most striking feature of this large Jewish cemetery is a round marble monument with six tall columns and a dome. The ceiling of the dome is decorated with a mosaic of Moses amidst clouds, holding the Ten Commandments. Familiar to countless commuters on the San Diego Fwy, the monument has become one of LA's most visible landmarks.

This large shrine came into being when the president of the mortuary commissioned famous architect Paul Williams to design a monument for Al Jolson, hoping to attract other celebrities to the site. Honoring Jolson's wish to be buried near the waterfall, water cascades from the tomb 120 feet (36 m) down the hill.

Grounds

Al Jolson (1886-1950)
Standing underneath the monument is the tomb of singer and actor Al Jolson, one of the most famous entertainers of all time. Born Asa Yoelson, this son of a Russ-

ian immigrant cantor started as a black-faced vaudeville singer and became the most popular recording artist in America. He made film history as the star of the first talkie, *The Jazz Singer* (1927) (➜ p329). Jolson died in room 1221 of the St Francis Hotel in San Francisco—the same room where young starlet Virginia Rappe was allegedly assaulted by comedian Roscoe "Fatty" Arbuckle in 1921.

Michael Landon (1936-1991)

The producer, writer, director and star of three popular television series—*Bonanza, Little House on the Prairie* and *Highway to Heaven*—rests in a locked family room in the mausoleum's central courtyard area. His crypt can be seen through a glass door. Born Eugene Maurice Orowitz, Landon picked his name out of the phone book.

Lorne Greene (1915-1987)

The headstone of the famous actor, head of the Ponderosa Ranch in television's long-running *Bonanza*, bears the name of his character in the series, Ben Cartwright. Greene is buried on the lawn behind the mausoleum, to the right of the entrance.

Max Factor (1877-1938)
Factor got his start as the wig-maker for Russian Emperor Nicholas II and make-up artist for the Royal Ballet. After moving to Hollywood in 1908, he introduced countless cosmetic products, first to the theater and motion pictures, and later to the general public (➜ p53). Factor founded the world-famous cosmetics giant that bears his name.

Moe Howard (1897-1975)
Born Moses Horwitz, Moe was the short-tempered Stooge with the famous bangs who initiated on-screen bopping and slapping. When Ted Healy left the Three Stooges in 1934, Moe became the leader of the group, making most of their business decisions. His leadership would last through the cinema's longest-running contract ever held by a comedy team—24 consecutive years with Columbia.

Mausoleum

Jack Benny (1894-1974)

The legendary comedian's black-marble crypt stands in the alcove at the end of the mausoleum's Hall of Graciousness. The son of a Russian immigrant, Benjamin Kubelsky was a talented young violin player before he discovered his gift for comedy and became one of the biggest stars of both radio and television. Among his most memorable movies are *Love Thy Neighbor* (1940) and *To Be or Not to Be* (1942).

Eddie Cantor (1892-1964)
Born Edward Israel Iskowitz, he was orphaned at three and began entertaining professionally as a teenager. Famous for his large, rolling eyes, he achieved a huge success as a vaudeville and Broadway performer. He had his Hollywood debut in 1926, and his popularity grew tremendously after the advent of sound, with such films as *Whoopee* (1930) and *Ali Baba Goes to Town* (1937). Cantor received a special Academy Award in 1956 for "distinguished service to the film industry."

Hillside Memorial Park

Al Jolson statue ①

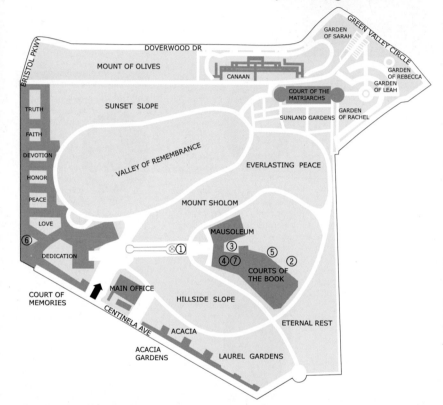

Courts of the Book, Outer Lawn, block 5, plot 800, grave 8 ②

Mausoleum, Memorial Court, Family Room ③

Mausoleum, Hall of Graciousness, sarcophagus F ④

Courts of the Book, Isaiah, Outer Court, wall U, crypt 314 ⑤

Garden of Memories, Alcove of Love, wall C, crypt 233 ⑥

Mausoleum, Hall of Graciousness, crypt 207 ⑦

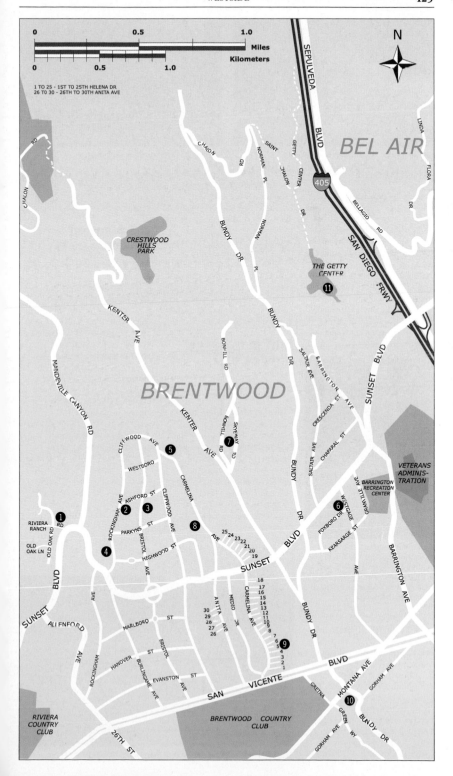

BEL AIR

1 TO 25 - 1ST TO 25TH HELENA DR
26 TO 30 - 26TH TO 30TH ANITA AVE

CRESTWOOD
HILLS
PARK

THE GETTY
CENTER ⓫

BRENTWOOD

VETERANS
ADMINIS-
TRATION

BARRINGTON
RECREATION
CENTER

⑤

⑦

② ③

④

⑧

⑥

25 24 23 22
21
20
19

18
17
16
15
14
13
12
11
10 9
8 7
6
5
9 ⑨
4
3
2
1

30
29
28
27
26

① RIVIERA
RANCH

OLD
OAK LN

RIVIERA
COUNTRY
CLUB

BRENTWOOD   COUNTRY
CLUB

⑩

Country-style atmosphere in the city

Shirley Temple childhood home

Brentwood

From its beginning in the early 1900s, Brentwood was intended as a home for the élite. This exclusive residential area was patterned after Golden Gate Park in San Francisco, with streets that avoided any resemblance to city formality. At one point it even had 34 landscaped traffic circles at intersections (of which only a few remain today), designed to slow down cars and trucks.

Brentwood's main thorough-fare, San Vicente Blvd, whose wide, green median is lined with mature coral trees (the official tree of Los Angeles), is popular with joggers

Brentwood is mainly a neighborhood of family-oriented professionals and the entertainment industry set. Some notable residents include Hollywood superagent Michael Ovitz, John Travolta and Kelly Preston, Meg Ryan and Dennis Quaid (before the split), Jim Carrey, Dustin Hoffman, Harrison Ford, former LA mayor Richard Riordan, conductor

Zubin Mehta and Monica Lewinsky's father.

Brentwood became a household name on June 12, 1994, the day of the slaying of Nicole Brown Simpson and Ron Goldman. The murder and the subsequent trial of Nicole's former husband, O J Simpson, turned this private ritzy community into a circus of paparazzi, television news crews, helicopters and curiosity seekers.

Cliff May Ranch Houses ❶

Riviera Ranch Rd and Old Oak Rd. Private residences.

This small community just north of Sunset Blvd is a showcase of one-story ranch residences, most of them designed by Cliff May, acknowledged master of the California ranch house. Characterized by low-pitched roofs, covered porches and low, extended wings, this popular house type embodies elements of the early California rancho and Craftsman bungalow. Although partially

obscured by the dense planting, you can still get a glimpse of some of the most representative examples.

O J Simpson Mansion (site) ❷

360 N Rockingham Ave.

Hidden behind the covered gate from gawkers who besieged it for several years, the former O J Simpson mansion stands at the southeast corner of Rockingham Ave and Ashford St in this 1998 photo. This was the place where O J returned after his nationally televised 60-mile (90-km) freeway chase, witnessed by almost 100 million viewers. It was also here that investigators later found a bloody glove and traces of the victims' blood.

The former football star was forced to move out of his estate after he defaulted on his mortgage payments. The five-bedroom Tudor mansion was sold in a foreclosure auction and razed by the new owner in the summer of 1998.

O J Simpson's former mansion was demolished in 1998

Joan Crawford Home

Joan Crawford Home ❸

426 N Bristol Ave.
Private residence.

With an advance of $40,000 from MGM head Louis B Mayer, Joan Crawford bought this 10-room mansion in 1929, shortly before her marriage to Douglas Fairbanks, Jr. The newlyweds called their chateau-style home El Jodo, a combination of the first syllables of their names. After she gained access to Hollywood's royal family, Joan immediately adopted the grand lifestyle of a superstar. She filled the house with Italian, Spanish and reproductions of 18th-century French furniture. Prominently displayed was her famous doll collection, said to number in the thousands.

For nearly five decades Crawford was the top ranking movie queen, winning an Oscar for best actress for her role as a sacrificing mother in *Mildred Pierce* (1945). Ironically, this was not the role she played in real life. One of her four adopted children,

Christina, wrote in her biography *Mommie Dearest* (1978) about the abuses she suffered while growing up in their Brentwood home. The film version of the book was released in 1981 under the same title, starring Faye Dunaway as Joan Crawford.

Shirley Temple Home ❹

John Byers, architect (1935-36).
231 N Rockingham Ave.
Private residence.

Shirley Temple was eight years old when her family moved from Santa Monica to their new home in Brentwood in 1936. Designed as a European farmhouse, the mansion featured fairy-tale chimneys, shuttered windows and a round tower with a weathervane—the perfect fantasy for the most famous child star ever. Shirley had her own cottage, called "the doll house," which contained her large doll collection and a famous soda fountain. The huge estate has since been divided into three large lots.

Schnabel House ❺

Frank O Gehry and Associates, architect (1989).
526 N Carmelina Ave.
Private residence.

Often described as a "village-like arrangement of forms," the Schnabel Residence is made-up of seven building–objects clustered within a garden. The central structure of the grouping is a three-story building that houses the entry, sheathed in lead-coated copper panels and lit by a skylight. Immediately to the right is a guest house topped by a dramatic copper dome. Unfortunately, a thick forest of olive trees partially blocks the view.

Lawson Westen House ❻

Eric Owen Moss Architects (1993).
167 S Westgate Ave.
Private residence.

One of the most important and inventive of Moss's designs, this hybrid house is a result of close collaboration between the architect and the clients. The entrance elevation view reveals some of the architect's fundamental ideas: the cylindrical central core with its cone-shaped roof; the vaulted roof supported by laminated timber beams, one of them fully extended at the entrance; and the bisected bent window in the front wall. This wall is concrete, while the rest of the house is covered with colored stucco.

Schnabel House

Lawson Westen House

Sturges House ❼

Frank Lloyd Wright, architect
(1939).
449 Skyewiay Rd.
Private residence.

Built as a model of low-cost design, the house represents Wright's response to the prevailing ideals of speed and movement in the 1930s, captured by the Streamline Moderne. Intended for "an ideal young married couple," the house occupies an ivy-covered hillside, to which it is tied by a carport. A large wooden terrace cantilevered from a windowless brick podium, embedded in the steep slope, floats over the street below.

Marilyn Monroe's last home remains virtually unchanged

Sturges House was built as a
model of affordable design

Greenberg House ❽

Legorreta Arquitectos (1991).
223 N Carmelina Ave.
Private residence.

The view through the gate reveals the graveled entry court and minimal façade of the Greenberg House, designed by LA-based Mexican architect Ricardo Legorreta. He was the first Latin American to receive the American Institute of Architects (AIA) highest honor, the Gold Medal. Reflecting the influence of traditional Mexican buildings, the house features the architect's signature tall, protective stucco walls, painted in shades of yellow, sand and mustard. Its serenity is emphasized by a group of 80-foot (24-m) tall palm trees.

Marilyn Monroe Suicide Home ❾

12305 5th Helena Dr.
Private residence. Ⓑ

This simple, three-bedroom Spanish-style house is the place where Marilyn Monroe died, reportedly of a drug overdose. She was found in her bedroom, laying nude in bed, with an empty bottle of the sedative Nembutal near her. The unpretentious, one-story house in which the movie star and the greatest sex symbol of the 20th century lived for six months has not changed much since her death on August 4, 1962.

Nicole Brown Simpson Condo ❿

875 (now 871) S Bundy Dr.
Private residence. Ⓑ

After the crime that shocked the world on June 12, 1994, the former condominium home of murdered Nicole Brown Simpson, at the corner of Bundy Dr and Dorothy St, became a huge

Nicole Brown Simpson condo,
the murder scene

tourist attraction. To divert the flood of lookie-loos, the new owner redesigned and re-landscaped the entrance to the three-story townhouse and changed the number from 875 to 871.

Greenberg House

Getty Center ⑪

Richard Meier, architect (1997).
1200 Getty Center Dr.
☎(310) 440-7360.
www.getty.edu.
🕘Tue-Thu, Sun 10am-6pm; Fri-Sat
10am-9pm. Closed: Mon and
major holidays.
Ⓢfree; parking fee.

After fourteen years of
planning and construction, at
a cost of $1 billion, the
world's richest museum and
Los Angeles' most exciting
cultural attraction opened in
1997. Situated on a hilltop
overlooking the city and the
Pacific Ocean, the new Getty
Center offers its 1.3 million
annual visitors unique opportunity to experience and
study art and cultural heritage. The six-building complex, designed by Pritzker
Prize winning architect
Richard Meier, features the
new J Paul Getty Museum,
Research and Conservation
Institutes and Foundation.

The Museum consists of
five interconnected, two-story
gallery pavilions which sur
round a large paved courtyard. Four pavilions contain
art of a specific period; the
fifth pavilion houses changing exhibitions.

Paintings are presented on
the upper level under ideal
conditions. They are illuminated by daylight entering
the galleries through a
sophisticated skylight system.
Computer-controlled louvers
and shades move every 20
minutes to adjust to the sun's
movement and keep out
direct sunlight.

The J Paul Getty Museum at the Getty Center

On the ground level the
permanent collections of
sculpture, illuminated manuscripts, decorative arts, drawings and photographs are
artificially lit and exhibited in
specially designed galleries.

The Getty Center campus
also comprises extensive formal and informal gardens,
including the three-acre Central Garden created by artist
Robert Irwin. The gardens
are planted with both California native and introduced
plants, including more than
500 varieties used in the
landscaping of the Central
Garden alone.

The European Paintings
collection, particularly rich in
French, Italian and Dutch
works, covers the period
from the early 14th to the
late 19th centuries. The most
important works include
Rembrandt's *Saint Bartholo-
mew* (1661), Jan Steen's
Drawing Lesson (ca. 1665),
Veronese's *Portrait of Man*
(ca. 1560), Monet's *Still Life
with Flowers* (1869), Renoir's

La Promenade (1870) and
Manet's *Rue Mosnier with
Flags* (1878).

The Decorative Arts collection contains mainly pieces
made in Paris between 1660
and 1815. It consists of furniture, tapestries, carpets,
clocks, porcelain, and small
objects—chandeliers, wall
lights and inkstands. Furniture made in Northern
Europe, Germany and Italy is
also on display.

The Drawings collection
features more than 400 works
spanning the period from the
second half of the 15th century to the end of the 19th
century. Works by Leonardo,
Raphael, Durer, Rubens, Goya,
Watteau, Ingres, Cézanne and
van Gogh are represented.

The core of the Manuscript
holdings consists of the Ludwig Collection of 144 illuminated manuscripts purchased
in 1983. Ranging from the
9th to the 17th centuries, collection highlights include
Ottonian, Byzantine,
Romanesque, Gothic and
Renaissance manuscripts.

The collection of Pho-
tographs, one of the best in
the US, covers the medium
from the early 1840s to the
1950s. Among the important
artists whose works are
included are Talbot, Nadar,
Cameron, Bayard, Cunning-
ham, Kertész and Man Ray.

European Sculpture from
the Middle Ages to the end
of the 19th century is represented by works of Bernini,
Giambologna, Clodion,
Houdon and Carpeaux,
among others.

Renaissance paintings gallery in the J Paul Getty Museum

The J Paul Getty Museum

Apollo Crowning Himself (1781-82) by Antonio Canova

Corner cupboard, by Jacques Dubois, French (ca. 1755)

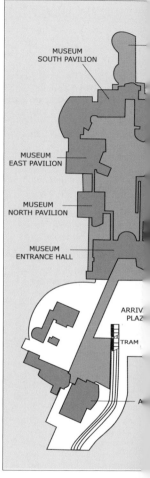

MUSEUM SOUTH PAVILION

MUSEUM EAST PAVILION

MUSEUM NORTH PAVILION

MUSEUM ENTRANCE HALL

ARRIV PLAZ

TRAM

The Holy Family with the Infant Saint John the Baptist (ca. 1530) by Michelangelo Buonarotti

Still Life with Apples (1893-94) by Paul Cézanne

Landscape with Calm (1651) by Nicolas Poussin

SOUTH PROMONTORY

MUSEUM
EST PAVILION

CENTRAL GARDEN

EXHIBITIONS
PAVILION

CAFE

RESEARCH INSTITUTE

RESTAURANT/CAFE

Lidded vase (1768-69) by Jean-Baptiste-Etienne Genest and Sevres Manufactory

The Story of Adam and Eve (ca. 1415) by Boucicaut Master and Workshop

Desert Sand Hills (1867) by Timothy H O'Sullivan

Venus and Adonis (ca. 1555-60) by Titian

The Return From War: Mars Disarmed by Venus (ca. 1610-12) by Peter Paul Rubens and Jan Brueghel the Elder

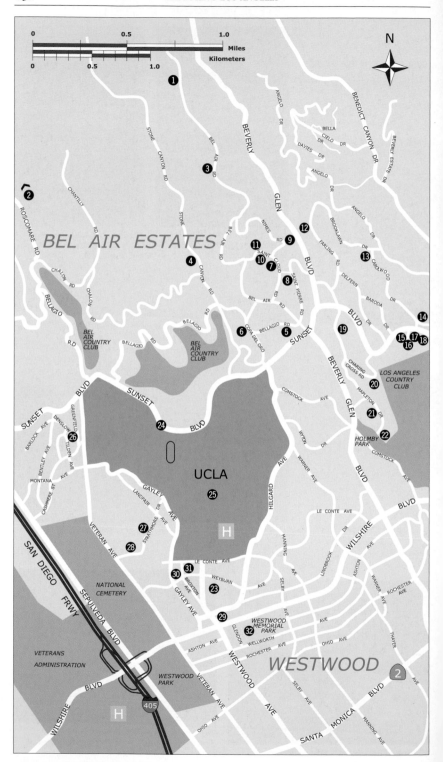

The west entrance to Bel Air

The hilly area of Bel Air offers views of the entire LA basin

Bel Air

The wooded hills just north of Sunset Blvd, between Beverly Hills and Brentwood, are the preferred home to movie celebrities or the very rich in general. In its early years, no movie people, blacks, Jews or Orientals were allowed in the enclave. This policy changed, however, during the Great Depression, when only Hollywood stars and movie moguls could afford Bel Air prices. Since then, anyone can take residence in the upper-crust retreat. The only requirement is money. Tons of money.

The area was developed in the 1920s by Alphonzo Bell, who was at the time one of the wealthiest men in California. He struck it rich when oil was discovered under his 200-acre (80-ha) ranch in Santa Fe Springs. This turned out to be one of the richest oil fields in the world, which brought in royalties of $100,000 a

month for years. He invested his fortune in a 2,000-acre (800-ha) tract of undeveloped land which he subdivided into generous lots and promoted under the name Bel Air. The name, coined by his wife, roughly means "beautiful place" in French, and also incorporates the Bell family name.

This tranquil area, with its winding narrow streets and green tunnels of lush foliage and mature trees is a perfect setting for a pleasant ride. The community's affluent residents hired the best architects of the time, including Wallace Neff, Gordon B Kaufmann and Paul Williams, to design their stately homes. Most of them are now hidden behind thick walls of overgrown landscaping.

When Alphonzo Bell erected two large entrance gates on Bel Air and Bellagio roads in the 1920s, Bel Air was an exclusive residential enclave. The gates were manned by uniformed guards, and

the area was protected by a private police force who patrolled the streets and escorted invited guests. Despite its off-limits appearance, the community is now open to the public and anybody can drive through or walk around.

A pioneer of security patrols, Bel Air was protected by a private service long before other exclusive communities found it necessary

Among the famous Bel Air residents are business tycoons Lee Iacocca, David Murdoch and Michael Eisner, musician Quincy Jones, producer Peter Guber, director Joel Schumacher, authors Neil Simon and Judith Krantz, fashion designer Tom Ford and actors Clint Eastwood, Robert Stack and Leonard Nimoy.

Symbolizing a glamorous lifestyle associated with its elegant namesake, the spirited Chevrolet Bel Air became one of the most desirable cars in America. In various permutations, hundreds of thousands of the popular Bel Air line cars were made during the 1950s.

The Chevy Bel Air was one of the most popular cars of the 1950s

Case Study House No. 16 is based upon 8-foot (2,4-m) modules

Case Study House No. 16 ❶

Craig Ellwood, architect (1951).
1811 Bel Air Rd.
Private residence.

This was the first of three houses designed by Craig Ellwood for the Case Study House program (➜ p97). Although without formal architectural training, Ellwood was eager to experiment and apply new technologies, as evident in this relatively small, steel-and-glass box. Situated in wooded hills and commanding splendid city views, the house is perfectly integrated into the environment, effectively blending indoor and outdoor spaces.

Wilt Chamberlain Home ❷

David Rich, architect (1971).
15216 Antelo Place. Not on map.
Private residence.

Built in 1971, this wood-and-glass pyramidal castle was custom designed to suit the 7-foot, 1-inch (216-cm) legendary Laker center. He named his house *Ursa Major* (the Latin name for the constellation called the Big Dipper, also Wilt's favorite nickname).

The focal point of the house is unquestionably the triangular bedroom, with mirrored walls, Cleopatra-inspired, 18-karat gold tile bathtub and retractable mirrored ceiling that reveals the sky. This was the favorite playground for a man who claimed to have slept with 20,000 women.

Chamberlain died here in 1999 of a heart attack after leaving behind an unsurpassed basketball legacy. He holds an all-time NBA record with 23,924 rebounds and was the only player ever to score 100 points in an NBA game. A man of diverse talents and interests, he starred along Arnold Schwarzenegger in the movie *Conan the Destroyer* (1984).

Wilt Chamberlain Home

Zsa Zsa Gabor Home ❸

1001 Bel Air Rd.
Private residence.

Former residence of eccentric filmmaker and aviator Howard Hughes, this is the home of actress Zsa Zsa Gabor and her ninth husband. During the 1950s and early 1960s, she was regarded as the epitome of femininity and one of the most glamorous women in America. Gabor has appeared in more than 75 movies, including *Moulin Rouge* (1952) and *Touch of Evil* (1958). Not so famous for her film roles as for many jewels and lovers, she made headlines again when she went to jail for slapping a Beverly Hills police officer in 1989.

Hotel Bel Air ❹

701 Stone Canyon Rd.
☎(310) 472-1211.

The hotel's main structure was built by oil millionaire Alphonzo Bell in 1922 as his office building, with stables and a riding ring. It was converted to a hotel in 1946, with a cluster of villas added around the original building. The hotel's 11.5-acre grounds are lavishly landscaped with over 200 plant species. Many of the garden's trees and shrubs are rarely seen in Southern California.

The secluded hotel has been a favorite hideaway for some of the greatest Hollywood stars, from Marlene Dietrich and Greta Garbo to Sharon Stone and Tom Cruise.

Brian Wilson Home ❺

10452 Bellagio Rd.
Private residence.

While residing in this villa during the 1960s, the Beach Boys' Brian Wilson painted it purple, infuriating the neighbors. He wrote here some of the group's most popular songs, and they recorded parts of their albums *Smiley Smile*, *Wild Honey*, *Sunflower* and *Surf's Up* in Wilson's home studio here. The house was once owned by author Edgar Rice Burroughs, author of the Tarzan books.

Fountain in the Hotel Bel Air

The Beatles stayed here in August 1964

Louis B Mayer Home

Nicolas Cage Home ❻

363 Copa De Oro Rd.
Private residence.

This ornate red-brick Tudor-style house is the residence of actor Nicolas Cage, who won an Academy Award as best actor for his performance as an alcoholic Hollywood agent in *Leaving Las Vegas* (1995). The 33 room mansion was the long-time home of English singer Tom Jones, who bought it from actor-singer Dean Martin, a popular entertainer of the 1950s and 1960s.

Nicolas Cage Home

Ronald Reagan Home ❼

668 St Cloud Rd.
Private residence.

After their departure from the White House, former President and First Lady Ronald and Nancy Reagan lived in this residence guarded by Secret Service agents. The original house number was 666, the sign of the beast in *The Book of Revelation*, but superstitious Nancy had it changed. The house is not visible from the road.

The Beatles Residence ❽

356 St Pierre Rd.
Private residence.

Fearing a cataclysm of teenage fans in the wake of their legendary concert at the Hollywood Bowl on August 23, 1964, Lockheed Airport in Burbank refused to let the Beatles' plane land.

After the Ambassador Hotel cancelled their reservations for the same reason, the Beatles rented an estate owned by British actor Reginald Owen for four days for $1,000. It was here where a fully clothed John Lennon jumped into the mansion's pool. Besieged by frenzied Beatlemaniacs, the group played cowboys and Indians on the estate's two-acre grounds with toy guns—a gift from Elvis Presley.

Elizabeth Taylor Home ❾

700 Nimes Rd.
Private residence.

Behind this unimpressive gate lives one of the most popular screen goddesses of the 20th century. Widely regarded as the most beautiful woman in the world, Elizabeth Taylor starred in *A Place in the Sun* (1951), *Cat on a Hot Tin Roof* (1958) and *Cleopatra* (1963). She won two best actress Academy Awards—for her performances in *Butterfield 8* (1960) and *Who's Afraid of Virginia Wolf?* (1966). Purchased by the actress in 1972, the two-story, 22-room house is not visible from the street.

Louis B Mayer Home ❿

332 St Cloud Rd.
Private residence.

Once the home of Louis B Mayer, MGM studio head from 1924 to 1951 and the most powerful man in Hollywood, this stately mansion was later owned by popular comedian Jerry Lewis.

Sonny and Cher Home ⓫

364 St Cloud Rd.
Private residence. 🏴

This was the one time residence of the popular singer duo Sonny and Cher. It was later owned by *Hustler* magazine publisher Larry Flynt.

The mansion was used as a backdrop in Milos Forman's film *The People vs. Larry Flynt* (1996), in a scene in which Woody Harrelson, who portrayed Flynt in the movie, was arrested. The house was also seen in the 1991 remake of the comedy *Father of the Bride*, as Steve Martin sneaks into the study of his affluent in-laws wishing to check the state of their bank account.

Sonny and Cher Home

Holmby Hills

The community of Holmby Hills is the most exclusive of all Westside districts, even more expensive than Bel Air and Beverly Hills. Conceived in the 1920s as the poshest residential neighborhood, it consists only of mansions and estates, without any commercial structures or smaller houses. The area was named after Holmby, England, the birthplace of its owner, Arthur Letts, Sr, founder of the Broadway Department Store. The hilly district is beautifully landscaped and contains many palatial older residences.

Claudette Colbert home

Claudette Colbert Home ⑫

Lloyd Wright, architect (1935).
615 N Faring Rd.
Private residence.

This amalgam of Moderne and Colonial Revival was the long-time home of actress and socialite Claudette Colbert. She was one of Hollywood's leading comediennes, who won the 1934 best actress Oscar for her role as a headstrong heiress in *It Happened One Night*.

Colbert, who wanted a Georgian house, was not quite pleased with the Wright's unconventional understanding of revival styles, and in 1937 hired the popular architect Wallace Neff to renovate the house.

In 1961 Colbert left Hollywood and lived in a plantation house on the Carribean island of Barbados.

Rod Stewart Home ⑬

391 N Carolwood Dr.
Private residence.

Behind the forbidding gate, tall walls and climbing vines is the former home of the popular rock singer Rod Stewart. He lived and partied here with his model wife, Rachel Hunter, until 1992.

Elvis Presley's last LA home

Elvis Presley Home ⑭

144 Monovale Dr.
Private residence.

This two-story, 25-room English house, barely visible behind a high wall, was a longtime residence of Elvis and Priscilla Presley. The king of rock 'n' roll and the most successful recording artist in history lived here between 1967 and 1975. This was the final of his several homes in Los Angeles (Elvis died at Graceland in Memphis, on August 16, 1977).

Rod Stewart home

Jayne Mansfield's Pink Palace (site) ⑮

10100 Sunset Blvd.

Originally built in the 1930s by singer-actor Rudy Vallee, this 7-bedroom, Mediterranean-style mansion gained the fame as the home of Jayne Mansfield, Hollywood bombshell of the 1950s and 1960s. It was nicknamed the Pink Palace after the actress had the whole house repainted in her favorite color. The wall surrounding the property, the façade, the rooms and wall-to-wall carpeting were all pink. Although it changed hands several times, including its owner from the mid-1970s to 2002, singer Engelbert Humperdinck, the Pink Palace remained pink. The house was razed in 2002.

Mansfield's second husband, muscleman Mickey Hargitay, built her a heart-shaped swimming pool in the backyard. On its bottom he inscribed "I Love You Jaynie" in gold-leaf mosaic.

Jayne Mansfield's famous Pink Palace was razed in 2002

Owlwood ⑯

Robert Farquhar, architect (1936).
141 S Carolwood Dr.
Private residence.

One of the most spectacular estates in the entire Los Angeles area can be seen from the end of a cul-de-sac, just south of Sunset Blvd. Through a tall, imposing iron-wrought gate is an impressive view of the main residence, sweeping lawns and manicured gardens.

The estate's focal point is an elegant Tuscan-style mansion, designed by noted architect Robert Farquhar. The property was purchased in the 1940s by film pioneer and later 20th Century Fox's chairman of the board, Joseph M Schenck. Young starlet Marilyn Monroe moved into the mansion's guest house in 1949 and stayed as Schenck's lover for more than a year. The residence was subsequently the home of actors Tony Curtis and Janet Leigh, then singer duo Sonny and Cher in the 1970s.

Marilyn Monroe lived once at the spectacular Owlwood estate

Plaque on the gate at Owlwood

Esther Williams Home ⑰

Gordon Kaufmann, architect (1925)
10060 Sunset Blvd.
Private residence.

Behind this gate is a Spanish-style villa designed by architect Gordon B Kaufmann and built in 1925 by Edwin Janss, the developer of Westwood Village. Today part of the Owlwood compound, the house, which remained virtually unchanged since the 1920s, was at one time the home of actress-swimmer Esther Williams. Known as the "Hollywood Mermaid," she starred in numerous musicals with

spectacular underwater ballet scenes in the 1940s and 1950s. MGM built her a large pool on the property, together with a special pedestal on a hydraulic lift, designed to raise the actress 50 feet (15m) out of the water in preparation for a dive.

Haderway Hall ⑱

Wallace Neff, architect (1939).
10000 Sunset Blvd.
Private residence.

Once owned by mysterious producer, director and aviator Howard Hughes, this was the home of actress Judy Garland and her second husband, director Vincente Minnelli in the late 1940s. Garland, who became world famous portraying Dorothy in *The Wizard of Oz* (1939), made the first in a series of suicide attempts in this house. Today, motorists who drive by the house are intrigued by numerous life-size statues installed in the front lawn.

Humphrey Bogart and Lauren Bacall Home ⑲

232 S Mapleton Dr.
Private residence.

This is the former home of the famous Hollywood couple, a perfect match both on- and off-screen. Bogart and Bacall met on the set of *To Have and Have Not* (1945), fell in love and soon married. This was his fourth marriage. He was 46 years old and at the peak of popularity. She was 21 and just started on her film career. They made three more films together, *The Big Sleep* (1946), *Dark Passage* (1947) and *Key Largo* (1948). The couple lived here with their two children between 1946 and 1957, when Bogart died of cancer.

The house was later owned by producer Ray Stark, whose films include *The Night of the Iguana* (1964) and *Funny Girl* (1968).

Humphrey Bogart and Lauren Bacall home

The Playboy Mansion became a synonym of a hedonistic lifestyle

The Playboy Mansion ⑳

10236 Charing Cross Rd. 🚩
Private residence.

The most renowned estate in Holmby Hills was built in 1927 for Arthur Letts Jr, whose father was the owner of the land now comprising a large part of West LA. *Playboy* publisher Hugh Hefner purchased the estate in 1971, after his girlfriend Barbi Benton picked out the 30-room Tudor-style mansion. The six-acre grounds contain a famous free-form swimming pool, a grotto with a waterfall, tennis court, fabulous gardens with the largest privately held stand of redwoods in Southern California, and a zoo with exotic birds and monkeys.

As the symbol of a bacchanalian lifestyle deeply seeded in popular imagination, the Playboy Mansion has no equal in the world. The stage for a never-ending series of parties, its mere mention immediately invokes images of buxom playmates frolicking in the pool or steamy grotto. You can get a glimpse of this exuberant world only if you are invited. And those invited (during the last 30 years, the list of guests includes almost every celebrity), apparently like it for some reason.

The mansion's dark wood interior was used as a setting on many *Playboy* centerfolds. It is Hefner's policy not to

allow his home to appear in the movies. However, in one of just a few exceptions, Hef played himself in *Beverly Hills Cop II* (1987), in a party scene filmed on the grounds. The mansion was also featured in Bob Fosse's movie *Star 80* (1983), a story of former Playmate of the Year Dorothy Stratten (played by Mariel Hemingway), who was brutally murdered by her estranged husband.

After their divorce in 1999, Hef purchased a house next door for his former wife Kimberly and their two sons.

Joan Bennett Home ㉑

Wallace Neff, architect (1936).
515 S Mapleton Dr.
Private residence.

Sitting atop a little knoll and featuring his signature tall chimneys, this whitewashed-brick house was designed by architect Wallace

Neff for glamorous star Joan Bennett. Originally a blonde, she changed color of her hair in 1938 following the advice from producer Walter Wanger, later her husband. As a brunette, Bennett made some of her best films, including Fritz Lang's *The Woman in the Window* (1944) and *Scarlet Street* (1946).

Aaron Spelling Manor ㉒

594 S Mapleton Dr.
Private residence.

Allegedly the biggest house in Southern California, this is the home of Emmy-winning producer Aaron Spelling, the man who created such popular television series as *The Mod Squad*, *Charlie's Angels*, *Fantasy Island*, *The Love Boat*, *Dynasty*, *Beverly Hills 90210* and *Melrose Place*.

The French Regency-style manor was erected on a six-acre site once occupied by singer-actor Bing Crosby's mansion, which was torn down to make room for this monstrous indulgence. Completed in 1991, the house is 56,000 sq ft (5.000m²)—about the size of a football field—and was built at a price of more than $40 million. Not counting domestic help, the 123-room house is usually inhabited only by Spelling, his wife and son. His daughter Tori, who starred in *Beverly Hills 90210*, moved out reportedly because she could not find a suitable room.

Aaron Spelling Manor is the largest residential property in LA

Westwood

Planned in the 1920s by the Janss Investment Company, Westwood is considered one of the most successful suburban real estate developments in the country. Its residential part consists of single-family homes built in a variety of historic styles, most frequently Spanish Colonial Revival.

Westwood Village, however, was developed as a business and commercial center. It was designed to resemble a Mediterranean village with its charming one- and two-story brick and stucco buildings. Although intended with the automobile in mind, the Village is one of only a few pedestrian-friendly areas in Los Angeles. It is especially busy on weekend nights, when a mostly younger crowd fills its avenues attracted by cafés, boutiques, record stores and movie theaters.

A vintage post card depicts Westwood Village in the 1940s

The Dome

The Dome ㉓

Allison and Allison, architects (1929).
1099 Westwood Blvd.

Built in 1929 as a sales office for the developers of Westwood, this Spanish-style landmark once housed a bank, several retail stores and now an upscale restaurant. The octagonal building, with its arched windows and colorful dome covered with glazed tiles arranged in zigzag pattern, still dominates the Village.

Dead Man's Curve ㉔

Sunset Blvd, west of Groverton Pl.

> Dead Man's Curve,
> it's no place to play
> Dead Man's Curve,
> you must keep away
> Dead Man's Curve,
> I can hear them say
> Won't come back from
> Dead Man's Curve.
> *Dead Man's Curve*
> by Jan & Dean (1964)

Immortalized by Jan & Dean's hit 1964 song, this difficult turn on Sunset Blvd was a site of numerous real-life accidents. Famous comedian Mel Blanc, best known as the voice of Bugs Bunny, was in critical condition in 1961 after a head-on collision at the curve.

Based on the hot rod culture that flourished among the LA youth at the time, the song describes the street race between a Corvette Stingray and Jaguar XKE that starts at Sunset and Vine, "all the way to Dead Man's Curve."

In a bizarre accident reminiscent of their song, singer Jan Berry was almost killed on April 12, 1966. He crashed his silver Stingray at 90 mph (145 km/h) into a parked truck on Whittier Dr in Beverly Hills, only a few miles from the real Dead Man's Curve. Berry suffered head injuries and was partially paralyzed for years while the duo's career was put on hold.

Wilshire high rises

Westwood's small-town ambience started to wane in the 1970s, when new developments along Wilshire Blvd transformed this thoroughfare into a canyon of tightly packed high-rises.

Known as the Wilshire Corridor, this is an area of luxury condominium buildings, where some penthouses sell for more than $15 million.

Tightly packed high rises along Wilshire Boulevard

University of California, Los Angeles (UCLA) ㉕

405 Hilgard Ave.
☎(310) 825-4321 (general info).
☛guided tours: 1147 Murphy
Hall, ☎(310) 825-8764 (reservations). Maps are available at any of the information booths located at the main entrances. Free Campus Shuttle buses circulate the grounds. Campus parking: Ⓢ
www.ucla.edu (UCLA is the birthplace of the Internet). ☛

The UCLA campus is beautifully landscaped with exotic plants

Established in 1919, UCLA is widely regarded as one of the leading academic institutions in the nation. The American Council on Education ranked UCLA among the top 10 universities in the country. Among UCLA faculty members were four Nobel Prize winners and seven recipients of the National Medal of Science. Today, the university boasts an enrollment of 35,000 students, the largest in California.

Joe Bruin, the UCLA mascot

Famous UCLA alumni include director Francis Ford Coppola, actors Carol Burnett and Tim Robbins, screenwriter Robert Towne, rockers Jim Morrison and Ray Manzarek of the Doors fame, composer John Williams, athletes Kareem Abdul-Jabbar and Jackie Joyner-Kersee. With its various concerts, performances, exhibits, lectures and other programs open to the public, UCLA is also an important cultural center.

The 419-acre (168-ha) campus is lavishly landscaped with remarkable mature trees and exotic plants and comprises more than 230 buildings. The master plan for the campus was developed by architect George W Kelham and the first four structures were constructed in 1929. These original buildings,

known as Royce Quad, or the historic center of the campus, are Royce Hall and Haines Hall on the north, and Powell Library and Kinsey Hall on the south. They are all built of red brick in an especially decorative Northern Italian, or Romanesque Lombardian style. However, most of the buildings that followed after the 1930s, with a few exceptions, are bland and undistinguished.

The UCLA campus is frequently used as a film location site. It has been the setting for UC Berkeley-based scenes in *The Graduate* (1967) and passed for Harvard in *Legally Blonde* (2001). Other movies filmed here include *The Sure Thing* (1985), *Final Analysis* (1992) and *The Nutty Professor* (1996).

Gordon and Virginia MacDonald Medical Research Laboratories
Venturi, Scott Brown, architects (1991).

Gonda (Goldschmied) Neuroscience and Genetics Research Center
Venturi, Scott Brown, architects (1998).

These new additions to the UCLA School of Medicine precinct were designed to correspond to other surrounding medical brick buildings and to the older Lombardian Romanesque structures in the central part of the campus.

The architects achieved an outstanding decorative effect on the façade with the rhythmic pattern of its bays and windows, along with multicolored brick ornaments.

Two new medical buildings designed by Venturi, Scott and Brown

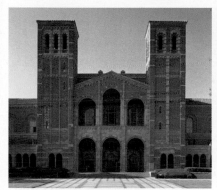

Royce Hall's auditorium is hailed for its acoustics **Italian Romanesque façade of the Powell Library**

Royce Hall
Allison and Allison, architects
(1928-29).

Two tall, unsymmetrical
towers with belfries at the
top are the main features of
Royce Hall, UCLA's landmark
building. It was based on the
Church of San Ambrogio in
Milan, Italy, and contains a
2,000-seat auditorium with an
antique pipe organ. Admired
for its acoustics, it is considered the best performance
hall in Los Angeles.

**Paintings decorate the vaults
in Royce Hall's portico**

Powell Library
George Kelham, architect (1928).

Patterned after the Church
of San Sepolcro in Bologna,
Italy, Powell Library serves as
UCLA's main undergraduate
library. It features a prominent octagonal central tower
and an arched entry with two
narrow towers on the sides.
Its striking interiors are noted
for a long, bifurcated stairway and a grand rotunda.

Schoenberg Hall
Welton Becket and Associates,
architects (1955).

One of the more important
examples of mid-century
architecture on the campus,
the building was named after
Austrian composer Arnold
Schoenberg. Considered one
of the greatest musical innovators, he taught music at
UCLA from 1936 to 1951.

Above the exterior foyer, a
16-panel mosaic by Richard
Haines depicts the history of
music. In the lobby is displayed a collection of non-
Western stringed musical
instruments.

Inverted Fountain
Jere Hazlett and Howard Troller
(1973).

About 10,000 gallons
(38,000 liters) of water per
minute rush from the fountain's perimeter to the center,
foaming over smooth stones.
It was inspired by the natural
hot springs of the Yellow-
stone National Park.

UCLA Fowler Museum of Cultural History
Arnold C Savrann, architect (1992)
405 Hilgard Ave.
☎ (310) 825-4361.
🕐: Wed-Sun noon-5pm, Thu noon-
8pm. Ⓞ free.

The Fowler Museum is con-
sidered one of the nation's
four leading university-based
anthropological museums. It
houses a collection of over
750,000 objects that represent
contemporary, historic and
pre-historic cultures.

The African art collection is
one of the largest in the
world. Works from Oceania
(primarily Melanesia) are also
very strongly featured. Mostly
European Neolithic and Pale-
olithic materials are extensive. The museum contains
folk art from around the
world, although the greatest
concentration is from Latin
America. There is also a
good collection of ethno-
graphic materials from the
tropical rain forests of South
America.

Schoenberg Hall

Tischler House ㉖

Rudolf M Schindler, architect (1949)
175 Greenfield Ave.
Private residence.

One of the architect's last projects, the complex geometric volume of the Tischler residence is among Schindler's most original works. The frontispiece of this stucco house is made of an inverted T-shaped base on which sit a skylight and a wooden gable roof. As an experiment in low-cost materials, the house was originally covered with blue corrugated fiberglass panels.

Tischler House

Strathmore Apartments ㉗

Richard Neutra, architect (1937).
11005 Strathmore Dr.
Private residences.

Designed as an International Style version of a Southern California bungalow court, this apartment complex consists of four separate buildings containing two units each. Constructed of wood and stucco, the buildings are grouped around a central garden and connected by a stairway that climbs a steep hill. With long bands of windows and balconies recessed from exterior walls, Neutra stresses the clean lines of rectangular volumes, now partially hidden behind thick foliage. Early tenants included architect/designer couple Charles and Ray Eames, and movie celebrities Dolores Del Rio and Orson Welles.

Richard Neutra's Strathmore Apartments

Sheats Apartments (L'Horizon) ㉘

John Lautner, architect (1948).
10919 Strathmore Dr.
Private residences.

In this unconventional fusion of regional spirit and futurism, Lautner used the concept of traditional LA garden apartments and clustered huge steel-and-redwood cylinders around the center court. Each of the apartment units is completely independent, with windows on all sides and its own terraces and outdoor spaces.

Façade of the Armand Hammer Museum of Art

Armand Hammer Museum of Art and Cultural Center ㉙

Edward Larabee Barnes, architect (1990).
10899 Wishire Blvd.
☎(310) 443-7000.
www.hammer.ucla.edu
🕘Tue-Wed, Fri-Sat 11am-7pm; Thu 11am-9pm, Sun 11am-5pm. $

The museum displays selections from its permanent collections, assembled by its founder, businessman Armand Hammer.

The Armand Hammer Collection consists of over 100 works, with an emphasis on Old Masters, French Impressionists and Post-Impressionists, with significant holdings of prints and drawings. Highlights of the collection include *Juno* by Rembrandt van Rijn, *View of Bordighera* by Claude Monet, *Bonjour M Gauguin* by Paul Gauguin and *Hospital at Saint Remy* by Vincent van Gogh.

The Grunwald Center for the Graphic Arts contains over 45,000 works on paper, including prints, artists' books, drawings and photographs dating from the 13th century to the present. Among the artists represented are Pablo Picasso, Albrecht Dürer, George Cruikshank, Jasper Jones and Käthe Kollwitz.

The Franklin D Murphy Sculpture Garden features a fascinating collection of pieces by some of the greatest European and American sculptors of the 19th and 20th centuries, including Jean Arp, Henry Moore, Auguste Rodin, David Smith and Francisco Zuñiga.

The Fox Village Theatre's tower, often compared to a tall wedding cake adorned with neon icing, dominates the Westwood Village skyline

The Fox Village auditorium features a golden feather motif

Fox Village Theatre ㉚

The first movie house in Westwood, the Village opened in 1931 as the flagship of a theater chain built by Fox Film Corporation. Designed in Spanish Colonial Revival style with Moderne details, the theater's exterior remains for the most part unchanged. Its striking features include an ornamented cornice and turrets topped with winged lions, as well as a four-sided marquee and an imposing, neon-lit tower. Designed to attract motorists driving along Wilshire Blvd, the tower top features the Fox nameplate and Art Deco metal patterns. One of the most remarkable of Los Angeles' movie theaters, the Village is still frequently used for movie premieres.

P P Lewis, architect (1931).
961 Broxton Ave.
☎(310) 248-6266.

A statue of golden maidens

Mann's Bruin Theatre ㉛

The Bruin was designed in 1937 by famous architect S Charles Lee, who completed more than four hundred different theaters in his career. The Streamline Moderne building, which contrasts to the predominantly Spanish Colonial style of the area, is noted for its signature semi-circular neon-lit marquee. The theater is mostly intact, but its original luminous murals have been painted over.

S Charles Lee, architect (1937).
948 Broxton Ave.
☎(310) 208-8998.

Mann's Bruin Theatre features an ornate, wrap-around marquee

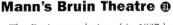

Jennifer Aniston attends a premiere in Westwood. With the largest concentration of first-run movie theaters in Los Angeles, Westwood has surpassed Hollywood as the city's cinema center. Major studio premieres and sneak previews are regularly staged at its large-screen theaters, making them places in town to see a movie on opening night.

Westwood Memorial Park 32

1218 Glendon Ave.
☎(310) 474-1579.
🕘8am-6pm daily.

This small, serene cemetery is not easy to locate, as it is tucked behind an office building, a parking structure and a movie house. From Wilshire Blvd, turn south on Glendon Ave and make an immediate left into the first driveway. At the end there is a small sign that reads "Pierce Brothers Westwood Village Memorial Park and Mortuary."

When the cemetery was founded in 1904, Westwood was a rural area on the outskirts of LA. For years the park served as burial grounds for veterans of America's many wars. After Marilyn Monroe was buried here in 1962, so many celebrities followed suit that it is now known as "the Cemetery to the Stars."

Interred here in unmarked graves are two famous rockers. **Roy Orbison** (1936-1988), whose best-known hits include *Only the Lonely*; *Oh, Pretty Woman* and *She's a Mystery to Me*, died on December 6, 1988 of a heart attack. **Frank Zappa** (1940-1993), the provocative and controversial leader of the Mothers of Invention, died of cancer on December 4, 1993. Also buried here are **Heather O'Rourke** and **Dominique Dunne**, the child stars from the *Poltergeist* films.

Burt Lancaster (1913-1994)

Close to the edge of the curb is the marker of famous actor Burt Lancaster, one of the greatest stars in the history of cinema. A former circus acrobat, he was equally successful in athletic and dramatic roles, giving major performances in *Come Back, Little Sheba* (1953), *From Here to Eternity* (1953), *Novecento/1900* (1976) and *Atlantic City* (1980). He won the 1960 best actor Academy Award for his role as a travelling salesman turned preacher in *Elmer Gantry*.

Darryl F Zanuck (1902-1979)

Head of 20th Century-Fox for 35 years, Darryl F Zanuck produced more than 160 movies, including such hits as *The Grapes of Wrath* (1940), *Gentleman's Agreement* (1947), *All About Eve* (1950) and *The Longest Day* (1962). His bronze plaque boasts the 20th Century-Fox logo and a list of his numerous accomplishments. At his funeral, the theme from *The Longest Day* was the only music played.

Donna Reed (1921-1986)

Before becoming a Hollywood leading lady in the 1940s and 1950s, Donna Reed won a high school beauty contest and was elected campus queen at college. She won an Academy Award as best supporting actress for her portrayal of Alma, the prostitute in *From Here to Eternity* (1953). However, she is best known for her role in the perennial holiday movie, *It's a Wonderful Life* (1946), and her own television series, *The Donna Reed Show* (1958-1966).

Dorothy Stratten (1960-1980)

Playboy's centerfold and 1980 Playmate of the Year, Dorothy Stratten was raped, tortured and murdered by her obsessive husband before he took his own life. At the time of the murder she was involved with director Peter Bogdanovich, who had cast her in his film *They All Laughed* (1981). Her marker is inscribed with a passage from Hemingway's *A Farewell to Arms*.

Natalie Wood (1938-1981)

Located in the central section, Natalie Wood's headstone is easy to spot as it is surrounded with pots of flowers. Born Natasha Gurdin, she made her film debut at age five and eventually became one of the most popular and beloved Hollywood stars. Among her memorable performances are *Rebel Without a Cause* (1955), *Splendor in the Grass* (1961), *West Side Story* (1961) and *Gypsy* (1962). She was married to actor Robert Wagner from 1957 to 1963, then again from 1972 onward. Wood drowned under mysterious circumstances off Catalina Island.

Mel Torme (1925-1999)

Popularly known as the "Velvet Fog" for his smooth voice, Torme was widely regarded as one of the best male jazz singers. He won Grammy Awards for best male jazz vocalist in 1982 and 1983. Among his best-remembered hits are *Careless Love* and *The Christmas Song* (*Chestnuts Roasting on an Open Fire*).

George C Scott (1927-1999)

An intense and forceful actor, Scott appeared in over one hundred films and was nominated for an Academy Awards three times, for *Anatomy of a Murder* (1959), *The Hustler* (1961) and *The Hospital* (1971). Scott made headlines as the first actor to decline an Oscar, which he won for his portrayal of the eccentric general in *Patton* (1970). He refused to show up and receive an award, denouncing the Academy Award ceremony as a "meat parade."

Jack Lemmon, Billy Wilder and Walter Matthau collaborated on such movies as *The Fortune Cookie* (1963), *The Front Page* (1974) and *Buddy Buddy* (1981)

Jack Lemmon (1925-2001)

One of the most admired Hollywood actors, gifted for both comedy and drama, Jack Lemmon was famous for his portrayals of frustrated and insecure middle-aged men. A two-time Oscar winner, he won an Academy Award as best supporting actor in *Mister Roberts* (1955) and the best actor Oscar in *Save the Tiger* (1973). Among more than 50 movies he made during his career are the classic *Some Like It Hot* (1959), *The Apartment* (1960), *The Front Page* (1974) and *Grumpy Old Men* (1993).

Walter Matthau (1920-2000)

A leading screen comedian, Walter Matthau is remembered for his signature poker face and slumped posture. Often teamed with Jack Lemmon in popular comedies, he starred in *The Odd Couple* (1967), *Charley Varrick* (1973) and *Grumpy Old Men* (1993). He won an Academy Award as best supporting actor for *The Fortune Cookie* (1966).

Billy Wilder (1906-2002)

Austrian-born director and screenwriter Billy Wilder got his start in the German movies as a scriptwriter. When Hitler came to power in 1933, Wilder, who was Jewish, fled Germany and went by way of France and Mexico to America. For several years he wrote or helped to write screenplays at Paramount.

Wilder received the Academy Award as best director for *The Lost Weekend* (1945), for which he also shared an Oscar for the screenplay with his long-time script collaborator Charles Brackett. They shared another Academy Award for the screenplay of *Sunset Boulevard* (1950). Wilder received his second Academy Award as best director for *The Apartment* (1960), sharing the Oscar for the film's screenplay with I A L Diamond.

Among Wilder's best-known films are *Double Indemnity* (1944), *Sabrina* (1954), *The Seven Year Itch* (1955) and *Some Like It Hot* (1959).

Dean Martin (1917-1995)

Actor, singer and all-round entertainer Dean Martin is laid to rest in the Sanctuary of Love. Well-known for his easy-going attitude, he teamed with Jerry Lewis in a series of wildly successful film comedies before his separate acting career flourished with such hits as *The Young Lions* (1958), *Some Came Running* (1958) and *Kiss Me, Stupid* (1964). Enormously popular as a singer, Dean's major hits include *Return To Me*, *Innamorata*, *That's Amore* and *Everybody Loves Somebody Sometime*.

John Cassavetes (1929-1989)

Academy Award-nominated actor, writer and director, Cassavetes appeared in *The Killers* (1964), *The Dirty Dozen* (1967) and *Rosemary's Baby* (1968). He is best known as the innovative, independent filmmaker of such works as *Shadows* (1961), *Faces* (1968) and *A Woman Under the Influence* (1974). His wife, Gena Rowlands, starred in many of his films.

Truman Capote (1924-1984)

An acclaimed novelist and prominent social figure, Capote is buried in an outdoor mausoleum crypt.

Among his major works are *Breakfast at Tiffany's* (1958), a novella about an amoral New York playgirl, which was filmed in 1961 with Audrey Hepburn, and *In Cold Blood* (1965), a "nonfiction novel" about a brutal multiple murder.

Marilyn Monroe (1926-1962)

Located in the Corridor of Memories, the crypt of Hollywood's most famous sex symbol is still swamped by fans daily. They leave photographs, letters, flowers and so many lipstick prints that marble stone on her vault have had to be replaced several times. For 20 years after Marilyn's death, her second husband, Joe DiMaggio, had six red roses placed on her tomb three times a week. Hugh Heffner has allegedly reserved for himself the crypt adjacent to the woman who appeared on the cover of his first *Playboy* magazine in November 1953.

On August 8, 1962, after a small ceremony attended by only a few of Marilyn's closest friends, the star of *Gentlemen Prefer Blondes* (1953), *How to Marry a Millionaire* (1953), *The Seven Year Itch* (1955) and *Some Like It Hot* (1959) was laid to rest. The eulogy was given by her acting coach, Lee Strasberg, who said: "Marilyn Monroe was a legend . . . For the entire world she became a symbol of the eternal feminine."

Every year on August 5, the anniversary of Marilyn's death, her devoted fans gather for a memorial service in the cemetery's chapel.

Westwood Memorial Park

New Mausoleum, outside ①

New Mausoleum, outside ②

Lot 308 ③

Section D, Lot 173 ④

Section D, Plot 60 ⑤

MAUSOLEUM

SANCTUARY OF TENDERNESS

③

①
②

④   ⑤

⑥

⑦

ROSE GARDEN

ESTATE GARDEN

⑫

OFFICE

CHAPEL

Section D, Lot 142 ⑥

Section D, Lot 189 ⑦

Section D, Lot 170 ⑧

Corridor of Memories, crypt 24
⑨

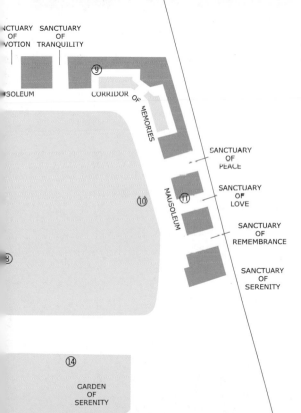

SANCTUARY
OF
DEVOTION

SANCTUARY
OF
TRANQUILITY

MAUSOLEUM

⑨

CORRIDOR OF MEMORIES

SANCTUARY
OF
PEACE

SANCTUARY
OF
LOVE

SANCTUARY
OF
REMEMBRANCE

SANCTUARY
OF
SERENITY

MAUSOLEUM

⑩

⑪

⑧

⑭

GARDEN
OF
SERENITY

Section D, urn garden ⑩

Sanctuary of Love ⑪

Garden of Serenity ⑫

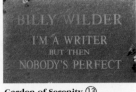

Garden of Serenity ⑬

Garden of Serenity ⑭

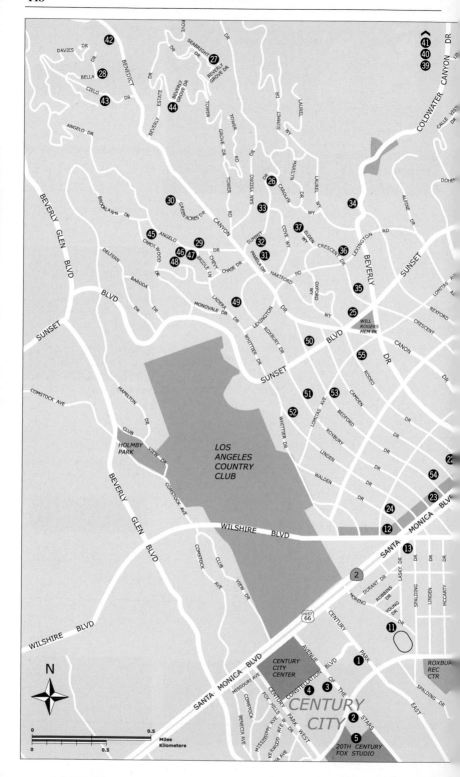

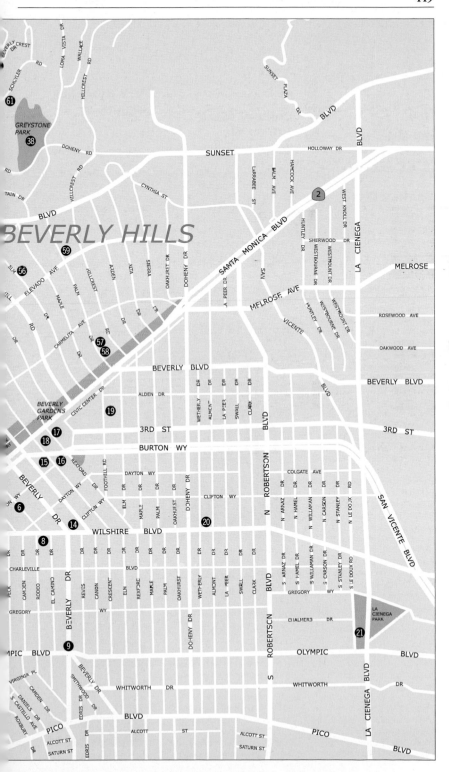

BEVERLY HILLS

Scenes from *Conquest of the Planet of the Apes* (1972) were filmed in Century City

Century City

This cluster of impressive office towers was built in the 1960s on land that used to be the back lot of the 20th Century-Fox motion picture studio. When it ran into huge debt during the production of its spectacle *Cleopatra* (1963), Fox sold the lot for $43 million to the Aluminum Company of America. ALCOA hired architect Welton Becket to design this massive highrise complex, which was to be the prototype of a twenty-first century city. The buildings include offices, hotels, theaters, apartments and shopping malls.

Critics called the design bland and soulless, lacking warmth and the human scale. Planned to attract businesses from downtown and so ease pressure on freeways, it seems that architects completely ignored pedestrians. With no parking on the streets and rare crosswalks, they were forced to go underground and use what was called the largest subterranean parking garage in the country.

Dissenting against its huge scale and coldness, Tom Petty sang *Don't Wanna Live in Century City*.

Because of its photogenic architecture, Century City has been seen in countless feature films, television movies and series. In *The Turning Point* (1977), a movie about the world of two ballet stars, Century City's ABC Entertainment Center (now demolished) doubled as New York's Lincoln Center. As a megalopolis of the future, Century City appeared in *Conquest of the Planet of the Apes* (1972), a sci-fi film about slave monkeys who revolt against the humans.

Century Plaza Towers ❶

Minoru Yamasaki, architect (1975). 2029, 2049 Century Park E. 🏃

Designed by famous architect Minoru Yamasaki, who also designed New York's World Trade Center, these two identical triangular skyscrapers dominate the Century City's skyline. They were featured in the popular television series of the 1980s, *Moonlighting*, as the locale where Bruce Willis and Cybill Shepherd's Blue Moon Detective Agency was situated.

Fox Plaza

Fox Plaza ❷

Johnson, Fain & Pereira, architects (1987). 2121 Ave of the Stars. 🏃

Clad in pink granite and gray-tinted glass, this office tower was used as the location of the high-tech Nakatomi Corporation, taken over by terrorists in the ultimate action movie *Die Hard* (1988). The building's 30th floor is the stage of Bruce Willis's heroic attempt to save employee hostages held during an attempted robbery.

After he left the White House, former President Ronald Reagan had his offices on the top floor of the building.

Park Hyatt Los Angeles ❸

2151 Ave of the Stars. ☎(310) 277-2777. 🏃

The hotel's pool was used for the jump scene in *Lethal Weapon 2* (1989). Protecting witness Joe Pesci, a former accountant who laundered drug smugglers' money, Mel Gibson and Danny Glover jump into the swimming pool. In *Point of No Return* (1992), a government assassin played by Bridget Fonda plants a bomb which destroys part of the building

MGM Tower ❹

Johnson Fain, architects (2003). 10250 Constellation Blvd.

Designed by renowned skyscraper architect Scott Johnson, the 34-story office complex boasts a skin of light-colored granite and a never-before-used surface material composed of a highly responsive thermal membrane of insulated glass and stainless steel. The tower's curved forms assume different looks throughout the day, reflecting changes in temperature and lighting conditions.

As the new corporate headquarters of MGM, the building's top signage features "Leo the Lion," the studio's famous roaring logo.

MGM Building

20th Century-Fox

20th Century-Fox was formed in 1935 after a merger between a major Hollywood studio, the Fox Film Corporation, and the new, but very successful 20th Century Pictures. Fox was controlled by a group of bankers after its founder, William Fox, had been forced to sell out his interest in the studio. Only two years old, 20th Century was a small production company established by Joseph M Schenck and Darryl F Zanuck. As head of production and later president, Zanuck would dominate the new firm for the next 35 years.

A pioneer in the field of technology, Fox developed the Movietone system in the late 1920s, the first successful sound-on-film process that set an industry standard that has lasted to this day. In 1953 it promoted another innovation, a wide-screen process called CinemaScope, that was introduced to counter the threat of television.

Fox was bought in 1981 by oil billionaire Marvin Davis. In 1985 it was acquired by Rupert Murdoch, chairman of the multinational communication giant, News Corporation.

Fox's first superstar during the late 1910s was Theda Bara (➔ p45), the first screen personality created by the studio publicity machinery. Another valuable resource was Shirley Temple in the 1930s, the most popular child star ever. Marilyn Monroe was launched into stardom in the 1950s. The studio's roster of stars also included Janet Gaynor, Will Rogers, Betty Grable, Sonja Henie, Tyrone Power, Henry Fonda and Gregory Peck.

With its main focus on musicals, westerns and dramas, the studio placed emphasis on the high technical quality of its movies, with brilliant photography and color. Its films were polished and glistening, and were popular at the box office. In 1977 the studio released the blockbuster *Star Wars*, the first part of the sci-fi series and the most profitable movie ever made. Fox repeated this success with *Titanic* (1997), which surpassed *Star Wars* as the biggest box office success in history.

Fox received an Oscar in the best picture category for the following movies: *Cavalcade* (1932-33); *How Green Was My Valley* (1941); *Gentleman's Agreement* (1947); *All About Eve* (1950); *The Sound of Music* (1965); *Patton* (1970); *The French Connection* (1971) and *Titanic* (1997).

The studio's logo with its famous beaming searchlights

The eldest of 13 children of a Jewish Hungarian immigrant, William Fox was a sweatshop worker and garment manufacturer before he developed a small chain of nickelodeons. He soon started his own film distribution and production entity, which he combined with his theater chain into the Fox Film Corporation in 1915. Ambitious and egocentric, he was on the verge of becoming the most powerful mogul in Hollywood by obtaining control of MGM in the late 1920s. However, the government antitrust action and the stock market crash forced him in 1930 to sell his shares in the company. The man who built a film empire worth over $300 million declared bankruptcy in 1936.

Star Wars (1977) is the most profitable film in history

Marilyn Monroe was Fox's biggest box-office attraction in the 1950s

20th Century-Fox Studios ❺

When the Fox Film Corporation outgrew its lot on Western Ave and Sunset Blvd (→ p131) in the mid 1920s, the company needed the additional space for shooting westerns, its principal product. Fox purchased the parcel of land stretching between Santa Monica and Pico boulevards that at one point comprised 286 acres (114 ha). Constructed in 1928, the new, highly departmentalized facility was Hollywood's first studio built for sound. After the merger with 20th Century Pictures in 1935, the new company made Movietone City, as the studio was known, its headquarters. At present, the studio occupies 63 acres (25 ha).

The eclectic blend of buildings, from the Spanish Colonial Revival Administration Building to ultramodern office structures, makes the Fox Studios the most impressive lot in Hollywood. With $6 billion spent on improvements since 1990, this is the most updated of all the studios. Today, between 60 and 70 percent of all Hollywood movies are made on this lot.

10201 W Pico Blvd.
☎(310) 369-1000.
Closed to the public. The studio does not offer public tours.
To get free tickets for live TV shows filming on the lot, call ☎(818) 753-3470 or (818) 506-0043, or visit www.tvtickets.com.

The original main entrance to the studio at Tennessee Ave was used over the years by throngs of major stars. Since it was closed in the early 1960s, the gate has been featured in several film and television productions, including Mel Brooks's *Silent Movie* (1976).

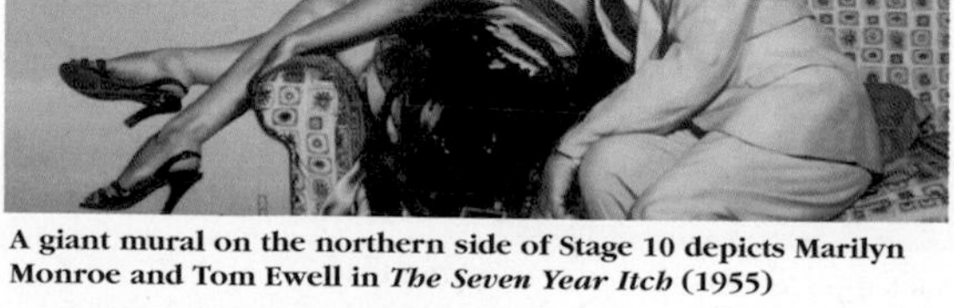

A giant mural on the northern side of Stage 10 depicts Marilyn Monroe and Tom Ewell in *The Seven Year Itch* (1955)

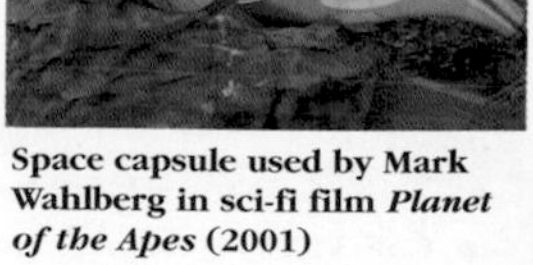

Space capsule used by Mark Wahlberg in sci-fi film *Planet of the Apes* (2001)

WPA-style Sound Stages 1 & 2, considered the top scoring facility in the world

Old Executive Building (1936)

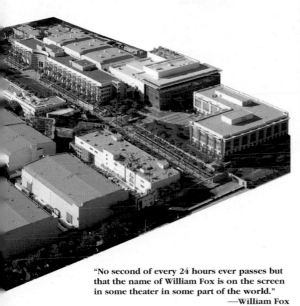

To catch a glimpse of the Fox lot, follow Steve Martin and Kevin Kline on their golf-cart tour in the final scenes of *Grand Canyon* (1991)

Fox Network Center. Michael White of HLW International, architect (1998). On the cutting edge of technology, this facility was said to be the most technically advanced building in the world at the time it was completed. Sheathed in glass that rises at an angle, the five-story structure houses broadcasting operations and is the nerve center of the Fox Television and Cable Sports Networks.

"No second of every 24 hours ever passes but that the name of William Fox is on the screen in some theater in some part of the world."
—William Fox

From the main gate on Pico Blvd it is still possible to glimpse the remains of the vast New York set used in *Hello, Dolly!* (1969). This landmark re-creation of an 1890s New York street was featured in the film's parade sequence and won an Oscar for Fox's designer team in the art direction category. The set was used in many later movie and television productions, before most of it was dismantled in the early 1980s. Its fake façades and colorful neighborhood streets recently turned up on the popular television series *NYPD Blue*.

Beverly Hills

What is today one of the most famous and fashionable places on earth, just a hundred years ago was land noted for its vast fields of lima beans.

The area was originally the 4,500-acre (1.800-ha) Spanish land grant known as El Rancho Rodeo de las Aguas or "the Ranch of the Gathering of the Waters." At the turn of the 20th century the land was purchased by an oil company, which started drilling in hopes of

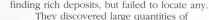

Seal of the city of Beverly Hills

finding rich deposits, but failed to locate any. They discovered large quantities of water instead and decided to enter the real estate business under the name of Rodeo Land and Water Company (hence Rodeo Drive). A dream town was conceiveded in 1906. The company's president, Burton Green, named the new development after his home in Beverly Farms, Massachusetts.

Gently winding Crescent, Canon, Beverly and Rodeo drives as they looked after opening in 1906

In order to attract new buyers and spur sales of his real estate, developer Burton Green erected the grand Beverly Hills Hotel in May 1912. Designed in the popular Mission Revival style, the white stucco structure was built even before Beverly Hills existed. The city was incorporated a year and a half later, in January 1914. Located "halfway between Los Angeles and the sea" and surrounded with vast bean fields, the hotel did well in the beginning, although land sales continued to be weak. That changed in 1919 when swashbuckling star Douglas Fairbanks moved to the area, followed by hordes of fellow movie people.

Beverly Hills was conceived from the beginning as an upscale community, its master plan calling for several districts in a town that balanced commercial and residential use. The commercial area, called the Golden Triangle, separates the modest

homes south of Wilshire Blvd from the upper-middle class neighborhood between Santa Monica and Sunset boulevards, called the flats. Above Sunset Blvd and in the hills and canyons to the north can be found large estates and the most expensive property.

The developers of Beverly Hills hired a landscape designer to devise a planting scheme for residential streets even before the first houses

were built. Each of the city's signature wide, curving streets was planted with a different type of tree—acacia, jacaranda, oak, palm and sycamore. The impressive rows of beautiful trees sometimes gave the streets their names.

Beverly Hills boasted a population of 634 in 1919, when Douglas Fairbanks bought a hunting lodge high in the hills above the bean fields. Named Pickfair (➜ p465), it was the first movie star home in the area, the one that popularized Beverly Hills and launched the celebrity migration to this vicinity. Pickfair was also the first movie star estate that served as a retreat and showplace where stars and moguls could entertain, hidden from gawking fans.

Charlie Chaplin, Gloria Swanson, Tom Mix, Harold Lloyd, Will Rogers and many others soon rushed to the neighborhood, making it a hometown for film industry people.

A vintage post card depicts palm-lined Beverly Dr

Beverly Hills Mystique

Frequently called the most fabulous six square miles on earth, Beverly Hills is invariably associated with fame, opulent lifestyle and extraordinary wealth. Its myth was born in the 1920s, when the city attracted Hollywood royalty and became the major concentration of the movie stars' "dream palaces." Its international image of a "rich people's play-

The shield signs mark the city limits

ground" has been created and constantly maintained by the mass media, as seen in movies and popular television series. Symbolizing glamorous shopping, fancy restaurants and luxury hotels, the 90210 zip code captured popular imagination, drawing millions of visitors from around the world looking for a glimpse of the dream town.

A place where you spend more than you make on things you don't need to impress people you don't like.

— Ken Murray

The "Golden Triangle" is Beverly Hills' main commercial district, named for its characteristic grid of streets running at a 45-degree angle north from Wilshire Blvd. Bordered by Wilshire and Santa Monica boulevards and Canon Dr, and cut through the middle by famous Rodeo Dr, it is dotted with upscale shops, restaurants, galleries and commercial buildings.

Wilshire Blvd is lined with luxurious hotels and most fashionable department stores, including Saks Fifth Avenue, Neiman-Marcus and Barneys New York. It was at Saks that Winona Ryder was arrested on December 12, 2001, with $5,560 of designer merchandise in her possession that she had not paid for. In a highly publicized shoplifting trial, she was convicted of felony grand theft and vandalism.

Beverly Hills status symbol

Holiday windows along Wilshire Blvd in Beverly Hills—elaborate displays often look like film sets

Among Beverly Hills' most famous draws are lavish residences of the rich and famous (➔ p465, 472). Many of them were at one time or another the homes of some of the greatest movie legends. Although celebrity watching is one of the main attractions here, do not expect to see many stars (➔ p68). Today they live in gated-off mansions, behind dense foliage and tight security.

Since the days of the silent screen Beverly Hills has been a favorite backdrop in films, from Laurel and Hardy silent comedies to more recent hits such as *Shampoo* (1975), the *Beverly Hills Cop* trilogy (1984, 1987, 1994) and *Pretty Woman* (1990). Its various locations have also been used in numerous television series, including the immensely popular *The Beverly Hillbillies* and *Beverly Hills 90210*.

The streets of Beverly Hills are packed with the world's most expensive and luxurious cars. It is quite common

to see Rolls-Royces, Ferraris, Bentleys and other ultimate status symbols on a scenic ride or parked in front of pricey boutiques.

Beverly Hills trolley

Beverly Hills Trolley Tours

Rodeo Dr and Dayton Way.
☎(310) 285-2438.
⊕between May and December, schedule varies. ⑤

Visitors interested in learning more about Beverly Hills' architecture and history may board a trolley for two city tours: the *Art and Architecture Trolley Tour* (90-minute) and the *Sites and Scenes Trolley Tour* (40-minute).

Models on a catwalk during the *Vogue* spring fashion show

Rodeo Drive ⑥

Constantly packed with tourists and affluent locals, this preeminent shopping street claims to be the most expensive in the world. With rents incredibly high, the commercial section of Rodeo Dr is concentrated in three legendary blocks containing a celebrated showcase of glamorous fashion and jewelry shops.

Julia Roberts and Richard Gere on Rodeo Dr in *Pretty Woman* (1990)

This is also a prime spot for celebrity watching, although they shop at odd times and don't hang out for too long—they quickly slip back into their limos waiting on the street. Sometimes celebrities enter stores from the alley side, unnoticed by the curious public.

For those who can't afford the luxury, window shopping is the best alternative, especially at night when the brightly lit store fronts are even more glittering.

In the 1990 movie *Pretty Woman*, wealthy businessman Richard Gere hires a young hooker played by Julia Roberts to be his beautiful escort for a week. While on a Rodeo Dr shopping spree, Roberts experiences some of the haughtiness for which salesgirls in Beverly Hills are famous.

For one Sunday in April, *Vogue* magazine closes Rodeo Dr for its spring fashion show, which includes designer fashion presentations, live musical performances, product displays and customized makeovers.

Every June on Father's Day Rodeo Dr closes to traffic to showcase the rarest as well as the most extravagant and eccentric cars imaginable. Called *Concours on Rodeo*, the show also displays automobiles owned by celebrities.

Prada Store
Rem Koolhaas and Ole Scheeren, architects (2004).
343 N Rodeo Dr.
☎(310) 278-8661.

Nine years after Uma Thurman's lavender gown worn during the Oscars made the name Prada famous around the world (➜ p51), the Italian fashion house opened its "epicenter" store in Beverly Hills.

Designed by the office of Dutch architect Rem Koolhaas, winner of the prestigious Pritzker Prize in 2000, the store reflects some dis-

Harrison Ford and Josh Hartnett film a scene on Rodeo Dr

tinct California themes. During the day, the 24,000-sq-ft (2.160-m²) boutique is entirely open to the street, taking advantage of the local climate that allows blending boundaries between interior and exterior. After hours, the store is completely shut-off by a bland aluminum door that does not bear the name or any trace of visual identity, resembling a gated community.

Turning their backs toward the street, larger-than-life headless male and female figures greet the visitors, while underfoot, three oblong glass display cases contain mannequins trapped in the sidewalk. Inside, shoppers can find such gimmicks as dressing rooms' glass walls that change from transparent to opaque at the touch of a finger.

Prada flagship store on Rodeo Dr

Anderton Court

Anderton Court
Frank Lloyd Wright, architect
(1953).
328 N Rodeo Dr.

Comprising a group of
shops organized around a
central courtyard, this striking
three-story structure is one of
Frank Lloyd Wright's last
works. It was commissioned
by ex-showgirl and wealthy
widow, Nina Anderton, to
house her favorite couturier's
shop. Conceived as a vertical
shopping center, the building's main features are the
angular ramp that winds
around the well of light and
the jagged central mast. The
structure has been subse-
quently changed, later additions being the canopy and
signage on the top level.

2 Rodeo
Kaplan/McLaughlin/Diaz, architects (1990).

A replica of the Spanish
Steps in Rome is part of a
high-end retail development
designed to resemble a European shopping village. Comprised of 24 two- and three-
story buildings, all individually designed with a unique
façade, it is home to exclusive designer and retail
shops. The site is bisected by
curved Via Rodeo, a cobbled
pedestrian lane and the first
new street built in Beverly
Hills since 1914. The outdoor
mall is a popular tourist
route, visited by 12 million
people annually.

To counter a widespread
perception that Rodeo Drive
merchants are snobbish, the

city hired an official Ambassador of Beverly Hills. Prop-
erly decked out, Gregg
Donovan greets visitors in 40
languages at 2 Rodeo.

Walk of Style
Established in 2003,
the Walk of Style Award
is the fashion world's
equivalent to Holly-
wood Walk of Fame. It
is given annually to
designers and style
icons for their contri-
butions to fashion and
entertainment. Each
honoree receives a
permanent plaque
embedded in the street
featuring a quote about fashion from the designer and his
personal signature, as well as
a bronze maquette of *Torso*,
both created by sculptor
Robert Graham.

A plaque on the Walk of Style

The celebrity-studded inaugural Walk of Style Awards
ceremony, held on Septem-
ber 9, 2003, honored leg-
endary Italian fashion designer Giorgio Armani. He was
one of the first designers to

understand that red carpet
exposure would be priceless,
dressing Jodie Foster in 1989
and Michelle Pfeiffer in 1990
for the Oscars (➔ p51).

Torso (2003) by
Robert Graham
Standing on a bronze
pedestal at the inter-
section of Rodeo Dr
and Dayton Way, the
14-foot-tall (4.2-m)
statue carved from
solid aluminum
blocks serves as the
symbol of the Rodeo
Drive Walk of Style.

Torso

Gagosian Gallery ❼
Richard Meier, architect (1995).
456 N Camden Dr.
☎(310) 271-9400.
🕐Tue-Sat 10am-5:30pm.

Designed to diffuse the
bright California light, the
west-looking façade is clad in
an expanse of clear and
frosted glass. The glazed
door can be rolled up to
allow a glimpse at the artworks inside, thus connecting
the sidewalk with the main
gallery. Clerestory windows
fill the soaring exhibit space
with indirect daylight.

The gallery displays the
works of such prominent
contemporary artists as Chris
Burden, Alexander Calder,
Frank Gehry, Arshile Gorky,
Jeff Koons, Ed Ruscha, Julian
Schnabel, Richard Serra,
Frank Stella, Cy Twombly
and Andy Warhol.

Gagosian Gallery displays the works of contemporary artists

Regent Beverly Wilshire Hotel

Regent Beverly Wilshire Hotel ❽

Walker & Eisen, architects (1928);
Welton Becket and Associates,
architects (1971).
9500 Wilshire Blvd.
☎(310) 275-5200.
www.regenthotels.com ⌐ NRHP

Located at the famous intersection of Rodeo Dr and Wilshire Blvd, this hotel is considered one of the grandest in Los Angeles. Designed in 1928 in the Italian Renaissance style with Beaux-Arts influences, the hotel's façade was built of white Carrera marble and Tuscan stone. Today called the Wilshire Wing, the refurbished 10-story structure still features an original series of arches and relief ornamentation, as well as a columned, marble lobby seen in a number of movies.

In 1971 a second structure was completed behind the original building. Called the Beverly Wing, the 14-story addition is linked with the main complex by a private cobblestone street named El Camino Real (King's Road). It is lined with 38 gaslight lanterns originally from a castle in Edinburgh, Scotland, and replicas of the mission-bell guideposts that once marked California's historic El Camino Real.

The pool in the Regent's Beverly Wing is a replica of the one on Sophia Loren's estate in Italy.

Catering to the world's royalty, nobility and celebrities, the hotel has been the host to countless famous visitors. Among its guests were Prince Charles, King Juan Carlos of Spain and King Gustav of Sweden. Legendary womanizer Warren Beatty lived in the hotel's Veranda Suite between 1972 and 1986. To celebrate their wedding anniversary, his wife Annette Bening reserved the suite, reportedly saying, "You've bedded everyone else in Hollywood in this room, now it's my turn!"

Elvis Presley, Carol Burnett and Steve McQueen also enjoyed prolonged stays in the hotel. This was the place where Sammy Davis Jr popped out of Frank Sinatra's birthday cake.

The Regent has had its share of scandals. Celebrating Ringo's birthday, the Beatles demolished one of the suites (they compensated the hotel for all damages). Upon their return to town from the filming of *Cleopatra* (1963), Elizabeth Taylor and Richard Burton shared the Presidential Suite, although she was still married to Eddie Fisher.

The hotel is legendary for its impeccable service—no request from a VIP guest goes unfulfilled. When Japanese Emperor Hirohito wanted his grapes peeled, his demand was promptly satisfied.

The stately Regent Beverly Wilshire is one of the favorite Hollywood movie locations. It has been used as a setting for numerous productions, including *American Gigolo* (1980), *Beverly Hills Cop* (1984), *Indecent Proposal* (1993), *Clueless* (1995) and *Wag the Dog* (1997).

Although many scenes in *Pretty Woman* (1990) were set in the hotel's Presidential Suite, where Richard Gere and Julia Roberts stayed, all the lobby and Presidential Suite scenes were actually shot on studio sound stages, since the hotel's interiors were undergoing restoration at the time and were not available for filming.

Monument to the Stars ❾

Intersection of Beverly Dr and Olympic Blvd.

Erected in 1959, this monument honors eight celebrities of the motion picture industry whose heroic struggle saved Beverly Hills from annexation. In 1923 Will Rogers, Douglas Fairbanks, Mary Pickford, Harold Lloyd, Rudolph Valentino, Tom Mix, Conrad Nagel and Fred Niblo led the effort to reject Los Angeles' merger plan, offering free autographs to residents willing to preserve the city's sovereignty. They are all shown here in bas-relief wearing costumes from their famous movies, topped by a huge spiral of movie film.

Monument to the Stars

Wosk House

Wosk House ❿

Frank O Gehry and Associates, architect (1984).
440 S Roxbury Dr
Private residence.

In one of his rare renovation projects, Gehry transformed the fourth floor of an existing apartment building into a large single-family residence. The new construction consists of a series of objects grouped together, including a greenhouse dining room, a blue dome above the kitchen, a gold-coated ziggurat for a den and a blue-tiled chimney. The owner requested that the first three floors, which remained essentially intact, be painted pink.

Beverly Hills High School ⓫

255 S Lasky Dr.
☎(310) 201-0661. 🏴

Established in 1927, Beverly Hills High has been the alma mater of such Hollywood celebrities as Nicolas Cage, Richard Chamberlain, Jamie Lee Curtis, Richard Dreyfuss, Rhonda Fleming, Gina Gershon, Joel Grey, Lenny Kravitz, Monica Lewinsky, Rob Reiner, David Schwimmer and Alicia Silverstone.

The popular television series *Beverly Hills 90210* was not, however, shot on the school premises. Exterior scenes were actually filmed on location at Torrance High School, which stood in for the fictitious West Beverly High.

Designed by Stiles O Clements in 1937, the school's Streamline Moderne swimming gym appeared in a famous scene in Frank Capra's classic *It's a Wonderful Life* (1946) When the basketball court floor on which James Stewart and Donna Reed are dancing suddenly is pulled out from under them, they fall into the swimming pool below.

Electric Fountain

Electric Fountain ⓬

Designed by Ralph Flewelling and Merrell Gage (1930)
Intersection of Wilshire and Santa Monica boulevards.

Built in 1930 as the first electric fountain in the nation, it still fascinates viewers with its cascading water jets and constantly changing colored lights. A kneeling figure at the top of the fountain represents an Indian praying for rain, while a circular frieze on the base depicts scenes from early California history.

This scene from *It's a Wonderful Life* (1946) was filmed in the swimming gym

Creative Artists Agency (formerly) ⓭

Pei Cobb Freed and Partners Architects (1989).
9830 Wilshire Blvd.

Generally considered the predominant power-broker in Hollywood, CAA was founded by Michael Ovitz and four other agents in 1975. The agency reached the height of its influence during the 1980s, when it represented most of the highest-paid stars. After Ovitz left in 1995, the company lost some of its power, but still remains the major player in the industry.

Located at the corner of busy Wilshire and Little Santa Monica boulevards, the former CAA headquarters dominates one of the most dangerous intersections in the nation. The sleek structure, with its curving façade wrapped in travertine marble and mirrored glass walls, was designed by architect I M Pei. A gigantic Lichtenstein mural can be seen through the glass entryway, overlooking the 56-foot-high (17 m) atrium.

Creative Artists Agency Building

MGM Building

(formerly) **⓮**

9441 Wilshire Blvd.

Movie mogul Louis B Mayer built this remarkable Art Deco (Zigzag Moderne) tower in 1929 as the headquarters of Metro-Goldwyn Mayer studio. Today called Sterling Plaza, the refurbished white and gold building is owned by businessman Donald Sterling, who also owns the Los Angeles Clippers basketball team.

Former headquarters of the Music Corporation of America (MCA)

Former MGM Building

Union 76 Gas Station **⓯**

Pereira and Luckman, architects (1965).
427 N Crescent Dr.

Originally designed for the Los Angeles airport, this monument to the space-age became a classic of the 1960s. With fluorescent lights illuminating its triangular white ceiling, a huge cantilevered concrete canopy successfully links two symbols of the American passion for speed—the car and space travel.

MCA Building **⓰**

Paul Williams, architect (1940).
360 N Crescent Dr. **NRHP**

Designed by renowned architect Paul Williams, this formal neo-Georgian structure was built as the headquarters for the Music Corporation of America. Williams's design, which included such details as white painted bricks, porches, gabled roofs, sculpted moldings, cornices, railings and paneling, bears resemblance to residential architecture. It is said that MCA's founder, Dr Jules Stein, bought columns from Marion Davies's Beach House at an auction and asked Williams to incorporate them at the rear of the building. The plaza, with its lush gardens, reflecting pools and fountains, is entered through massive antique iron gates that were bought in Scotland.

Litton Industries acquired the property in 1964 and commissioned Williams to add an additional structure. The three-building complex was bought in 1998 for $41.5 million by telecommunications giant Global Crossing Ltd. The company's owner, Gary Winnick, who was the richest man in Los Angeles in 1999 (before Global Crossing filed for bankruptcy in 2002), installed a replica of the Oval Office inside the building.

Beverly Hills Civic Center

Beverly Hills Civic Center **⓱**

Charles Moore, architect (1990).
455 N Rexford Dr.

Originally envisioned as a public gathering place similar to those in European urban centers, the Civic Center's design was significantly changed due to financial cutbacks. A cafeteria, an art gallery and a theatre were abandoned and today the courtyards, as well as balconies and open corridors on the upper levels, remain empty. The new additions—a library, police and fire stations, and parking garage—are linked by three diagonal elliptical courtyards to the old City Hall.

Resembling a spaceship, Union 76 Station is a classic of the 1960s

Beverly Hills City Hall ⑱

William Gage and Harry Koerner, architects (1932).
450 N Crescent Dr.
☎(310) 285-1000.

City Hall is a two-story, H-shaped Spanish Renaissance-style building, with a third story in the center and an ornate, eight-story tower topped by a colorfully tiled dome. In a plan frequently used for public structures during the Great Depression, the tower rises from a base symbolizing business growth on a strong government foundation.

This splendid edifice was featured in numerous movies, including *Citizen Kane* (1951), where it stood in for Hearst Castle, *In A Lonely Place* (1950) and *Six Days, Seven Nights* (1998). In all three *Beverly Hills Cop* films (1984, 1987, 1994), City Hall passes for the Beverly Hills Police Station where a Detroit police detective played by Eddie Murphy meets the local cops.

Virgin Records ⑲

Franklin Israel Design Associates, architect (1991).
338 N Foothill Rd.

A translucent canopy supported by steel columns designates the entrance to this remodeled former warehouse, now home to a recording company. A swelling red stucco wall thrusts forward encircling a desert garden, partially visible through rectangular holes.

Beverly Hills City Hall

Academy of Motion Picture Arts and Sciences ⑳

8949 Wilshire Blvd.
☎(310) 247-3000.
⊕galleries: Tue-Fri 10am-5pm; Sat-Sun noon-6pm. ⑤free

Since 1975, this undistinguished seven-story glass building has housed the headquarters of the Academy of Motion Picture Arts and Sciences (AMPAS). This honorary association of film industry professionals was founded in Hollywood in 1927 by Douglas Fairbanks, Mary Pickford, Louis B Mayer, Conrad Nagel and other film dignitaries. Membership in the Academy is by invitation of the Board of Governors only and at present consists of more than 6,000 persons. Established to improve the image of the film industry, it is best known today as the organization that presents the annual Academy Awards (Oscars).

Two galleries show changing exhibitions of photographs, posters, lobby cards, sets, costumes and other artifacts related to the movie industry. The splendid Samuel Goldwyn Theater frequently offers screenings open to the public.

Margaret Herrick Library ㉑

333 S La Cienega Blvd.
☎(310) 247-3000; recorded message (310) 247-3035; reference (310) 247-3020.
www.oscars.org/mhl/sc/index.html
⊕Mon-Tue; Thu-Fri 10am-5:30pm.

Founded in 1931, the world-renowned Library has one of the most extensive collections of film-related materials in the world. It contains rare books, periodicals and pamphlets, posters, screenplays, still photographs, files of clippings and archival materials.

Margaret Herrick Library

It was named for the former librarian and the Academy's executive director who, as legend has it, gave the Oscar statue its name (➜ p48).

The Library building is converted from the former Beverly Hills waterworks, originally built in 1928 by Salisbury, Bradshaw and Taylor and inspired by La Giralda in Seville, Spain. The Academy took over the building in 1988 and hired architect Francis Offenhauser to extensively remodel the structure and add a new wing.

Virgin Records

O'Neill House ㉒

Don M Ramos, architect (1978-89). 507 N Rodeo Dr. Private residence.

One of the most unusual designs in Los Angeles, this stunning residence was built as a memorial to antique collector and dealer Don O'Neill. In praise of mother nature, all rooms are round or oval in shape, mimicking organic forms. With its writhing stucco details and colored tiles, the house is one of the best local examples of Art Nouveau architecture, but the real gems are hidden behind the building. Visible only from the rear alley, the pavilion and the guest house feature blue mosaic tiles, dancing figures, intricate balconies and stained-glass windows— Gaudíesque extravagance at its finest.

O'Neill House is a rare example of Art Nouveau in Los Angeles

The funeral ceremonies for Rudolph Valentino were held at Good Shepherd Catholic Church in 1926

Good Shepherd Catholic Church ㉓

505 N Bedford Dr. ⚑

Nicknamed "Our Lady of the Cadillacs" by actress Rosalind Russell, this church was the site of a number of celebrity weddings, most notably Elizabeth Taylor and her first husband, hotelier Nicky Hilton in 1950. Taylor wore a wedding gown designed by Edith Head, a gift from MGM. The studio used the occasion to promote the release of the superstar's new film, *Father of the Bride*, conveniently scheduled to coincide with the wedding. Actress Loretta Young was also married here, as was rocker Rod Stewart (whose bride was model Rachel Hunter).

Many celebrity funerals were also held in the church, including those of Rudolph Valentino (1926), Carmen Miranda (1955), Gary Cooper (1961), Alfred Hitchcock (1980), Vincente Minnelli (1986), Rita Hayworth (1987) and Eva Gabor (1995). The funeral of Frank Sinatra took place here in 1998, with myriad stars in attendance and over a thousand fans lining the surrounding streets.

Good Shepherd was the location for Norman Maine's (played by James Mason) funeral ceremonies in the 1954 remake of the 1937 classic *A Star Is Born*. After emerging from the church, Maine's wife, Vicki Lester (played by Judy Garland), collapses on the entrance when encountered by fans and reporters.

Spadena House ㉔

Harry Oliver, architect (1921). 516 N Walden Dr. Private residence. ⚑

With its sharply pitched shingled roof, leaded windows with tilted shutters, a witch's broom on the roof and a wooden bridge across a moat, this is the quintessential Hansel and Gretel cottage. Inspired by fairy tales, this architectural style was especially popular in Los Angeles during the 1920s.

Called the "witch's house," the structure was originally built in 1921 as the office for Irvin Willat Productions, a movie studio located at 6509 Washington Blvd in Culver City. The studio closed in the mid 1920s and the building was later transported to its present location.

The cottage appeared in many of Willat's films and was also used in *The Loved One* (1965) as the home of the character played by Sir John Gielgud.

Good Shepherd Church

Spadena House

Beverly Hills Hotel ㉕

The signature pink façade and striking bell towers of the Beverly Hills Hotel are widely recognized symbols of one of the world's most celebrated hotels. Although the original Mission Revival-style design by renowned architects Myron Hunt and Elmer Grey was altered over the years, the building still evokes a nostalgic sense of early California. Set among 12 acres of lushly landscaped grounds, the hotel's bungalows, suites, pools and restaurants are rich in Hollywood history and imbued with an aura of mystique and glamour.

The Beverly Hills Hotel instantly became a posh meeting place for the Hollywood elite, a legendary playground where film people socialized, romanced and made deals. For those who wanted to appear as part of the scene, it was the right place to see and be seen. Nicknamed the "Pink Palace," the hotel played host to countless social events.

The Polo Lounge has been the favorite gathering place for generations of celebrities and Hollywood dealmakers. It got its name when the hotel's director displayed a trophy silver bowl, won by his friend's championship polo team. It was also the favorite watering hole of polo players Will Rogers, Darryl F Zanuck and Spencer Tracy, who regularly gathered there for their post-game drinks. Marlene Dietrich, a regular at the bar, challenged a strict dress code when she showed up one day in slacks. The only table here with an exclusive reservation was held for Charlie Chaplin; if he did not appear, no one else could sit there. After years of absence, Chaplin stayed at the hotel when he returned to accept a special Oscar in 1972. Oscar-winning actor Peter Finch was on his way to a promotional breakfast conference for *Network* (1976), when he collapsed in the hotel lobby and died in 1977.

The Beverly Hills Hotel has appeared in numerous films before the management introduced a strict no-filming policy. Neil Simon, a frequent hotel guest, adapted his Broadway play for the film *California Suite* (1978). The movie takes place entirely at the hotel in the wake of the Academy Awards. Also filmed on the premises were *The Way We Were* (1973), *Shampoo* (1975) and *American Gigolo* (1980).

The signature pink and green Mission-style towers of the legendary "Pink Palace"

Myron Hunt and Elmer Grey, architects (1912).
9641 Sunset Blvd.
☎(310) 276-2251.
www.beverlyhillshotel.com
♿ ⚑

One of the first movies filmed on the premises was Harold Lloyd's feature-length comedy *A Sailor-Made Man* (1921)

The arrival of glamorous guests at the porte cochère in the 1950s

Marlene Dietrich at the bar in the fabled Polo Lounge in 1940

At the Beverly Hills Hotel you do not get just any professional as a tennis instructor. It is often a champion, such as tennis pro Harvey Snodgrass, shown here giving a lesson to actress Jean Harlow. Since 1965, the hotel's tennis courts have been supervised by Wimbledon champion Alex Olmedo.

Cover of the Eagles' *Hotel California* (1976) album showing the top of the hotel's three bell towers

Many celebrities came to the hotel's pool to play, relax and take a dip. During the 1950s and 60s, starlets lounged in the chairs on one side of the pool, while on the opposite side, in cabanas, were the deal makers. Katharine Hepburn once jumped fully clothed into the pool after a tennis game. Raquel Welch was "discovered" while frolicking here. The Beatles had to be sneaked in through the back way to avoid teenage fans. The pool manager taught Faye Dunaway to swim for her role of Joan Crawford in the movie *Mommie Dearest* (1981). A famous scene from *Designing Woman* (1957), with Lauren Bacall and Gregory Peck, was shot at the hotel's pool and the cabana club.

In 1949 a new Crescent Wing was added by noted architect Paul Williams, who redecorated the Polo Lounge and introduced the now famous pink-and-green motif. The hotel had several famous owners before it was purchased by the Sultan of Brunei in 1987 for an alleged $176 million. An additional $100 million were spent for an extensive two-year restoration, completed in 1995.

The hotel's luxurious suites and bungalows have hosted celebrities and royalty alike, from Gloria Swanson, Greta Garbo and Rudolph Valentino, to Prince Philip, the Duke and Duchess of Windsor, Grace Kelly and Prince Rainier.

In the 1930s, Clark Gable and Carole Lombard used to discreetly meet in bungalow 4 before their marriage. Marilyn Monroe and her co-star Yves Montand stayed in bungalows 20 and 21, conducting a secret affair while filming *Let's Make Love* (1960). It is said that John Kennedy entertained Angie Dickinson in the hotel's bungalow in 1960. Frank Sinatra and Ava Gardner were another famous couple who romanced here.

Elizabeth Taylor's father had an art gallery in the hotel, and she got so accustomed to the place that she honeymooned here with six of her eight husbands.

Since 1942 reclusive billionaire Howard Hughes lived in the hotel on and off for almost 30 years, renting three bungalows on a daily basis. Notorious for his obsession with germs and pursuit of privacy, Hughes communicated with his staff through countless memos, which gave instructions down to the smallest details. He would have room service hide roast beef sandwiches in the trees, so he could eat undisturbed at the time of his choosing. His paranoia went so far that he had an assistant wave a folded newspaper for at least one minute before opening the door of his bungalow 1-C to prevent flies from entering the room. A simple procedure such as opening a can of fruit was to be accomplished in nine steps, using sterilized equipment and only after the staff member thoroughly washed and rinsed his hands four times!

The hotel's music heritage was established in the 1950s by drinking pals Frank Sinatra, Dean Martin and the rest of the "Rat Pack." The Beatles stayed here in the 1960s, and during the 1970s John Lennon and Yoko Ono secluded themselves in a bungalow.

The Beverly Hills Hotel's legendary pool and cabanas, a place where the world's richest and most famous come to socialize

Legendary Estates of Beverly Hills

Some of the world's most glamorous and famous residences were built in this fashionable city during Hollywood's Golden Age. Here the newly rich of the booming film industry created dream palaces to suit their extravagant lifestyles, giving birth to the myth of Beverly Hills. Their grand estates symbolized the magic, fantasy and opulence of the alluring film world,

Greystone gate

capturing the popular imagination of millions of movie fans worldwide.

"In those days, the public wanted us to live like kings and queens," recalls silent screen legend Gloria Swanson. "So we did—and why not? We were in love with life. We were making more money than we ever dreamed existed, and there was no reason to believe it would ever stop."

Harold and Mildred Lloyd, leaving a party at Pickfair (1932)

Pickfair 🅰

1143 Summit Dr.
Private residence

Purchased in 1919 for $35,000, Pickfair was the first movie star home in Beverly Hills. Its name was invented by the press by combining the names of its famous residents, Mary Pickford and Douglas Fairbanks, Hollywood's biggest star couple Originally a six-room hunting lodge on 14 acres (5,6 ha) remodeled for the newlyweds, the estate was redesigned in 1932 by famous architect Wallace Neff. He replaced its mock-Tudor façade with a Georgian one, more appropriate for the pompous playground of Hollywood royalty.

During the 1920s and 1930s Pickfair gained a worldwide reputation for the endless entertainment that took place there. Among the house's famous guests were major Hollywood stars, as well as royalty and celebrities from around the world, including the King of Spain Alfonso XIII, the Crown Prince of

Japan, the King and Queen of Siam, the Duke of York, along with F Scott Fitzgerald, H G Wells, Henry Ford and Albert Einstein.

Pickfair's 100-foot-long (30-m) swimming pool, with a sandy beach on one side, was the first one in Beverly Hills. As a fan of canoeing, Doug also added a series of ponds where he could enjoy his favorite pastime. The private life of the "King and Queen of Hollywood," as Doug and Mary were called by the press, was well publicized for millions of their

Doug and Mary canoeing in the Pickfair's swimming pool

adoring fans, Pickfair was turned into a carefully designed stage where the nation's most popular couple played their well choreographed roles.

Following Mary's death in 1979, the estate was purchased in 1980 by Los Angeles Lakers owner Jerry Buss for $5.36 million. He, in turn, sold it in 1988 for $7 million to financier Meshulam Riklis and his wife, singer Pia Zadora. They razed the old landmark in 1990 and erected a massive, three-story Mediterranean-style mansion.

New mansion built on the site of former Pickfair estate

Belle Vista ㉗

1400 Seabright Pl.
Private residence.

When legendary actor John Barrymore bought director King Vidor's three-acre estate on Tower Rd in 1927, the unassuming Spanish-style house was its only structure. During the next 10 years, the estate grew to 16 buildings with 55 rooms, all extravagantly decorated with antique furnishings in a mixture of styles. The seven-acre grounds comprised a bowling green, tennis courts, a pool stocked with trout, a skeet-shooting range and a large aviary with 300 different bird species, including Barrymore's vulture, Maloney.

Falcon Lair, Rudolph Valentino's fabled estate

John Barrymore in his trophy room

Since Barrymore's death in 1942, the estate has been subdivided into several properties. The hacienda-style house (at 9876 Beverly Grove Dr) has been called Bella Vista since the 1940s, when it was purchased by ventriloquist Edgar Bergen (father of actress Candice Bergen). The remodeled former aviary (at 9898 Beverly Grove Dr) was later the home of Katharine Hepburn, Marlon Brando and Candice Bergen.

Falcon Lair ㉘

1436 Bella Dr.
Private residence.

When Rudolph Valentino bought this Spanish-style house in 1925 for $175,000, it was under constant siege by his fervent female fans. To protect his privacy, the screen's first great Latin lover erected a 9-foot wall (2,7-m), installed floodlights and let loose his dogs overnight.

He named the 16-room, 4,700-square-foot mansion Falcon Lair, after the screenplay *The Hooded Falcon*, written by his second wife, Natacha Rambova (the movie was never made). The estate's name can still be seen on the pillars of the front gate. Valentino died in 1926, after living in his extravagantly decorated house for less than a year.

Valentino at home, suitably dressed for his role as a perfect country gentleman

As described by a contemporary fan magazine, Valentino's extensive wardrobe included 30 business suits, 124 shirts, 60 pairs of gloves, 59 pairs of shoes, 24 pairs of riding boots, 44 hats, 37 vests and 110 silk handkerchiefs (all monogrammed RGV). An avid collector of medieval armor and antique weapons, he displayed some of his favorite pieces on the wall above the fireplace.

The estate was owned by tobacco heiress Doris Duke for 40 years, from 1953 until her death in 1993. Although she rarely stayed here, Duke, who was a noted collector of art and antiques, installed Napoleon Bonaparte's original war room at the house.

A vintage post card depicts John Barrymore's residence in 1929

The symbol of the Hollywood Golden Age, former Jack Warner estate was bought by record mogul David Geffen for $47.5 million

Jack Warner Estate ㉙

1801 Angelo Dr.
Private residence.

This magnificent nine-acre estate once belonged to Hollywood mogul Jack Warner, co-founder of the Warner Bros studio. Its 13,600-sq-ft (1,220-m²) mansion was originally a 15 room Spanish-style house that looked inadequate after his *The Jazz Singer* (1927) hit and the talkies that followed. He enlarged the property by purchasing several surrounding mansions, which he demolished, adding additional parcels of land to his estate. The stately Georgian-style mansion, with beautiful gardens and terraces with panoramic city views, swimming pool, nine-hole golf course, tennis court, and even its own service shop and gas pumps, was the stage of fabled entertaining for the Hollywood elite. Symbolizing the grandeur of the Hollywood Golden Age, it is the only Beverly Hills celebrity estate of the 1920s and 1930s that survives to this day virtually unchanged.

After the death of Warner's widow in 1990, the estate, complete with museum-quality antique furnishings, was purchased by record mogul and DreamWorks co-founder David Geffen for $47.5 million. It was at the time the highest price ever paid for a private residence in the US.

Greenacres ㉚

1740 Green Acres Dr.
Private residence. ⟁ NRHP

Completed in 1929 at a cost of $2 million, Greenacres was the largest and most impressive of all the movie stars' estates. Set on a reclining hillside, the two-story, 40-room Italian Renaissance villa was the home of legendary comedian Harold Lloyd, the star of such silent hits as *Safety Last* (1923), *Girl Shy* (1924) and *The Freshman* (1925).

Lloyd's unsurpassed extravaganza included 12 different formal gardens, an Olympic-size swimming pool, an 800-foot-long (240-m) canoe pond complete with a 120-foot (36-m) waterfall, a nine-hole golf course, tennis and handball courts, and even its own telephone system with operator.

After Lloyd's death in 1971, the estate was converted into a short-lived museum, and soon after most of its 22-acre (9-ha) grounds were subdivided into building lots. The restored main house is currently occupied by billionaire grocery mogul Ron Burkle, owner of the Ralphs and Food 4 Less supermarket chains, who paid nearly $18 million for the estate in 1993.

The majestic Greenacres gardens were used as the backdrop for orgy scenes in the movie *Westworld* (1973), starring Yul Brynner, where

Greenacres entry hall (ca. 1930). The magnificent room had a 16-foot (5-m) ceiling and a circular oak staircase. As was the rest of the estate, it was decorated with custom-made furniture.

they stood in for Roman-world theme park. The estate was also used for the interior of the Grayle residence in *Farewell, My Lovely* (1975).

Comedian Harold Lloyd by the cypress-lined cascading fountain in one of the 12 formal gardens on his stately Greenacres estate

A vintage post card depicts Buster Keaton's villa

Buster Keaton in his bedroom in 1929

Buster Keaton Estate ③

Gene Verge, architect (1925).
1018 Pamela Dr.
Private residence. 🏳

Built in 1925 for the astronomical sum of $300,000, this two-story Italian Renaissance-style villa was one of Hollywood's famous showplaces, where one of the greatest comedians in history, Buster Keaton, and his wife, Natalie Talmadge, threw fabulous parties. The grounds encompassed expansive gardens, fountains, an artificial brook stocked with trout, and an aviary on a three-acre knoll.

After their divorce in 1933 Talmadge sold the villa, whose subsequent tenants or owners included Marlene Dietrich, Peter O'Toole, Richard Burton, Cary Grant and his second wife, Barbara Hutton, and James and Pamela Mason. It was Mason who discovered in the 1950s the old 35-mm nitrite prints of Keaton's best comedies in a secret panel to a film storage vault in the projection room. Long considered lost, these prints were transferred onto safety stock and showed at retrospectives and international festivals, thus sparking a worldwide resurrection of the Keaton legend.

The 22-room house is featured in Keaton's film *Parlor, Bedroom and Bath* (1931), in a scene where Keaton jumps from his bedroom balcony into the yard.

The mansion was bought in 2002 by infomercial makeup queen Victoria Jackson and her husband for $20 million.

Tom Mix Estate ㉜

1018 Summit Dr.
Private residence.

Silent screen cowboy Tom Mix was one of the most popular and highest-paid stars of the 1920s. Best-known as a skillful rider who performed his own stunts, Mix sometimes rode his famous horse, Tony, up the stairs to the second floor of his mansion. Built on the six-acre estate, his large Mediterranean-style, pretentiously decorated house was the site of extravagant parties. The mansion was filled from floor to 20-foot-high ceilings with exotic objects, animal heads, saddles and guns. Mix placed an illuminated fountain display in the entrance hall and even installed a 10-feet-high (3-m) neon sign spelling his name on the roof.

His wife pioneered in 1924 what would become an obsession of Beverly Hills housewives and a steady source of income for Beverly Hills cosmetic surgeons ever since—she got a nose job. A former actress, Vicki Mix explained: "I didn't do this because I'm contemplating a return to the screen, but I felt that my nose could be improved and I believe a woman should look her best for her husband."

Western star Tom Mix standing in his living room decorated with animal skins, trophies, rare handguns and cowboy paraphernalia

In the 1960s the house was completely modernized, losing its tile roof and all decorative elements.

A vintage post card of Tom Mix's Mediterranean-style mansion

Charlie Chaplin Estate ㉝

1085 Summit Dr.
Private residence.

Called "the only genius developed in motion pictures," Charlie Chaplin will be forever remembered for the screen character he invented and immortalized—the Little Tramp. Creator of masterpieces *The Gold Rush* (1925), *City Lights* (1931), *Modern Times* (1936) and co-founder of the United Artists studio, he received two special Academy Awards, in 1928 and 1972.

A photograph from the 1920s shows the modestly decorated living room of Charlie Chaplin's residence

Notoriously penny-pinching, he built in 1922 this "Californian Gothic" house reportedly employing studio carpenters to save money on construction. Since they were not skilled in erecting permanent buildings, soon after the completion the two-story house began to fall apart. Chaplin's friends dubbed it "Breakaway House."

A vintage post card depicts Charlie Chaplin's "Breakaway House"

Designed by Chaplin himself, the 14-room house sat on a hilltop on six and a half acres (2,6 ha) of land which included a swimming pool and tennis court. Among the players who enjoyed the Saturday afternoon games here were Douglas Fairbanks, Greta Garbo and tennis champion Bill Tilden.

During the 1980s, the estate was the home of actor George Hamilton.

Marion Davies and William Randolph Hearst Estate ㉞

Gordon B Kaufmann, architect (1927).
1011 N Beverly Dr.
Private residence.

Designed by famous architect Gordon Kaufmann, this pink stucco mansion was built on a seven-acre estate for banker Milton Getz in 1927 for over $1 million. The 27-room residence was purchased in 1947 for $120,000 by actress Marion Davies and her long-time companion, newspaper magnate William Randolph Hearst. They both died there: Hearst in 1951, Davies in 1961.

Built in a combination of Spanish and Italian styles, the three-story mansion has been beautifully restored. It features a long reflecting pool which cascades down the hill in a series of waterfalls and formal gardens with statuary from San Simeon.

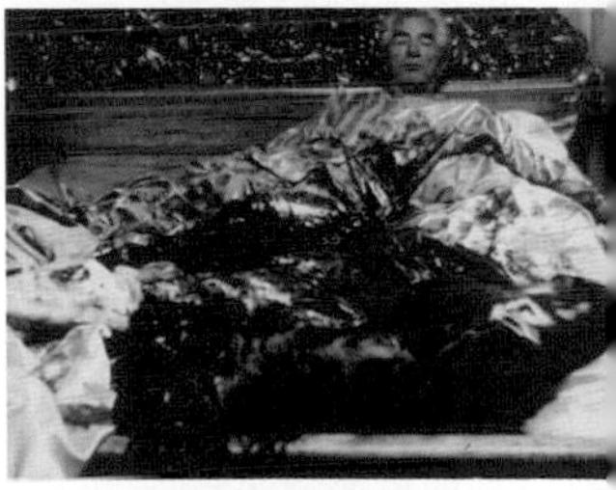

After refusing to give a movie role to Don Corleone's godson, a Hollywood producer experiences a rude awakening in *The Godfather* (1972)

The estate is frequently used as a location for film and television productions, including *The Bodyguard* (1992). It is also seen in the memorable dawn scene in *The Godfather* (1972), in which an uncooperative movie producer awakens to find the severed head of his favorite horse in his blood-soaked bed.

Aerial view of Marion Davies and William Randolph Hearst Estate

Gloria Swanson in front of her Italian Renaissance-style palace

in 1923. The magazine reported that she spent $10,000 a year on lingerie, $9,000 on stockings, $5,000 on shoes, $25,000 on fur coats, $50,000 on gowns and an extra $6,000 on perfume, using several bottles of her favorite brand, Forbidden Fruit, each week. The median annual income of an American household at the time was $1,600.

Gloria Swanson Estate ㉟

904 N Crescent Dr.
Private residence.

Gloria Swanson achieved great fame after starring in DeMille's comedies *Male and Female* (1919) and *Why Change Your Wife?* (1920). Only 23 years old and already a major star, Swanson bought in 1919 a 22-room, five-bath Italian Renaissance villa previously owned by razor-blade mogul King C Gillette. Set on four-acre grounds with sweeping lawns and mature palm and acacia trees, the mansion was thoroughly redecorated for the reigning Hollywood queen with such extravagances as peacock silk wallcoverings, tapestries and paintings. She surrounded herself with her trademark luxury, including an automatic electric elevator, a small movie theater, a

black marble bathroom with golden tub and lavish gardens which seemed "to flower in profuse."

Swanson's royal palace became a stage set for her extravagant parties. On one occasion, each of her 300 invited guests was attended by a liveried butler and received gifts of solid gold compacts and cigarette cases.

Swanson pioneered what became a lavish and eccentric movie star lifestyle, never missing an opportunity to publicize her private life. The glamorous *femme fatale* declared: "I have decided that while I am a star, I will be every inch and every moment a star. Everyone from the studio gatemen to the highest executive will know it."

"There is no star in Hollywood who lives in such gilded luxury as Gloria Swanson," announced *Photoplay*

Gloria Swanson relaxes in her sitting room in 1922

Harry Cohn Estate ㊱

Robert Farquhar, architect (1927).
1000 N Crescent Dr.
Private residence.

Built in 1927 by the architect Robert Farquhar and combining Italian and Spanish elements, this stylish mansion was not as extravagant as other residences owned by Hollywood luminaries. It was the home of movie mogul Harry Cohn, co-founder and head of Columbia Pictures for more than 30 years. Cohn bought the house in 1945 and lived here until his death in 1958.

This landmark was the site of glamorous weekly parties attended by Hollywood's most famous stars. In an elaborate screening room located in the basement, Cohn showed the newest Columbia films to his famous guests.

During the 1980s, the mansion was the home of talk show host Mike Douglas.

Harry Cohn Estate can be glimpsed behind wrought iron gates

Virginia Robinson Gardens ㊲

Nathaniel Dryden, architect (1911).
1008 Elden Way.
☎(310) 276-5367.
☞open for guided walking tours by appointment only: Tue-Thu 10am and 1pm; Fri 10am. Ⓢ NRHP

This is the oldest estate in Beverly Hills, built in 1911 for Harry Robinson, heir to the Robinsons department store chain, and his wife, Virginia. The house was designed by the bride's father, architect Nathaniel Dryden, as a wedding gift. The 6,000-square-foot (540 m²) Mediterranean Classic Revival house was the site of Mrs Robinson's fabulous parties, with famous guests such as Clark Gable, Carole Lombard, Mary Pickford and Charlie Chaplin. The interiors remain as they were when Mrs Robinson lived there, with all of its original furnishings and memorabilia.

Covering more than six acres (2,4 ha), the gardens contain over 1,000 varieties of plants, mainly subtropicals, including azaleas, gardenias, kaffir lilies, southern magnolias, roses and various fruit and citrus trees. Over 50 varieties of Mr Robinson's favorite flower, the camellia, grow in the garden. A magnificent palm grove features several hundred mature palms, including the largest stand of king palms outside Australia.

The 55-room English Tudor Greystone Mansion

Interior of the Robinson house

Greystone Mansion ㊳

Gordon B Kaufmann, architect (1927).
905 Loma Vista Dr.
☎(310) 550-4796
⏱grounds only: daily 10am-5m (winter), 10am 6pm (summer).
Closed: Thanksgiving, Christmas, New Year's Day. Ⓢ free.
Ⓦ 🏳 ↔ NRHP

In his youth, Edward L Doheny was an adventurer and gold miner. With his friend Charles Canfield, he was the first to discover oil in Los Angeles in 1892 (➔ p39). Their local holdings, together with later discoveries in southern California and Mexico, eventually made them the largest oil producers in the world. Having amassed a fortune in the oil business, Doheny began to purchase land, and his 429-acre (172-ha) ranch was the largest estate in the history of Beverly Hills. In 1925 he gave 12.58 acres to his only son, Edward Jr (called Ned), to be the site of his residence, called Greystone.

On February 16, 1929, the bodies of 35-year-old heir Ned Doheny and his male secretary, Hugh Plunkett, were found in the first-floor guest room, both dead of bullet wounds. Although the investigators ruled that Plunkett first shot his employer and then killed himself, the rumors persist that they died in a lovers' quarrel.

Greystone is continually rented as a filming location.

It was Gracie Mansion in *Ghostbusters* (1984) and home to the Green Goblin (Willem Dafoe) in *Spider-Man* (2002). Its great hall and marble staircase were seen in a dance scene with Steve Martin and Lily Tomlin in *All of Me* (1984) and its kitchen was the place where Cher, Susan Sarandon and Michelle Pfeiffer performed their magic as *The Witches of Eastwick* (1987). Other movies filmed here include *The Bodyguard* (1992), *Death Becomes Her* (1992), *Nixon* (1995), *X-Men* (2000) and *Austin Powers III* (2002).

Kitchen scenes in *The Witches of Eastwick* (1987) were filmed in Greystone Mansion

Raymond Chandler's fictional Sternwood mansion in his novel *The Big Sleep* (1939) was patterned after Greystone.

Although the mansion is not open to the public on a regular basis, it hosts a variety of cultural activities, chamber concerts, events and weddings. For information and reservations, call ☎(310) 550-4654.

Celebrity Homes

No place on earth is more strongly accociated with celebrities than Beverly Hills. Notorious for its expensive real-estate and independent of Los Angeles, the city has its own set of laws and regulations to accomodate the rich and famous. Some of the city's priciest residences are located on the winding streets in the hills north of Sunset Blvd. Hidden behind landscaping and tall walls, they are equipped with every possible security device.

Jack Nicholson Home ㊴

12850 Mulholland Dr.
Private residence (not visible from the street). Not on map. ⓐ

Since 1969, the celebrated three-time Oscar winner has lived in this 10-room house under tight security. Nicholson won two Academy Awards for best actor (*One Flew Over the Cuckoo's Nest*, 1975, and *As Good As It Gets*, 1997) and one for best supporting actor (*Terms of Endearment*, 1983). He has been nominated for an Oscar a record 12 times—more than any other actor in history.

It was at this house that director Roman Polanski brought a 13-year-old girl to take photographs of her in March 1977. While Nicholson was away, Polanski gave the girl champagne and the pow-

erful sedative methaqualone, or quaaludes, and then had sex with her in the jacuzzi. Accused of rape, he pleaded guilty to a charge of unlawful sexual intercourse with a minor. Upon the completion of a court-ordered diagnostic study at Chino State Prison, Polanski jumped bail and fled to Europe to avoid sentencing. He now lives in permanent exile in Paris, where he continues to direct. For his film *The Pianist* (2002), he received, in absentia and amid the standing ovation of Academy members, an Oscar as best director.

Marlon Brando Home (site) ㊵

12900 Mulholland Dr.
Not on map. ⓐ ♠

The rebellious leading man who changed the style of movie acting in the 1950s, Brando lived in this semi-reclusive estate from 1960 until his death in 2004 from lung disease at age 80. His ashes were scattered over Tahiti and California's Death Valley. Brando was nominated seven times and won two best actor Oscars—for his performances in *On the Waterfront* (1954) and *The Godfather* (1972).

This was the compound where in May 1990 Brando's son Christian shot and killed Dag Drollet, the lover of his half-sister Cheyenne, who was seven months pregnant

with their child. Although Christian initially claimed that the shooting was an accident, he pleaded guilty to voluntary manslaughter and was sentenced to ten years. Cheyenne committed suicide by hanging in Tahiti in 1995. Christian was released from prison in 1996 on parole.

Brando's neighbor for 30 years, Jack Nicholson, bought the house in 2005 for $5 million and demolished it.

Charlton Heston Home ㊶

2859 Coldwater Canyon Dr.
Private residence. Not on map. 🐾

Throughout most of his career, Heston played larger-than-life characters in such spectacles as *The Ten Commandments* (1956), *El Cid* (1961), *The Agony and Ecstasy* (1965) and *Earthquake* (1974). An actor with a dominating physical presence, Heston won the best actor Oscar for his title role in the 1959 remake of *Ben-Hur*. He also won the 1977 Jean Hersholt Humanitarian Award. Heston was president of the Screen Actors Guild from 1965 to 1971 and was chairman of the American Film Institute.

The house, which Heston built in 1959, is seen in Michael Moore's film *Bowling for Columbine* (2002), where Moore interviews the famous actor and a National Rifle Association spokesman.

Jack Nicholson hilltop estate. The empty pool on the far right is the only remnant of the former Marlon Brando home. Nicholson purchased the compound of his longtime friend and neighbor and demolished it, claiming that Brando's ghost visited him at night.

George Reeves Suicide Home ㊷

1579 Benedict Canyon Dr.
Private residence. 🖐 ♠

This is where the star of television's *Adventures of Superman* (1952-57) was found dead with a gunshot wound to the head on June 16, 1959. Supposedly despondent over his stagnating career, he killed himself with a .30 Luger found by his side. His mother never accepted the official ruling, trying for years to prove that he was murdered. It has been reported that his ghost still haunts the house. Reeves's death provoked a memorable quote: "George Reeves accomplished the impossible—he killed Superman."

Sharon Tate Murder House (site) ㊸

10050 Cielo Dr. 🖐

The horrific Manson murders occurred here on August 9, 1969, when actress Sharon Tate (who was eight months pregnant) and her guests, celebrity hairstylist Jay Sebring, coffee heiress Abigail Folger, her lover Wojtek Frykowski and student Steven Parent, who was visiting the estate caretaker, were savagely slaughtered. Tate and her husband, director Roman Polanski (who was out of the country at the time), rented the rambling farmhouse shortly before the tragic events. Its previous occupants were music producer Terry Melcher (the son of actress Doris Day) and his girlfriend, actress Candice Bergen. It is widely believed that ex-convict Charles Manson was infuriated when Melcher refused to publish his songs, and in an apparent act of revenge, sent four members of his "family" to terrify the producer. The murderers scrawled the word "Pig" on the front door of the house with the victims' blood.

The "Tate House," which was impossible to sell, was

Fleur de Lys is the most expensive mansion in Los Angeles

torn down in 1994 and replaced with a palatial, Mediterranean-style mansion called Villa Bella. To discourage gawkers, its address was changed to 10066 Cielo Dr.

Cary Grant Home ㊹

9966 Beverly Grove Dr.
Private residence.

It was Cary Grant at whom Mae West's famous line, "Come up and see me some time," was directed in *She Done Him Wrong* (1933). Hollywood's top romantic lead for more than three decades, Grant starred in such classics as Capra's *Arsenic and Old Lace* (1944), Hawks's *Bringing Up Baby* (1938) and *His Girl Friday* (1940), and Hitchcock's *North by Northwest* (1959). He was nominated for an Academy Award for *None But the Lonely Heart* (1944) and received an honorary Oscar for 1969 "for his unique mastery of the art of screen acting."

Grant was married five times, including Woolworth heiress Barbara Hutton (the couple was referred to as "Cash and Cary") and actress Dyan Cannon, the mother of his only child, Jennifer. This estate, where he lived with his fifth wife, Barbara Harris, was his last home. The actor who turned down the role of James Bond 007 died in 1986 after suffering a stroke while on tour with his one-man show in Iowa. His ashes were scattered over the Pacific.

Fleur de Lys ㊺

Richardson Robertson III, architect (2002).
1800 block of Angelo Dr.
Private residence.

With a price tag estimated at $100 million, this is the most expensive mansion in Los Angeles. The 45,000-square-foot (4,000-m²) house is the second largest residential property in LA (TV producer Aaron Spelling's palace holds the record with 55,000 square feet). Built for media mogul David Saperstein, the founder and former chairman and CEO of Metro Networks, a nationwide radio traffic syndicator, Fleur de Lys was inspired by the royal châteaux of France.

The real driving force behind this unequalled extravagance was David's flamboyant wife Suzanne, whose obsession with authenticity did not stop with such details as a ballroom that seats 250 dinner guests, modeled after Versailles's Hall of Mirrors. She also wanted the genuine furnishings, amassing along the way one of the most exquisite collections of the 18th-century furniture in the world, including pieces from Carl Lagerfeld's personal collection. In cases where they could not purchase the original piece they wanted, the Sapersteins had it reproduced —for example, an exact replica of Marie Antoinette's bed for the master bedroom.

Hedy Lamarr Home

Busby Berkeley Home

Hedy Lamarr Home ④⑥

1802 Angelo Dr.
Private residence.

Austrian-born Hedy Lamarr won notoriety when she starred totally nude in the Czech film *Ecstasy* (1933), becoming the first actress to appear naked in a commercially distributed movie and also the first to perform an orgasm on screen. A ravishing and exotic beauty, she was frequently typecast in roles of mysterious, sultry women. Billed as the most beautiful woman in the world when she arrived in Hollywood in 1938, Lamarr considered her beauty a curse, blaming it for six failed marriages and countless affairs.

Independent and remarkably intelligent, she co-invented and patented in 1942 a technology, known as frequency hopping, by which frequencies could be randomly changed and thus codified to avoid jamming.

The method, which was used by the military in a torpedo guidance system, is still in use today, in devices such as wireless phones.

Busby Berkeley Home ④⑦

Wallace Neff, architect (1926).
1800 Angelo Dr.
Private residence.

This Spanish-style villa was designed by Wallace Neff as he was gaining notoriety among the "movie colony" of Beverly Hills. Between 1930 and 1935, it was the home of Hollywood legend Busby Berkeley, director and choreographer of spectacular dancing sequences featuring dozens of uniformly dressed (or undressed) long-legged beauties. He worked on such lavish musicals as *42nd Street* (1933) and *Footlight Parade* (1933), and received Oscar nominations for dance direction for *Gold Diggers of 1935*, *Gold Diggers of 1936* and *Varsity Show* (1937). Another

famous resident was writer John L Balderston, a two-time Oscar nominee (for *The Lives of a Bengal Lancer*, 1935 and *Gaslight*, 1944). He lived here from 1935 to 1942.

Brad Pitt and Jennifer Aniston Home ④⑧

Wallace Neff, architect (1934).
1026 Ridgedale Dr.
Private residence.

This French Normandy-style residence was built at the height of the Depression for actor Fredric March and his wife, actress Florence Eldridge. March was a highly respected actor, both of stage and screen, who won best actor Oscars for *Dr Jekyll and Mr Hyde* (1932) and *The Best Years of Our Lives* (1946).

Designed by the famous architect to the stars, the six-bedroom house features whitewashed brick walls, overhanging eaves and weathered wood trim. Its focal point is a distinctive octagonal dovecot tower, which contained Eldridge's dressing room and bath.

The restored home, which still retains its original landscaping and color scheme, was bought in 2001 by Brad Pitt and Jennifer Aniston for a reported $14 million. Pitt, who is an architecture aficionado, starred in such films as *Ocean's Eleven* (2001) and *Troy* (2004). Aniston portrayed Rachel Green on the NBC sitcom *Friends*. The pair lived here until their widely publicized split in 2005.

A vintage post card depicts Fredric March home. The restored house was later owned by Brad Pitt and Jennifer Aniston.

Madonna Home ㊾

Wallace Neff, architect (1926).
1015 N Roxbury Dr.
Private residence (not visible from the street).

Diane Keaton lived in this house before selling it to Madonna

Surrounded by mature landscaping and hidden from the street, this private gated estate designed by famous architect Wallace Neff was the home of pop icon Madonna and her husband, director Guy Ritchie. During a career spanning more than two decades, the multiple Grammy Award-winning singer/actress has had five albums reach No. 1 on the Billboard 200. Madonna, who also has a home in London, sold the house for $8.9 million in 2004.

The house's previous owner was actress Diane Keaton, who won the best actress Oscar for her performance in *Annie Hall* (1977). Known for her passion for restoring elegant old residences, Keaton totally refurbished the eight-bedroom, Spanish-style house before selling it to Madonna in 2000 for $6.5 million.

Greta Garbo Home ㊿

904 N Bedford Dr.
Private residence.

The greatest myth in the history of cinema, the Swedish-born actress was surrounded by an aura of mystique unequalled by any other movie legend. Adored by both male and female audiences around the globe, Garbo starred in such classics as *Mata Hari* (1931), *Queen Christina* (1933), *Anna Karenina* (1935) and *Ninotchka* (1939). Although she was nominated for Academy Awards three times, Garbo never won an Oscar. The Academy, however, voted to give her a special 1954 Oscar for "her unforgettable screen performances."

One of Garbo's numerous residences in Los Angeles, this 11-room, English country-style mansion was owned by the elusive star between 1945 and 1955. At one time or another, this was also the home of Gene Kelly, Rex Harrison, Ringo Starr, Pat Boone and Barbra Streisand.

Marlene Dietrich Home (51)

822 N Roxbury Dr.
Private residence.

Dietrich gained international fame as sexy vamp Lola Lola in the German sensation *The Blue Angel* (1930). Upon her arrival in Hollywood, Paramount transformed her from a voluptuous, plain girl into a slender, glamorous woman of mystery. With her fabulous legs and intense sex appeal she became an instant legend. Dietrich was promoted as Paramount's response to MGM's Greta Garbo. She starred in such hits as *Morocco* (1930), for which she was Oscar-nominated, *Blonde Venus* (1932), *Shanghai Express* (1932) and *The Devil Is a Woman* (1935). Her habit of wearing slacks in public created a national craze among American women that is still in full swing.

Dietrich moved into this Art Deco house with her daughter, Maria, in 1932. At that time Hollywood was besieged by a series of attempted kidnappings and criminal threats, triggered by the kidnapping of the Lindbergh baby. Concerned for their safety after receiving a threatening note, Dietrich had bars installed on all the windows in the house.

Greta Garbo Home

Marlene Dietrich Home

Bugsy Siegel Murder House 52

810 N Linden Dr.
Private residence. (♿)

In this Spanish-style house mobster Benjamin "Bugsy" Siegel, referred to by J Edgar Hoover as "the most dangerous man in America," was murdered on the night of June 20, 1947. Siegel is widely credited for his role in the development of the modern city of Las Vegas. He recognized its potential as a gambling resort and persuaded Mafia bosses to finance his vision of the first luxury hotel-casino, the Flamingo, in what was then a sleepy desert town.

When he was killed, Siegel was relaxing on a sofa in the living room of the house his girlfriend Virginia "Sugar" Hill was renting. He was reading the early edition of next day's *Los Angeles Times*. The barrage of bullets, which gauged both his eyes, came from the garden shattering the window. The shooting remained unsolved. According to one theory, Siegel was gunned down because he spent millions more building the Flamingo than the Mafia allowed him to spend. The other stated that he was killed by the crime rival Jack Dragna, who ran a profitable betting wire service Siegel wanted a piece of.

A romanticized version of Siegel's story was told in the movie *Bugsy* (1991), starring Warren Beatty in the title role.

In this house Lana Turner's lover was stabbed to death

Lana Turner Home 53

730 N Bedford Dr.
Private residence. (♿)

This house made headlines just three days after the star of such films as *The Postman Always Rings Twice* (1946) and *Peyton Place* (1957) moved in.

Early in 1958, screen goddess Lana Turner was trying unsuccessfully to break a year-long affair with her lover, small-time gangster Johnny Stompanato. Notorious for his short temper, he repeatedly beat the star and threatened to kill her or cut up her face so she would never work again. This torrid and exploitive affair ended at this mansion on April 4, 1958, when Turner's 14-year-old daughter, Cheryl Crane, stabbed Stompanato to death in an upstairs bedroom with an eight-inch kitchen knife. Although many wondered how a teenage girl could overwhelm a 175-pound mobster and ex-Marine, the killing was ruled a justifiable homicide. The theory circulated that Turner killed her abusive lover herself, and Cheryl, the minor, stepped in to protect her mother.

The media had their day when gangster Mickey Cohen leaked Turner's love letters to Stompanato to the press, which revealed details of her love life. Cohen, who once hired Stompanato as his bodyguard, commented upon the acquittal, "It's the first time I ever saw a man convicted of his own murder."

Clara Bow Home 54

512 N Bedford Dr.
Private residence.

In this one-story Spanish-style home, the red-headed actress and one of cinema's first sex symbols lived up to her reputation as "the Hottest Jazz Baby in Films." According to Bow's secretary, Daisy DeVoe, the "It" girl entertained scores of men in her Chinese-themed den, including Eddie Cantor, Gary Cooper, John Gilbert, Bela Lugosi and the entire starting lineup of the USC football team, including tackle Marion Morrison, later known as John Wayne. Coach Howard Jones reportedly posted a sign in the USC locker room that warned that the actress was off limits to the members of his team.

Gangster Bugsy Siegel was murdered in this house

Lupe Velez Suicide Home ⑤⑤

732 N Rodeo Dr.
Private residence.

Known as "Whoopee Lupe" and the "Mexican Spitfire," Lupe Velez played tempestuous leads opposite such stars as Douglas Fairbanks and Gary Cooper in a number of films during the 1920s and 1930s. As temperamental and volatile in her private life as in her films, she had romantic affairs with Gary Cooper, John Gilbert, Charlie Chaplin and Randolph Scott.

Called "Casa Felicitas" (Spanish for "happy house"), this pink mansion was the home of Velez and movie Tarzan Johnny Weissmuller during their stormy, five-year marriage. The Spanish-style home was the site of one of the most theatrical suicides in Hollywood history.

After learning that her lover, an indifferent bit actor, did not want to marry her, four-month pregnant Velez undertook elaborate preparations on December 13, 1944. After seeing her hairdresser and makeup man, Velez wrote suicide notes, arranged flowers and lighted candles in her boudoir. She then swallowed almost a full bottle of Seconal tablets. Newspapers reported that her maid found the actress next morning dead in her satin bed. However, rumors spread that Velez actually died in the bathroom, where she lost consciousness while vomiting and drowned in the toilet bowl.

Actress Lupe Velez commited suicide in this house

Menendez Murders House ⑤⑥

722 N Elm Dr.
Private residence.

This is the site where on August 20, 1989, wealthy executive Jose Menendez and his wife Kitty were brutally killed by their sons. Eric Menendez was 19 and his brother Lyle was 22 when they shot their parents to death with multiple shotgun blasts to the heads—Jose was shot five times and Kitty ten.

The brothers were arrested after a former lover of their psychiatrist taped their confession and reported it to the police. The two testified in court that they were sexually and psychologically abused by their father. After two trials Eric and Lyle were each convicted on two counts of first degree murder and sentenced to life in prison with no possibility of parole.

The house had formerly been rented to rock legend Elton John.

Jean Harlow Last Home ⑤⑦

512 N Palm Dr.
Private residence.

With her roles opposite Hollywood leading men James Cagney in *Public Enemy* (1931), Clark Gable in *Red Dust* (1932) and Wallace Beery in *Dinner at Eight* (1934), platinum blonde sensation Jean Harlow quickly reached superstardom.

Harlow fell ill on the set while filming *Saratoga* and was sent home to recover. Her mother, who was a Christian Scientist, kept doctors away for several days. When the studio finally managed to get medical help, it was too late. The Baby, as Harlow was affectionately called by her piers, died the next day at age 26.

Rita Hayworth, another Hollywood love goddess and glamorous star of *Gilda* (1946) and *The Lady from Shanghai* (1948), later lived in this house.

The Menendez murders took place here

Platinum blonde Jean Harlow's last home

Marilyn Monroe and Joe DiMaggio Home

Rock Hudson died of AIDS in this house

Marilyn Monroe "Honeymoon Home" 58

508 N Palm Dr.
Private residence.

Three months after their wedding, Marilyn Monroe and her second husband, baseball legend Joe DiMaggio, rented this eight-bedroom house in April of 1954. After completing the filming of *There's No Business Like Show Business* in Los Angeles, Marilyn flew to New York for the location shooting of *The Seven Year Itch*. Joe was present during the filming of the iconic scene on Lexington Ave on September 15. While she was standing over the grate, Marilyn's white dress was blown upward, revealing her panties in front of estimated several thousand cheering onlookers. The jealous husband was so infuriated that he reportedly beat Marilyn in their hotel room that night and returned to Los Angeles alone. In early October, Marilyn told Joe that their marriage was over. Surrounded by reporters and fans, he moved out of the house on October 6; Marilyn moved out in November.

Marilyn Monroe Home 59

718 N Palm Dr.
Private residence

During 1949 and 1950, William Morris agent Johnny Hyde rented this house to live with Marilyn. Twenty years her senior and madly in love, Hyde left his wife to be with the young actress,

helping her get crucial roles in *The Asphalt Jungle* and *All About Eve* (both 1950). As a cover-up, Marilyn kept a room at the Beverly Carlton Hotel (now called Avalon).

Rock Hudson Last Home 60

9402 Beverlycrest Dr.
Private residence.

Hudson started his career with bit parts in adventure films and became a leading man in popular bedroom comedies. He was nominated for the best actor Academy Award for *Giant* (1956). The first film celebrity to became a victim of AIDS, Hudson died at this Spanish-style mansion in 1985 at the age of 59. His body was cremated and his ashes scattered at sea.

The sprawling estate, which Hudson called "the Castle," was later purchased by John Landis, director of such hits as *The Blues Brothers* (1980) and *Spies Like Us* (1985). Its next owner was Microsoft cofounder Paul Allen, ranked by *Forbes* magazine as the fifth richest man in the world.

Elizabeth Taylor Home 61

1330 Schuyler Rd.
Private residence.

This was the home of one of the most popular screen goddesses of the 20th century. Widely regarded as the most beautiful woman in the world, Elizabeth Taylor lived here with her third husband, Michael Todd, until his death in a plane crash in 1958.

Known for her scandalous private life (she was married seven times) as much as for her acting, Taylor's first breakthrough role was in *A Place in the Sun* (1951). She starred in such hits as *Cat on a Hot Tin Roof* (1958), *Suddenly Last Summer* (1959) and *Cleopatra* (1963). Taylor won two best actress Academy Awards, first for her performance in *Butterfield 8* (1960), and again for *Who's Afraid of Virginia Wolf?* (1966).

Recently she is been active in helping victims of AIDS, and for this work she received the Jean Hersholt Humanitarian Award in 1993.

Elizabeth Taylor lived here with her third husband, Michael Todd

Visitors' Information

Hotels

$	under $100
$$	$100-200
$$$	$200-325
$$$$	over $325

Hollywood

Best Western Hollywood Hills
$-$$
6141 Franklin Ave.
☎(323) 464-5181.
www.bestwesterncalifornia.com

Highland Gardens Hotel
$-$$
7047 Franklin Ave. (➔ p143)
☎(323) 850-0536.
www.highlandgardenshotel.com

Hollyday Inn Hollywood
$$
2005 N Highland Ave.
☎(323) 876-8600.
www.holiday-inn.com

Hollywood Roosevelt Hotel
$$
7000 Hollywood Blvd. (➔ p115)
☎(323) 466-7000.
www.hollywoodroosevelt.com

Magic Castle Hotel
$$
7025 Franklin Ave. (➔ p143)
☎(323) 851-0800.
www.magiccastlehotel.com

Orange Drive Manor Hostel
$
1764 N Orange Dr.
☎(323) 850-0350.
www.orangedrivehostel.com

Renaissance Hollywood Hotel
$$-$$$
1775 N Highland Ave.
☎(323) 856-1200.
www.renaissancehollywood.com

The Galeria at the Millenium Biltmore Hotel

West Hollywood

Banana Bungalow
$
7950 Melrose Ave.
☎(323) 655-1510.
www.bananabungalow.com

Chateau Marmont
$$$-$$$$
8221 Sunset Blvd. (➔ p183)
☎(323) 626-1010.
www.chateaumarmont.com

Elan Hotel Modern
$$
8435 Beverly Blvd.
☎(323) 658-6663.
www.elanhotel.com

Grafton on Sunset
$$$
8462 Sunset Blvd.
☎(323) 654-4600.
www.graftononsunset.com

Hyatt West Hollywood
$$-$$$
8401 Sunset Blvd. (➔ p186)
☎(323) 656-4101.
www.westhollywood.hyatt.com

Le Montrose Suite Hotel
$$$
900 Hammond St.
☎(310) 657-9192.
www.lemontrose.com

Le Parc Suite Hotel
$$$$
733 W Knoll Dr.
☎(310) 659-7812.
www.leparcsuites.com

Mondrian
$$$-$$$$
8440 Sunset Blvd.
☎(323) 650-8999.
www.ianschragerhotels.com

Sofitel
$$-$$$
8555 Beverly Blvd.
☎(310) 278-5444.
www.hotelsofitel.com

Standard
$$
8300 Sunset Blvd.
☎(323) 654-2800.
www.standardhotel.com

Sunset Marquis
$$$-$$$$
1200 N Alta Loma Rd.
☎(310) 657-1333.
www.sunsetmarquishotel.com

Sunset Tower
$$$-$$$$
8358 Sunset Blvd. (➔ p186)
☎(323) 654-7100.
www.argylehotel.com

Wyndham Bel Age Hotel
$$$
1020 N San Vicente Blvd.
☎(310) 854-1111.
www.wyndham.com

Downtown

Downtown LA Standard
$$
550 S Flower St.
☎(213) 892-8080.
www.standardhotel.com

Figueroa Hotel
$$
939 S Figueroa St.
☎(213) 627-8971.
www.figueroahotel.com

Hilton Checkers
$$$
535 S Grand Ave.
☎(213) 624-0000.
www.hiltoncheckers.com

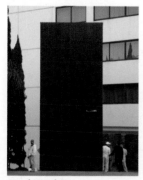

Hotel Mondrian

Hyatt Regency
$$
711 S Hope St.
☎(213) 683-1234.
www.losangelesregency.hyatt.com

Marriott Downtown
$$
333 S Figueroa St.
☎(213) 617-1133.
www.mariott.com

Millenium Biltmore
$$$
506. S Grand Ave. (➜ p255)
☎(213) 624-1011.
www.thebiltmore.com

New Otani
$$
120 S Los Angeles St.
☎(213) 629-1200.
www.newotani.com

Omni Los Angeles
$$$
251 S Olive St.
☎(213) 617-3300.
www.omnilosangeles.com

Stillwell Hotel
$
838 S Grand Ave.
☎(213) 627-1151.
www.stillwell-la.com

Westin Bonaventure
$$$
404 S Figueroa St.
☎(213) 624-1000.
www.westin.com

Pasadena/Valley

Ritz-Carlton Huntington
$$$$
1401 S Oak Knoll Ave, Pasadena.
☎(626) 568-3900. (➜ p287)
www.ritzcarlton.com

Westin Pasadena
$$
191 N Los Robles Ave, Pasadena.
☎(626) 792-2727.
www.westin.com

Safari Inn
$$
1911 W Olive St, Burbank.
☎(818) 845-8586.
www.safariburbank.com

Hilton Universal City
$$$
555 Universal Ter, Universal City.
☎(818) 506-2500.
www.hilton.com

Sheraton Universal
$$$
333 Universal Ter, Universal City.
☎(818) 980-1212.
www.starwood.com/sheraton

Beach Cities

Casa Malibu Inn
$$
22752 PCH, Malibu.
☎(310) 456-2219.

Bayside Hotel
$$
2001 Ocean Ave, Santa Monica.
☎(310) 396-6000.
www.baysidehotel.com

Casa del Mar
$$$$
1910 Ocean Way, Santa Monica.
☎(310) 581-5533.
www.hotelcasadelmar.com

Fairmont Miramar
$$$$
101 Wilshire Blvd, Santa Monica.
☎(310) 576-7777. (➜ p379)
www.fairmont.com

Georgian
$$$
1415 Ocean Ave, Santa Monica.
☎(310) 395-9945.
www.georgianhotel.com

Hotel California
$$
1670 Ocean Ave, Santa Monica.
☎(310) 393-2363.
www.hotwlca.com

Le Merigot Beach Hotel
$$$-$$$$
1740 Ocean Ave, Santa Monica.
☎(310) 395-9700.
www.lemerigothotel.com

Loews Santa Monica Beach Hotel
$$$$
1700 Ocean Ave, Santa Monica.
☎(310) 458-6700.
www.loewshotels.com

Georgian Hotel

Sea Shore Motel
$
2637 Main St, Santa Monica.
☎(310) 392-2787.
www.seashoremotel.com

Shutters on the Beach
$$$$
1 Pico Blvd, Santa Monica.
☎(310) 458-0030.
www.shuttersonthebeach.com

Cadillac Hotel
$-$$
8 Dudley Ave, Venice.
☎(310) 399-8876
www.thecadillachotel.com

Inn at Venice Beach
$$
327 Washington Blvd, Venice.
☎(310) 821-2557.
www.innatvenicebeach.com

Ritz-Carlton Marina del Rey
$$$
4375 Admiralty Way.
☎(310) 823-1700.
www.ritzcarlton.com

View of the pool at the Loews Santa Monica Beach Hotel

LAX/Culver City

Hilton Los Angeles Airport
$$
5711 W Century Blvd.
☎(310) 410-4000.
www.hilton.com

Marriott Los Angeles Airport
$$$
5855 W Century Blvd.
☎(310) 641-5700.
www.marriott.com

Sheraton Gateway
$$$
6101 W Century Blvd.
☎(310) 642-1111.
www.sheraton.com

Travelodge Hotel at LAX
$
5547 W Century Blvd.
☎(310) 649-4000.
www.travelodgelax.com

Westin Los Angeles Airport
$$$-$$$$
5400 W Century Blvd.
☎(310) 216-5858.
www.westin.com

Culver Hotel
$$
9400 Culver Blvd, Culver City.
☎(310) 838-7963. (➔ p410)
www.culverhotel.com

Radisson Los Angeles Westside
$$
6161 Centinela Ave, Culver City.
☎(310) 649-1776.
www.radisson.com

Westside/Century City

Century Plaza Hotel & Spa
$$$$
2025 Ave of the Stars.
☎(310) 277-2000.
www.westin.com

Doubletree Hotel
$$
10740 Wilshire Blvd.
☎(310) 475-8711.
www.doubletreelawestwood.com

Holiday Inn Brentwood
$$
170 N Church Lane.
☎(310) 476-6411.
www.holiday-inn.co/brentwoos-bel

Hotel Bel Air
$$$$
701 Stone Canyon Rd. (➔ p434)
☎(310) 472-1211.
www.hotelbelair.com

Luxe Hotel Sunset Blvd
$$$
11461 Sunset Blvd.
☎(310) 476-6571.
www.luxehotels.com

Park Hyatt Los Angeles
$$$
2151 Ave of the Stars.
☎(310) 277-1234.
www.parklosangeles.hyatt.com

St Regis Los Angeles
$$$$
2055 Ave of the Stars.
☎(310) 277-6111.
www.stregis.com

W Los Angeles
$$$$
930 Hilgard Ave.
☎(310) 208-8765.
www.whotels.com

Beverly Hills

Avalon
$$
9400 Olympic Blvd.
☎(310) 277-5221.
www.avalonbeverlyhills.com

Beverly Hills Hotel
$$$$
9641 Sunset Blvd. (➔ p463)
☎(310) 276-2251.
www.beverlyhillshotel.com

Beverly Hilton
$$$
9876 Wilshire Blvd.
☎(310) 274-7777.
www.beverlyhills.hilton.com

Four Seasons Beverly Hills
$$$$
300 S Doheny Dr.
☎(310) 385-4927.
www.fourseasons.com/losangeles

Hotel Bel Air's garden pond

Le Meridien
$$$$
465 S La Cienega Blvd.
☎(310) 247-0315.
www.lemeridienbeverlyhills.com

Luxe Hotel Rodeo Drive
$$$$
360 N Rodeo Dr.
☎(310) 273-0300.
www.luxehotels.com

Maison 140
$$
140 S Lasky Dr.
☎(310) 281-4000.
www.maison140beverlyhills.com

Peninsula Beverly Hills
$$$$
9882 S Santa Monica Blvd.
☎(310) 551-2888.
www.peninsula.com

Raffles L'Ermitage
$$$$
9291 Burton Way.
☎(310) 278-3344.
www.raffle-lermitagehotel.com

Regent Beverly Wilshire
$$$$
9500 Wilshire Blvd. (➔ p458)
☎(310) 275-5200.
www.regenthotels.com

Lobby of the Hotel Regent Beverly Wilshire

Restaurants

$ under $20
$$ $20-35
$$$ $35-50
$$$$ over $50

Hollywood

Ca Brea Italian
$$
346 S La Brea Ave.
☎(323) 938-2863.

Café des Artistes French
$$
1534 McCadden Pl.
☎(323) 469-7300.

Campanile Italian
$$$
624 S La Brea Ave.
☎(323) 938-1447.

Canter's Deli
$
419 N Fairfux Ave.
☎(323) 651-2030.

Chan Dara Thai
$$
310 N Larchmont.
☎(323) 467-1052.

Dar Maghreb Moroccan
$$$
7651 Sunset Blvd.
☎(323) 876-7651.

Musso and Frank American
$$-$$$
6667 Hollywood Blvd. (➔ p119)
☎(323) 467-7788.

Sonora Café Mexican
$$$
180 S La Brea Ave.
☎(323) 857-1800.

Tantra Indian
$$
3705 Sunset Blvd.
☎(323) 663-8268.

Yamashiro Japanese
$$
1999 N Sycamore. (➔ p146)
☎(323) 466-5125.

West Hollywood

A.O.C. French/Cal
$$
8022 W 3rd St.
☎(323) 653-6359.

Bastide French
$$$$
8475 Melrose Ave.
☎(323) 651-5950.

Tower Bar at the Sunset Tower

Chaya Brasserie French/Asian
$$$
8741 Alden Dr.
☎(310) 859-8833.

Dan Tana's Italian
$$
9071 Santa Monica Blvd.
☎(310) 275-9444.

Diaghilev Russian
$$$$
Wyndham Bel Age Hotel
1020 N San Vicente Blvd.
☎(310) 854-1111.

Grace American
$$$$
7360 Beverly Blvd.
☎(323) 934-4400.

La Boheme Cal/French
$$$
8400 Santa Monica Blvd.
☎(323) 848-2360.

Lucques French/Med
$$$
8474 Melrose Ave.
☎(323) 655-6277.

The Palm Steaks
$$$
9001 Santa Monica Blvd.
☎(310) 550-8811.

Sofi Greek
$$
8030 3/4 W 3rd St.
☎(323) 651-0346.

Tower Bar California
$$$
Sunset Tower, 8358 Sunset Blvd.
☎(323) 848-6677. (➔ p186)

Urth Café Wholefood
$
8565 Melrose Ave.
☎(310) 659-0628.

Downtown

Checkers Cal/Continental
$$$
Hilton Checkers Hotel
535 S Grand Ave.
☎(213) 624-0000.

Cicada Italian
$$$
617 S Olive St. (➔ p256)
☎(213) 488-9188.

Ciudad Latin
$$$
445 S Figueroa St.
☎(213) 486-5171.

Empress Pavilion Chinese
$$
988 N Hill St.
☎(213) 617-9898.

Pacific Dining Car American
$$$
1310 W 6th St.
☎(213) 483-6000.

Seoul Jung Korean
$$$
Wilshire Grand Hotel
930 Wilshire Blvd.
☎(213) 688-7880.

Patina French/Cal
$$$$
Walt Disney Concert Hall
141 S Grand Ave.
☎(213) 972-3331.

Thousand Cranes Japanese
$$$
New Otani Hotel
120 S Los Angeles St.
☎(213) 253-9255.

Water Grill Seafood
$$$
544 S Grand Ave.
☎(213) 891-0900.

Beach Cities

Beau Rivage   Mediterranean
$$$
26025 PCH, Malibu.
☎(310) 456-5733.

Taverna Tony   Greek
$$
23410 Civic Center Way, Malibu.
☎(310) 317-9667.

Saddle Peak Lodge   Game
$$$$
419 Cold Canyon Rd, Calabasas.
☎(818) 222-3888.

Border Grill   Mexican/Latin
$$-$$$
1445 4th St, Santa Monica.
☎(310) 451-1655.

Chinois on Main   Chinese/
$$$-$$$$ French
2709 Main St, Santa Monica.
☎(310) 392-9025.

Drago   Italian
$$
2628 Wilshire Blvd, S. Monica.
☎(310) 828-1585.

The Hump   Japanese
$$$$
3221 Donald Douglas Loop S.
☎(310) 313-0977.

JiRaffe   French
$$$
502 S. Monica Blvd, S. Monica.
☎(310) 917-6671.

The Lobster   Seafood
$$-$$$
1602 Ocean Ave, Santa Monica.
☎(310) 458-9294.

Mélisse   French
$$$$
1104 Wilshire Blvd.
☎(310) 395-0881.

Michael's   California
$$-$$$
1147 3rd St, Santa Monica.
☎(310) 451-0843.

Valentino   Italian
$$$
3115 Pico Blvd, Santa Monica.
☎(310) 829-4313.

Joe's Restaurant   California
$$
1023 Abbot Kinney Blvd, Venice.
☎(310) 399-5811.

L'Opera   Italian
$$$
101 Pine Ave, Long Beach.
☎(562) 491-0066.

Polo Lounge at the Beverly Hills Hotel

Westside

Beacon   Asian
$$
3280 Helms Ave, Culver City.
☎(310) 838-7500.

Four Oaks   French
$$$$
2181 N Beverly Glen Blvd, Bel Air.
☎(310) 470-2265.

La Cachette   French
$$$
10506 S Santa Monica Blvd.
☎(310) 470-4992.

Mori Sushi   Japanese
$$$$
11500 Pico Blvd.
☎(310) 479-3939.

Versailles   Cuban
$-$$
10319 Venice Blvd, Culver City.
☎(310) 558-3168.

Beverly Hills

The Belvedere   California
$$$$
Peninsula Hotel
9882 S Santa Monica Blvd.
☎(310) 788-2306.

Crustacean   Vietnamese
$$$-$$$$
9646 S Santa Monica Blvd.
☎(310) 205-8990.

Enoteca Drago   Italian
$$-$$$
410 N Canon Dr.
☎(310) 786-8236.

Kate Mantilini   American
$$$
9101 Wilshire Blvd.
☎(310) 278-3699.

Lawry's   Steak
$$$-$$$$
100 N La Cienega Blvd.
☎(310) 652-2827.

Matsuhisa   Japanese
$$$
129 N La Cienega Blvd.
☎(310) 659-9639.

Mastro's   Steak
$$$
246 N Canon Dr.
☎(310) 888-8782.

Nate 'n' Al's Deli   Deli
$
414 N Beverly Dr.
☎(310) 274-0101.

Polo Lounge   California
$$$$
Beverly Hills Hotel (➜ p.463)
9641 Sunset Blvd.
☎(310) 276-2251.

Spago   California
$$$$
176 N Canon Dr.
☎(310) 385-0880.

Chaya Brasserie

Nightlife

Bars

Hollywood

4100 Bar
4100 Sunset Blvd, Silver Lake.
☎(323) 666-4460.

Beauty Bar
1638 N Cahuenga Blvd.
☎(323) 468-3800.

Big Foot Lodge
3172 Los Feliz Blvd, Los Feliz.
☎(323) 662-9227.

Burgundy Room
1621 1/2 N Cahuenga Blvd.
☎(323) 465-7530.

Cat and Fiddle Pub
6530 Sunset Blvd.
☎(323) 468-3800.

Daddy's
1610 N Vine St.
☎(323) 463-7777.

Good Luck Bar
1514 Hillhurst Ave, Los Feliz.
☎(323) 666-3524.

Formosa Café
7156 Santa Monica Blvd.
☎(323) 850-9050. (➔ p193)

Frolic Room
6245 Hollywood Blvd.
☎(323) 462-5890.

Lava Lounge
1533 N La Brea Ave.
☎(323) 876-6612.

Red Lion Tavern
2366 Glendale Blvd, Silver Lake.
☎(323) 662-5337.

Star Shoes
6364 Hollywood Blvd.
☎(323) 462-7827.

Three Clubs
1123 N Vine St.
☎(323) 462-6441.

West Hollywood/Midtown

Bar Marmont
Château Marmont Hotel adjacent
8171 Sunset Blvd. (➔ p183)
☎(323) 650-0575.

El Coyote
7312 Beverly Blvd.
☎(323) 939-2255.

El Carmen
8138 W 3rd St.
☎(323) 852-1552.

Frolic Room

Sky Bar
Mondrian Hotel
8440 Sunset Blvd.
☎(323) 848-6025.

Snake Pit
7529 Melrose Ave.
☎(323) 852-9390.

Molly Malone's Irish Pub
575 S Fairfax Ave.
☎(323) 935-1577.

HMS Bounty
3357 Wilshire Blvd.
☎(213) 385-7275.

Jones
7205 Santa Monica Blvd.
☎(323) 850-1727.

The Rainbow Bar and Grill
9015 Sunset Blvd. (➔ p189)
☎(310) 278-4232.

Standard
Standard Hotel
8300 Sunset Blvd.
☎(323) 650-9090.

Whiskey Bar
Sunset Marquis Hotel
1200 N Alta Loma Rd.
☎(310) 657-1333.

Downtown

BonaVista Lounge
Westin Bonaventure Hotel
404 S Figueroa St. (➔ p259)
☎(213) 624 1000.

Casey's Bar
613 S Grand Ave..
☎(213) 629-2353.

Gallery Bar
Millenium Biltmore Hotel
506 S Grand Ave. (➔ p255)
☎(213) 624-1011.

Golden Gopher
417 W 8th St.
☎(213) 614-8001.

Hank's
Stillwell Hotel
838 S Grand Ave.
☎(213) 623-7718.

Mountain
473 Gin Ling Way.
☎(213) 625-7500.

Beach Cities

Rooftop Bar
Standard Downtown Hotel
550 S Flower St.
☎(213) 892-8080.

217 Lounge
217 Broadway, Santa Monica.
☎(310) 394-6336.

The Brig
1515 Abbot Kinney Blvd, Venice.
☎(310) 399-7537.

Circle Bar
2926 Main St, Venice
☎(310) 450-0508.

Monsoon
1212 3rd St Promenade, S Monica.
☎(310) 576-9996.

Library Alehouse
2911 Main St, Santa Monica.
☎(310) 314-4855.

Voda
1449 2nd St, Santa Monica
☎(310) 394-9774.

Westside/Beverly Hills

Bar Noir
Maison 140 Hotel
140 Lasky Dr, Beverly Hills.
☎(310) 271-2145.

Liquid Kitty
11780 W Pico Blvd, West LA.
☎(310) 473-3707.

Whiskey Blue
W Hotel
930 Hilgard Ave, Westwood.
☎(310) 443-8232.

Biltmore's Gallery Bar

Dance Clubs

1650
1650 Schrader Blvd, Hollywood.
☎(323) 871-1650.

A.D.
836 N Highland Ave, Hollywood.
☎(323) 467-3000.

Arena
6655 Santa Monica Blvd, Hollywood.
☎(323) 462-0714.

Avalon
1735 N Vine St, Hollywood.
☎(323) 462-3000. (➔ p122)

Boardner's
1652 Cherokee Ave, Hollywood.
☎(323) 462-9621.

Century Club
10131 Constellation Blvd, Century City.
☎(310) 553-6000.

Club 7969/Peanuts
7969 Santa Monica Blvd, West Hollywood.
☎(323) 654-0280.

Club Lingerie
6507 Sunset Blvd, Hollywood.
☎(323) 466-3416.

Cinespace
6356 Hollywood Blvd, Hollywood.
☎(323) 817-FILM.

Dragonfly
6510 Santa Monica Blvd, Hollywood.
☎(323) 466-6111.

The Echo
1822 Sunset Blvd, Echo Park.
☎(213) 413-8200.

Element
1642 Las Palmas Ave, Hollywood.
☎(323) 460-4632.

The Factory/Ultra Suede
661 N Robertson Blvd, West Hollywood.
☎(310) 659-4551.

Gabah
4658 Melrose Ave, LA.
☎(323) 664-8913.

Garden Of Eden
7080 Hollywood Blvd, Hollywood.
☎(323) 465-3336.

Highlands
6810 Hollywood Blvd, Hollywood.
☎(323) 461-9800.

Ivar
6356 Hollywood Blvd, Hollywood.
☎(323) 465-4827.

House of Blues

King King
6555 Hollywood Blvd, Hollywood.
☎(213) 427-3982.

Little Temple
4515 S Monica Blvd, Silver Lake.
☎(323) 660-4549.

Nacional
1645 Wilcox Ave, Hollywood.
☎(323) 962-7712.

The Ruby
7070 Hollywood Blvd, Hollywood.
☎(323) 467-7070.

The Space
2020 Wilshire Blvd, Santa Monica.
☎(310) 829-1933 .

The Stock Exchange
618 S Spring St, downtown.
☎(213) 489-3877.

Tempest
7323 Santa Monica Blvd, West Hollywood.
☎(323) 850-5115.

XES
1716 Cahuenga Blvd, Hollywood.
☎(323) 461-8190.

Zanzibar
1301 Fifth St, Santa Monica.
☎(310) 451-2221.

Live Music

Rock/Pop

14 Below
1348 14th St, Santa Monica.
☎(310) 451-5040.

The Cat Club
8911 Sunset Blvd, West Hollywood.
☎(310) 657-0888.

The Derby
4500 Los Feliz Blvd, Los Feliz.
☎(323) 663-8979.

El Rey Theater
5515 Wishire Blvd. (➔ p208)
☎(323) 936-4790.

Fais Do-Do
5257 W Adams Blvd, LA.
☎(323) 954-8080.

Genghis Cohen
740 N Fairfax Ave, LA.
☎(323) 653-0640.

The Gig
7302 Melrose Ave, Hollywood.
☎(323) 936-4440.

House of Blues
8430 Sunset Blvd, West Hollywood.
☎(323) 848-5100.

Key Club
9039 Sunset Blvd, West Hollywood. (➔ p189)
☎(310) 274-5800.

The Knitting Factory
7021 Hollywood Blvd, Hollywood.
☎(323) 463-0204.

Largo
432 N Fairfax Ave, LA.
☎(323) 852-1073.

The Mint
6010 W Pico Blvd, LA.
☎(323) 954-9400.

Rainbow Bar and Grill
9015 Sunset Blvd, West Hollywood. (➔ p189)
☎(323) 278-4232.

Roxy
9009 Sunset Blvd, West Hollywood. (➔ p189)
☎(310) 276-2222.

The Smell
247 S Main St, downtown.
☎no phone.

Spaceland
1717 Silverlake Blvd, Silver Lake.
☎(323) 661-4380.

Temple Bar
1026 Wilshire Blvd, Santa Monica.
☎(310) 393-6611.

The Troubadour
9081 Santa Monica Blvd, West Hollywood. (➔ p190)
☎(310) 276-6168.

Viper Room
8852 Sunset Blvd, West Hollywood. (➔ p188)
☎(310) 358-1880.

Whisky-A-Go-Go
8901 Sunset Blvd, West Hollywood. (➔ p189)
☎(310)652-4202.

Jazz

The Baked Potato
3787 Cahuenga Blvd, Studio City.
☎(818) 980-1615.

Catalina Bar & Grill
6725 Sunset Blvd, Hollywood.
☎(323) 466-2210.

Jax
339 N Brand Ave, Glendale.
☎(818) 500-1604.

The Jazz Bakery
3233 Helms Ave, Culver City,
☎(310) 271-9039.

Spazio
14755 Ventura Blvd, Sherman
Oaks.
☎(818) 728-8400.

Vibrato Grill & Jazz
2930 Beverly Glen Circle, Bel Air.
☎(310) 474-9400.

The World Stage
4344 Degnan Blvd, South Central
☎(323) 293-2451.

Blues

Babe & Ricky's Inn
4339 Leimert Blvd, South Central.
☎(323) 295-9112.

Café Boogaloo
1238 Hermosa Ave, Hermosa
Beach.
☎(310) 318-2324.

Cozy's Bar & Grill
14058 Ventura Blvd, Sherman
Oaks.
☎(818) 986-6000.

Harvelle's
1432 4th St, Santa Monica.
☎(310) 395-1676.

Country/Folk

Boulevard Music
4316 Sepulveda Blvd, Culver City.
☎(323) 398-2583.

Cowboy Country
3321 E South St, Long Beach.
☎(562) 630-3007.

Viva Cantina
900 Riverside Dr, Burbank.
☎(818) 845-2425.

Latin

El Floridita
1253 N Vine St, Hollywood.
☎(323) 871-0936.

Zabumba
10717 Venice Blvd, Culver City.
☎(310) 841-6525.

The Arts

Classical Music

Da Camera Society
different venues throughout LA.
☎(213) 477-2929.
www.dacamera.org

Long Beach Symphony
Terrace Theater
300 E Ocean Blvd, Long Beach.
☎(562) 436-3203.
www.lbso.org

**Los Angeles Chamber
Orchestra**
different venues throughout LA.
☎(213) 622-7001 ext 215.
www.laco.org

**Los Angeles Master
Chorale**
Walt Disney Concert Hall
151 S Grand Ave, downtown.
☎(800) 787-LAMC.
www.lamc.org

Los Angeles Philharmonic
Walt Disney Concert Hall
151 S Grand Ave, downtown.
☎(213) 850-2000.
www.laphil.org

Musica Angelica
different venues throughout LA
☎(310) 458 4504.
www.musicaangelica.org

Pacific Serenades
different venues throughout LA.
☎(213) 534-3434.
www.pacser.org

Pasadena Symphony
Pasadena Civic Auditorium
300 E Green St, Pasadena.
☎(626) 584-8833.

Southwest Chamber Music
different venues throughout LA.
☎(800) 726-7147.
www.swmusic.org

Opera

Casa Italiana Opera
1051 N Broadway, downtown.
☎(818) 559-8696.
www.casaitaliana.org

Los Angeles Opera
Music Center (➔ p271)
135 N Grand Ave, downtown.
☎(213) 972-8001.
www.losangelesopera.com

Long Beach Opera
Carpenter Center
6200 Atherton St, Long Beach.
☎(562) 439-2580.
www.lbopera.com

Dance

**Cerritos Center for the
Performing Arts**
12700 Center Court Dr, Cerritos.
☎(562) 467-8820.
www.cerritoscenter.com

Cal State, Los Angeles
Luckman Fine Arts Complex
5151 State University Dr.
☎(323) 343-5124.
www.luckmanarts.org

John Anson Ford Theatre
2850 Cahuenga Blvd, Hollywood.
☎(323) 461-3673.
www.fordamphitheatre.org

REDCAT
631 W 2nd St, downtown.
☎(213) 237-2800.
www.redcat.org

Pasadena Dance Theater
1985 Locust Ave, Pasadena.
☎(626) 683-3459.
www.pasadenadance.org

**UCLA Center for the
Performing Arts**
405 N Hilgard Ave, Westwood.
☎(310) 825-4401.
www.performingartsucla.edu

Dorothy Chandler Pavilion, home of the Los Angeles Opera

Theater

Ahmanson Theatre
Music Center (➜ p271)
135 N Grand Ave, downtown.
☎(213) 628-2772.
www.centertheatregroup.com

Geffen Playhouse
10886 Le Conte Ave, Westwood.
☎(310) 208-5454.
www.geffenplayhouse.com

Kirk Douglas Theatre
9820 Washington Blvd, Culver
City. (➜ p410)
☎(213) 628-2772.
www.centertheatregroup.com

Mark Taper Forum
Music Center (➜ p271)
135 N Grand Ave, downtown.
☎(213) 628-2772.
www.centertheatregroup.com

Pantages Theater
6233 Hollywood Blvd, Hollywood.
☎(323) 468-1770. (➜ p113)
www.nederlander.com

Pasadena Playhouse
39 S El Molinio Ave, Pasadena.
☎(626) 792-8672. (➜ p296)
www.pasadenaplayhouse.org

Ricardo Montalbán Theatre
1615 N Vine St, Hollywood.
☎(323) 462-6666.
www.nosotros.org

**Will Geer Theatricum
Botanicum**
1419 N Topanga Canyon Blvd,
Topanga.
☎(310) 455-3723.
www.theatricum.com

Edgemar Center
2437 Main St, Santa Monica.
☎(310) 399-3666.
www.edgemarcenter.org

Hudson Theatre
6539 Santa Monica Blvd.
☎(323) 856-4252.
www.hudsontheatre.com

Knightsbridge Theatre
1944 Riverside Dr, Silver Lake.
☎(323) 667-0955.
www.knightsbridgetheatre.org

Odyssey Theater Ensemble
2055 S Sepulveda Blvd, West LA.
☎(310) 477-2055.
www.odysseytheatre.com

Powerhouse Theatre
3116 2nd St, Santa Monica.
☎(310) 396-3680.
www.powerhousetheatre.com

MET Theatre
1089 N Oxford Ave, Hollywood.
☎(323) 957-1152.
www.themettheatre.com

Zephyr Theatre
7456 Melrose Ave, Hollywood.
☎(323) 852-9111.

Acme Comedy Theater
135 N La Brea Ave, Midtown.
☎(323) 525-0202.
www.acmecomedy.com

Comedy Store
8433 Sunset Blvd, West Hollywood.
☎(323) 656-6225
www.thecomedystore.com

Groundlings Theater
7307 Melrose Ave, Hollywood
☎(323) 934-9700.
www.groundlings.com

I.O. West
6366 Hollywood Blvd, Hollywood.
☎(323) 962-7560.
www.iowest.com

Laugh Factory
8001 Sunset Blvd, West Hollywood.
☎(323) 656-1336.
www.laughfactory.com

Cinegrill
7000 Hollywood Blvd, Hollywood.
☎(323) 466-7000.
www.hollywoodroosevelt.com

The Dresden Room
1760 N Vermont Ave, Hollywood.
☎(323) 665-4294.
www.thedresden.com

Forty Deuce
5574 Melrose Ave.
☎(323) 465-4242.
www.fortydeuce.com

ArcLight and Cinerama Dome

Film

ArcLight and Cinerama
6360 Sunset Blvd, Hollywood.
☎(323) 464-4226. (➜ p126)
www.arclightcinemas.com

Bridge Cinema de Lux
6081 Center Dr, Culver City.
☎(310) 568-3375.
www.thebridgecinema.com

IMAX Theater
600 State Dr, Exposition Park.
☎(323) 724-3623.
www.californiasciencecenter.org

Pacific Theatres
189 The Grove Dr, Midtown.
☎(323) 692-0829.
www.thegrovela.com

AMC Century City 15
10250 Santa Monica Blvd,
Century City.
☎(310) 289-4AMC.
www.amctheatres.com

Mann Beverly Center 13
8522 Beverly Blvd, West Hollywood.
☎(310) 652-7760.
www.manntheatres.com

Universal Studio Cinemas
Universal CityWalk, Universal City.
☎(818) 508-0711.
www.citywalkhollywood.com

American Cinemateque
Egyptian Theater (➜ p108)
6712 Hollywood Blvd, Hollywood.
Aero Theater (➜ p378)
1328 Montana Ave, Santa Monica.
☎(323) 466-3456.
www.americancinemateque.com

Bing Theater
LACMA (➜ p205)
5905 Wilshire Blvd, Midtown.
☎(323) 857-6010.
www.lacma.org

Cinespace
6356 Hollywood Blvd.
☎(323) 817-3456.

Cecchi Gori Fine Arts
8556 Wilshire Blvd, Beverly Hills.
☎(310) 281-8223.
www.landmarktheaters.com

Nuart Theatre
11272 Santa Monica Blvd, LA.
☎(310) 281-8223.
www.landmarktheaters.com

Silent Movie Theatre
611 N Fairfax Ave, Midtown.
☎(323) 655-2520.
www.silentmovietheatre.com

Theme Parks

Knott's Berry Farm
8039 Beach Blvd, Buena Park,
Orange County. Not on map.
☎(714) 220-5200.
www.knotts.com
🕐Jun-mid Sep daily 9am-midnight;
mid Sep-May weekdays 10am-
6pm, Sat 10am-10pm, Sun 10am-
8pm. Ⓢ

Started during the Depression when Mrs Knott began selling chicken dinners and Mr Knott built an Old West town to entertain hungry customers waiting in line, this 150-acre complex now boasts more than 160 rides.

Ghost Town features cowboys, cancan dancers and gold panning in the authentic Wild West setting comprised of old buildings moved here from deserted mining towns.

Fiesta Village, inspired by California's Mexican heritage, features *mariachis,* festive markets and a hand-carved antique Dentzel carousel.

Among the most popular thrill rides are roller coasters Montezooma's Revenge, which spins through a 360-degree loop, and Jaguar!, which mimics a big cat's motions pursuing its prey.

Six Flags Magic Mountain
26101 Magic Mountain Pkwy,
(off I-5), Valencia. Not on map.
☎(661) 255-4100.
www.sixflags.com
🕐mid Mar-mid-Sep daily; mid
Sep-mid March weekends; open at
10am; call for closing hours. Ⓢ

Experience enormous adrenaline rushes in this thrill ride heaven, featuring some of the world's largest, fastest and scariest roller coasters. You can thunder through Viper's seven lightening loops before dropping 18 stories or "fly at the speed of fear" on Tatsu, a dragon-themed coaster.

For those who like to swim, raft or just get wet in a tropical paradise, nearby Hurricane Harbor offers towering speed slides, interactive water play zones and dozens of water adventures for thrill seakers of all ages.

Guests visiting Disneyland's Fantasyland whirl in a Mad Tea Party

Disneyland
1313 S Harbor Blvd, Anaheim,
Orange County. Not on map.
☎(714) 781 4565; 781-7290.
www.disneyland.com Ⓖ
🕐daily, year-round; call for hours.

Conceived by Walt Disney and advertised as the "happiest place on Earth," Disneyland opened in 1955 with 18 ticketed attractions. Fifty years later, with 63 attractions and nearly 500 million visitors, it is still the world's most popular amusement park.

Sometimes criticized as an artificial, utopian world that offers escapism to the masses, the idealized park permeated American culture and influenced the modern way of life in many ways (family entertainment, shopping malls, corporate branding and cross-promotions).

The Magic Kingdom today is comprised of eight realms, each organized around a dominant theme.

Main Street, USA is a recreation of an early 20th-century small town and was inspired by Walt Disney's hometown.

Fantasyland is a magical realm inhabited by some of the most popular Disney characters. Behind Sleeping Beauty Castle await such rides as the King Arthur Carousel and Peter Pan's Flight.

Mickey's Toontown is a kid's playground place where they can visit their favorite animated mouse in his own house and take a ride on Roger Rabbit's Car Toon Spin.

Frontierland offers a ride on the Big Thunder Mountain Railroad roller coaster. Guests can also enjoy a dance hall-style revue, complete with cancan dancers, board authentic replicas of two 19th-century ships and explore Tom Sawyer's Island.

Critter Country is inhabited by stuffed animal characters who sing and dance in the famous Country Bear Jamboree show. Winnie the Pooh and Splash Mountain ride are its main draws.

New Orleans Square features a sanitized version of the city's French Quarter, a Haunted Mansion with "999 happy haunts," as well as Pirates of the Caribbean, the park's most popular ride.

Adventureland features exotic locales waiting to be explored in such rides as Jungle Cruise and Indiana Jones Adventure.

Tomorrowland provides a chance to join *Star Wars* droids R2-D2 and C-3PO in a high-tech travel through outer space. Thrill seekers will love a ride to the stars on Space Mountain roller coaster.

California Adventure is the new theme park next to Disneyland. It pays tribute to the history and natural beauty of the Golden State with such attractions as the Sun Wheel (a giant Ferris wheel), a replica of the Golden Gate bridge, a stylized Hollywood Boulevard and the California Screamin' roller coaster.

Index

LOS ANGELES AS SEEN
COR. WILDER ST.

★ SOUTHERN PA
LOOKING SOUTH FRO

EXPLANATORY.

LOS AN
CALIFOR

PUBLISHED BY
SEMI-TROPIC HOMESTEAD CO.
TEMPLE BLOCK.